FORECASTING FOR ECONOMICS AND BUSINESS

Gloria González-Rivera
University of California–Riverside

Routledge
Taylor & Francis Group
LONDON AND NEW YORK

First published 2013 by Pearson Education, Inc.

Published 2016 by Routledge
2 Park Square, Milton Park, Abingdon, Oxon OX14 4RN
711 Third Avenue, New York, NY, 10017, USA

Routledge is an imprint of the Taylor & Francis Group, an informa business

ISBN 13: 978-0-13-147493-2 (pbk)

Cover Designer: Suzanne Behnke

Library of Congress Cataloging-in-Publication Data

González-Rivera, Gloria.
Forecasting for economics and business / Gloria González-Rivera.
p. cm.
ISBN-13: 978-0-13-147493-2
1. Economic forecasting. 2. Economic forecasting—United States. I. Title.
HB3730.G57 2013
338.5'44—dc23

2011049940

To a very special undergraduate,
Vasilios A. Morikis González,
with love

Brief Contents

Contents

Preface

Knowledge of forecasting methods is among the most demanded qualifications for professional economists and business people working in either the private or public sectors of the economy. This textbook provides an introduction to forecasting for junior and senior undergraduates in a variety of fields such as economics, business administration, applied mathematics and statistics, and for graduate students in quantitative masters programs such as MBA and MA/MS in economics. The general aim is the development of sophisticated professionals, able to critically analyze time series data and forecasting reports because they have experienced the merits and shortcomings of forecasting practice.

Features

This book comes as the outcome of continuous feedback from several cohorts of advanced undergraduate students in a forecasting course for economics and business that I have taught at University of California, Riverside over the years. The book is written in a conversational style because this is my approach to teaching and because I find that engaging conversation promotes an active learning environment. Many iterations, from the classroom-as-playground to the writing desk and from the writing desk to the classroom, have shaped the methodological and pedagogical approach of the textbook. As a result, three classroom-tested features define this book: (i) visualization, (ii) engagement with real-life data and simulated data, and (iii) a modern hands-on approach.

Pictures, graphs, and plots engage the students' minds and are useful tools to motivate and to develop forecasting intuition in anticipation of formal, more technical, concepts. Never underestimate the value of a visual. A meaningful context to place forecasting ideas is necessary to bring the discipline alive. Therefore, all chapters in the textbook are motivated by real-life data. The same data sets that professional forecasters examine are also at the fingertips of the students. Examining these data sets provides an immediate immersion in the practice of forecasting. In all chapters, the introduction of a new concept, model, or procedure is immediately followed by a real data exercise. No concept will be fully understood until it comes alive in a real-life scenario. Simulated data also helps with the understanding of forecasting models. Short computer programs are provided in all chapters to simulate the models under study. These programs and all real-life data exercises bring a hands-on experience to the understanding of forecasting. Students can then appreciate forecasting as a quantitative side of the micro and macroeconomic theories that they are concurrently learning, which will help with the delivery of business and economics curriculum as an integrated discipline with complementary qualitative and quantitative strands.

Audience and Technical Background

Nowadays forecasting is a technical field, and as such, it requires some mathematics and statistics knowledge. However, a principle of this textbook is that the introduction of technical concepts must be triggered by a specific and immediate practical need. Having said so, some technical background is necessary. The textbook should be accessible to students with a basic background in algebra, statistics, and linear regression. In a few instances, some introductory calculus is used to facilitate the exposition, but it is not absolutely necessary for the comprehension of the material. A brief review of fundamental statistical concepts is provided in the book Appendix A. Chapter 2 offers a concise review of the linear regression model focusing on ordinary least squares estimation and hypothesis testing, and emphasizing the necessary regression tools to be used in forecasting. Some chapters contain more technical material that is either specifically labeled as advanced sections, or relegated to the chapter appendix and footnotes. As a general rule, skipping this material will not interrupt the flow of the chapter and will not be detrimental to its understanding. It will be up to the instructor to decide whether or not to skip these sections depending on the technical background of the audience.

Organization

The organization of most forecasting books has followed the classical decomposition of a time series: trend, cycles and seasonal components. First, the trend component is modeled followed by the modeling of the non-seasonal cycle, which is considered the residual information left in a time series after the trend is analyzed. If there is some seasonality, this is added after the trend and non-seasonal cycle have been modeled. The organization of this textbook differs from the traditional approach by introducing the analysis of the cycle first followed by the trend. This is because pedagogically we need to introduce very early in the course the time series concepts of stationary/non-stationarity and the autocorrelation functions as foundational tools for the understanding of model-based forecasting. Therefore, the organization of the book is framed along two coordinates: the first deals with the properties of time series data (stationarity or non-stationarity), and the second with general properties of the model (linear or non-linear). The following figure explains our forecasting world:

FIGURE 1
Parametric Time Series World

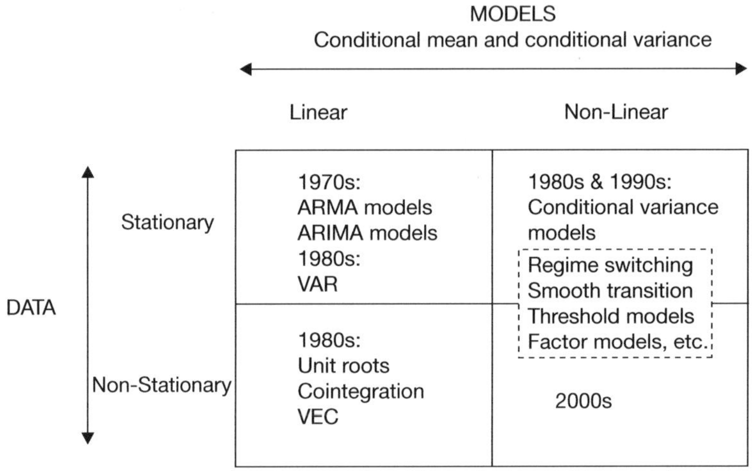

This figure also classifies advances in time series modeling historically. In the 1970s we have the seminal contributions of Box and Jenkins who brought the development of ARIMA models; in the late 1970s and 1980s we have critical developments in the analysis of unit roots (Dickey and Fuller), spurious regressions (Granger and Newbold), Vector Autoregressions (Sims), and cointegration and vector error correction models (Engle and Granger). In the 1980s and 1990s, we witness extensive literature on models for the conditional variance (ARCH, Engle). Finally, during the last two decades, numerous developments have been made in non-linear modeling such as smooth transitions, threshold model, factor models, etc., which may represent stationary or non-stationary data (the dashed rectangle strides between the stationary and non-stationary coordinate).

The organization of the textbook follows the four entries of the aforementioned matrix with particular emphasis on the following three combinations: stationary data with linear models, non-stationary data with linear models, and stationary data with non-linear models. Within these coordinates trends, cycles, and seasonal components will be modeled jointly.

The book contains sixteen chapters grouped in three modules. Although there is a more detailed explanation (a road map) of the book in Chapter 1, a succinct description of the modules follows.

- Module I (Chapters 1 to 3) is introductory. It sets the forecaster's final objective and introduces foundational concepts like stochastic process, time series, stationarity, and autocorrelation functions. Although the students are expected to have a basic background in statistics and linear regression, Chapter 2 and the book Appendix A offer a review of the linear regression model and basic statistics concepts respectively.
- Module II (Chapters 4 to 12) introduces the modeling methodology and the construction of optimal forecasts for univariate and multivariate stationary linear

models, e.g. ARMA and VAR models; univariate non-stationary linear models, e.g. stochastic and deterministic trends; and multivariate non-stationary linear models, e.g. cointegrated systems and vector error correction models. *Forecasting Practice* is a set of chapters presenting techniques for in-sample and out-of-sample evaluation of models and their forecasts within the context of real life data sets.

- Module III (Chapters 13 to 16) introduces more complex dependence. It deals with the modeling of the conditional variance, volatility forecast, and relevant empirical applications. Univariate non-linear models for the conditional mean are also introduced at a basic level.

Academic terms are scheduled either in quarters (10 weeks of instruction) or semester (12-14 weeks of instruction). In any case, the core of the textbook—material that must be covered in a serious forecasting course—consists of eight chapters: Chapters 1, 3, 4, 6, 7, 8, 9 and10. The instructor may choose to skip some sections within these chapters depending on the students' background. Once the core is taught, it is up to the instructor which chapters and sections to add to round out the course. Business students tend to prefer Chapters 13, 14, and 15, while economics students are more inclined towards Chapters 5, 11, 12, and 16.

Pedagogy

The student will find common features in each chapter that facilitate the navigation and comprehension of the material.

- Motivation sections introduce each chapter by explaining the context in which new learning will take place and the objectives to accomplish within the chapter. In between chapters the student will find summary sections entitled "A Pause: Where are we and where are we going?" that summarize the main ideas learned up to that point and the new objectives to be accomplished.
- "Real data" sections immediately put into practice the concept, model, test or procedure that has been just explained.
- Website addresses facilitate downloading the most updated data to replicate the "Real data" sections or any other example in the book.
- Short computer programs are provided to simulate the models under study. They can be easily modified to the taste of the instructor and to the needs of the students. These are simple logical programs written in EViews and easily translated into any other computer language.
- Guidance is included to recreate the computer tables and figures in the textbook and commentary in all computer output.
- Key Words are inserted in the main text alerting the student about the introduction of a new concept. These words are collected at the end of the chapter and are briefly defined again in the Glossary.

Two additional pedagogical aids have worked very well in the classroom. Start the lecture with a short reading of some forecast from the daily press and throw open questions to the student audience. There is no shortage of forecasts these days! The instructor may want to complement the lectures with forecasting reports from the business press and forecasting centers. The second pedagogical resource is the introduction of a forecasting game to be carried out over the academic term. The instructor may select the time series to forecast, and the students, working in groups or individually, would produce the best reasoned forecasts given the methods that they are currently learning. Incentives are up to the instructor.

Acknowledgments

Writing a textbook is a communal enterprise because of the many generous contributions to the author, some of which are explicit and some implicit. Many UC-Riverside undergraduate and graduate students over the years have contributed to this manuscript by providing willing or unwilling feedback. Numerous questions, exams, grimaces, smiles, exercises, silences, noises, chatter, all kind of "hints" through which I have kept the pulse of the book have proven to be of value. To all my students, my most sincere thanks. They were a necessary condition for this book to exist.

I do not teach alone, I teach with my team. I have been fortunate to have wonderful teaching assistants in econometrics and forecasting, who conducted discussion sessions and apprised me about what is easy or difficult in the students' minds. My special thanks to Emre Yoldas (Federal Reserve, Board of Governors), a former graduate student of mine and my teaching assistant, who patiently read earlier versions of the textbook, contributed with multiple data sets and exercises, and provided constructive criticism on what worked and what did not. Conversations with my econometrics colleagues at UC-Riverside, Aman Ullah and Tae-Hwy Lee, enlightened me not only about substantive econometrics but also about their classroom experiences, both reflected in my writings.

I could not have written this textbook if I had not had great teachers myself. From my undergraduate years, when for first time I heard the word "time series" from my energetic teachers Antoni Espasa (Universidad Carlos III, Madrid) and Antonio García-Ferrer (Universidad Autónoma, Madrid), to my graduate years when revolutionary words like "ARCH" and "cointegration" were taught by Robert Engle and

Clive Granger (UC-San Diego, 2003 Nobel laureates), my gratitude goes to all these men who taught me with generosity.

A textbook is "distilled knowledge". How to distill it is a personal choice shaped by our own perception of so many research contributions. I would not have enough space to name all the time series and forecasting people who explicitly through conversations, or implicitly through their writings, have helped me to distill. To name a few more contemporary, in addition to the already mentioned researchers, my most appreciative thanks go to Tim Bollerslev (Duke University), Frank Diebold (University of Pennsylvania), Jesús Gonzalo (Universidad Carlos III, Madrid), Jim Hamilton (UC-San Diego), Esther Ruiz (Universidad Carlos III, Madrid), Timo Teräsvirta (Aarhus University), Allan Timmermann (UC-San Diego), Mark Watson (Princeton University), Halbert White (UC-San Diego), among many others.

Multiple drafts were reviewed at different stages by the following reviewers who offered their critical and constructive comments that helped to cut or add material. Their experiences in the classroom were also valuable and are reflected somehow in the final output. My thanks to:

Rokon Bhuiyan, California State University, Fullerton
Jen-Chi Cheng, Wichita State University
Prakash L. Dheeriya, California State University, Dominguez Hills
Martha F. Evans, Florida State University
Dennis Jansen, Texas A&M University
Junsoo Lee, University of Alabama
Haizheng Li, Georgia Institute of Technology
Hassan Mohammadi, Illinois State University
Tanya Molodtsova, Emory University
Lucjan T. Orlowski, Sacred Heart University
Huaming Peng, State University of New York at Albany
Elena Pesavento, Emory University
Ryan Ratcliff, University of San Diego
Aaron Smallwood, University of Texas, Arlington
Allan Timmermann, University of California, San Diego
Wei-Choun Yu, Winona State University

My team at Pearson kept me on schedule. All through this project, I counted on their professional guidance and sound advice. In addition, their cheerful attitude made the completion of this book much easier. My thanks to Adrienne D'Ambrosio (Executive Acquisitions Editor), Sarah Dumouchelle (Editorial Project Manager), Kathryn Dinovo (Senior Production Project Manager), and John Shannon (Senior Project Manager at Jouve).

If my students were a necessary condition for the conception and initial drafts of this textbook, my husband Professor Dimitrios Morikis was the ultimate necessary condition for the delivery. He kept on challenging me to "eat the tail" or something to this effect, and so I did, although I have to admit that at some point I got stomachache! I am so lucky to have such unconditional support. To him, whose commitment and dedication to undergraduate and graduate education is unsurpassed.

Final Thought

Teaching a forecasting course, or for that matter any course, is more than teaching forecasting methods. Appropriately summarized in the word ***ORACLE***, some principles to promote in our lectures are:

1. **O***rdinary common sense by which to develop forecasting intuition.*
2. **R***eal world connection by constructing models that replicate the features in real data.*
3. **A***cademic innovation by appreciating the need to develop new methods.*
4. **C***uriosity as the incentive to learn.*
5. **L***eading by opening the latest research to the undergraduate classroom.*
6. **E***nthusiasm for innovations to come.*

MODULE I

STATISTICS AND TIME SERIES

CHAPTER 1

Introduction and Context

1.1 What Is Forecasting?

Most people have an intuitive notion of what forecasting means. In our daily lives, we refer very frequently to *future* events, we look *forward*, we have the *foresight* to do something, we are able to *foretell,* we *foresee* an event, and we say that something is *forthcoming*. Forecasting, implicit or explicitly, is embedded in all our planning activities from the beginning of our history.

1.1.1 The First Forecaster in History: The Delphi Oracle

The first forecaster recorded in history was in the city of Delphi in ancient Greece (6th century BC until 2nd century AD) known as the **Delphi Oracle**[1] to which pilgrims from all over the world came to seek advice from the oracle in the temple of Apollo. This is a brief description of how this forecaster worked and one of its most famous predictions.

The pilgrims submitted questions to the oracle through emissaries, and every month, Pythia, the priestess of the god Apollo, spoke the prophecies (in our jargon, conveyed forecasts). According to history, Pythia sat on a tripod chewing bay leaves, drinking water from the Kassotis spring, and inhaling the fumes that sent her into a trance. Then she spoke the forecast, which purposely was ambiguous and subject to interpretation because the Gods cannot be wrong! (Perhaps there is some lesson here for professional forecasters.)

A famous oracle came around 480 BC during the Persian wars when the Athenians were fighting the Persians, who had an enormous float of wooden boats and a large army of men. Emissaries were sent to the Oracle of Delphi to solicit a prediction on the outcome of the war. The Oracle spoke these words "Only wooden walls will save Athens." Obviously, this forecast needed interpretation. Thank god for the wisdom of Themistocles, who understood the prediction: If the Athenians could construct flexible

[1]Hellenic Tourism Organization.

small fast boats that fit the geographical configuration of the gulf of Athens, they would outmaneuver Persia's large and slow boats and win the war.

This is an example of a historical *forecast,* which required some skills to be understood. Not much has changed in modern times. We do not have a physical place to go to listen to the oracle, but we have an army of professional forecasters in the public and private sectors whose job is to foretell the future.

1.1.2 Examples of Modern Forecasts

All socioeconomic issues of the day require some level of prediction. Open the newspaper and just read some headlines: the exit strategy of the Federal Reserve, health care reform, financial regulation, systemic risk, network traffic, the fear of inflation, job creation, and so on. The following are some examples of how the daily business press presents forecasting. As you read them, think about three questions:

1. What is the predicted event?
2. What is the magnitude of the predicted event?
3. What is the future date of the predicted event?

- *On the bond and stock markets:* On March 22, 2010, a *Fortune* magazine journalist asked Wilbur Ross, an American investor, how he saw 2010. Ross answered that the year would be volatile and that some stocks would perform well despite the environment.
- *In U.S. industrial production:* On March 16, 2010, *The New York Times* published an article claiming that production would rise in 2010 citing, among others, John Ryding, chief economist for RDQ Economics, who forecast 7% growth in industrial production in 2010 as a consequence of improvements in the labor market and more spending on capital goods in foreign countries.
- *On network traffic:* On February 27, 2010, *The Economist* published a special report on managing information stating that, according to *Cisco*, annual Internet traffic by 2013 would reach 667 exabytes (one exactabyte equals one billion gigabites).
- *On U.S. bank bailouts:* On March 22, 2010, *Fortune* magazine published an article on the state of bank bailouts, citing a prediction by the U.S. Treasury Department that the cost of the Troubled Asset Relief Program (TARP) to taxpayers would eventually be $117 billion (adjusted for inflation).
- *On U.S. real estate:* On April 2010, *Kiplinger's* magazine ran an article on the state of the rental real estate market in which experts expected that the national vacancy rate would be 7.8% by the end of 2010, would rapidly recover beginning in 2011, and would experience strong rent growth from 2011 to 2015.
- *On India's economic growth:* *The Economist* published a report on India on March 2010 stating that the Indian economy would grow by 7.2% by the end of the 2010 fiscal year (March 31) with the expectation of 9% growth rate in the medium term.
- *On small business:* On March 15, 2010, *The Wall Street Journal* published predictions by Raj Date who expected a shortfall of $250 to $500 billion in lending to small business when the economy begins to recover.

What we gather from these examples is that some predictions are detailed and some are sketchy concerning either the magnitude of the future event or its date of occurrence. Examples 2, 3, 5, and 6 are very precise on the magnitude and timing of the prediction: 7% growth in industrial production in 2010; 667 exabytes by 2013; 7.8% vacancy rate by year-end 2010; and 7.2% growth in the Indian economy by March 31, 2010. Examples 1, 4, and 7 are fuzzier predictions: 2010 would be a volatile year (how much volatility?), TARP eventually (when?) would cost taxpayers $117 billion, and lending shortfall for small business would be as much as $250 billion to $500 billion as the economy recovered (when?). Furthermore, a common feature to these examples is that we, the readers, do not have any information about how certain or uncertain the forecaster is about the predictions. Only when time passes can we judge who was right and who was wrong.

These introductory examples show the relevant features to answer the question, "What is forecasting?"

1.1.3 Definition of Forecasting

We define **forecasting** as the *science* and the *art* to predict a *future* event with some degree of *accuracy*.

1.1.3.1 Why Is Forecasting a Science?

You may be wondering how it is possible to state a precise statement such as "we expect 7% growth in U.S. industrial production in 2010." To produce such statements, we need a methodological approach to summarize and analyze the information that is available. Statistical and mathematical methods are very useful in discovering time patterns in historical data. We will construct models that synthesize the past and will explain how today is related to yesterday, yesterday to the day before yesterday, and so on. This time dependence is the key to making statements about the future. The mastery of these statistical methods will enable us to construct forecasts that have a logical consistency.

1.1.3.2 Why Is Forecasting an Art?

Statistical methods have limitations. They depend on a set of assumptions, which may or may not be satisfied by the available data. Models, by construction, are limited representations of the economic and business environments. In addition, there is also a technological limitation given by the frontier of statistical and mathematical research. Professional forecasters also accumulate soft human capital, that is, knowledge and experiences, which we do not know yet how to quantify or formalize but nevertheless are useful in modifying the forecast provided by a statistical model. In this sense, the forecaster needs judgment and when exercising it, forecasting becomes an art.

1.1.3.3 Why Do We Care About the Future?

This seems to be obvious. The past is known to a certain extent, and although statistical models can also be used for backcasting or backtesting, forecasting eventually is always an activity that involves an assessment of future events.

1.1.3.4 Why Does Accuracy Matter?

Professional forecasters succeed by making accurate forecasts. They need to establish a performance record for their activities to be relevant and useful. Broadly speaking, we should not expect a forecast to be exactly accurate in a mathematical sense, that is, hitting the exact future value of the variable of the interest, but we should expect the forecast to be statistically sound and, when possible, also to offer a measure of the uncertainty of the predictions.

1.1.4 Two Types of Forecasts

Customarily, we distinguish between event forecast and time series forecast, although both can be related.

An **event forecast** refers to the future occurrence of an outcome and/or the timing of such an occurrence. For instance, read the following questions and provide your best event forecast:

- Will the Federal Reserve raise interest rates at its next board meeting?
- When will the recession end?
- When will the stock market recover?
- Will the euro keep appreciating?

Some questions will require just "yes" or "no" answers, and some others will require a future date or a timeline.

The term **time series forecast** refers to the use of time series information in the prediction of the variable of interest. In a time series data set, the information is arranged according to time. For instance, the annual time series of U.S. GDP is the dollar amount of domestic production in United States from 1955 to 2009. For each year, we attach a production dollar amount, and these amounts are reported chronologically starting in 1995 and ending in 2009. Time series data will be the necessary input to construct statistical models and eventually build a time series forecast, which is an estimate of the future value of the variable of interest at a specific date, jointly with a measure of uncertainty. In light of this discussion, it is clear that we can produce an event forecast based on a time series forecast.

1.2 Who Are the Users of Forecasts?

Planning and preparing for the future requires some forecasting because today's decisions are functions of what we can foresee today. Broadly speaking, let us think about the economy as a collection of agents—firms, consumers/investors, and government—engaging in productive activities. Why should they be interested in forecasting?

1.2.1 Firms

Although the activities of firms depend on industry specifics, some are common to all of them: capacity investments and capital allocation (size and units), operations planning (personnel, production, inventory, sales, innovation), budgeting (costs and revenues), and marketing (pricing, clients, advertisement). In each of these areas, decisions that depend on the forecasting of the relevant variables must be made. For instance, if a firm is contemplating a business expansion or planning to launch a new product, it must have forecasts of future revenues, new sales, potential new markets, and so forth. Financial firms such as banks and investment companies are in the business of allocating financial capital and managing risk, but to do so, they need forecasts of asset prices (stocks, bonds, exchange rates, swaps, etc.) and of their volatility not only in the domestic market but also in international markets. Every industry has idiosyncratic features and requests forecasts that differ from those of the other industries. You may want to consider different sectors of the economy—energy, pharmaceuticals, technology, financials, information technology, natural commodities, transportation, services—and consider what forecasts would be most relevant to the firms in that industry.

1.2.2 Consumers and Investors

Households play two roles in the economy: They are consumers providing demand for the products and services produced by firms, and they are investors providing savings (in bank deposits, saving accounts, stock and bond purchases, and so on) to the firms to engage in production. In both roles, household decisions are informed by the forecasts of the relevant economic variables. For instance, household revenues depend on the business cycle in the economy, the state of labor markets, and the state of capital markets. For most households, a large proportion of revenues come from labor income, so early decisions about investment in education rely on the prospects of employment. As the life cycle unfolds, capital income becomes important, and household decisions about capital investments rely on forecasts of interest rates, earnings, dividends, and so forth. As consumers and investors, households are concerned about the forecasts of inflation because high inflation will be beneficial if the household is a net borrower or detrimental if the household is a net lender.

1.2.3 Government

Government is a large producer and consumer of forecasts. Many federal and state agencies have armies of professional forecasters concerned about domestic and international macroeconomic variables such as gross domestic product, consumption, investment, exports, imports, employment, prices, interest rates, and exchange rates. These forecasts are key to making major decisions in fiscal and monetary policies. For instance, every month, all economic agents in the U.S. economy wait with anticipation for the statement of the Federal Reserve (Fed) regarding changes in the federal fund rate and guidance on the state of the economy. For all economic agents, this statement is a reading in expectations and is the closest account in modern times to the Oracle of Delphi! This is an excerpt from the Federal Open Market Committee meeting on March 16, 2010:

> Although the pace of economic recovery is likely to be moderate for a time, the Committee anticipates a gradual return to higher levels of resource utilization in a context of price stability. . . . With substantial resource slack continuing to restrain cost pressures and longer-term inflation expectations stable, inflation is likely to be subdued for some time . . . .The Committee will continue to monitor the economic outlook and financial developments and will employ its policy tools as necessary to promote

> economic recovery and price stability . . . . The Committee will continue to monitor the economic outlook and financial developments and will employ its policy tools as necessary to promote economic recovery and price stability. (*Source:* http://www.federalreserve.gov/newsevents/press/monetary/20100316a.htm)

Embedded in this statement are several forecasts: a prediction of resource utilization, which is expected to grow; a prediction of price inflation, which is expected to be moderate; and a prediction of GDP growth, which is expected to be slow. Of course, the timing is an open question, but very likely, the professional forecasters at the Fed produced several forecasts for the short and long terms.

1.3 Becoming Familiar with Economic Time Series: Features of a Time Series

Let us introduce the basic object of analysis in this book: *a time series.* A time series is a sequence of numerical values *ordered* according to time. See the table included in Figure 1.1, which is a time series of the U.S. population from 1790 to 2000 at 10-year intervals.

For each year from 1790 to 2000, we read the population of the United States. For instance, in 1990, the number of people was 248.7 million. A time series plot is a graphical representation of the time series. It always has the same structure: in the horizontal axis, we plot time, and in the vertical axis, we plot the value of the variable. A time

FIGURE 1.1 Population of the United States at 10-Year Intervals (1790–2000)

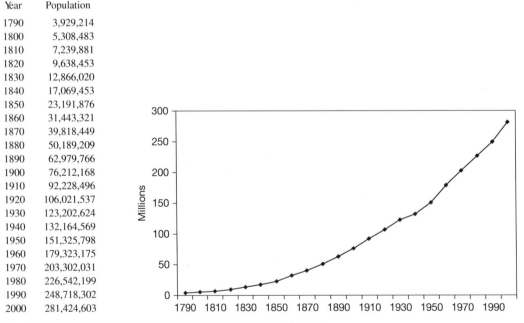

Year	Population
1790	3,929,214
1800	5,308,483
1810	7,239,881
1820	9,638,453
1830	12,866,020
1840	17,069,453
1850	23,191,876
1860	31,443,321
1870	39,818,449
1880	50,189,209
1890	62,979,766
1900	76,212,168
1910	92,228,496
1920	106,021,537
1930	123,202,624
1940	132,164,569
1950	151,325,798
1960	179,323,175
1970	203,302,031
1980	226,542,199
1990	248,718,302
2000	281,424,603

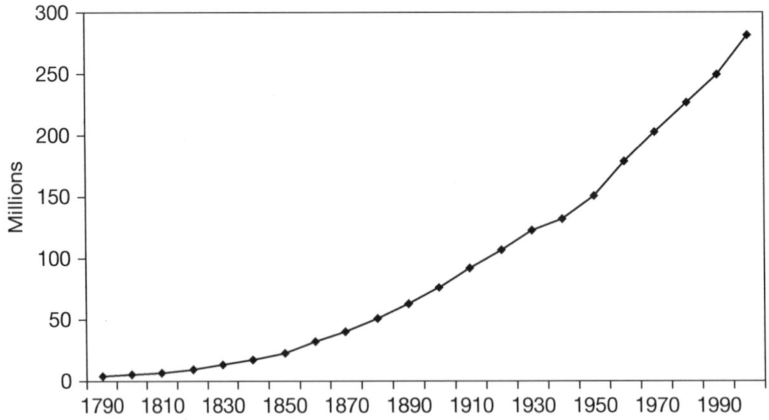

Source: http://www.census.gov/compendia/statab/cats/population.html

series data point is a pair (t, y_t). For instance, for $t = 1990$, the U.S. population was about 248.7 million, and we write $y_{1990} = 248.7$. It is important to visualize time series, particularly business and economic time series, because these are key elements in this book. Visual skills help to foster intuition about the data and to spot features that will guide us in the search for a model. Do not underestimate the value of a graph!

Some general features in economic time series can be classified within three broad categories: **trends, cycles, and seasonality**. Time series can exhibit one or several of these features. For instance, the time series of U.S. GDP (http://research.stlouisfed.org/fred2/) exhibits a general upward trend, but there are also deviations around this trend. Sometimes the time series goes above the trend (indicating expansions) and sometimes below (suggesting recessions) forming a cycle around the trend.

1.3.1 Trends

When a time series evolves slowly and smoothly over time, we say that it shows a *trend*, which is a long-run feature of the data. We should have a great deal of data before identifying any trend. The graph in Figure 1.1 showed a clear upward trend in the U.S. population for the last two centuries. In Figure 1.2, the graph shows an upward trend in U.S. productivity—defined as output per hour worked—and in the output time series. The number of hours worked remained fairly stable for the 10-year period 1997:Q1 to 2007:Q1. As we visualize the time series plots, it is necessary to understand the measurement units of the variables of interest. In Figure 1.2, all variables are reported as indexes. Dealing with an index, we always need the base year to interpret the plot. The base year is the year for which the value of the index is equal to 100. The base year for the series in Figure 1.2 is the first quarter of 1992. Now let us choose any number in the plot, say the output index is 120 in 1997:Q1. Given that the base is in 1992:Q1, the index says that there has been a 20% increase in output from 1992 to 1997 (Q1).

FIGURE 1.2 Quarterly Productivity, Output, and Hours (Non-Farm Business Sector)

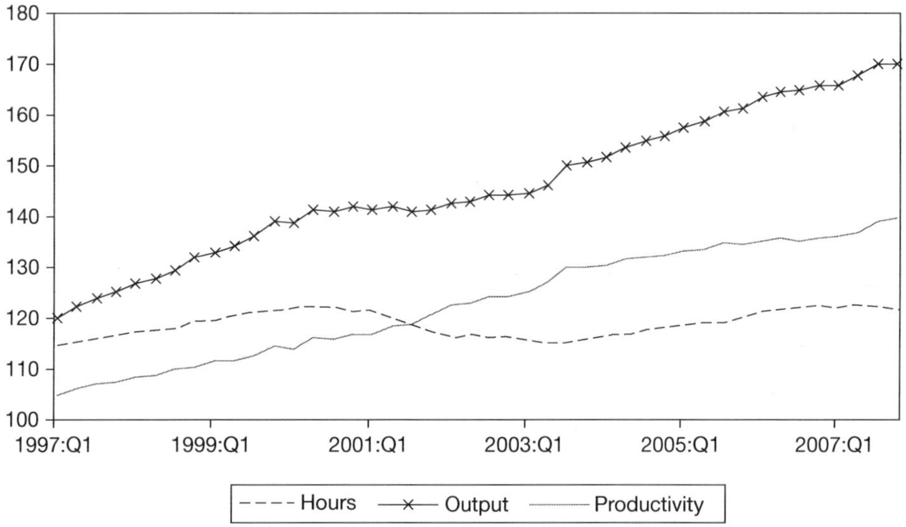

Source: Bureau of Labor Statistics. Productivity is output per hour. Index, 1st quarter 1992=100.

FIGURE 1.3
Annual Hours Worked in the OECD Countries, 1979–2006

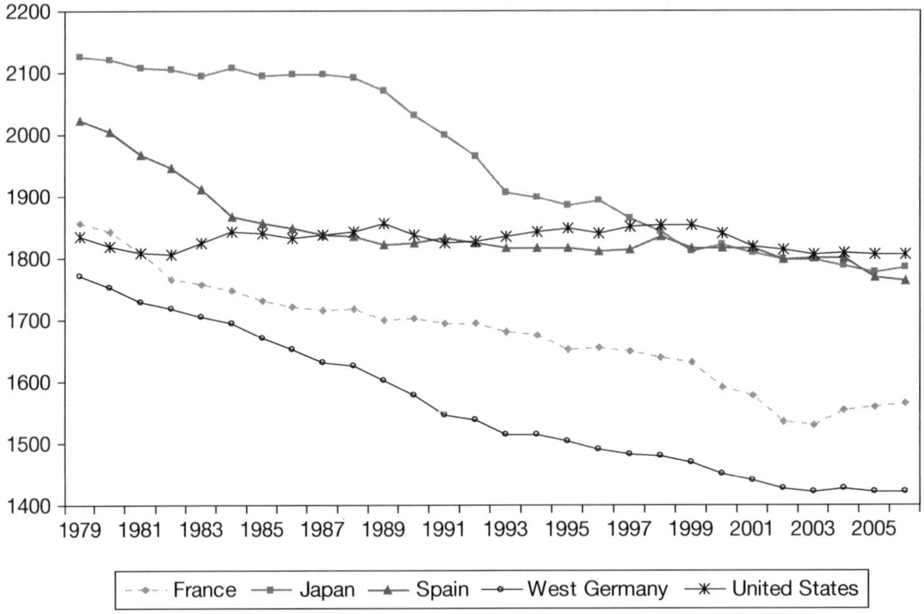

Source: OECD (2016), Hours worked (indicator). https://data.oecd.org/emp/hours-worked.htm (Accessed on 24 February 2016).

See Figure 1.3 for an example of a downward trend describing the annual hours worked in some Organization for Economic Cooperation and Development (OECD) countries. There is a downward trend in the number of annual hours worked in Japan, Germany, France, and to a lesser extent in Spain. In contrast, hours worked in the United States remained quite stable from 1979–2006. The unit for all variables in Figure 1.3 is the number of hours per year.

1.3.2 Cycles

When a time series exhibits periodic fluctuations, we say that it has a *cycle*. The cycle may be seasonal or nonseasonal. In Figure 1.4, the time series for unemployed persons 1988–2008 exhibits a nonseasonal cycle. Observe that unemployment rises during recessions and drops during expansions creating a cycle, so that every X number of years, we observe similar peaks and troughs. The units of unemployment are millions of unemployed people in a month. Figure 1.5 graphs a nonseasonal cycle in the time series for the number of people in poverty and the poverty rate. These two measures tend to rise in recessions and fall or stabilize during expansions. Both series are pictured within the same graph but have different units. The time series for number in poverty is measured in millions of people per year, and the time series for the poverty rate is measured in percentage as the ratio of the number of people in poverty to the number of people in the United States.

FIGURE 1.4 Unemployed Persons (Seasonally Adjusted), Monthly Data 1988–2008

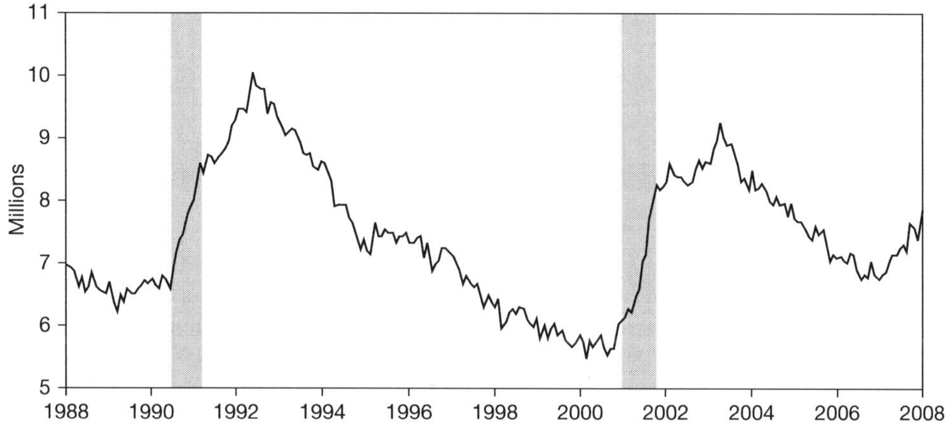

Note: Shaded areas represent recessions.

Source: St. Louis Federal Reserve Bank. FRED.

1.3.3 Seasonality

A cycle is *seasonal* when specific fluctuations occur within the calendar year, for instance activities that peak in summer months (or in specific quarters, days, hours, etc.) . The time

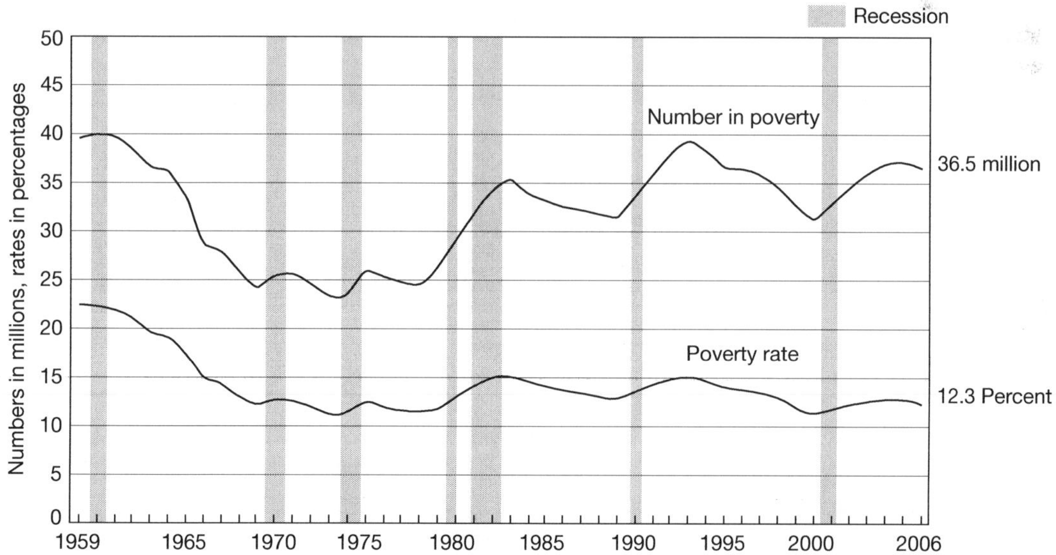

Note: The date points are placed at the midpoints of the respective years.

Source: U.S. Census Bureau, Current Population Survey, 1960 to 2007 Annual Social and Economic Supplements.

FIGURE 1.5 Number of People in Poverty and Poverty Rate, Yearly Data 1959–2006

FIGURE 1.6 Revenue Passenger Emplanements, Monthly Data 2000–2008

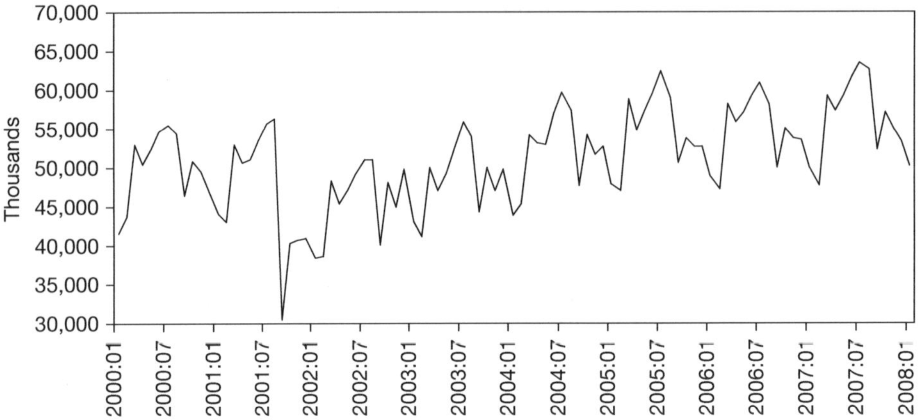

Note: Total number of passengers boarding an aircraft.

Source: Bureau of Transportation Statistics.

series for revenue passenger enplanements (the total number of passengers boarding an aircraft) in Figure 1.6 exhibits a strong seasonal cycle with pronounced peaks in the summer months of July and August and dips in the winter months of January and February. The measurement unit is 1,000 passengers traveling by plane in a month.

Three features, trend, cycle, and seasonal cycle, may come together in a time series. For instance, in Figure 1.7, the time series for new home sales exhibits a seasonal cycle and a trend. Home sales rise during the spring months (Q2) and fall during the winter

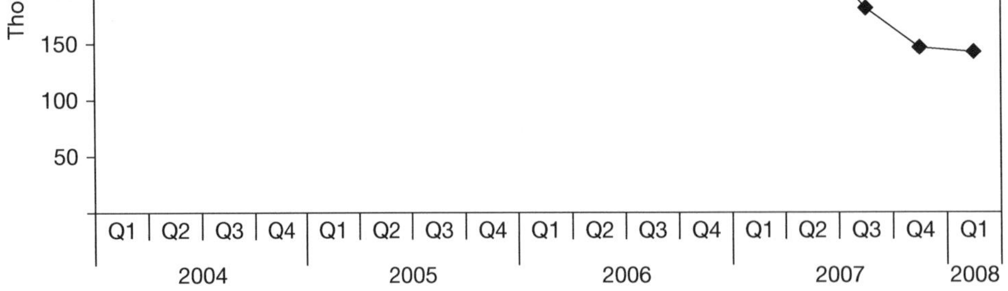

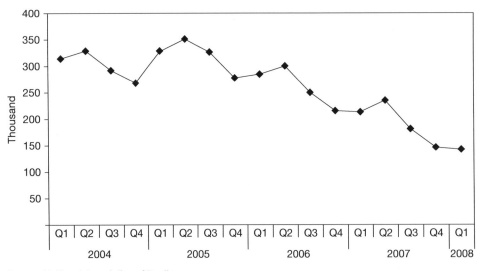

Source: National Association of Realtors.

FIGURE 1.7 New Home Sales in the United States, Quarterly Data 2004–2008

months (Q4). The seasonal cycle is intertwined with an unambiguous downward trend. In 2004, sales per quarter were about 300,000 houses and in 2008 about 150,000.

For pedagogical reasons, we analyze cycles (seasonal and nonseasonal) and trends separately, but eventually the forecaster's objective is to produce a forecast for a given time series for which cycles and trends are embedded within each other.

1.4 Basic Notation and the Objective of the Forecaster

To start talking the language of a professional forecaster, we need to introduce some preliminary jargon and some notation.

1.4.1 Basic Notation

The following table summarizes the forecaster's basic jargon:

Description	**Technical name**	**Notation**
Object to analyze:	Time series	$\{y_t\}$
Value at present time *t*:	Known value of the series	y_t
Future at time *t+h*:	Random variable	Y_{t+h}
Value at future time *t+h*:	Unknown value of the random variable	y_{t+h}
Collection of information:	Univariate information set Multivariate information set	$I_t = \{y_1, y_2, \ldots, y_t\}$ $I_t = \{y_1, y_2, \ldots, y_t, x_1, x_2, \ldots, x_t\}$
Final objective:	Forecast 1-step ahead *h*-step ahead	 $f_{t,1}$ $f_{t,h}$
Uncertainty:	Forecast error	$e_{t,h} = y_{t+h} - f_{t,h}$

The data to analyze are a *time series* that is a collection of realizations ordered according to time $\{y_t\} = \{y_1, y_2 \ldots y_t \ldots\}$. When we analyze just one time series, we say that the analysis is *univariate,* and when we analyze several time series *jointly*, for instance two time series $\{y_t\} = \{y_1, y_2 \ldots y_t \ldots\}$ and $\{x_t\} = \{x_1, x_2 \ldots x_t \ldots\}$, the analysis is called *multivariate.*

We denote the *present time* by *t*, and y_t is the known value of the time series at time *t*. The *future* time is denoted by $t + h$ with *h* being the **forecast horizon** or the step. The future is completely unknown and is represented by a random variable Y_{t+h} with many possible realizations or values. As with any random variable, we characterize Y_{t+h} by specifying its (conditional) probability density function. A future *unknown* value of this random variable is denoted by y_{t+h}. The step *h* could be one minute, day, month, or so on, depending on the frequency of the time series. For instance, if the time series is monthly interest rates and $h = 2$, we are interested in forecasting the 2-month-ahead interest rates. The h-step-ahead forecast $f_{t,h}$ is based on an **information set**, denoted by I_t, meaning the history or information known to us to the present time t. The information set can be *univariate* if it contains only the history of one time series $I_t = \{y_0, y_1, y_2, \ldots y_t\}$ or *multivariate* if it contains the information of several time series $I_t = \{y_0, y_1, \ldots y_t; x_0, x_1, \ldots x_t; \ldots\}$.

When time passes and we are able to observe the realized value y_{t+h}, we can measure how accurate the forecast was. The h-step **forecast error** is the difference between the actual realized value and the forecast, that is, $e_{t,h} = y_{t+h} - f_{t,h}$.

1.4.2 The Forecaster's Objective

At the present time t, we wish to forecast Y_{t+h}. The information set is all past history of the series $I_t = \{y_0, y_1, y_2, \ldots\ldots y_t\}$. Based on this information (we say "conditional on the information set"), we will produce three types of forecast:

1. **Point forecast** $f_{t,h}$. This is just a single value. For instance, we may say the 2-month-ahead forecast (h =2) for the short-term interest rate will be 3%.
2. **Interval forecast.** This is a range of values. We could construct intervals such as $(f_{t,h} - k\sigma, f_{t,h} + k\sigma)$ where σ is the (conditional) standard deviation of the random variable Y_{t+h}, and k is a constant related to the probability (or confidence) attached to the interval, which in turn depends on the probability density function of Y_{t+h}. For instance, we may say that in two months, the short-term interest rate will be between 2% and 4% with a 70% confidence.
3. **Density forecast.** This is a probability density function. We could construct the (conditional) probability density function of Y_{t+h}, and by doing that, we will know in a probabilistic sense all future realizations of interest rates. For instance, we may say that in 2 months, the probability for the short-term interest rate to be below 5% is 0.85; that is, $P(Y_{t+h} \leq 5\%) = 85\%$.

See Figure 1.8 for the graphic description of the univariate forecasting problem.

In Figure 1.8, the known information runs up to time t. Based on the information set, we would like to forecast Y_{t+h} at time t+h. At this future time, we picture the (conditional)

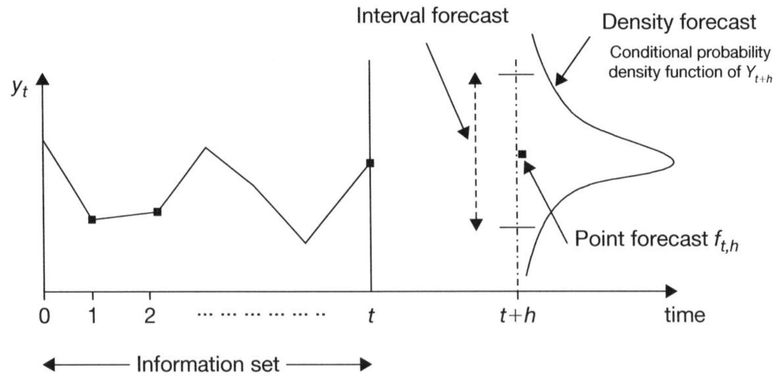

FIGURE 1.8
The Forecasting Problem

probability density function of Y_{t+h} to acknowledge that many values of this random variable are possible; some will be more likely than others. The forecast $f_{t,h}$, constructed at the present time t, is one of these values. In Figure 1.8, we chose the central value of the random variable as a point forecast, and the interval centered on the point forecast as the interval forecast. The final objective in this textbook is to construct three types of forecasts—point, interval, and density—based on the analysis of past information.

The multivariate forecasting problem is more complex but conceptually is defined in similar terms to those in the univariate forecasting. Now the time series data set contains more than one time series, say $\{y_t\},\{x_t\},\{z_t\}$. For instance, we may be interested in forecasting jointly interest rates, output, and money demand. Economic models postulate that output depends on money demand and interest rates; thus, a forecast of output benefits greatly from the information on interest rates and money demand. The information set contains the histories of all time series considered, $I_t = \{y_1 \ldots y_t, x_1 \ldots x_t, z_1 \ldots z_t\}$, and the final objective is to produce the h-step-ahead forecast for the three series $f^y_{t,h}, f^x_{t,h}, f^z_{t,h}$ corresponding to the future values y_{t+h}, x_{t+h}, z_{t+h}, respectively.

1.5 A Road Map for This Forecasting Book

This book is concerned with model-based forecasting. We call our models *time series models* meaning that, by analyzing the statistical properties of time series data sets, we can discover the time dependence in the data, and we will express it by means of a mathematical model. If we understand *dependence,* that is, how the present relates to the past, we will be able to project our information from the present to the future.

We proceed to describe broadly the organization of this book. A distinctive feature is that after the introduction of a new concept and/or a new model, an empirical illustration follows. Practical implementation with real data and with simulated data is paramount to the understanding of the most theoretical ideas. We strongly recommend replicating every empirical application because it will help to master these forecasting methods.

The book contains 16 chapters grouped in three large modules. Module I, Chapters 1 to 3, introduces the field of forecasting by providing context and setting the forecaster's final objective. Regression analysis is a prerequisite for model-based forecasting, so we offer a brief review of regression techniques. Chapter 3 presents foundational time series concepts, paying special attention to the concept of stationarity. It also provides a fundamental tool of analysis, the autocorrelation functions.

Module II, Chapters 4 to 12, focuses on forecasting with *linear* time series models introduced across two dimensions: univariate versus multivariate and stationary versus nonstationary. Traditionally, the teaching of forecasting starts with the introduction of trends followed up by the introduction of cycles, which are understood as whatever is left in the series after dealing with the trend. In this book, the pedagogical division is *stationary versus nonstationary* processes. We start by introducing *univariate stationary linear* time series models, which are very well suited to model (nonseasonal and seasonal) cycles in the data. This set of models is characterized as autoregressive and moving average models (Chapters 6 and 7). These models constitute the workhorse of **time series**

forecasting because they are benchmarks against more complex models should be measured. Chapter 11 introduces *multivariate* versions: vector autoregression. Chapters 10 and 12 introduce *nonstationary linear* models, univariate and multivariate, respectively. These models capture trends in the data. We introduce the analysis of trends after the analysis of cycles because we show that a stochastic trend is a limiting case of autoregressive models.

Our final objective is to construct a forecast based on the best model(s) that we can find in the data. To this end, the forecaster faces two important tasks. A priori, before the search for the model starts, the forecaster needs a set of basic tools: a loss function, which drives the optimal forecast; the information set; and the forecast horizon. These are introduced in Chapter 4. A posteriori, once the model(s) have been selected, the forecaster needs to evaluate them. In-sample evaluation (Chapter 8) assesses the logical consistency of the model with the data, and out-of-sample evaluation (Chapter 9) measures the performance of the model-based forecast. Both Chapters 8 and 9 provide forecasting practice based on real time series data.

Chapter 5 offers a link between macro and microeconomic theories and the time series models that we propose. Though understanding this link is not necessary for the construction of a sound forecast, it provides a rich background on how the behavior of consumers, producers, investors, and institutions generates time dependence in the data.

Module III, Chapters 13 to 16, contains advanced material. We introduce more complex dependence across two dimensions. The first extension deals with dynamics of *volatility*. All models in Module II seek to specify the dynamics of the conditional mean of the process. In Module III, Chapters 13 and 14, we aim to specify the dynamics of the conditional variance. In Chapter 15, we provide several financial applications for which forecasting volatility is crucial. The second extension deals with *nonlinear dependence* in the conditional mean (Chapter 16). Nonlinear features of time series, such as different dynamics in economic expansions or recessions or different asset dynamics in a bull or in a bear market, require the introduction of more sophisticated models, which are at the frontier of forecasting research.

Between chapters, you will find short sections, "A pause: Where are we and where are we going?" that serve as a compass to navigate the book. We summarize our learning as we go along and set up the next objective. In this way, we position ourselves in the forecasting map so that we do not lose our north.

1.6 Resources

Websites. Because this textbook offers a hands-on approach, the first step to it is to locate time series data to which to apply the techniques that you will be learning. Fortunately, data are at our fingertips with so many websites offering free access. The following is a list of organizations with plenty of on-line time series information. Our advice is to go each website and become familiar with its content:

http://www.bloomberg.com (daily market data and news)
http://www.bea.gov/ (U.S. Bureau of Economic Analysis)

http://www.bls.gov/ (U.S. Bureau of Labor Statistics)
http://www.census.gov/ (U.S. Census Bureau)
http://sdw.ecb.europa.eu (European Central Bank's data warehouse)
http://www.economagic.com (historical data on economic and financial time series)
http://www.ers.usda.gov/ (U.S. Department of Agriculture Economic Research Service)
http://www.federalreserve.gov/releases/ (Federal Reserve, Board of Governors Database)
http://finance.yahoo.com (current and historical financial data)
http://www.imf.org/external/data.htm (International Monetary Fund—IMF—data)
http://www.freddiemac.com/news/finance/ (data and reports on the housing market)
http://mba.tuck.dartmouth.edu/pages/faculty/ken.french/data_library.html (Kenneth French's Equity Data Library)
http://www.oecd.org/statsportal (OECD Statistics Portal)
http://research.stlouisfed.org/fred2/ (St. Louis Federal Reserve Bank, Economic Data)
http://uclaforecast.com (UCLA Forecasting Center)
http://www.worldbank.org/ (World Bank)
http://epp.eurostat.ec.europa.eu/portal/page/portal/eurostat/home/ (statistical database of the European Commission)
http://online.thomsonreuters.com/datastream/ (Thomson Reuters financial statistical database)
http://www.eia.doe.gov/ (U.S. Energy Information Administration, independent statistics and analysis)

Daily press and specialized magazines. Reading the daily press and specialized magazines is important to grasp how predictions are reported. When you read, take a critical approach to examine the information provided. Ask yourself what information is missing and how you can improve upon the publication. The following is a nonexhaustive list of periodicals:

The Wall Street Journal
Financial Times
The Economist
The New York Times
BusinessWeek (*Bloomsberg Businessweek* after 2009)
Fortune
Barron's
Money
Forbes

Academic journals. Forecasting is an active field of academic research. Methodological advances are published first in academic journals. Although the level of exposition in these outlets is highly technical, you may want to browse some issues and read the introduction and the economic and business applications of some articles. You will be surprised how much you will understand once you have studied the material in this textbook. The following is a list of specialized academic journals:

International Journal of Forecasting
Journal of Forecasting
Journal of Time Series Analysis
Journal of Business & Economic Statistics
Journal of Applied Econometrics
Journal of Econometrics
Journal of Financial Econometrics
Review of Economics and Statistics

Software packages. Because the goal of this book is learning by doing, you will need to be proficient in using at least one software package. In the following chapters, you will be exposed to many exercises with real and simulated data that are solved with EViews. This package is very well suited for time series modeling and forecasting, is user friendly, and for most of the chapters, provides "click-and-see" for immediate results. However, the methods in this book can be implemented with any other software. Other great packages for time series analysis are on the market, but they will require some programming skills on your part. The following list contains the most popular software for quantitative analysis:

EViews
GAUSS
Matlab
R
SAS
S-Plus
Stata

KEY WORDS

Delphi Oracle p. 1
density forecast p. 12
event forecast p. 4
forecast error p. 12
forecast horizon p. 11
forecasting p. 3
information set p. 12
interval forecast p. 12
point forecast p. 12
time series forecast p. 4
trends, cycles, and seasonality p. 7

EXERCISES

The following exercises provide a nonexhaustive collection of time series describing some aspects of the U.S. economy. The series are classified within three large categories: the *real economy* that deals with the generation of income and determination of prices; the *financial economy* that deals with financial prices such as interest rates, stock indexes, exchange rates; and the *social economy* that deals with social aspects of the U.S. population. For each time series, please answer the following fundamental questions:

- Definition of the time series: *What is it measured?*
- Measurement units (special attention should be paid to indexes): *How is it measured*?
- Frequency of the series: *What is the periodicity (i.e., daily, monthly)?*
- Features of the series (trends, nonseasonal cycle, seasonal cycle): *What is the immediate message*?

Other specific questions are posed after each time series plot, which will be helpful for comprehension. Micro- and macroeconomic theories as well as U.S. economic history may provide context to these time series.

Time Series of the U.S. Real Economy

FIGURE E.1 Median Household Income (2006 Dollars) by Race, Yearly Data 1967–2006

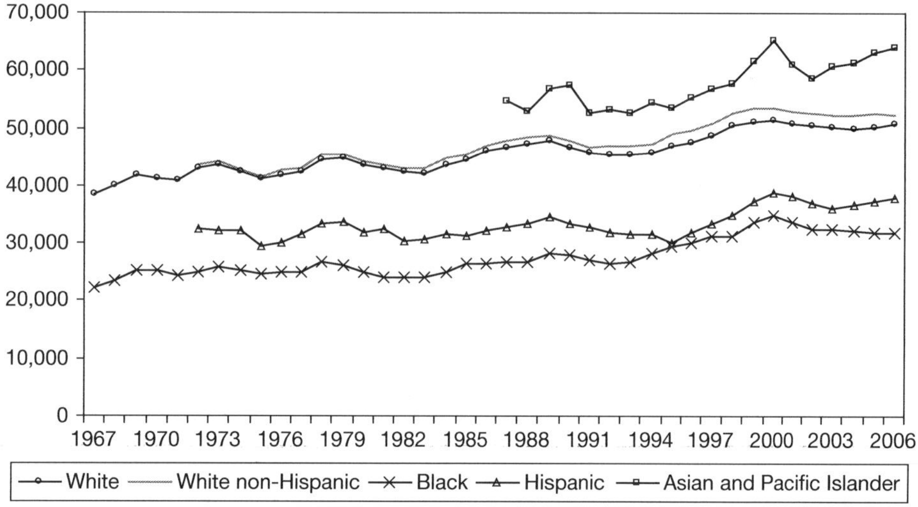

Source: U.S. Census Bureau, Current Population Survey.

a. What does "median income" mean?
b. What is the definition of "household" according to the Census Bureau?
c. What is the difference between "real dollars" and "nominal dollars"?
d. What may explain the upward trend for most groups?

FIGURE E.2
Saving Rate (%), Monthly Data 1988/01–2008/02

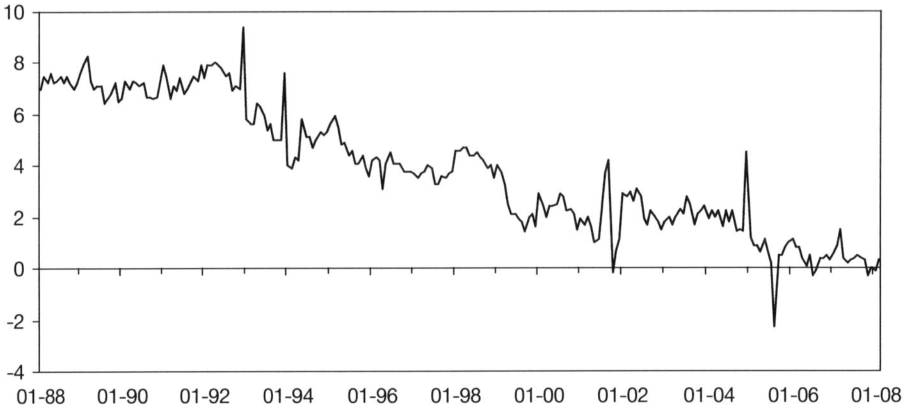

Source: St. Louis Federal Reserve Bank. FRED.

a. What is the definition of "saving rate"?
b. What does *negative saving rate* mean, and when does it occur?
c. What is contributing to the downward trend?

FIGURE E.3
Inflation Rate (12-Month Percentage Change), Monthly Data 1998/01–2008/03

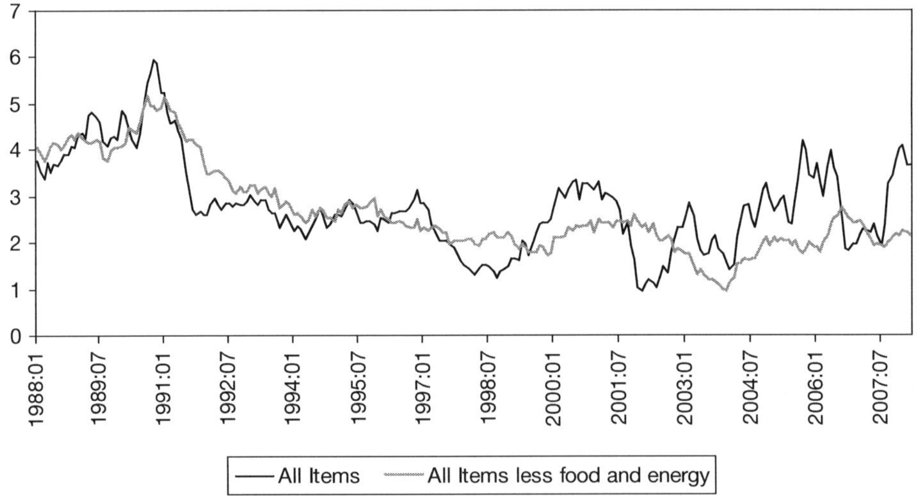

Source: St. Louis Federal Reserve Bank. FRED.

a. What is the definition of *inflation rate*?
b. How would you compute the 12-month percentage change?
c. What is the main difference between the two time series of the inflation rate?
d. What is the purpose of excluding the prices of food and energy?
e. How does the U.S. inflation rate compare to that of other countries?

FIGURE E.4 Home Price Index (12-Month Percentage Change), Monthly Data 1988–2008/02

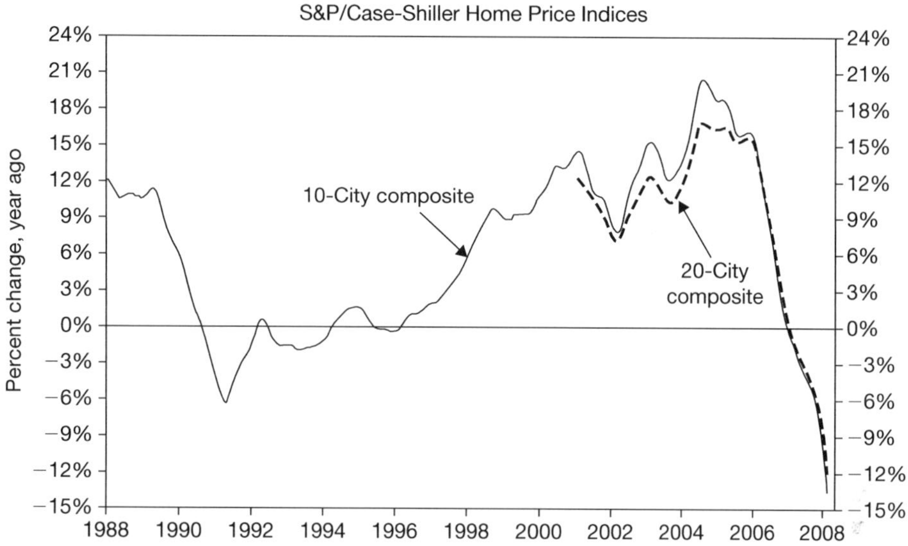

Source: Standard and Poor's and Fiserv.

a. What does the Case-Shiller Index measure?
b. Was there "a housing market bubble" or just an economic cycle from 1996 to 2006?
c. What was going on in the U.S. economy from 1996 to 2006?

Time Series of the U.S. Financial Economy

FIGURE E.5 Dow Jones Industrials Index, Monthly Data 1988/01–2008/04

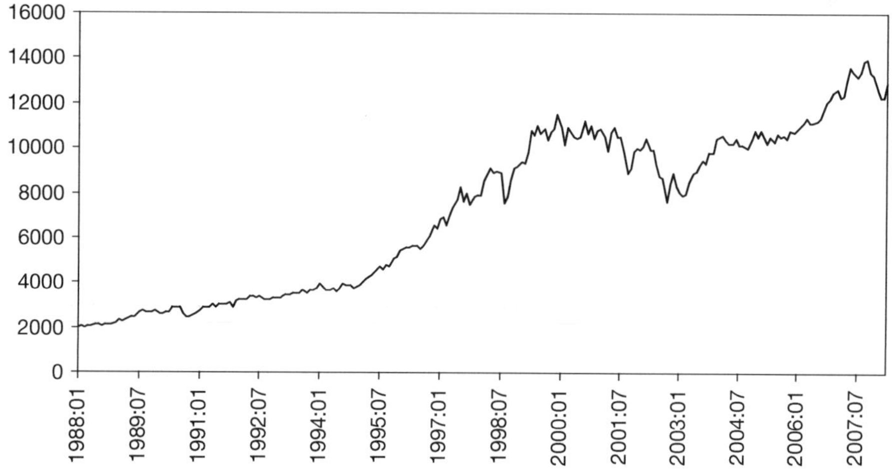

Source: Yahoo Finance.

a. What does this index measure?
b. What is the total return over this 20-year period?
c. Why is there a trend?
d. Do similar indexes for other countries exhibit a corresponding trend?

FIGURE E.6 Exchange Rate U.S.$/Euro, Monthly 1999/01–2008/03

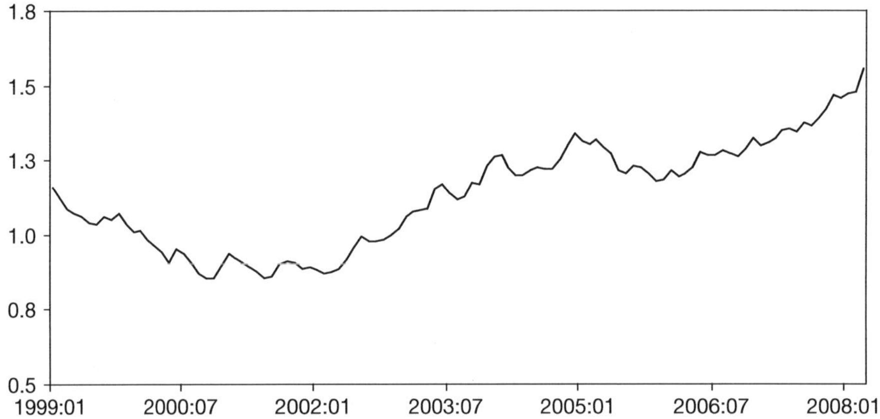

Source: St. Louis Federal Reserve Bank. FRED.

a. What is an exchange rate? What does the value of U.S. $/euro = 1.5 mean?
b. In which years is the euro appreciating?
c. In which years is the dollar depreciating?

FIGURE E.7 Exchange Rate, Japanese Yen/U.S. $, Monthly 1988/01–2008/03

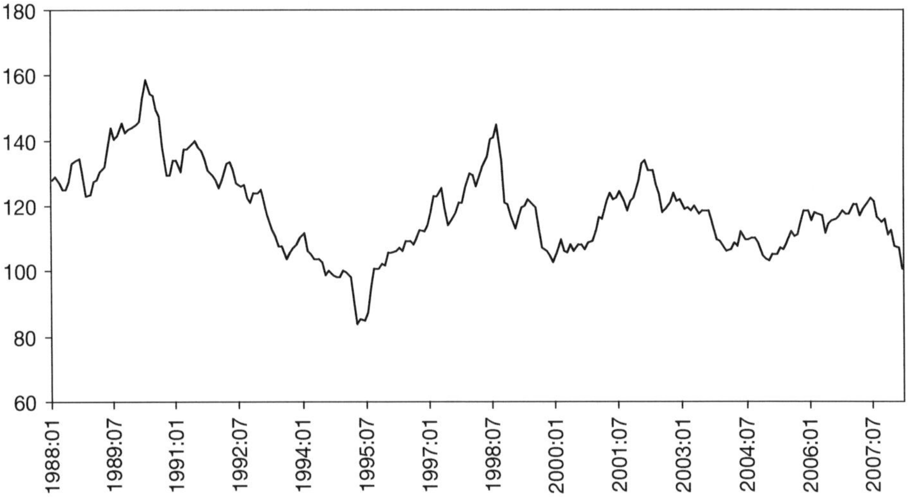

Source: St. Louis Federal Reserve Bank. FRED.

a. What does the value of the yen/$ = 120 mean?
b. In which years is the yen appreciating?

c. In which years is the dollar depreciating?
d. Would you be able to construct the series yen/euro with the information in Figures E.6 and E.7?

FIGURE E.8 Mortgage Rates: 30-Year Fixed Loan, Monthly 1988/01–2008/03

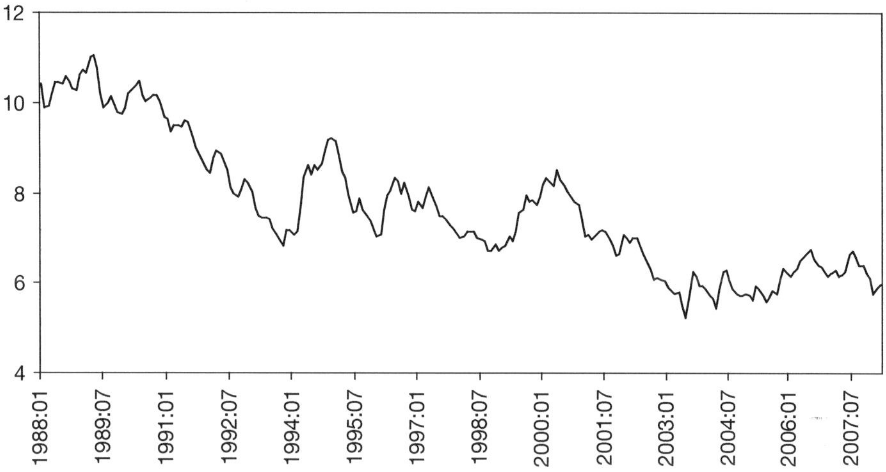

Source: St. Louis Federal Reserve Bank. FRED.

a. What is a mortgage rate?
b. What rate should be higher, that of a 30-year or of a 15-year loan?
c. What are the economic factors affecting mortgage rates?
d. What is the effect of monetary policy on mortgage rates?

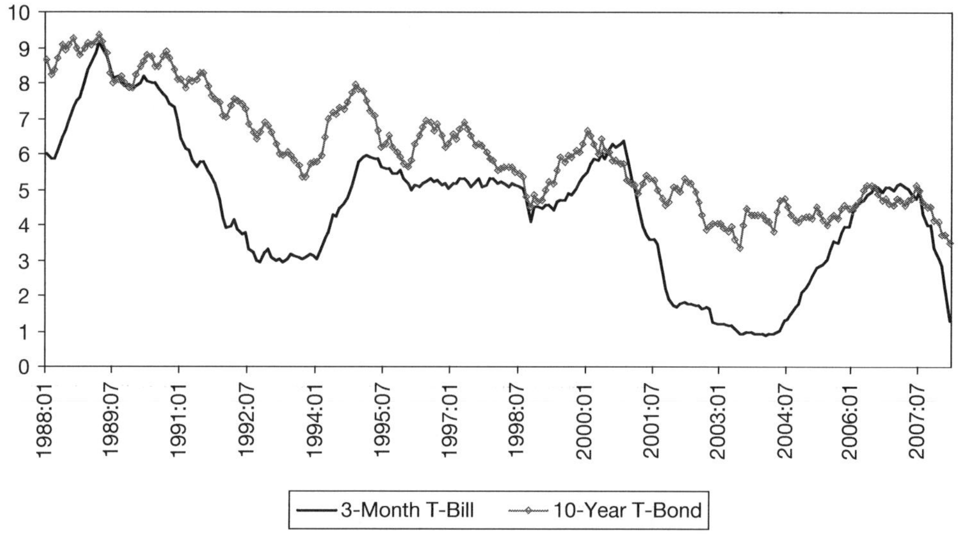

Source: St. Louis Federal Reserve Bank. FRED.

FIGURE E.9 Treasury Rates: Short-Term Rate (3-Month T-Bill) and Long-Term Rate (10-Year T-Bond), Monthly 1988/01–2008/03

FIGURE E.10 Spread (Long–Short Term Rates), Monthly 1988/01–2008/03

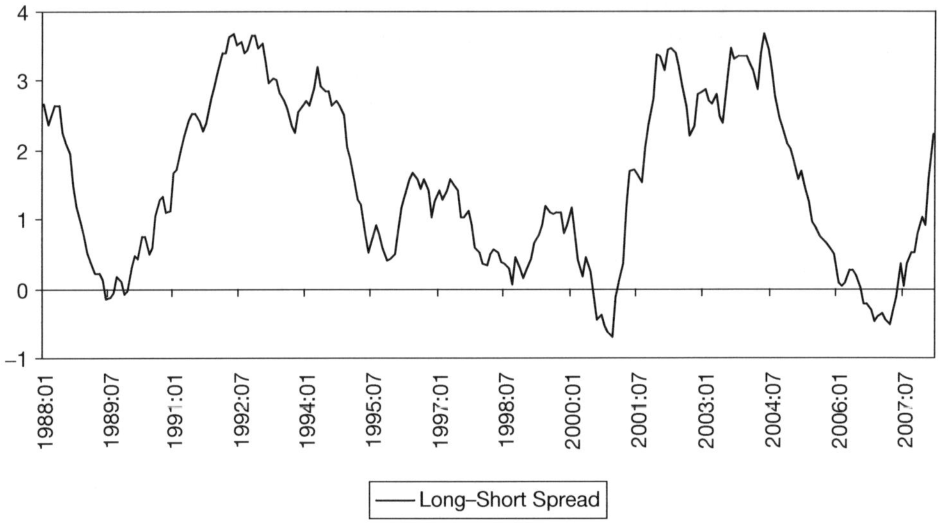

Source: St. Louis Federal Reserve Bank. FRED.

a. What is a Treasury bill?
b. Is the long-term rate always higher than the short-term rate?
c. What is the yield curve?
d. In which years does the spread widen? Why?

Time Series of the U.S. Society

FIGURE E.11 Birth, Infant Mortality, and Life Expectancy, Yearly Data 1980–2002

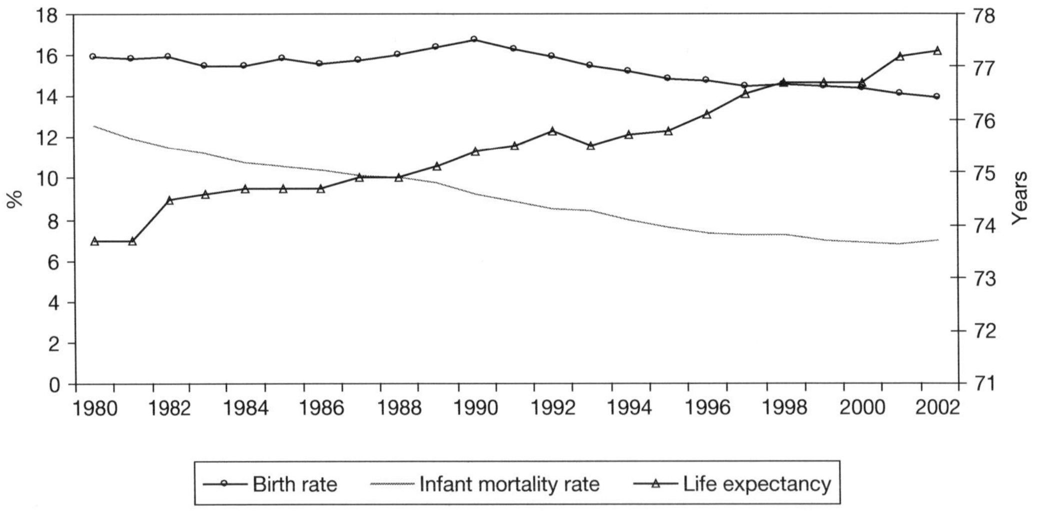

Source: National Center for Health Statistics. http://www.cdc.gov/nchs

a. What is the meaning of the terms *birth rate* and *mortality rate*?
b. How is *life expectancy* defined?
c. What are the factors that affect all three time series?
d. Why is there an upward trend in life expectancy and a downward trend in infant mortality?

FIGURE E.12 Mathematics Scores, 1973–2004

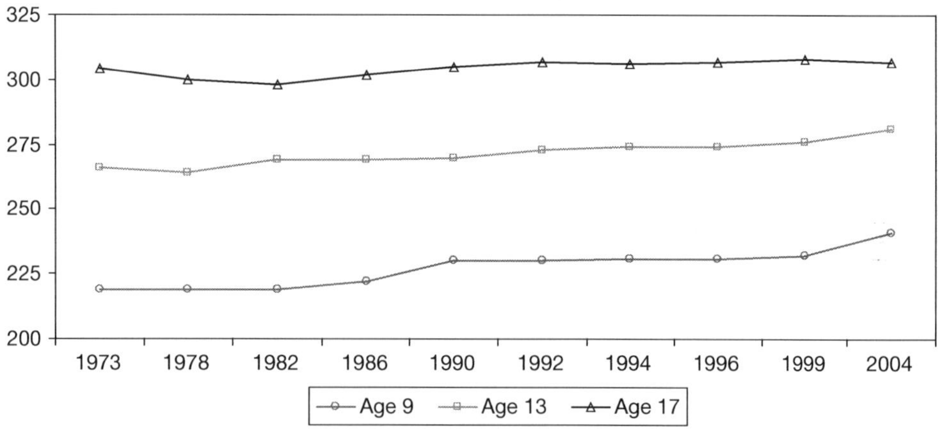

Source: Department of Education, National Center for Education Statistics. http://nces.ed.gov/programs

a. What do these scores mean and measure?
b. Do all three series exhibit an upward trend?

CHAPTER 2

Review of the Linear Regression Model

The primary aim of this chapter is to refresh concepts that you have already learned in your introductory econometrics course. We will review the linear regression model, which is a foundational tool to understand the forthcoming time series models. We will start by introducing conditional density and conditional moments of a random variable. These notions provide a natural background to introduce the idea of regression. We will provide basic concepts on estimation and testing of a regression model using ordinary least squares (OLS).

Be aware that this is a review chapter, and as such, it is not a substitute for your statistics and econometrics textbooks; thus, we highly recommend that you keep your books by your side.

If you need to refresh basic statistics, prior to the review of regression, it is advisable that you go directly to the Appendix (at the end of book) in which we explain basic concepts such as random variable, probability density function, expected value, variance, and so on.

2.1 Conditional Density and Conditional Moments

Consider two random variables, Y and X, say consumption (Y) and income (X), for which we would like to understand the relation between both. It is of interest to analyze how useful the information contained in X is to describe the behavior of Y. Suppose that we ask the following three questions:

1. For people with a level of income of \$40,000 per year, what is the probability of spending at most \$30,000 a year?
2. For people with a level of income of \$60,000 per year, what is the expected average consumption?
3. For people with a level of income of \$80,000 per year, what is the expected variability in consumption?

In all three questions, observe that we single out a set of the population that has a specific level of income: We consider only people in (1) with income of \$40,000, in (2) with income of \$60,000, and in (3) with income of \$80,000 per year; and in all questions, we are interested in some statistical measure. To answer (1), we need the **conditional probability density function** of consumption given income, that is, $f(Y|X)$, to calculate

$P(Y \leq 30{,}000 \mid X = 40{,}000) = \int_{-\infty}^{30{,}000} f(Y \mid X)dY$; in (2) we need to find the **conditional expectation** of consumption given income, that is, $\mu_{Y|X=60K} = E(Y \mid X = 60{,}000)$; and in (3), we need to find the **conditional variance** of consumption given income, that is, $\sigma^2_{Y|X=80K} = Var(Y \mid X = 80{,}000)$.

Now suppose that we collect a random sample of consumption and income. We calculate the sample conditional moments of Y as sample statistics for fixed values of X. Consider the example in Table 2.1.

There are 50 observations corresponding to 50 households. Income has five brackets $\{\leq\$20, 21\text{–}40, 41\text{–}60, 61\text{–}80, 81\text{–}100\}$ in thousands of dollars. Each household reports its income bracket and its corresponding consumption. The last two rows show the conditional mean of consumption and the conditional standard deviation for different levels of income. We calculate the sample conditional mean by adding up all the observations in each column and dividing by the number of observations in each column. For instance, $\bar{y}_{Y|X=40} = (25 + 32 + 37 + \cdots + 18 + 26)/10 = 27.8$. Likewise, the sample conditional standard deviation is the square root of the conditional variance, which is also calculated for each column. For instance, $\hat{\sigma}^2_{Y|X=40} = \left[(25 - 27.8)^2 + (32 - 27.8)^2 + \cdots (26 - 27.8)^2\right]/9 = 53.28$ and $\hat{\sigma}_{Y|X=40} = 7.29$. In this example, we observe that the conditional mean of consumption increases with higher levels of

TABLE 2.1 Sample Conditional and Unconditional Moments of Consumption

Income (thousand of $)	**≤ 20**	**21-40**	**41-60**	**61-80**	**81-100**	
Consumption (thousand of $)	19	25	44	55	55	
	15	32	35	60	77	Unconditional mean of consumption = $43.60
	11	37	55	75	88	
	13	19	57	45	42	
	9	20	58	68	82	
	8	32	59	73	90	Unconditional standard deviation of consumption = $23.31
	18	31	42	71	77	
	16	38	38	49	67	
	12	18	33	56	60	
	11	26	47	71	43	
Conditional Mean of Consumption	13.20	27.80	46.80	62.30	68.10	
Conditional Standard Deviation of Consumption	3.70	7.29	9.90	10.71	17.56	

income as well as the conditional standard deviation. If we do not condition on the values of X, by averaging over all the observations, we calculate the unconditional mean of consumption, $\bar{y} = 43.6$, and the unconditional standard deviation $\hat{\sigma}_Y = 23.31$.

In summary, the conditional pdf and any *conditional* moment, that is mean, variance, and so on, are statistical notions in which the outcome of X is fixed, so that when X takes on a different value the conditional probability of Y, the conditional mean of Y, and the conditional variance of Y will vary as a function of X. We call X the conditioning set, and we can write (in population) $E(Y|X) = g_1(X)$ or $Var(Y|X) = g_2(X)$ where g_1 and g_2 are functions (linear or nonlinear) of the conditioning set X. For instance, $E(Y|X) = 2.3 + 3X$ means that the conditional expectation is a linear function of X, so that for a given value of X, say $X = 10$, $E(Y|X = 10) = 2.3 + 3 \times 10 = 32.3$. In the same lines, if $Var(Y|X) = \exp(-X)$, we say that the conditional variance is a nonlinear function of the conditioning set; for example for $X = 2$, $Var(Y|X = 2) = \exp(-2) = 0.135$.

If Y and X are independent, then X does not affect the random behavior of Y. In this case, the conditional density is equal to the marginal density, that is, $f(Y|X) = f(Y)$, and the conditional moments are equal to the unconditional moments, that is, $E(Y|X) = E(Y)$, and $Var(Y|X) = Var(Y)$. Finally, if $E(Y|X) = E(Y)$, then the correlation is zero, that is, $\rho_{YX} = 0$. The converse result, however, is not always true. Correlation refers only to linear dependence; thus, if $\rho_{YX} = 0$, the conditional mean still may depend on X in a nonlinear fashion, for instance, $E(Y|X) = a + bX^2$.

In Figure 2.1, we describe a stylized version of conditional density and conditional mean and variance. The main point is to understand that conditional moments are functions of the conditioning set. The modeling problem in econometrics and in forecasting is to find the best functions that describe the conditional mean, the conditional variance, or any other conditional moment. In the next section, we will review the linear regression

FIGURE 2.1 Conditional Density and Conditional Moments

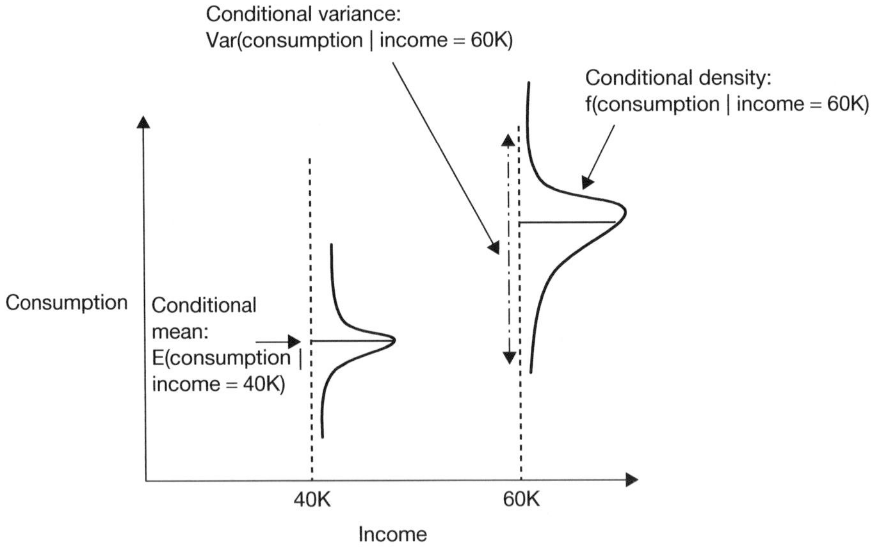

model that postulates that the conditional mean of a random variable is a linear function of the conditioning set. In the forthcoming chapters, you will learn how to construct time series models for the conditional mean and for the conditional variance, which in turn will be exploited for forecasting the random variable of interest.

2.2 Linear Regression Model

In the last section, we defined relations between two random variables, Y and X, by constructing the conditional moments of Y, mean and variance. We saw that the conditional moments are functions of the conditioning set, that is, $E(Y|X) = g_1(X)$ or $Var(Y|X) = g_2(X)$. In this section, we will review further the conditional mean $E(Y|X)$; in particular, we will focus on the **linear regression model**. Suppose that we collect data on consumption (Y) and income (X) for the population in SoCal (recall the example in Table 2.1). Our interest is to answer questions about the average consumption for people with different levels of income. In other words, we are interested in the conditional mean of consumption given a level of income $E(Y|X = x)$. Suppose that we fix $X = 40{,}000$ a year. For those people with approximately this level of income, we will observe some spending most of their income, say $Y = 39{,}000$, some spending little, say $Y = 10{,}000$, and some spending an average amount, say $Y = 32{,}000$. This is a rough description of the conditional density of consumption for a fixed level of income. Now observe Figure 2.2, which is a description of the conditional density of Y for different values of X.

For each value of $X = \{x_1, x_2, x_3, x_4\}$, we plot a conditional density of Y, which we draw along the vertical axis in order to read the values of Y. For each density, we single

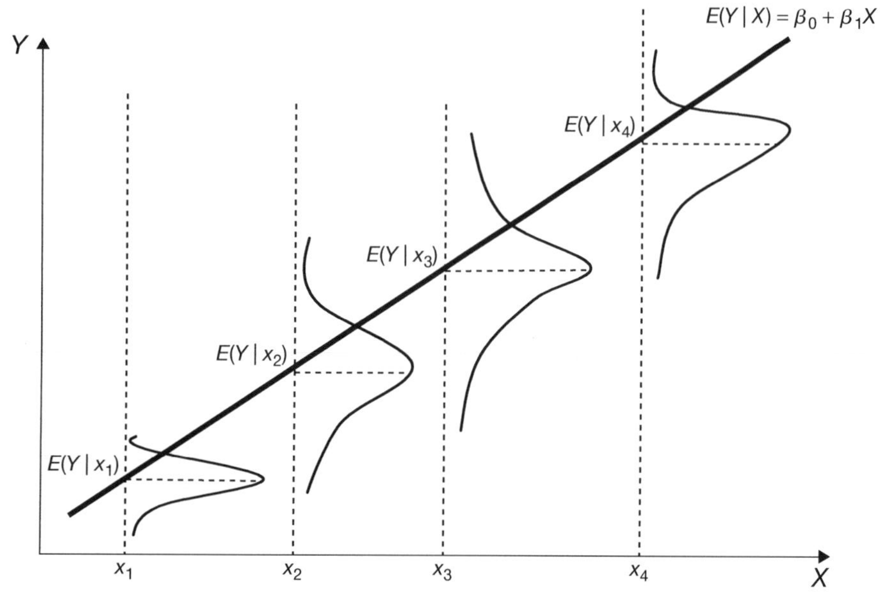

FIGURE 2.2 Population Linear Regression Model

out the conditional mean $E(Y|X=x)$. Observe the behavior of $E(Y|X=x)$: All conditional means fall on a line; thus, $E(Y|X) = g_1(X) = \beta_0 + \beta_1 X$, where β_0 is the intercept and β_1 is the slope of the line.

We define a *simple linear regression model* as the relation between Y and X given by the following expression:

$$Y = \beta_0 + \beta_1 X + u \tag{2.1}$$

We use the following terminology: Y is the dependent variable or response variable or regressand; X is the independent variable or explanatory variable or regressor; β_0 and β_1 are the regression coefficients, which are constant; and u is the stochastic disturbance or error term. From (2.1), it is evident that the dependence between Y and X is given by the coefficient β_1. If $\beta_1 = 0$, X has no effect on Y. If you know calculus, you will recognize that the derivative of Y with respect to X is the regression coefficient β_1, that is, $dY/dX = \beta_1$. This means that a marginal change in X generates a change in Y equal to β_1. As an approximation, we also write $\Delta Y \cong \beta_1 \Delta X$.

We observe Y and X, but the error term is unobservable. The role of the error term is to account for other variables that may affect Y but are not explicitly accounted for in the model. For instance, interest rates may affect consumption as people may want to defer present consumption in favor of future consumption when the interest rate on savings is high enough. The error term may also account for any measurement errors in X and Y. As far as we include an intercept in the model β_0, we could safely assume that any omitted or unobservable variables contained in the error term, taken together, have on average no impact on the dependent variable Y. Thus, we write $E(u) = 0$.

A more important assumption is that the error term should not depend on the regressor X, that is, $E(u|X) = E(u)$. In the previous example, this assumption implies that interest rates, implicitly contained in the error term u, are not correlated with different levels of income of the population, which seems to be a sensible assumption. Putting together the two assumptions, $E(u|X) = E(u)$ and $E(u) = 0$, we conclude that $E(u|X) = 0$. Using the properties of the expectation, we take conditional expectation on the equation (2.1)

$$E(Y|X) = E(\beta_0 + \beta_1 X + u) = \beta_0 + \beta_1 X \tag{2.2}$$

to obtain the *population regression line* that we have discussed in Figure 2.2.

The simple regression model can be extended to include many regressors, that is, $X_1, X_2, \ldots. X_k$. For instance, consumption may be explained not only by income but also by personal net worth, interest rates, preferences, and so on. To account for multiple factors, we need to define a model with more than one regressor. Thus, a *multiple regression model* is defined as

$$Y = \beta_0 + \beta_1 X_1 + \beta_2 X_2 + \beta_3 X_3 + \cdots + \beta_k X_k + u \tag{2.3}$$

Extending the same set of assumptions as in the single regression model, that is, $E(u|X_1, X_2, \ldots. X_k) = E(u) = 0$, we write the population regression as

$$E(Y|X_1, X_2, \ldots X_k) = \beta_0 + \beta_1 X_1 + \beta_2 X_2 + \cdots + \beta_k X_k \tag{2.4}$$

It is difficult to draw the multiple regression line as we did in Figure 2.2 because we do not deal anymore with a two-dimension problem (Y versus X); now we have a $k + 1$ dimension problem (Y versus $X_1, X_2, \ldots . X_k$). However, the main feature that defines regression remains: The conditional expectation of Y given fixed values for all k regressors is a linear function of the regressors.

In a multiple regression model, the interpretation of the regression coefficients should be understood under the "ceteris paribus" clause, which is very common in comparative statics exercises in macro and microeconomics courses. For instance, if in the consumption function we include X_1 = income and X_2 = net worth, the effect of a marginal change in income on consumption is β_1, $\Delta Y/\Delta X_1 \cong \beta_1$ holding X_2 (the net worth regressor) fixed. Because net worth is likely to be positively correlated with income, we need to include it explicitly in the model to control for its effect on consumption. By controlling for all these additional effects, the interpretation of the coefficient β_1 is purely the effect of marginal changes in income. In other words, β_1 is not contaminated by any other variable that may be highly correlated with income. Thus, the interpretation of a regression coefficient in a multiple regression model is the *partial* marginal effect of its regressor on the dependent variable keeping the remaining regressors fixed.

In summary:

- The linear regression model postulates that the conditional expectation of Y given $X_1, X_2, \ldots . X_k$ is a linear function of $X_1, X_2, \ldots . X_k$
- β_j is the expected change in Y when there is a marginal change in the regressor X_j keeping other regressors fixed.
- As far as $E(u \mid X_1, X_2, \ldots . X_k) = 0$, the linear regression model, either simple or multiple, can be decomposed in two parts,

$$Y = E(Y \mid X_1, X_2, \ldots . X_k) + u \tag{2.5}$$

which means that random variable Y is explained by a predictable or systematic component, $E(Y \mid X_1, X_2, \ldots . X_k)$, and by an unpredictable or unsystematic component, u.

2.3 Estimation: Ordinary Least Squares

In the linear regression model, the regression coefficients $\beta_0, \beta_1, \beta_2, \ldots . \beta_k$ are unknown. The question is how to estimate them. In this section, we will review a very important estimation methodology that is known as **ordinary least squares (OLS)**. We will focus first on the simple regression model to review the most fundamental concepts. Their extension to a multiple regression model will easily follow.

Let us start by collecting data on the variables of interest. Suppose that we draw a random sample of n observations on Y and X. Let us call (x_i, y_i), $i = 1, 2, \ldots . n$ the data corresponding to each unit in our sample. Following with the example in section 2.2, x_i is the \$ income and y_i is the \$ consumption of household i, and we have this

FIGURE 2.3 Sample Linear Regression Model

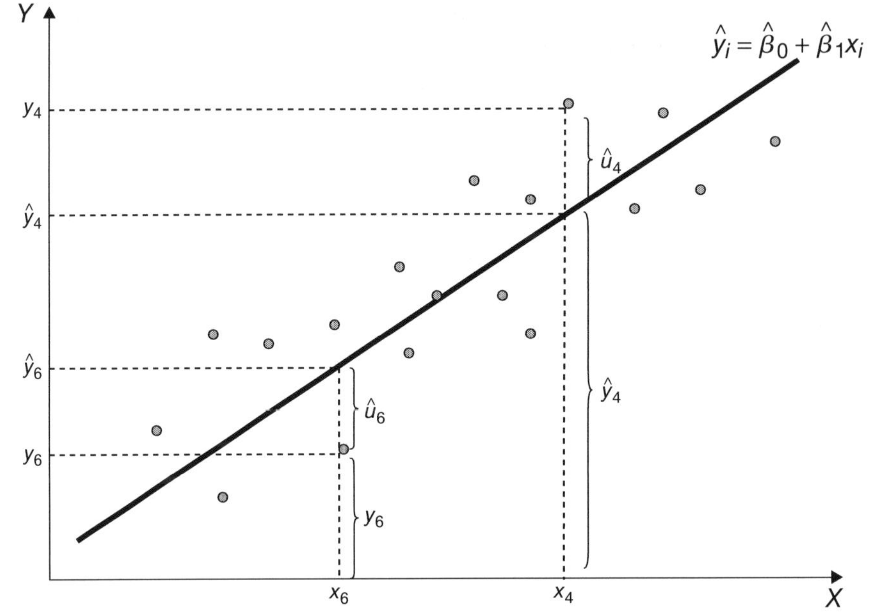

information for each of the n households in our sample. In Figure 2.3, we plot the data. Each dot represents a unit as the pair (x_i, y_i). In total, we have n dots.

Just from observing the scatter plot, we can see that there is a positive relation between Y and X: When values of X increase, values of Y also increase. This is a positive correlation between the two variables. Now the objective is to find the best line that describes the sample conditional mean. We could draw many lines over the scatter plot. Our intuition tells us that the line cannot be well above or well below the set of dots. If we want to represent the average behavior of Y for different levels of X, the prospective line must cross through the dots. But because there are many potential lines, we will need a notion of optimality to guide us on the search for the "best" line. Before we present the optimality criterion, let us go back to Figure 2.3 and choose any dot, say (x_4, y_4). Let us assume a hypothetical line that reads as

$$\hat{y}_i = \hat{\beta}_0 + \hat{\beta}_1 x_i \tag{2.6}$$

If we plug x_4 into the line, we obtain *the fitted value* through the line $\hat{y}_4 = \hat{\beta}_0 + \hat{\beta}_1 x_4$. The vertical distance between the data y_4 and the fitted value $\hat{y}_4$ is called *the residual* $\hat{u}_4$; that is, $y_4 - \hat{y}_4 = \hat{u}_4$. For each dot, we can do the same exercise so that we collect a set of residuals $\hat{u}_i$ for $i = 1, 2, \ldots n$. Some of the residuals will be above the line, like $\hat{u}_4$, and some will be below the line, like $\hat{u}_6 = y_6 - \hat{y}_6$. Observe that those residuals above the line will be positive and those below negative. We would like to find a line so that the distance between the fitted values $\hat{y}_i$ and the data y_i is the smallest possible. In other words, the best line should produce the smallest possible residuals (in magnitude, that is, disregarding the sign).

Ordinary Least Squares is the methodology that estimates $\hat{\beta}_0$ and $\hat{\beta}_1$ by minimizing the sum of squared residuals, that is

$$\min_{\hat{\beta}_0, \hat{\beta}_1} \sum_{i=1}^{n} \hat{u}_i^2 = \min_{\hat{\beta}_0, \hat{\beta}_1} \sum_{i=1}^{n} (y_i - \hat{\beta}_0 - \hat{\beta}_1 x_i)^2 \tag{2.7}$$

Observe that we choose the square of the residuals because we are interested in minimizing the magnitude of the residuals, that is, the distance between the data and the line regardless of the sign. There are other estimation methodologies with different optimality criteria, such as minimizing the sum of absolute residuals, but the solution to this is much more complicated.

The solution to the optimization problem stated in Equation (2.7) can be easily obtained if you know calculus. In the appendix, we provide the derivation. Here it suffices to state the solution for $\hat{\beta}_0$ and $\hat{\beta}_1$, which is

$$\hat{\beta}_1 = \frac{\sum_{i=1}^{n} (x_i - \bar{x})(y_i - \bar{y})}{\sum_{i=1}^{n} (x_i - \bar{x})^2} \tag{2.8}$$

$$\hat{\beta}_0 = \bar{y} - \hat{\beta}_1 \bar{x} \tag{2.9}$$

For $\hat{\beta}_1$, if we divide both numerator and denominator by $n - 1$, we will not change the value of $\hat{\beta}_1$. Then observe that the numerator is the sample covariance of X and Y and the denominator is the sample variance of X. This means that $\hat{\beta}_1$ will have the same sign as the covariance. If X and Y move in the same (opposite) direction, the covariance will be positive (negative) and $\hat{\beta}_1$ will be positive (negative). Once we obtain the estimate $\hat{\beta}_1$, we plug it in (2.9) to obtain the estimate $\hat{\beta}_0$, so that we obtain the optimal *sample regression line* described in Figure 2.3,

$$\hat{y}_i = \hat{\beta}_0 + \hat{\beta}_1 x_i \tag{2.10}$$

In a multiple regression model, the optimization problem is identical to that of a simple regression model:

$$\min_{\hat{\beta}_0, \hat{\beta}_1, \hat{\beta}_2 \ldots \hat{\beta}_k} \sum_{i=1}^{n} \hat{u}_i^2 = \min_{\hat{\beta}_0, \hat{\beta}_1, \hat{\beta}_2 \ldots \hat{\beta}_k} \sum_{i=1}^{n} (y_i - \hat{\beta}_0 - \hat{\beta}_1 x_{1i} - \hat{\beta}_2 x_{2i} \ldots . \hat{\beta}_k x_{ki})^2 \tag{2.11}$$

but the solution is more complex because we need to solve for $k + 1$ unknowns $(\hat{\beta}_0, \hat{\beta}_1, \hat{\beta}_2 \ldots . \hat{\beta}_k)$. The analogous formulas to (2.8) and (2.9) are more complicated and not as easy to read as those in the simple regression model, but suffice it to say that they exist and any regression software will be able to compute them. Once the $\hat{\beta}$'s are estimated, the optimal sample regression function is

$$\hat{y}_i = \hat{\beta}_0 + \hat{\beta}_1 x_{1i} + \hat{\beta}_2 x_{2i} \cdots + \hat{\beta}_k x_{ki} \tag{2.12}$$

It is important to understand that the *sample* (simple or multiple) regression line $\hat{y}_i = \hat{\beta}_0 + \hat{\beta}_1 x_{1i} + \hat{\beta}_2 x_{2i} \cdots + \hat{\beta}_k x_{ki}$ is an *estimate* of the *population* regression line $E(Y|X) = \beta_0 + \beta_1 X_1 + \beta_2 X_2 + \cdots + \beta_k X_k$. In population $\beta_0, \beta_1, \ldots \beta_k$ are unknown coefficients or constants or fixed parameters, but in sample $\hat{\beta}_0, \hat{\beta}_1, \hat{\beta}_2 \ldots \hat{\beta}_k$ are **estimators**, which in econometrics means "random variables." Given a different sample, we will perform an OLS estimation and we will very likely obtain different values or **estimates** for $\hat{\beta}_0, \hat{\beta}_1, \hat{\beta}_2 \ldots \hat{\beta}_k$. Conceptually, we could imagine going back to the population and drawing many different samples, and for each sample, we will obtain OLS estimates $\hat{\beta}_0, \hat{\beta}_1, \hat{\beta}_2 \ldots \hat{\beta}_k$, which will be different for each sample. We will end up with a collection of estimates that are the realizations of the random variables $\hat{\beta}_0, \hat{\beta}_1, \hat{\beta}_2 \ldots \hat{\beta}_k$. As with any random variable, we would like to learn their statistical characteristics. In other words, we would like to know some of their moments, such as mean and variance, or/and their probability density functions. This is the objective of the forthcoming sections. By characterizing the random variables $\hat{\beta}_0, \hat{\beta}_1, \hat{\beta}_2 \ldots \hat{\beta}_k$, we will learn about the population regression coefficients $\beta_0, \beta_1, \ldots \beta_k$, which is our ultimate objective.

2.3.1 *R*-squared and Adjusted *R*-squared

We mention that the random variable Y can be decomposed into both a systematic component and an unsystematic component, that is, $Y = E(Y|X) + u$. A question of interest is how much of the variability of Y is explained by the systematic component $E(Y|X) = \beta_0 + \beta_1 X_1 + \beta_2 X_2 + \cdots + \beta_k X_k$, which is the linear regression model. Suppose that for a sample of observations, this regression model has been estimated by OLS and $y_i = \hat{\beta}_0 + \hat{\beta}_1 x_{1i} + \hat{\beta}_2 x_{2i} \cdots + \hat{\beta}_k x_{ki} + \hat{u}_i$. Then the sample counterpart of the decomposition $Y = E(Y|X) + u$ is $y_i = \hat{y}_i + \hat{u}_i$. A measure of *goodness of fit* —how good the model is on explaining the variability of Y—is provided by the **R-squared** of the regression, which is also known as the *coefficient of determination*. Let us define the following quantities:

- The total sum of squares SST as

$$SST \equiv \sum_{i=1}^{n} (y_i - \bar{y})^2 \tag{2.13}$$

  that is the total sample variation in the dependent variable y with respect to the sample average $\bar{y}$.
- The sum of squares explained by the model SSE as

$$SSE \equiv \sum_{i=1}^{n} (\hat{y}_i - \bar{y})^2 \tag{2.14}$$

  that is the sample variation in the fitted values $\hat{y}$ with respect to the sample average $\bar{y}$.
- The sum of squared residuals SSR as

$$SSR \equiv \sum_{i=1}^{n} \hat{u}_i^2 \tag{2.15}$$

  that is the sample variation in the residuals $\hat{u}$ with respect to their sample mean, which is zero. It can be proven that $SST = SSE + SSR$ so that the total variation can be decomposed into the explained variation (due to the model) and the unexplained variation (due to the residual). Based on this relation, the R-squared is defined as the ratio

$$R^2 = \frac{SSE}{SST} = 1 - \frac{SSR}{SST} \tag{2.16}$$

which is the proportion of the sample variation of the dependent variable explained by the regressor(s) in the model. Because $SSE \leq SST$ and both quantities are non-negative, the R-squared is bounded between zero and one, that is, $0 \leq R^2 \leq 1$. If the model is a good fit and it fully explains the total variation of the dependent variable, then $SSE = SST$ and $R^2 = 1$; on the contrary, if the model is a very poor fit and it does not at all explain the total variation, then $SSE = 0$ and $R^2 = 0$.

The R-squared can be computed for a simple or multiple regression model; its interpretation is exactly the same regardless the number of regressors included in the model. In practice, we will be wondering whether to add new regressors to the model. By adding more independent variables, the residuals may decrease or may stay the same, but they never will increase; thus, SSR can never go up. This means that the R-squared, at worst, will be unchanged and, at best, it will increase so that it seemingly provides a better fit when more regressors are added to the model. However, adding new regressors may not be a sound practice unless that the regressors are significant enough and provide new information to the model. To guard against an R-squared that may increase in the presence of irrelevant regressors, we have another measure of goodness of fit, known as the **adjusted R-squared** ($\overline{R}^2$), that is defined as

$$\overline{R}^2 = 1 - \frac{SSR/(n-k-1)}{SST/(n-1)} \tag{2.17}$$

Observe that SSR and SST have been divided by their respective degrees of freedom (number of observations in the regression minus the number of parameters to be estimated). The degrees of freedom for SSR are $n-(k+1)$ and for SST, $n-1$. Now if we were to include an irrelevant regressor in the model, k will go up and the ratio $SSR/(n-k-1)$ will go up so that the adjusted R-squared will go down, which will indicate that the new regressor is worthless. On the contrary, if we were to include a relevant regressor, k still goes up but SSR will go down significantly (residuals are smaller) so that the ratio $SSR/(n-k-1)$ eventually will go down and the adjusted R-squared up. Thus, this regressor is informative and it provides a better fit. In this sense, the introduction of degrees of freedom can be interpreted as a penalty function that balances the inclusion of more regressors against the quality of the information that they provide to explain the variability of the dependent variable. The adjusted R-squared can be negative; in this instance, the regressors considered are very poor on explaining the dependent variable. Comparing both R-squared, we can see that $\overline{R}^2 \leq R^2$.

2.3.2 Linearity and OLS

We have seen that a linear regression model postulates that the conditional expectation of Y given $X_1, X_2, \ldots. X_k$ is a linear function of $X_1, X_2, \ldots. X_k$. This statement should be interpreted in the following sense. Suppose that we claim that consumption (Y) is a quadratic function of income (X), such as $Y = \beta_0 + \beta_1 X + \beta_2 X^2$. This implies that the marginal propensity to consume depends on the level of income: $dY/dX = \beta_1 + 2\beta_2 X$ and, for $\beta_1 > 0$ and $\beta_2 < 0$, the higher the level of income, the lower is the marginal propensity to consume. Can this model be written as a regression model and be estimated by OLS? You may be inclined to answer no because $Y = \beta_0 + \beta_1 X + \beta_2 X^2$ is a nonlinear function of X and this is true. However, it is easy to incorporate some nonlinearities into a regression model by redefining the regressors and/or the dependent variable. Suppose that we call $W \equiv X^2$, then $Y = \beta_0 + \beta_1 X + \beta_2 X^2$ can be written as $Y = \beta_0 + \beta_1 X + \beta_2 W$, which is now a linear function of W. A regression model as $Y = \beta_0 + \beta_1 X + \beta_2 W + u$ is suitable for estimation with OLS; it only requires, prior to running the OLS routine, the inclusion of two regressors X and X^2 in the data set instead of just one X.

Other nonlinear specifications such as the log-log function $\log Y = \beta_0 + \beta_1 \log X + u$ or semilog $\log Y = \beta_0 + \beta_1 X + u$ or $Y = \beta_0 + \beta_1 \log X + u$ are also considered regression models. Observe that once the dependent variable Y is transformed into, say $\log Y$, it becomes a new dependent variable, and a new interpretation of the model should be given. For instance, in $\log Y = \beta_0 + \beta_1 \log X + u$, what is the response of Y when there is a marginal change in X? From the model, we read the answer by considering the properties of the log-function. In particular, we need to know the derivative of the log: $d\log Y = dY/Y$. Thus,

$$\frac{d\log Y}{d\log X} = \frac{dY/Y}{dX/X} = \beta_1 \tag{2.18}$$

which means that 1% change in X (i.e., dX/X) translates into a percent change in Y equal to β_1 ($dY/Y = \beta_1 dX/X$). This is the *elasticity* concept that is so prevalent in micro- and macroeconomics theories. In the same fashion, if the model is $\log Y = \beta_0 + \beta_1 X + u$, then

$$\frac{d\log Y}{dX} = \frac{dY/Y}{dX} = \beta_1 \tag{2.19}$$

and note that now we do not deal with a marginal percent change in X but just a marginal change in X. Finally, if the model is $Y = \beta_0 + \beta_1 \log X + u$, then

$$\frac{dY}{d\log X} = \frac{dY}{dX/X} = \beta_1 \tag{2.20}$$

so that a 1% change in X produces a change in Y by the amount β_1.

It is important to understand what all these nonlinear specifications have in common: All the βs' regression coefficients enter linearly into the model. For instance, if we were to have a model such $Y = 1/(1 + \beta_0 \exp(\beta_1 X))$, the dependent variable Y is neither a linear function of the regressor X nor a linear function of the regression coefficients β_0 and β_1. These models cannot be estimated by OLS, so we need more advanced methodologies.

In summary, many nonlinear specifications fall into the realm of linear regression analysis as far as the dependent variable (or a transformation of the dependent variable) is a linear function of the regression coefficients. We need only to take care of the appropriate interpretation of these coefficients.

2.3.3 Assumptions of OLS: The Gauss–Markov Theorem

Recall that the OLS estimators are random variables. Conceptually, we could draw as many samples of (X,Y) as we wish from a given population. If we were to calculate the OLS estimates for each sample, we would have found that these estimates vary from sample to sample; we say that they are subject to sample variation. In other words, the OLS estimates are realizations of a random variable that we call the OLS estimator. In reality, given the nature of the (nonexperimental) data in economics and business, we mostly work with only one sample. We will estimate a sample regression model but from that sample, we would like to infer some characteristics of the population regression model. The Gauss–Markov theorem is a very powerful result that will explain how well we approximate the *population* regression coefficients $(\beta_0, \beta_1, \ldots \beta_k)$ when we estimate a *sample* regression model $(y_i = \hat{\beta}_0 + \hat{\beta}_1 x_i + \hat{\beta}_2 x_{2i} \cdots + \hat{\beta}_k x_{ki} + \hat{u}_i)$ by OLS. Most importantly, the Gauss–Markov theorem will characterize the mean and variance of the OLS estimators.

We start by stating the set of assumptions under which the Gauss–Markov theorem holds.

A1 Linearity: The population regression model is linear in the regression coefficients:

$$Y = \beta_0 + \beta_1 X_1 + \beta_2 X_2 + \beta_3 X_3 + \cdots + \beta_k X_k + u \tag{2.21}$$

We have already explained the meaning of linearity, and we have seen that we can entertain a wide set of nonlinear models, but in all these specifications (linear and nonlinear), OLS estimation always requires that the regression coefficients $(\beta_0, \beta_1, \ldots \beta_k)$ enter linearly into the model.

A2 Zero Conditional Mean: Conditioning on the regressors, the expected value of the error term is zero:

$$E(u \mid X_1, X_2, \ldots X_k) = 0 \tag{2.22}$$

This is the most important assumption in the population regression model. We have already seen why the error term should not be correlated with the regressors. Each regression coefficient β_j should convey by itself, as cleanly as possible, the effect of the associated regressor X_j on the dependent variable Y.

A3 Homoscedasticity: Conditioning on the regressors, the variance of the error term is constant:

$$Var(u \mid X_1, X_2, \ldots X_k) = \sigma_u^2 \tag{2.23}$$

or equivalently, the conditional variance of the dependent variable is constant.

Because $Var(Y|X) = E\left[(Y - E(Y|X))^2|X\right]$ and $E(Y|X_1, X_2, \ldots X_k) = \beta_0 + \beta_1 X_1 + \beta_2 X_2 + \beta_3 X_3 + \cdots + \beta_k X_k$, then $Var(Y|X_1, X_2, \ldots X_k) = E(u^2|X_1, X_2, \ldots X_k)$. With homoscedasticity, we can write

$$Var(Y|X_1, X_2, \ldots X_k) = Var(u|X_1, X_2, \ldots X_k) = \sigma_u^2 \tag{2.24}$$

The variance σ_u^2 is also known as the **error variance**. In Figure 2.2 for each value of X, we have pictured a conditional density. Under the assumption of homoscedasticity, each density should show the same dispersion, that is to say, the variance of Y is the same regardless of the value of X. For instance, in the consumption example, homoscedasticity implies that the variance of consumption should be the same for each level of income, rich or poor.

A4 No Serial Correlation: This assumption refers to a regression model for which the data are gathered over time so that the model reads as $y_t = \beta_0 + \beta_1 x_{1t} + \beta_2 x_{2t} + \cdots + \beta_k x_{kt} + u_t$. The absence of serial correlation in the error term means that the errors are not correlated over time; thus,

$$cov(u_t, u_{t-l}) = 0 \qquad l = \pm 1, \pm 2, \ldots \tag{2.25}$$

If the errors were serially correlated $cov(u_t, u_{t-l}) \neq 0$, we could have used past information to predict the present. For instance, in the consumption example, if there is serial correlation, past consumption Y_{t-l} may explain present consumption Y_t and, as such, Y_{t-l} needs to be incorporated into the regression model as an additional regressor. The idea of serial correlation and, in general, of time dependence is the subject of this book. In subsequent chapters, we will provide detailed explanations. At this time, suffice it to say that this is a necessary assumption for the Gauss–Markov theorem to hold.

A5 No Perfect Collinearity: There is not an exact linear relation among the regressors. For instance, if $X_1 = 1000 \times X_2$, then the regressors X_1 and X_2 are perfectly colinear. Suppose that in the consumption example, we introduce the regressor "income in dollars" and again "income in thousands of dollars." Both regressors convey the same information but in different units. This is an extreme case of collinearity because the correlation between X_1 and X_2 is exactly 1. With perfect collinearity, the model cannot be estimated by OLS. One of the regressors needs to be removed.

A6 Sample Variation in Regressors: All the regressors must have positive variances, that is to say, no regressor can take a constant value for all the units in the sample:

$$var(X_j) > 0 \qquad j = 1, 2 \ldots k \tag{2.26}$$

Now we can state the **Gauss–Markov theorem**:

Under assumptions **A1** through **A6**, the OLS estimators $(\hat{\beta}_0, \hat{\beta}_1, \ldots \hat{\beta}_k)$ are the **b**est **l**inear **u**nbiased **e**stimators (**BLUE**) of their respective population regression coefficients $(\beta_0, \beta_1, \ldots \beta_k)$.

Let us explain succinctly the meaning of BLUE:

- *Linear.* The estimator $\hat{\beta}$ is a linear function of the dependent variable. Recall the simple regression model and the OLS estimators (2.8) and (2.9). Let us work with $\hat{\beta}_1$. If we call $w_i \equiv \frac{(x_i - \bar{x})}{\sum_{i=1}^{n}(x_i - \bar{x})^2}$, then

$$\hat{\beta}_1 = \frac{\sum_{i=1}^{n}(x_i - \bar{x})(y_i - \bar{y})}{\sum_{i=1}^{n}(x_i - \bar{x})^2} = \sum_{i=1}^{n} w_i(y_i - \bar{y}), \tag{2.27}$$

  which says that $\hat{\beta}_1$ is a liner function of y. The same argument applies to the OLS estimators of a multiple regression model.
- *Unbiased.* The expected value of the OLS estimator $\hat{\beta}$ is the corresponding population regression coefficient β,

$$E(\hat{\beta}_j) = \beta_j \qquad j = 1, 2 \ldots k \tag{2.28}$$

  This result says that *on average,* the OLS estimator approximates the population parameter. Not all the assumptions are needed to guarantee **unbiasedness**. The key assumptions are **A1**, **A2**, **A5**, and **A6.** This means that even in the presence of heteroscedasticity and serial correlation, the OLS estimator is still unbiased.
- *Best.* This is a property concerned with the variance of the OLS estimator. There may be other estimators, say $\tilde{\beta}_j$, obtained with techniques different from OLS that also are linear and unbiased. Being "best"means that the variance of the OLS estimator $\hat{\beta}_j$ is the smallest among those of any other linear and unbiased estimators:

$$var(\hat{\beta}_j) \leq var(\tilde{\beta}_j) \qquad j = 1, 2 \ldots k \tag{2.29}$$

  This property is also known as the **efficiency** property. In addition to assumptions **A1**, **A2**, **A5**, and **A6**, assumptions **A3**, and **A4** are key for this property to hold.

In summary, the Gauss–Markov theorem is a powerful result that characterizes the mean and the variance of the OLS estimator.

In the chapter appendix, we provide the formulas for the variance of the OLS estimator. It is important to stress that these formulas will be valid only when assumptions **A3** and **A4**—homoscedasticity and no serial correlation—are satisfied. Unfortunately, economic data are in many instances heteroscedastic and serially correlated. It is possible to modify the variance of the OLS estimator to account for heteroscedasticity and serial correlation. This procedure is out of the scope of this review chapter, but suffice it to say that most econometrics software packages can compute **robust** variances against heteroscedasticity and serial correlation (Newey-West HAC standard errors) as we will show in the following example. It is important to understand that the **best** property (minimum variance estimators) claimed by the Gauss–Markov theorem is lost when we use robust variances, but fortunately, the OLS estimator remains unbiased. There are advanced estimation methodologies that provide more efficient estimators than the OLS in the presence of heteroscedasticity and/or serial correlation. In later chapters, we will introduce "maximum likelihood estimation" in the context of time series data.

Finally, if **A3** and **A4** hold, we obtain an estimator of the error variance σ_u^2 based on the residuals $\hat{u}_i$ by calculating the following average:

$$\hat{\sigma}_{\hat{u}}^2 = \frac{\sum_{i=1}^{n} \hat{u}_i^2}{n - (k + 1)} \tag{2.30}$$

$\hat{\sigma}_{\hat{u}}^2$ is known as the **residual variance**. The denominator $n - (k + 1)$ is known as the *degrees of freedom*, defined as the number of observations n minus the number of parameters to estimate, which in the multiple regression model are $k + 1$. An important property of this estimator is unbiasedness, that is, $E(\hat{\sigma}_{\hat{u}}^2) = \sigma_u^2$.

2.3.4 An Example: House Prices and Interest Rates

An important question in housing economics is whether house prices are responsive to interest rates. Low mortgage rates provide an incentive for consumers and investors to buy real estate. If the supply of houses is stable or if it grows slowly, a strong demand for homes will put upward pressure on house prices. Our claim is that low mortgage rates will push up the demand for houses and will drive prices up.

We start by collecting data on house prices and mortgage interest rates. On Freddie Mac's website, http://www.freddiemac.com, we find time series for regional and national quarterly house price indexes and 30-year fixed rate on conventional mortgage loans. We download annual data from 1971 to 2007. Notice that the data have a time series format, that is, (x_t, y_t) $t = 1, 2, \ldots T$, where the sample consists of T observations, one for each time period. We have replaced the subindex i for the subindex t, so that in those equations with a summation sign, (2.1) throught (2.30) the summation will read $\sum_{t=1}^{T}$ instead of $\sum_{i=1}^{n}$. Observe what the data looks like in Table 2.2.

There are five columns. In column (1), we have the year t, in (2) the national house price index p_t, in (3) the percentage change in the index Δp_t, in (4) the 30-year fixed mortgage rate r_t, and (5) the percentage change in the rate Δr_t. For instance, let us take observation $t = 1988$. For this year, the value of the index is $p_t = 110.73$, and the annual growth rate with respect to the previous year is $\Delta p_t = 6.47\%$. The mortgage rate is $r_t = 10.34\%$, and the percentage change with respect to the previous year is $\Delta r_t = 1.26\%$. In EViews, you can import data from Excel and other file formats. Open EViews and create a new workfile. Click on **File**, select **Import**, and follow the instructions.

The next step is the estimation of a multiple regression model with time series data. We propose the following linear regression model:

$$\Delta p_t = \beta_0 + \beta_1 \Delta p_{t-1} + \beta_2 \Delta r_{t-1} + u_t \tag{2.31}$$

TABLE 2.2 House Prices and Interest Rates. Multiple Regression: The Data

(1) Obs	(2) Price index (P)	(3) %change price (D_P)	(4) Rate (R)	(5) %change rate (D_R)
1971	33.50000	NA	7.550000	NA
1972	35.94000	7.283582	7.380000	−2.277392
1973	39.45000	9.766277	8.040000	8.565544
1974	42.58000	7.934094	9.190000	13.36869
1975	44.90000	5.448567	9.050000	−1.535118
1976	48.55000	8.129176	8.870000	−2.008996
1977	55.09000	13.47065	8.850000	−0.225734
1978	62.62000	13.66854	9.640000	8.550365
1979	69.42000	10.85915	11.20000	14.99927
1980	74.36000	7.116105	13.74000	20.43975
1981	78.38000	5.406132	16.63000	19.08970
1982	79.30000	1.173769	16.04000	−3.612269
1983	82.44000	3.959647	13.24000	−19.18431
1984	86.31000	4.694323	13.88000	4.720640
1985	91.10000	5.549762	12.43000	−11.03360
1986	97.93000	7.497256	10.19000	−19.87061
1987	104.0000	6.198305	10.21000	0.196078
1988	110.7300	6.471154	10.34000	1.265224
1989	118.1500	6.700984	10.32000	−0.193611
....	....	....	....	....

where the dependent variable is $Y \equiv \Delta p_t$, and the two regressors are $(X_1, X_2) \equiv (\Delta p_{t-1}, \Delta r_{t-1})$. We include Δp_{t-1} to acknowledge that house prices move slowly and the changes from one period to the next are not abrupt. This idea of persistence is an important concept for modeling economic data, and it will be explained in detail within the context of the time series models that will be developed in later chapters. You may be wondering why we do not work directly with the level of house price index and the level of interest rates. The answer is technical in nature and relates to issues of stationarity of the time series, which is a concept to be explained in Chapter 3. However, Equation (2.31) per se has a nice interpretation because we are interested in how changes in interest rates affect changes in house prices.

We proceed with OLS estimation of Equation (2.31).

TABLE 2.3 House Prices and Interest Rates. Multiple Regression: OLS Estimation

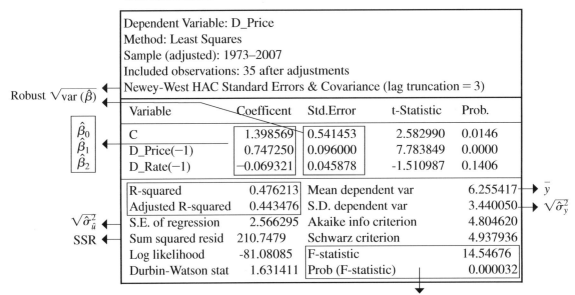

Dependent Variable: D_Price
Method: Least Squares
Sample (adjusted): 1973–2007
Included observations: 35 after adjustments
Newey-West HAC Standard Errors & Covariance (lag truncation = 3)

Variable	Coefficent	Std.Error	t-Statistic	Prob.
C	1.398569	0.541453	2.582990	0.0146
D_Price(−1)	0.747250	0.096000	7.783849	0.0000
D_Rate(−1)	−0.069321	0.045878	-1.510987	0.1406

R-squared	0.476213	Mean dependent var	6.255417
Adjusted R-squared	0.443476	S.D. dependent var	3.440050
S.E. of regression	2.566295	Akaike info criterion	4.804620
Sum squared resid	210.7479	Schwarz criterion	4.937936
Log likelihood	-81.08085	F-statistic	14.54676
Durbin-Watson stat	1.631411	Prob (F-statistic)	0.000032

Annotations: Robust $\sqrt{var(\hat{\beta})}$ (Std.Error column); $\hat{\beta}_0$, $\hat{\beta}_1$, $\hat{\beta}_2$ (coefficients); $\sqrt{\hat{\sigma}^2_{\hat{u}}}$ (S.E. of regression); SSR (Sum squared resid); $\bar{y}$ (Mean dependent var); $\sqrt{\hat{\sigma}^2_y}$ (S.D. dependent var); *F*-test for overall significance of the regression (F-statistic, Prob (F-statistic)).

In your EViews workfile, click on the following sequence

Object
New Object
Equation

In the specification screen, write the following command:

D_Price c D_Price(−1) D_Rate(−1)

where **D_Price** $= \Delta p_t$, **c** is a constant, **D_Price(−1)** $= \Delta p_{t-1}$, and **D_Rate(−1)** $= \Delta r_{t-1}$. The estimation results are in Table 2.3. The main concepts that we reviewed in the previous sections—estimates, robust HAC standard errors, residual variance and standard error of the regression, sum of squared residuals SSR, *R*-squared, Adjusted *R*-squared, mean of the dependent variable, and standard deviation of the dependent variable—are underlined or in a box.

From the results in Table 2.3, the sample regression line is

$$\Delta p_t = 1.40 + 0.75\Delta p_{t-1} - 0.07\Delta r_{t-1} + \hat{u}_t \tag{2.32}$$

Because $\hat{\beta}_2$ is negative ($\hat{\beta}_2 = -0.07$), there is an inverse relation between house price growth and changes in interest rates. In addition, the regressors explain a large proportion of the variation of house price growth because the adjusted *R*-squared is 44%. The *R*-squared is 48% that, as expected, is higher than the adjusted. At this stage, we can say that our claim has been validated. However, we need to explain how statistically significant these findings are. This is the subject of the next section that deals with statistical inference or hypothesis testing.

2.4 Hypothesis Testing in a Regression Model

Once we have estimated a regression model, it is of interest to test the statistical significance of the regression coefficients. For instance, in Table 2.3, we have obtained that the marginal effect of interest rates on house prices is negative with $\hat{\beta}_2 = -0.07$. We could ask whether, statistically speaking, β_2 is zero, and by that, conclude that on average, house prices do not react to changes in interest rates. Hypothesis testing is the branch of statistical inference that deals with this type of question. In this section, we will review two test statistics: the t-ratio and the F-test.

We need an additional assumption in the linear regression model to proceed with the construction of our tests.

A7 The Error Term *u* Is Normally Distributed: We have already assumed that the mean of u is zero (A2) and its variance is constant σ_u^2 (A3); thus, $u \rightarrow N(0, \sigma_u^2)$.

This assumption is very important because it permits the full characterization of the OLS estimator $\hat{\beta}$. The Gauss–Markov theorem provides the mean and the variance of $\hat{\beta}$. Now assumption A7 implies that the OLS estimator $\hat{\beta}$ is also a normal random variable; thus,

$$\hat{\beta}_j \rightarrow N(\beta_j, \sigma_{\hat{\beta}_j}^2) \quad j = 1, 2 \ldots k \tag{2.33}$$

By standardizing $\hat{\beta}_j$ (subtract its mean and divide by its standard deviation), we obtain a standard normal pdf, that is,

$$\frac{\hat{\beta}_j - \beta_j}{\sigma_{\hat{\beta}_j}} \rightarrow N(0, 1) \qquad j = 1, 2 \ldots k \tag{2.34}$$

This result is the basis of the forthcoming test statistics.

2.4.1 The *t*-ratio

The denominator in Equation (2.34)—the standard deviation of the OLS estimator $\sigma_{\hat{\beta}_j}$ —is a function of the error variance σ_u^2, which is not directly observable and needs to be estimated. We have proposed to estimate σ_u^2 by the residual variance $\hat{\sigma}_{\hat{u}}^2$. When we replace σ_u^2 by $\hat{\sigma}_{\hat{u}}^2$ in the formulas of the variances of the OLS estimators, we will be able to calculate the variances of the OLS estimators. We will denote these by $\hat{\sigma}_{\hat{\beta}_j}^2$ where the "hat" notation acknowledges that we are now using sample information. On doing this, we affect the pdf of $\hat{\beta}_j$, which now is a Student-t with $(n - k - 1)$ degrees of freedom:

$$\frac{\hat{\beta}_j - \beta_j}{\hat{\sigma}_{\hat{\beta}_j}} \to t_{n-k-1} \qquad j = 1, 2 \ldots k \tag{2.35}$$

In a regression model, it is of interest to test a single hypothesis such as $H_0: \beta_j = c$ where c is a constant. This is the case for which the **t-ratio** is a suitable statistic to assess whether we reject the hypothesis or fail to reject it. In hypothesis testing, when we postulate a claim, we write the *null* hypothesis H_0—the claim that we would like to disprove—and the *alternative* hypothesis H_1—the hypothesis to accept when the null is rejected. We can test against one-sided or two-sided alternative hypothesis, so that we consider the following three cases:

Case (1): One-sided alternative: The regression coefficient is larger than c,

$$\begin{aligned} H_0 &: \beta_j = c \\ H_1 &: \beta_j > c \end{aligned} \tag{2.36}$$

Case (2): One-sided alternative: The regression coefficient is smaller than c,

$$\begin{aligned} H_0 &: \beta_j = c \\ H_1 &: \beta_j < c \end{aligned} \tag{2.37}$$

Case (3): Two-sided alternative, the regression coefficient is different from c,

$$\begin{aligned} H_0 &: \beta_j = c \\ H_1 &: \beta_j \neq c \end{aligned} \tag{2.38}$$

Once we have chosen the hypothesis to test, we need a test statistic and a decision rule. Let us start with Case (3). Under the null hypothesis, we claim that the value of the regression coefficient is c. Equation (2.35) provides the basis to construct the test statistic. If the null is true, then $\beta_j = c$. Then by substituting the OLS estimate $\hat{\beta}_j$, the standard deviation of $\hat{\beta}_j$, $\hat{\sigma}_{\hat{\beta}_j}$, and the value under the null $\beta_j = c$ in Equation (2.35), we construct the t-ratio, $t_{\hat{\beta}_j}$, which will be Student-t distributed only when the null is true, that is:

$$t_{\hat{\beta}_j} = \frac{\hat{\beta}_j - c}{\hat{\sigma}_{\hat{\beta}_\xi}} \to t_{n-k-1} \qquad \text{(under } H_0\text{)} \tag{2.39}$$

Suppose that $\beta_j = c$ is not true. Then the ratio $t_{\hat{\beta}_j}$ will not be centered around zero and the value of $t_{\hat{\beta}_j}$ will be far from zero indicating a rejection of the null. The question becomes how to evaluate how far from zero the ratio should be in order to reject the null hypothesis. This is why we need a decision rule in conjunction with the claim stated in the alternative hypothesis.

In Case (3), when we have a two-sided alternative hypothesis, we do not care about the sign of $t_{\hat{\beta}_j}$. To reject the null, the value of the t-ratio could be very far from zero in the direction of positive or negative numbers. A decision rule should be stated in probabilistic terms because $\hat{\beta}_j$ is a random variable. We choose a **significance level** α for the test. This means that we need to decide the probability of mistakenly rejecting the null

FIGURE 2.4 Rejection Rules for the *t*-Ratio

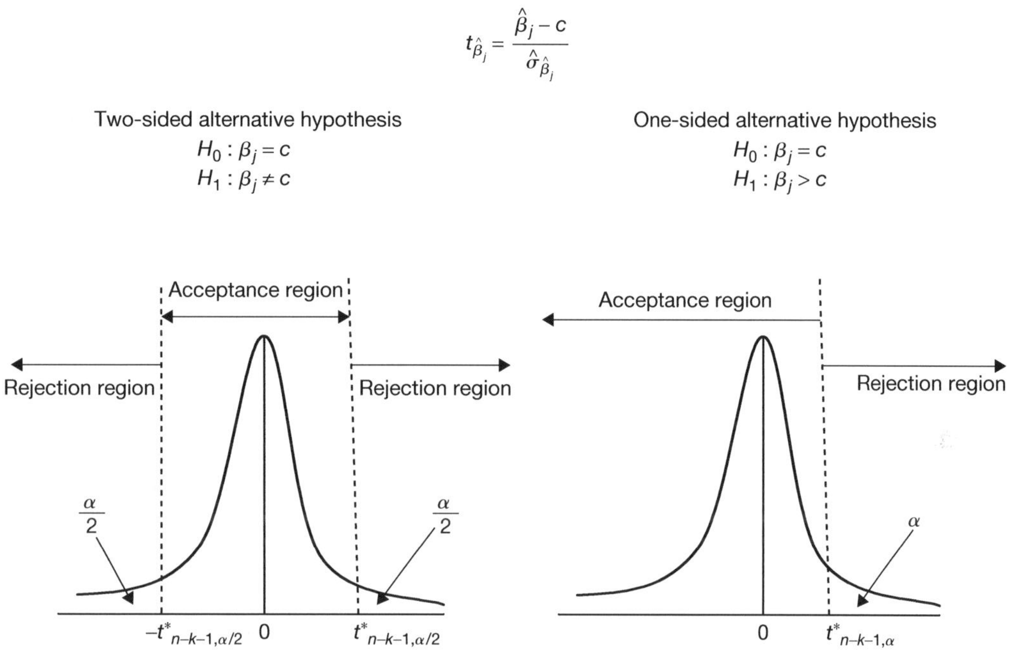

hypothesis when this is true (Type I error). It is customary to choose 5% or 1% significance level, but the researcher could choose any other. Now since we could reject the null either because $t_{\hat{\beta}_j}$ may be well above zero or well below zero, we will split the significance level equally between the two tails of the Student-*t* pdf. The left panel of Figure 2.4 describes the rejection and acceptance regions for Case (3). The value $t^*_{n-k-1,\alpha/2}$ is known as the **critical value** associated with a two-sided alternative hypothesis at the α significance level. This value can be found in the tables of the Student-*t*.

In Case (1), the null hypothesis will be rejected in favor of the alternative when the value of $t_{\hat{\beta}_j}$ is large and positive. The right panel of Figure 2.4 describes the rejection region for this one-sided alternative hypothesis. Similarly, for Case (2), the null hypothesis will be rejected when the value of $t_{\hat{\beta}_j}$ is large (in magnitude) and negative. In this instance, the rejection region will be in the lower tail of the Student-*t* pdf.

A hypothesis of great interest is $H_0 : \beta_j = 0$. If we fail to reject this null, then the regressor X_j is not important to explain the dependent variable Y. Thus, a very first exercise when confronted with the estimation results of a linear regression model is to assess this hypothesis. Going back to the results reported in Table 2.3, the computer software generates the *t*-ratios for all the regressors when the null hypothesis is of this type $H_0 : \beta_j = 0$. The fourth column in the EViews output named "t-Statistic" is this *t*-ratio,

$$t_{\hat{\beta}_1} = \frac{0.747}{0.096} = 7.783 \qquad (2.40)$$

$$t_{\hat{\beta}_2} = \frac{-0.069}{0.046} = -1.510 \tag{2.41}$$

For β_1, let us test against a two-sided alternative hypothesis $H_0: \beta_1 = 0; H_1: \beta_1 \neq 0$ at the 5% significance level. Because we have two regressors and a constant, $k + 1 = 2 + 1 = 3$. The number of observations is $n = 35$. We obtain the critical value from the Student-t tables, $t^*_{32,0.05/2} \approx 2.040$. Because $t_{\hat{\beta}_1} > t^*_{32,0.05/2}$ $(7.783 > 2.040)$, the t-ratio falls clearly into the rejection region, and so we reject the null hypothesis at the 5% significance level. We conclude that past information contained in Δp_{t-1} is statistically relevant to explain Δp_t.

For β_2, let us test against a one-sided alternative hypothesis $H_0: \beta_2 = 0; H_1: \beta_1 < 0$ at the 5% significance level. In this case, note that the rejection region is placed in the lower tail of the Student-t pdf. The critical value is $t^*_{32,0.05} \approx -1.693$. Because $t_{\hat{\beta}_2} > t^*_{32,0.05}$ $(-1.510 > -1.693)$, the ratio $t_{\hat{\beta}_2}$ falls into the acceptance region, and we fail to reject the null, concluding that changes in interest rates do not affect house prices. However, this failure to reject is not as strong as we would like it to be. Suppose that the researcher is willing to entertain a significance level of 10%. Then the critical value is $t^*_{32,0.10} \approx -1.308$, and because $t_{\hat{\beta}_2} < t^*_{32,0.10}$ $(-1.510 < -1.308)$, we will reject the null hypothesis. Hence, we can say that the statistical significance of interest rates is marginal.

The computer output also provides the **p-values** associated with $H_0: \beta_j = 0$. The p-value is the smallest significance level at which the null hypothesis can be rejected. This probability is provided in the last column ("Prob.") of the EViews output. This is the p-value for testing $H_0: \beta_j = 0$ against the two-sided alternative, $H_1: \beta_j \neq 0$:

$$p\text{-}value = P(|t_{n-k-1}| > |t_{\hat{\beta}_j}|) = 2P(t_{n-k-1} > t_{\hat{\beta}_j}) \tag{2.42}$$

Then we will reject the null hypothesis whenever we encounter smaller p-values than the chosen significance level; and on the contrary, we will fail to reject whenever the p-values are larger than the significance level. Going back to the results of Table 2.3, we read that for β_1:

$$p\text{-value} = 0.000 = P(|t_{32}| > |7.783|) = 2P(t_{32} > 7.783)$$

Thus, we have plenty of evidence against the null $H_0: \beta_1 = 0$.

For β_2,

$$p\text{-value} = 0.140 = P(|t_{32}| > |-1.510|) = 2P(t_{32} > 1.510) \rightarrow$$
$$P(t_{32} > 1.510) = 0.140/2 = 0.07$$

Thus, we will fail to reject the null $H_0: \beta_2 = 0$ at the 5% significance level, but we will reject it at the 10% level.

2.4.2 The *F*-test

The t-ratio is useful when there is a single hypothesis to test. A multiple or *joint hypothesis* involves several regression coefficients. For instance, the null hypothesis $H_0: \beta_2 = \beta_4 = 0$ involves two restrictions ($\beta_2 = 0$ and $\beta_4 = 0$) and two regression coefficients. Other examples are $H_0: \beta_2 + \beta_4 = 1$ and $H_0: \beta_2 = 2, \beta_4 = 0$. Because several restrictions are involved, it is enough that at least one is false to reject the null. Thus, the alternative hypothesis is formulated as the negation of H_0. The F-ratio is the statistic to test for a joint hypothesis.

To construct the F-ratio, we distinguish between the *unrestricted model* and the *restricted model*. Suppose that we work with the following regression model:

$$Y = \beta_0 + \beta_1 X_1 + \beta_2 X_2 + \beta_3 X_3 + \beta_4 X_4 + u \tag{2.43}$$

and we entertain the null hypothesis $H_0: \beta_2 = \beta_4 = 0$. The unrestricted model is the most general regression model (2.43) with no restrictions imposed. The restricted model is the resulting model when the null hypothesis is imposed on the unrestricted model. In this example,

$$Y = \beta_0 + \beta_1 X_1 + \beta_3 X_3 + \varepsilon \tag{2.44}$$

After estimating both models, restricted and unrestricted, we gather the SSR for each model. We call SSR_u the sum of squared residuals of the unrestricted model, and SSR_r the sum of squared residuals of the restricted model. If the null hypothesis is true, the estimation results of the unrestricted and restricted models should be very similar, and hence SSR_u and SSR_r will not be very different from each other. Then if the difference $SSR_r - SSR_u$ is significantly large, we will conclude that there is evidence against the null hypothesis. The F-ratio is the statistic that measures statistically the difference in the sum of squared residuals. The statistic is defined as

$$F_{m,n-k-1} = \frac{(SSR_r - SSR_u)/m}{SSR_u/(n-k-1)} \tag{2.45}$$

where m is the number of restrictions under the null (in Equation (2.44) $m = 2$) and $n - k - 1$ is the number of degrees of freedom in the unrestricted model. The ratio is distributed as an F random variable with $(m, n - k - 1)$ degrees of freedom. As with the t-ratio, we will need a decision rule to reject or fail to reject the null hypothesis. In

FIGURE 2.5 Rejection Rules for the *F*-Ratio

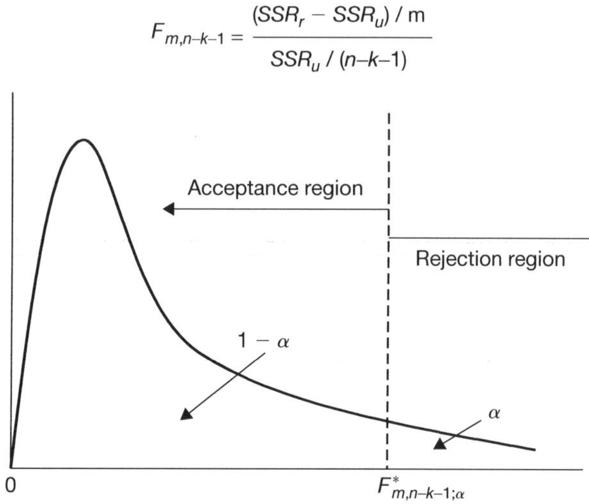

Figure 2.5, we show the F pdf with the rejection and acceptance regions. The value $F^*_{m,n-k-1;\alpha}$ is the critical value associated with the $\alpha\%$ significance level, and it is found on the tables for the F-distribution. The null hypothesis will be rejected when $F_{m,n-k-1} > F^*_{m,n-k-1;\alpha}$; otherwise $F_{m,n-k-1}$ will fall in the acceptance region, and by that we will fail to reject the null.

Going back to the results reported in Table 2.3, we find the value of an F-statistic ($F = 14.546$) and its p-value ($= 0.000$). We call this statistic the **F-test** for *overall significance of the regression* because it assesses the joint significance of all regressors in the model excluding the constant. Thus, the null hypothesis for this test is

$$H_0 : \beta_1 = \beta_2 = \cdots\cdot = \beta_k = 0 \tag{2.46}$$

This test is computed following (2.45). The SSR_r is calculated by running the restricted model, which regresses the dependent variable on just a constant. The value of this test is provided by all or most econometrics computer packages. From reading its p-value, we will decide whether or not to reject the null. Since the p-value is zero, we have strong evidence against the null, and we conclude that interest rates and/or past prices are informative enough to explain current changes in house prices. If the p-value is not provided, then we need to find $F^*_{m,n-k-1;\alpha}$. Suppose that we choose $\alpha = 5\%$. We now have $m = 2$ and $n - k - 1 = 35 - 2 - 1 = 32$. From the tables of the F-distribution, $F^*_{2,32,0.05} \approx 3.30$. Because $F_{2,32} = 14.546 > 3.30 \approx F^*_{2,32,0.05}$, the F-ratio falls into the rejection region, and clearly the null hypothesis is rejected at the 5% significance level.

Depending on the researcher's interest, there are many other linear restrictions for which the F-test is not directly provided by the econometrics software. The important step is to formulate and estimate the restricted model. Once this is accomplished, the F-test is easily calculated by following Equation (2.45).

KEY WORDS

adjusted R-squared p. 33
conditional expectation p. 25
conditional probability density function p. 24
conditional variance p. 25
critical value p. 43
efficiency p. 37
error variance p. 36
estimator and estimate p. 32
F-test p. 44
Gauss–Markov theorem p. 36
homoscedasticity p. 35
linear regression model p. 27
linearity p. 35
ordinary least squares (OLS) p. 29
p-value p. 44
residual variance p. 38
R-squared p. 32
serial correlation p. 36
significance level p. 42
t-ratio p. 42
unbiasedness p. 37

APPENDIX

A2.1 OLS Derivation

In this section, we present the solution to the OLS optimization problem by using multivariate calculus. Let us focus on the simple regression model and derive the Equations (2.8) and (2.9):

$$\min_{\hat{\beta}_0, \hat{\beta}_1} S \equiv \sum_{i=1}^{n} \hat{u}_i^2 = \min_{\hat{\beta}_0, \hat{\beta}_1} \sum_{i=1}^{n} (y_i - \hat{\beta}_0 - \hat{\beta}_1 x_{1i})^2 \tag{A2.1}$$

We derive the first order conditions (FOC) by taking the partial derivatives of the function S with respect to $\hat{\beta}_0$ and $\hat{\beta}_1$ and setting them equal to zero:

$$\frac{\partial S}{\partial \hat{\beta}_0} = -2 \sum_{i=1}^{n} (y_i - \hat{\beta}_0 - \hat{\beta}_1 x_{1i}) = 0 \tag{A2.2}$$

$$\frac{\partial S}{\partial \hat{\beta}_1} = -2 \sum_{i=1}^{n} x_{1i}(y_i - \hat{\beta}_0 - \hat{\beta}_1 x_{1i}) = 0 \tag{A2.3}$$

This a system of two equations with two unknowns, $\hat{\beta}_0$ and $\hat{\beta}_1$. The system is known as the *normal equations,* and the solution to the system delivers the OLS estimators. Dividing all the terms in Equation (A2.2) by n, we obtain

$$\bar{y} = \hat{\beta}_0 + \hat{\beta}_1 \bar{x}_1 \Rightarrow \hat{\beta}_0 = \bar{y} - \hat{\beta}_1 \bar{x}_1 \tag{A2.4}$$

To solve for $\hat{\beta}_1$, we multiply Equation (A2.2) by $\sum_i x_{1i}$,

$$\sum_{i=1}^{n} y_i \sum_{i=1}^{n} x_{1i} = \hat{\beta}_0 \sum_{i=1}^{n} x_{1i} - \hat{\beta}_1 \left(\sum_{i=1}^{n} x_{1i} \right)^2, \tag{A2.5}$$

and together with (A2.3)

$$\sum_{i=1}^{n} y_i x_{1i} = \hat{\beta}_0 \sum_{i=1}^{n} x_{1i} + \hat{\beta}_1 \sum_{i=1}^{n} x_{1i}^2 \tag{A2.6}$$

we subtract one equation from the other, side by side, to obtain

$$\sum_{i=1}^{n} y_i x_{1i} - \sum_{i=1}^{n} y_i \sum_{i=1}^{n} x_{1i} = \hat{\beta}_1 \left[\sum_{i=1}^{n} x_{1i}^2 - \left(\sum_{i=1}^{n} x_{1i} \right)^2 \right] \tag{A2.7}$$

Finally, solving for $\hat{\beta}_1$,

$$\hat{\beta}_1 = \frac{\sum_{i=1}^{n} y_i x_{1i} - \sum_{i=1}^{n} y_i \sum_{i=1}^{n} x_{1i}}{\sum_{i=1}^{n} x_{1i}^2 - \left(\sum_{i=1}^{n} x_{1i} \right)^2} = \frac{\sum_{i=1}^{n} (y_i - \bar{y})(x_{1i} - \bar{x}_1)}{\sum_{i=1}^{n} (x_{1i} - \bar{x}_1)^2} \tag{A2.8}$$

we obtain Equations (2.8) and (2.9).

A2.2 Review of Some Formulas of Interest

Although all econometrics software will calculate the OLS estimators and their variances, it is of interest to review what is behind these formulas. We will focus on the simple regression model because the formulas are easier to interpret, but our conclusions will also hold for the multiple regression model. At the same time, this review will summarize the main ideas behind OLS estimation.

The starting point is the linear regression model

$$Y = \beta_0 + \beta_1 X + u \tag{A2.9}$$

for which, under the assumptions of the Gauss–Markov theorem, the conditional mean and variance of the dependent variable are

$$E(Y|X) = \beta_0 + \beta_1 X \tag{A2.10}$$

$$Var(Y|X) = \sigma_u^2 \tag{A2.11}$$

For a random sample of n observations (x_i, y_i) for $i = 1, 2 \ldots n$, the OLS estimators are

$$\hat{\beta}_1 = \frac{\sum_{i=1}^{n}(x_i - \overline{x})(y_i - \overline{y})}{\sum_{i=1}^{n}(x_i - \overline{x})^2} \tag{A2.12}$$

$$\hat{\beta}_0 = \overline{y} - \hat{\beta}_1 \overline{x} \tag{A2.13}$$

for which their means and variances are

$$E(\hat{\beta}_0) = \beta_0 \quad \text{and} \quad E(\hat{\beta}_1) = \beta_1 \tag{A2.14}$$

$$\sigma_{\hat{\beta}_0}^2 \equiv var(\hat{\beta}_0) = \frac{\sigma_u^2 \sum_{i=1}^{n} x_i^2}{n \sum_{i=1}^{n}(x_i - \overline{x})^2} \tag{A2.15}$$

$$\sigma_{\hat{\beta}_1}^2 \equiv var(\hat{\beta}_1) = \frac{\sigma_u^2}{\sum_{i=1}^{n}(x_i - \overline{x})^2} \tag{A2.16}$$

These are some important conclusions:

- The OLS estimators $\hat{\beta}$ are centered on the population parameters β.
- The variance of $\hat{\beta}$ is directly proportional to the error variance σ_u^2; this is to say, the larger the error variance, the more disperse the OLS estimator is.
- The variance of $\hat{\beta}$ is inversely proportional to the sample variance of the regressor $n^{-1}\sum_{i=1}^{n}(x_i - \overline{x})^2$; thus, a regressor with a large variance reduces the variance of the estimator.

- The error variance needs to be estimated to be able to compute the (A2.15) and (A2.16) formulas. The estimator of σ_u^2 is based on the residuals $\hat{u}_i = y_i - \hat{\beta}_0 - \hat{\beta}_1 x_i$ and looks like

$$\hat{\sigma}_{\hat{u}}^2 = \frac{\sum_{i=1}^{n} \hat{u}_i^2}{n-2} \tag{A2.17}$$

  $\hat{\sigma}_{\hat{u}}^2$ is the residual variance that is plugged in (A2.15) and (A2.16) to calculate the variances of the estimators. The denominator $n - 2$ is known as the *degrees of freedom,* defined as the number of observations n minus the number of parameters to estimate, in this case, two parameters (β_0 and β_1). In the multiple regression model, the degrees of freedom are $n - (k + 1)$ and will be the denominator of the estimated error variance. A further property of this estimator is unbiasedness, that is, $E(\hat{\sigma}_{\hat{u}}^2) = \sigma_u^2$.
- The variance of $\hat{\beta}$ is only valid when assumptions **A3** and **A4**—homoscedasticity and no serial correlation—are satisfied. Because heteroscedasticity and serial correlation are regularly present in economic data, we will not use the formulas (A2.15) and (A2.16) but instead the HAC robust version (taking care to some extent of heteroscedasticity and/or serial correlation), which is provided by most econometric software packages.

EXERCISES

1. Suppose that you have information on interest rates $\{X\}$ and in savings $\{Y\}$ for a sample of 50 households:

	***X* in %**				
	1.0	**2.0**	**3.0**	**4.0**	**5.0**
	0.0	10.0	15.0	0.0	20.0
	5.0	0.0	10.0	15.0	16.0
	1.0	2.0	4.0	6.0	6.0
***Y* in**	1.0	3.0	4.0	5.0	7.0
thousands $	0.5	1.0	2.0	2.0	5.0
	1.6	2.0	2.5	2.0	5.0
	0.8	1.0	2.0	2.0	4.0
	0.2	0.5	1.0	2.0	6.0
	1.0	1.0	2.0	2.0	8.0
	0.0	1.0	1.5	6.0	16.0

Compute the following

a. Conditional sample mean $\bar{y}_{Y|X=4}$.
b. Conditional sample variance $\hat{\sigma}^2_{Y|X=5}$.
c. Conditional histogram when $X = 2$.
d. Unconditional mean and standard deviation of Y.

2. Download the U.S. GDP quarterly growth rates and the Standard & Poor's (SP) 500 quarterly returns. For both series, compute their descriptive statistics and their histograms. Are these two series contemporaneously correlated? Comment on your findings.

3. The stock market is said to be a leading indicator for GDP growth. Because the stock market prices the expectations of future earnings, a bullish market may predict future economic growth and vice versa. Let Y_t be GDP growth and X_t be SP500 returns. (both series collected at the quarterly frequency as in the previous exercise). Run OLS for the following models:

a. $Y_t = \beta_0 + \beta_1 X_t + u_t$ (contemporaneous correlation).
b. $Y_t = \beta_0 + \beta_1 X_{t-1} + u_t$ (one-quarter leading indicator).
c. $Y_t = \beta_0 + \beta_1 X_{t-1} + \beta_2 X_{t-2} + \beta_3 X_{t-3} + \beta_4 X_{t-4} + u_t$ (four-quarter leading indicator).
d. $Y_t = \beta_0 + \beta_1 X_{t-1} + \beta_2 X_{t-2} + \beta_3 X_{t-3} + \beta_4 X_{t-4} + \beta_5 Y_{t-1} + u_t$ (leading indicator with GDP inertia).

For each model, assess the R-squared and the adjusted R-squared. Which model do you prefer?

4. In models (a) and (b), conduct t-ratio tests for the null $H_0 : \beta_1 = 0$ versus $H_1 : \beta_1 \neq 0$, and $H_1 : \beta_1 > 0$, and $H_1 : \beta_1 < 0$. Choose your own significance level. What are your conclusions? Is the stock market a leading indicator?

5. For model (c), conduct a t-ratio test for every single coefficient; that is, $H_0 : \beta_j = 0$ versus $H_1 : \beta_j \neq 0$ for $j = 1, 2, 3, 4$. Perform an F-test for overall significance of the regression; that is, $H_0 : \beta_1 = \beta_2 = \beta_3 = \beta_4 = 0$. Choose your own significance level.

6. For model (d), conduct a t-ratio test for every single coefficient, that is, $H_0 : \beta_j = 0$ versus $H_1 : \beta_j \neq 0$ for $j = 1, 2, 3, 4, 5$. Perform an F-test for overall significance of the regression, that is, $H_0 : \beta_1 = \beta_2 = \beta_3 = \beta_4 = \beta_5 = 0$. Choose your own significance level.

7. You have already downloaded some of the time series described in Chapter 1. Take the time series "'unemployed persons'" from the FRED database and the "'number of people in poverty'" from the U.S. Census Bureau. Calculate the growth rates for both series and compute their respective descriptive statistics. What is their correlation coefficient? Comment on your findings.

8. We would like to investigate whether changes in unemployment is one of the causes of changes in poverty. Propose at least three regression models relating unemployment and poverty changes. You may want to follow similar specifications as those in Exercise 3. For each model, comment on the R-squared and adjusted R-squared. Which model(s) do you prefer?

9. For each model proposed in Exercise 8, conduct a t-ratio for every single coefficient, and perform an F-test for overall significance of the regression. Choose your own significance level. Are changes in unemployment producing changes in poverty?
10. Run similar models to those in Exercise 8 but now use both series in levels instead of growth rates. Perform similar t-ratios and F-tests as in Exercise 9. Comment on your results in comparison with those in Exercises 8 and 9.

CHAPTER 3

Statistics and Time Series

In Chapter 2, we reviewed several statistical concepts, which were already familiar to you from your introductory courses in statistics and econometrics. At the core of statistics is always a random experiment or mechanism that gives rise to different outcomes. Remember the popular example of throwing a die into the air and recording the outcomes. Sometimes you get 1, sometimes 3, and so on. You can perform this experiment over and over and gather a sample as large as you wish. Based on a sample, you can always compute a sample mean, a sample variance, and any other moment. In addition, you may ask questions regarding how well the sample moments approximate the population moments. This analysis does not mention time. Your samples are cross-sectional and to a certain extent, you could repeat the experiment at will should you desire to gather more samples.

In this chapter, we confront a different scenario—we call it a **time series** *scenario*—where at the most basic level, we will not be able to repeat the random experiment as many times as we want, and consequently, our sample information will be limited. In fact, our sample will be just one observation per unit of time with no option for more. Because of such a meager sample, you may be wondering how to compute a sample average with just one observation, much less a sample variance, and certainly, you can forget about approximating population moments with sample moments. It seems that we have a difficult problem ahead of us.

Let us start by introducing a time series sample and some time series plots. A *time series sample* is a collection of records ordered by time. We write $\{y_t, t = 1, 2 \ldots. T\} = \{y_1, y_2, \ldots.. y_T\}$, where T is the number of periods. A *time series plot* is the graphical representation of the time series sample. Look at Figure 3-1a–3-1c. On the horizontal axis, we read "time." Time appears in an ordered fashion moving only forward. On the vertical axis, we read the values or records of the variable of interest. For instance, in Figure 3.1a, we read that in June 2001, the value of the Dow Jones (DJ) Index, which is a basket of stocks of the largest companies in the United States, was 10,502 (indexes do not have units). Likewise, in Figure 3.1c, we read that in 1999, there were 200 property crimes per 1,000 households in the United States. For every period of time (months in the DJ Index, years in the property crimes series), there is one and only one observation. How do we interpret these numbers?

FIGURE 3.1
Examples of Time Series

(a) Stock Prices: Dow Jones Index monthly data. Closing price at the end of the month, January 1988 to April 2008.

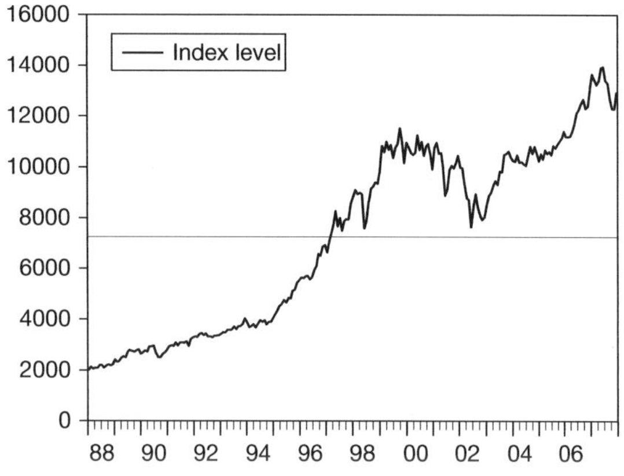

(a)

(b) Returns to the Dow Jones Index. Monthly returns, February 1988 to April 2008.

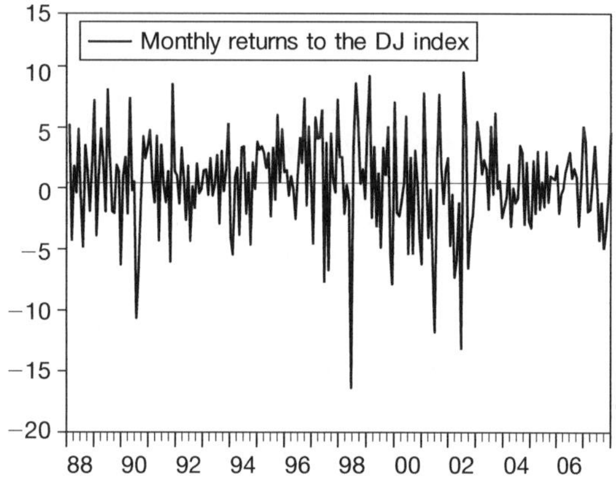

(b)

(c) Property crimes include burglary, theft, and motor vehicles. Yearly data from 1973 to 2000. (*Source:* From Bureau of Justice Statistics website: http://bjs.ojp.usdoj.gov/index.cfm?ty=tp&tid=32)

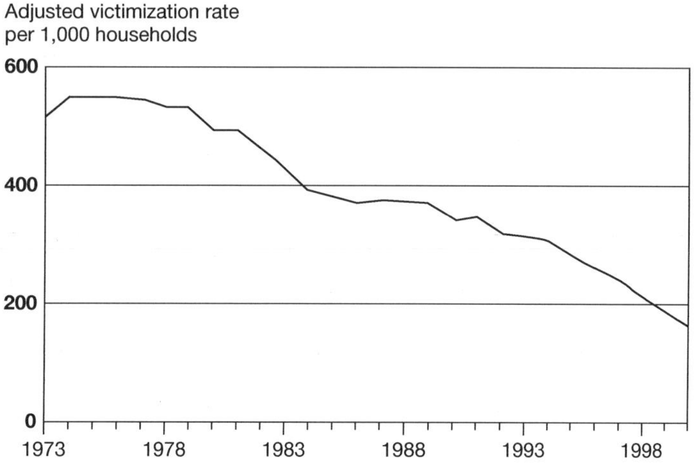

(c)

Let us go back to the DJ Index. In April 30, 2007, its value was 13,264. Why not 10,400 or 14,000, or any other number? How are these numbers generated? Think about the economic mechanism that drives stock prices. A large system of economic agents make decisions, almost every minute, on why, when, what, and how much to buy or sell. We can think of the economy as a big experiment such that before the end of April 2007, many outcomes were possible but when all is settled (allegorically, the die falls to the ground, and we can see its side), we observe a realization of 13,264. This is the only outcome that we have, and we cannot observe any other because we cannot go back in time and run another experiment under the same circumstances that happened during the month of April. Next month, the economic machinery will run again, most likely under different circumstances, and by the end of the month, we will observe another outcome, and that continues month after month. We eventually collect many outcomes, or in other words, a time series sample. The important point is that a potentially different experiment goes on in every period of time, and although a priori, many values of the variable of interest are possible, eventually only one value is realized.

Informative as these numbers are, they represent just a data point. Now take each time series plot as a whole and observe that there is even more information. For instance, there is an upward tendency in plot 3-1a, or a reverting behavior toward a central value (the horizontal solid line) in plot 3-1b, or a downward trend in plot 3-1c. These features are specific to the study of time series; they do not appear in a cross-sectional setting.

With a time series sample $\{y_1, y_2, \ldots. y_T\}$, we could compute the following average $\bar{\bar{y}} = \sum_{t=1}^{T} y_t / T$. This is *a time mean*, which differs from a cross-sectional mean. In a time mean, we aggregate over time periods, but in a cross-sectional mean, we aggregate over units or individuals. Take the DJ Index time series again (Figure 3.1a) and think what you would learn if you were to calculate $\bar{\bar{y}}$. What are we estimating when we compute $\bar{\bar{y}}$? Is there a population mean? If so, is $\bar{\bar{y}}$ a good estimator for the population mean? Is it possible that the population mean changes over time? If so, is $\bar{\bar{y}}$ a meaningful statistic? Do we observe any pattern in the time series of Figure 3.1a–3.1c? How is the DJ value in April 2007 related to that of April 2008? Can we predict next year's DJ returns? None of these questions occurred in the cross-sectional setting. They arise because we introduce a new dimension: *time*. Time series analysis and model-based forecasting are concerned with these questions. Over the subsequent chapters, you will find the answers. For now, in this chapter, we are going to start with foundational concepts, which will support the construction of good forecasting models. Our goal is to answer three fundamental questions in time series analysis:

1. What is a stochastic process and what is a time series?
2. What is the interpretation of a time average or any other time moment?
3. What are the new tools of analysis?

3.1 Stochastic Process and Time Series

Recall that random variables can be characterized in two ways. If we wish to fully characterize a random variable, we need to know its *probability density function (pdf)*. Alternatively, a partial characterization of a random variable can be obtained by calculating its moments: mean μ, variance σ^2, and so forth. If we know the pdf, we can calculate the moments, but knowing the moments is not enough to find the pdf. Following conventional notation, random variables are written with uppercase letters, and the possible outcomes or events of the random variable are written with lowercase letters:

Random variable: Y

Outcomes: $\{y_1, y_2, y_3, \ldots\ldots\} = \{y_i, i = 1, 2, 3 \ldots\}$

In Figure 3.2, we plot the pdf of the random variable Y, for instance, yearly income in the United States in 2008. On the horizontal axis, we have all possible outcomes of this variable, and, for a given event, say that $y = \$10{,}000$ we read the area under the curve to obtain the probability of such an outcome. For instance, we say that 12% of the U.S. population has at most a yearly income of \$10 thousand. We can also select a cross-sectional sample $\{y_1, y_2, \ldots.. y_n\}$ by drawing individuals from the population and computing sample moments such as the sample mean $\bar{y} = \sum_{i=1}^{n} y_i/n$, sample variance $\hat{\sigma}^2 = \sum_{i=1}^{n}(y_i - \bar{y})^2 > (n-1)$, and so on. We also know that these sample moments are good estimators of the population moments.

3.1.1 Stochastic Process

Now let us formalize the time series scenario. How do we introduce the new *time* dimension in the study of random variables? We need to introduce a new concept: **stochastic process**, which we denote as $\{Y_t\} = \{Y_1, Y_2, \ldots.\ Y_T\}$. Note that we use capital letters. According to our notation, we must have a collection of random variables, but each random variable has a subindex that runs from time 1 to time T. Look at Figure 3.3 to help you visualize a stochastic process.

FIGURE 3.2 Probability Density Function

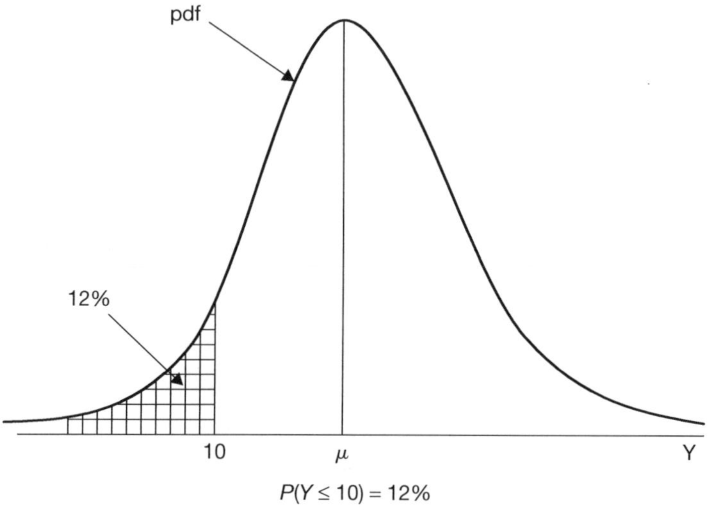

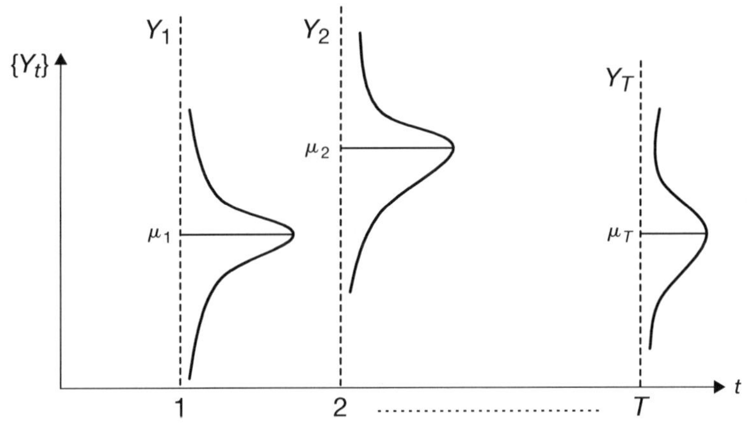

FIGURE 3.3 Graphical Representation of a Stochastic Process

On the horizontal axis, we have discrete time. The unit of time can be days, weeks, months, years, and so forth, and time increases at a unit interval, for instance with monthly data, $t = 1$ could be November, $t = 2$ December, and so on. For each period of time, we vertically represent a random variable $Y_1, Y_2, \ldots. Y_T$, and each random variable is characterized by its pdf and its moments (you may want to turn the page 90° to visualize the pdfs of Figure 3.3 as being those of Figure 3.2). In Figure 3.3, we explicitly picture the population means $\mu_1, \mu_2, \ldots.. \mu_T$ but we also could have referred to any other moment of the random variables. For instance, going back to the DJ Index, we can think conceptually about how to represent all possible outcomes that the economic engine could have produced in each period of time. It is natural to think of a random variable with outcomes summarized by its pdf, and in doing so, we could read the pdf of the DJ Index at $t = 1$ (say April 2007), the pdf of the DJ Index at $t = 2$ (say May 2007), and so on. Observe that we draw different shapes for the pdfs and different population means for different periods of time.

We define:

A stochastic process is a collection of random variables indexed by time.

3.1.2 Time Series

Recall Figure 3.1a. We have 244 realizations $\{y_t; t = 1, 2 \ldots 244\} = \{y_1, y_2, \ldots.. y_{244}\}$: y_1 is the outcome corresponding to the random variable Y_1 (monthly DJ Index on January 1988), y_2 is the outcome corresponding to the random variable Y_2 (monthly DJ Index on February 1988) and going forward to the last period, we observe y_{244} that is an outcome from the random variable Y_{244} (monthly DJ Index on April 2008). We say that the collection $\{y_1, y_2, \ldots.. y_{244}\}$ is a time series sample corresponding to the stochastic process $\{Y_t\} = \{Y_1, Y_2, \ldots. Y_{244}\}$.

From a visual perspective, what is the relation between the stochastic process and the time series? Look at Figure 3.4 that has a time series superimposed on the stochastic process.

FIGURE 3.4
Graphical Representation of a Stochastic Process and a Time Series (Thick Line)

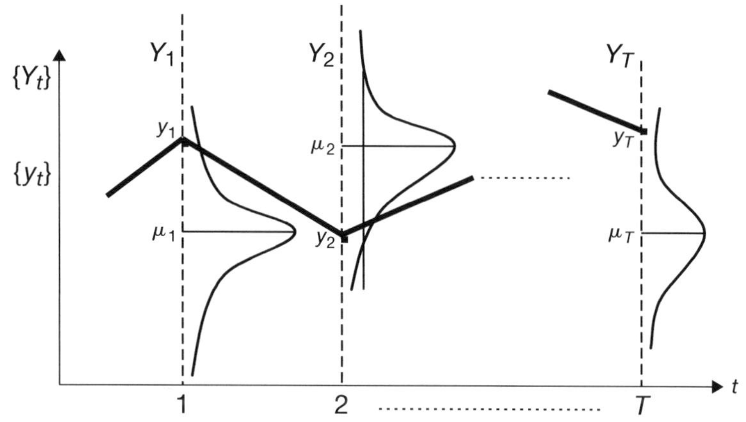

The squares represent, for instance, the value of the DJ Index in each month. Joining these points, we obtain the thick line, which represents the time series $\{y_t; t = 1, 2 \dots T\} = \{y_1, y_2, \dots\dots y_T\}$. Each element y_t in the time series is *one and only one* outcome of the random variable Y_t. We never observe the stochastic process: this is a conceptual construction that is a fundamental key for the analysis of our data. The data that we find in real life are time series, and our task is to infer the characteristics of the stochastic process behind the time series data in order to build forecasting models.

We define:

A time series is a sample realization of a stochastic process.

3.2 The Interpretation of a Time Average

At this stage, what is the most striking feature of a time series scenario compared to a cross-sectional scenario? A cross-sectional sample has *several* observations of the random variable, and we use these observations to compute a sample mean, a sample variance, and so on. A time series sample has *one and only one* observation of the random variable, and we cannot go back in time to draw additional realizations. In this situation, you may be wondering how we could compute a sample average with just one observation, much less a sample variance. As we mentioned in the introduction to this chapter, this seems to be a difficult problem.

In a time series scenario, because we only have a time series sample, that is, one observation per period, the **cross-sectional averages** are not feasible. You may think that instead we could take averages over time. For a time series $\{y_1, y_2, \dots\dots y_T\}$ we can compute a *time mean* as

$$\bar{\bar{y}} = \frac{\sum_{t=1}^{T} y_t}{T}$$

or a *time variance* as

$$\overline{\overline{\sigma}}^2 = \frac{\sum_{t=1}^{T}(y_t - \overline{\overline{y}})^2}{T}$$

Consider these two questions:

1. Do these time averages make sense? Does it matter that we aggregate realizations over time rather than over individuals? Think that the realizations may come from a random variable with potentially different pdfs over time (see Figure 3.3 or 3.4).
2. Do these two time averages $\overline{\overline{y}}$ and $\overline{\overline{\sigma}}^2$ estimate a population mean and a population variance, respectively? If so, are the population mean and the population variance the same for all the random variables in the stochastic process?

So far, we have not imposed any condition in the stochastic process. In Figure 3.3, we pictured a stochastic process with different population means $\{\mu_1, \mu_2, \ldots.. \mu_T\}$ and different population variances $\{\sigma_1^2, \sigma_2^2, \ldots.. \sigma_T^2\}$. Then which μ is approximated by $\overline{\overline{y}}$? Which σ^2 is approximated by $\overline{\overline{\sigma}}^2$?

All these questions prompt us to think that some conditions must be imposed on the behavior of the stochastic process, such that time averages are meaningful estimators of population averages. The first condition, known as *stationarity*, focuses on the stochastic process (population information). It requires that, at least, the random variables that form the stochastic process have the same population mean and the same population variance. Stationarity will rule out a process such as that of Figure 3.3 because it is very heterogeneous, meaning that there are different means and variances or even different pdfs over time. The second condition, known as *ergodicity,* requires that when stationarity is in place, a time average approximates well the population average, and in doing so, time averages are good substitutes for cross-sectional averages, which as we have already seen are not feasible with just one time series. Thus, ergodicity makes a bridge between sample information (time series) and population information (stochastic process).

Next we analyze the idea of stationarity in more detail. The idea of ergodicity is rather technical; we provide an introductory explanation in the appendix to this chapter. Skipping ergodicity for now will not interrupt the flow of the chapter. You may want to keep on reading and move to the appendix once you grasp the following ideas on stationary.

3.2.1 Stationarity

Let us look at Figure 3.1 and contrast the time series plot of the DJ Index (3.1a) with the plot of Index returns (3.1b). What is the average value of the Index from January 1988 to April 2008? What is the average Index return in the same period? In both cases, we can compute a time average and say that the mean value of the Index was 7,201 (Figure 3.1a) and that the monthly average return was 0.77% (Figure 3.1b). Do these numbers make sense?

Look at the plots 3.1a and 3.1b. The solid horizontal line is the time mean. In which plot is the time mean a more representative statistic of the entire series? In the first case, the mean of 7,201 is meaningless. This value happened only once, approximately in May 1997 and never again in the period of time under study. But a mean statistic is a measure of centrality; thus, in any given month, one should expect the value of the Index to be around the mean value. However, the Index had been running well above 10,000 in the last 5 years of the sample and well below 4,000 in the first four years of the sample. It seems that there may be different mean values at the beginning and toward the end of the time series. In contrast, the mean return of 0.77% is meaningful because in any given month, the realized return could be above or below the mean, but again, there is a tendency to revert to the mean. The time series does not remain for long periods of time around any particular value other than the mean. We say that the time series of the DJ Index seems to come from a nonstationary stochastic process and the time series of Index returns from a stationary process.

Figure 3.5a pictures a theoretical stochastic process in which each random variable has a different mean value. The mean depends on the time index *t*, and we write μ_t to

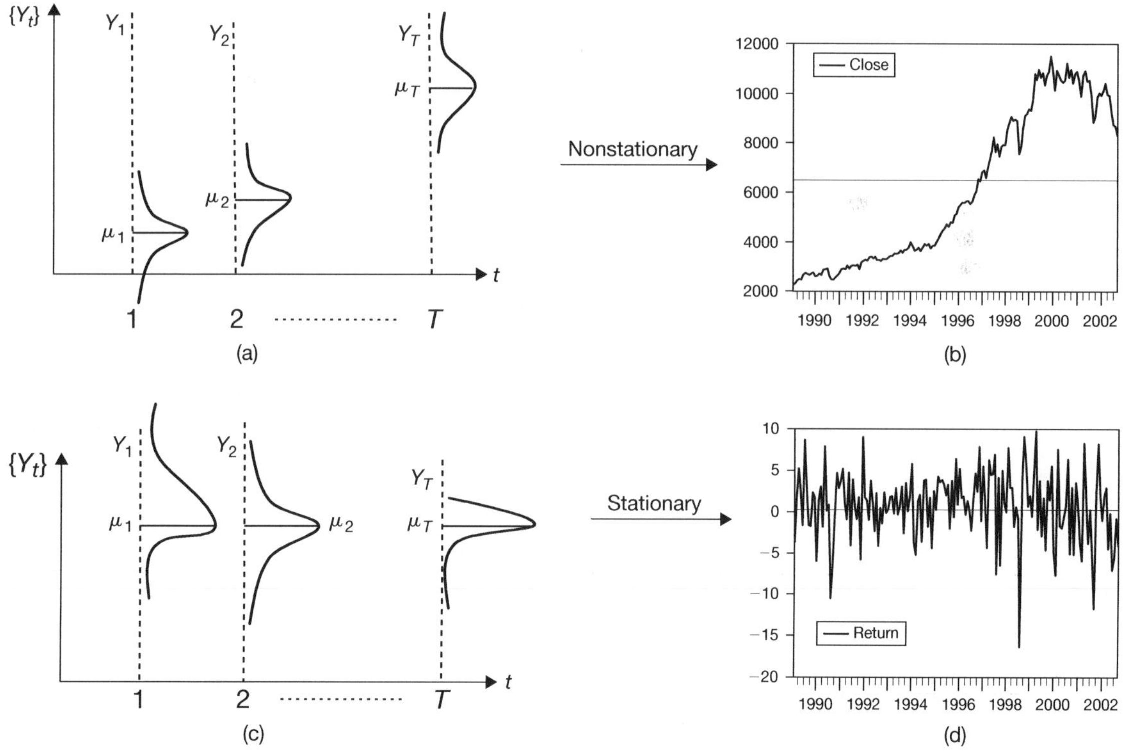

FIGURE 3.5 Nonstationary and Stationary Stochastic Process

indicate that we have different mean values over time. The DJ Index is a time series that most likely comes from a nonstationary process. In contrast, Figure 3.5c pictures a process that has a constant mean for all t, which we write as μ. The time series of returns to the DJ Index seems to come from a stationary process.

Observe that if we require the process to be stationary, we are asking for some degree of homogeneity or similarity in the random variables. How much homogeneity do we need? We distinguish between **strong stationarity** and **weak stationarity.**

We define:

A stochastic process is said to be first order strongly stationary if all random variables have the same probability density function.[1]

This definition is very strict because it imposes a very high degree of homogeneity among the random variables. It requires that all pdf's be identical. That is,

$$P(Y_1 \leq y) = P(Y_2 \leq y) = \cdots\cdots = P(Y_T \leq y)$$
$$f_{Y_1}(y) = f_{Y_2}(y) = \cdots\cdots\cdots f_{Y_T}(y)$$

Graphically, we can picture a first order strongly stationary stochastic process as in Figure 3.6.

If we focus on the first and second moments of the random variables—mean and variance—as opposed to the entire probability density function, we can define a milder form of stationarity. In Figure 3.5c, you can see that the probability density functions are very different: Some are skewed, some are symmetric, and some have a larger variance than others. However, all random variables have the same mean μ.

We define:

A stochastic process is said to be first order weakly stationary if all random variables have the same mean.

FIGURE 3.6 Strongly Stationary Stochastic Process

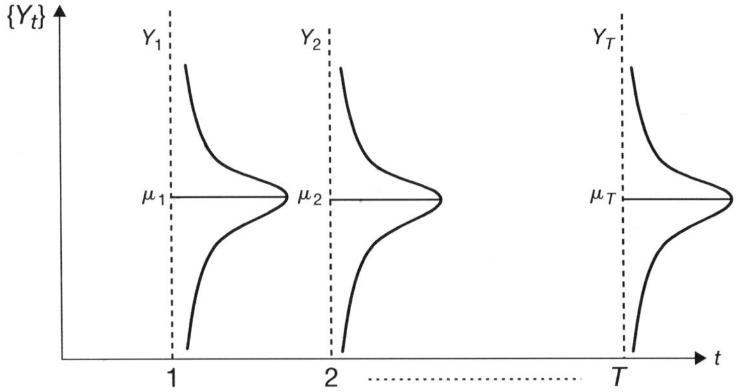

[1] We can also define 2nd, 3rd, 4th,. . . . order strongly stationary processes, but that requires the introduction of more advanced multivariate statistics that we do not pursue in this book.

That is,

$$\mu_{Y_1} = \mu_{Y_2} = \cdots\cdots = \mu_{Y_T} = \mu$$

We could require higher moments to be identical and define a higher order of weakly stationarity:

A stochastic process is said to be second order weakly stationary if all random variables have the same mean and the same variance and the covariances do not depend on time.

That is,

$$\text{i. } \mu_{Y_1} = \mu_{Y_1} = \cdots\cdots = \mu_{Y_T} = \mu$$
$$\text{ii. } \sigma^2_{Y_1} = \sigma^2_{Y_2} = \cdots\cdots = \sigma^2_{Y_T} = \sigma^2$$
$$\text{iii. } \rho_{Y_t, Y_{t-k}} = \rho_{|k|}$$

Condition (i.) is pictured in Figure 3.5c. Condition (ii.) requires the variance of each random variable to be identical to each other. You can easily think of two random variables with the same mean and variance, but one can have a symmetric probability density function and the other can have a skewed density function. For instance, plot the density of a chi-square random variable with 1 degree of freedom. The mean of this variable is 1 and the variance is 2. Contrast this density with that of a normal random variable with a mean of 1 and variance equal to 2. Condition (iii.) deals with the correlation of two random variables dated at different times, Y_t and Y_{t-k}. This condition is explained in more detail in Section 3.3 when we introduce the concept of autocorrelation. However, you can see that these two random variables are k periods apart. Condition (iii.) says that the strength of the linear relation (correlation) between any two random variables is a function of how distant in time they are from each other.

Variances, covariances, and correlations are all second moments. Thus, second order weakly stationary processes are concerned with the properties of only first and second moments and because of this, they are also called *covariance-stationary processes*. The most important feature of these processes is that the mean, the variance, and the covariances (and correlations) *do not depend on the time index*; they are time invariant, and this is why we write μ, σ^2, and $\rho_{|k|}$ in conditions (i.), (ii.), and (iii.), respectively.

By now, we have learned that a covariance-stationary process imposes fewer requirements in the random variables than a strongly stationary process, but you may wonder how we know when a process is stationary or nonstationary. The question is extremely relevant. Strongly stationary processes are difficult, if not impossible, to test for. Our focus is on weakly stationary processes and, in particular, on covariance-stationary processes. We have statistical testing procedures to detect nonstationarity in the mean and in the variance, which you will study in subsequent chapters. As a first resource, time series plots are good tools to hint the existence of a nonstationary mean and variance as we saw with the data of the DJ Index. In practice, model-based forecasting relies very often on **covariance-stationary** processes. Historically, until the late 1980s, time series econometricians and model-based forecasters worked almost exclusively with covariance-stationary models. The introduction and development of the idea of cointegration by Nobel laureates Granger and Engle, which allows for the combination of stationary and nonstationary processes, revolutionized the practice of forecasting. Economic and business data come from stationary and nonstationary processes. In this book, you will learn how to work with both types of processes.

3.2.2 Useful Transformations of Nonstationary Processes

We have seen that the DJ Index is likely a nonstationary process. The time series comes from a process with at least different means across time. The questions that we wish to analyze in this section are: (1) Can we find a transformation of the Index such that the resulting process is first order weakly stationary? (2) Is there any transformation that can make the process second order weakly stationary?

The answer to both questions is yes. In the first instance, a very helpful transformation is to take **first differences** of the data; and in the second instance, a *logarithmic transformation* helps to stabilize the variance of the time series. Thus, taking natural logs and taking first differences of the log time series makes a nonstationary process covariance stationary. We will see that these transformations also have economic meaning.

Let us start with *differencing* the data. Table 3.1 has a small sample of the DJ Index from January 2001 to September 2002. In the first column, we write the monthly date

TABLE 3.1 Dow Jones Index and Returns

Date	Index	Index(-1)	First difference index-index(-1)	Return = 100* (index-index(-1)/ index(-1)	Return = 100* (log(index)-log (index(-1))
2001:01	10887.400	10788.000	99.40000	0.921394	0.917175
2001:02	10495.300	10887.400	-392.10000	-3.601411	-3.667862
2001:03	9878.800	10495.300	-616.50000	-5.874058	-6.053649
2001:04	10735.000	9878.800	856.20000	8.667045	8.311838
2001:05	10911.900	10735.000	176.90000	1.647881	1.634451
2001:06	10502.400	10911.900	-409.50000	-3.752784	-3.825013
2001:07	10522.800	10502.400	20.40000	0.194241	0.194053
2001:08	9949.800	10522.800	-573.00000	-5.445319	-5.599188
2001:09	8847.600	9949.800	-1102.20000	-11.077610	-11.740620
2001:10	9075.100	8847.600	227.50000	2.571319	2.538816
2001:11	9851.600	9075.100	776.50000	8.556380	8.209948
2001:12	10021.600	9851.600	170.00000	1.725608	1.710889
2002:01	9920.000	10021.600	-101.60000	-1.013810	-1.018984
2002:02	10106.100	9920.000	186.10000	1.876008	1.858628
2002:03	10403.900	10106.100	297.80000	2.946735	2.904153
2002:04	9946.200	10403.900	-457.70000	-4.399312	-4.499017
2002:05	9925.300	9946.200	-20.90000	-0.210131	-0.210352
2002:06	9243.300	9925.300	-682.00000	-6.871329	-7.118809
2002:07	8736.600	9243.300	-506.70000	-5.481808	-5.637787
2002:08	8663.500	8736.600	-73.10000	-0.836710	-0.840230
2002:09	8312.690	8663.500	-350.81000	-4.049287	-4.133554

and in the second column the corresponding value of the Index. The third column has the one-period-**lag** of the Index, indicated as Index(−1). For instance, look at 2001:05; the Index is equal to 10,911.90 and the corresponding lag value is 10,735.00, which is the value of the Index in the previous period 2001:04.

We define:

A lag operator L applied to Y_t has the property $L\,Y_t = Y_{t-1}$.

This is to say that when L is applied to a random variable, the operator returns the 1-period lagged random variable.

The first difference of a time series is the change in the value of the series from one period to the next. Look at the fourth column of Table 3.1. What is the first difference of the series at 2001:05? It is 176.90, which is obtained as the difference 10911.90 – 10,735.00. The Index jumped up 176.90 points in 2001:05.

We define:

The first difference of a time series is calculated as $\Delta Y_t = Y_t - L\,Y_t = Y_t - Y_{t-1}$.

In Figure 3.7, compare the time series of the first differences of the Index (3.7b) with the Index (3.7a) itself. What do you observe? We have removed a time-varying mean. The differenced time series (3.7b) has a mean that is constant over time. We can say that, at least, the first differences of the Index come from a first order weakly stationary process. This is the expected effect when we difference a nonstationary time series.

However, the first difference of the Index seems to have a variance that changes with time. You can see that the series became much more volatile from 1997 to 2008 compared to the variance at the beginning of the sample. The process does not seem to be second order weakly stationary because it violates the second condition of our definition. The logarithmic transformation helps to stabilize the variance. In Figure 3.7c and 3.7d, you can observe the effect of this transformation. We apply natural log to the Index itself. Observe that the log transformation does not affect the trending behavior of the Index, and it cannot help with the mean of the series, but by taking first differences of the log (Index), we obtain a time series (3.7d) that has a more homogenous variance than the original series and a mean that is constant over time. Hence, the time series in Figure 3.7d, which is the first differences of the logarithmic transformation of the DJ Index, seems to come from a covariance-stationary process. In the last column of Table 3.1, you can read the values of this time series. For instance, in 2001:05, log(Index) = log(10911.90) = 9.297609, and in 2001:04, log(Index) = log(10735) = 9.281264. The first difference in log(Index) is equal to 9.2976 − 9.2812 = 0.016344, and multiplying by 100, we have the value of 1.6344%, as stated in Table 3.1. This number has also economic meaning: it is a monthly return.

To understand the economic meaning of the first differences of a logarithmic transformation, observe that the values in the fifth and sixth columns of Table 3.1 are not very different. Suppose that you want to compute the monthly return to the Index. The question is: How much money (in percentage terms) would you make if you were to buy the Index in a given month and sell it in the next month? If you buy in 2001:04, you will pay 10,735.00 points, and if you sell it in 2001:05, you will get 10,911.90. The

FIGURE 3.7 Dow Jones Index and Its Transformation to Returns

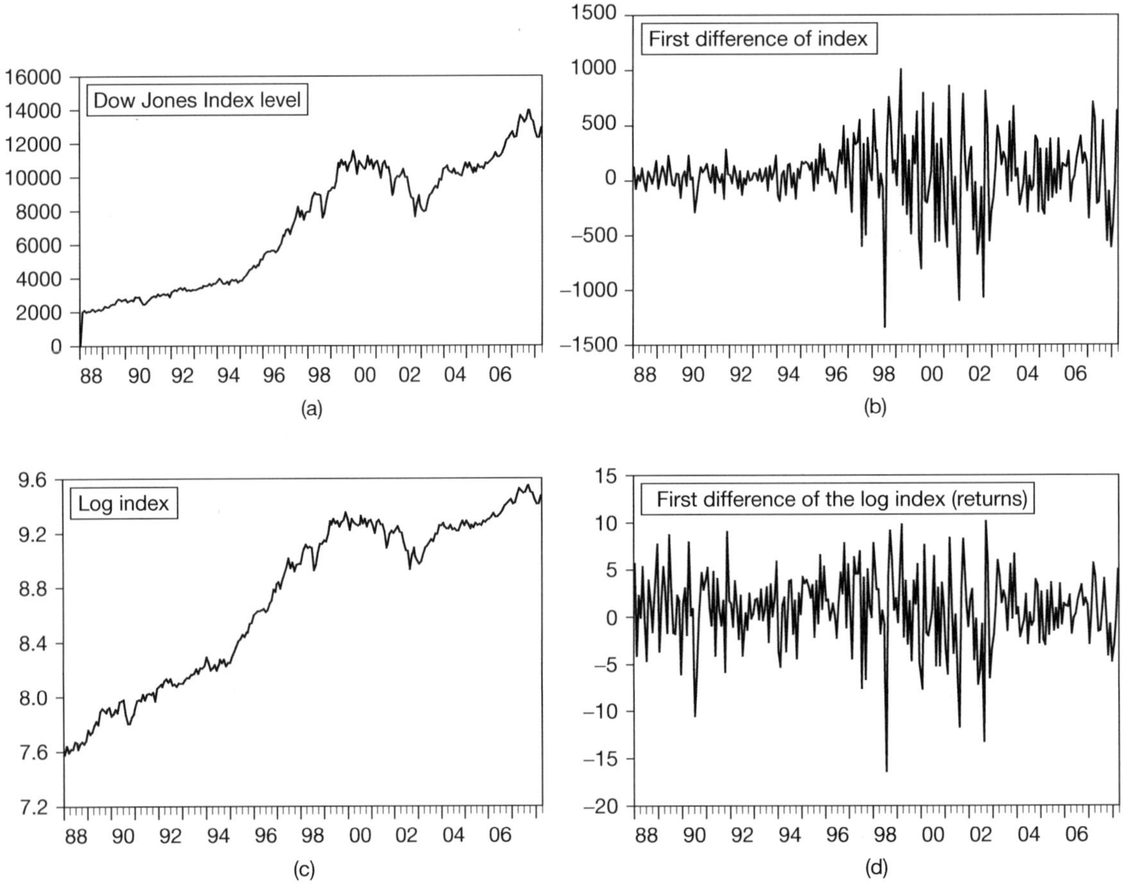

percentage monthly return to your investment will be 100 × (10,911.90 − 10,735.00) / 10,735 = 1.6478%. In general, the percentage return R_t is computed as

$$R_t = \frac{Y_t - Y_{t-1}}{Y_{t-1}} \times 100 = \frac{\Delta Y_t}{Y_{t-1}} \times 100$$

If R_t is not very large, the **natural logarithm** has the following property: $\log[1+(R_t/100)] \cong R_t/100$, where the symbol $\cong$ means "almost equal." Then we can write

$$\frac{R_t}{100} \cong \log\left(1 + \frac{R_t}{100}\right) = \log \frac{Y_t}{Y_{t-1}} = \log Y_t - \log Y_{t-1} = \Delta \log Y_t$$

which is the return to the Index approximated by taking the first differences of its logarithm. This is why the values in the fifth and sixth column of Table 3.1 are very similar.

In practical applications in economics and business, it is very common to transform a nonstationary process by computing the first difference of the logarithm of the series. It is also very convenient because such transformation has the interpretation of economic returns or, equivalently, growth rates.

We have now learned the theoretical framework in which forecasting models are built. We have introduced new statistical concepts, mainly the idea of stationarity, which is fundamental in the analysis of time series. The remainder of this chapter focuses on very useful tools to detect time patterns: the **autocorrelation function** and the **partial autocorrelation function**. Additionally, we revisit the difference between conditional and unconditional moments and their importance for time series forecasting.

3.3 A New Tool of Analysis: The Autocorrelation Functions

Recall the correlation coefficient. Given two random variables, say $Y$and X, the correlation coefficient is a measure of linear association defined as the ratio of their covariance to the product of their standard deviations:

$$\rho_{YX} = \frac{\sigma_{YX}}{\sigma_Y \sigma_X}$$

This coefficient has a very useful property: $-1 \leq \rho_{YX} \leq 1$. The association is stronger the closer ρ_{YX} is either to 1 or –1. Its sign will be positive when the two random variables move in the same direction and negative when they move in opposite directions.

In time series, we can also define a correlation coefficient. We have learned that a stochastic process is a collection of random variables $\{Y_1, Y_2, \ldots. Y_t \ldots\ldots Y_T\}$. Thus, if we select any two random variables, we could ask how they are related to each other, and we could construct their correlation coefficient. For instance, choose two random variables that are 1 period apart, say Y_t and Y_{t-1}. Their correlation coefficient is

$$\rho_{Y_t, Y_{t-1}} = \frac{\text{cov}(Y_t, Y_{t-1})}{\sqrt{\text{var}(Y_t)}\sqrt{\text{var}(Y_{t-1})}}$$

Choose again any two random variables that are k periods apart, say Y_t and Y_{t-k}. Their correlation coefficient is

$$\rho_{Y_t, Y_{t-k}} = \frac{\text{cov}(Y_t, Y_{t-k})}{\sqrt{\text{var}(Y_t)}\sqrt{\text{var}(Y_{t-k})}}$$

These expressions are, properly speaking, correlation coefficients, but they are called *autocorrelation coefficients* because they measure the linear association of random variables that belong to the same stochastic process. The numerator is called the *autocovariance* for the same reason. We say that $\rho_{Y_t, Y_{t-1}}$ is the autocorrelation of order 1 because the random variables are 1 period apart; $\rho_{Y_t, Y_{t-k}}$ is the autocorrelation of order k because the random variables are k periods apart, and so on. In general, we can choose any distance between any two random variables and calculate their autocorrelation.

We define:

The autocorrelation function is a function that assigns to any two random variables that are k periods apart their correlation coefficient, that is $\rho: k \rightarrow \rho_{Y_t,Y_{t-k}}$.

Distance	1	2	....	k
Function ρ	$\rho_{Y_t,Y_{t-1}}$	$\rho_{Y_t,Y_{t-2}}$	....	$\rho_{Y_t,Y_{t-k}}$

$\rho_{Y_t,Y_{t-k}}$ maintains the property of any correlation coefficient, that is $-1 \leq \rho_{Y_t,Y_{t-k}} \leq 1$.

For a covariance stationary process, the autocorrelation function can be simplified. Recall the conditions (i.), (ii.), and (iii.) mentioned in Section 3.2.1. For a covariance stationary process, the first and second moments are time invariant. Thus, $\text{var}(Y_t) = \text{var}(Y_{t-k}) = \sigma^2$ and the autocovariance $\text{cov}(Y_t, Y_{t-k}) = \sigma_k$, and then the autocorrelation of order k can be written as

$$\rho_k = \frac{\sigma_k}{\sqrt{\sigma^2}\sqrt{\sigma^2}} = \frac{\sigma_k}{\sigma^2} \equiv \frac{\gamma_k}{\gamma_0}$$

where the last equality is just a change of notation. In time series notation, it is customary to write the autocovariance of order k as γ_k, and the variance of the process, which is the autocovariance of order zero, as γ_0. Because the autocorrelation depends only on the distance between the two random variables, we can write that $\rho_{Y_t,Y_{t-k}} = \rho_{Y_t,Y_{t-(-k)}} = \rho_{Y_t,Y_{t+k}}$ and

$$\rho_k = \rho_{-k} = \rho_{|k|}$$

Thus, the *autocorrelation function* (ACF) of a covariance stationary process can be written as $\rho : k \rightarrow \rho_{|k|}$.

How do we compute this function? Let us examine the time series in Figure 3.8, Annual hours worked per person employed in Germany from 1977–2006, published by the Organization for Economic Cooperation and Development (OECD) (http://www.oecd.org).

In Figure 3.8a, we plot the time series. We observe that German employees reduced their annual working hours from 1,801 hours in 1977 to 1,421 in 2006. As we saw in the previous section, this time series is likely to come from a nonstationary process, and we are going to transform it by taking the first differences the logarithm of the original series. The resulting time series, which is the percentage annual change in working hours, is plotted in Figure 3.8b. Now the time series is more likely to come from a covariance-stationary process. As expected, most of the annual changes are negative with the exception of the changes in 1994 and 2004.

The autocorrelation function of the percentage annual changes in working hours is presented in the middle panel of Figure 3.8.

Note that we write the symbol ^ to denote that the autocorrelation is a sample estimate (the requirements of stationarity and ergodicity are at work here!). These numbers are customarily plotted in a diagram called the *autocorrelogram*.

You can see that the autocorrelations are not very strong. This means that there is not much time dependence on how working hours have changed over time. Let us show

FIGURE 3.8 Annual Hours Worked per Person Employed in Germany

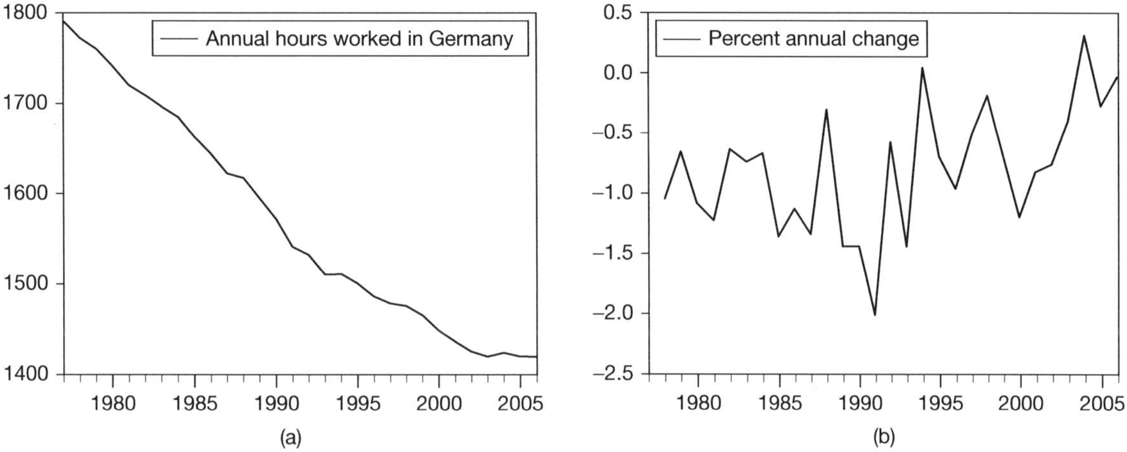

Source: "Annual hours worked per person employed" in Germany from 1977-2006, published by the OECD, Organization for Economic Cooperation and Development (http://www.oecd.org).

Autocorrelation Function										
κ	1	2	3	4	5	6	7	8	9	10
$\hat{\rho}_\kappa$	.22	.29	−.10	.16	−.01	0.19	−.06	−.04	.09	.20

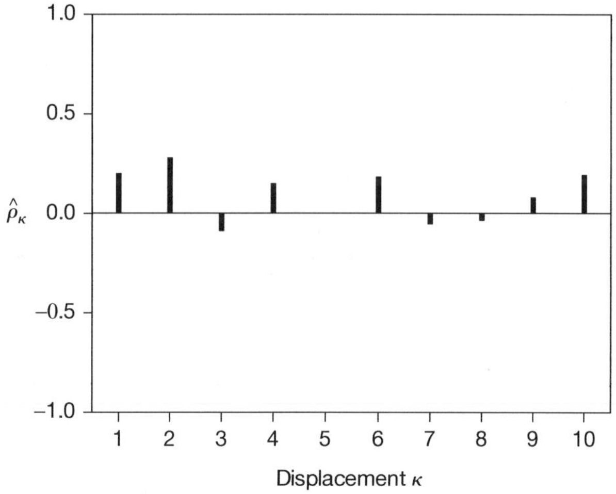

how to compute these numbers focusing, for instance, on $\hat{\rho}_1 = 0.22$ and $\hat{\rho}_3 = -0.10$. See Table 3.2 for the calculations. First, compute the sample mean and sample variance of the series Y_t. Next lag the time series 1 period to obtain Y_{t-1} and 3 periods to

TABLE 3.2 Percentage Change in Working Hours in Germany: Calculation of the Autocorrelation Coefficients

	Y_t	Y_{t-1}	Y_{t-3}
1978	-1.0604		
1979	-0.6699	-1.0604	
1980	-1.1018	-0.6699	
1981	-1.2413	-1.1018	-1.0604
1982	-0.6497	-1.2413	-0.6699
1983	-0.7536	-0.6497	-1.1018
1984	-0.6826	-0.7536	-1.2413
1985	-1.3733	-0.6826	-0.6497
1986	-1.1438	-1.3733	-0.7536
1987	-1.3533	-1.1438	-0.6826
1988	-0.3196	-1.3533	-1.3733
1989	-1.4574	-0.3196	-1.1438
1990	-1.4536	-1.4574	-1.3533
1991	-2.0234	-1.4536	-0.3196
1992	-0.5904	-2.0234	-1.4574
1993	-1.4550	-0.5904	-1.4536
1994	0.0264	-1.4550	-2.0234
1995	-0.7087	0.0264	-0.5904
1996	-0.9752	-0.7087	-1.4550
1997	-0.5249	-0.9752	0.0264
1998	-0.2026	-0.5249	-0.7087
1999	-0.7057	-0.2026	-0.9752
2000	-1.2126	-0.7057	-0.5249
2001	-0.8375	-1.2126	-0.2026
2002	-0.7745	-0.8375	-0.7057
2003	-0.4141	-0.7745	-1.2126
2004	0.2950	-0.4141	-0.8375
2005	-0.2879	0.2950	-0.7745
2006	-0.0492	-0.2879	-0.4141
Mean: $\hat{\mu}$	-0.8026		
Variance: $\hat{\gamma}_0$	0.2905		
$\hat{\gamma}_k$ **(*k*= 1, 3)**		0.0651	-0.0282
$\hat{\rho}_k$ **(*k*= 1, 3)**		0.2240	-0.0970

obtain Y_{t-3}. Proceed to compute the sample covariances between Y_t and Y_{t-1} and between Y_t and Y_{t-3}. Finally, compute the autocorrelation coefficients.

Another way to understand the meaning of autocorrelation is to plot the series Y_t against Y_{t-1}, and Y_t against Y_{t-3}, as in Figure 3.9. In the first case, Figure 3.9a, you expect to find a direct relation (thick line) because the autocorrelation is positive, meaning that observations that are 1 year apart move in the same direction. When Germans reduce

FIGURE 3.9 Percentage Change in Working Hours in Germany: Autocorrelations of Order 1 and 3

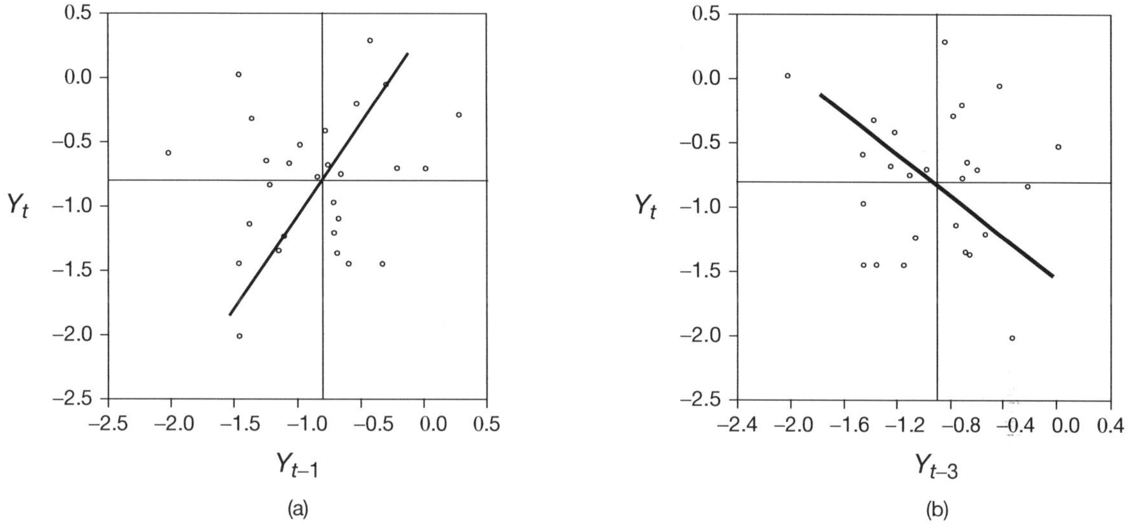

(increase) their working hours, one year later we will expect a subsequent reduction (increase). However, this relation is not very strong because the correlation is small, just in the neighborhood of 0.2. Observe that there are observations in the four quadrants (below and above, right and left of the mean of the process). In the second plot, Figure 3.9b, we expect to find an inverse relation (the autocorrelation is negative) between observations three years apart but, again, this relation is not very strong. If Germans now reduce (increase) their working hours, three years later we will expect an increase (decrease).

For comparison purposes, we have plotted the annual working hours per employee in the United States in Figure 3.10. The differences with the German data are very substantial. The U.S. plot does not exhibit the downward trending behavior of the German data. Go ahead and analyze the autocorrelation function, draw the autocorrelogram, study the plot of Y_t against Y_{t-1}, and comment on the differences with the German data.

3.3.1 Partial Autocorrelation

When we calculate the autocorrelation between Y_t and Y_{t+k}, information flows from t to $t+k$, so that indirectly $\rho_{|k|}$ accounts for the contribution of the random variables between t and $t+k$, that is $Y_{t+1}, Y_{t+2}, \ldots\ldots. Y_{t+k-1}$. Suppose that we wish to learn the autocorrelation between Y_t and Y_{t+k} if we had removed the information in between. In the statistical jargon, we say that we wish to "control" for the effects of $Y_{t+1}, Y_{t+2}, \ldots\ldots. Y_{t+k-1}$. This type of correlation is given by the *partial autocorrelation coefficient*. The best way to understand partial autocorrelation is in the context of a regression model, which was reviewed in Chapter 2. Consider a linear regression with k regressors

$$Y_{t+k} = \beta_0 + \beta_1 Y_{t+k-1} + \beta_2 Y_{t+k-2} + \cdots\cdot \beta_{k-1} Y_{t+1} + \beta_k Y_t + \varepsilon_{t+k}$$

FIGURE 3.10 Annual Working Hours per Employee in the United States

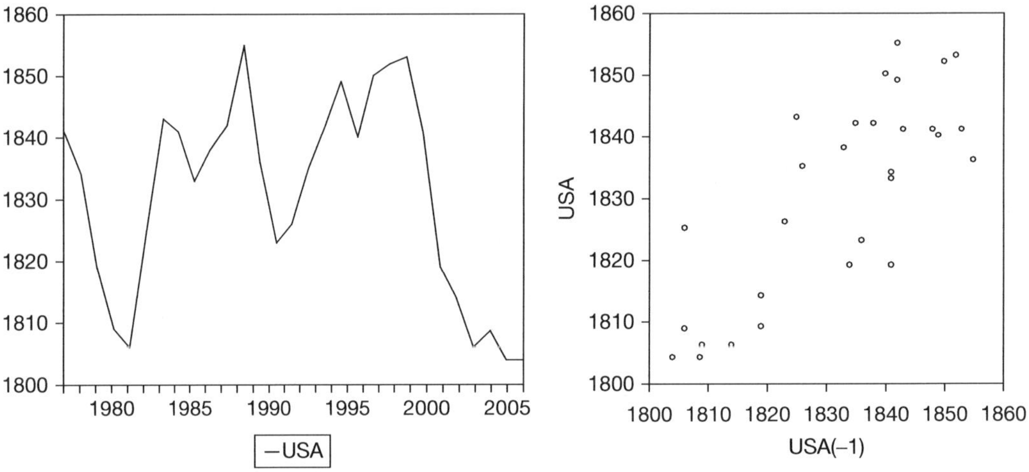

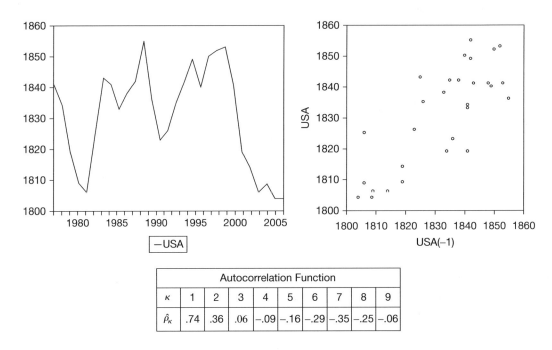

Autocorrelation Function									
κ	1	2	3	4	5	6	7	8	9
$\hat{\rho}_\kappa$	.74	.36	.06	−.09	−.16	−.29	−.35	−.25	−.06

On writing explicitly the variables $Y_{t+1}, Y_{t+2}, \ldots\ldots\, Y_{t+k-1}$ in the model, we control for their effect on Y_{t+k}. Then the linear relation between Y_t and Y_{t+k} must be contained in the regression coefficient β_k, which must be already "cleaned" from the contribution of any other variable $Y_{t+1}, Y_{t+2}, \ldots\ldots\, Y_{t+k-1}$ to Y_{t+k}. The regression coefficient β_k is the partial autocorrelation between Y_t and Y_{t+k}. Similar to the autocorrelation function, the *partial autocorrelation function*(PACF) assigns to every k the corresponding partial autocorrelation coefficient, that is, $r : k \rightarrow r_k$

An easy way to compute the autocorrelation function is to run several regressions as follows:

Distance k	**Regression**	**Partial autocorrelation coefficient r_k**
1	$Y_{t+k} = \beta_0 + \beta_1 Y_{t+k-1} + \varepsilon_{t+k}$	β_1
2	$Y_{t+k} = \beta_0 + \beta_1 Y_{t+k-1} + \beta_2 Y_{t+k-2} + \varepsilon_{t+k}$	β_2
3	$Y_{t+k} = \beta_0 + \beta_1 Y_{t+k-1} + \beta_2 Y_{t+k-2} + \beta_3 Y_{t+k-3} + \varepsilon_{t+k}$	β_3
.....	....	......
k	$Y_{t+k} = \beta_0 + \beta_1 Y_{t+k-1} + \beta_2 Y_{t+k-2} + \cdots\cdot\, \beta_{k-1} Y_{t+1} + \beta_k Y_t + \varepsilon_{t+k}$	β_k

For instance, let us look at the second regression ($k = 2$). We regress Y_{t+2} on a constant, Y_{t+1}, and Y_t. The OLS estimate $\hat{\beta}_2$ is the partial autocorrelation coefficient of order 2 that we call $\hat{r}_2$. We can interpret $\hat{r}_2$ in two ways, either as a correlation coefficient or, by applying the customary OLS interpretation, as the effect of a marginal change in Y_t on Y_{t+2}. Both interpretations are equivalent, and both are measuring the degree of linear association between the random variables Y_{t+2} and Y_t once we control for the information contained in Y_{t+1}.

In practical terms, we will not run so many regressions because the econometrics software calculates the partial autocorrelations at the touch of a key.[2] However, the preceding argument based on regression highlights the interpretation of the partial correlation coefficients.

The ACF and the PACF summarize all linear dependence of a stochastic process. ACF and PACF could be very different or somewhat similar. In subsequent chapters, we analyze the shape and values of the autocorrelation functions. These tools are necessary to propose different models on which we base our predictions.

Going back to the time series Figure 3.8b Percentage change in annual working hours per employee in Germany, we estimate the partial autocorrelation function:

Partial Autocorrelation Function										
κ	1	2	3	4	5	6	7	8	9	10
$\hat{\rho}_\kappa$	.22	.26	−.22	.17	.02	.09	−.09	−.13	.27	.14

Note that for $k = 1$, the autocorrelation and partial autocorrelation coefficients are identical. This is expected because there is no information to consider between times t and $t + 1$. In this series, the PACF is similar to the ACF in that the correlations are low. There is not much linear dependence in this time series. It is possible that the autocorrelations in the ACF and PACF are zero. Can we test it? Yes, this is the subject of the next section.

3.3.2 Statistical Tests for Autocorrelation Coefficients

We would like to test the following null hypothesis $H_0: \rho_k = 0$. Observe that the null always refers to a population parameter. When we compute the ACF, we obtain an estimate of the population parameter that we denote $\hat{\rho}_k$. To test the null hypothesis, we need to know the probability density function of the estimator $\hat{\rho}_k$. For a large sample, $\hat{\rho}_k$ is a normal random variable with mean 0 and variance $1/T$ when the null hypothesis is true:

$$\hat{\rho}_k \rightarrow N\left(0, \frac{1}{T}\right)$$

---

[2]The partial autocorrelation function can also be obtained by solving a system of equations known as the *Yule-Walker equations*. This is the approach programmed in econometrics software.

Our task is to assess how far, statistically speaking, the estimate of $\hat{\rho}_k$ is from zero. This is an exercise in hypothesis testing like those we reviewed in Chapter 2. We form the *t*-ratio as $\hat{\rho}_k/\sqrt{1/T} \rightarrow N(0, 1)$ and state the following decision rule: At the customary 5% significance level, we reject the null hypothesis (i.e., the autocorrelation is different from zero) whenever $|\hat{\rho}_k/\sqrt{1/T}| > 1.96$, and we fail to reject otherwise. Equivalently, a 95% confidence interval is $(-1.96/\sqrt{T}, 1.96/\sqrt{T})$, which says that whenever the value of $\hat{\rho}_k$ falls within the interval, the autocorrelation is statistically zero, and when it is outside, the autocorrelation is different from zero.

In Figure 3.11, we show the ACF and PACF of the time series described in Figure 3.10 as well as the autocorrelograms. In the appendix to this chapter, you will find computer help on how to obtain these functions in EViews.

The dashed lines running vertically in both autocorrelograms are the bands corresponding to a 95% confidence interval, centered at zero, *for each individual autocorrelation coefficient*, that is $(-1.96/\sqrt{T}, 1.96/\sqrt{T})$. Reading the autocorrelograms, we learn that ρ_1 and ρ_2 in the ACF and r_1 and r_2 in the PACF are different from zero as the corresponding values fall outside the 95% bands. The remaining autocorrelations fall within the bands, so they are statistically zero.

The last two columns of Figure 3.11, *Q-Stat* and *Prob*, provide additional information about the statistical significance of the autocorrelation coefficients. The *Q-statistic* seeks to test the following null joint hypothesis

$$H_0: \rho_1 = \rho_2 = \cdots\cdots = \rho_k = 0$$

Rejecting this hypothesis means that some or all autocorrelations up to order *k* are different from zero. The Q-statistic, known as the *Ljung-Box Q-statistic,* has the following formula

$$Q_k = T(T+2)\sum_{j=1}^{k} \frac{\hat{\rho}_j^2}{T-j} \hat{\rho}_j^2 \rightarrow \chi_k^2$$

and, under the null, its probability density function is a chi-square with as many degrees of freedom as the number of autocorrelations stated in the null. In Figure 3.11, if we wish to test the null $H_0: \rho_1 = \rho_2 = \rho_3 = 0$, the corresponding *Q-statistic* is $Q_3 = 22.676$, which is calculated by using the preceding formula and involves the first three autocorrelation coefficients ρ_1, ρ_2, and ρ_3. Because Q_3 is distributed chi-squared

FIGURE 3.11
Time Series: Annual Working Hours per Employee in the United States—Autocorrelation Function

Sample: 1977 2006
Included observations: 30

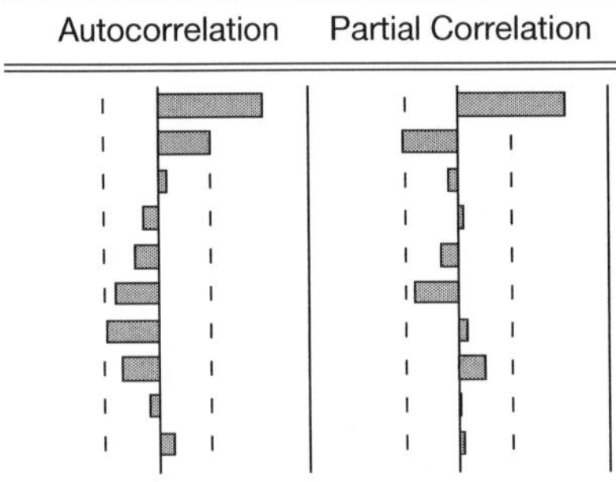

	AC	PAC	Q-Stat	Prob
1	0.737	0.737	17.987	0.000
2	0.364	-0.392	22.537	0.000
3	0.062	-0.058	22.676	0.000
4	-0.086	0.039	22.951	0.000
5	-0.162	-0.126	23.957	0.000
6	-0.288	-0.295	27.270	0.000
7	-0.352	0.052	32.432	0.000
8	-0.253	0.185	35.229	0.000
9	-0.064	0.001	35.416	0.000
10	0.114	0.034	36.035	0.000

with 3 degrees of freedom, we need only to gather the critical value of the chi-squared at the 5% or 1% significance lever to decide on the null. However, the last column *Prob* in Figure 3.11 helps to evaluate the null hypothesis so that there is no need to search for the corresponding critical values. This column is a p-value or probability associated with the value of the *Q-statistic*; it tells the probability Prob $= \Pr(Q \geq q)$. For $Q_3 = 22.676$, we should read that Prob $= \Pr(Q_3 \geq q) = \Pr(Q_3 \geq 22.676) = 0.0$, which means that the value $Q_3 = 22.676$ is large enough to be above the corresponding critical value, or in other words, the significance level associated with $Q_3 = 22.676$ is zero, so that we are able to strongly reject the null. We conclude that there are strong autocorrelations or, equivalently, that there is substantial time dependence in the data.

3.4 Conditional Moments and Time Series: What Lies Ahead

Recall the regression analysis that we reviewed in Chapter 2. In regression, we have one dependent variable and at least one regressor, say Y and X, and the topic of interest is to find out the expected value of Y for a given value of X; we write $E(Y|X)$. This is the **conditional mean** of Y, which is a function of X, that is, $E(Y|X) = g(X)$, such that for different values of X, the expected value of Y will be different. In model-based forecasting, the idea of regression plays an important role because the forecast is a function of conditional moments; most of the time, the forecast is constructed as a conditional mean, but sometimes it also depends on the **conditional variance**.

For a stochastic process $\{Y_t\}$ and for an **information set** I_t (or conditioning set) $I_t = \{y_1, y_2, \ldots\ldots y_t\}$, our objective is to construct a forecast for a future value of Y_t, say Y_{t+h}, as a function of the information set, that is,

$$f_{t,h} = g(I_t)$$

The function $g(.)$ is a function of conditional moments. For instance, look at the following cases:

$$\text{Case (i): } f_{t,h} = g_1(I_t) = E(Y_{t+h}|I_t) = E(Y_{t+h}|y_t, y_{t-1}, \ldots\ldots y_1)$$

In this case, the function $g_1(.)$ is a conditional mean. We need to calculate the conditional mean, and for this, a well-constructed regression model is very useful. As an example, suppose that we come up with a model as

$$E(Y_t|Y_{t-1}, Y_{t-2}, \ldots\ldots Y_1) = \beta_0 + \beta_1 Y_{t-1} + \beta_2 Y_{t-2}$$

This is a linear regression model where the conditioning variables are $\{Y_{t-1}, Y_{t-2}\}$, that is, $Y_t = \beta_0 + \beta_1 Y_{t-1} + \beta_2 Y_{t-2} + \varepsilon_t$. If the forecast is constructed as in (i), then for known values of β_0, β_1, and β_2 (OLS estimation is handy here), we write the 1-period-ahead forecast ($h = 1$) of Y_{t+1} as

$$f_{t,1} = \beta_o + \beta_1 y_t + \beta_2 y_{t-1}$$

It is enough to know the two most recent values of Y in the information set (y_t and y_{t-1}) to predict the expected value of Y_{t+1}.

Let us consider a second case where

$$\text{Case (ii): } f_{t,h} = g_2(I_t) = E(Y_{t+h}|I_t) + \text{var}(Y_{t+h}|I_t)$$
$$= E(Y_{t+h}|y_t, y_{t-1}, \ldots.. y_1) + \text{var}(Y_{t+h}|y_t, y_{t-1}, \ldots.. y_1)$$

In this case, the function $g_2(.)$ involves the conditional mean and the conditional variance. Consequently, now we need models for both conditional moments. Let us assume that the model for the conditional mean is given by a linear regression as in case (i) and suppose that a model for the conditional variance (models of this type are analyzed in the last chapters) is given by

$$\text{var}(Y_t|Y_{t-1}, Y_{t-2}, \ldots.. Y_1) = \alpha_0 + \alpha_1 Y_{t-1}^2$$

If the forecast is constructed as in (ii), then for known values of β_0, β_1, and β_2, and α_o and α_1, we write the 1-period-ahead forecast $(h-1)$ of Y_{t+1} as

$$f_{t,1} = (\beta_0 + \alpha_0) + \beta_1 y_t + \beta_2 y_{t-1} + \alpha_1 y_t^2$$

It is enough to know the two most recent values of Y in the information set (y_t and y_{t-1}) to predict the future value of Y_{t+1}. Note that this forecast is a nonlinear function of the information set (y_t is squared) as opposed to the linear forecast that we constructed in (i).

In subsequent chapters, we will learn how to use the information contained in the ACF and PACF to construct time series models from which we will be able to calculate the conditional mean and the conditional variance. The forecast will be built on these moments.

KEY WORDS

autocorrelation function, p. 65
conditional mean, p. 73
covariance stationary, p. 61
cross-sectional average, p. 57
first differences, p. 62
lag, p. 63
natural logarithm, p. 64
partial autocorrelation function, p. 65
stochastic process, p. 55
strong stationarity, p. 60
time series, p. 52
weak stationarity, p. 60

APPENDIX

A3.1 An Introduction to Ergodicity

A covariance stationary stochastic process is characterized by time invariant first and second moments. We refer to μ, σ^2, and $\rho_{|k|}$ as the population mean, population variance, and population correlation, respectively. The statistical problem at hand is the estimation of these population moments based on sample information. Recall that the only sample information that we have is one realization of the stochastic process: a time series $\{y_1, y_2, \ldots y_t, \ldots . y_T\}$. How can we estimate μ (σ^2 and $\rho_{|k|}$) with a time series? The answer to this question deals with a property of the stochastic process known as *ergodicity,* where the Greek root *ergo* means "work."

Ergodicity is the required property that links the population to sample information.

In simple words, it brings the concept of "stationary stochastic process," which deals with population information, to the real world, in which we deal only with sample information or time series data.

In this chapter, we have distinguished between a cross-sectional mean $\bar{y}$ and variance $\bar{\sigma}^2$ and a time mean $\bar{\bar{y}}$ and variance $\bar{\bar{\sigma}}^2$. Let us focus on the mean, but the following arguments also apply to the variance. We know that a sample average is a good approximation to the population mean. In statistical jargon, we say:

The sample average is a consistent estimator of the population mean, and we write

$$\bar{y} = \frac{\sum_{i=1}^{n} y_i}{n} \xrightarrow{p} \mu$$

where the symbol '$\xrightarrow{p}$' means convergence in probability. This is an asymptotic property, meaning that when the sample size is very large ($n \rightarrow \infty$), the probability of the sample average being different from the population mean is almost zero. In this sense, we talk about the sample average being a representative statistic of the population mean. Note that we are referring to the *cross-sectional average.*

In time series, the only sample average that we can compute is a time average, which is a sum over realizations that come from random variables with potentially different statistical properties. Let us assume that all random variables in the process have the same mean: The process is, at least, first order weakly stationary. Ergodicity is the property that links the time average moments with the population moments.

We define:

A stochastic process is ergodic for the mean if the time average is a consistent estimator of the mean of the process, and we write

$$\bar{\bar{y}} = \frac{\sum_{t=1}^{T} y_t}{T} \xrightarrow{p} \mu$$

This is to say that the time average is also a good approximation to the population mean when the time series sample is large, $T \rightarrow \infty$. Intuitively, we can think of ergodicity as collecting many realizations over time that bring new information. Because the process is mean stationary, over time, all these realizations provide the full set of outcomes associated with the random variable. Hence, pooling all time realizations is a good device to approximate the population mean.

A3.2 Computer Help

Many computer packages can help you to practice the concepts you have learned in this chapter. We mention the main functions that you can use in EViews. We assume that you are familiar with opening a Workfile with the data.

1. To plot a time series, click the series and choose **View/Graph**.
2. To calculate unconditional moments of a time series and a histogram, click the series and choose **View/Descriptive Statistics**.
3. To generate a scatter plot, say Y_t against $Y_{\{t-1\}}$, type **scat usa(-1) usa** in the command line or click on **View/Graph/Scatter/Simple Scatter** after selecting both series.
4. To generate the first differences of the logarithmic transformation of the series "Germany," click **Genr** and type difger=(log(germany)-log(germany(-1)))×100
5. To calculate the autocorrelation (AC) and partial autocorrelation (PAC) functions of a series, click the series and choose **View/Correlogram.**

EXERCISES

1. Download monthly data on real personal consumption expenditures and real disposable personal income from the Federal Reserve Economic Database (FRED) of the St. Louis Fed (http://research.stlouisfed.org/fred2). Take a sample starting on 1959:01 and continuing to the most recent month.
   a. Calculate the growth rates of real consumption and disposable personal income and plot the data (simply calculate changes in natural-log). How do you compare the level of volatility on consumption growth with that of income growth? Can you explain it with your knowledge of macroeconomics? (*Hint:* Consider the *permanent income* model.)
   b. Regress consumption growth on disposable income growth. Interpret the estimated equation and discuss statistical significance.
   c. Add a lag of the growth in disposable income to the equation that you estimated in b. Based on your estimates, comment on the possibility of an adjustment lag in consumption growth.
2. From the same website as that in Exercise 1, download Consumer Price Index (for all items), and the 3-month T-bill interest rate (secondary market rate). Calculate monthly inflation (i.e., growth rate of monthly CPI) and then obtain ex post real interest rate as the difference between the 3-month T-bill rate and the monthly inflation rate. Add the real interest rate to the equation that you estimated in Exercise 1b. Interpret the economic and statistical significance of the real interest rate in this new equation.
3. Visit again the website of the Federal Reserve Bank in St. Louis (http://research.stlouisfed.org) and download the following data:
   a. U.S. real GDP.
   b. The exchange rate of the Japanese yen against the U.S. dollar.
   c. The 10-year U.S. Treasury constant maturity yield.
   d. The U.S. unemployment rate.

For each data set, plot the time series, and write the exact definition, periodicity, and units. Judge whether the underlying stochastic process may be first and second order weakly stationary. Explain your rationale.

4. Perform the following lag operations (Y_t and X_t are stochastic processes and c is a constant):

a. $LY_t =$
b. $Lc =$
c. $L^2 Y_t =$
d. $L^k Y_t =$ for some integer k > 0
e. $Y_t - LY_t =$
f. $Y_t = \alpha + (1 - \rho L)Y_t =$
g. $Y_t = \alpha + (1 - \rho_1 L + \rho_2 L^2)Y_t + LX_t =$

5. The following table contains quarterly nominal GDP in U.S. (billions of dollars). Let Y_t denote the GDP at time t and let $y_t = \ln(Y_t)$.
(Show your calculations in a spreadsheet, e.g., in Microsoft Excel.)

a. Plot the time series (Y_t). Can the underlying stochastic process be weakly stationary of any order? Explain why or why not.
b. Calculate the growth rate of nominal GDP by computing the percentage changes of the series, that is, $g_{1t} = 100 \times (Y_t - Y_{t-1})/Y_{t-1}$.
c. Plot the natural logarithm of the series (y_t) and compare with part i., commenting on stationarity and smoothness.
d. Repeat part ii. by taking the first log-differences (in percentage), that is, $g_{2t} = 100 \times (y_t - y_{t-1})$.
e. Do you observe any significant differences between g_{1t} and g_{2t} computed in ii. and iv, respectively?

Date	**GDP**
2001-01-01	10021.5
2001-04-01	10128.9
2001-07-01	10135.1
2001-10-01	10226.3
2002-01-01	10338.2
2002-04-01	10445.7
2002-07-01	10546.5
2002-10-01	10617.5
2003-01-01	10744.6
2003-04-01	10884.0
2003-07-01	11116.7
2003-10-01	11270.9
2004-01-01	11472.6
2004-04-01	11657.5
2004-07-01	11814.9
2004-10-01	11994.8

6. Following with the same data as in Exercise 5,
   a. Compute the sample moments $\hat{\mu}$ (mean) and $\hat{\gamma}_0$ (variance) of g_{2t}.
   b. Compute the autocorrelation function of g_{2t}, that is, ρ_k for $k = 1, 2, 3, 4$. Interpret the autocorrelations by plotting g_{2t} against the lagged values of g_{2t}. Give an economic interpretation.

7. Download the daily S&P500 Index from January 2, 2006, and continuing to the most recent date. Let P_t denote the SP500 time series and $p_t = \ln(P_t)$.
   a. Compute the daily return (i.e., $R_t = p_t - p_{t-1}$).
   b. Compute the sample moments of returns: mean, variance, skewness, and kurtosis. Plot the histogram.
   c. Plot R_t against R_{t-1}, R_{t-2}, R_{t-3}, and R_{t-4}. Can you discern any pattern in any of the four graphs?

8. Following with the same data as in Exercise 7, and using the EViews software,
   a. Calculate the sample autocorrelation functions, ACF and PACF of R_t for $k = 1, 2, \ldots, 12$.
   b. Compute the following conditional means (assume linearity): $E(R_t | R_{t-1})$, $E(R_t | R_{t-1}, R_{t-2})$, and $E(R_t | R_{t-1}, R_{t-2}, R_{t-4})$. Do you think that it will be possible to predict future returns based on linear combinations of past returns? Why or why not?

9. Analyze the ACF and PACF that you calculated in Exercise 8b. Are the autocorrelation and partial autocorrelation coefficients statistically different from zero? State a single hypothesis and a joint hypothesis, and implement t-ratios and Q-statistics. Interpret your results.

10. For the four series that you downloaded in Exercise 3, calculate the ACF and PACF using EViews. Comment on the shapes of these functions. Are the autocorrelation and partial autocorrelation coefficients statistically different from zero? State a single hypothesis and a joint hypothesis, and implement t-ratios and Q-statistics. Interpret your results.

MODULE II

MODELING LINEAR DEPENDENCE FORECASTING WITH TIME SERIES MODELS

CHAPTER 4

Tools of the Forecaster

In Chapter 1, we have learned that our objective is to construct forecasts based on time series models. These are representations (equations) that link past information with the present, and by doing so, they summarize the time dependence in the data. Time dependence is the key to predicting future values of the variable of interest. However, before constructing a time series model, the forecaster needs to consider three basic elements that will guide the production of the forecast. These are:

1. The information set.
2. The forecast horizon.
3. The loss function.

These elements are *a priori* choices that the forecaster must make. In this sense, we call them *tools*. If you are ready to build a dining table, you need to choose nails, hammers, wood, glues, machine saws, and so on. In the same fashion, if you are ready to build a time series model, you need to choose at least the three basic elements just listed. For instance, suppose that you wish to forecast the number of new homes in Riverside County. You will need to collect information related to the construction sector in the area, the state of the local economy, the population inflows, the actual supply of houses, and so on. You are constructing the *information set* by gathering relevant and up-to-date information for the problem at hand. This information will be fed into the time series models. Because different models will process information differently, it may happen that some information is more important than others or that some information may be irrelevant for the forecast of interest.

The forecaster needs to choose how far into the future she wishes to predict. Do we want a 1-month-ahead, a 1-day-ahead, or a 1-year-ahead prediction? It depends on the use of the forecast. For instance, think about policy makers who plan to design or revamp the transportation services of the area or any other infrastructure. It is likely that they will be more interested in long-term predictions of new housing (i.e., forecasts for 1 year, 2 years, 5 years) than in short-term predictions (i.e., forecasts for 1 day, 1 month, 1 quarter). The *forecast horizon* influences the choice of the frequency of the time series data. If our interest is a 1-month-ahead prediction, we may wish to collect monthly data, or if our interest is a 1-day-ahead forecast, we may collect daily data. Of course, it is possible to forecast 1 month ahead with daily observations but, in some instances, this may not be desirable.

The forecaster must deal with uncertainty, which is inherent in any exercise involving the future. Only when time passes and the future becomes a reality does the forecaster know whether her prediction was right or wrong, and if it is wrong, by how much. In other words, forecast errors will happen but more importantly, they will be costly. The *loss function* is a representation of the penalties associated with forecast errors. Suppose that based on the forecast of new housing construction, some policy makers decide to invest in a system of new highways. If the forecast happens to overestimate the construction of new housing and, as a result, new construction is less than expected, the highways likely will be underutilized. On the contrary, if the forecast underestimates the construction of new housing and construction is more than expected, the highways will be overcrowded and congested. Either case has a cost. In the first case, more was invested than needed; thus, resources were wasted. In the second case, there were costs associated with traffic congestion, air pollution, longer commuting times, and so on. The costs of underestimation and of overestimation may be of different magnitude. It is sensible to assume that the forecaster may want to avoid forecast errors that are costly and to choose a forecast that minimizes the forecaster's losses. This is deemed an **optimal forecast**.

In the following sections, let us analyze in more detail the issues concerning the information set, the forecasting horizon, and the loss function.

4.1 The Information Set

The information set can contain *qualitative and/or quantitative information*. **Qualitative information** refers to a collection of experiences and knowledge that, not being readily quantifiable, are difficult to model. A qualitative information set may arise from the forecaster's professional experience. For instance, a seller of coats may know the clientele's preferences in taste, color, and fabric, which will be helpful in predicting the demand of coats for next winter. Most frequently, the information set is **quantitative**; it is a collection of historical time series. The seller of coats may have a time series of previous sales that will be helpful in forecasting the demand for coats next winter.

Within a quantitative information set, we distinguish between univariate and multivariate information sets. For a stochastic process $\{Y_t\}$,

- a **univariate information set** I_t is the historical time series of the process up to time t:

$$I_t = \{y_0, y_1, y_2, \ldots y_t\}$$

- a **multivariate information set** I_t is the collection of several historical time series up to time t:

$$I_t = \{y_0, y_1, y_2, \ldots y_t, x_0, x_1, x_2 \ldots x_t, z_0, z_1, z_2, \ldots z_t\}$$

For instance, to produce a 1-year-ahead forecast for new housing in Riverside County, the univariate information set is the time series of new houses built in the previous years. In addition, a multivariate information set may contain the time series of inflows of population, the time series of unemployment in the area, the time series of building permits in the county, and so on.

In any case, whether the information set is qualitative or quantitative or univariate or multivariate, the information set is important because any forecast $f_{t,h}$ is constructed as a function of the information set:

$$f_{t,h} = g(I_t)$$

The function $g(.)$ represents the time series model that processes the known information up to time t and from which we produce the forecast of the variable of interest at a future date $t+h$. Observe the following examples of 1-step-ahead forecasts of a process $\{Y_t\}$, say the construction of new housing.

i. $f_{t,1} = 0.8y_t$

ii. $f_{t,1} = 0.2y_t - 0.9y_{t-1}$

iii. $f_{t,1} = \dfrac{4}{1 + 0.5y_t}$

iv. $f_{t,1} = 1.2y_t - 0.5y_{t-1} + 0.4x_t + 0.3x_{t-1} + 0.6x_{t-2}$

In the first forecast, (i), the information set is univariate, and the most relevant piece of information is the previous level of construction, which indicates that the 1-period-ahead prediction of new construction will be 80% of the construction in the previous period. In the second forecast, (ii), we are dealing with a univariate information set, but now the previous two levels of construction y_t and y_{t-1} (with different weights) are relevant for the next year's prediction. Observe that in (i) and (ii), the forecast is a linear function of the information set. In the third forecast, (iii), the prediction is a nonlinear function of the previous level of construction because y_t appears in the denominator of the right-hand side of the equation. Forecast (iii) indicates that the 1-period-ahead construction is inversely related to the present construction. In this case, we also have a univariate information set. In the last example, (iv), the forecast is a linear function of the information set, which is a bivariate set because it contains information not only about past levels of construction y_t and y_{t-1} but also about past values of an additional time series, say inflows of population, x_t, x_{t-1} and x_{t-2}.

4.1.1 Some Information Sets Are More Valuable Than Others

The predictability of a time series depends on how useful the information set is. Sometimes univariate information sets are not very helpful, and we need to resort to multivariate information sets. For instance, stock returns are very difficult to predict on the basis of past stock returns alone, but when we add other information such as firm size, price-earnings ratio, cash flows, and so on, we find some predictability.

Let our knowledge of linear regression illustrate the use of the information set.

REAL DATA: Housing Prices and Interest Rates

In the heat of the last housing bubble, on April 26, 2004, the *New York Times* included the article "Consumers are wary but housing remains hot." Federal Reserve governor Donald L. Kohn was quoted as saying, "Low interest rates, in turn, have been a major force driving the phenomenal run-up in residential real estate prices over the past few years." From a forecasting point of view, we can interpret this statement as saying that interest rates must be an important part of the information set, and, furthermore, if interest rates keep dropping, we should observe higher housing prices. In other words, will interest rate movements help to predict movements in house prices?[1] Let us collect data on housing prices and mortgage interest rates. On Freddie Mac's website http://www.freddiemac.com, we find time series for regional and national quarterly house price indexes and 30-year fixed-rate on conventional mortgage loans. We work with annual data from 1971 to 2007. Because we are interested in the relation between changes in prices and interest rates, we compute the percentage changes in the price index, Δp_t, and the changes in mortgage rates, Δr_t. We run two regression models: (i) a model with a univariate information set, which consists of past information on price changes $\{\Delta p_{t-1}, \Delta p_{t-2}, \ldots\}$ and (ii) a model with a multivariate information set, which consists of past price and interest rates movements $\{\Delta p_{t-1}, \Delta p_{t-2}, \ldots \Delta r_{t-1}, \Delta r_{t-2} \ldots\}$:

i. $\Delta p_t = \alpha_0 + \alpha_1 \Delta p_{t-1} + \alpha_2 \Delta p_{t-2} + u_t$
ii. $\Delta p_t = \alpha_0 + \alpha_1 \Delta p_{t-1} + \alpha_2 \Delta p_{t-2} + \beta_1 \Delta r_{t-1} + \beta_2 \Delta r_{t-2} + \varepsilon_t$

The OLS estimation results are presented in Table 4.1. The notation is as follows: DP $= \Delta p_t$ and DR $= \Delta r_t$ so that DP(-1) $= \Delta p_{t-1}$ and DR(-1) $= \Delta r_{t-1}$, and so on.

Model (i) has two regressors—the last two lagged price changes—and model (ii) has added the last two lagged interest rate changes. Observe that the regression estimates associated with interest rates are negative, providing some evidence for Mr. Kohn's statement; lower interest rates lead to higher housing prices. However, the statistical significance of interest rates is more dubious. In model (ii), let us interpret the *t*-ratios corresponding to Δr_{t-1} and Δr_{t-2}: They are rather small with large *p*-values (0.55 and 0.60, respectively) indicating that interest rates do not affect house prices and confirm

[1] This is also a question that relates to the concept of Granger causality, which will be explained in detail in the subsequent chapters.

TABLE 4.1 OLS Regression Results: House Prices and Mortgage Rates

Model (i)

Dependent Variable: DP
Method: Least Squares
Sample (adjusted): 1974 2007
Included observation: 34 after adjustments
Newey-West HAC Standard Errors & Covariance (lag truncation = 3)

Variable	Coefficient	Std. Error	t-Statistic	Prob.
C	2.507576	0.772012	3.248103	0.0028
DP(-1)	0.949125	0.158163	6.000914	0.0000
DP(-2)	-0.380643	0.207324	-1.835982	0.0760

R-squared	0.512796	Mean dependent var	6.152156
Adjusted R-squared	0.481363	S.D. dependent var	3.436283
S.E.of regression	2.474689	Akaike info criterion	4.734204
Sum squared resid	189.8467	Schwarz criterion	4.868883
Log likelihood	-77.48147	F-statistic	16.31416
Durbin-Watson stat	1.906822	Prob(F-statistic)	0.000014

Model (ii)

Dependent Variable: DP
Method: Least Squares
Sample (adjusted): 1974 2007
Included observations: 34 after adjustments
Newey-West HAC Standared Errors & Covariance (lag truncation = 3)

Variable	Coefficient	Std. Error	t-Statistic	Prob.
C	2.220667	0.939448	2.363800	0.0250
DP(-1)	0.914249	0.187557	4.874509	0.0000
DP(-2)	-0.303738	0.276051	-1.100296	0.2803
DR(-1)	-0.227373	0.373079	-0.609449	0.5470
DR(-2)	-0.155855	0.295756	-0.526970	0.6022

R-squared	0.520419	Mean dependent var	6.152156
Adjusted R-squared	0.454270	S.D. dependent var	3.436283
S.E. of regression	2.538503	Akaike info criterion	4.836079
Sum squared resid	186.8759	Schwarz criterion	5.060544
Log likelihood	-77.21334	F-statistic	7.867378
Durbin-Watson stat	1.867714	Prob(F-statistic)	0.000201

that interest rates did not play an important role in the increase of house prices. Gathering further evidence for this statement, we could construct the F-statistic corresponding to the joint null hypothesis $H_0 : \beta_1 = \beta_2 = 0$ (two restrictions):

$$F = \frac{(SSR_0 - SSR_1)/k_0}{SSR_1/k_1} = \frac{(189.85 - 186.88)/2}{186.88/(34 - 5)} = 0.23$$

The denominator is divided by the number of degrees of freedom, which is the number of observations minus the number of estimated parameters in model (ii). The p-value associated with $F_{2,\,29} = 0.23$ is 79%, from which we strongly fail to reject the joint null hypothesis and confirm that interest rates did not play such an important role in the rise of house prices. In addition, observe that the adjusted R-squared of model (i) is larger than that of model (ii): 0.48 versus 0.45. In conclusion, model (i), which exploits a univariate information set, is as good as model (ii), which exploits a multivariate information set.

4.1.2 Some Time Series Are More Forecastable Than Others

It may happen that regardless of the complexity of the information sets, some time series are very difficult to predict. For instance, financial prices such as stock returns, interest rates, exchange rates, and so on are difficult to predict. Why is that? Some reasons are:

- *Lack of understanding of the phenomenon.* Thus, advances in theoretical models explaining the complexity of interactions among economic agents will help with the production of better forecasting models.
- *Lack of statistical methods.* Thus, advances in econometric and statistical methodology help to increase the predictability of some series.
- *High uncertainty* to the extent that it is difficult to separate information from noise and *high complexity* to the extent that parsimonious statistical models are difficult to design.
- *Lack of integration of skills (i.e., economic theory, statistics, mathematics) in the research community.*

In some instances, transformations of the original time series happen to be more predictable than the original series itself. For example, financial returns R_t are difficult to predict but transformations such as squared returns R_t^2 or absolute returns $|R_t|$ are more predictable. These two transformations also have economic meaning because both speak about the volatility of returns, which is of interest to economists, investors, government agencies, and other economic agents.

4.2 The Forecast Horizon

The forecaster needs to choose the horizon of the prediction. Often we distinguish between a short-term forecast and a long-term forecast. Most economists agree that up to a 1-year-ahead prediction is a short-term forecast, and a 10-year-ahead (and longer) prediction is a long-term forecast. Forecasts between 1 and 10 years are considered short/medium term or medium/long term. However, in model-based forecasting, the terms *short-, medium-,* and *long-term* forecast are functions of the frequency of the data and of the properties of the model.

We distinguish between (i) 1-step ahead forecast $f_{t,1}$ and (ii) multistep forecast $f_{t,h}$ for $h > 1$. One-step ahead seems to point toward a short-term forecast and a multistep forecast toward a medium-/long-term forecast. However, this language may be deceiving because the step depends on the frequency of the data. If we work with low-frequency time series data, that is, data that are sampled at long periods of time, for instance, yearly, quinquennial (5-year intervals), or 10-year intervals (as with census data), the 1-step-ahead prediction is either a 1-year-ahead prediction, a 5-year-ahead prediction, or a 10-year-ahead prediction. These are long-term predictions even though they are 1 step ahead. On the contrary, if we work with high-frequency time series data that is, data sampled at short and very short intervals of time, such as daily data or half-hour data, a multistep forecast may refer to a short run prediction. With daily data, a 30-step-ahead forecast is 1-month-ahead prediction; with half-hour data, a 48-step-ahead forecast is a 1-day-ahead prediction. In both cases, we are predicting the short and the very short term although it is a multistep forecast.

Depending on the characteristics of the data, some time series models are better suited for forecasting the short/medium term, and some others are better at forecasting the long term. For instance, covariance stationary processes (defined in Chapter 3) have a limited ability to forecast the long term. These processes are also known as *short memory* processes because the most recent information is weighted more heavily than the older information. For covariance stationary processes, we find that the predictive ability of the model at long horizons is severely reduced because, under certain conditions, we will see that the multistep forecast converges to the unconditional mean of the process ($f_{t,h} \rightarrow \mu$ as $h \rightarrow \infty$). Suppose that we construct a 1-month-ahead forecast based on a daily time series. This is a 30-day-ahead forecast. If the memory of the process is short, a 30-day-ahead forecast may well be the unconditional mean of the process. In this case, the time series model is not helpful; at such a horizon, the model does not have any more predictive ability than what is already contained in the unconditional moments of the process. In this sense, we say that covariance stationary processes, although well suited to capture the short- and medium-term characteristics of the data, do not have much ability to forecast the long term. On the contrary, for nonstationary processes, also known as *long memory* processes, the most recent information is as important as the oldest information. By nature, these processes capture the long-term features of the data, which will be incorporated in the 1-step-ahead and in the multistep forecasts. In this sense, they are better suited to model the long term.

Now suppose that a forecaster needs a long-term forecast. Two ways to go about this are either to choose a time series with the same frequency as the forecast horizon or to choose high-frequency data to produce a low-frequency forecast. The question is: Are these two approaches equivalent, and if so, do they produce the same forecast? The answer is not necessarily. The issue at stake is *aggregation*. Consider the following example. We have two time series: a monthly series of prices and a weekly series of prices. We wish to forecast the monthly change in prices Δp^m_{t+1}. There are at least two options:

i. Use the monthly series to produce 1-step-ahead forecast.
ii. Use the weekly series and aggregate over the 1-, 2-, 3-, and 4-step-ahead forecasts.

Graphically,

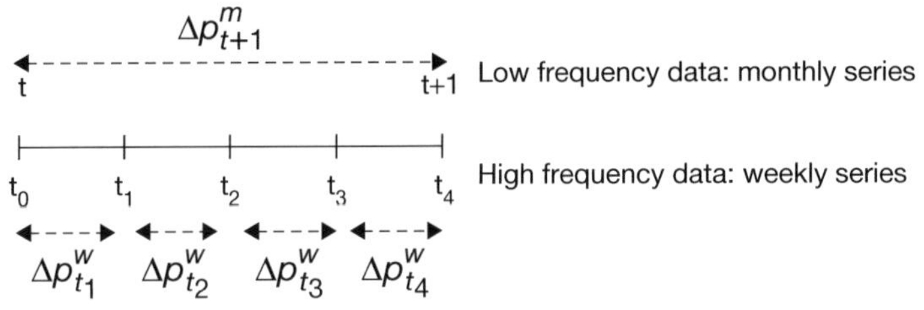

With monthly data, we need only to compute the 1-step-ahead forecast $f^m_{t,1}$ to predict $\Delta p^m_{t+1} = p^m_{t+1} - p^m_t$. However, the price change can also be written using weekly data as the sum of the four weekly changes:

$$\begin{aligned}\Delta p^m_{t+1} &= p^m_{t+1} - p^m_t = p^w_{t_4} - p^w_{t_0} \\ &= (p^w_{t_4} - p^w_{t_3}) + (p^w_{t_3} - p^w_{t_2}) + (p^w_{t_2} - p^w_{t_1}) + (p^w_{t_1} - p^w_{t_0}) \\ &= \Delta p^w_{t_4} + \Delta p^w_{t_3} + \Delta p^w_{t_2} + \Delta p^w_{t_1}\end{aligned}$$

Hence, with weekly data, we need the multistep forecasts (4, 3, 2, and 1 step) $f^w_{t_0,4}, f^w_{t_0,3}, f^w_{t_0,2}$, and $f^w_{t_0,1}$ for $\Delta p^w_{t_4}$, $\Delta p^w_{t_3}$, $\Delta p^w_{t_2}$, and $\Delta p^w_{t_1}$, respectively.

The question becomes: Do $f^w_{t_0,4} + f^w_{t_0,3} + f^w_{t_0,2} + f^w_{t_0,1} = f^m_{t,1}$? Not necessarily. The reason is that the functional form of the time series model for **low-frequency data** may not be the same as that for **high-frequency data** although we are modeling the same variables. A practical recommendation is to use the same data frequency as the forecast horizon of interest. If you need a monthly forecast, model the monthly time series and construct the 1-step-ahead forecast. For instance, stock returns seem to be more predictable at long horizons (5 years and longer) than at short horizons (daily, weekly). This is so because the statistical properties of the time series are different across frequencies and because there are different statistical models for different frequencies. In the exercises at the end of this chapter, you will be asked to estimate regression models at the annual and quarterly frequencies and observe their differences.

4.2.1 Forecasting Environments

In the practice of model-based forecasting, we first assess the performance of the model(s) in what we call *in-sample* and *out-of-sample* environments. Let us assume that we have a time series with T observations. We divide the sample into two parts: the **estimation sample** and the **prediction sample**. We estimate the model with the observations in the estimation sample $\{y_1, y_2, \ldots . y_t\}$, which has t observations. We could assess the "in-sample" goodness of the model by performing specification tests within the sample of t observations. But, from a forecasting perspective, this is tantamount to "cheating" because in real life, we want to predict the future, which by nature is not part of the estimation sample. This is why we would like to reserve some observations, from the $t+1$ to the T observations, to fairly assess the forecasting ability of the model. This is what we call the *out-of-sample* assessment. By proceeding this way, our goal is to recreate a "real" forecasting environment. Without loss of generality, suppose that we are interested in the 1-step-ahead forecast $f_{t,1}$. The objective is to produce a sequence of 1-step-ahead forecasts $\{f_{t+j,1}$ for $j = 0, 1, \ldots T - t - 1\}$ for $\{Y_{t+1}, Y_{t+2}, \ldots Y_T\}$. Observe that now we can assess the accuracy of the forecast because in the prediction sample, we have the observations $\{y_{t+1}, y_{t+2}, \ldots . y_T\}$, and we will be able to compute the 1-step-ahead forecast errors $e_{t+j,1} = y_{t+j+1} - f_{t+j,1}$ for $j = 0, 1, \ldots T - t - 1$.

The forecaster will choose among the following three forecasting schemes: recursive, rolling, and fixed. Let us proceed to describe them.

In Figure 4.1, we describe the **recursive forecasting environment**. We start with our first prediction at time t. The model is estimated with t observations and the 1-step-ahead forecast is produced. For the next period $t+1$, the estimation sample increases by 1 more observation, and the model is estimated again with $t+1$ observations. At time $t+1$, we again produce the 1-step-ahead forecast. We keep repeating the same procedure

FIGURE 4.1
Forecasting Environments: Recursive Scheme

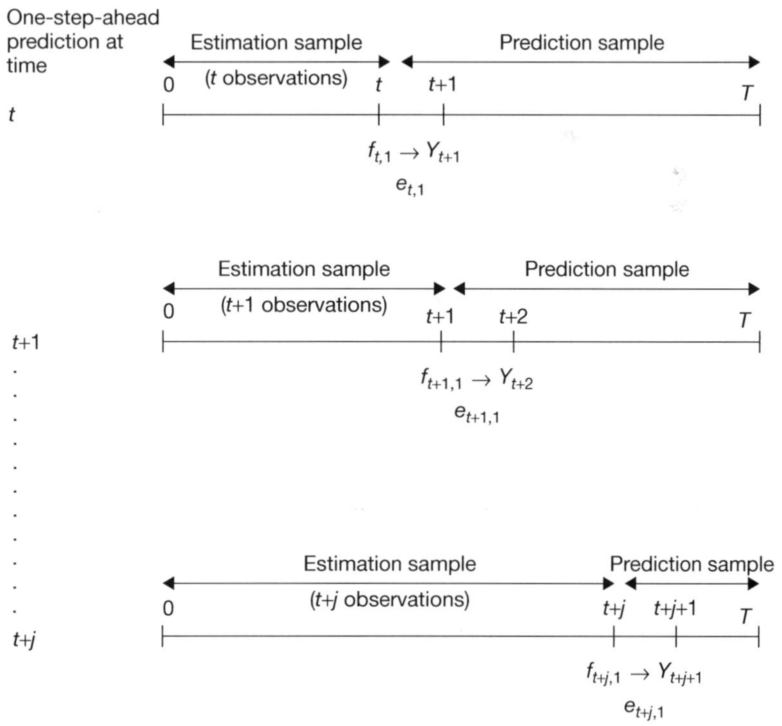

until we exhaust the prediction sample. Observe that the estimation sample keeps expanding one observation at a time, and the model is estimated again when one new observation is added to the estimation sample. Once the prediction sample is exhausted, we have collected a sequence of 1-step-ahead forecasting errors $\{e_{t,1}, e_{t+1,1}, \ldots\ldots e_{t+j,1}, \ldots\ldots e_{T-1,1}\}$, which will be evaluated within the context of a loss function (to be introduced in the next section).

In Figure 4.2, we describe the **rolling forecasting environment**. The starting point is the same as in the previous scheme. The difference is that the estimation sample always contains the same number of observations. At time t, the estimation sample has t observations; at time $t+1$, it contains observations 2 to $t+1$; at time $t+2$, it contains observations 3 to $t+2$, and so on. The estimation sample is rolling until the prediction sample is exhausted. The model is estimated within each rolling sample, and the 1-step-ahead forecast is produced along the way. As before, we have a collection of 1-step-ahead forecasting errors $\{e_{t,1}, e_{t+1,1}, \ldots\ldots e_{t+j,1}, \ldots\ldots e_{T-1,1}\}$.

In Figure 4.3, we describe the **fixed forecasting environment**. The main difference is that the model is estimated only once using the estimation sample that contains the first t observations. When time passes, the information set is updated, but there is no new estimation of the model as in the recursive and rolling schemes. For instance, at time $t+1$, the information set contains one more observation, which will contribute to

FIGURE 4.2 Forecasting Environments: Rolling Scheme

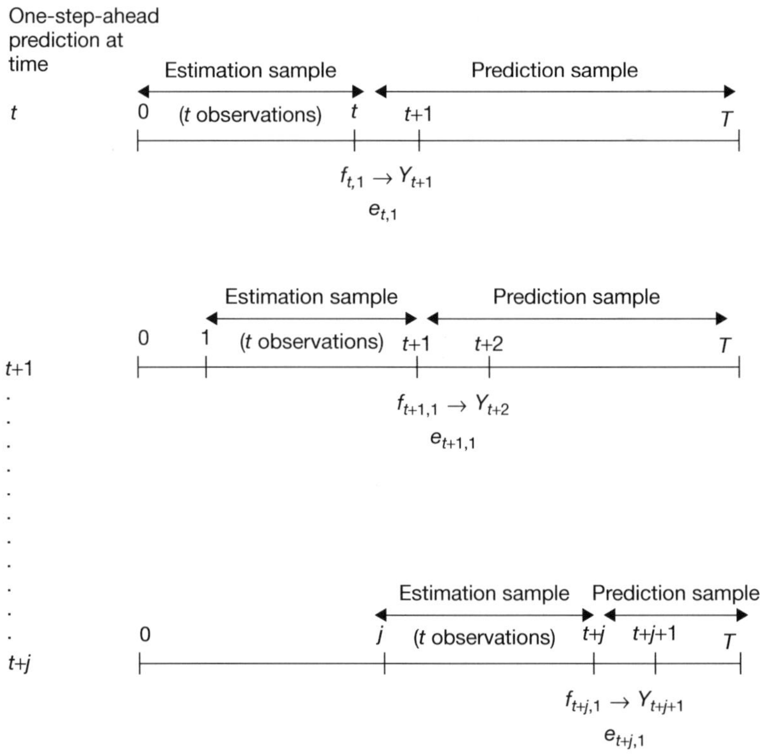

FIGURE 4.3
Forecasting Environments: Fixed Scheme

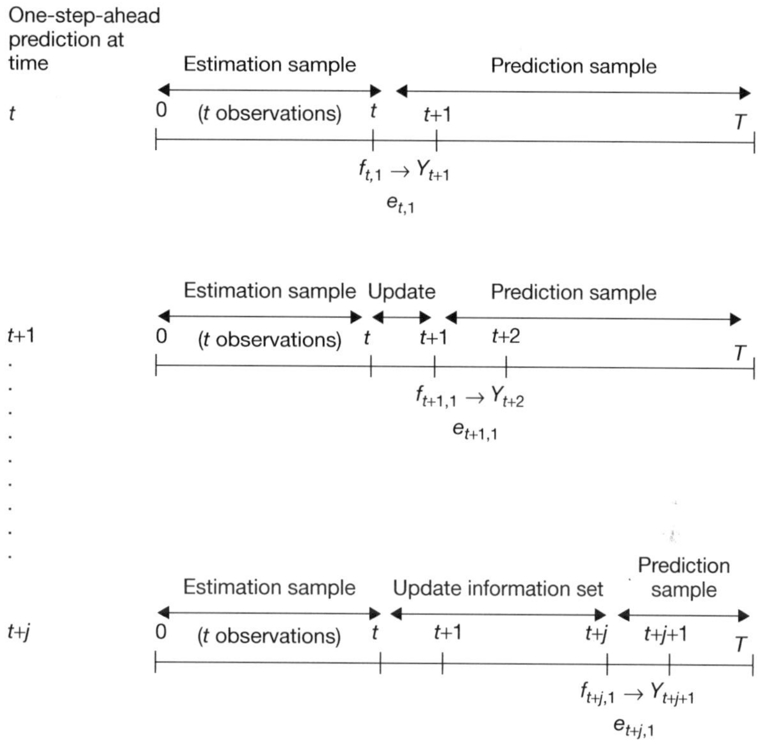

the construction of the 1-step-ahead forecast but will not contribute to the estimation of the model's parameters. The information set is updated period by period until the prediction sample is exhausted. As in the previous schemes, we have a collection of 1-step-ahead forecasting errors $\{e_{t,1}, e_{t+1,1}, \ldots\ldots e_{t+j,1}, \ldots\ldots e_{T-1,1}\}$ that will be properly evaluated.

Each scheme has advantages and disadvantages. The recursive scheme incorporates as much information as possible in the estimation of the model. This scheme will be advantageous if the model is stable over time, but if the data have structural breaks, the model's stability is in jeopardy and so is the forecast. The rolling scheme avoids the potential problem with the model's stability, and it is more robust against structural breaks in the data. The fixed scheme is fast and convenient because there is one and only one estimation, but it does not allow for parameter updating.

4.3 The Loss Function

Consider the following scenario. You are in Riverside, a city in Southern California, about 90 miles east of Los Angeles. Tomorrow you are departing on a business trip to the East Coast from Los Angeles International Airport (LAX). You wish to forecast how many hours you will need to travel from Riverside to LAX, and, of course, you would not like to miss your plane. Your information set will contain the following information: the distance between Riverside and LAX, the rush hours in the area highways, the construction work in the area, the access to the airport, the airport parking, the weather conditions (always sunny!), the lines at the check-in counters, the time for luggage inspection, and so on. Suppose that your forecast is $f_{t,1} = 4$ hours and that the actual time could be either 5 hours or 3 hours with equal probability, that is,

$$f_{t,1} = 4 \quad y_{t+1} = \begin{cases} 5 \\ 3 \end{cases} \quad \Rightarrow \quad e_{t,1} = y_{t+1} - f_{t,1} = \begin{cases} 1 \\ -1 \end{cases}$$

Suppose that tomorrow comes, and for some unexpected reason, it takes you 5 hours to reach the airport and therefore you miss your plane. Your forecast error is $e_{t,1} = 1$. What are the potential costs associated with a positive forecast error? Either you have to go back to Riverside, spend the night in Los Angeles, or wait seven hours in the airport to catch the next plane to your destination. You may spend extra money on food, taxi rides, and so on. You mood would likely be rotten for the rest of the day. You may wonder whether your professional reputation and your prospective business deal would be damaged because you will miss your evening meeting with your client on the East Coast. Contrast these costs with those associated with a negative forecast error $e_{t,1} = -1$. This is the case in which you arrive at LAX in three hours and have 1 hour to spare before boarding your plane. Some costs may be unpleasant: noisy environments, uncomfortable chairs, crowded spaces, and so on. Which scenario is more costly to you? Obviously, the first one in which $e_{t,1} = 1$. The positive and negative errors are of the same magnitude but different signs have very different costs. The bottom line: You have an asymmetric loss *(cost)* function! And what would you do next time? You will revise your forecast upward (allocate more time) to avoid positive forecast errors. Suppose now that an external observer collects your forecast errors over time and computes their mean. What is the expected sign of the mean forecast error? If you are avoiding positive errors, negative errors will be more prevalent, and the sign of the average of the forecast errors will be most likely negative.

Because uncertainty cannot be avoided, the forecaster is bound to commit forecast errors, which in turn are costly. From the previous example, we have learned that the prediction will be adjusted accordingly to the loss function that the forecaster is facing. Thus, *a priori,* the forecaster must know the loss function.

We define:

A loss function $L(e_{t,h})$ is the evaluation of costs associated with the forecast errors.[2]

There are three properties that a loss function should satisfy:

i. If the forecast error is zero, the loss is zero:

$$e_{t,h} = 0 \rightarrow L(e_{t,h}) = 0$$

[2] In some instances, the loss function is also written as a function of the future value and the forecast, that is, $L(y_{t+h}, f_{t,h})$.

ii. The loss function is a non-negative function with minimum value equal to zero:

$$e_{t,h} \neq 0 \rightarrow L(e_{t,h}) \geq 0$$
$$\min L(e_{t,h}) = 0$$

iii. For positive errors, the function is monotonically increasing, and for negative errors, monotonically decreasing:

$$\text{if } e_{t,h}^{(1)} > e_{t,h}^{(2)} > 0 \rightarrow L(e_{t,h}^{(1)}) > L(e_{t,h}^{(2)})$$
$$\text{if } e_{t,h}^{(1)} < e_{t,h}^{(2)} < 0 \rightarrow L(e_{t,h}^{(1)}) > L(e_{t,h}^{(2)})$$

4.3.1 Some Examples of Loss Functions

Symmetric Loss Functions

In Figure 4.4, we offer two examples of symmetric loss functions. For these functions, the sign of the forecast errors is irrelevant, that is, positive or negative errors of the same magnitude have identical costs.

Observe that both functions satisfy requirements (i) to (iii). The constant a must be positive in order to have a non-negative loss. The lower the value of a, the flatter the function becomes.

Asymmetric Loss Functions

In Figure 4.5, we picture the two most popular asymmetric loss functions: the linex function and the lin-lin function. In the *linex function,* positive forecast errors have a larger (smaller) penalty than negative errors when $a > 0$ ($a < 0$). In the *lin-lin function,* negative errors are more (less) costly than positive errors when $|b| > a$ ($|b| < a$).

4.3.2 Examples

In practice, the quadratic loss function is the most prevalent because it is mathematically tractable, but it is also the most unrealistic. Most of the time, economic agents

FIGURE 4.4
Symmetric Loss Functions

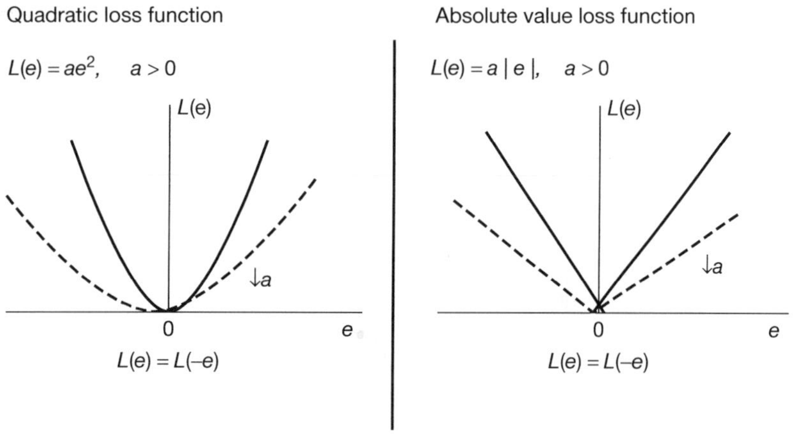

FIGURE 4.5
Asymmetric Loss Functions

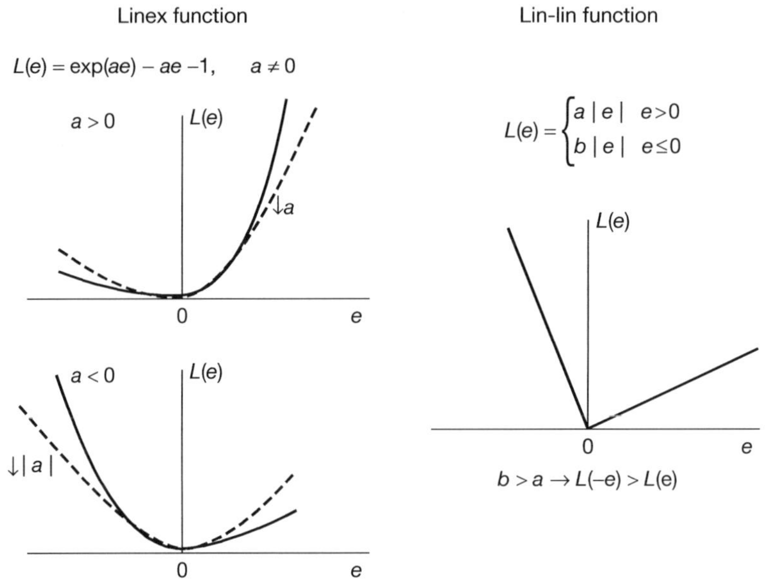

have asymmetric loss functions. Think about the earlier example of your trip to LAX. For most of us, it is less costly to wait in the airport than to miss a flight. Think about consumers deciding to allocate money between present consumption and future consumption. To do so, they will be interested in forecasting their future level of income. Depending on this forecast, today they decide to save or consume more. If consumers are very optimistic and predict more future income than the actual realized income, they might not have saved enough, jeopardizing their future standard of living. If they predict less income than the actual income, they find a windfall. In this example, it is obvious that overprediction of future income is more costly than underprediction.

Think about a government budget that must allocate funds for different government programs and expenditures that are financed by tax revenues. Forecasting tax revenues is very important because government runs either a surplus (higher tax revenues than expenditures) or a deficit (lower tax revenues than expenditures). Running big deficits could mean the end of politicians' careers whereas a surplus may guarantee reelection. Once again, the cost of underpredicting tax revenues (realized tax revenue is higher than predicted) is smaller than the cost of overpredicting (realized tax revenue is less than predicted and a deficit is likely to happen).

The financial meltdown of 2008 tested the effectiveness of monetary policy on revitalizing the U.S. economy, which was on the verge of a great recession. In normal times, the Federal Reserve (Fed) conducts monetary policy by controlling the federal fund rate through open market operations; in extraordinary times, such as 2008, an additional major concern of the Fed is maintaining enough liquidity in the banking system by buying huge amounts of assets of different maturities. These activities by nature are short-term injections and sooner or later will end. The difficult question for the Fed is how and when to stop, the so-called exit strategy. The short answer is that stopping will depend on future economic growth. If growth is slow, the Fed will continue its expansionary policy, but if growth is fast, it will start withdrawing its support. A forecast of GDP growth must be of great importance in guiding the Fed's decisions. Suppose that the Fed decides to raise interest rates because it predicts fast growth ahead. If fast growth is not realized and the economy remains sluggish, higher interest rates will aggravate the state of the economy further. Now suppose that the Fed continues its expansionary policy by keeping rates down because the forecast is almost zero GDP growth. In this case, if growth occurs faster than the Fed's prediction, it is likely that inflation will develop. Which scenario is more costly, more painful? Arguably, a recession has a higher human cost than an inflationary economy; thus, the loss function of the Fed is surely asymmetric, attaching higher costs to overpredicting GDP growth than to underpredicting it.

Banking regulations require financial intermediaries to make capital provisions as a preventive measure against insolvency caused by loan defaults. Bank failures can trigger financial crisis in the economy. Banks and other financial intermediaries need to judge the consequences of allocating too much or too little capital. Depending on their line of business (i.e., commercial loans, consumer loans, real estate investments, mortgages), the banking sector needs forecasts of interest rates, economic recessions and expansions, house prices, and so on. A level of capital provision that is too large is costly because the banks face opportunity costs for the funds set aside. A level of capital provision that is too low is also costly because the banks may face massive loan defaults in the future, which could jeopardize their survival. Which costs are more onerous? Again, an asymmetric loss function should guide the forecast of the variables of interest.

Fund managers build their reputations by delivering high returns for the funds they manage. Stocks and other financial assets go up and down as do their returns. To make optimal investment decisions, a fund manager needs accurate predictions of asset returns. If fund performance turns out to be poor, investors will withdraw their money and the manager's bonus will be reduced. Furthermore, with long-lasting negative returns, most investors will liquidate their investments in the fund, and the manager will be fired. Think about the loss function of this fund manager. It must be asymmetric because the consequences of consistently delivering negative returns are much more costly than those of delivering positive returns or some negative returns here and there.

4.3.3 Optimal Forecast: An Introduction[3]

Knowing the loss function is crucial to the design of the best forecast. We introduce the definition of *optimal forecast* to stress the importance of the loss function in the forecaster's tool kit. Optimality will be studied in additional detail after we have more experience with the construction of time series models. For now, an introduction will suffice.

[3] This section can be skipped without affecting the flow of the chapter. It introduces more advanced concepts that will be revisited again after the chapters on time series models. If the students are familiar with calculus, they will benefit from understanding the link between loss function and optimal forecast now.

Putting all our tools together—information set I_t, forecast horizon h, and loss function $L(e)$—we write

$$L(e_{t,h}) = L(y_{t+h} - f_{t,h})$$

It is reasonable to assume that by choosing $f_{t,h}$, the forecaster would like to minimize the costs associated with potential forecast errors. Thus, minimizing the loss function seems a sensible criterion to guide the forecast choice. Observe that y_{t+h} is a potential realization (future value unknown at time t) of the random variable Y_{t+h}, which has a conditional probability density function, say $f(y_{t+h}|I_t)$. Because the loss function depends on a random variable, it is also a random variable. Thus, we can talk about the statistical moments of the loss function. In particular, we are interested in the expected loss or, in other words, the average of the loss function

$$E(L(y_{t+h} - f_{t,h})) = \int L(y_{t+h} - f_{t,h}) f(y_{t+h}|I_t)dy$$

for Y_{t+h} being a continuous random variable.

Accordingly, the optimality criterion has to be rephrased slightly: The forecaster would like to minimize the *expected* loss function. We define:

Optimal forecast $f^*_{t,h}$ is the forecast that minimizes the expected loss

$$\min_{f_{t,h}} E(L(y_{t+h} - f_{t,h}))$$

From this definition, there are two components that affect the optimal forecast:

i. The conditional probability density function $f(y_{t+h}|I_t)$.
ii. The functional form of the loss function $L(y_{t+h} - f_{t,h})$.

4.3.3.1 Conditional Density of Y_{t+h}

Graphically, the optimal forecast $f^*_{t,h}$ will be a potential outcome of the random variable Y_{t+h} (some value along the vertical dashed line in Figure 4.6).

We assume that the conditional density is a normal density with conditional mean $\mu_{t+h|t} \equiv E(Y_{t+h}|I_t)$ and conditional variance $\sigma^2_{t+h|t} \equiv Var(Y_{t+h}|I_t)$,

$$f(y_{t+h}|I_t) = N(\mu_{t+h|t}, \sigma^2_{t+h|t})$$

4.3.3.2 Functional Form of the Loss Function: The Case of a Quadratic Loss

Suppose that the forecaster has a symmetric quadratic loss function $L(e_{t,h}) = ae^2_{t,h}$ for $a > 0$. Let us construct the expected value of the loss,

$$E(L(e_{t,h})|I_t) = aE(e^2_{t,h}) = aE(y_{t+h} - f_{t,h})^2 = aE(y^2_{t+h} - 2f_{t,h}y_{t+h} + f^2_{t,h})$$
$$= a(E(y^2_{t+h}) - 2f_{t,h}E(y_{t+h}) + f^2_{t,h})$$

FIGURE 4.6
The Forecasting Problem

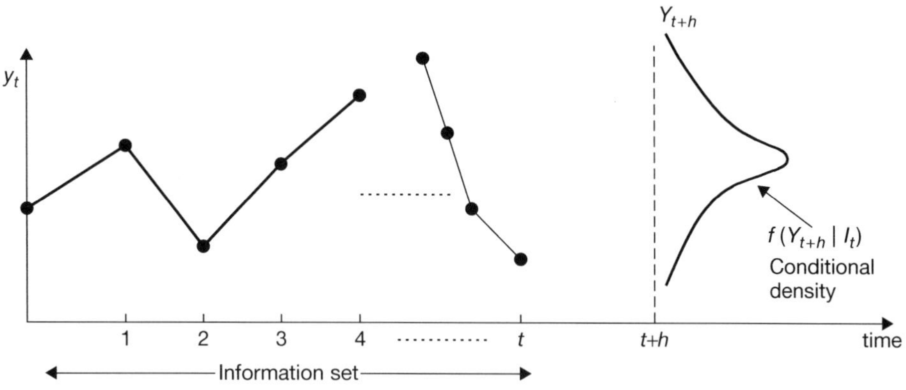

Observe that we consider the expectation conditional on the information set; thus, $E(f_{t,h}) = f_{t,h}$. To simplify notation, the conditioning set has been suppressed after the first equal sign, but it should be understood that all the expectations are conditional expectations.

The objective is to choose $f^*_{t,h}$ such that the expected loss is minimized.[4] By solving the optimization problem, we find that the optimal forecast is the conditional mean of y_{t+h}

$$f^*_{t,h} = E(y_{t+h} \mid I_t) \equiv \mu_{t+h|t}$$

See Figure 4.7 for the graphic position of the optimal forecast.

FIGURE 4.7
Optimal Forecast Under Quadratic Loss

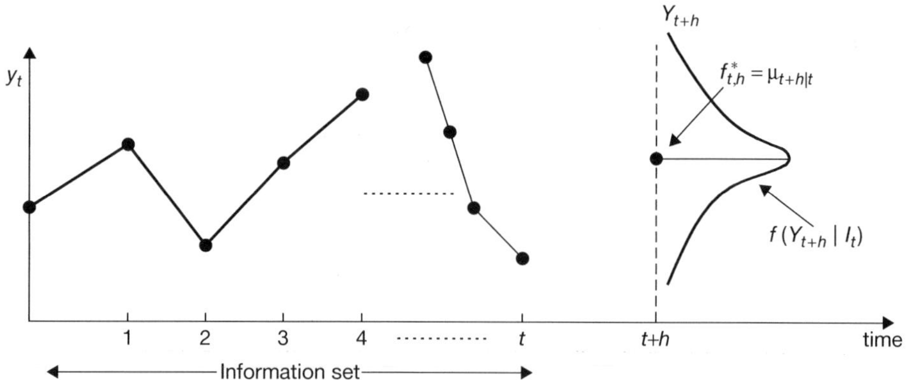

[4] For those of you familiar with calculus, the solution is found by solving the first-order conditions of the optimization problem. Take the first derivative of the expected loss with respect to the forecast and make it equal to zero:

$$\frac{\partial\, E(L(e_{t,h} \mid I_t)}{\partial f_{t,h}} = -2aE(y_{t+h} \mid I_t) + 2af_{t,h} = 0 \quad \Rightarrow f^*_{t,h} = E(y_{t+h} \mid I_t)$$

If the conditional density $f(y_{t+h}|I_t)$ is a normal density function, a 95% confidence interval for the optimal forecast is

$$\mu_{t+h|t} \pm 1.96\sigma_{t+h|t} = (\mu_{t+h|t} - 1.96\sigma_{t+h|t}, \mu_{t+h|t} + 1.96\sigma_{t+h|t})$$

In addition, the conditional density $f(y_{t+h}|I_t)$ is also known as the *density forecast*. Under the assumption of normality, once we know the conditional mean and the conditional variance, we fully know the density forecast,

$$f(y_{t+h}|I_t) = N(\mu_{t+h|t}, \sigma^2_{t+h|t})$$

Constructing the optimal forecast under quadratic loss is an easy exercise once we have a model. Go back to the example in Section 4.1.1, "Housing prices and interest rates" where we estimated two regression models. We concluded that model (i) was preferred to model (ii). Let us take advantage of these results to illustrate how to construct the optimal forecast. Recall that model (i) was specified as $\Delta p_t = \alpha_0 + \alpha_1 \Delta p_{t-1} + \alpha_2 \Delta p_{t-2} + u_t$ and that in regression, we model the *conditional mean* of the variable of interest. Thus, by interpreting model (i) , we write

$$E(\Delta p_t | \Delta p_{t-1}, \Delta p_{t-2}) = \alpha_0 + \alpha_1 \Delta p_{t-1} + \alpha_2 \Delta p_{t-2}$$

Observe that the information set is $I_{t-1} = \{\Delta p_{t-1}, \Delta p_{t-2}\}$ containing information up to time $t-1$, and that the 1-step-ahead optimal forecast will be

$$f^*_{t-1,1} = E(\Delta p_t | I_{t-1}) = E(\Delta p_t | \Delta p_{t-1}, \Delta p_{t-2}) = \alpha_0 + \alpha_1 \Delta p_{t-1} + \alpha_2 \Delta p_{t-2}.$$

By plugging in the OLS estimates in Table 4.1, the 1-year-ahead forecast, with information up to 2007, is

$$\begin{aligned} f^*_{t-1,1} &= 2.51 + 0.95\Delta p_{t-1} - 0.38\Delta p_{t-2} \\ f^*_{2007,1} &= 2.51 + 0.95\Delta p_{2007} - 0.38\Delta p_{2006} \end{aligned}$$

From the information set, we gather that $\Delta p_{2007} = 0.25\%$ and $\Delta p_{2006} = 6.23\%$, thus $f^*_{2007,1} = 0.38\%$; in other words, the expected house price growth for 2008 is 0.38%.

KEY WORDS

asymmetric loss function, p. 91
estimation sample, p. 86
fixed forecasting environment, p. 88
high-frequency data, p. 86
loss function, p. 90
low-frequency data, p. 86
multivariate information set, p. 81
optimal forecast, p. 80
prediction sample, p. 86
qualitative information set, p. 80
quantitative information set, p. 80
recursive forecasting environment, p. 87
rolling forecasting environment, p. 88
symmetric loss function, p. 91
univariate information set, p. 81

APPENDIX

EViews computer program to implement the fixed, rolling, and recursive schemes.

The following program uses the data set "House price growth in California 1975Q2-2002Q4" for three hypothetical forecasts: (F1)$f_{t,1} = 0.21 + 0.74y_t + 0.16y_{t-2}$, (F2)$f_{t,1} = y_t$, (F3) $f_{t,1} = \dfrac{y_t + y_{t-1} + y_{t-2} + y_{t-3}}{4}$.

```
' Alternative Forecasting Schemes
load c:\EViews3\112_S08\ca_hp.wf1
' Fixed Scheme
smpl 1975q2 2002q4
coef(3) prms1
ls g = prms1(1) + prms1(2)*g(-1)+prms1(3)*g(-3)
vector(20) frcst1
for !i = 1 to 20
        frcst1(!i) = prms1(1) + prms1(2)*g(111+!i)+prms1(3)*g(109+!i)
next
' Recursive Scheme
vector(20) frcst2
for !i = 1 to 20
        smpl 1975q2 2002q4+(!i-1)
        coef(3) prms2
        ls g = prms2(1) + prms2(2)*g(-1)+prms2(3)*g(-3)
        frcst2(!i) = prms2(1) + prms2(2)*g(111+!i)+prms2(3)*g(109+!i)
next
' Rolling Scheme
vector(20) frcst3
for !i = 1 to 20
        smpl 1975q2+(!i) 2002q4+(!i-1)
        coef(3) prms3
        ls g = prms3(1) + prms3(2)*g(-1)+prms3(3)*g(-3)
        frcst3(!i) = prms3(1) + prms3(2)*g(111+!i)+prms3(3)*g(109+!i)
next
' Model II
vector(20) frcst4
for !i = 1 to 20
        frcst4(!i) = g(111+!i)
```

```
next
' Model III
vector(20) frcst5
for !i = 1 to 20
        frcst5(!i) = (g(111+!i)+g(110+!i)+g(109+!i)+g(108+!i))/4
next
```

EXERCISES

1. Update the data set on *annual* house prices and interest rates analyzed in Section 4.1.1. Compute the ACF and PACF functions of house prices, interest rates, house price growth, and interest rate changes. Comment on the differences across autocorrelation functions. In which series do you find stronger time dependence?
2. With the new data from Exercise 1, replicate models (i) and (ii) of Section 4.1.1. Run different regression models by adding two more lags for price and interest rate movements. Compare your results with models (i) and model (ii). Is a univariate information set more valuable than a multivariate information set to explain housing prices? Are the new models better than models (i) and (ii) at explaining price growth?
3. Download the same data as in Exercise 1, but at the *quarterly* frequency. Compute the ACF and PACF functions of quarterly house prices, interest rates, house price growth, and interest rates changes. Comment on the differences across autocorrelation functions. In which series do you find stronger time dependence? Examine the differences in the autocorrelation functions of quarterly data versus annual data.
4. Using the same data set as in Exercise 3 and for house price growth, run several regression models with one, two, three, and four lags of price growth in the right-hand side of the model. Analyze the regression results. Compare the regression models at the quarterly frequency with the models at the annual frequency that you estimated in Exercise 2. Choose your favorite model and implement a recursive and a rolling estimation scheme. Plot the time series of the estimates of the regression coefficients and observe how much they change over time.
5. Consider the manager of a large department store. Among other responsibilities, she is in charge of inventory control so that she needs good forecasts of department sales. Think about the costs of overstocking and understocking merchandise, and recommend a loss function that she should use to produce her forecast.
6. The Board of Governors of the Federal Reserve publishes the 1-quarter-ahead forecasts of real GDP growth. These are known as the *Greenbook forecasts*. Download the realized values of GDP growth (from the website of the Federal

Reserve Bank of Philadelphia, http://www.phil.frb.org/econ/forecast) and compare with the Fed forecasts. Compute the 1-quarter-ahead forecast errors. Plot the time series of realized values, forecasts, and forecast errors. What do you observe in these time series? Compute the descriptive statistics of the three series. Compute the ACF and PACF of the realized values, forecasts, and forecast errors. Do you observe time dependence?

7. Following with the same data as in Exercise 6, plot the realized values against the forecasts and run a regression such as $y_{t+1} = \beta_0 + \beta_1 f_{t,1} + u_{t+1}$ where y_{t+1} is the realized GDP growth and $f_{t,1}$ is the 1-quarter-ahead forecast. Are the values scattered around a 45-degree line? What are the estimates $\hat{\beta}_0$ and $\hat{\beta}_1$? The forecast will be called *unbiased* under a quadratic loss function if $\beta_0 = 0$ and $\beta_1 = 1$. Perform a t-ratio for the individual hypothesis and an F-test for the joint hypothesis to determine whether the forecast is unbiased. What do you conclude?

8. Let us call $e_{t,1} = y_{t+1} - f_{t,1}$ the 1-quarter-ahead forecast error that you have computed in Exercise 6. Is the expected value of the forecast errors equal to zero? If not, what do you conclude? Run the regression of the forecast errors on several lags, that is, $e_{t,1} = \beta_0 + \beta_1 e_{t-1,1} + \beta_2 e_{t-2,1} + \cdots u_{t+1}$. Comment on the regression results. Perform an F-test for the joint hypothesis $H_0: \beta_1 = \beta_2 = \cdots \beta_k = 0$ for your choice of k. What do you conclude? Is the forecast error predictable from its own past?

9. With the forecast errors of Exercise 8, run the following regression: $e_{t,1} = \beta_0 + \beta_1 e_{t-1,1} + \beta_2 e_{t-2,1} + \beta_3 f_{t,1} + \beta_4 f_{t-1,1} + u_{t+1}$. Comment on the regression results. Perform an F-test for the joint hypothesis $H_0: \beta_1 = \beta_2 = \beta_3 = \beta_4 = 0$ and another F-test for $H_0: \beta_3 = \beta_4 = 0$. Is the forecast error predictable in any way?

10. Exercises 7, 8, and 9 are all tests of forecast optimality under quadratic loss function. Summarize all previous results and write a brief report explaining whether the Fed produces optimal forecasts (under the assumption that it has a quadratic loss function).

A PAUSE

WHERE ARE WE AND WHERE ARE WE GOING?

From this point, our main objective is to learn how to build time series models that summarize as parsimoniously as possible the dependence between the present time and the past with the expectation that this dependence will extend to the future. Consequently, a time series model will serve as a good device to construct the best forecast. But before embarking in model building, let us summarize the three main ideas that *we have learned so far* in the previous four chapters:

1. Our focus is on model-based forecasting (Chapter 1). We are searching for functional forms (equations) that relate past history to the present. Our premise is that if there is dependence between the past and the present, we should expect this dependence to hold between the present and the future. In other words "history repeats itself," and we could take advantage of it. The forthcoming question is whether we can uncover and formalize this dependence.
2. The introduction of time requires new statistical concepts that go beyond the fundamentals of regression analysis (Chapter 2). We have introduced the fundamental concept of stochastic process. We have learned that a very important property of the data is stationarity, which brings a degree of homogeneity within the random variables that form the stochastic process (Chapter 3). But we have already seen that economic and business data sometimes are stationary and sometimes are not. Thus, the forthcoming question is whether we need different methods of analysis for stationary versus nonstationary data.
3. A notion of optimality should guide the construction of the forecast (Chapter 4). We have learned that there are losses associated with forecast errors. A sensible principle for any forecaster is to know and minimize potential losses and upon doing so, the resulting forecast will be optimal. Consequently, forecasters with different loss functions may produce different forecasts for the same variable of interest.

Where Are We Going from Here?

Our main objective is to formalize the notion of time dependence. We have already seen that the autocorrelation functions are key tools that summarize the linear dependence in the data. Look at the four different autocorrelograms that correspond to four simulated (artificial) time series (see Figure P.1). They exhibit different shapes, different decay

FIGURE P.1 Autocorrelation Functions of Four Simulated Time Series

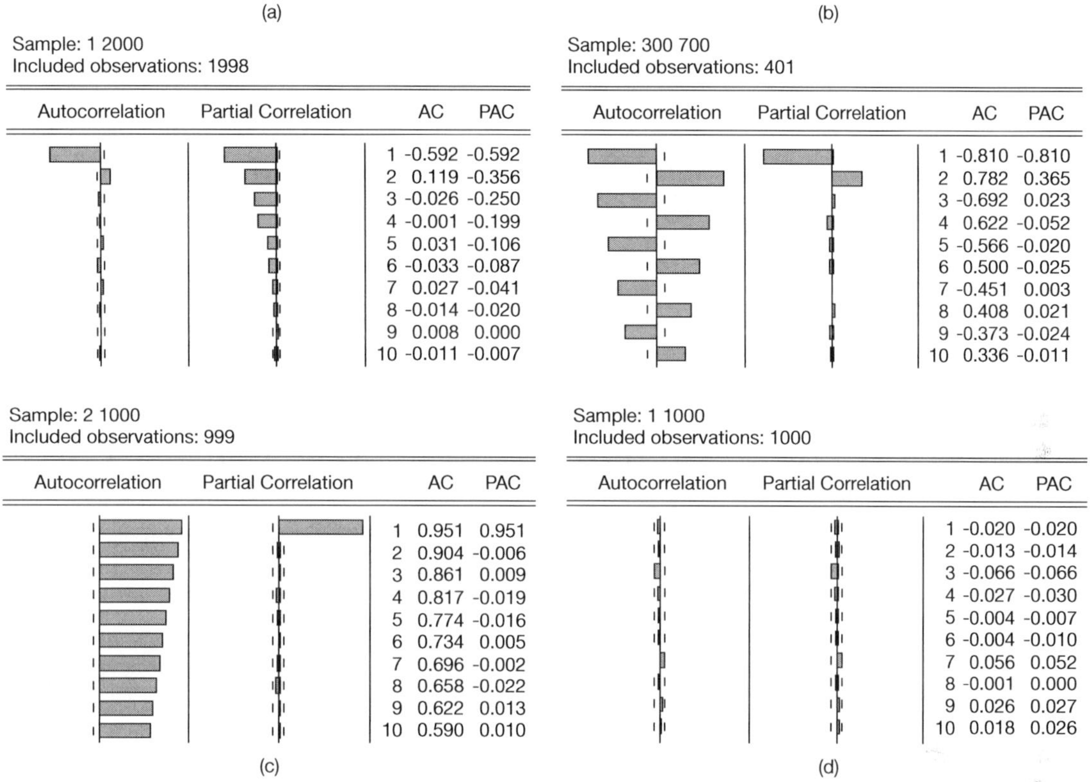

toward zero, and different memory (number of autocorrelations statistically different from zero). Why are they so different? The answer is that every time series has its own generating mechanism. Our objective is to unveil this mechanism, and in order to do so, we proceed to construct models that can explain different patterns of linear dependence.

(a)
Sample: 1 2000
Included observations: 1998
Autocorrelation Partial Correlation AC PAC
1 -0.592 -0.592
2 0.119 -0.356
3 -0.026 -0.250
4 -0.001 -0.199
5 0.031 -0.106
6 -0.033 -0.087
7 0.027 -0.041
8 -0.014 -0.020
9 0.008 0.000
10 -0.011 -0.007
(b)
Sample: 300 700
Included observations: 401
Autocorrelation Partial Correlation AC PAC
1 -0.810 -0.810
2 0.782 0.365
3 -0.692 0.023
4 0.622 -0.052
5 -0.566 -0.020
6 0.500 -0.025
7 -0.451 0.003
8 0.408 0.021
9 -0.373 -0.024
10 0.336 -0.011
Sample: 2 1000
Included observations: 999
Autocorrelation Partial Correlation AC PAC
1 0.951 0.951
2 0.904 -0.006
3 0.861 0.009
4 0.817 -0.019
5 0.774 -0.016
6 0.734 0.005
7 0.696 -0.002
8 0.658 -0.022
9 0.622 0.013
10 0.590 0.010
(c)
Sample: 1 1000
Included observations: 1000
Autocorrelation Partial Correlation AC PAC
1 -0.020 -0.020
2 -0.013 -0.014
3 -0.066 -0.066
4 -0.027 -0.030
5 -0.004 -0.007
6 -0.004 -0.010
7 0.056 0.052
8 -0.001 0.000
9 0.026 0.027
10 0.018 0.026
(d)

However, before embarking in model building, you may wonder about the connection between the many macro- and microeconomic models analyzed in your economics and business courses and the time series models that we are ready to analyze. Economic models are stylized representations of either the structure of the macroeconomy (e.g., models of income determination, models of investment, open economy models) or the structure of microunits such as firms, investors, markets (e.g., models of profit maximization, asset pricing models, monopoly models). In general, these models are known as *structural models* because, as the name indicates, they analyze the workings of the economic structure of interest. At an introductory level, these models are static, which means that time does not play any role in them. We do not learn how economic variables, such as income, prices, rates, and so on move from one period to the next. In contrast, time series models are intrinsically dynamic: Time is the main ingredient. We will learn how variables evolve over time. For most part, time series models are not structural models because they are not designed to explain the workings of economic units. Uncovering the dynamics of an economic variable is a statistical exercise, and in this sense, time series models are ad hoc representations. Nevertheless, in Chapter 5, we will present very simple economic models that have implications for the dynamics of the variables of interest, and, on doing so we will justify the autocorrelation that characterizes many economic and business data. You will learn that the behavior of economic agents (consumers, investors, institutions, etc.) explains why time dependence may arise in the data. In this sense, Chapter 5 is a "bridge" between economic and quantitative/forecasting reasoning.

Our main objective—model building—starts in Chapter 6 and Chapter 7 where we study the statistical properties of Moving Average (MA) and Autoregressive (AR) Models, respectively. In Chapter 8 and Chapter 9, we introduce the practice of forecasting with a hands-on exercise based on real data. Chapter 8 provides a step-by-step *in-sample* evaluation of time series models, and Chapter 9 provides a step-by-step *out-of-sample* evaluation.

With these expectations in mind, there are several, not mutually exclusive, paths to:

How to Organize Your Reading of the Forthcoming Chapters

1. If you are anxious to put your hands into model building, skip Chapter 5 and go directly to Chapters 6 and 7 where you will learn how to model linear dependence with simple equations and analyze the relations between the autocorrelation functions and the models. After that, come back to Chapter 5 and read at least one of the economic models. We would recommend reading section 5.1 on the cob-web model. Then proceed to read Chapters 8 and 9.
2. If you wish to have a complete exercise in forecasting practice, skip Chapter 5, and read Chapters 6, 7, 8, and 9 in this order. After that, come back to Chapter 5, and read any or all of the following three economic models:

   a. The cob-web model of price formation (beginner level).
   b. Nonsynchronous trading and portfolio returns (intermediate level).
   c. The bid-ask bounce and asset prices (advanced level).

   These are ordered from less to more mathematical complexity. These models are not exhaustive, but they describe very well why linear dependence may arise in the data. These are theoretical models that will require understanding the assumptions, algebraic manipulation, operating with expectations to compute mean, variance, and autocovariances and autocorrelation coefficients of several orders.
3. If you feel curious about how the economy generates time dependence but are also anxious to start with model building, we would recommend reading section 5.1 (cob-web model) in Chapter 5 and then jump to Chapters 6, 7, 8, and 9. Section 5.1 will provide an introduction to the models in Chapter 6 and 7 within the context of an economic question.
4. Alternatively, you could follow the natural order of Chapters 5, 6, 7, 8, and 9 so that you feel that this quantitative forecasting course offers a rational link to theoretical macro- and microeconomic models that you have already experienced.

CHAPTER 5

Understanding Linear Dependence: A Link to Economic Models

This chapter is designed as a bridge between economic models analyzed in standard macro- and microeconomics courses and the empirical time-series models to be analyzed in subsequent chapters. The objective is to show that the observed time dependence in the data has roots in the behavior of economic agents (consumers, investors, institutions, etc.). Model building starts in Chapters 6 and 7. Please refer to "A pause: Where are we and where are we going?" at the end of Chapter 4 for different suggestions on how to read the following sections and chapters.

The first **economic model**—the **cob-web model**—describes how the price of a commodity evolves over time. The second economic model—the **nonsynchronous trading**—shows how the lack of synchronization in economic decisions gives rise to autocorrelated portfolio returns. The third model—**the bid/ask bounce**—illustrates how institutional rules can affect the time dependence of asset prices. For every model, we will describe first the behavior of the economic agents, and then we will translate such a behavior either into a time series model or into properties of the autocorrelation function. These three models are presented in increasing order of mathematical complexity and they will provide practice on working with the expectation operator to calculate theoretical autocorrelation coefficients of any order.

5.1 Price Dynamics: The Cob-Web Model (Beginner Level)

This section provides an introduction to moving average and autoregressive models within the context of an economic model. A simulation of an AR(1) is introduced.

Suppose that we are studying the market of a given product and our objective is to analyze the price formation. Consumers have a demand schedule so that they are willing to consume more (less) when the price is low (high). Producers have a supply schedule such that they will be willing to produce more (less) when the price is high (low). We say that there is equilibrium when consumers and producers agree on the price and quantity to buy and sell respectively. We talk about the equilibrium price p^* as the price that clears the market. We summarize this behavior with a simple model:

$$\begin{aligned} &\text{Demand equation: } q^D = \alpha_1 - \beta_1 p \\ &\text{Supply equation: } q^S = \alpha_2 + \beta_2 p \\ &\text{Equilibrium: } q^D = q^S \end{aligned} \tag{5.1}$$

where q^D is the quantity demanded at price p and q^S is the supplied quantity at price p. In equilibrium, supply equals demand (i.e., $q^D = q^S$), and solving for the equilibrium price p^*, we have

$$p^* = \frac{\alpha_1 - \alpha_2}{\beta_1 + \beta_2}$$

for $\alpha_2 < \alpha_1$ and $\beta_1, \beta_2 > 0$. This model is static (time does not play any role) and delivers a static equilibrium. In Figure 5.1, the point (q^*, p^*) represents the static market equilibrium. The set of equations in (5.1) characterizes the structure of the market, and in this sense, the model is structural, and the αs and the βs are the structural parameters of the model. We learn that there is a price, the equilibrium price, at which the desires of buyers and sellers are fulfilled. However, demand and supply schedules are not readily observable; it is only a posteriori when we observe the realized price and the realized quantity, which may not be the equilibrium price and quantity. More importantly, markets are subject to shocks and uncertainties that throw the market out of its equilibrium. When equilibrium is disturbed, Equations (5.1) do not provide information on what the expected reaction in prices will be. In most markets, prices do not adjust instantaneously; on the contrary, it may be several periods until the price incorporates all the information concerning the supply and the demand sides of the market. In this case, understanding price dynamics is paramount to understanding the market itself.

However, the aforementioned static supply-demand model will be useful as a starting point. By adding some additional assumptions to the model, mainly some dynamic features, which will explain how time dependence arises in prices. In other words, we are asking where the dynamics of the price come from. *Assume that only the supply side of the market is subject to unpredictable shocks.* For instance, in agricultural markets, the weather may be an unpredictable shock as unexpected storms, hurricanes, flooding, and so on are risk factors that influence the amount of produce; in manufacturing markets, a technological innovation may help to increase the productivity of labor by allowing the manufacture of more products with the same number of employees; in the service markets, a new sophisticated software may allow processing consumers' requests faster. In addition, because production does not take place overnight, suppliers need to decide how much to produce today based on the price that is expected to prevail in the market tomorrow. Thus, production takes place under uncertain conditions. *Assume that suppliers expect tomorrow's price to be today's price.* Let us start with a

FIGURE 5.1
The Cob-Web Model: Price Dynamics (One Supply Shock)

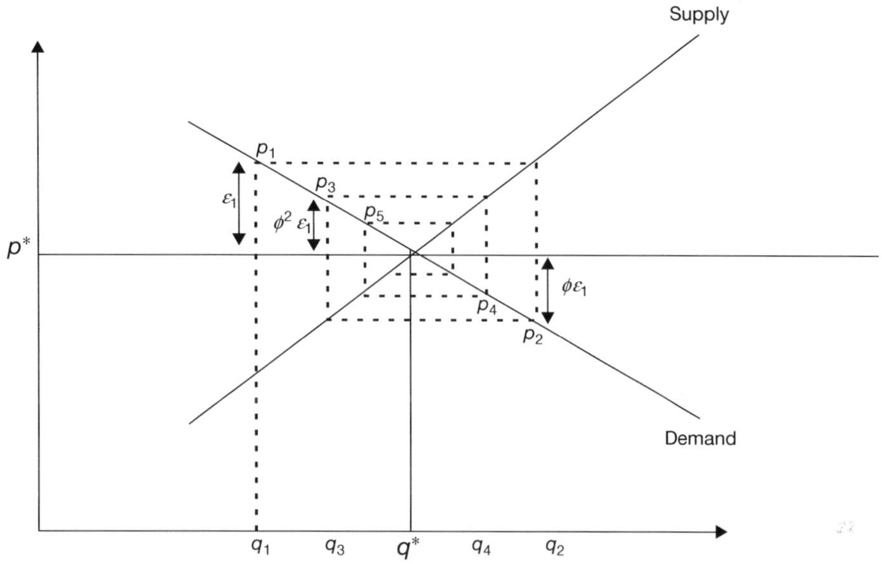

shock to the supply side that moves the market away from the equilibrium point (q^*, p^*) and follow the price movements over time as pictured in Figure 5.1.

5.1.1 The Effect of Only One Supply Shock

Suppose that the supply shock is such that producers can supply only quantity q_1, lower than q^*. This may happen, for example, when a severe storm affects the production of an agricultural commodity. Consumers are willing to pay a price p_1 for quantity q_1 so that the price in the first period is equal to

$$p_1 = p^* + \varepsilon_1$$

Naturally, the scarcity of production pushes the price of the commodity up; p_1 is higher than the equilibrium price by an amount ε_1, which represents the unpredictable supply shock. Can we ever come back to the equilibrium price p^*? In the second period, suppliers plan production assuming that the future price will be p_1. Accordingly, they produce quantity q_2 for which consumers are willing to pay p_2. This price is below the equilibrium price because suppliers have overproduced, $q_2 > q^*$. A reduction in price is the mechanism to sell the overproduction. Thus, the price in the second period is equal to

$$p_2 = p^* + \phi\varepsilon_1 \tag{5.2}$$

for $-1 < \phi < 0$. We introduce the parameter ϕ to indicate corrections to the equilibrium price. Note that the parameter ϕ is not related to the structural parameters αs and

βs, which are the determinants of the equilibrium price p^*. As an example, suppose that $\phi = -0.6$. Expression (5.2) says that 60% of the original supply shock remains in the price of the second period, or alternatively, that the market has corrected 40% of the original shock. In the third period, suppliers consider p_2 too low of a price and produce an amount q_3, which is lower than the equilibrium quantity, now $q_3 < q^*$. Consumers willing to buy the commodity bid the price up to p_3 so that the price in the third period is

$$p_3 = p^* + \phi^2 \varepsilon_1$$

which is higher than the equilibrium price by an amount $\phi^2\varepsilon_1$. If, for instance, $\phi = -0.6$, 36% of the original shock remains in the price of the third period, so that the market has absorbed 64% of the shock in three periods. If we continue with the same reasoning for future periods, it is easy to see that price at time t will be

$$p_t = p^* + \phi^{t-1} \varepsilon_1$$

if t is even $\phi^{t-1} < 0$ and $p_t < p^*$; and if t is odd, $\phi^{t-1} > 0$ and $p_t > p^*$.

Because $|\phi| < 1$, higher powers of ϕ deliver smaller numbers ($\phi^{t-1} \to 0$ for t large), so that, from one period to the next, the market price moves toward the equilibrium price p^*. In other words, $|p_1 - p^*| > |p_2 - p^*| > |p_3 - p^*| > \cdots\cdots |p_t - p^*|$ and eventually $p_t \to p^*$. How fast the market price reaches the equilibrium price depends on the magnitude of ϕ. It will take more time to reach the equilibrium price when ϕ is large in magnitude because the shocks are absorbed more slowly.

5.1.2 The Effect of Many Supply Shocks

In Figure 5.2, we assumed that there is only one shock ε_1 at time $t = 1$. However, every subsequent period may have additional shocks. Remember that these are unpredictable. Let us modify the model to allow for one additional shock in each period. We start at time $t = 1$ with $p_1 = p^* + \varepsilon_1$. Now in the second period, the market price will account for (5.2) plus a potential new shock ε_2 i.e. $p_2 = p^* + \phi\varepsilon_1 + \varepsilon_2$; in the third period, the market price will correct the overall shock of the second period at the rate ϕ, that is, $\phi(\phi\varepsilon_1 + \varepsilon_2)$, and it will account for an additional unpredictable shock ε_3, that is, $p_3 = p^* + \phi(\phi\varepsilon_1 + \varepsilon_2) + \varepsilon_3 = p^* + \phi^2\varepsilon_1 + \phi\varepsilon_2 + \varepsilon_3$; and so on. If, from one period to the next, the market is correcting only a fraction of the previous shock and there is a new shock in each period, the time series of observable market prices will be formed as follows:

$$\begin{aligned}
p_1 &= p^* + \varepsilon_1 \\
p_2 &= p^* + \phi\varepsilon_1 + \varepsilon_2 \\
p_3 &= p^* + \phi^2\varepsilon_1 + \phi\varepsilon_2 + \varepsilon_3 \\
p_4 &= p^* + \phi^3\varepsilon_1 + \phi^2\varepsilon_2 + \phi\varepsilon_3 + \varepsilon_4 \\
&\cdots \cdots \cdots \cdots \cdots \cdots \cdots \\
p_t &= p^* + \phi^{t-1}\varepsilon_1 + \phi^{t-2}\varepsilon_2 + \cdots\cdots \phi^2\varepsilon_{t-2} + \phi\varepsilon_{t-1} + \varepsilon_t
\end{aligned}$$

Now we can see how dynamics arise. The market price at time t is a function of the past shocks $\{\varepsilon_t, \varepsilon_{t-1}, \varepsilon_{t-2}, \ldots\ldots \varepsilon_1\}$, which are weighted according to the powers of the parameter ϕ. When $|\phi| < 1$, the most recent shocks weigh more than the old shocks, which eventually are fully absorbed and disappear from the system.

In reality, market participants observe the time series $\{p_1, p_2, p_3, \ldots\ldots p_t\}$ and the forecaster's objective is to uncover its dynamics. A time series model like $p_t = p^* + \phi^{t-1}\varepsilon_1 + \phi^{t-2}\varepsilon_2 + \cdots\cdots \phi^2\varepsilon_{t-2} + \phi\varepsilon_{t-1} + \varepsilon_t$ is just one specification among many derived under a set of assumptions on the behavior of the producers and consumers. Note that the collection of observable prices $\{p_1, p_2, p_3, \ldots\ldots p_t\}$ are not necessarily equilibrium prices. Given the observed prices over time, our next task is to discover dynamic models like $p_t = p^* + \phi^{t-1}\varepsilon_1 + \phi^{t-2}\varepsilon_2 + \cdots\cdots \phi^2\varepsilon_{t-2} + \phi\varepsilon_{t-1} + \varepsilon_t$. We are not interested in discovering structural models such as (5.1) although in the cob-web example, the dynamic model has been built in reference to (5.1). Note that in the time series model, the equilibrium price p^* shows up as a constant; we know that p^* depends on the structural parameters, the αs and βs of Equation (5.1), but we will not be able to provide any information about them based on the estimation of **time series models**. Our interest will be directed only toward the parameters of the dynamic specification, in this example, the parameter ϕ.

5.1.3 A Further Representation of the Dynamics in the Cob-Web Model

We can exploit further the model $p_t = p^* + \phi^{t-1}\varepsilon_1 + \phi^{t-2}\varepsilon_2 + \cdots\cdots \phi^2\varepsilon_{t-2} + \phi\varepsilon_{t-1} + \varepsilon_t$. First, note that the magnitude of the shock ε is discovered a posteriori once the market price is realized. For instance, at time $t = 1$, we can solve for $\varepsilon_1 = p_1 - p^*$. Then, in the second period, knowing ε_1, we can insert it in p_2 to write the market price as

$$p_2 = p^* + \phi\varepsilon_1 + \varepsilon_2 = p^* + \phi(p_1 - p^*) + \varepsilon_2 = p^*(1 - \phi) + \phi p_1 + \varepsilon_2$$

which says that the price in period 2, p_2, depends on a fraction ϕ of the price in period 1, ϕp_1, plus the unpredictable shock ε_2. In addition, we can solve for $\varepsilon_2 = p_2 - p^*(1 - \phi) - \phi p_1$, and write the market price in period 3 as

$$p_3 = p^* + \phi^2\varepsilon_1 + \phi\varepsilon_2 + \varepsilon_3$$

$$= p^* + \phi^2(p_1 - p^*) + \phi(p_2 - p^*(1 - \phi) - \phi p_1) + \varepsilon_3$$

This expression may seem messy, but with a slight algebraic manipulation, it is straightforward to find that

$$p_3 = p^*(1 - \phi) + \phi p_2 + \varepsilon_3$$

which says that the price in period 3 depends on a fraction ϕ of the price in period 2. In addition, we can solve for $\varepsilon_3 = p_3 - p^*(1 - \phi) - \phi p_2$. We could proceed in the same fashion to obtain $p_4, p_5, \ldots. p_t$ to find that the price in a given period of time depends on a fraction ϕ of the price in the previous period. In summary, we have obtained an equivalent and simple model that captures the dynamics of market prices as

$$p_1 = p^* + \varepsilon_1$$
$$p_2 = p^*(1-\phi) + \phi p_1 + \varepsilon_2$$
$$p_3 = p^*(1-\phi) + \phi p_2 + \varepsilon_3$$
$$p_4 = p^*(1-\phi) + \phi p_3 + \varepsilon_4$$
$$\ldots \ldots \ldots \ldots \ldots \ldots \ldots$$
$$p_t = p^*(1-\phi) + \phi p_{t-1} + \varepsilon_t$$

More importantly we have developed two representations of the dynamics of market prices that are equivalent:

i. Price as a function of past shocks:

$$p_t = p^* + \phi^{t-1}\varepsilon_1 + \phi^{t-2}\varepsilon_2 + \cdots\cdots \phi^2\varepsilon_{t-2} + \phi\varepsilon_{t-1} + \varepsilon_t \tag{5.3}$$

This model is known as a **moving average (MA) representation** because it is a sum of weighted shocks and it is "moving" because the shocks ε are different in each period t.

ii. Price as a function of past prices:

$$p_t = p^*(1-\phi) + \phi p_{t-1} + \varepsilon_t \tag{5.4}$$

This model is known as an **autoregressive (AR) representation** because it looks like a regression model in which the regressor p_{t-1} belongs to the same stochastic process as the dependent variable p_t. This is why we say that p_t is regressed on itself or it is autoregressive. In particular, this model is an autoregressive process of order 1, that is, AR(1) because there is only one lag in the right-hand side of the equation.

These two types of models, moving average and autoregressive, are the most important representations within the class of linear models to explain time dependence in economic and business data. They are the foundation for the development of more sophisticated models of time dependence. They will be studied in detail in Chapters 6 and 7.

At this point, we may wonder whether the observed market prices conform to this model. The MA and AR models in (5.3) and (5.4) are based on the adjustment of prices over time to the equilibrium price described in Figure 5.1. Suppose that we gather a time series of agricultural prices. We can plot it and calculate its autocorrelation functions. What profile should we expect to find in the time series plot and in the shape of the autocorrelation functions if the prices were generated according to our assumptions about the cob-web model? To answer this question, we resort to a *simulation exercise:* We will generate artificial data under a very specific model specification, we will plot the artificial time series, and we will compute its autocorrelation function. From here, we will confront our findings with those based on real data, and we will be able to conclude whether or not the cob-web model is a good explanation of the dynamics of agricultural prices.

Let us start by generating artificial data. We can choose either the MA or the AR representation. Suppose that we choose the AR representation.

5.1.4 Simulation of the Model, $p_t = p^*(1 - \phi) + \phi p_{t-1} + \varepsilon_t$, and Autocorrelation Function

Start by choosing the values of the parameters of the model and the nature of the shocks:

- Equilibrium price: $p^* = 14$.
- Adjustment or persistence coefficient: $\phi = -0.6$; recall that one implication of the model is that this coefficient should be negative in order to generate price movements less than and more than the equilibrium price (see Figure 5.1).
- Random shock: ε_t is a random variable for which we assume that is normally distributed with zero mean and variance 0.25, that is, $\varepsilon_t \rightarrow N(0, 0.25)$.

Within this setting, we type a little program in EViews as follows:

smpl @first @first	(initialize the model: the first observation)
series p=14	(we start from equilibrium: first observation is 14)
smpl @first+1 @last	(from the second to the last observation)
series p=22.4 -0.6*p(-1) +0.5*nrnd	(the series p_t is generated according to the proposed model $p_t = p^*(1 - \phi) + \phi p_{t-1} + \varepsilon_t$)

The command **nrnd** generates a normal random variable with zero mean and variance 1; thus, multiplying by 0.5 is necessary to obtain a random variable with variance 0.25 ($\sigma^2 = 0.25 \rightarrow \sigma = 0.5$). The constant 22.4 comes from $p^*(1 - \phi) = 14 \times (1 + 0.6)$.

Plotting 100 observations of the time series p_t in Figure 5.2, we observe that the price oscillates around a value of 14, which is the equilibrium price, and that the series is very ragged, which is expected because our model predicts that, from one period to the next, the market price jumps higher or lower than the equilibrium price. By alternating in sign, the shape of the autocorrelation function is also consistent with the zigzaggy behavior of the price series. The autocorrelation is positive for those observations with even distances ($k = 2, 4, \ldots.$) and negative for those with odd distances ($k = 1,3, \ldots.$). Note two additional features: first, $\hat{\rho}_1 = \hat{r}_1 = \phi = -0.6$, and second, the partial autocorrelation function has only one large spike. These are characteristics of autoregressive processes, which will be studied in more detail in the following chapters. The bottom line of this simulation exercise is to show that the profile of the time series and the corresponding shape of the autocorrelation functions are in agreement with the dynamics that we have analyzed in the cob-web model.

REAL DATA: Monthly Producer Prices of Oranges in Florida

Do we observe the previously mentioned simulated behavior in the real data? If we gather real data and we observe that the time series and the autocorrelation functions resemble those of the simulated data, we could conclude that the assumed price dynamics are consistent with real data and hence, the dynamic model may offer an explanation on how market prices are formed.

Let us retrieve some time series of prices. The U.S. Department of Agriculture's National Agricultural Statistics Service reports price information on an extensive collection of agricultural commodities. In Figure 5.3, we report the time series of monthly producer prices of oranges ($ per box) in the state of Florida from October 1991 to June 2003. Many other prices can be downloaded from http://www.usda.gov. The shaded areas in the time series plot represent the summer months (from July to September)

FIGURE 5.2
Time Series and Auto-Correlation Functions of the AR Model

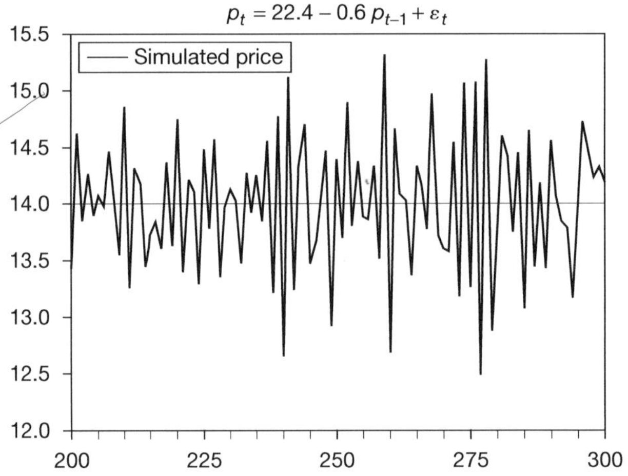

Sample: 1 1000
Included observations: 1000

Lag	AC	PAC
1	-0.636	-0.636
2	0.407	0.004
3	-0.284	-0.039
4	0.197	0.001
5	-0.129	0.011
6	0.060	-0.043
7	-0.005	0.033
8	-0.056	-0.068

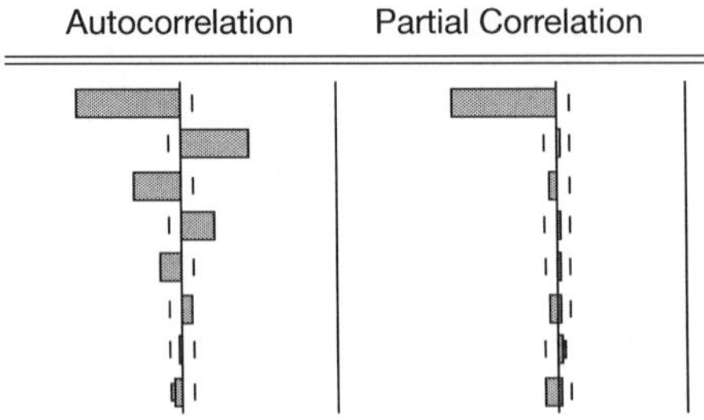

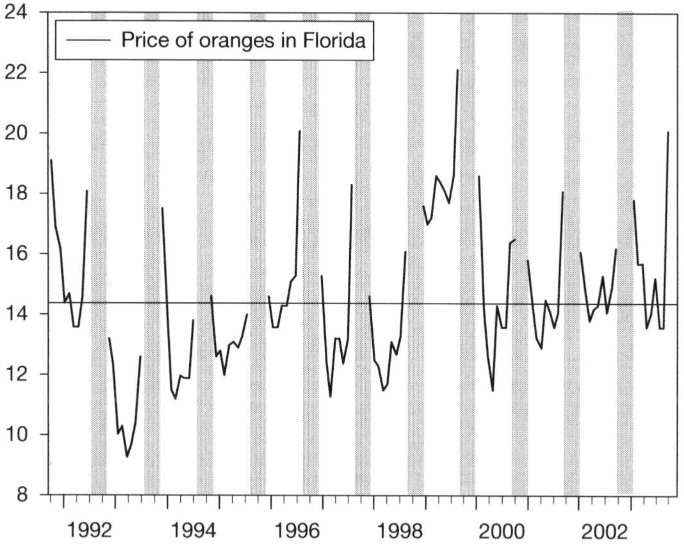

FIGURE 5.3 Time Series and Auto-Correlation Functions of Producer Prices of Oranges in Florida

Sample: 1991:10 2003:08
Included observations: 104

Autocorrelation	Partial Correlation		AC	PAC
		1	0.551	0.551
		2	0.371	0.098
		3	0.298	0.087
		4	0.248	0.050
		5	0.107	-0.116
		6	-0.005	-0.101
		7	0.024	0.071
		8	0.067	0.082

when there is no production of oranges and, thus, no producer price reported. Observe that the price of oranges is the lowest in the winter months (when production is in full swing), starts rising in the spring, and reaches the highest level at the beginning of summer. Compare this plot with that of simulated data in Figure 5.2. There are both similarities and differences. Among the similarities, we point out that the price oscillates around an average price of \$14 per box. However, the main difference is that the time series is smoother. The price slowly goes up from the winter months to the spring and beginning of the summer months or slowly goes down from October to the winter months; we do not observe the zigzaggy behavior of the simulated price in Figure 5.2. These different dynamics, abrupt versus smooth price changes, must show up in the shape of the autocorrelation function.

Let us look at the autocorrelation functions in Figure 5.3. Again, assess the similarities and the differences with those of Figure 5.2. Two features are similar: First, the autocorrelation function decays slowly to zero, and second, there is only one prominent spike in the partial autocorrelation function. The most striking difference is that the autocorrelation function is positive for any even or odd distance. There is no alternating sign as in Figure 5.2. However, this is not surprising because the time series has already shown that the price moves slowly up or down. The autocorrelation function shows that there is time dependence and the question becomes whether an AR process as in Equation (5.4) is a good representation of the real data and whether the proposed price adjustment (Figure 5.1) is a good explanation to describe the market for oranges in Florida.

Let us start with the first question: is an AR model a good representation of the data? If an AR model were appropriate, the persistence coefficient ϕ would be positive because otherwise (i.e., with ϕ negative), we would have observed an alternating behavior in the autocorrelation function. What would it happen if we had considered a positive persistence parameter? Go ahead and simulate, as we did in the section, 5.1.4 a model like

$$p_t = 14.3 \times 0.45 + 0.55 p_{t-1} + \varepsilon_t$$

This model produces a time series that is smoother than the model with a negative persistence coefficient, and its autocorrelation function is very similar to that of Figure 5.3. Thus, this AR model may be a good representation of the real data.

Now, let us turn to the second question: Is the AR model $p_t = 6.4 + 0.55 p_{t-1} + \varepsilon_t$ consistent with the cob-web model that describes the dynamics of prices? The straight answer is no. Then how can we reconcile the properties of the real data with the cob-web price adjustments? Should we abandon completely the economic model? After all, the AR representation seems to be consistent with the real data. The way out of this puzzle is to understand the assumptions behind the model. There are two main assumptions in which the supply/demand interactions are predicated:

- There are shocks only to the supply side of the market, but in reality, markets may be exposed to shocks on both sides of the market, demand and supply.
- The supply side shows a somewhat myopic behavior; on planning production, suppliers assume that the prevailing future price will be today's price, which gives rise to either overproduction or underproduction. The direct consequence is that the dynamics of the market price exhibits a zigzaggy behavior; from one period to the next, the price jumps from higher to lower than the equilibrium price and vice versa. This behavior implies that the persistence (or adjustment) parameter ϕ must be negative.

In agricultural markets such as the market for oranges in Florida, the first assumption may be acceptable because supply shocks (i.e., weather conditions) are very important. The second assumption may be less realistic because one can think of different adjustment mechanisms to equilibrium: Suppliers may have different rules for planning production; for instance, when possible, they may rely on inventories to avoid abrupt price

FIGURE 5.4 Alternative Price Dynamics (Smooth Adjustment to Equilibrium)

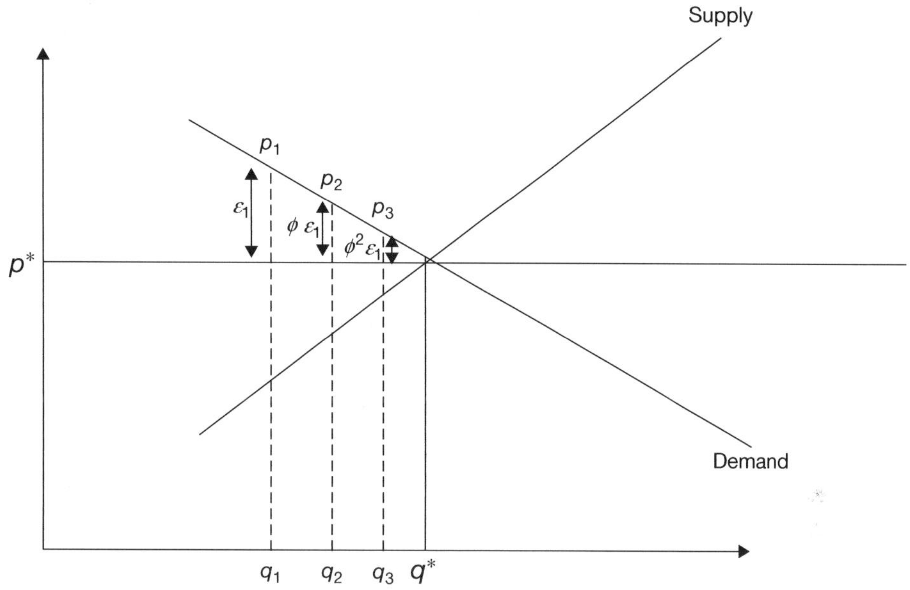

fluctuations. Because we have obtained a positive ϕ for the AR model of prices of oranges, we need to think about smoother adjustments to equilibrium. Suppliers may think that once the initial shock has passed, production will start rising again but being cautious about overproduction, they will plan a production level q_2 (as in Figure 5.4). At this level, the price that buyers are willing to pay is p_2, which is slightly lower than the previous price. This behavior produces a smooth adjustment to equilibrium, which implies a positive ϕ. The convergence to the equilibrium (p^*, q^*) is pictured in Figure 5.4.

5.2 Portfolio Returns and Nonsynchronous Trading (Intermediate Level)

This section illustrates that we can generate autocorrelation by aggregating time series that share common information. We will show that time dependence may also arise because economic agents do not synchronize their economic decisions, that is, not all of us consume the same good at the same time nor do we invest in the same assets at the same time. Let us consider the case of an equally weighted portfolio of assets that are traded with different frequency. For simplicity, we assume that the portfolio has two assets i and j with asset i trading less frequently than asset j. Our question is this: Which time dependence should we expect on the returns to this portfolio? We are asking for the autocorrelation of portfolio returns. We will show that the autocorrelation is different from zero raising the question of which time series model can capture this time dependence.

FIGURE 5.5 Two Assets Trading at Different Frequencies (Nonsynchronous Trading)

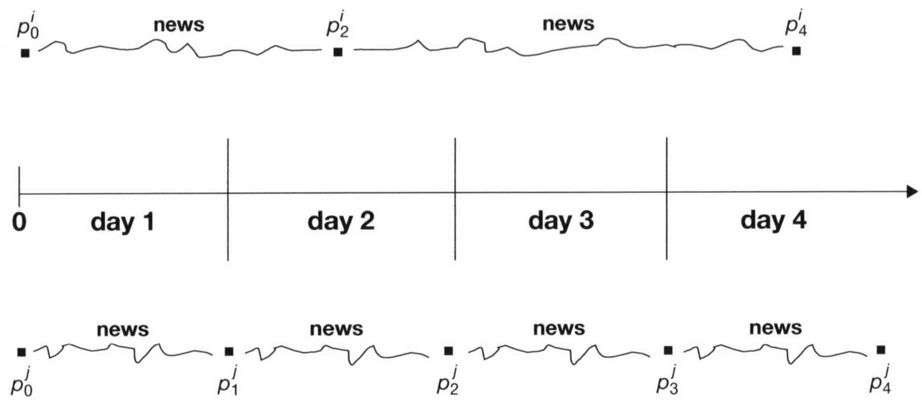

The description of our economic problem follows. In Figure 5.5, we consider four trading days. Both assets have traded at time 0 with closing prices (recorded at the end of the trading day) p_0^i and p_0^j. Subsequently, asset i trades only on day 2 and day 4, and asset j trades in every single day. The market reports the closing price for each asset at the end of the day.

We calculate the daily asset return as the daily change in prices (i.e., $R_t = p_t - p_{t-1}$). In Table 5.1, we summarize the daily returns of each asset and the absorption of news.

Observe that because asset i does not trade on day 1 or day 3, its daily returns are zero in these two days. However, the news keeps accumulating over time, and when the asset trades in day 2, the price reflects the news from day 1 and day 2; when it trades in day 4, the price is the result of the information accumulated over days 2, 3, and 4. On the other hand, asset j is trading daily, so its daily price reflects the information of the day. Within this setting, suppose that we form an equally weighted portfolio of both assets and compute the daily portfolio return R_t as the simple average of the return to asset i, R_t^i and of the return to asset j, R_t^j:

$$R_t = \frac{R_t^i + R_t^j}{2}$$

TABLE 5.1 Returns and Their News Content

	Return to asset j	**News content in returns to j**	**Return to asset i**	**News content in returns to asset i**
End of day 1	$R_1^j = p_1^j - p_0^j$	News of day 1	$R_1^i = p_0^i - p_0^i = 0$	
End of day 2	$R_2^j = p_2^j - p_1^j$	News of day 2	$R_2^i = p_2^i - p_0^i$	News of days 1 and 2
End of day 3	$R_3^j = p_3^j - p_2^j$	News of day 3	$R_3^i = p_2^i - p_2^i = 0$	
End of day 4	$R_4^j = p_4^j - p_3^j$	News of day 4	$R_4^i = p_4^i - p_2^i$	News of days 2, 3, and 4

Now we will show that the nonsynchronous trading of asset i and j generates autocorrelation in the portfolio returns. To simplify the computation of the autocovariance function, we assume the following:

- The unconditional means of assets i and j are equal to zero, that is, $E(R_t^i) = E(R_t^j) = 0$.
- Asset i and asset j are not autocorrelated at any lag k, that is, $E(R_t^i R_{t-k}^i) = E(R_t^j R_{t-k}^j) = 0$.
- Asset i and asset j belong to the same industry; thus, any "news" tends to impact both assets in the same fashion. For instance, suppose that both assets are financial stocks of vehicle manufacturers (i.e., GM and Ford) and that there is a decrease in the price of gas. This news will positively impact both companies because their prices will move up in anticipation of a push-up in the market demand for cars.

Under this set of assumptions, we compute the first order autocovariance of the portfolio returns:

$$\gamma_1 \equiv \text{cov}(R_t, R_{t-1}) = E(R_t R_{t-1}) - E(R_t)E(R_{t-1}) = E(R_t R_{t-1})$$

$$= \frac{1}{4}E(R_t^i + R_t^j) \times (R_{t-1}^i + R_{t-1}^j) = \frac{1}{4}(E(R_t^i R_{t-1}^i) + E(R_t^j R_{t-1}^i) + E(R_t^i R_{t-1}^j)$$

$$+ E(R_t^j R_{t-1}^j)) = \frac{1}{4}(E(R_t^j R_{t-1}^i) + E(R_t^i R_{t-1}^j))$$

Let us think about the terms $E(R_t^j R_{t-1}^i)$ and $E(R_t^i R_{t-1}^j)$ within the context of Figure 5.5. For instance, the returns R_2^i and R_1^j, which are one day apart, have in common the news of day 1; the returns R_4^i and R_3^j, which are also one day apart, have in common the news of day 3. Hence, $E(R_t^i R_{t-1}^j)$ must be different from zero. Because we have assumed that both assets belong to the same industry, the impact of news will be either positive or negative for both assets so that their returns will move in the same direction and the autocorrelation will be positive $E(R_t^i R_{t-1}^j) > 0$. The term $E(R_t^j R_{t-1}^i)$ will be zero because there is not common news between the returns R_t^j and the lag returns of asset i, R_{t-1}^i. Then $\gamma_1 > 0$. Because $\rho_1 = \gamma_1/\gamma_0$, the first order autocorrelation must be positive $\rho_1 > 0$.

By the same reasoning, we can calculate the autocovariances of higher order. For instance, the second order autocovariance is

$$\gamma_2 \equiv \text{cov}(R_t, R_{t-2}) = E(R_t R_{t-2}) = \frac{1}{4}E(R_t^i + R_t^j)(R_{t-2}^i + R_{t-2}^j)$$

$$= \frac{1}{4}(E(R_t^j R_{t-2}^i) + E(R_t^i R_{t-2}^j))$$

Within the context of Figure 5.5, observe that the returns R_4^i and R_2^j, which are two days apart, share the information of day 2; then $E(R_t^i R_{t-2}^j)$ must be different from zero and positive according to assumption iii. The nonsynchronous trading has produced at least first and second order positive autocorrelations in the portfolio returns.

Observe that the less frequently an asset trades, the larger the autocorrelation of the portfolio return will be. This happens because the news is accumulating over time and when the asset trades, its price will reflect not only the present day information but also all the lagged information of the previous days. On the contrary, when both assets trade in every single day, there is no lagged information to account for in the asset prices and the autocorrelation of the portfolio returns will be zero. Hence, we conclude that the strength of the autocorrelation is inversely proportional to the frequency of trading: The more trading, the less autocorrelation we should expect.

REAL DATA: Daily Stock Portfolio Prices: AMEX and the SP500

Let us check real data to analyze whether the autocorrelation predicted by nonsynchronous trading is present in the data. We choose two portfolios of stocks: the American Stock Exchange (AMEX) and the SP500 at the daily frequency. The first is a portfolio of the companies traded on AMEX, which is a small market in comparison to the New York Stock Exchange. The Standard and Poor's (SP) 500 portfolio is formed by the largest 500 companies in the United States. There is strong correlation between size and frequency of trading. In general, size is a good proxy for trading frequency: The largest firms trade daily while the smallest tend to trade less frequently. Comparing the AMEX portfolio with the SP500 portfolio, the former has a mixture of firms of different sizes; thus, we expect that some of the firms are thinly traded while others trade on a daily basis. According to the prediction of the nonsynchronous trading model, we expect positive autocorrelations, and the strength of the autocorrelation is an indirect measure of the trading frequency. In contrast, all firms in the SP500 portfolio trade on a daily basis, so we expect zero autocorrelations. In Figure 5.6, we present the autocorrelation functions of the portfolio returns to the AMEX and SP500 portfolios. The AMEX portfolio exhibits first order autocorrelation, $\hat{\rho}_1 = 0.142$, and higher autocorrelations that are virtually zero. The financial literature provides sophisticated models of nonsynchronous trading that claim that the first order autocorrelation coefficient is equal to the nontrading probability. According to this claim, $\hat{\rho}_1 = 0.142$ means that, on average, of 100 days, the securities in the AMEX portfolio trade in 86 days or equivalently, there is just one nontrading day in seven days. This is a small nontrading frequency. The SP500 portfolio exhibits zero autocorrelation, which was expected because the largest firms tend to trade daily. In probability terms, the nontrading probability is zero.

5.3 Asset Prices and the Bid–Ask Bounce (Advanced Level)

This section provides an introduction to moving average dynamics within the context of an economic problem and a simulation of a MA(1).

FIGURE 5.6 Auto-Correlation Functions of Daily Portfolio Returns

AMEX portfolio

Sample: 12/27/1995 10/25/2004
Included observations: 2212

Autocorrelation	Partial Correlation		AC	PAC
		1	0.142	0.142
		2	-0.009	-0.030
		3	0.021	0.027
		4	0.001	-0.006
		5	-0.009	-0.007
		6	0.007	0.009
		7	-0.013	-0.016
		8	0.025	0.030
		9	0.028	0.019
		10	-0.009	-0.014

SP500 portfolio

Sample: 1/22/1990 10/26/2004
Included observations: 3721

Autocorrelation	Partial Correlation		AC	PAC
		1	-0.001	-0.001
		2	-0.024	-0.024
		3	-0.037	-0.037
		4	0.009	0.008
		5	-0.036	-0.038
		6	-0.025	-0.026
		7	-0.043	-0.044
		8	0.002	-0.002
		9	0.011	0.008
		10	0.011	0.007

In this section, we will analyze how institutional rules governing the organization of markets can also produce time dependence in prices. We consider a securities exchange and show that the behavior of the market makers induces time dependence in asset prices. By analyzing the basic autocorrelation function of price moves, we will raise an important question: Is there any time series model that can reproduce the observed autocorrelation?

One of the functions of the securities exchange is to provide liquidity to market participants so that sellers are able to sell and buyers to buy anytime they wish to. In the exchange place, the job of the market makers is to provide liquidity. Their incentive is to sell securities at a high price (ask price) and to buy at a lower price (bid price). The difference between the ask price p_{ask} and the bid price p_{bid} is called the **bid-ask spread**: $s = p_{ask} - p_{bid}$. An investor who wishes to buy will pay the ask price and an investor who wishes to sell will do so at the bid price. Thus, the transaction price of a security will be sometimes the ask price and sometimes the bid price, depending on whether a buyer or a seller initiates the transaction. This institutional feature of the securities exchange creates time dependence on prices. Let us see how time dependence arises within the framework of a simple model.

We distinguish between the *fundamental price* and the *transaction price*. The fundamental price p_t^* reflects the economic value of the security based on the fundamentals of the company such as earnings, potential growth, investment strategies, etc. The transaction price p_t is the final price at which the transaction takes place. Suppose that the fundamental price is equidistant between the bid price and the ask price, i.e. $p_{bid} \leq p_t^* \leq p_{ask}$, and that the market maker takes in the full spread by charging one-half to each side of the trade. Now, if the transaction is initiated by an investor who wants to buy shares of the security, the transaction price charged by the market maker will be $p_t = p_t^* + (s/2)$. On the other hand, if the transaction is initiated by an investor who wants to sell shares, the market maker will charge a transaction price $p_t = p_t^* - (s/2)$. Buyers and sellers come to the exchange randomly, and we assume that, in a given period of time, the probability of a transaction being buyer initiated is equal to the probability of the transaction being seller initiated, and equal to ½. In summary, we write the transaction price as

$$p_t = \begin{cases} p_t^* + \dfrac{s}{2} & \text{if buyer initiated, with probability } \dfrac{1}{2} \\ p_t^* - \dfrac{s}{2} & \text{if seller initiated, with probability } \dfrac{1}{2} \end{cases}$$

or, in a more compact fashion, as

$$p_t = p_t^* + I_t \frac{s}{2}$$

where I_t takes the value 1 with probability 0.5 if the transaction is buyer initiated, and –1 with probability 0.5 if the transaction is seller initiated. Then the change in the transaction price from period t to period $t+1$ is $\Delta p_{t+1} \equiv p_{t+1} - p_t$, and is equal to

$$\Delta p_{t+1} = \Delta p_{t+1}^* + (I_{t+1} - I_t)\frac{s}{2} \tag{5.5}$$

From Equation (5.5), we see that the autocorrelation function of Δp_{t+1} will depend on the statistical properties of the fundamental price and those of the indicator variable I_t. Under a set of simple assumptions, we can prove (see the chapter appendix) that the autocorrelation function of Δp_{t+1} is

$$\begin{aligned} \rho_1 &= -\frac{1}{2}\frac{s^2/2}{\sigma^2 + s^2/2} > -\frac{1}{2} \\ \rho_2 &= \rho_3 = \cdots\cdots = \rho_k = 0 \end{aligned} \tag{5.6}$$

where $\sigma^2 = \text{var}(\Delta p_{t+1}^*)$. Changes in transaction prices are negatively autocorrelated so that, on average, up movements are followed by down movements. This is expected as the transaction price bounces back and forth between the bid price and the ask price.

REAL DATA: Monthly Stock Prices of Banco Bilbao Vizcaya Argentaria

Let us analyze some real data to check whether the predictions of the bid-ask bounce model are granted. In Figure 5.7, we plot the monthly stock returns to one of the largest banking institutions in Europe, Banco Bilbao Vizcaya Argentaria (BBVA). The time series runs from January 1999 to October 2004. We also calculate its autocorrelation function.

Observe that the shape of the estimated autocorrelation function is very similar to the one predicted by the bid-ask spread model because $-0.5 < \hat{\rho}_1 = -0.21 < 0$ and the remaining autocorrelations are practically zero (i.e. $\hat{\rho}_2 = \hat{\rho}_3 = \hat{\rho}_4 \approx 0$). Hence, the data are consistent with the predictions of this economic model.

More importantly for our purposes, if we would like to summarize this economic behavior in a time series model that describes the movements in transaction prices, what will this model look like? This is the claim: A first order moving average, that is, MA(1) model, that is, $\Delta p_t = \theta\varepsilon_{t-1} + \varepsilon_t$ with $\theta < 0$, will replicate the autocorrelation function predicted by a bid-ask bounce model.

FIGURE 5.7
Time Series and Auto-Correlation of Monthly Returns to BBVA

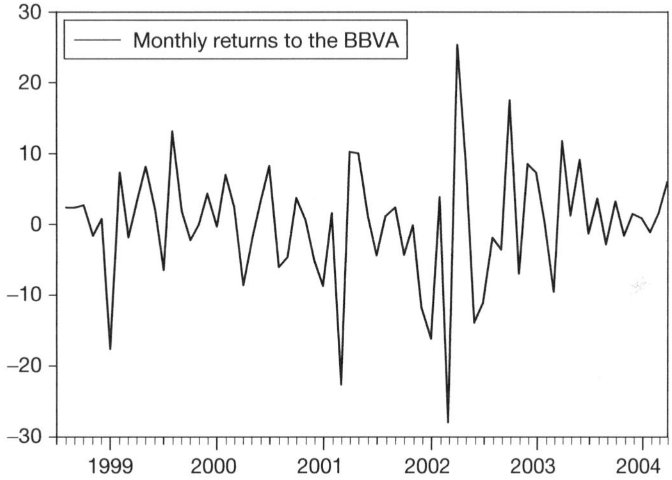

Sample: 1999:01 2004:10
Included observations: 69

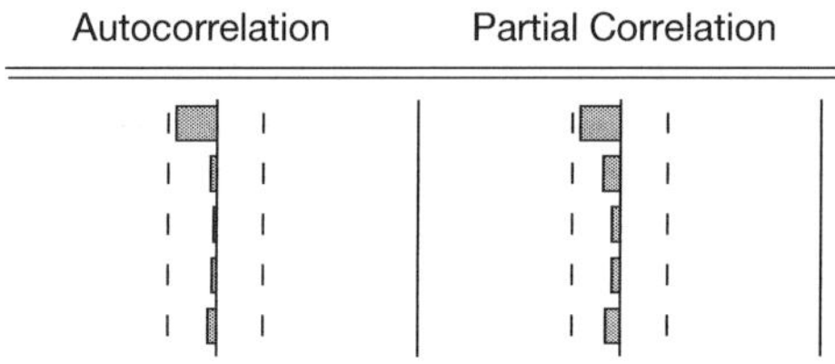

	AC	PAC
1	-0.208	-0.208
2	-0.029	-0.075
3	-0.015	-0.039
4	-0.032	-0.048
5	-0.042	-0.065

Let us simulate a MA(1) model like $\Delta p_t = \theta\varepsilon_{t-1} + \varepsilon_t$. For instance, we choose $\theta = -0.2$, and ε_t is a normal random variable with zero mean and variance 64.

The following two commands in EViews will suffice to generate a series of simulated returns:

series e=8*nrnd	(normal random variable ε_t with mean zero and variance 64)
series ret_sim=e-0.2*e(-1)	(simulated return that follows the model $\Delta p_t = -0.2\varepsilon_{t-1} + \varepsilon_t$)

In Figure 5.8, we plot 100 observations of the simulated returns and their corresponding autocorrelograms. Observe the similarities between the shapes of the autocorrelation functions in Figures 5.7 and 5.8. The main feature is that there is only one large spike in the autocorrelation function at lag 1, and the remaining lags are virtually zero. This a characteristic feature of a MA(1) model. We conclude that our claim seems to be consistent with the implications of a simple bid-ask bounce model.

FIGURE 5.8
Time Series and Auto-Correlation Functions of the Simulated Series

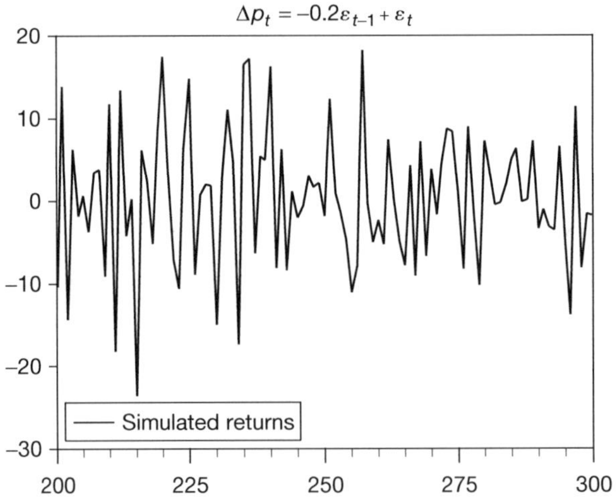

Sample: 1 1000
Included observations: 999

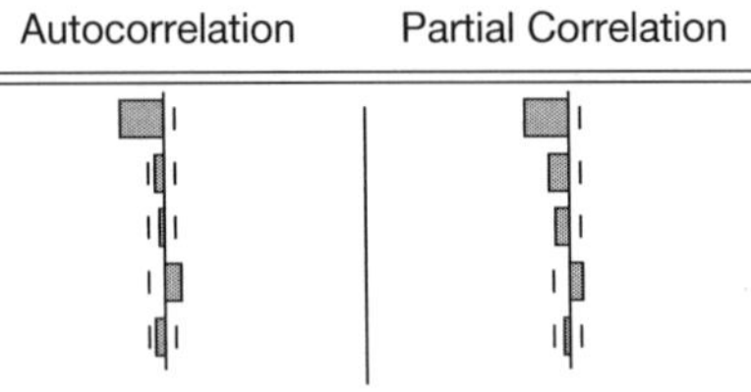

	AC	PAC
1	-0.231	-0.231
2	-0.043	-0.102
3	-0.028	-0.067
4	0.083	0.059
5	-0.049	-0.021

5.4 Summary

Let us put in perspective the lessons that we can draw from the previous models. Time dependence is a common feature of economic and business data. We have seen that dependence may arise because of many different reasons. Without being exhaustive, we have explored three economic examples that give rise to autocorrelation functions of different shapes and signs. In the cob-web model for price dynamics, the behavior of consumers and producers produce positively and negatively autocorrelated prices. In the bid-ask bounce model, institutional features of the market are responsible for negative autocorrelation in asset returns. In the nonsynchronous trading model, aggregation (i.e., formation of portfolios with assets of different trading frequencies) produces positive autocorrelation in the portfolio returns.

The autocorrelation functions are very useful tools to understand time dependence. Representations such as moving average (MA) models and autoregressive (AR) models will summarize the shape and sign of the autocorrelations functions. Simulating a model is a good technique for understanding the profile of a time series and the shapes of the autocorrelation functions. In subsequent chapters, we will analyze in detail MA and AR models and develop our understanding by using simulated time series and real world time series data.

KEY WORDS

autoregressive (AR) representation, p. 108

bid/ask bounce, p. 103

bid-ask spread, p. 117

cob-web model, p. 103

economic model, p. 103

moving average (MA) representation, p. 108

nonsynchronous trading, p. 103

simulation of a model, p. 109

time series model, p. 107

APPENDIX

Computation of the autocorrelation function (5.6) in the bid-ask bounce model.

The objective is to find the autocorrelation of the movements in the transaction price (i.e. Δp_{t+1}), which is given by

$$\Delta p_{t+1} = \Delta p^*_{t+1} + (I_{t+1} - I_t)\frac{s}{2}$$

I_t is a binary indicator that takes the value 1 if the transaction is buyer initiated, and –1 if it is seller initiated:

$$I_t = \begin{cases} 1 & \text{with probability } \dfrac{1}{2} \\ -1 & \text{with probability } \dfrac{1}{2} \end{cases}$$

Let us start by computing the mean and the variance of this binary random variable:

$$E(I_t) = 1 \times \frac{1}{2} - 1 \times \frac{1}{2} = 0$$

$$\text{var}(I_t) = E(I_t^2) - [E(I_t)]^2 = 1 \times \frac{1}{2} + 1 \times \frac{1}{2} = 1$$

Because we have assumed that buyers and sellers come randomly to the exchange, it is natural to assume that there is no time dependence (no autocorrelation) in I_t, that is, $\text{cov}(I_{t+k}, I_t) = 0$. For instance, I_t may exhibit time dependence if buyers were followed by buyers or sellers by sellers in a consistent way. Furthermore, let us assume that

i. Δp^*_{t+1} has zero mean and constant variance, that is, $E(\Delta p^*_{t+1}) = 0$, $\text{var}(\Delta p^*_{t+1}) = \sigma^2$.
ii. Δp^*_{t+1} is serially uncorrelated, that is, $E(\Delta p^*_{t+k} \times \Delta p^*_t) = 0$.
iii. Δp^*_{t+1} is independent of the indicator variable I_{t+1} at all leads and lags, that is, $E(\Delta p^*_{t+k} \times I_t) = E(\Delta p^*_t \times I_{t+k}) = E(\Delta p^*_t \times I_t) = 0$.

With these assumptions in place:

- Compute the mean and variance of the transaction price:

$$E(\Delta p_{t+1}) = E(\Delta p^*_{t+1}) + (E(I_{t+1}) - E(I_t))\frac{s}{2} = 0$$

$$\text{var}(\Delta p_{t+1}) = \sigma^2 + (\text{var}(I_{t+1}) + \text{var}(I_t))\frac{s^2}{4} = \sigma^2 + \frac{s^2}{2}$$

and recall that I_t is serially uncorrelated, so that $\text{cov}(I_{t+1}, I_t) = 0$.

- Compute the autocovariances:

$$\gamma_1 \equiv \text{cov}(\Delta p_{t+1}, \Delta p_t) = E(\Delta p_{t+1} \times \Delta p_t) - E(\Delta p_{t+1}) \times E(\Delta p_t)$$

$$= E(\Delta p_{t+1} \times \Delta p_t) = E\left(\left(\Delta p^*_{t+1} + \frac{s}{2}(I_{t+1} - I_t)\right) \times \left(\Delta p^*_t + \frac{s}{2}(I_t - I_{t-1})\right)\right)$$

$$= E\left(\Delta p^*_{t+1} \times \Delta p^*_t + \frac{s^2}{4}(I_{t+1} - I_t)(I_t - I_{t-1}) + \frac{s}{2}\Delta p^*_{t+1}(I_t - I_{t-1})\right.$$

$$\left. + \frac{s}{2}\Delta p^*_t(I_{t+1} - I_t)\right) = \frac{s^2}{4}E(I_{t+1}I_t - I_tI_t - I_{t+1}I_{t-1} + I_tI_{t-1})$$

$$= -\frac{s^2}{4}E(I_tI_t) = -\frac{s^2}{4}$$

and recall that Δp^*_{t+1} is uncorrelated, so $E(\Delta p^*_{t+1} \times \Delta p^*_t) = 0$ and that Δp^*_{t+1} is independent of the indicator variable, so $E(\Delta p^*_{t+1}(I_t - I_{t-1})) = E(\Delta p^*_t (I_{t+1} - I_t)) = 0$.

Applying the same arguments, we compute higher order autocovariances:

$$\begin{aligned}\gamma_2 &\equiv \text{cov}(\Delta p_{t+2}, \Delta p_t) = E(\Delta p_{t+2} \times \Delta p_t) - E(\Delta p_{t+2}) \times E(\Delta p_t)\\ &= E(\Delta p_{t+2} \times \Delta p_t) = E\Big(\Delta p^*_{t+2} \times \Delta p^*_t + \frac{s^2}{4}(I_{t+2} - I_{t+1})(I_t - I_{t-1})\\ &\quad + \frac{s}{2}\Delta p^*_{t+2}(I_t - I_{t-1}) + \frac{s}{2}\Delta p^*_t (I_{t+2} - I_{t+1})\Big)\\ &= \frac{s^2}{4}E(I_{t+1}I_t - I_{t+1}I_t - I_{t+2}I_{t-1} + I_{t+1}I_{t-1}) = 0\end{aligned}$$

and $\gamma_3 = \gamma_4 = \cdots\cdots \gamma_k = 0$.

- Compute the autocorrelation function:

$$\rho_1 \equiv \frac{\gamma_1}{\gamma_0} = \frac{-s^2/4}{\sigma^2 + s^2/2} = -\frac{1}{2}\frac{s^2/2}{\sigma^2 + s^2/2} > -\frac{1}{2}$$

$$\rho_2 = \rho_3 = \cdots\cdots = \rho_k = 0$$

EXERCISES

1. Simulate the model $p_t = 14.3 \times 0.45 + 0.55 p_{t-1} + \varepsilon_t$. Assume that ε_t is a normally distributed random variable $\varepsilon_t \to N(0, \sigma^2)$ and consider different values for the variance $\sigma^2 = 0.25$, 1, 2. In the three cases, plot the resulting time series of prices and compute its autocorrelation functions. Compare your results with those of Figures 5.2 and 5.3. What is the effect of increasing the variance of the random shock?
2. Update the time series of producer prices of oranges in Florida in Figure 5.3 and download a similar series for California (http://www.usda.gov). Calculate the autocorrelation functions for both California and Florida oranges and compare them with those in Figure 5.3.
3. Download prices of other agricultural products and determine whether a cobweb model may explain the time dependence in prices.
4. Update the time series of AMEX and SP500 returns in Section 5.2. Compute their autocorrelation functions and analyze how different or similar they are to those in Figure 5.6.
5. Download other prices of national and international portfolios (Dow Jones, NASDAQ, FTSE, N225, IBEX, etc.) and compute the autocorrelation functions of their returns. From these, what is your assessment of the frequency of trading of the assets in these portfolios?

6. Simulate the following model $\Delta p_t = \theta\varepsilon_{t-1} + \varepsilon_t$. Assume that ε_t is a normally distributed random variable $\varepsilon_t \rightarrow N(0, \sigma^2)$ and consider different values for the parameter $\theta = -0.4, 0.4, -0.7, 0.7$. In each of the four cases, plot the resulting time series of Δp_t and compute its autocorrelation functions. Compare your results with those of Figure 5.7. What difference does it make when θ is negative or positive?
7. Update the time series of BBVA in Section 5.3. Compute the autocorrelation functions and analyze how different or similar they are to those in Figure 5.7. Download other stock prices and assess whether their autocorrelation functions can be explained by the bid-ask bounce model.
8. Under the assumptions stated in Section 5.2, calculate the theoretical autocorrelation coefficients of orders 3 and 4.
9. Under the assumptions stated in Section 5.3 and the appendix, calculate the theoretical autocorrelation coefficients of orders 3 and 4.
10. Suppose that in the model of Section 5.3 we assume that the binary indicator I_t is positively autocorrelated of order 1, (i.e., $\rho_1 > 0$). That is to say that when a buyer (seller) comes to the market, it is likely that the next customer will also be a buyer (seller)? What are the consequences of this assumption for the calculation of the autocorrelation function of price changes?

CHAPTER 6

Forecasting with Moving Average (MA) Processes

We start this chapter with time series model building. We first introduce a basic process called white noise that is characterized by the absence of linear dependence. This process is important because it will appear as a "residual" process in the forthcoming time series models. We will follow with a foundational theorem, known as the **Wold decomposition**, which justifies the study of moving average (MA) and autoregressive (AR) time series models. After the Wold decomposition, we will focus on the statistical properties of MA processes and their forecasts. The properties of AR and (ARMA) models in general will be the subject of Chapter 7.

6.1 A Model with No Dependence: White Noise

If you have read Chapter 5, you have already seen two simple models: a moving average model as $\Delta p_t = \theta\varepsilon_{t-1} + \varepsilon_t$, and an autoregressive model as $p_t = p^*(1-\phi) + \phi p_{t-1} + \varepsilon_t$. In both models, the random variable ε_t has been referred as an unpredictable shock. If you have not read Chapter 5, you are now introduced to a process, ε_t, which in time series jargon, is called a *white noise process*. The main characteristic of such a process is that it is unpredictable because it does not exhibit any linear dependence. In other words, the autocorrelations are zero, meaning that there is no link between past and present observations. There is no dependence to exploit and, consequently, we cannot predict future realizations of the process.

We define:

A white noise process is characterized by autocorrelation and partial autocorrelation functions that are equal to zero:

$$\rho_k = 0 \quad k \geq 1$$
$$r_k = 0 \quad k \geq 1$$

6.1.1 What Does This Process Look Like?

Let us generate an artificial time series that behaves like a white noise process. Consider the following model $Y_t = 1 + \varepsilon_t$ where ε_t is a random variable normally distributed with zero mean and variance 4, that is $\varepsilon_t \rightarrow N(0, 4)$. Generate a time series from the process Y_t: in EViews, choose the **Genr** function of your workfile and type the following command:

```
ynoise = 1+2*nrnd
```

You are already familiar with the meaning of 2*nrnd. This is the command that generates random numbers from a normal distribution with zero mean and standard deviation equal to 2 (variance equal to 4). Proceed to plot the time series y_t and calculate the descriptive statistics of the series. See Figure 6.1 for the results.

The time series looks very ragged, and the histogram of the series has the expected bell shape corresponding to a normal distribution. The white noise process is a covariance stationary process. You can observe that the realizations bounce around a mean value of 1 (the horizontal line in the time series plot). This is not surprising when you look at the model. Compute the unconditional mean of the process. Take expectations to obtain and compute the variance of the process to obtain $\sigma^2 \equiv \text{var}(Y_t) = \text{var}(\varepsilon_t) = 4$. Thus, the first two moments are time invariant. The corresponding sample moments are very close to the population moments as expected. The sample mean is 0.96, close enough to 1, and the sample standard deviation is 2.03, close enough to 2. In addition, the Jarque-Bera test indicates that normality is not rejected because the skewness coefficient is approximately zero and the kurtosis coefficient approximately 3.

What do the autocorrelation functions of this process look like? You can read from the autocorrelograms that the autocorrelation and partial autocorrelation are practically zero for any displacement.

Go back to the introductory time series models in Chapter 5, $\Delta p_t = \theta\varepsilon_{t-1} + \varepsilon_t$ or $p_t = p^*(1 - \phi) + \phi p_{t-1} + \varepsilon_t$, and observe the role of ε_t. In $\Delta p_t = \theta\varepsilon_{t-1} + \varepsilon_t$, the dependence between the variable at the present time (Δp_t) and the past is explicitly modeled by the component $\theta\varepsilon_{t-1}$; in $p_t = p^*(1 - \phi) + \phi p_{t-1} + \varepsilon_t$, the link between the present and the past is modeled by the component $p^*(1 - \phi) + \phi p_{t-1}$. Thus, the remainder in both examples is the component ε_t, which must be unpredictable (otherwise it would have been modeled). This process ε_t must be white noise.

REAL DATA: Monthly Returns to the Dow Jones Index and to Microsoft

In business and economics, some data behave very similarly to a white noise process. Financial data such as the Dow Jones (DJ) Index, Standard & Poor's (SP) 500 Index, individual stocks, interest rates, exchange rates, and so on have correlograms that very closely resemble a white noise process. This is the reason why these data are so difficult to predict. They do not exhibit any temporal linear dependence that could be consistently exploited. See Figure 6.2 for the plot of the monthly returns to Microsoft and to the DJ Index with their respective autocorrelation functions from April 1986 to July 2004.

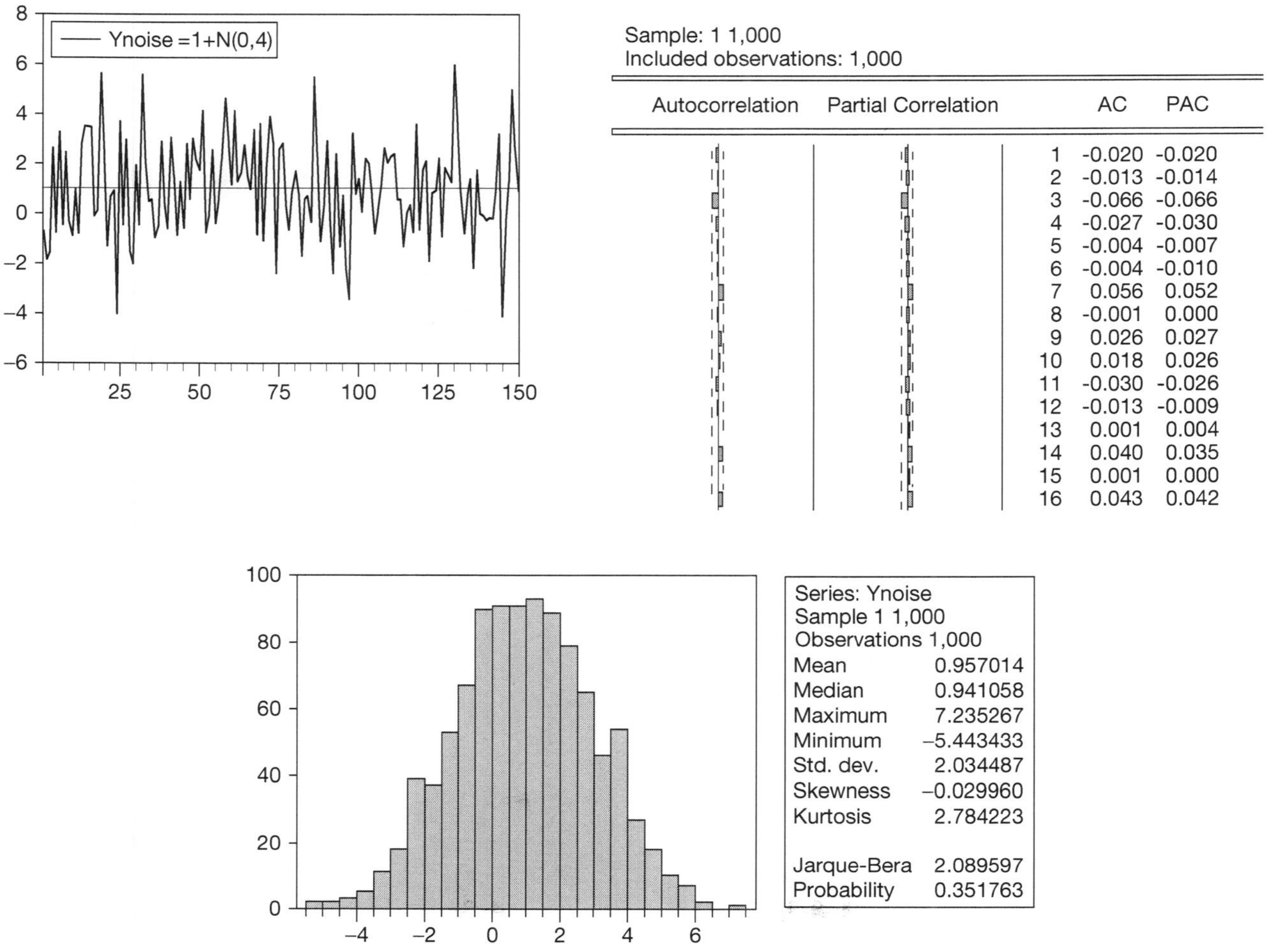

FIGURE 6.1 Time Series and Autocorrelation Functions of a Simulated White Noise Process

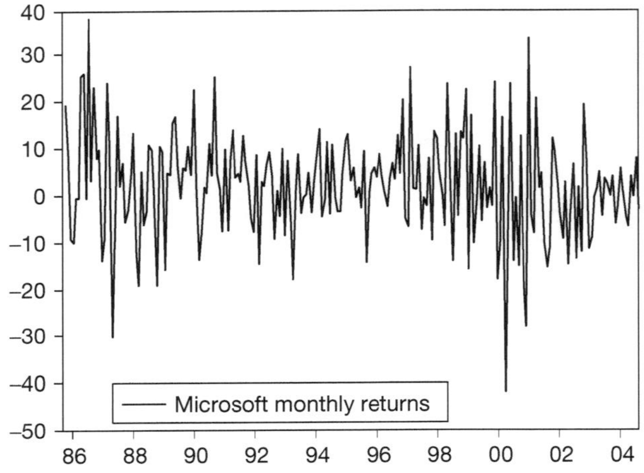

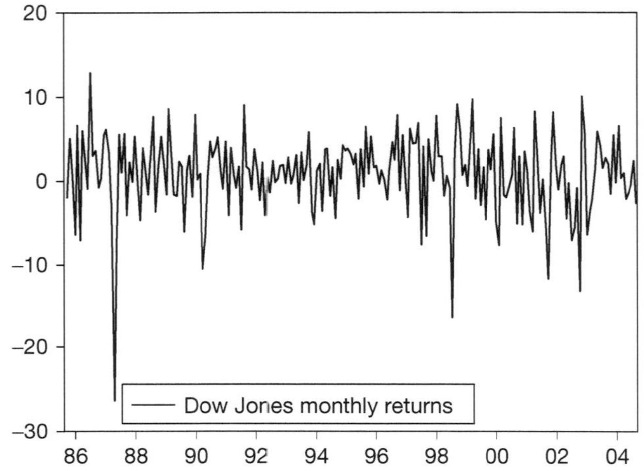

Sample: 1986:03 2004:07
Included observations: 220

Autocorrelation	Partial Correlation		AC	PAC
		1	-0.081	-0.081
		2	-0.094	-0.101
		3	0.132	0.117
		4	-0.017	-0.006
		5	0.008	0.030
		6	-0.013	-0.029
		7	0.106	0.113
		8	0.015	0.023
		9	-0.006	0.024
		10	0.131	0.112
		11	0.013	0.035
		12	-0.016	0.005
		13	-0.020	-0.045
		14	0.030	0.013
		15	-0.075	-0.091
		16	0.064	0.068
		17	0.085	0.051
		18	-0.094	-0.064
		19	-0.049	-0.079
		20	0.046	0.005

Sample: 1986:03 2004:07
Included observations: 220

Autocorrelation	Partial Correlation		AC	PAC
		1	-0.021	-0.021
		2	-0.044	-0.044
		3	-0.056	-0.058
		4	-0.126	-0.131
		5	0.048	0.037
		6	-0.031	-0.045
		7	0.092	0.081
		8	-0.044	-0.057
		9	-0.043	-0.030
		10	0.043	0.035
		11	-0.012	0.006
		12	0.015	-0.006
		13	-0.003	0.003
		14	-0.034	-0.034
		15	-0.059	-0.060
		16	0.039	0.042
		17	0.031	0.012
		18	0.079	0.076
		19	-0.026	-0.028
		20	-0.016	0.005

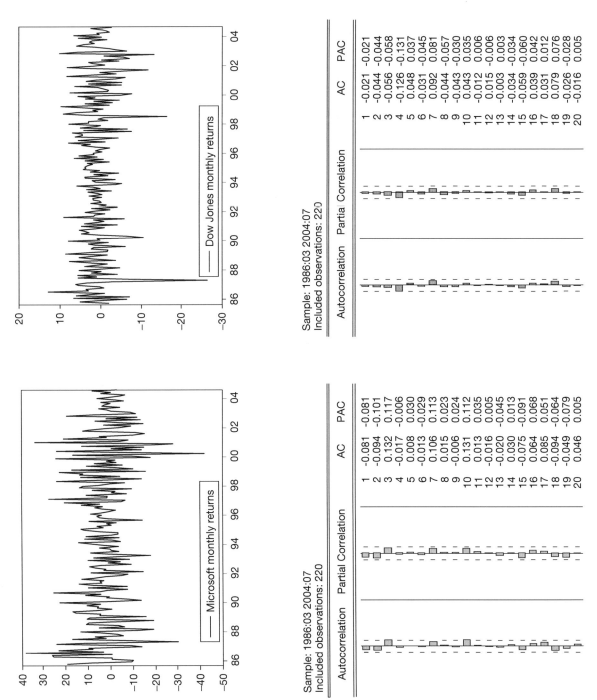

FIGURE 6.2 Autocorrelation Functions of Monthly Returns to Microsoft and the Dow Jones Index

Observe that the autocorrelations are very close to zero for any displacement. We can safely say that stock returns are white noise processes and as such, they are linearly unpredictable. You may retrieve more financial data from http://www.yahoo.com and compute autocorrelations functions. You will find that white noise processes are very common among financial series.

6.2 The Wold Decomposition Theorem: The Origin of AR and MA Models (Advanced Section)[1]

Recall from Chapter 3 the definition of covariance stationary process. This is a process for which the unconditional mean and unconditional variance are time invariant and the autocorrelation function does not depend on time. The Wold decomposition is a theoretical result concerning *only covariance stationary* processes. However, it is very powerful because regardless of how the true process has been generated, the theorem claims that there is always a *linear* approximation to the true process, which implies that at least we will be able to construct a linear forecast.

The Wold decomposition theorem states the following:

If $\{Y_t\}$ is a covariance stationary process and $\{\varepsilon_t\}$ is a white noise zero-mean process, then there exists a unique linear representation as

$$Y_t = V_t + \varepsilon_t + \psi_1\varepsilon_{t-1} + \psi_2\varepsilon_{t-2} + \psi_3\varepsilon_{t-3}\cdots\cdots = V_t + \sum_{j=0}^{\infty}\psi_j\varepsilon_{t-j}$$

where V_t is a deterministic component and $\sum_{j=0}^{\infty} \psi_j\varepsilon_{t-j}$ is the stochastic component with $\psi_0 = 1, \sum_{j=0}^{\infty}\psi_j^2 < \infty$.

The five main important points of the theorem are:

1. The process $\{\varepsilon_t\}$ is white noise and, as defined in Section 6.1, it is a sequence of uncorrelated random variables.
2. The sequence $\{\varepsilon_t\}$ is also known as a sequence of *innovations* or *one-step-ahead linear prediction* errors. Suppose that we run a linear regression of Y_t on the past available information $Y_{t-1}, Y_{t-2}, \ldots\ldots.,$ such as $Y_t = \beta_0 + \beta_1 Y_{t-1} + \beta_2 Y_{t-2} + \cdots + \varepsilon_t$. Then ε_t is the error term or the shock that contains unpredictable information. The error ε_t is also known as an *innovation*, which by definition we could not predict based on the available

[1]The content of this section is more technically demanding. Moving directly to section 6.3 will not interrupt the flow of the chapter.

information; it is a prediction error. In this context, the Wold decomposition says that today's value Y_t is a *linear* combination of all those innovations that were happening over time. You can think of $\{\varepsilon_t\}$ as informational shocks coming over time and being processed within Y_t. At time t, the shock ε_t comes as a surprise to Y_t, but the shock ε_{t-1} is already known and somehow processed in Y_t so that only $\psi_1\varepsilon_{t-1}$ remains in Y_t. Similar arguments will apply for $\psi_2\varepsilon_{t-2}$, $\psi_3\varepsilon_{t-3}$, and so on. Because $\sum_{j=0}^{\infty} \psi_j^2 < \infty$, there must be a j from which all subsequent $\psi_{j+1}, \psi_{j+2}, \ldots.$ are necessarily smaller and smaller; consequently, the corresponding shocks $\varepsilon_{t-(j+1)}, \varepsilon_{t-(j+2)}, \ldots$ will have almost negligible effect on Y_t.

3. Although ε_t very frequently is assumed to be normally distributed, the Wold decomposition does not require normality.
4. The deterministic component V_t refers to nonrandom components in the process; it may refer to a deterministic cycle or a deterministic trend, which will be introduced in the forthcoming chapters. At this point, we will assume that Y_t does not contain any deterministic component (or that it has been removed) and we state the Wold decomposition as a linear combination of past innovations or white noise shocks

$$Y_t = \varepsilon_t + \psi_1\varepsilon_{t-1} + \psi_2\varepsilon_{t-2} + \psi_3\varepsilon_{t-3}\cdots\cdots = \sum_{j=0}^{\infty}\psi_j\varepsilon_{t-j}$$

5. The approximation of the linear model to the true model is understood in a mean-square sense, that is, $E\left(Y_t - \sum_{j=0}^{n}\psi_j\varepsilon_{t-j}\right)^2 \to 0$ as $n \to \infty$, which means that on average, the (squared) distance between a linear model and the true model is negligible when we account for *all* past information. In the appendix to this chapter, we offer a sketch of the proof of this result.

The Wold decomposition is very important because it guarantees that there is always a linear model that can represent the dynamics of a covariance stationary stochastic process. There may be other more complicated representations, such as nonlinear models, but we can always *approximate* the stochastic process by a linear representation. This is the starting point in any time series modeling strategy.

In Chapter 5, we encountered a model very similar to what the Wold theorem states. Recall the cob-web model of price dynamics

$$p_t = p^* + \varepsilon_t + \phi\varepsilon_{t-1} + \phi^2\varepsilon_{t-2} + \cdots\cdots + \phi^{t-2}\varepsilon_2 + \phi^{t-1}\varepsilon_1 + \cdots\cdots$$

and compare it to the Wold decomposition

$$Y_t = \varepsilon_t + \psi_1\varepsilon_{t-1} + \psi_2\varepsilon_{t-2} + \psi_3\varepsilon_{t-3}\cdots\cdots + \psi_{t-1}\varepsilon_1 + \psi_t\varepsilon_0 + \psi_{t+1}\varepsilon_{-1} + \cdots\cdots\cdots$$

Both representations are identical for $\psi_1 = \phi$, $\psi_2 = \phi^2 \ldots.., \psi_j = \phi^j$ (in addition to the constant p^*); and both representations, the Wold decomposition and the cob-web model of price dynamics, are linear combinations of past shocks. In fact, we already have a name for these representations: moving average (MA) models. Thus, the Wold decomposition is an MA process of infinite order, that is, **MA(∞)**; we need to consider an infinite number of parameters $\psi_1, \psi_2, \psi_3, \ldots..$ in order to represent the dynamics of the process. In practice, this feature is not very appealing because we have a limited number of observations; thus, a question of interest is whether there is an equivalent linear representation of the process with a finite number of parameters. This is the subject of the next subsection.

6.2.1 Finite Representation of the Wold Decomposition

In Chapter 3, we introduced the lag operator L. Recall that when the operator is applied to a random variable, it delivers the one-period lagged random variable, that is, $LY_t = Y_{t-1}$ and, in general, $L^jY_t = Y_{t-j}$. Let us write the Wold decomposition in terms of the lag operator:

$$Y_t = \varepsilon_t + \psi_1\varepsilon_{t-1} + \psi_2\varepsilon_{t-2} + \psi_3\varepsilon_{t-3} \cdots\cdots\cdots = (1 + \psi_1 L + \psi_2 L^2 + \psi_3 L^3 + \cdots\cdots)\varepsilon_t = \Psi(L)\varepsilon_t$$

where $(1 + \psi_1 L + \psi_2 L^2 + \psi_3 L^3 + \cdots\cdots\cdots) \equiv \Psi(L)$.

The infinite polynomial in the lag operator $\Psi(L)$ can be approximated by the ratio of two finite lag polynomials:

$$\Psi(L) \approx \frac{\Theta_q(L)}{\Phi_p(L)}$$

where $\Theta_q(L) = 1 + \theta_1 L + \theta_2 L^2 + \cdots\cdot \theta_q L^q$ and $\Phi_p(L) = 1 - \phi_1 L - \phi_2 L^2 - \cdots \phi_p L^p$.

Now the Wold decomposition can be written as

$$Y_t = \Psi(L)\varepsilon_t \approx \frac{\Theta_q(L)}{\Phi_p(L)}\varepsilon_t$$

or

$$\Phi_p(L)Y_t = \Theta_q(L)\varepsilon_t$$

$$(1 - \phi_1 L - \phi_2 L^2 - \cdots\cdots \phi_p L^p)Y_t = (1 + \theta_1 L + \theta_2 L^2 + \cdots\cdots \theta_q L^q)\varepsilon_t$$

$$\underbrace{Y_t - \phi_1 Y_{t-1} - \cdots\cdots \phi_p Y_{t-p}}_{AR(p)} = \underbrace{\varepsilon_t + \theta_1\varepsilon_{t-1} + \theta_2\varepsilon_{t-2} + \cdots\cdots \theta_q\varepsilon_{t-q}}_{MA(q)}$$

The stochastic process Y_t now has a linear representation that is characterized by a finite number of parameters, $p + q$, as opposed to the infinite number of parameters contained in the original Wold decomposition. Furthermore, we observe that Y_t is represented by an **autoregressive AR(p)** component (in the left-hand side of the equation) and a **moving average MA(q)** component (in the right-hand side of the equation): The overall representation is called an *ARMA model.* Solving for Y_t, we obtain a general linear model (ARMA) that describes the dynamics of the process:

$$Y_t = \phi_1 Y_{t-1} + \phi_2 Y_{t-2} + \cdots\cdots \phi_p Y_{t-p} + \varepsilon_t + \theta_1 \varepsilon_{t-1} + \theta_2 \varepsilon_{t-2} + \cdots\cdots \theta_q \varepsilon_{t-q}$$

EXAMPLE 1

We have already encountered particular cases of the general ARMA model. In Chapter 5, the cob-web model implies that the price dynamics can be summarized by a model such as

$$p_t = p^*(1 - \phi) + \phi p_{t-1} + \varepsilon_t$$

with $|\phi| < 1$. This is an ARMA model for which $\phi_1 = \phi$; $\phi_2 = \phi_3 = \cdots\cdots = \phi_p = \theta_1 = \theta_2 = \cdots\cdots = \theta_q = 0$; that is, there is no MA structure, and the AR component consists only of the most recent lag; thus, the model is called an AR(1). Now let us understand why there is an equivalent MA representation for this model. Write the model in polynomial form (to simplify the exposition, ignore the constant) and solve for p_t:

$$(1 - \phi L)p_t = \varepsilon_t$$

$$p_t = \frac{1}{1 - \phi L}\varepsilon_t$$

The term $1/(1 - \phi L)$ is a ratio of two finite lag polynomials: $\Theta_q(L) = 1$, $\Phi_p(L) = 1 - \phi L$.

For $|\phi| < 1$, we define

$$\frac{1}{1 - \phi L} = \lim_{j \to \infty}(1 + \phi L + \phi^2 L^2 + \phi^3 L^3 + \cdots\cdots + \phi^j L^j + \cdots\cdots)$$

Hence,

$$p_t = (1 + \phi L + \phi^2 L^2 + \phi^3 L^3 + \cdots\cdots)\varepsilon_t = \varepsilon_t + \phi \varepsilon_{t-1} + \phi^2 \varepsilon_{t-2} + \phi^3 \varepsilon_{t-3} + \cdots\cdots$$

that is the same cob-web model, now written as a linear function of all past shocks.

EXAMPLE 2

Recall the bid-ask bounce model of Chapter 5. According to this model, changes in asset prices have the following dynamic representation:

$$\Delta p_t = \theta \varepsilon_{t-1} + \varepsilon_t$$

with $|\theta| < 1$. This is an ARMA model for which $\phi_1 = \phi_2 = \phi_3 = \cdots\cdots = \phi_p = \theta_2 = \cdots\cdots = \theta_q = 0$, and $\theta_1 = \theta$; that is, there is no AR structure and the MA component contains only the most recent lag, and thus, we refer to it as an MA(1). How do we obtain the equivalent AR representation? Once again, let us write the model in lag polynomial form and solve for ε_t:

$$\Delta p_t = (1 + \theta L)\varepsilon_t$$

$$\frac{1}{(1 + \theta L)}\Delta p_t = \varepsilon_t$$

For $|\theta| < 1$, the term $1/(1 + \theta L)$ is equal to an infinite lag polynomial:

$$\frac{1}{1 - (-\theta)\,L} = \lim_{j \to \infty} (1 - \theta L + \theta^2 L^2 - \theta^3 L^3 + \cdots\cdots\cdots + (-1)^j \theta^j L^j + \cdots)$$

$$(1 - \theta L + \theta^2 L^2 - \theta^3 L^3 + \cdots\cdots\cdots)\Delta p_t = \varepsilon_t$$

Hence, Δp_t can be written as

$$\Delta p_t = \theta\,\Delta p_{t-1} - \theta^2\,\Delta p_{t-2} + \theta^3 \Delta p_{t-3} - \cdots\cdots\cdots + (-1)^t \theta^{t-1} \Delta p_1 \cdots\cdots\cdots + \varepsilon_t$$

which is the bid-ask bounce model now written in an infinite autoregressive form.

In summary, the Wold decomposition justifies the analysis of linear models, which are represented in general by ARMA specifications. Understanding linear models is the foundation of any time series analysis and subsequent forecasting exercises. Our next objective is to analyze the forecasting properties of MA and AR models.

6.3 Forecasting with Moving Average Models

For a process that is covariance stationary, moving average and autoregressive models are very well suited to describe short-term dynamics of a time series. In time series analysis, the short-, medium-, and long-term characteristics of a time series are defined according to the properties of the forecast produced by a given model. Remember that the ultimate objective of any time series model is to construct a forecast based on an information set that contains past histories. In the next sections, we will show that *covariance stationary* processes have the property that their multi-period forecasts converge to the unconditional mean of the process. Given this property, we say that covariance stationary processes have a limited ability to exploit the information set because, sooner or later, the forecast reverts to the unconditional mean, which does not depend on the information set. We also say that these processes have a **short memory**, indicating that they exploit the most recent histories in the information set. On the contrary, processes with a *long memory* tend to incorporate very distant histories in the formation of their forecast. Moving-average and covariance-stationary autoregressive models are examples of processes with short memory and, as such, they cannot capture long-term features of the data because their forecasts exploit only the most recent information. In this sense, we say that they are better suited to model the short and medium terms. In this chapter and Chapter 7, we will study short memory processes. In Chapters 10 and 12, we will study processes with long memory. Because these incorporate distant history, we say that they are suited to model the long term.

In addition, the meaning of short, medium, and long term depends on the frequency of the time series that we are analyzing. For instance, if we study a daily time series, a short-term forecast could be a 1-day-ahead forecast. If we study a monthly time series of prices, a 1-month-ahead forecast is also a short-term forecast. However, 1-month-ahead forecast based on a daily time series may be considered a medium-/long-term forecast because, with daily information, it is a 30-day-ahead forecast. Depending on the memory of the process, a 30-day-ahead forecast may well be the unconditional mean of the process for which no time series model is needed.

In this section, we will study the statistical properties of a pure MA model with the ultimate objective of constructing the optimal forecast. The short memory property of these processes will be evident.

We have already introduced some moving average models as good representations of the price dynamics induced by the cob-web model or by the bid-ask bounce. Now, we define:

A moving average process of order $q \geq 0$, referred as MA(q), has the following functional form:

$$Y_t = \mu + \theta_1\varepsilon_{t-1} + \theta_2\varepsilon_{t-2} \cdots + \theta_q\varepsilon_{t-q} + \varepsilon_t$$

where ε_t is a zero-mean white noise process.

The order of the model is given by the largest lag, not by the number of lag variables in the right-hand side. For instance, the model $Y_t = \mu + \theta_2\varepsilon_{t-2} + \varepsilon_t$ is an MA(2) because the largest lag is 2 although there is only one lagged variable (i.e., ε_{t-2}). The model $Y_t = \mu + \theta_1\varepsilon_{t-1} + \theta_2\varepsilon_{t-2} + \varepsilon_t$ is also an MA(2) because the largest lag is 2 but in this case, there are two lagged variables (i.e. ε_{t-2} and ε_{t-1}).

We can relate this functional form to a regression model. In a regression, we are concerned with the conditional mean of the variable of interest, conditioning on a set of regressors. Suppose that we ask the following question: What is the conditional mean of Y_t based on the information up to time $t-1$? Given the MA(q) model, up to time t-1 the conditioning set is $\{\varepsilon_{t-1}, \varepsilon_{t-2}, \ldots\ldots \varepsilon_{t-q}\}$, and the conditional mean will be:

$$E(Y_t | \varepsilon_{t-1}, \varepsilon_{t-2}, \ldots\ldots\ldots \varepsilon_{t-q}) = \mu + \theta_1\varepsilon_{t-1} + \theta_2\varepsilon_{t-2} \cdots + \theta_q\varepsilon_{t-q}$$

and ε_t plays the role of the regression error. However, we should note that the regressors $\{\varepsilon_{t-1}, \varepsilon_{t-2}, \ldots\ldots \varepsilon_{t-q}\}$ are not directly observable, which will make estimating the model slightly more complicated. Nevertheless the basic idea of regression (i.e., modeling the conditional mean) stands.

To familiarize ourselves with moving average processes, we will analyze the lowest order process MA(1). The generalization to MA(q) will be straightforward. For each process, there are three questions to answer:

1. What does a time series of an MA process look like?
2. What do the corresponding autocorrelation functions look like?
3. What is the optimal forecast?

6.3.1 MA(1) Process

Let us proceed to answer Question 1 by simulating some time series of a process such as

$$Y_t = \mu + \theta\varepsilon_{t-1} + \varepsilon_t$$

for different values of the parameter θ. In Chapter 5, we simulated an MA(1) with $-1 < \theta < 0$. Now let us simulate for positive values of θ. We need to choose some distributional assumption for the white noise error ε_t, for instance, $\varepsilon_t \rightarrow N(0, 0.25)$ (i.e., a normal random variable with zero mean and variance equal to 0.25). In EViews, we type the following commands:

series e=0.5*nrnd	(normal random variable ε_t with mean zero and variance 0.25)
series y=2+0.5*e(-1) +e	(simulated time series from the process $Y_t = 2 + 0.5\varepsilon_{t-1} + \varepsilon_t$)

6.3.1.1 What Does a Time Series of an MA(1) Process Look Like?

In Figure 6.3, we present 200 observations of four time series for different values of $\theta = 0.05$, 0.5, 0.95, and 2.0. For all of them, we will assume that $\mu = 2$ and $\varepsilon_t \rightarrow N(0, 0.25)$.

Let us comment on the similarities and differences across the four time series plots:

- The profiles of the time series are very ragged. This is not very surprising because we are dealing with averages of white noise processes. Observe that when $\theta \rightarrow 0$, the MA(1) process becomes a white noise process. On the other hand, when θ is large (i.e., $\theta = 0.95$), we observe some dependence from one period to the next. This will be evident on analyzing the autocorrelation functions of the process.
- The four time series seem to be weakly stationary. All of them fluctuate around a central value of 2. Why is that? Note that the unconditional mean of the process is exactly the value of the constant in the model (i.e., $\mu = 2$). Calculate the unconditional mean of the process by taking expectations in the left- and

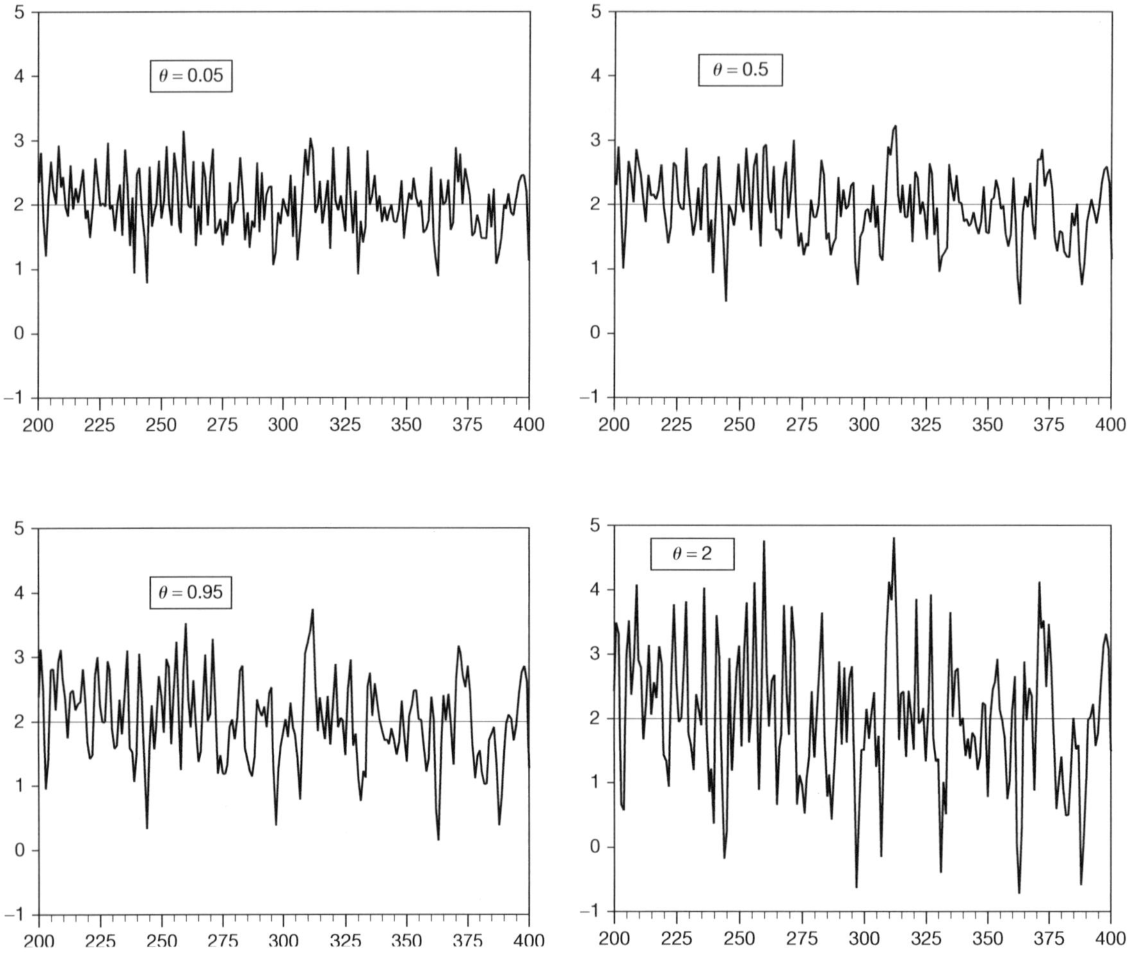

FIGURE 6.3 Simulated MA(1) Processes

right-hand sides of the model: $E(Y_t) = \mu + \theta E(\varepsilon_{t-1}) + E(\varepsilon_t) = \mu$. Recall that ε_t is a zero-mean white noise process; thus, $E(\varepsilon_{t-1}) = E(\varepsilon_t) = 0$. Because the unconditional mean of the process is time invariant, MA(1) is a first order weakly stationary process.

- The variance of the process is directly proportional to the magnitude of θ. Visually, you can compare the variability of the four time series because the scale in the vertical axis is the same across the four plots. More formally, let us compute the unconditional variance of the process:

$$\sigma_Y^2 \equiv E(Y_t - \mu)^2 = E(\theta\varepsilon_{t-1} + \varepsilon_t)^2$$
$$= E(\theta^2\varepsilon_{t-1}^2 + 2\theta\varepsilon_{t-1}\varepsilon_t + \varepsilon_t^2) = (1 + \theta^2)\sigma_\varepsilon^2$$

recall that $E(\varepsilon_{t-1}\varepsilon_t) = 0$ (because of white noise properties) and $E(\varepsilon_{t-1}^2) = E(\varepsilon_t^2) = \sigma_\varepsilon^2$. Thus, the unconditional variance is also time invariant. Is the process covariance stationary? Although the variance is time invariant, we still need to verify that the autocorrelation function does not depend on time in order to claim that the process is covariance stationary.

6.3.1.2 What Do the Corresponding Autocorrelation Functions Look Like?

See Figure 6.4 for the plots of the corresponding autocorrelograms of the processes in Figure 6.3.

The most prominent features of the autocorrelation functions of a MA(1) process are:

- There is only one spike in the AC function that is different from zero $\rho_1 \neq 0$; the remaining spikes are equal to zero $\rho_k = 0$ for $k > 1$. The magnitude of the spike is directly proportional to the magnitude of θ for $|\theta| < 1$, and its sign is

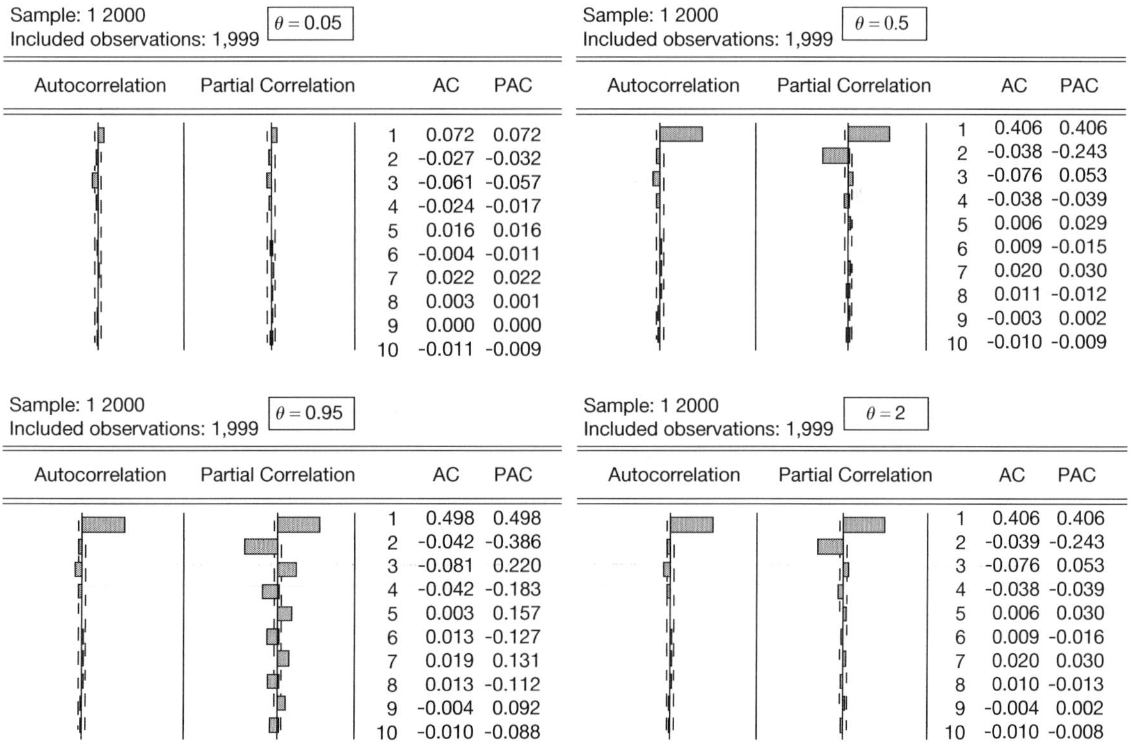

FIGURE 6.4 Autocorrelation Functions of Simulated MA(1) Processes

the same as the sign of θ. Why is this? Let us compute the autocorrelation function. Start with the autocovariance of order 1:

$$\gamma_1 \equiv E\{(Y_t - \mu)(Y_{t-1} - \mu)\} = E\{(\theta\,\varepsilon_{t-1} + \varepsilon_t)(\theta\,\varepsilon_{t-2} + \varepsilon_{t-1})\} = \theta\,\sigma_\varepsilon^2$$

recall that ε_t is a white noise process, that is, $E(\varepsilon_{t-1}\varepsilon_{t-2}) = E(\varepsilon_{t-2}\varepsilon_t) = E(\varepsilon_{t-1}\varepsilon_t) = 0$ and $E(\varepsilon_{t-1}^2) = \sigma_\varepsilon^2$. Then the autocorrelation of order 1 is

$$\rho_1 = \frac{\gamma_1}{\gamma_0} = \frac{\theta\sigma_\varepsilon^2}{(1+\theta^2)\sigma_\varepsilon^2} = \frac{\theta}{(1+\theta^2)}$$

Observe that because the denominator of this expression is positive, the sign of the autocorrelation is the sign of the numerator. The theoretical autocorrelation for different values of θ are for $\theta = 0.05$, $\rho_1 = 0.0498$; for $\theta = 0.5$, $\rho_1 = 0.40$; for $\theta = 0.95$, $\rho_1 = 0.499$; and for $\theta = 2$, $\rho_1 = 0.40$. These numbers are virtually identical to the numbers that we read in the AC functions in Figure 6.4. Autocorrelations of higher order can be computed in the same fashion. For instance, for the second order autocovariance:

$$\gamma_2 \equiv E\{(Y_t - \mu)(Y_{t-2} - \mu)\} = E\{(\theta\,\varepsilon_{t-1} + \varepsilon_t)(\theta\,\varepsilon_{t-3} + \varepsilon_{t-2})\} = 0$$

which implies that $\rho_2 = 0$. This is in agreement with the estimated autocorrelations in Figure 6.4. The same zero autocorrelation is obtained for any other displacement $k > 1$.

These results confirm that the autocorrelation function does not depend on time. Because we have already proved that the unconditional mean and the unconditional variance are time invariant, we conclude that the MA(1) process is covariance stationary.

- The partial autocorrelation function (PAC) decreases toward zero in an alternating fashion. The shape is more obvious when θ is large and $\theta < 1$. The partial autocorrelation is positive for odd displacements and negative for even displacements. The alternating sign in the PAC function is a consequence of the sign of θ. When $\theta < 0$, as it was in the case of the monthly stock returns to the BBVA in Chapter 5, the PAC function decreases toward zero in a very smooth fashion, and all partial autocorrelations are negative. Check the PAC in Figure 5.7. (Chapter 5).

  A property of the partial autocorrelation function is that $r_1 = \rho_1$ for any process. Read that this is the case for the MA(1) in Figure 6.4 and Figure 5.7
- Compare the autocorrelation functions for the MA(1) processes with $\theta = 0.5$ and $\theta = 2$. They are identical. Is this possible? Yes. Check the value of ρ_1 for $\theta = 0.5$ and $\theta = 2$:

$$\rho_t = \frac{\theta}{(1+\theta^2)} = \begin{cases} \dfrac{2}{1+4} = 0.4 & \text{for } \theta = 2 \\[2ex] \dfrac{0.5}{1+0.25} = 0.4 & \text{for } \theta = 0.5 \end{cases}$$

and observe that $\theta = 0.5$ is the inverse of $\theta = 2$. The same will happen for any other value of θ. Choose any θ and check that the first autocorrelation coefficient will be the same for θ and for the inverse of θ (i.e., $1/\theta$). This means that we have two MA processes that produce the same autocorrelation. Now the question becomes: which process we should choose. To answer this question, let us introduce a new concept: *invertibility.*

We say that:

An MA(1) process is invertible if $|\theta| < 1$

On the contrary, if $|\theta| \geq 1$, the process is noninvertible. What is the meaning of invertibility?

Recall the MA(1) process written in lag-polynomial form

$$Y_t = \mu + \varepsilon_t + \theta\varepsilon_{t-1} = \mu + (1 - (-\theta)L)\varepsilon_t$$

and solve for ε_t as

$$\frac{1}{1-(-\theta)L}(Y_t - \mu) = \varepsilon_t$$

In Section 6.2.1, we have defined that for $|\theta| < 1$,

$$\frac{1}{1-(-\theta)\,L} = \lim(1 - \theta L + \theta^2 L^2 - \theta^3 L^3 + \cdots\cdots\cdots)$$

Thus, we can write the MA(1) process as

$$(1 - \theta L + \theta^2 L^2 - \theta^3 L^3 + \cdots\cdots\cdots)(Y_t - \mu) = \varepsilon_t$$

and, solving for Y_t, we have that

$$\begin{aligned} Y_t - \mu &= \theta(Y_{t-1} - \mu) - \theta^2(Y_{t-2} - \mu) + \theta^3(Y_{t-3} - \mu) - \cdots\cdots\cdot \\ &\quad + (-1)^t\theta^{t-1}(Y_1 - \mu)\cdots\cdots\cdot + \varepsilon_t. \end{aligned}$$

In other words, we have converted an MA(1) process into an autoregressive process where Y_t is a function of its own past. Since $|\theta| < 1$, the recent past has more weight than the distant past because, for t large, $\theta^t \to 0$. This is the meaning of **invertibility**: If the MA process is invertible, we can always find an autoregressive representation in which the present is a function of the past. This is very important for forecasting purposes because in order to predict the future we need the information contained in the past.

You may wonder what happens when the MA is not invertible, that is, $|\theta| \geq 1$. What happens to the ratio $\frac{1}{1-(-\theta)\,L}$? To simplify the exposition, let us work with the ratio $\frac{1}{1-\theta L}$. Suppose that $\theta > 1$. Then the ratio $\frac{1}{1-\theta L}$ does not have a limit. However, if $\theta > 1$, then $1/\theta < 1$. Let us multiply the numerator and the denominator of $\frac{1}{1-\theta L}$ by $(1/\theta L)$:

$$\frac{1}{1-\theta L} = -\frac{\frac{1}{\theta L}}{1-\frac{1}{\theta L}} = -\frac{1}{\theta L}\left(1 + \frac{1}{\theta L} + \left(\frac{1}{\theta L}\right)^2 + \left(\frac{1}{\theta L}\right)^3 + \cdots\cdots\right)$$

Now this infinite lag polynomial is bounded because $1/\theta < 1$, but what is $1/L$? It is the inverse of the lag operator, which we call the *forward operator* (i.e., $F \equiv 1/L$). This operator has the following property when applied to a random variable $FY_t = Y_{t+1}$, that is, it delivers the process at a future date, and as with any inverse operator, it will be required that $F \times L = \frac{1}{L} \times L = 1$. For instance, $(F \times L)Y_t = F(LY_t) = FY_{t-1} = Y_t$.

Then for $\theta > 1$ and using the forward operator, the ratio $\frac{1}{1-\theta L}$ is written as

$$\frac{1}{1-\theta L} = -\frac{1}{\theta}F\left(1 + \frac{1}{\theta}F + \frac{1}{\theta^2}F^2 + \frac{1}{\theta^3}F^3 + \cdots\cdots\right)$$

Consequently, the noninvertible MA process written in the autoregressive representation will have the following form

$$\varepsilon_t = \frac{1}{1-\theta L}Y_t = -\frac{1}{\theta}F\left(1 + \frac{1}{\theta}F + \frac{1}{\theta^2}F^2 + \frac{1}{\theta^3}F^3 + \cdots\cdots\right)Y_t$$

and solving for Y_{t+1}, we will have

$$-\frac{1}{\theta}Y_{t+1} = \frac{1}{\theta^2}Y_{t+2} + \frac{1}{\theta^3}Y_{t+3} + \cdots\cdots + \varepsilon_t$$

In order words, the present is a function of the future! Obviously, in this environment, forecasting does not make any sense.

In summary, of the two possible MA processes, we always choose the invertible MA representation.

REAL DATA: 5-Year Constant Maturity Yield on Treasury Securities

In Figure 6.5, we plot the *percentage monthly changes* in the 5-year constant maturity yield on **U.S. Treasury securities** (TCM5Y) from April 1953 to April 2008 and its corresponding estimated autocorrelation functions. The U.S. Treasury Department constructs

FIGURE 6.5
Percentage Changes in the 5-Year Treasury Note Yield

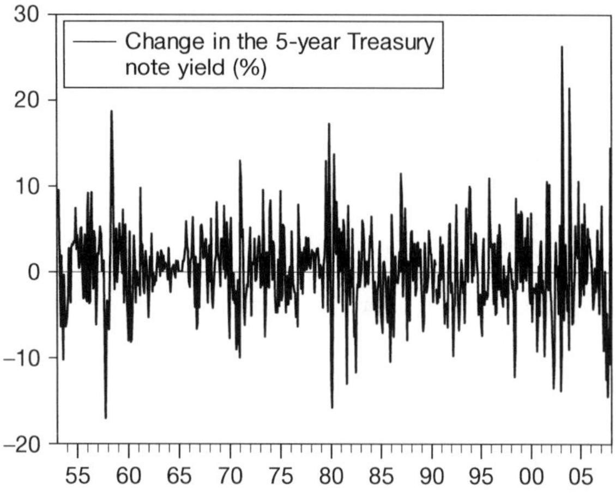

Sample: 1953M04 2008M04
Included observations: 660

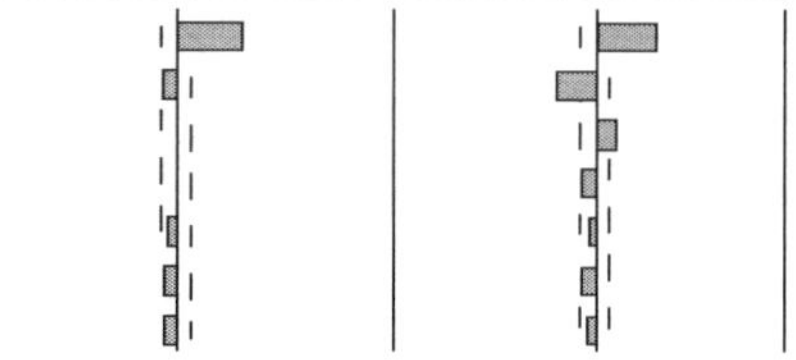

	AC	PAC
1	0.339	0.339
2	-0.073	-0.213
3	0.007	0.129
4	0.014	-0.063
5	-0.043	-0.017
6	-0.073	-0.060
7	-0.069	-0.035

the time series of daily, weekly, monthly, and yearly yields on Treasury securities with different maturities (1, 2, 3, 5, 7, 10, 20, and 30 years). U.S. Treasury securities are considered the least risky assets in the U.S. economy and constitute an asset of reference to monitor the level of risk of other fixed-income securities such as grade bonds and certificates of deposit. It is customary to quote the asset spread to Treasury, which is the difference between the yield of the fixed-income security and the yield of a corresponding Treasury security with the same maturity. When the spread is large, the fixed-income security is considered risky.

The profile of the time series is very ragged and fluctuates around zero. The yield changes have a mean of zero approximately. The most striking feature of this time series is its volatility. There are abrupt (positive and negative) changes in this series of approximately 20%. Compare the autocorrelation function with those in Figure 6.4. They are very similar. The AC function has only one positive spike $\hat{\rho}_1 > 0$ with the remaining autocorrelations practically equal to zero. The partial autocorrelation function is alternating in sign. These are features that characterize an MA(1) process with $\theta > 0$. In addition, from $\hat{\rho}_1 = 0.339$, we can estimate the parameter, which is $\hat{\theta} \cong 0.4$. Many more time series of yields on Treasury securities can be downloaded from the Federal Reserve Board website http://www.federalreserve.gov.

6.3.1.3 What Is the Optimal Forecast Corresponding to an MA(1) Process?

Recall from Chapter 4 that the optimal forecast $f_{t,h}$ depends on the loss function chosen by the forecaster. Let us choose a quadratic loss function. Accordingly, the optimal point forecast is a conditional expectation: $f_{t,h} = \mu_{t+h|t} = E(Y_{t+h}|I_t)$. For MA(1), we will compute this expectation for different forecast horizons $h = 1, 2, \ldots . s$. We proceed in two steps: First to write the process at the desired horizon and second to take the conditional expectation. For instance,

FORECASTING HORIZON $h = 1$

Write the process at time $t + 1$

$$Y_{t+1} = \mu + \theta \varepsilon_t + \varepsilon_{t+1}$$

Take expectation conditioning on the information set up to time t. Observe that ε_t belongs to the information set; because its value is known, it is not a random variable any more: $E(\varepsilon_t | I_t) = \varepsilon_t$. Additionally, ε_{t+1} is a mean zero white noise process uncorrelated with the information set; thus, $E(\varepsilon_{t+1} | I_t) = E(\varepsilon_{t+1}) = 0$. Putting these pieces together, we ask the following questions:

i. *What is the optimal point forecast $f_{t,1}$?*

$$f_{t,1} = \mu_{t+1|t} = E(Y_{t+1} | I_t) = E(\mu + \theta\varepsilon_t + \varepsilon_{t+1}) = \mu + \theta\varepsilon_t$$

Note that even though ε_t belongs to the information set, it is not readily observable. It needs to be retrieved from the past data. This is not a major problem because we have an invertible MA(1), which permits us to write ε_t as a function of past observations. For instance, solving for ε_t, and substituting backward, we obtain

$$\begin{aligned}\varepsilon_t &= Y_t - \mu - \theta \varepsilon_{t-1} = Y_t - \mu - \theta (Y_{t-1} - \mu - \theta \varepsilon_{t-2}) \\ &= (Y_t - \mu) - \theta (Y_{t-1} - \mu) + \theta^2 \varepsilon_{t-2} = \cdots\cdots\cdots = (Y_t - \mu) \\ &\quad - \theta (Y_{t-1} - \mu) + \theta^2 (Y_{t-2} - \mu) - \cdots\cdots\cdots + (-1)\theta^j (Y_{t-j} - \mu) \\ &\quad + \cdots\cdots\cdots\end{aligned}$$

ii. *What is the one-period-ahead forecast error $e_{t,1}$?*
It must be the difference between the realized value Y_{t+1} and the forecast value $f_{t,1}$:

$$e_{t,1} = Y_{t+1} - f_{t,1} = \mu + \theta \varepsilon_t + \varepsilon_{t+1} - \mu - \theta\varepsilon_t = \varepsilon_{t+1}$$

It is not very surprising to find out that the forecast error is the component of the process that is not predictable.

iii. *What is the uncertainty associated with the forecast?*
It must be a function of the unpredictability of the process, which is summarized in the variance of the forecast error

$$\sigma^2_{t+1|t} = \text{var}(Y_{t+1}|I_t) = E(Y_{t+1} - f_{t,1}|I_t)^2 = E(e^2_{t,1}) = E(\varepsilon^2_{t+1}) = \sigma^2_\varepsilon$$

iv. *What is the density forecast?*
It is the conditional probability density function of the process at the future date. If we assume that $\{\varepsilon_t\}$ is a normally distributed white noise process,

$$f(Y_{t+1}|I_t) \to N(\mu_{t+1|t}, \sigma^2_{t+1|t}) = N(\mu + \theta\varepsilon_t, \sigma^2_\varepsilon)$$

From the density forecast, we construct confidence intervals. For instance, a 95% confidence interval is

$$\mu_{t+1|t} \pm 1.96\sigma_{t+1|t} = (\mu_{t+1|t} - 1.96\sigma_{t+1|t}, \mu_{t+1|t} + 1.96\sigma_{t+1|t})$$

where $1.96 = \Phi^{-1}(0.975)$, and $\Phi^{-1}(.)$ is the inverse of the cumulative distribution function of a $N(0,1)$ random variable. To understand the latter statement, remember the bell-shaped density function of a standardized normal random variable $Z \to N(0, 1)$; allow for 2.5% probability in each of the upper and lower tails so that 95% probability lies in the middle body of the density function; then $\Pr(-1.96 \le Z \le 1.96) = 0.95$.

Forecasting Horizon $h = 2$

We follow the same steps as in the previous case.

i. *What is the optimal point forecast $f_{t,2}$?*

$$f_{t,2} = \mu_{t+2|t} = E(Y_{t+2}|I_t) = E(\mu + \theta\varepsilon_{t+1} + \varepsilon_{t+2}|I_t) = \mu$$

Observe that ε_{t+1} and ε_{t+2} are future innovations uncorrelated with past information; thus, they that cannot be forecasted given the information set I_t. For an MA(1), past history is not useful when we wish to forecast beyond one period. The optimal forecast becomes the unconditional mean of the process because the process cannot further exploit the information set. This agrees with the properties of the autocorrelation function for which only the first autocorrelation coefficient ($\rho_1 \neq 0$) is different from zero. After one period, the process does not exhibit any more time dependence, and consequently, the best forecast is the mean of the process. We say that the MA(1) model is a process with very *short memory.*

ii. *What is the two-period-ahead forecast error $e_{t,2}$?*
It must be the difference between the realized value Y_{t+2} and the forecast value $f_{t,2}$:

$$e_{t,2} = Y_{t+2} - f_{t,2} = \mu + \theta\varepsilon_{t+1} + \varepsilon_{t+2} - \mu = \theta\varepsilon_{t+1} + \varepsilon_{t+2}$$

iii. *What is the uncertainty associated with the forecast?*

It must be a function of the unpredictability of the process, which is summarized in the variance of the forecast error:

$$\sigma^2_{t+2|t} = \text{var}(Y_{t+2}|I_t) = E(Y_{t+2} - f_{t,2}|I_t)^2 = E(e^2_{t,2})$$
$$= E(\theta\varepsilon_{t+1} + \varepsilon_{t+2})^2 = \sigma^2_\varepsilon(1+\theta^2) = \sigma^2_Y$$

For this result, it is important to recall the no-autocorrelation property that characterizes a white noise process. Observe that now the uncertainty of the forecast is the unconditional variance of the process. This is again a consequence of the short memory of the MA(1) process.

iv. *What is the density forecast?*

It is the conditional probability density function of the process at the future date. If we assume that $\{\varepsilon_t\}$ is normally distributed white noise process, the density forecast is

$$f(Y_{t+2}|I_t) \rightarrow N(\mu_{t+2|t}, \sigma^2_{t+2|t}) = N(\mu, \sigma^2_Y)$$

Now the conditional probability density function has collapsed to the unconditional density function of the process. Since for $h = 2$, the optimal forecast, the forecast uncertainty, and the density forecast have already converged to the unconditional mean, unconditional variance, and unconditional density, respectively, we should not expect a different behavior for longer forecasting horizons. In general, for $h > 1$:

Forecasting Horizon $h = s$

i. *What is the optimal point forecast $f_{t,s}$?*

$$f_{t,s} = \mu_{t+s|t} = E(Y_{t+s}|I_t) = \mu$$

ii. *What is the s-period-ahead forecast error $e_{t,s}$?*

$$e_{t,s} = Y_{t+s} - f_{t,s} = \varepsilon_{t+s} + \theta\,\varepsilon_{t+s-1}$$

iii. *What is the uncertainty associated with the forecast?*

$$\sigma^2_{t+s|t} = \text{var}(Y_{t+s}|I_t) = E(Y_{t+s} - f_{t,s}|I_t)^2 = E(e^2_{t,s}) = \sigma^2_\varepsilon(1+\theta^2) = \sigma^2_Y$$

iv. *What is the density forecast?*

$$f(Y_{t+s}|I_t) \rightarrow N(\mu_{t+s|t}, \sigma^2_{t+s|t}) = N(\mu, \sigma^2_Y)$$

In summary, forecasting with an MA(1) is limited by the very short memory of the process. In this sense, we say that these models forecast the short term; in the longer term, the optimal forecast is identical to the unconditional mean of the process.

REAL DATA: Forecasting 5-year Constant Maturity Yield on Treasury Securities

We go back to the real data in Figure 6.5 and practice the ideas that we have learned so far about forecasting with MA models. This exercise is a warm-up to the practice of forecasting; in the next chapters we will explain step-by-step how to conduct a full forecasting exercise once we have augmented our library of time series models.

The autocorrelation functions in Figure 6.5 are typical of an MA(1) process. We proceed by estimating such a model. In your EViews workfile click on the following sequence:

Object

New Object

Equation

In the Specification window choose the method LS – Least Squares (NLS and ARMA) and write the following command: dy c MA(1) where "dy" is the monthly change in the 5-year Treasury yield, "c" is a constant, and "MA(1)" is the number of lags in the moving average model. The estimation output is displayed in Table 6.1.

The estimation sample runs from May 1953 to November 2007 for a total of 655 observations. The estimated parameters are $\hat{\theta} = 0.485$, which is very close to our educated guess in Section 6.3.1.2, $\hat{\mu} = 0.160$, and $\hat{\sigma}_\varepsilon = 4.449$. Then we write the time series model as

$$Y_t = 0.160 + 0.485\,\varepsilon_{t-1} + \varepsilon_t$$

We proceed to use this model to forecast from December 2007 to April 2008; thus, we will be constructing from 1-step to 5-step forecasts. Observe that the forecasting sample is not included in the estimation exercise of Table 6.1.

Two features are relevant. First, for $h = 1$, we need the value of $\hat{\varepsilon}_t$. As we mentioned in the preceding section, this value is retrieved indirectly from the formula $\varepsilon_t = (Y_t - \mu) - \theta(Y_{t-1} - \mu) + \theta^2(Y_{t-2} - \mu) - \cdots\cdots\cdots + (-1)\theta^j(Y_{t-j} - \mu) + \cdots\cdots\cdots$ by substituting the estimates of θ and μ and gathering the past values of the time series $\{Y_t, Y_{t-1}, \ldots\ldots\}$. Second, the short memory of the MA(1) process is evident because, for $h > 1$, the best forecast is the unconditional mean of the process $\hat{\mu} = 0.160$ and the variance of the forecast is the unconditional variance of the process $\hat{\sigma}^2_Y = 23.683$. We have also assumed that ε_t is normally distributed; thus, the density forecast is readily available given that we know the first and second moments at each forecasting horizon.

In EViews, the multistep forecasts are generated by clicking the following sequence

Equation

Proc

Forecast

TABLE 6.1 Estimation Output: 5-Year Treasury Yield (Monthly Percentage Changes)

Dependent Variable: DY
Method: Least Squares
Sample (adjusted): 1953M05 2007M11
Included observations: 655 after adjustments
Convergence achieved after 7 iterations
Backcast: 1953M04

Variable	Coefficient	Std. Error	t-Statistic	Prob.
C	0.160159	0.258095	0.620544	0.5351
MA(1)	0.485011	0.034468	14.07130	0.0000

R-Squared	0.165370	Mean dependent var	0.168613
Adjusted R-squared	0.164092	S.D. dependent var	4.866609
S.E. of regression	4.449443	Akaike info criterion	5.826484
Sum squared resid	12927.79	Schwarz criterion	5.840177
Log likelihood	-1906.173	F-Statistic	129.3829
Durbin-Wastson stat	2.055799	Prob(F-statistic)	0.000000
Inverted MA Roots	-.49		

TABLE 6.2 December 2007–April 2008 Forecasts of 5-year Treasury Yield Changes

$h=1$ 12/2007	$f_{t,1}=\hat{\mu}+\hat{\theta}\varepsilon_t= =0.160+0.485\hat{\varepsilon}_t =-6.276\%$	$\sigma^2_{t+1\|t}=\hat{\sigma}^2_\varepsilon=4.449^2$	$f(Y_{t+1}\|I_t)\rightarrow N(\mu_{t+1\|t},\sigma^2_{t+1\|t}) =N(-6.276, 4.449^2)$
$h=2$ 1/2008	$f_{t,2}=\hat{\mu}=0.160\%$	$\sigma^2_{t+2\|t}=\hat{\sigma}^2_\varepsilon(1+\hat{\theta}^2) =4.449^2(1+0.485^2) =23.683=\hat{\sigma}^2_Y$	$f(Y_{t+2}\|I_t)\rightarrow N(0.16, 23.683)$
$h=3$ 2/2008	$f_{t,3}=\hat{\mu}=0.160\%$	$\sigma^2_{t+3\|t}=23.683=\hat{\sigma}^2_Y$	$f(Y_{t+3}\|I_t)\rightarrow N(0.16, 23.683)$
$h=4$ 3/2008	$f_{t,4}=\hat{\mu}=0.160\%$	$\sigma^2_{t+4\|t}=23.683=\hat{\sigma}^2_Y$	$f(Y_{t+4}\|I_t)\rightarrow N(0.16, 23.683)$
$h=5$ 4/2008	$f_{t,5}=\hat{\mu}=0.160\%$	$\sigma^2_{t+5\|t}=23.683=\hat{\sigma}^2_Y$	$f(Y_{t+5}\|I_t)\rightarrow N(0.16, 23.683)$

FIGURE 6.6
Multistep Forecast of Monthly Changes of 5-year Treasury Yield

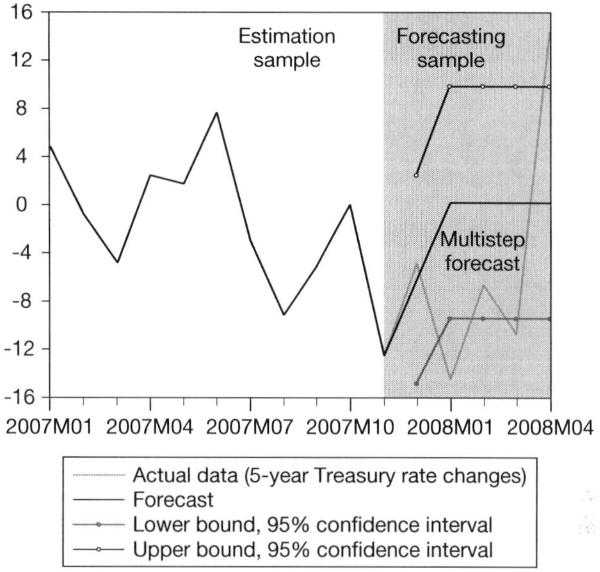

and selecting in the forecast window the "**dynamic**" method. You need to state the forecasting horizon and the name of the forecast series.

In Figure 6.6, we graph the multistep forecast with a 95% confidence interval (based on the normality assumption), which measures the uncertainty of the forecast. To compute the 95% confidence bands, perform the following calculations $(\mu_{t+h|t} - 1.96\sigma_{t+h|t}, \mu_{t+h|t} + 1.96\sigma_{t+h|t})$. For instance, for $h = 1$, the interval will be $(-6.276 - 1.96 \times 4.449, -6.276 + 1.96 \times 4.449) = (-14.997, 2.444)$. Observe that for $h > 1$, the bounds and the forecasts are constant because of the previously mentioned convergence of the forecast toward the unconditional mean and variance of the process.

Compare the actual realizations with the forecasts. The 1-step-ahead forecast (for December 2007) is very accurate but for later horizons, most of the realizations fall outside of the 95% confidence bands. A formal evaluation of forecast accuracy will be conducted in subsequent chapters. At this point, the important task is to familiarize yourself with the construction of the forecast, the interval forecast, and the density forecast.

6.3.2 MA(q) Process

The analysis of an MA(q) process proceeds in the same fashion as that of an MA(1). For any q, a good starting point is to simulate the process to get acquainted with the features of the corresponding time series. The autocorrelation functions will show how much time dependence is in the process, and finally, the construction of the optimal forecasts will exploit the dependence (memory) of the process. Let us focus on an MA(2) process to illustrate that the generalization of MA processes is straightforward. We proceed by simulating time series of a process such as

$$Y_t = \mu + \theta_1 \varepsilon_{t-1} + \theta_2 \varepsilon_{t-2} + \varepsilon_t$$

for different values of the parameter θ_1 and θ_2. We keep the same distributional assumption for the white noise error term ε_t as in the previous section: $\varepsilon_t \rightarrow N(0, 0.25)$ (i.e., a normal random variable with zero mean and variance equal to 0.25). In EViews, we type the following commands:

series e=0.5*nrnd	(normal random variable ε_t with zero mean and variance 0.25)
series y=2-e(-1)+0.25*e(-2) +e	(simulated time series from $Y_t = 2 - \varepsilon_{t-1} + 0.25\varepsilon_{t-2} + \varepsilon_t$)

6.3.2.1 What Does a Time Series of an MA(2) Process Look Like?

In Figure 6.7, we present 200 observations of two time series for different values of $\theta_1 = 1.70, -1$ and for $\theta_2 = 0.72, 0.25$. For both processes, we assume $\mu = 2$ and $\varepsilon_t \rightarrow N(0, 0.25)$.

On comparing time series (a) and (b), we observe the following similarities and differences:

- The profiles of both series are very ragged, but the series (a) is "smoother". Once it is above (below) the mean, it tends to remain there for a longer period of

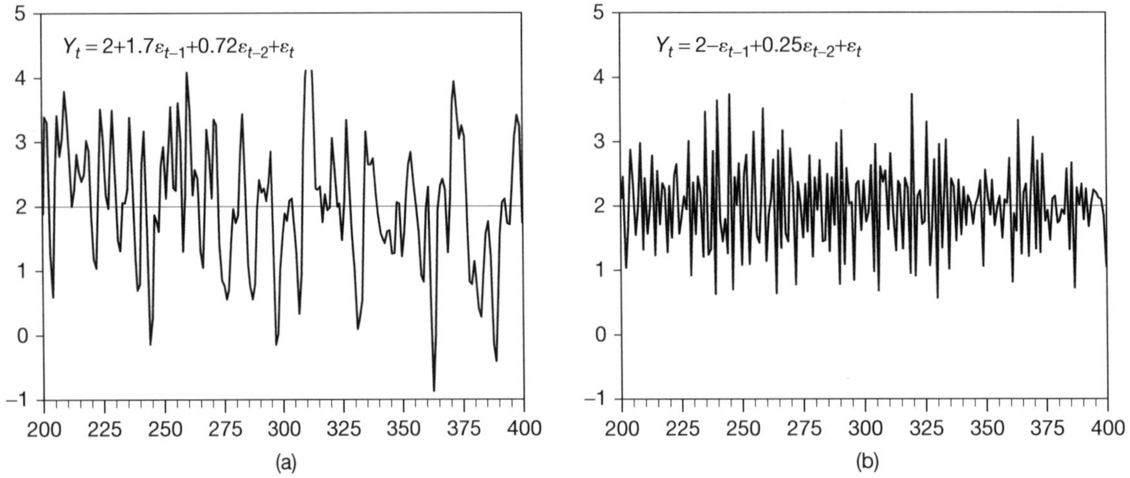

FIGURE 6.7 Simulated MA(2) Processes

time than the series (b). From one period to the next, the series (a) seems to exhibit positive dependence while the dependence in the series (b) seems to be negative. This feature will be more evident when we analyze the autocorrelation functions of both processes.

- Both series fluctuate around a central value of 2, which is the unconditional mean of the process. As we did with the MA(1) case, we calculate the unconditional mean by taking expectations on the left- and right-hand sides of the model

$$E(Y_t) = \mu + \theta_1 E(\varepsilon_{t-1}) + \theta_2 E(\varepsilon_{t-2}) + E(\varepsilon_t) = \mu$$

Recall that ε_t is a zero-mean white noise process, so $E(\varepsilon_{t-1}) = E(\varepsilon_t) = 0$. The constant in any MA(q) specification is the unconditional mean of the process, which is time invariant. Thus, any MA(q) is first order weakly stationary.

- The variance of the series (a) is larger than that of the series (b). Visually, you can observe that the variability of the series (a) is larger than that of the series (b). On computing the unconditional variance of the process, we observe that it will be large when the magnitudes of θ_1 and θ_2 are large, everything else equal:

$$\sigma_Y^2 \equiv E(Y_t - \mu)^2 = E(\theta_1 \varepsilon_{t-1} + \theta_2 \varepsilon_{t-2} + \varepsilon_t)^2 = (1 + \theta_1^2 + \theta_2^2)\sigma_\varepsilon^2$$

recall that $E(\varepsilon_{t-i}\varepsilon_t) = 0$ for $i \neq 0$ and $E(\varepsilon_{t-2}^2) = E(\varepsilon_{t-1}^2) = E(\varepsilon_t^2) = \sigma_\varepsilon^2$. Thus, the unconditional variance is also time invariant.

6.3.2.2 What Do the Corresponding Autocorrelation Functions Look Like?

In Figure 6.8, we plot the corresponding autocorrelograms of the two processes of Figure 6.7. The most prominent features of the autocorrelation functions of an MA(2) process are:

- Only two spikes in the AC function are different from zero $\rho_1 \neq 0$, $\rho_2 \neq 0$, and the remaining autocorrelations are equal to zero $\rho_k = 0$ for $k > 2$. In time series (a), we have $\rho_1 > 0$ and $\rho_2 > 0$ while in time series (b), $\rho_1 < 0$ and $\rho_2 > 0$. To understand these signs, we need to compute the autocorrelation function. Start with the autocovariance of order 1:

$$\begin{aligned}
\gamma_1 &\equiv E\{(Y_t - \mu)(Y_{t-1} - \mu)\} \\
&= E\{(\theta_1 \varepsilon_{t-1} + \theta_2 \varepsilon_{t-2} + \varepsilon_t)(\theta_1 \varepsilon_{t-2} + \theta_2 \varepsilon_{t-3} + \varepsilon_{t-1})\} \\
&= (\theta_1 + \theta_1\theta_2)\,\sigma_\varepsilon^2
\end{aligned}$$

recall that ε_t is a white noise process, that is, $E(\varepsilon_{t-i}\varepsilon_t) = 0$ for $i \neq 0$ and $E(\varepsilon_t^2) = \sigma_\varepsilon^2$. Then the autocorrelation of order 1 is

$$\rho_1 = \frac{\gamma_1}{\gamma_0} = \frac{(\theta_1 + \theta_1\theta_2)\,\sigma_\varepsilon^2}{(1 + \theta_1^2 + \theta_2^2)\sigma_\varepsilon^2} = \frac{(\theta_1 + \theta_1\theta_2)}{(1 + \theta_1^2 + \theta_2^2)}$$

FIGURE 6.8 Autocorrelation Functions of Simulated MA(2) Processes

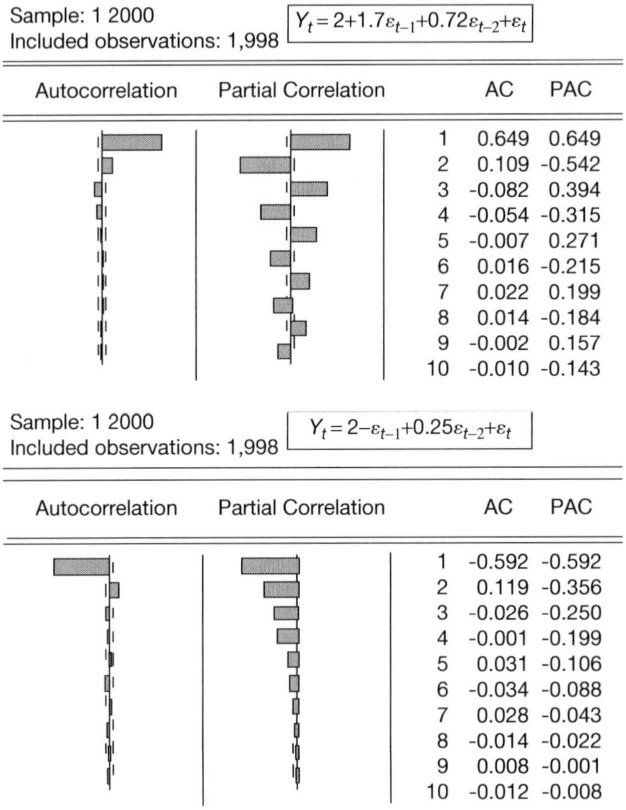
Sample: 1 2000
Included observations: 1,998
Yt=2+1.7εt-1+0.72εt-2+εt
Autocorrelation
Partial Correlation
AC
PAC
1 0.649 0.649
2 0.109 -0.542
3 -0.082 0.394
4 -0.054 -0.315
5 -0.007 0.271
6 0.016 -0.215
7 0.022 0.199
8 0.014 -0.184
9 -0.002 0.157
10 -0.010 -0.143
Sample: 1 2000
Included observations: 1,998
Yt=2-εt-1+0.25εt-2+εt
Autocorrelation
Partial Correlation
AC
PAC
1 -0.592 -0.592
2 0.119 -0.356
3 -0.026 -0.250
4 -0.001 -0.199
5 0.031 -0.106
6 -0.034 -0.088
7 0.028 -0.043
8 -0.014 -0.022
9 0.008 -0.001
10 -0.012 -0.008

which can be positive or negative depending on the signs of θ_1 and θ_2. Now we calculate the autocovariance of order 2:

$$\gamma_2 \equiv E\{(Y_t - \mu)(Y_{t-2} - \mu)\}$$

$$= E\{(\theta_1 \varepsilon_{t-1} + \theta_2 \varepsilon_{t-2} + \varepsilon_t)(\theta_1 \varepsilon_{t-3} + \theta_2 \varepsilon_{t-4} + \varepsilon_{t-2})\} = \theta_2 \sigma_\varepsilon^2$$

Then the autocorrelation of order 2 is

$$\rho_2 = \frac{\gamma_2}{\gamma_0} = \frac{\theta_2 \sigma_\varepsilon^2}{(1 + \theta_1^2 + \theta_2^2)\sigma_\varepsilon^2} = \frac{\theta_2}{(1 + \theta_1^2 + \theta_2^2)}$$

and its sign depends on the sign of θ_2. Autocorrelations of higher order will be equal to zero. For instance, calculate the third order autocovariance: $\gamma_3 \equiv E\{(Y_t - \mu)(Y_{t-3} - \mu)\} = E\{(\theta_1 \varepsilon_{t-1} + \theta_2 \varepsilon_{t-2} + \varepsilon_t)(\theta_1 \varepsilon_{t-4} + \theta_1 \varepsilon_{t-5} + \varepsilon_{t-3})\} = 0$ which implies that $\rho_3 = 0$. In the same fashion, you can check that the fourth, fifth, and so on autocorrelations are zero. In Figure 6.8, observe that high order autocorrelations are virtually zero compared to the first and second autocorrelations.

In general, a distinctive feature of the autocorrelation function of any MA(q) is that $\rho_k = 0$ for $k > q$. Thus, by counting the number of spikes that are different from zero in the AC function, we learn the order of the MA process. In addition, these results confirm that the autocorrelation function does not depend on time. Because we have already shown that the unconditional mean and the unconditional variance are time invariant, we conclude that the MA(q) process is covariance stationary.

- The partial autocorrelation function PAC decreases toward zero in an alternating fashion for time series (a) and in a smooth fashion for time series (b). This behavior depends on the signs of θ_1 and θ_2. The speed of the decay toward zero depends on the magnitudes of θ_1 and θ_2, and the shape of the PAC depends on the magnitudes and signs of θ_1 and θ_2. A common feature to all MA processes is that there is not a cut-off point in the PAC function as we have observed in the AC function. As in the MA(1) case, the general property of the partial autocorrelation function $r_1 = \rho_1$ holds. Read that this is the case for the MA(2) processes in Figure 6.8.
- As in the MA(1) case, the issue of invertibility is present in any high order MA process. We need to choose between the two MA representations that generate the same autocorrelation functions. For instance, generate a time series from the following process:

$$Y_t = 2 - 4\varepsilon_{t-1} + 4\varepsilon_{t-2} + \varepsilon_t$$

Type these familiar commands into EViews:

series e=0.5*nrnd	(normal random variable ε_t with zero mean and variance 0.25)
series y=2-4*e(-1)+4*e(-2) +e	(simulated time series from $Y_t = 2 - 4\varepsilon_{t-1} + 4\varepsilon_{t-2} + \varepsilon_t$)

Compute the autocorrelations functions. You should obtain the autocorrelograms in Figure 6.9.

FIGURE 6.9 Autocorrelation Functions of MA Process $Y_t = 2 - 4\varepsilon_{t-1} + 4\varepsilon_{t-2} + \varepsilon_t$

Sample: 1 2000
Included observations: 1,998

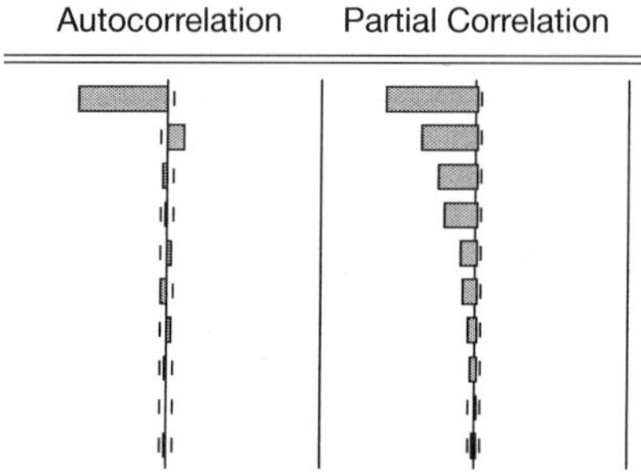

	AC	PAC
1	-0.592	-0.592
2	0.119	-0.356
3	-0.026	-0.250
4	-0.001	-0.199
5	0.031	-0.106
6	-0.033	-0.087
7	0.027	-0.041
8	-0.014	-0.020
9	0.008	0.000
10	-0.011	-0.007

Observe that these autocorrelograms are identical to those generated by the process $Y_t = 2 - \varepsilon_{t-1} + 0.25\varepsilon_{t-2} + \varepsilon_t$ (Figure 6.8). Then given that there is the same time dependence, which of the following models should we choose?

$$Y_t = 2 - 4\varepsilon_{t-1} + 4\varepsilon_{t-2} + \varepsilon_t \quad \text{or} \quad Y_t = 2 - \varepsilon_{t-1} + 0.25\varepsilon_{t-2} + \varepsilon_t?$$

We always choose the invertible representation because it guarantees that there exists an autoregressive representation for which the present is always a function of the past. This feature is necessary to produce a sensible model-based forecast. Fortunately, most time series computer programs will alert us when the process is not invertible. In the previous example, the invertible representation is $Y_t = 2 - \varepsilon_{t-1} + 0.25\varepsilon_{t-2} + \varepsilon_t$.[2]

REAL DATA: Stock Prices and Technical Analysis

In **technical analysis**, financial analysts tend to **smooth prices** in order to detect potential trends. A very simple and popular smoothing tool is the moving average method. For instance, a simple 20-day moving average price is obtained as the average of the current price and the previous 19 daily prices, that is,

$$p_t^{MA20} = \frac{p_t + p_{t-1} + p_{t-2} + \cdots\cdots p_{t-19}}{20}$$

In Figure 6.10, we plot the time series of daily stock prices of Microsoft from January 8, 2003, to April 13, 2005 (solid line), and the 20-day moving average price (dashed line). Observe that the latter is smoother than the former. By construction, smoothing generates autocorrelation in the data because information between consecutive smoothed prices overlaps. For instance, p_t^{MA20} and p_{t-1}^{MA20} have $p_{t-1}, p_{t-2}, \ldots\ldots p_{t-19}$ in common.

Suppose that we are interested in constructing the time series of returns based on the smoothed price p_t^{MA}. For simplicity, we construct the 3-day moving average price and calculate the corresponding time series of returns. The smoothed returns must inherit the induced autocorrelation in prices. In Figure 6.11, we show the time series of returns based on the closing price and on the smoothed price (3-day moving average price).

It is evident that the smoothed returns have less volatility than the original returns. What type of autocorrelation is induced in the smoothed returns? In Figure 6.12, we present the autocorrelation functions of the daily returns based on the original price and on the 3-day smoothed price.

---

[2] If you are versed in calculus and algebra, you will solve for the roots of the following characteristic equations (observe that the equation coefficients are equal to the MA parameters θ_1 and θ_2):

$$\text{(a) } 1 - 4x + 4x^2 = 0 \rightarrow x_1 = x_2 = 0.5$$
$$\text{(b) } 1 - x + 0.25x^2 = 0 \rightarrow x_1 = x_2 = 2$$

The invertible representation has always roots greater than 1. Observe that the roots of the invertible representation are the inverse of the roots of the noninvertible representation.

FIGURE 6.10 Microsoft Daily Stock Prices

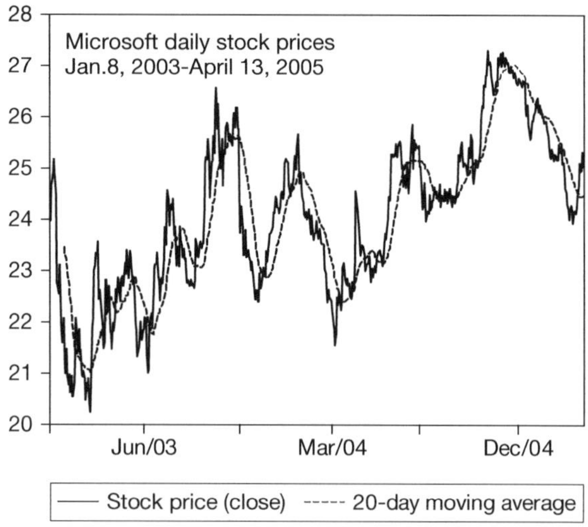

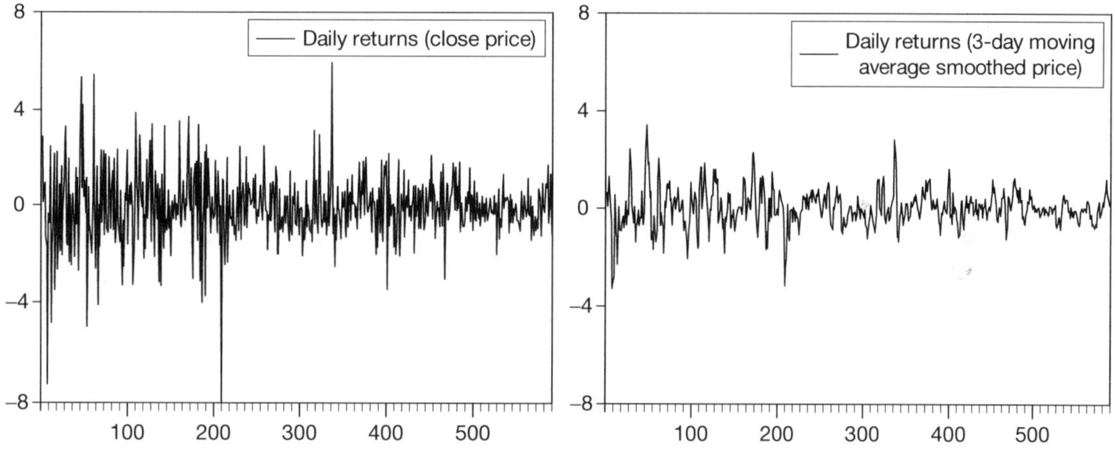

FIGURE 6.11 Daily Returns to Microsoft

The autocorrelation functions are very different. The returns based on the original closing price behave like a white noise process while the returns based on the smoothed price have substantial autocorrelation. Their AC function exhibits two significant spikes, which are both positive, and their PAC function exhibits a decay toward zero in a cyclical alternating fashion. These features point toward an MA(2) process with positive parameters θ_1 and θ_2. Their autocorrelograms are very similar to those in Figure 6.8.

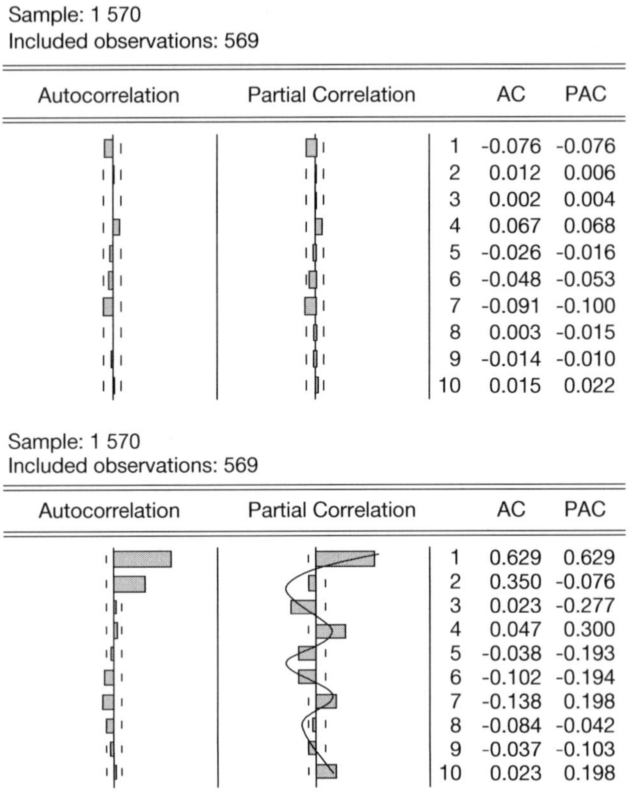
Sample: 1 570
Included observations: 569
Autocorrelation
Partial Correlation
AC
PAC
1 -0.076 -0.076
2 0.012 0.006
3 0.002 0.004
4 0.067 0.068
5 -0.026 -0.016
6 -0.048 -0.053
7 -0.091 -0.100
8 0.003 -0.015
9 -0.014 -0.010
10 0.015 0.022
Sample: 1 570
Included observations: 569
Autocorrelation
Partial Correlation
AC
PAC
1 0.629 0.629
2 0.350 -0.076
3 0.023 -0.277
4 0.047 0.300
5 -0.038 -0.193
6 -0.102 -0.194
7 -0.138 0.198
8 -0.084 -0.042
9 -0.037 -0.103
10 0.023 0.198

FIGURE 6.12 Autocorrelograms of Microsoft Daily Returns Based on the Closing Price (top) and on the 3-day Moving Average Price (bottom)

The process is $Y_t = 0.95\varepsilon_{t-1} + 0.94\varepsilon_{t-2} + \varepsilon_t$. Check that by substituting $\hat{\theta}_1 = 0.95$ and $\hat{\theta}_2 = 0.94$ in the formulas that we have derived in this section

$$\rho_1 = \frac{(\theta_1 + \theta_1\theta_2)}{(1 + \theta_1^2 + \theta_2^2)} \quad \text{and} \quad \rho_2 = \frac{\theta_2}{(1 + \theta_1^2 + \theta_2^2)}$$

you will obtain the estimated autocorrelations $\hat{\rho}_1 = 0.66$ and $\hat{\rho}_2 = 0.34$, which are very close to those that you read from the autocorrelograms in Figure 6.12.

6.3.2.3 What Is the Optimal Forecast Corresponding to an MA(2) Process?

We follow the same steps as in the MA(1) case. For a quadratic loss function, the optimal point forecast is a conditional expectation: $f_{t,h} = \mu_{t+h|t} = E(Y_{t+h}|I_t)$. For an MA(2), we compute this expectation for different forecast horizons $h = 1, 2, \ldots.\ s$. We proceed in two steps: first, write the process at the desired horizon, and second, take the conditional expectation. For instance,

Forecasting Horizon $h = 1$

Write the process at time $t + 1$,

$$Y_{t+1} = \mu + \theta_1 \varepsilon_t + \theta_2 \varepsilon_{t-1} + \varepsilon_{t+1}$$

Take expectation conditioning on the information set up to time t. Observe that ε_t and ε_{t-1} belong to the information set; their values are known at time t; thus, there are no random variables, that is, $E(\varepsilon_t | I_t) = \varepsilon_t$ and $E(\varepsilon_{t-1} | I_t) = \varepsilon_{t-1}$. Additionally, ε_{t+1} is a mean zero white noise process uncorrelated with the information set; thus, $E(\varepsilon_{t+1} | I_t) = E(\varepsilon_{t+1}) = 0$. Putting these pieces together, we ask the following questions:

i. *What is the optimal point forecast $f_{t,1}$?*

$$f_{t,1} = \mu_{t+1|t} = E(Y_{t+1} | I_t) = E(\mu + \theta_1 \varepsilon_t + \theta_2 \varepsilon_{t-1} + \varepsilon_{t+1})$$
$$= \mu + \theta_1 \varepsilon_t + \theta_2 \varepsilon_{t-1}$$

Note that although ε_t and ε_{t-1} belong to the information set, they are not readily observable. They need to be retrieved from past data. This is not a major problem because we have an invertible MA(2), which permits us to write ε_t and ε_{t-1} as a function of past observations, as we did in the case of the MA(1) process.

ii. *What is the one-period-ahead forecast error $e_{t,1}$?*

It must be the difference between the realized value Y_{t+1} and the forecast value $f_{t,1}$

$$e_{t,1} = Y_{t+1} - f_{t,1} = \mu + \theta_1 \varepsilon_t + \theta_2 \varepsilon_{t-1} + \varepsilon_{t+1} - \mu - \theta_1 \varepsilon_t - \theta_2 \varepsilon_{t-1} = \varepsilon_{t+1}$$

It is not very surprising to find out that the forecast error is the component of the process that is not predictable.

iii. *What is the uncertainty associated with the forecast?*

It must be a function of the unpredictability of the process, which is summarized by the variance of the forecast error

$$\sigma^2_{t+1|t} = \mathrm{var}(Y_{t+1} | I_t) = E(Y_{t+1} - f_{t,1} | I_t)^2 = E(e^2_{t,1}) = E(\varepsilon^2_{t+1}) = \sigma^2_\varepsilon$$

iv. *What is the density forecast?*

It is the conditional probability density function of the process at the future date. If we assume that $\{\varepsilon_t\}$ is normally distributed white noise process, the density forecast is

$$f(Y_{t+1} | I_t) \rightarrow N(\mu_{t+1|t}, \sigma^2_{t+1|t}) = N(\mu + \theta_1 \varepsilon_t + \theta_2 \varepsilon_{t-1}, \sigma^2_\varepsilon)$$

From the density forecast, we construct confidence intervals. For instance, a 95% confidence interval is

$$\mu_{t+1|t} \pm 1.96\sigma_{t+1|t} = (\mu_{t+1|t} - 1.96\sigma_{t+1|t}, \mu_{t+1|t} + 1.96\sigma_{t+1|t}),$$

where $1.96 = \Phi^{-1}(0.975)$.

FORECASTING HORIZON $h > 1$

The same steps can be followed to construct the forecast for any desired horizon. As a practice exercise, compute the forecast for $h = 2$ for an MA(2). It is important to understand that, because the MA(q) is also a short memory process, the forecast at a horizon longer than the order of the process collapses to the unconditional moments of the process. For instance let us compute the forecast in the case of an MA(2), for $h = 3$,

i. *What is the optimal point forecast $f_{t,3}$?*

$$f_{t,3} = \mu_{t+3|t} = E(Y_{t+3} | I_t) = E(\mu + \theta_1 \varepsilon_{t+2} + \theta_2 \varepsilon_{t+1} + \varepsilon_{t+3} | I_t) = \mu$$

The future innovations ε_{t+1}, ε_{t+2}, and ε_{t+3} are uncorrelated with past information; thus, they cannot be forecasted given the information set I_t. Past information is not useful when we wish to forecast beyond two periods, and the optimal forecast becomes the unconditional mean of the process because the process cannot further exploit the information set. This is in agreement with the properties of the autocorrelation function in which only the first two autocorrelation coefficients differ from zero: $\rho_1 \neq 0$, $\rho_2 \neq 0$. After two periods, the process does not exhibit any more time dependence, and consequently, the best forecast is the unconditional mean of the process.

ii. *What is the three-period-ahead forecast error $e_{t,3}$?*

It must be the difference between the realized value Y_{t+3} and the forecast value $f_{t,3}$

$$\begin{aligned} e_{t,3} &= Y_{t+3} - f_{t,3} = \mu + \theta_1 \varepsilon_{t+2} + \theta_2 \varepsilon_{t+1} + \varepsilon_{t+3} - \mu \\ &= \theta_1 \varepsilon_{t+2} + \theta_2 \varepsilon_{t+1} + \varepsilon_{t+3} \end{aligned}$$

iii. *What is the uncertainty associated with the forecast?*

It must be a function of the unpredictability of the process, which is summarized by the variance of the forecast error

$$\begin{aligned} \sigma^2_{t+3|t} &= \text{var}(Y_{t+3} | I_t) = E(Y_{t+3} - f_{t,3} | I_t)^2 = E(e^2_{t,3}) \\ &= E(\theta_1 \varepsilon_{t+2} + \theta_2 \varepsilon_{t+1} + \varepsilon_{t+3})^2 = \sigma^2_\varepsilon (1 + \theta_1^2 + \theta_2^2) = \sigma^2_Y \end{aligned}$$

Observe that the uncertainty of the forecast is the unconditional variance of the process. This is again a consequence of the short memory of the MA(2) process.

iv. *What is the density forecast?*

It is the conditional probability density function of the process at the future date. If we assume that $\{\varepsilon_t\}$ is normally distributed white noise process, the density forecast is

$$f(Y_{t+3} | I_t) \rightarrow N(\mu_{t+3|t}, \sigma^2_{t+3|t}) = N(\mu, \sigma^2_Y)$$

The conditional probability density function has collapsed to the unconditional density function of the process.

In summary, forecasting with an MA(q) is limited by the short memory of the process, which depends on the order of the process itself.

KEY WORDS

autoregressive : AR(p), p. 131
invertibility, p. 139
moving average : MA(q), MA(∞), p. 131
short memory, p. 133
smoothed prices, p. 152
technical analysis, p. 152
U.S. Treasury securities, p. 140
white noise, p. 125
Wold decomposition, p. 125

APPENDIX

Wold Decomposition

Sketch of the Proof: The Meaning of Linear "Approximation."

Let us assume that there is not deterministic component, so that the Wold decomposition reduces to $Y_t = \sum_{j=0}^{\infty} \psi_j \varepsilon_{t-j}$. We will show that this linear representation approximates the true process in *a mean-squared sense*. This is to say

$$E\left(Y_t - \sum_{j=0}^{\infty} \psi_j \varepsilon_{t-j}\right)^2 \rightarrow 0$$

Suppose that we start with a finite representation: $Y_t = \sum_{j=0}^{n} \psi_j \varepsilon_{t-j}$, where ε_t are the prediction errors (errors from linear regressions of the process on the information set) explained in point 2 of section 6.2. Because Y_t is linearly regressed on ε_t, ε_{t-1}, ε_{t-2}, ε_{t-3}, ... ε_{t-n} and these are uncorrelated regressors, the regression coefficients are equal to $\psi_j = E(Y_t \varepsilon_{t-j})/\sigma^2$, where $\sigma^2 = E\varepsilon_t^2$. Then,

$$0 \leq E\left(Y_t - \sum_{j=0}^{n} \psi_j \varepsilon_{t-j}\right)^2 = EY_t^2 - 2\sum_{j=0}^{n} \psi_j E(Y_t \varepsilon_{t-j}) + \sigma^2 \sum_{j=0}^{n} \psi_j^2 = EY_t^2 - \sigma^2 \sum_{j=0}^{n} \psi_j^2.$$

Now, as $n \rightarrow \infty$, the quantity $\sigma^2 \sum_{j=0}^{n} \psi_j^2$ cannot exceed EY_t^2 because otherwise the above inequality will not hold. Thus,

$$E\left(Y_t - \sum_{j=0}^{n} \psi_j \varepsilon_{t-j}\right)^2 \rightarrow 0 \text{ as } n \rightarrow \infty$$

and the result follows.

EXERCISES

1. Answer the following questions:

a. Give an example of an economic time series that behaves like a white noise process.

b. Generate 100 observations from a white noise process which is normally distributed with zero mean and variance equal to 4. Compute the sample autocorrelation functions up to lag 10 and comment on their behavior.

c. Download the daily stock indexes for **three** U.S. industries from 2004 to the present. Plot the time series. Compute the autocorrelation functions of the indexes. Compute the returns to the indexes and their corresponding autocorrelation functions. Do you think that an MA process is appropriate to model the index returns? Propose an MA model and forecast 1-day, 2-day, 3-day, and 4-day-ahead index returns. Compute your forecast error, and a 95% confidence interval for your forecasts.

2. Consider the following two MA (1) processes

$$y_t = 1.2 + 0.8\varepsilon_{t-1} + \varepsilon_t$$
$$y_t = 1.2 + 1.25\varepsilon_{t-1} + \varepsilon_t$$

What similarities/differences do you expect to see in their autocorrelations? Now, simulate 100 observations from each of these processes. Compute their sample autocorrelation functions up to lag 10 and observe that they exhibit the same pattern. Which representation is invertible?

3. Consider the following MA(1) process

$$y_t = 2.3 - 0.95\varepsilon_{t-1} + \varepsilon_t, \quad \varepsilon_t \rightarrow i.i.d. \quad N(0,1)$$

Given a quadratic loss function, calculate the optimal forecast for $h = 1, 2, 3$, variance of the forecast error and density forecast. Your information set contains information up to time t. It may be useful to know that $\varepsilon_t = 0.4$, $\varepsilon_{t-1} = -1.2$.

4. Consider the following MA(2) process

$$y_t = 0.7 - 2\varepsilon_{t-1} + 1.35\varepsilon_{t-2} + \varepsilon_t$$

ε_t is a white noise process, normally distributed with zero mean and unit variance.

a. Obtain the *theoretical* autocorrelation function up to lag 10.

b. Now, simulate the process for $t = 1, 2, \ldots, 100$ and compute the *sample* autocorrelation function up to lag 10. Comment and compare with your results in a.

5. Consider the same MA(2) process in exercise 4.

a. Estimate an MA(2) process with the artificial data generated in exercise 4. Comment on the differences with the theoretical model.

b. Compute the 1, 2, and 3-step ahead forecasts. Your information set contains information up to time t. It may be useful to know that $\varepsilon_t = 0.4$, $\varepsilon_{t-1} = -1.2$.

6. Obtain the corresponding autoregressive representation of the processes

$$y_t = 1.2 + 0.8\varepsilon_{t-1} + \varepsilon_t$$
$$y_t = 1.2 + 1.25\varepsilon_{t-1} + \varepsilon_t$$

Based on these representations, which process do you prefer for forecasting purposes? Explain.

7. Update the data set "5-year constant maturity yield on Treasury securities" in section 6.3.1. Conduct a similar analysis to that in section 6.3.1: propose an MA process, estimate an MA model, and forecast at several horizons. What differences or similarities do you find?

8. Download different Treasury yields (shorter and longer than 5-year term) and analyze their autocorrelations. Are they different from those in exercise 7?

9. Update the data set on Microsoft prices in section 6.3.2. With these prices, construct a smoothed price based on a moving average of order four, calculate the returns based on the smoothed prices, compute the autocorrelation functions, and comment on your findings.

10. Download financial prices of your favorite stocks. Obtain the autocorrelation functions. Which process(es) will fit the financial returns to these stocks? Propose a model, estimate it, and forecast at several horizons.

CHAPTER 7

Forecasting with Autoregressive (AR) Processes

In this chapter, we introduce the autoregressive processes that are very well suited to model cyclical fluctuations. A *cycle* is defined as fluctuations in the data that happen at periodic intervals. All of us can relate very well to the concept of cycles. For instance, in U.S. economic history, we find episodes referred as *expansions* (positive growth in economic output, e.g., 1992–2000) as opposed to *recessions* (negative or slow growth, e.g., 2001–2003, 2008–?), *bubbles* (exuberant prices, e.g., the technology bubble of the late 1990s or the housing bubble of the late 2000s) as opposed to *busts* (rapid price decline, e.g., the 1929 stock market crash or the market crash of 2008); *inflation* (rapid price growth, e.g., in the United States in 1980s) as opposed to *deflation* (severe price decline, e.g., the Japanese experience of the 1990s). In moving from expansions to recessions, from bubbles to busts, from inflation to deflation, history is creating time series data characterized by cycles.

Examine the four time series plots in Figure 7.1. Plots 7.1a, 7.1b, and 7.1d provide information on a variety of economic issues in the United States such as unemployment, poverty, and house sales. Plot 7.1c is a signal delivered by a physical device. What do the four time series have in common? In all four, we detect a cyclical pattern although the pattern is more predictable in some than in others. Additionally, the cycles have different durations: Some are longer than others. The unemployment plot (7.1a) exhibits a long cycle (10 years) from the 1991 recession to the 2001 recession. As the economy expands, the number of unemployed people decreases, and as the economy enters in a recession, unemployment increases. The *poverty plot* (7.1b) contains two time series: One is the number of people in poverty, and the other is the poverty rate. In both of them, we detect cyclical movements. The poverty plot exhibits a longer history than that of plot (7.1a) (from 1959) and shows several cycles amid a soft downward secular trend in the poverty rate. During recessions (expansions), the poverty rate and the number of people living in poverty increase (decrease). The house sales plot (7.1d) describes the real estate cycle in California in the 1990s. The 1991 recession was longer in California than in the rest of the United States. The real estate sector was depressed until 1995 when the economic activity of the state entered into an expansion phase. Finally, the fourth plot (7.1c) pictures a physical signal. Focus on the labeled "adjusted

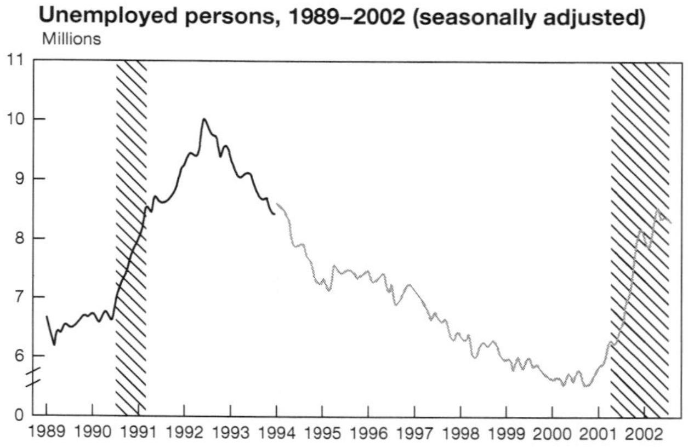

(a)

Note: Shaded areas represent recessions. Break in series in January 1994 is due to the redesign of the survey.

Source: Bureau of Labor Statistics. Current Population Survey.

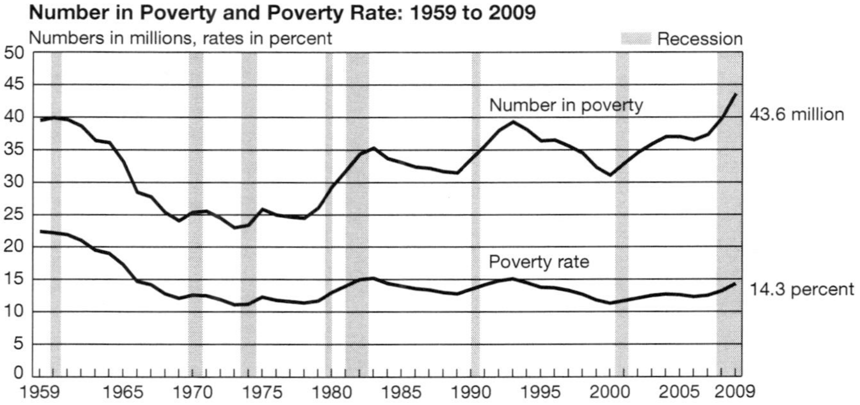

(b)

Note: The data points represent the midpoints of the respective years. The latest recession began in June 1990 and ended in March 1991.

Source: U.S. Census Bureau. Current Population Survey, March 1960–2001.

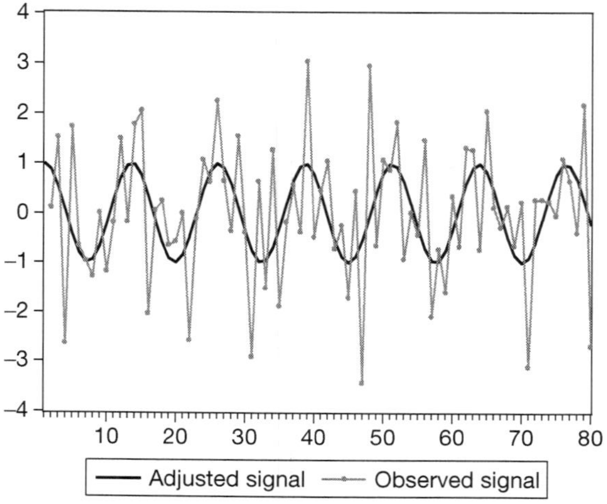

(c)

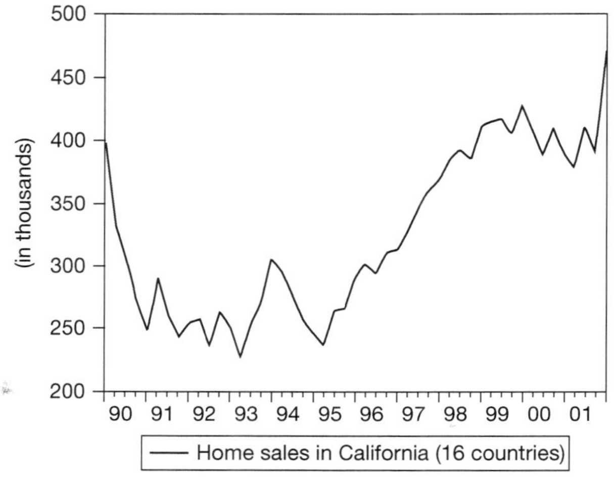

(d)

FIGURE 7.1 A Variety of Time Series Cycles

signal" lines. This is a signal extracted from a "noisy" device. The cycle in plot (7.1c) differs from those of the other three plots. The main difference is its predictability. Every thirteen periods, the series repeats itself, and the cycle keeps its shape forever.

We conclude that, if the cycles are different across plots, there must be different mechanisms to generate them. How can we uncover the mechanism? How can we take advantage of it? These are the broad questions that this chapter will answer. We introduce a set of time series models that will replicate cycles such as those in Figure 7.1 and will explain the pattern of time dependence. Ultimately, we exploit the time dependence to construct a forecast.

7.1 Cycles

The time series plots in Figure 7.1 have different cycles. Some are more predictable, longer, and deeper than others, but in all cases, we detect periodicity or repetition of events. Thus, we define

A cycle is a time series pattern of periodic fluctuations.

We distinguish between deterministic and stochastic cycles. In Figure 7.1, the signal detection plot (7.1c) is an example of a deterministic cycle, and the unemployment time series plot (7.1a) is an example of a stochastic cycle.

A **deterministic cycle** is common in the physical sciences, engineering, geophysics, and so on, and the stochastic cycle is very prevalent in economics and business data. Although we will focus on stochastic cycles, let us briefly introduce an example of the deterministic cycle to observe how a fixed-periodic pattern emerges. Simulate artificial data from the following model:

$$Y_t = 2\cos(0.5t + 0.78) + \varepsilon_t \quad \text{for } t = 1, 2, \ldots 40$$

where t is time (running in a predictable fashion, $t = 1, 2, 3 \ldots$), ε_t is a random variable that is normally distributed with mean zero and variance equal to 0.64, $\varepsilon_t \rightarrow N(0, 0.64)$, and "cos(. . .)" is the *cosine* function that generates cycles with a fixed periodicity. This is a model that has a deterministic component given by the cosine function of a deterministic variable ($t = 1, 2, 3 \ldots$) and an unpredictable component (or noisy component) given by ε_t. Type the following statement in the command line of EViews and plot the generated series y_t (Figure 7.2): `y = 2*(cos(0.5*@trend(1)+0.78))+0.8*nrnd`

Note that `0.8*nrnd` is the normal random variable with standard deviation equal to 0.8, and the function `@trend(1)` generates a time index starting at 1 and increasing by one unit at a time. The time series in Figure 7.2 looks very similar to that in Figure 7.1c. In Figure 7.2, the deterministic cycle has been overlaid on the time series y_t. Observe that for each t, the vertical distance between the deterministic component and the time series is the contribution of the unpredictable component. When the variance of the unpredictable component ε_t is larger, we will observe a time series with larger deviations from the deterministic component.

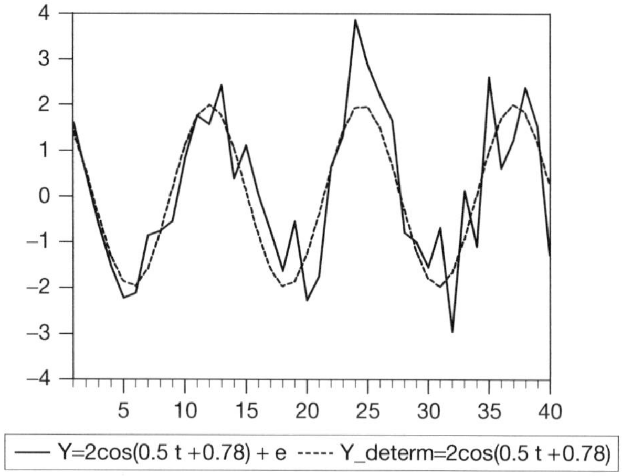

FIGURE 7.2 Deterministic Cycle

Most importantly for economic and business data is the **stochastic cycle**. We say that *a cycle is stochastic when it is generated by random variables*. The process at time t, Y_t, is a function of previous random variables such as $Y_{t-1}, Y_{t-2}, \ldots$. An example of a stochastic cycle is a model such as $Y_t = 0.5Y_{t-1} + 0.3Y_{t-2} + \varepsilon_t$, which will be analyzed in following sections. Observe that in the right-hand side of the model, we have random variables. By contrast, in a model with a deterministic cycle like that of Figure 7.2, the right-hand side is a function of a time index, which is purely a deterministic variable.

The main tools to discover the model that gives rise to stochastic cycles are the autocorrelation and partial autocorrelation functions. Recall that the autocorrelation functions inform about the dependence between random variables in different periods of time. For instance, ρ_5 is the autocorrelation between Y_t and Y_{t-5}, that is, between today and five periods ago, but ρ_5 is also the autocorrelation between Y_t and Y_{t+5}, that is, between today and five periods into the future (assuming that the process is stationary). Thus, the autocorrelation functions, which help us to understand the past dependence, also help us to predict the dependence between today's information and the future.

Let us start by developing some intuition. In Figure 7.3, we show a time series of unemployment in which we have selected four sections: A, B, C, and D. You can find these data at the Bureau of Labor Statistics website, http://data.bls.gov. Look at the plot and answer the following three questions:

1. What is the sign of the autocorrelation between observations located within section A (or B or C or D)?
2. What is the sign of the autocorrelation between the observations in section A and those in section B (or in C and D)?
3. What is the sign of the autocorrelation between the observations in section A and those in section D?

FIGURE 7.3 Unemployed Persons, 1989–2002 (Seasonally Adjusted)

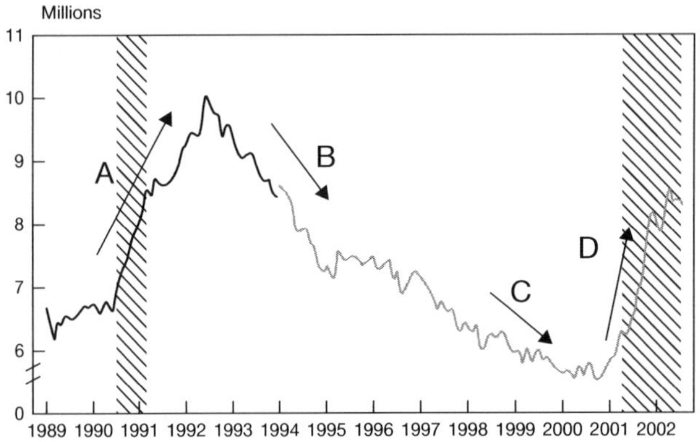

Note: Shaded areas represent recessions. Break in series in January 1994 is due to the redesign of the survey.

Source: Bureau of Labor Statistics. Current Population Survey.

If you answered (1) positive, (2) negative, (3) positive, you were right. Let us analyze why it is so.

1. *Positive.* Observations within A (or B or C or D) are one or two years apart and we observe that, in this *short interval* of time, the unemployment keeps increasing (section A and section D) or keeps decreasing (section B and section C). Computing the autocorrelation between observations one and two years apart, we obtain $\rho_1 = 0.67$ and $\rho_2 = 0.14$.
2. *Negative.* Observations in A and B (or C and D) are four or five years apart and, in this *medium interval* of time, when unemployment goes up in A, unemployment in B goes down, or when unemployment goes down in C, it goes up in D. Thus, the autocorrelation between observations in A and B (or C and D) is negative. The autocorrelation coefficients are $\rho_4 = -0.32$ and $\rho_5 = -0.35$.
3. *Positive.* Observations in A and D are 10 or 11 years apart. In this *long interval,* the unemployment in A and B moves in the same direction; in both sections, it goes up. The autocorrelation coefficients are $\rho_{10} = 0.26$ and $\rho_{11} = 0.31$.

Depending on the time horizon, the autocorrelation could be positive or negative as is expected in a cycle. We just calculated the autocorrelation function but we did not find the mechanism/model that generates this function. This is our next goal, which is summarized in the following question: *Which statistical model(s) can generate the observed autocorrelation functions?*

Our task ahead is to associate different models with different shapes of the autocorrelation function. In doing so, we generate a library of autocorrelation functions with their corresponding models. When facing a real time series, we compute its autocorrelation, we will search our library, and we will retrieve the model(s) that most closely approximates the estimated autocorrelation function.

7.2 Autoregressive Models

Recall a regression model. As we saw in Chapter 2, the question of interest in a linear regression is to find out the conditional mean of the variable of interest, say Y. In a linear regression, we model $E(Y|X) = \beta_0 + \beta_1 X_1 + \beta_2 X_2 + \cdots + \beta_k X_k$. The conditional mean of Y is a linear function of a set of regressors or explanatory variables $X = \{X_1, X_2, \ldots X_k\}$. Suppose that the set of regressors is $X = \{Y_{t-1}, Y_{t-2}, \ldots Y_{t-p}\}$, which in previous chapters we called the *information set;* then we write $E(Y_t | Y_{t-1}, Y_{t-2}, \ldots Y_{t-p}) = c + \phi_1 Y_{t-1} + \phi_2 Y_{t-2} + \cdots + \phi_p Y_{t-p}$ (the change of notation from βs to ϕs is innocuous). Now it is easy to understand the word *autoregressive (AR)*: it means a regression model in which the dependent variable and the regressors belong to the same stochastic process, and Y_t is regressed on itself (Y_t on $Y_{t-1}, Y_{t-2}, \ldots Y_{t-p}$).

We define:

An autoregressive model of order $p \geq 0$, referred as AR(p), has the following functional form

$$Y_t = c + \phi_1 Y_{t-1} + \phi_2 Y_{t-2} + \cdots + \phi_p Y_{t-p} + \varepsilon_t$$

where ε_t is a white noise process.

The order is given by the largest lag in the right-hand side of the model. For instance, a model such as $Y_t = c + \phi_2 Y_{t-2} + \varepsilon_t$ is an **autoregressive process AR(2)** even though it has only one regressor in the right-hand side.

To familiarize ourselves with autoregressive process, we start with the lowest order **autoregressive process AR(1)** and AR(2). Once we understand the issues, we will generalize to an **autoregressive process AR(*p*)**. For each process, there are three questions to answer:

1. What does a time series of an AR process look like?
2. What do the corresponding autocorrelation functions look like?
3. What is the optimal forecast?

7.2.1 The AR(1) Process

Let us proceed to answer Question (1) by simulating some time series of a process such as

$$Y_t = c + \phi Y_{t-1} + \varepsilon_t$$

for different values of the parameter ϕ. In the command line of EViews, type a little program as follows:

```
smpl @first @first
series y=0
smpl @first+1 @last
series y=1+0.4*y(-1)+0.5*nrnd
```

FIGURE 7.4 Autoregressive Processes AR(1)

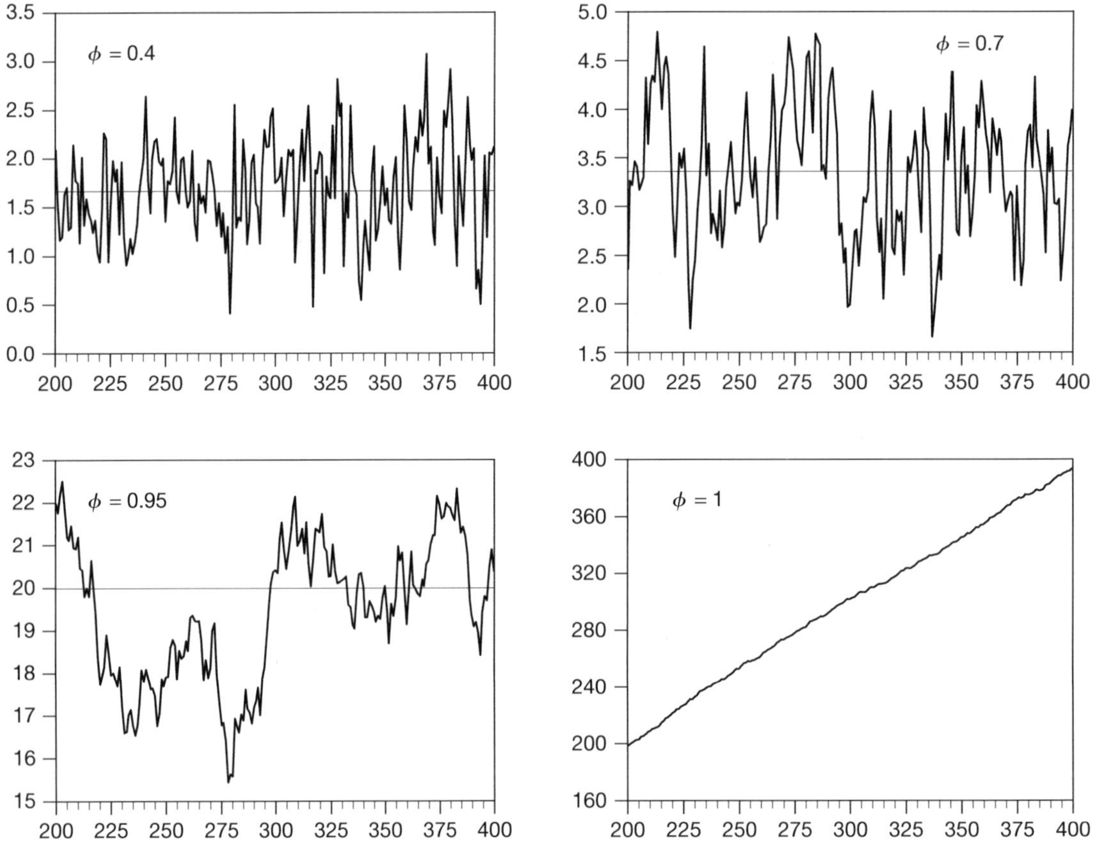

This program means that the initial observation of the process is zero and the parameters are $c = 1$ and $\phi = 0.4$. The white noise has zero mean and standard deviation 0.5. In Figure 7.4, we present four time series for different values of $\phi = 0.4$, 0.7, 0.95, 1.0. All of them have the same constant $c = 1$ and the same white noise process $\varepsilon_t \rightarrow N(0, 0.25)$.

7.2.1.1 What Does a Time Series of an AR(1) Process Look Like?

Observe that different values of the autoregressive parameter ϕ can generate very different time series. When ϕ becomes larger, the series becomes smoother. The time series with $\phi = 0.4$, 0.7, 0.95 are more similar to each other than to the time series with $\phi = 1$. The parameter ϕ is called the **persistence** parameter. Contrast the plot for

$\phi = 0.4$ with the plot for $\phi = 0.95$. Note that in the latter, the series remain for longer periods of time either above or below the unconditional mean of the process (the horizontal line). We say that the process with $\phi = 0.95$ is more persistent than the process with $\phi = 0.4$. The plot for $\phi = 0.7$ is an intermediate case between the previous two. Then what can we say about the process with $\phi = 1$? Is it extremely persistent? The obvious feature of this process is that it exhibits an upward trend and does not mean revert because there is not a constant unconditional mean to which to revert. As we saw in Chapter 3, this is the case of a nonstationary process. In time series, this process is also known as a *random walk with drift*, which we will analyze in Chapter 10, *Forecasting the Long Term*. In this chapter, we focus exclusively on covariance-stationary processes. In light of the preceding, we establish the following property:

A necessary and sufficient condition for an AR(1) process $Y_t = c + \phi Y_{t-1} + \varepsilon_t$ to be covariance stationary is that $|\phi| < 1$.

We proceed to answer the following question:

7.2.1.2 What Do the Corresponding Autocorrelation Functions Look Like?

In Figure 7.5, we plot the corresponding autocorrelograms of the three stationary processes in Figure 7.4.

The autocorrelation functions of an AR(1) process have three distinctive features:

1. $\rho_1 = r_1 = \phi$. Note that the autocorrelation (AC) and partial autocorrelation (PAC) functions are just estimated autocorrelations based on only one time series; thus, we should expect some sampling error. This is why we have in the first plot $\hat{\rho}_1 = 0.33$, which is close enough to the population parameter 0.4. In the other two plots, the estimated parameters are numerically close to the population parameters: $\hat{\rho}_1 = 0.73$ and $\hat{\rho}_1 = 0.95$.
2. The autocorrelation function, AC decreases exponentially toward zero, and the decay is faster when the persistence parameter is smaller. A more persistent process has larger autocorrelations. The exponential decay is given by the formula $\rho_k = \phi^k$. For instance, check the process with persistence parameter $\phi = 0.95$: $\rho_1 = 0.95$, $\rho_2 = 0.95^2 = 0.90$, $\rho_3 = 0.95^3 = 0.86$, and so on. Read the AC and confirm that the estimated correlations are practically the same as the population autocorrelations.
3. The partial autocorrelation function is characterized by only one spike $r_1 \neq 0$, and the remaining $r_k = 0$ for $k > 1$. Read the estimated PAC values and confirm that r_k for $k > 1$ is practically zero.

You may be wondering what happens when $\phi < 0$. Simulate a time series from an AR(1) process with $\phi = -0.9$ and calculate its autocorrelation functions. You will obtain plots similar to those in Figure 7.6.

The process in Figure 7.6 is covariance-stationary (why?), and the autocorrelation functions exhibit the three features that we just discussed. Note that the alternating

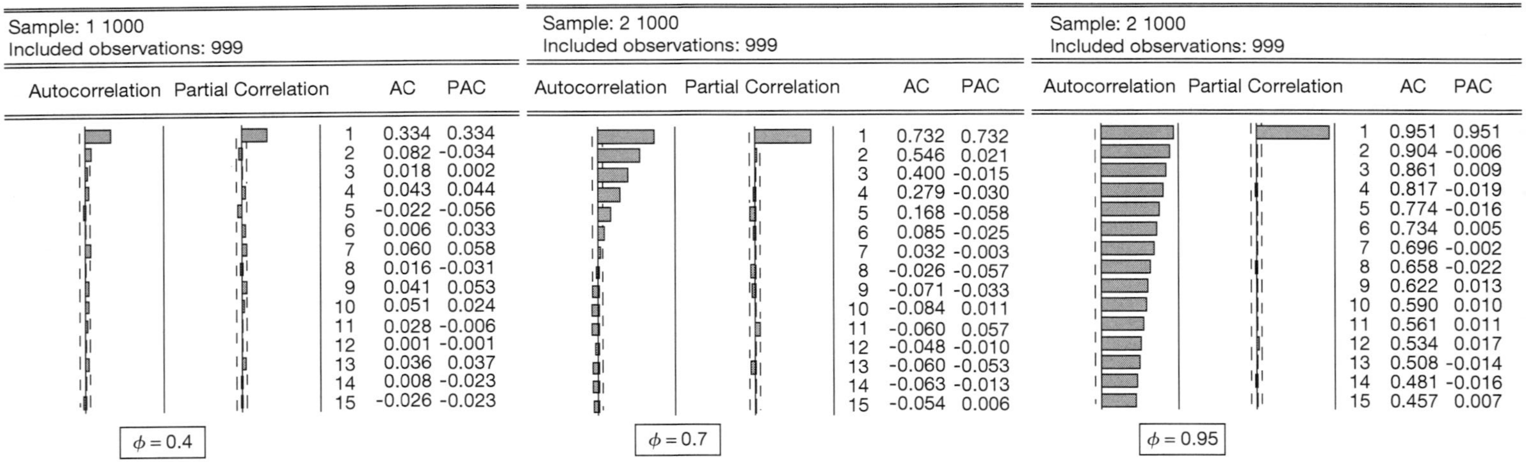

FIGURE 7.5 Autocorrelation Functions of Covariance-Stationary AR(1) Processes

FIGURE 7.6 Time Series Plot and Autocorrelation Functions of AR(1) with Negative Parameter

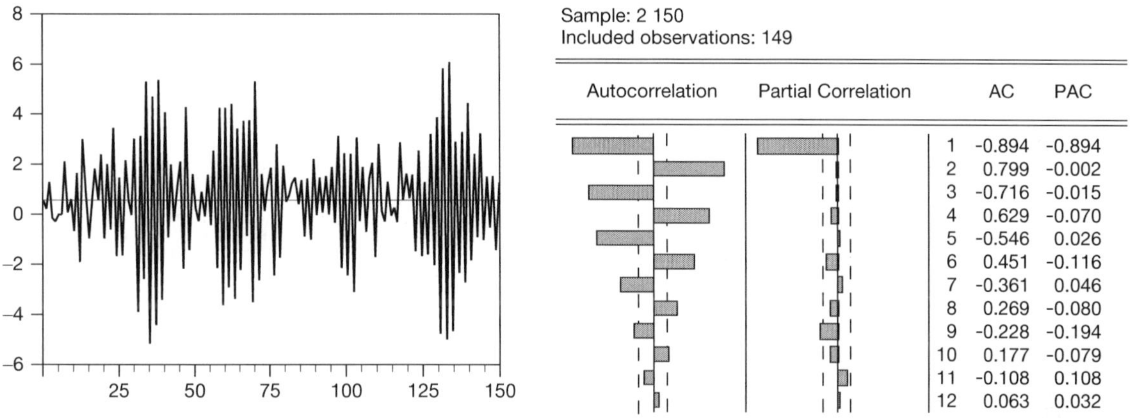

	AC	PAC
1	-0.894	-0.894
2	0.799	-0.002
3	-0.716	-0.015
4	0.629	-0.070
5	-0.546	0.026
6	0.451	-0.116
7	-0.361	0.046
8	0.269	-0.080
9	-0.228	-0.194
10	0.177	-0.079
11	-0.108	0.108
12	0.063	0.032

FIGURE 7.7 Per Capita Income Growth (California, 1969–2002)

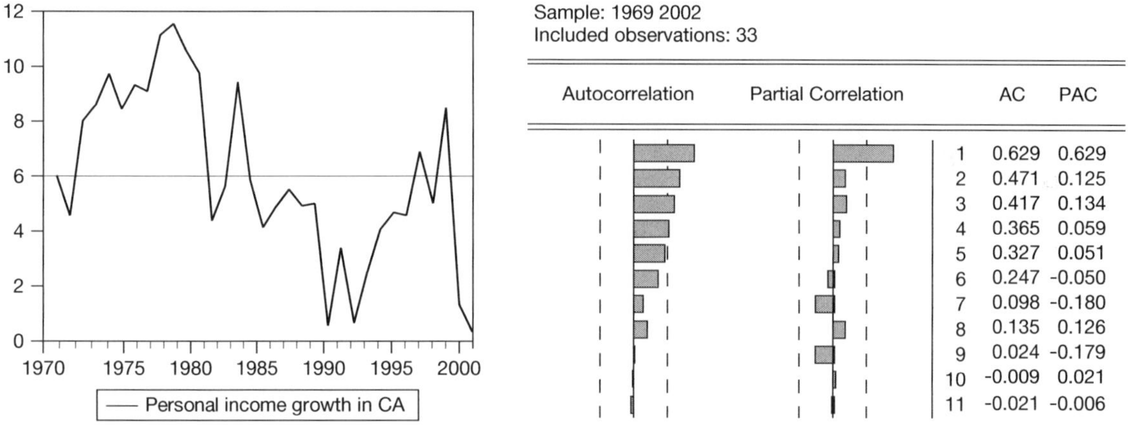

	AC	PAC
1	0.629	0.629
2	0.471	0.125
3	0.417	0.134
4	0.365	0.059
5	0.327	0.051
6	0.247	-0.050
7	0.098	-0.180
8	0.135	0.126
9	0.024	-0.179
10	-0.009	0.021
11	-0.021	-0.006

autocorrelations (negative for odd lags and positive for even lags) are consequences of the negative sign of the persistence parameter, which also causes the zigzaggy behavior that we observe in the time series plot.

REAL DATA: Per Capita Personal Income Growth in California, 1969–2002

Autoregressive processes are common in economic and business data. In Figure 7.7, we plot the growth of per capita personal income in California from 1969 to 2002 (the data are not adjusted by inflation) and its estimated autocorrelation functions. In the recession at the beginning of the 1990s, California income grew at a low rate of 0.5% and in the recession of 2001–2002 at 0.3%, well below the average growth of 6% in this period.

Compare Figure 7.7 with Figures 7.4 and 7.5. Does Figure 7.7 look like an autoregressive process AR(1)? Yes, the AC decays smoothly toward zero, and the PAC has one relevant spike.

Is the process persistent? What is the persistence parameter? It is mildly persistent, so we read from the AC or PAC that $\hat{\phi} = 0.63$.

Investigate whether personal income in other states follows a similar process. You will find a wealth of economic data for the United States and for regional and local economies in the site of the Bureau of Economic Analysis, http://www.bea.gov.

7.2.1.3 What Is the Optimal Forecast Corresponding to an AR(1) Process?

Recall from Chapter 4 that the **optimal forecast** $f_{t,h}$ depends on the loss function chosen by the forecaster. Let us choose a quadratic loss function. Accordingly, the optimal point forecast is a conditional expectation: $f_{t,h} = \mu_{t+h|t} = E(Y_{t+h} | I_t)$. For AR(1), we compute this expectation for different forecast horizons $h = 1, 2, \ldots . s$. We proceed in two steps: first, we write the process at the desired horizon, and second, we take the conditional expectation. For instance,

FORECASTING HORIZON $h = 1$

Write the process at time $t + 1$,

$$Y_{t+1} = c + \phi Y_t + \varepsilon_{t+1}$$

Take expectation conditioning on the information set up to time t. Observe that Y_t belongs to the information set and its value is known; thus, it is not a random variable any more: $E(Y_t | I_t) = Y_t$. Additionally, ε_{t+1} is a mean zero white noise process uncorrelated with the information set; thus, $E(\varepsilon_{t+1} | I_t) = 0$. Putting these pieces together, we ask the following questions:

i. *What is the optimal point forecast $f_{t,1}$?*

$$f_{t,1} = \mu_{t+1|t} = E(Y_{t+1} | I_t) = E(c + \phi Y_t + \varepsilon_{t+1}) = c + \phi Y_t$$

ii. *What is the 1-period-ahead forecast error $e_{t,1}$?*
It must be the difference between the realized value Y_{t+1} and the forecast value $f_{t,1}$:

$$e_{t,1} = Y_{t+1} - f_{t,1} = c + \phi Y_t + \varepsilon_{t+1} - c - \phi Y_t = \varepsilon_{t+1}$$

It is not very surprising to find out that the forecast error is the component of the process that is not predictable.

iii. *What is the uncertainty associated with the forecast?*
It must be a function of the unpredictability of the process, which is summarized in the variance of the forecast error

$$\sigma^2_{t+1|t} = \text{var}(Y_{t+1} \,|\, I_t) = E(Y_{t+1} - f_{t,1} \,|\, I_t)^2 = E(e^2_{t,1}) = E(\varepsilon^2_{t+1}) = \sigma^2_\varepsilon$$

iv. *What is the density forecast?*

The **density forecast** is the conditional probability density function of the process at the future date. If we assume that $\{\varepsilon_t\}$ is a normally distributed white noise process, the density forecast is

$$f(Y_{t+1} \,|\, I_t) \rightarrow N(\mu_{t+1|t}, \sigma^2_{t+1|t}) = N(c + \phi Y_t, \sigma^2_\varepsilon)$$

From the density forecast, we construct confidence intervals. For instance, a 95% confidence interval is

$$\mu_{t+1|t} \pm 1.96\sigma_{t+1|t} = (\mu_{t+1|t} - 1.96\sigma_{t+1|t}, \mu_{t+1|t} + 1.96\sigma_{t+1|t})$$

where $1.96 = \Phi^{-1}(0.975)$, and $\Phi^{-1}(.)$ is the inverse of the cumulative distribution function of a $N(0, 1)$ random variable. To understand the latter statement, remember that the bell-shaped density function of a standardized normal random variable $Z \rightarrow N(0, 1)$ allows for 2.5% probability in each of the upper and lower tails so that 95% probability lies in the middle body of the density function, and then $\Pr(-1.96 \leq Z \leq 1.96) = 0.95$.

Forecasting Horizon $h = 2$

We follow the same step as in the previous case. The algebra is slightly more complicated but straightforward.

i. *What is the optimal point forecast $f_{t,2}$?*

$$\begin{aligned} f_{t,2} = \mu_{t+2|t} &= E(Y_{t+2} \,|\, I_t) = E(c + \phi Y_{t+1} + \varepsilon_{t+2} \,|\, I_t) \\ &= c + \phi E(Y_{t+1} \,|\, I_t) = c(1 + \phi) + \phi^2 Y_t \end{aligned}$$

The last equality follows from direct substitution of the 1-period-ahead forecast calculated in the previous case. Observe that if the information set is I_t, the forecast must be a function of known information up to time t.

ii. *What is the 2-period-ahead forecast error $e_{t,2}$?*
It must be the difference between the realized value Y_{t+2} and the forecast value $f_{t,2}$:

$$e_{t,2} = Y_{t+2} - f_{t,2} = c + \phi Y_{t+1} + \varepsilon_{t+2} - (c + \phi f_{t,1}) = \phi\varepsilon_{t+1} + \varepsilon_{t+2}$$

iii. *What is the uncertainty associated with the forecast?*
It must be a function of the unpredictability of the process, which is summarized by the variance of the forecast error:

$$\sigma^2_{t+2|t} = \text{var}(Y_{t+2}|I_t) = E(Y_{t+2} - f_{t,2}|I_t)^2 = E(e^2_{t,2}) = E(\phi\varepsilon_{t+1} + \varepsilon_{t+2})^2$$
$$= \sigma^2_\varepsilon(1 + \phi^2)$$

The last equality uses the no autocorrelation property that characterizes a white noise process.

iv. *What is the density forecast?*

It is the conditional probability density function of the process at the future date. Under the normality assumption, the density forecast is:

$$f(Y_{t+2}|I_t) \rightarrow N(\mu_{t+2|t}, \sigma^2_{t+2|t})$$

Generalizing for any horizon, we can say

FORECASTING HORIZON $h = s$

i. *What is the optimal point forecast $f_{t,s}$?*

$$f_{t,s} = \mu_{t+s|t} = E(Y_{t+s}|I_t) = c(1 + \phi + \phi^2 + \ldots\ldots \phi^{s-1}) + \phi^s Y_t$$

ii. *What is the s-period-ahead forecast error $e_{t,s}$?*

$$e_{t,s} = Y_{t+s} - f_{t,s} = \varepsilon_{t+s} + \phi\,\varepsilon_{t+s-1} + \phi^2\,\varepsilon_{t+s-2} + \ldots\ldots \phi^{s-1}\varepsilon_{t+1}$$

iii. *What is the uncertainty associated with the forecast?*

$$\sigma^2_{t+s|t} = \text{var}(Y_{t+s}|I_t) = E(Y_{t+s} - f_{t,s}|I_t)^2 = E(e^2_{t,s})$$
$$= \sigma^2_\varepsilon(1 + \phi^2 + \phi^4 + \ldots \phi^{2(s-1)})$$

iv. *What is the density forecast?*

$$f(Y_{t+s}|I_t) \rightarrow N(\mu_{t+s|t}, \sigma^2_{t+s|t})$$

It is of interest to understand what the forecast looks like when the forecasting horizon is very large. Remember that we deal with a covariance-stationary process for which $|\phi| < 1$; thus, ϕ^s will converge to zero for large values of s. For $s \rightarrow \infty$, the optimal forecast does not depend on the information set, so it converges to a constant value[1]:

$$f_{t,s} = c(1 + \phi + \phi^2 + \phi^3 + \cdots) = \frac{c}{1 - \phi}$$

$$\sigma^2_{t+s|t} = \sigma^2_\varepsilon(1 + \phi^2 + \phi^4 + \phi^6 + \cdots) = \frac{\sigma^2_\varepsilon}{1 - \phi^2}$$

[1]For $\phi < 1$, $S = 1 + \phi + \phi^2 + \phi^3 + \cdots = \frac{1}{1 - \phi}$.

Note that the optimal forecast is the *unconditional mean* of the process and that the variance of the forecast error is the *unconditional variance* of the process. To see these results, take expectations in the model to obtain:

$$E(Y_t) = c + \phi E(Y_{t-1}) + E(\varepsilon_t)$$

The process is stationary; thus, $\mu \equiv E(Y_t) = E(Y_{t-1})$, and ε_t is a zero mean white noise process. Then $\mu = c + \phi\mu$, and solving for $\mu = \frac{c}{1-\phi}$, we have the unconditional mean of the process. We proceed likewise to calculate the variance of the process. Using the properties of the variance and recalling that the white noise is uncorrelated with the information set, we write

$$\text{var}(Y_t) = \phi^2 \text{var}(Y_{t-1}) + \text{var}(\varepsilon_t)$$

Because the process is covariance stationary, we know that $\sigma_Y^2 \equiv \text{var}(Y_t) = \text{var}(Y_{t-1})$. Then $\sigma_Y^2 = \phi^2\sigma_Y^2 + \sigma_\varepsilon^2$, and solving for $\sigma_Y^2 = \frac{\sigma_\varepsilon^2}{1-\phi^2}$, we obtain the unconditional variance of the process.

For long horizons, the convergence of the optimal forecast to the unconditional moments of the process is a consequence of the *short memory* of the AR(1), which is linked to the condition $|\phi| < 1$ required for the process to be covariance stationary. The convergence is faster when the parameter ϕ is smaller. In summary, forecasting with an AR(1) is limited by the magnitude of the persistence parameter. In this sense, we say that these models are well suited to forecast the short/medium term; in the long term, the forecast converges to the unconditional mean of the process.

7.2.2 AR(2) Process

The analysis of the AR(2) process proceeds in the same fashion as the AR(1) does. The functional form of an AR(2) process is:

$$Y_t = c + \phi_1 Y_{t-1} + \phi_2 Y_{t-2} + \varepsilon_t$$

Let us start by simulating this process for different values of the parameters c, ϕ_1, ϕ_2.

In the command line of EViews, type the following small program:

```
smpl @first @first + 1
series y = 0
smpl @first + 2 @last
series y = 1 + y(-1)-0.5*y(-2) + nrnd
```

We have set the two initial observations of the process to zero and the parameters are $c = 1$, $\phi_1 = 1$, and $\phi_2 = -0.5$. The white noise has zero mean and standard deviation 1. See three simulated time series from three different AR(2) processes in Figure 7.8. In all of them, the white noise process is distributed as $\varepsilon_t \rightarrow N(0, 1)$.

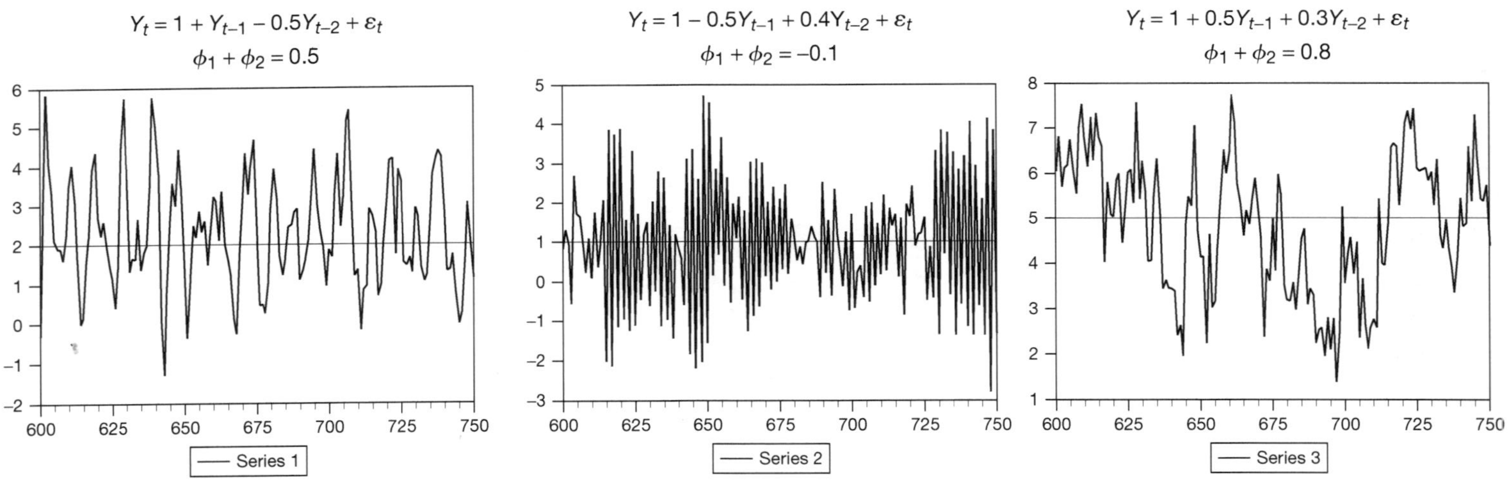

FIGURE 7.8 Autoregressive Processes AR(2)

7.2.2.1 What Does a Time Series of an AR(2) Process Look Like?

Let us analyze the differences among these three plots. What can we say about the persistence of the process? Compare the three series and observe their behavior around their respective unconditional means (horizontal lines). It seems that series 3 is more persistent than series 1, and this in turn is more persistent than series 2. Series 3 remains either above or below its mean for longer periods than series 1, but the three cases have a mean-reverting behavior. The persistence measure in an AR(2) is $\phi_1 + \phi_2$; this sum is larger in series 3 than in series 1 and series 2.

The issue of stationarity in AR(2) is more complex than that in the AR(1) case. It is not enough to require the persistence of the process to be less than 1 (i.e., $\phi_1 + \phi_2 < 1$) to guarantee that the process is covariance stationary. We need the following restrictions:

The necessary conditions for an AR(2) process to be covariance stationary are

$$-1 < \phi_2 < 1$$

$$-2 < \phi_1 < 2$$

and the sufficient conditions are

$$\phi_1 + \phi_2 < 1$$

$$\phi_2 - \phi_1 < 1$$

How are these conditions used? Once the parameters of the AR(2) are known, we proceed as follows. First, we check whether the necessary conditions are satisfied. If they are, we check the sufficient conditions. If they are satisfied, the process is covariance stationary. If the necessary conditions are not satisfied, the process is not covariance stationary. The three processes in Figure 7.8 satisfy the necessary and sufficient conditions for covariance stationarity. We can simulate processes for which these conditions are not satisfied and analyze the results. For instance, simulate a process for which $\phi_1 = \phi_2 = 0.5$. The necessary conditions are satisfied, but one of the sufficient conditions ($\phi_1 + \phi_2 = 1$) is not. A simulated time series from this process looks like series 4 in Figure 7.9. The time series exhibits an upward tendency. There is not a constant unconditional mean; thus, the process is not covariance stationary.[2]

---

[2]If you are versed in algebra, you could solve for the roots of the following equation (known as the *characteristic equation*):

$$1 - \phi_1 x - \phi_2 x^2 = 0$$

An AR(2) process is covariance stationary if the absolute value of the roots of the characteristic equation are strictly greater than 1. For the example where $\phi_1 = \phi_2 = 0.5$, the absolute values of the roots are equal to 2 and 1. Because 1 is exactly equal to 1, the process is *not* covariance stationary.

FIGURE 7.9 Nonstationary AR(2)

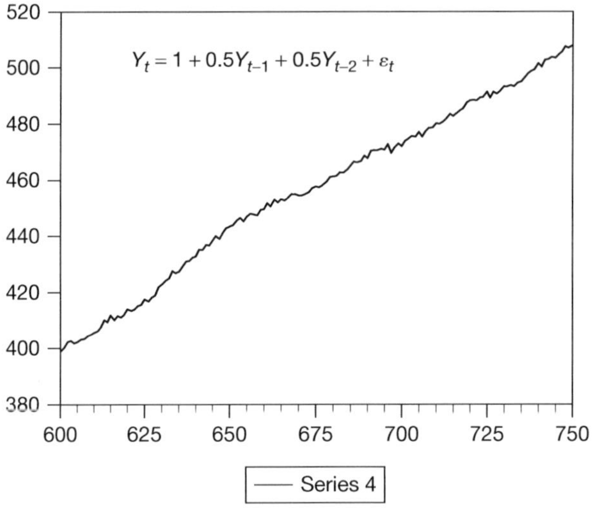

The unconditional mean of a stationary AR(2) process is obtained by taking expectations in the model

$$E(Y_t) = c + \phi_1 E(Y_{t-1}) + \phi_2 E(Y_{t-2}) + E(\varepsilon_t)$$

Because the process is stationary, we know that $\mu \equiv E(Y_t) = E(Y_{t-1}) = E(Y_{t-2})$. In addition, ε_t is a zero mean white noise process. Then $\mu = c + \phi_1\mu + \phi_2\mu$, and solving for $\mu = \dfrac{c}{1 - \phi_1 - \phi_2}$, we have the unconditional mean of the process, which is a constant. Observe that if $\phi_1 + \phi_2 = 1$, the unconditional mean is not defined.

7.2.2.2 What Do the Corresponding Autocorrelation Functions of the AR(2) Processes Look Like?

In Figure 7.10, we plot the autocorrelograms of the three stationary processes in Figure 7.8. These three shapes of the autocorrelation functions are representative of those generated by any AR(2) process in general.

There are three distinctive features in the autocorrelation functions of an AR(2) process:

1. $\rho_1 = r_1$. This result is always valid for any process. Additionally, for an AR(2), $r_2 = \phi_2$. Note that the AC and PAC are just estimated correlations based on only one time series; thus, we should expect some sampling error. This is why in the first PAC $\hat{r}_2 = \hat{\phi}_2 = -0.537$, which practically is the value of the population parameter –0.5; in the second PAC, $\hat{r}_2 = \hat{\phi}_2 = 0.365$, which is close to 0.4; and in the third PAC, $\hat{r}_2 = \hat{\phi}_2 = 0.286$, which is close to 0.3.

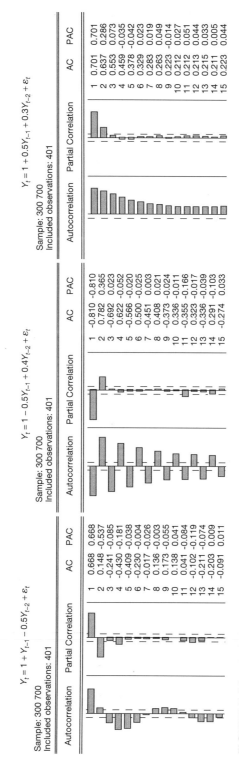

$Y_t = 1 + Y_{t-1} - 0.5Y_{t-2} + \varepsilon_t$

Sample: 300 700
Included observations: 401

Autocorrelation / Partial Correlation

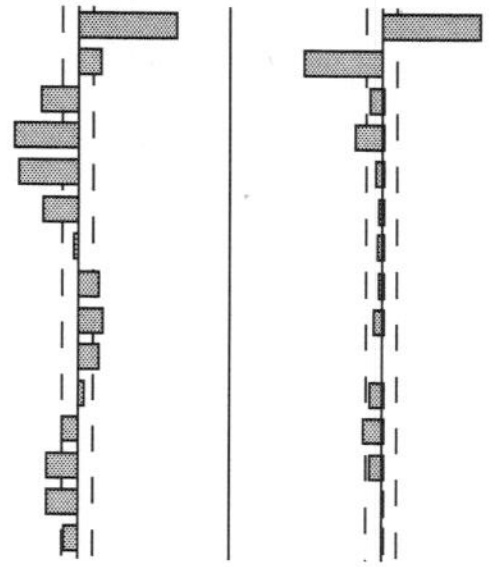

	AC	PAC
1	0.668	0.668
2	0.148	-0.537
3	-0.241	-0.085
4	-0.430	-0.181
5	-0.409	-0.038
6	-0.230	-0.004
7	-0.017	-0.026
8	0.136	-0.003
9	0.173	-0.055
10	0.138	0.041
11	0.041	-0.084
12	-0.102	-0.119
13	-0.211	-0.074
14	-0.203	0.009
15	-0.091	0.011

$Y_t = 1 - 0.5Y_{t-1} + 0.4Y_{t-2} + \varepsilon_t$

Sample: 300 700
Included observations: 401

Autocorrelation / Partial Correlation

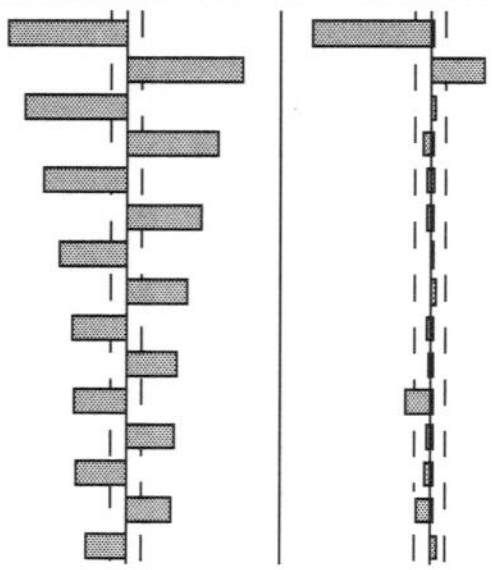

	AC	PAC
1	-0.810	-0.810
2	0.782	0.365
3	-0.692	0.023
4	0.622	-0.052
5	-0.566	-0.020
6	0.500	-0.025
7	-0.451	0.003
8	0.408	0.021
9	-0.373	-0.024
10	0.336	-0.011
11	-0.355	-0.166
12	0.323	-0.017
13	-0.336	-0.039
14	0.291	-0.103
15	-0.274	0.033

$Y_t = 1 + 0.5Y_{t-1} + 0.3Y_{t-2} + \varepsilon_t$

Sample: 300 700
Included observations: 401

Autocorrelation / Partial Correlation

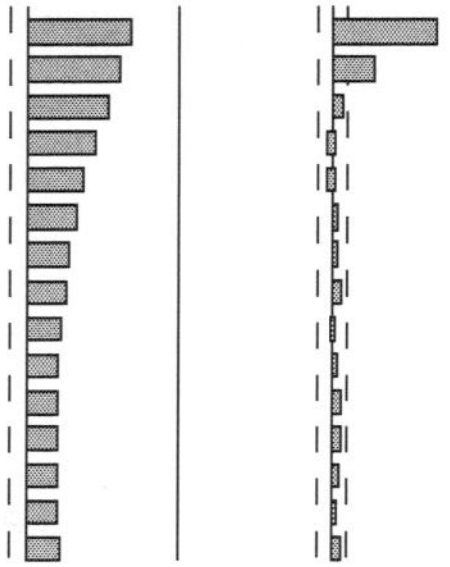

	AC	PAC
1	0.701	0.701
2	0.637	0.286
3	0.553	0.073
4	0.459	-0.035
5	0.378	-0.042
6	0.329	0.023
7	0.283	0.019
8	0.263	0.049
9	0.223	-0.014
10	0.212	0.027
11	0.212	0.051
12	0.213	0.044
13	0.215	0.033
14	0.211	0.005
15	0.223	0.044

FIGURE 7.10 Autocorrelation Functions of Covariance–Stationary AR(2) Processes

2. The autocorrelation function AC decreases toward zero but in different fashions. In the first AC, we observe a sinusoidal decay. There is a stochastic cycle of approximately nine periods. Also observe this cycle in time series 1 of Figure 7.8. In the second AC, the decay toward zero happens in an alternating mode. At odd lags, the autocorrelation is negative, and at even lags, the autocorrelation is positive. This is a consequence of the zigzagging behavior of time series 2. In the third AC, the decay is exponential with all autocorrelations positive. This is a consequence of high persistence as displayed in time series 3.
3. The partial autocorrelation function is characterized by only two spikes, $r_1 \neq 0$ and $r_2 \neq 0$, and the remaining $r_k = 0$ for $k > 2$. Read the estimated PAC values, which are practically zero for $k > 2$. In general, the order of an AR process is detected by the number of spikes that are different from zero in the PAC function.

REAL DATA: U.S. Consumer Price Index Growth Rate, 1913–2003

See Figure 7.11 for the time series and the autocorrelation functions of the last century's inflation rate (not seasonally adjusted) in the United States measured as the

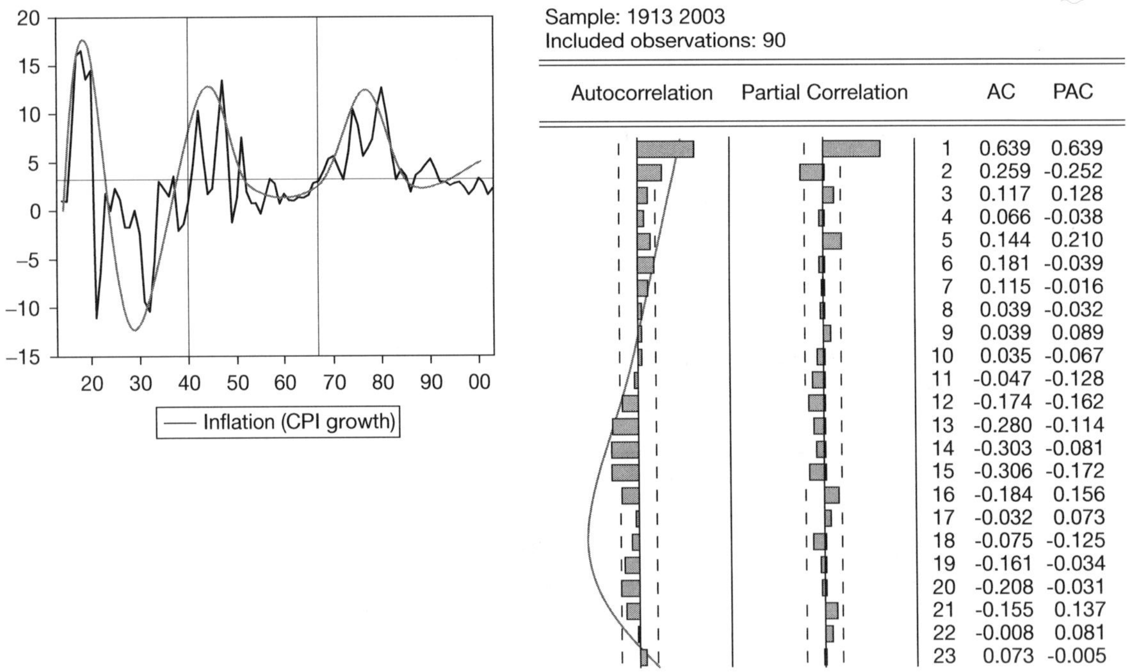

	AC	PAC
1	0.639	0.639
2	0.259	-0.252
3	0.117	0.128
4	0.066	-0.038
5	0.144	0.210
6	0.181	-0.039
7	0.115	-0.016
8	0.039	-0.032
9	0.039	0.089
10	0.035	-0.067
11	-0.047	-0.128
12	-0.174	-0.162
13	-0.280	-0.114
14	-0.303	-0.081
15	-0.306	-0.172
16	-0.184	0.156
17	-0.032	0.073
18	-0.075	-0.125
19	-0.161	-0.034
20	-0.208	-0.031
21	-0.155	0.137
22	-0.008	0.081
23	0.073	-0.005

FIGURE 7.11 U.S. Inflation Rate

growth rate in the Consumer Price Index (CPI), from 1913 to 2003. The Bureau of Labor Statistics (BLS) publishes these data (http://www.bls.gov).

The most prominent feature of this time series is that it contains a cycle (the smooth line) with larger amplitude at the beginning of the 20th century than at the end of it. The average inflation rate over the century has been around 3%. Prior to the 1920s, the U.S. economy withstood inflation rates of 15% to be followed by deflation rates of –10% in the depression years after the crisis of 1929. In the post-World War II years, there were no deflation episodes, but during the 1940s and late 1970s/early 1980s, the economy ran double-digit inflation rates. The latest years of the century experienced milder inflation rates, primarily because of a better understanding of the instruments of monetary policy to control economic activity.

The corresponding autocorrelation functions reinforce the existence of a cycle. Do these autocorrelograms look like any of those in Figure 7.10? Yes. In the AC function, we observe a sinusoidal decay toward zero with an approximated cycle of 25 years. This is in agreement with the time series information. There are three cycles (the horizontal lines in the time series plot separate one cycle from the next). Approximately, one cycle runs from 1913 to the late 1930s, another from 1940 to late 1960s, and the last one from 1970 to present time. The PAC function has two prominent spikes, indicating that an AR(2) processes may be a good linear model for this time series. From the PAC, we gather that $\hat{\phi}_2 = -0.25$. Additional information about the process will be obtained by using estimation, which will be explained in following sections.

Download some of the components of the CPI such as housing, food, and transportation from the BLS site and analyze whether they can also be modeled as AR(2) processes.

7.2.2.3 What Is the Optimal Forecast Corresponding to an AR(2) Process?

We proceed as in the case of an AR(1). Recall that under a quadratic loss function, the optimal forecast is $f_{t,h} = \mu_{t+h|t} = E(Y_{t+h} | I_t)$. To compute this conditional expectation for different forecast horizons $h = 1, 2, \ldots. s$, we proceed in two steps: first, write the process at the desired horizon, and second, take the conditional expectation. For instance,

FORECASTING HORIZON $h = 1$

Write the process at time $t + 1$,

$$Y_{t+1} = c + \phi_1 Y_t + \phi_2 Y_{t-1} + \varepsilon_{t+1}$$

Take expectation conditioning on the information set up to time t. Observe that Y_t and Y_{t-1} belong to the information set and their values are known at time t; thus, $E(Y_t | I_t) = Y_t$ and $E(Y_{t-1} | I_t) = Y_{t-1}$. Additionally, ε_{t+1} is a mean zero white noise process uncorrelated with the information set; thus, $E(\varepsilon_{t+1} | I_t) = 0$. Putting these pieces together, we ask the following questions:

i. *What is the optimal point forecast $f_{t,1}$?*

$$\begin{aligned} f_{t,1} &= \mu_{t+1|t} = E(Y_{t+1} | I_t) = E(c + \phi_1 Y_t + \phi_2 Y_{t-1} + \varepsilon_{t+1}) \\ &= c + \phi_1 Y_t + \phi_2 Y_{t-1} \end{aligned}$$

ii. *What is the 1-period-ahead forecast error $e_{t,1}$?*

It is the difference between the realized value Y_{t+1} and the forecast value $f_{t,1}$

$$\begin{aligned} e_{t,1} &= Y_{t+1} - f_{t,1} = c + \phi_1 Y_t + \phi_2 Y_{t-1} + \varepsilon_{t+1} - c - \phi_1 Y_t - \phi_2 Y_{t-1} \\ &= \varepsilon_{t+1} \end{aligned}$$

As in the AR(1) case, the 1-period-ahead forecast error is the innovation of the process. In general, for any AR process of any order, the 1-period ahead forecast error is always equal to the innovation of the model.

iii. *What is the uncertainty associated with the forecast?*

It must be a function of the unpredictability of the process, which is summarized in the variance of the forecast error:

$$\sigma^2_{t+1|t} = \text{var}(Y_{t+1} | I_t) = E(Y_{t+1} - f_{t,1} | I_t)^2 = E(e^2_{t,1}) = E(\varepsilon^2_{t+1}) = \sigma^2_\varepsilon$$

iv. *What is the density forecast?*

It is the conditional probability density function of the process at the future date. If we assume that white noise process $\{\varepsilon_t\}$ is normally distributed, the density forecast is:

$$f(Y_{t+1} | I_t) \rightarrow N(\mu_{t+1|t}, \sigma^2_{t+1|t})$$

From the density forecast, we construct confidence intervals. For instance, a 95% confidence interval is:

$$\mu_{t+1|t} \pm 1.96\sigma_{t+1|t} = (\mu_{t+1|t} - 1.96\sigma_{t+1|t}, \mu_{t+1|t} + 1.96\sigma_{t+1|t}),$$

where $1.96 = \Phi^{-1}(0.975)$ and $\Phi^{-1}(.)$ is the inverse of the cumulative distribution function of a $N(0, 1)$ random variable.

FORECASTING HORIZON $h = 2$

We follow the same steps as in the previous case. The algebra is slightly more complicated but straightforward.

i. *What is the optimal point forecast $f_{t,2}$?*

$$\begin{aligned} f_{t,2} &= \mu_{t+2|t} = E(Y_{t+2} | I_t) = E(c + \phi_1 Y_{t+1} + \phi_2 Y_t + \varepsilon_{t+2} | I_t) \\ &= c + \phi_1 E(Y_{t+1} | I_t) + \phi_2 Y_t = c + \phi_1 f_{t,1} + \phi_2 Y_t \end{aligned}$$

Observe that $f_{t,1}$ has already been calculated. A direct substitution of this expression in the last equality makes the forecast a function of the information set.

ii. *What is the 2-period-ahead forecast error $e_{t,2}$?*

It is the difference between the realized value Y_{t+2} and the forecast value $f_{t,2}$,

$$\begin{aligned} e_{t,2} &= Y_{t+2} - f_{t,2} = c + \phi_1 Y_{t+1} + \phi_2 Y_t + \varepsilon_{t+2} - (c + \phi_1 f_{t,1} + \phi_2 Y_t) \\ &= \phi_1 \varepsilon_{t+1} + \varepsilon_{t+2} \end{aligned}$$

iii. *What is the uncertainty associated with the forecast?*

It must be a function of the unpredictability of the process, which is the variance of the forecast error

$$\sigma^2_{t+2|t} = \text{var}(Y_{t+2}|I_t) = E(Y_{t+2} - f_{t,2}|I_t)^2 = E(e^2_{t,2}) = E(\phi_1 \varepsilon_{t+1} + \varepsilon_{t+2})^2$$
$$= \sigma^2_\varepsilon(1 + \phi_1^2)$$

The last equality uses the no-autocorrelation property that characterizes a white noise process:

iv. *What is the density forecast?*

It is the conditional probability density function of the process at the future date. If we assume that $\{\varepsilon_t\}$ is normally distributed white noise process, the density forecast is:

$$f(Y_{t+2}|I_t) \rightarrow N(\mu_{t+2|t}, \sigma^2_{t+2|t})$$

Now we can generalize for any horizon. Observe that the optimal forecast is computed in a recursive fashion. For any horizon s, you need to calculate the forecast of the previous horizons $s-1$, $s-2$, and so on. Following the same arguments you will be able to find the answers for

Forecasting Horizon $h = s$

i. *What is the optimal point forecast* $f_{t,s}$*?*

$$f_{t,s} = \mu_{t+s|t} = E(Y_{t+s}|I_t) = c + \phi_1 f_{t,s-1} + \phi_2 f_{t,s-2}$$

ii. *What is the* s*-period-ahead forecast error* $e_{t,s}$*?*

$$e_{t,s} = Y_{t+s} - f_{t,s} = \varepsilon_{t+s} + \phi_1 e_{t,s-1} + \phi_2 e_{t,s-2}$$

iii. *What is the uncertainty associated with the forecast?*

$$\sigma^2_{t+s|t} = \text{var}(Y_{t+s}|I_t) = E(Y_{t+s} - f_{t,s}|I_t)^2 = E(e^2_{t,s})$$
$$= E(\varepsilon_{t+s} + \phi_1 e_{t,s-1} + \phi_2 e_{t,s-2})^2 = \sigma^2_\varepsilon + \phi_1^2 \text{var}(e_{t,s-1})$$
$$+ \phi_2^2 \text{var}(e_{t,s-2}) + 2\phi_1\phi_2 \text{cov}(e_{t,s-1}, e_{t,s-2})$$

Note that when $s > 1$, the forecast errors are correlated because they share common information. As an example, compare the forecast errors for $h = 2$ and for $h = 3$: $e_{t,2} = \phi_1 \varepsilon_{t+1} + \varepsilon_{t+2}$ and $e_{t,3} = (\phi_1^2 + \phi_2)\varepsilon_{t+1} + \phi_1\varepsilon_{t+2} + \varepsilon_{t+3}$, respectively. Two innovations ε_{t+1} and ε_{t+2} are common to both forecast errors; hence, their covariance must be different from zero: $\text{cov}(e_{t,3}, e_{t,2}) = (\phi_1^3 + \phi_1\phi_2 + \phi_1)\sigma^2_\varepsilon$.

iv. *What is the density forecast?*

$$f(Y_{t+s}|I_t) \rightarrow N(\mu_{t+s|t}, \sigma^2_{t+s|t})$$

As in the case of the AR(1), the AR(2) process is a short memory process. When the forecasting horizon is very large, $s \rightarrow \infty$, the optimal forecast converges to the unconditional mean of the process, and the variance of the forecast error to the unconditional variance of the process.

REAL DATA: Forecasting U.S. Consumer Price Index Growth Rate (U.S. Inflation Rate)

Let us go back to the real data described in Figure 7.11 and practice constructing a **multistep forecast** based on AR models. The autocorrelation functions in Figure 7.11 are typical of an AR(2) process. We proceed by estimating such a model. As we mentioned in Chapter 6, *Forecasting with Moving Average (MA)* processes, click on the following sequence once you have an EViews workfile in place:

Object

New Object

Equation

In the Specification window, choose the method LS – Least Squares (NLS and ARMA) and write the following command: cpi_gr c AR(1) AR(2) where "cpi_gr" is the yearly inflation rate, c is a constant, and AR(1) and AR(2) are the number of lags of the autoregressive model. The estimation output is displayed in Table 7.1.

The estimation sample is from 1916 to 2003 for a total of 88 observations. The estimated parameters are $\hat{\phi}_1 = 0.799$ and $\hat{\phi}_2 = -0.251$, which is very close to our educated guess in Section 7.2.2.2, $\hat{c} = \hat{\mu}(1 - \hat{\phi}_1 - \hat{\phi}_2) = 3.31(1 - 0.79 + 0.25) = 1.498$,[3] and $\hat{\sigma}_\varepsilon = 3.737$. Then we write the time series model as:

$$Y_t = 1.498 + 0.7995\, Y_{t-1} - 0.251\, Y_{t-2} + \varepsilon_t$$

TABLE 7.1 Estimation Results, U.S. Inflation Rate, AR(2) Model

Dependent Variable: CPI_GR
Method: Least Squares
Sample (adjusted): 1916 2003
Included observations: 88 after adjustments
Convergence achieved after 3 iterations

Variable	Coefficient	Std. Error	t-Statistic	Prob.
C	3.311924	0.880693	3.760588	0.0003
AR(1)	0.799420	0.104934	7.618326	0.0000
AR(2)	-0.251858	0.104879	-2.401413	0.0185

R-squared	0.445779	Mean dependent var	3.298182
Adjusted R-squared	0.432739	S.D. dependent var	4.962744
S.E. of regression	3.737777	Akaike info criterion	5.508356
Sum squared resid	1187.533	Schwarz criterion	5.592810
Log likelihood	-239.3676	F-statistic	34.18425
Durbin–Watson stat	1.904683	Prob(F-statistic)	0.000000
Inverted AR Roots	.40-.30i	.40+.30i	

We proceed to use this model to forecast from 2004 to 2009; we will construct 1-step to 6-step forecasts. Observe that the forecasting sample is not included in the estimation exercise of Table 7.1.

Three features are relevant. First, for $h = 1$, we retrieve the values of Y_t (year 2003) and Y_{t-1} (year 2002) from the information set. Second, observe that for $h \geq 2$, the forecast is constructed following a recursive relation. Once we obtain $f_{t,1}$, the forecast for any horizon $s > 2$ is obtained recursively, $f_{t,s} = \hat{c} + \hat{\phi}_1 f_{t,s-1} + \hat{\phi}_2 f_{t,s-2}$. Third, observe that as the forecast horizon increases, the forecast approaches the unconditional moments of the process. For instance, for $h = 6$ (year 2009), $f_{t,6} = 3.32$ and $\sigma^2_{t+6|t} = 5.04^2$. The unconditional mean of inflation is 3.30% and the unconditional

TABLE 7.2 Multistep Forecast of U.S. Inflation Rate

$h=1$ 2004	$f_{t,1} = \hat{c} + \hat{\phi}_1 Y_t + \hat{\phi}_2 Y_{t-1}$ $= 1.49 + 0.79 \times 2.25 - 0.25 \times 1.56$ ≈ 2.90	$\sigma^2_{t+1\|t} = \hat{\sigma}^2_\varepsilon = 3.74^2$	$f(Y_{t+1} \| I_t) \rightarrow N(\mu_{t+1\|t}, \sigma^2_{t+1\|t})$ $= N(2.90, 3.74^2)$
$h=2$ 2005	$f_{t,2} = \hat{c} + \hat{\phi}_1 f_{t,1} + \hat{\phi}_2 Y_t$ $= 1.49 + 0.79 \times 2.90 - 0.25 \times 2.25$ ≈ 3.25	$\sigma^2_{t+2\|t} = \hat{\sigma}^2_\varepsilon(1 + \hat{\phi}_1{}^2)$ $= 3.74^2(1 + 0.79^2)$ $\approx 4.81^2$	$f(Y_{t+2} \| I_t) \rightarrow N(3.25, 4.81^2)$
$h=3$ 2006	$f_{t,3} = \hat{c} + \hat{\phi}_1 f_{t,2} + \hat{\phi}_2 f_{t,1}$ $= 1.49 + 0.79 \times 3.25 - 0.25 \times 2.90$ ≈ 3.36	$\sigma^2_{t+3\|t} = \hat{\sigma}^2_\varepsilon(1 + \hat{\phi}_1^2$ $+ (\hat{\phi}_2 + \hat{\phi}_1^2)^2)$ $\approx 5.03^2$	$f(Y_{t+3} \| I_t) \rightarrow N(3.36, 5.03^2)$
$h=4$ 2007	$f_{t,4} = \hat{c} + \hat{\phi}_1 f_{t,3} + \hat{\phi}_2 f_{t,2}$ $= 1.49 + 0.79 \times 3.36 - 0.25 \times 3.25$ ≈ 3.37	$\sigma^2_{t+4\|t} \approx 5.04^2$	$f(Y_{t+4} \| I_t) \rightarrow N(3.37, 5.04^2)$
$h=5$ 2008	$f_{t,5} = \hat{c} + \hat{\phi}_1 f_{t,4} + \hat{\phi}_2 f_{t,3}$ $= 1.49 + 0.79 \times 3.37 - 0.25 \times 3.36$ ≈ 3.34	$\sigma^2_{t+5\|t} \approx 5.04^2$	$f(Y_{t+5} \| I_t) \rightarrow N(3.34, 5.04^2)$
$h=6$ 2009	$f_{t,6} = \hat{c} + \hat{\phi}_1 f_{t,5} + \hat{\phi}_2 f_{t,4}$ $= 1.49 + 0.79 \times 3.34 - 0.25 \times 3.37$ ≈ 3.32	$\sigma^2_{t+6\|t} \approx 5.04^2$	$f(Y_{t+6} \| I_t) \rightarrow N(3.32, 5.04^2)$

[3]EViews estimates the AR process following a nonlinear algorithm; see the "EViews Help Manual." The important point is that the constant C in the estimation output refers to the estimate of the unconditional mean of the process $\hat{\mu}$.

variance is about 25. For this reason, we call the AR process a *short memory process:* Once the dependence contained in the model is fully exploited, the best forecast we can construct is the unconditional mean of the process. Because we have assumed that ε_t is normally distributed, the density forecast is readily available given that we know the first and second moments at each forecasting horizon.

In EViews, you can generate the preceding multistep forecasts by clicking the following sequence:

Equation

Proc

Forecast

and selecting in the forecast window the **dynamic** method. You need to state the forecasting horizon and the name of the forecast series.

In Figure 7.12, we graph the multistep forecast with a 95% confidence interval (based on the normality assumption), which measures the uncertainty of the forecast. To compute the 95% confidence bands, perform the following calculations $(\mu_{t+h|t} - 1.96\sigma_{t+h|t}, \mu_{t+h|t} + 1.96\sigma_{t+h|t})$. For instance, for $h = 1$, the interval will be $(2.90 - 1.96 \times 3.76, 2.90 + 1.96 \times 3.76) = (-4.47, 10.28)$. Observe that the confidence bands and the forecasts tend to stabilize after 2006 because of the previously mentioned convergence of the forecast toward the unconditional mean and variance of the

FIGURE 7.12
U.S. Inflation Rate, Multistep Forecast

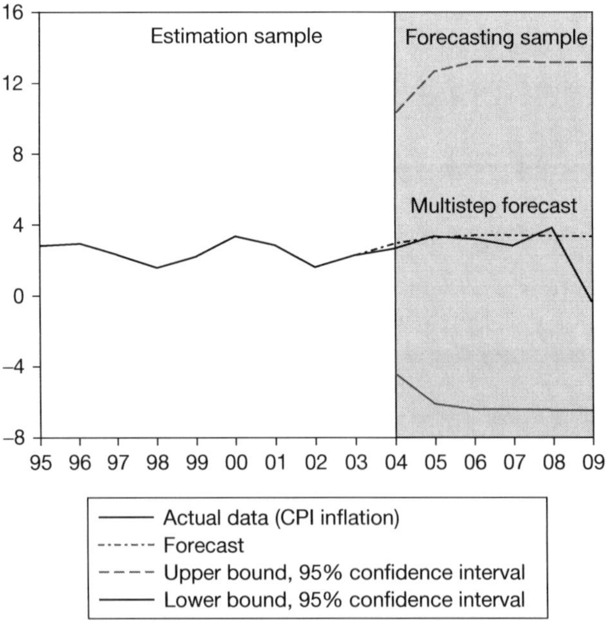

process. The AR(2) model seems to forecast quite well from 2004 to 2008, but in 2009, the forecast (3.32%) is far from the realized value (–0.37%). However, when we evaluate the forecast together with its associated uncertainty (check the confidence bands), we recognize that negative inflation rates are possible. In fact, inflation rates are notoriously difficult to predict. They have a large variance (about $4.96^2 \approx 25$) and although the AR(2) model is successful in capturing linear dependence, the residual variance is still large (about $3.737^2 \approx 14$), which translates into large forecast error variances.

7.2.3 AR(p) Process

The analysis of an AR(p) process does not bring new questions. By now, you have enough tools to familiarize yourself with a higher order autoregressive process.

The functional form of an AR(p) is:

$$Y_t = c + \phi_1 Y_{t-1} + \phi_2 Y_{t-2} + \phi_3 Y_{t-3} + \ldots + \phi_p Y_{t-p} + \varepsilon_t$$

Choose $p > 2$ and write a small program in EViews to generate some time series from this process. You have the freedom to experiment with different values of ϕs. As we have seen in the AR(1) and AR(2) cases, the values of the ϕs determine whether the process is covariance stationary. In a high-order AR(p), it is extremely cumbersome to identify the conditions that the ϕs should satisfy to guarantee that the process is covariance stationary. We need advanced calculus, which is out of the scope of this book. Fortunately, you can obtain enough information from most econometric software to decide on the stationarity of the process. At this point, you should randomly choose values of ϕs and by examining the resulting time series, judge whether or not the simulated process is covariance stationary.

REAL DATA: U.S. Unemployed Looking for Part-Time Work, 1989/1–2004/6

Let us introduce some economic data that can be represented by a high-order AR. We present the time series and the autocorrelation functions of the "unemployed looking for part-time work" (seasonally adjusted) in the United States in Figure 7.13. This is a monthly time series from January 1989 to June 2004 that includes people 16 years of age and older. The Bureau of Labor Statistics published the data.

The time series plot shows reversion to the mean (the horizontal line) although there is high persistence. We observe a steady decline during the 1992–2000 economic expansion and a rise in the 2000–2003 recession.

Is this time series generated by an AR process? Let us look at the autocorrelation functions.

The AC function exhibits a smoothly slow decay toward zero, indicating high persistence, which is consistent with the time series plot. On the contrary, the PAC function decays quickly to zero. These features are familiar to us from the shapes of the PAC corresponding to the AR(1) and AR(2) processes. In the PAC, we distinguish four spikes different from zero, indicating an AR(4) process.

FIGURE 7.13 Number of Unemployed People Looking for Part-Time Work

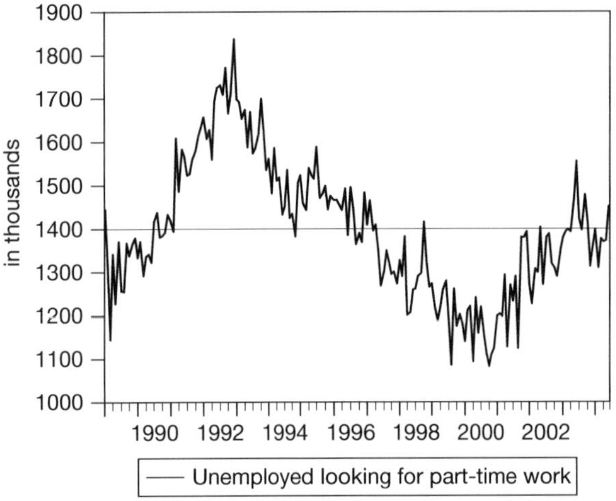

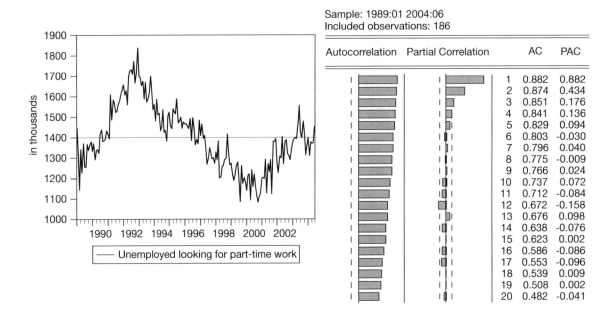

Sample: 1989:01 2004:06
Included observations: 186

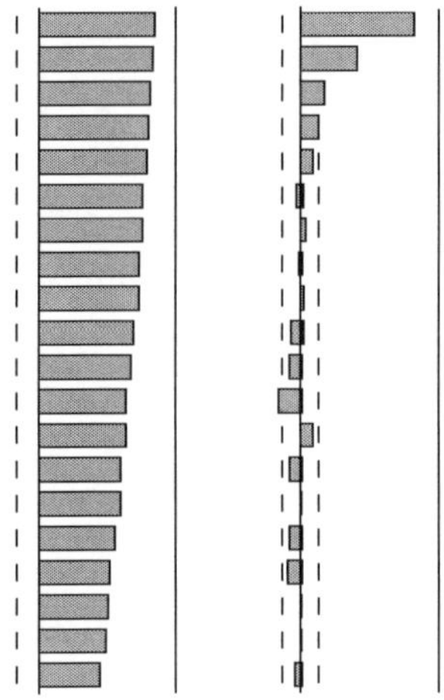

	AC	PAC
1	0.882	0.882
2	0.874	0.434
3	0.851	0.176
4	0.841	0.136
5	0.829	0.094
6	0.803	-0.030
7	0.796	0.040
8	0.775	-0.009
9	0.766	0.024
10	0.737	0.072
11	0.712	-0.084
12	0.672	-0.158
13	0.676	0.098
14	0.638	-0.076
15	0.623	0.002
16	0.586	-0.086
17	0.553	-0.096
18	0.539	0.009
19	0.508	0.002
20	0.482	-0.041

Simulate a time series and calculate its autocorrelation functions from the following process:

$$Y_t = 112 + 0.43Y_{t-1} + 0.35Y_{t-2} + 0.14Y_{t-4} + \varepsilon_t \quad \text{with } \varepsilon_t \rightarrow N(0, 4052)$$

Note that this is an AR(4) process even though there is not any direct effect from Y_{t-3}. Additionally, note that the persistence is high: $\phi_1 + \phi_2 + \phi_3 + \phi_4 = 0.92$. How do your results compare to those in Figure 7.13?

Let us summarize the three distinctive features of the autocorrelation functions of AR(p) processes:

1. $\rho_1 = r_1$. This result is always valid for any process. Additionally, on AR(p) processes, $r_p = \phi_p$.
2. The autocorrelation function AC decays toward zero but in different fashions. We find smooth exponential decays, alternating decays, sinusoidal decays, and any combination of these. The speed of decay depends on the persistence of the process defined as $\phi_1 + \phi_2 + \cdots + \phi_p$. The less persistence the process has, the fastest is the decay to zero. If $\phi_1 + \phi_2 + \cdots + \phi_p = 1$, the process is not covariance stationary. Hence, a necessary condition for covariance stationarity is $\phi_1 + \phi_2 + \cdots + \phi_p < 1$.
3. The partial autocorrelation function PAC is characterized by the first p spikes $r_1 \neq 0, r_2 \neq 0, \ldots. r_p \neq 0$ and the remaining $r_k = 0$ for $k > p$. In general, the order of an AR process is detected by the number of spikes that are different from zero in the PAC function.

To compute the forecast of an AR(p), we proceed in a similar fashion as in the AR(1) and AR(2) processes. The algebra is slightly more elaborate, but conceptually, the same ideas hold. Assuming a quadratic loss function, now the familiar questions to ask are:

i. *What is the optimal point forecast* $f_{t,s}$?

$$f_{t,s} = \mu_{t+s|t} = E(Y_{t+s} \mid I_t) = c + \phi_1 f_{t,s-1} + \phi_2 f_{t,s-2} + \cdots + \phi_p f_{t,s-p}$$

Recall that the forecast is computed recursively; that is, given a horizon s, you need to compute the previous p forecasts at the shorter horizons $s-1$, $s-2, \ldots, s-p$.

ii. *What is the* s*-period-ahead forecast error* $e_{t,s}$?

$$e_{t,s} = Y_{t+s} - f_{t,s} = \varepsilon_{t+s} + \phi_1 e_{t,s-1} + \phi_2 e_{t,s-2} + \cdots + \phi_p e_{t,s-p}$$

iii. *What is the uncertainty associated with the forecast?*

$$\begin{aligned}\sigma^2_{t+s|t} &= \text{var}(Y_{t+s} \mid I_t) = E(Y_{t+s} - f_{t,s} \mid I_t)^2 = E(e^2_{t,s}) \\ &= E(\varepsilon_{t+s} + \phi_1 e_{t,s-1} + \phi_2 e_{t,s-2} + \cdots + \phi_p e_{t,s-p})^2 \\ &= \sigma^2_\varepsilon + \sum_{i=1}^{p} \phi_i^2 \text{var}(e_{t,s-i}) + 2\sum_{i \neq j} \phi_i \phi_j \text{cov}(e_{t,s-i}, e_{t,s-j})\end{aligned}$$

iv. *What is the density forecast?*

$$f(Y_{t+s} \mid I_t) \rightarrow N(\mu_{t+s|t}, \sigma^2_{t+s|t})$$

All these formulas summarize in a very compact fashion the optimal forecast of an AR(p). Eventually, they need to be developed further to obtain the forecast as a function of the information set. To practice your knowledge, select a horizon, say $s = 3$, and proceed sequentially to answer the preceding four questions.

7.2.4 Chain Rule of Forecasting

Under a quadratic loss function and for any autoregressive process, the multistep forecast is obtained in a recursive fashion. For any horizon $h > 1$, the forecast $f_{t,h}$ can be calculated from the 1-step-ahead forecast $f_{t,1}$ alone. This rule is known as the **chain rule of forecasting**, which we used in Sections 7.2.2 and 7.2.3—AR(2) and AR(p), respectively.

For a general AR(p) $Y_t = c + \phi_1 Y_{t-1} + \phi_2 Y_{t-2} + \phi_3 Y_{t-3} + \cdots\cdots\cdots \phi_p Y_{t-p} + \varepsilon_t$, we calculate the 1-step-ahead forecast, which is a function of the information set

$$f_{t,1} = c + \phi_1 Y_t + \phi_2 Y_{t-1} + \cdots\cdots + \phi_p Y_{t+1-p}$$

from here, the multistep forecast $h = 2, 3 \ldots, p$ is based on the previous forecasts and realized values of the process in the information set:

$$f_{t,2} = c + \phi_1 f_{t,1} + \phi_2 Y_t + \cdots + \phi_p Y_{t+2-p}$$

$$\cdots$$

$$f_{t,p} = c + \phi_1 f_{t,p-1} + \phi_2 f_{t,p-2} + \cdots + \phi_p Y_t$$

finally, for $h > p$, the forecast is a function of the previous p forecasts:

$$f_{t,p+1} = c + \phi_1 f_{t,p} + \phi_2 f_{t,p-1} + \cdots + \phi_p f_{t,1}$$

$$\cdots$$

$$f_{t,s} = c + \phi_1 f_{t,s-1} + \phi_2 f_{t,s-2} + \cdots + \phi_p f_{t,s-p}$$

Observe that the primary base of this recursion is the 1-step-ahead forecast $f_{t,1}$.

7.3 Seasonal Cycles

A **seasonal cycle** is defined as a periodic fluctuation in the data associated with the calendar. Generally speaking, economic activity has seasons. Let us think about different industries in relation to the calendar. Retail sales enjoy a high season during holidays. In November and December, consumers increase their expenditures in items including clothing, toys, small appliances, and other gadgets. In the travel industry, the summer months are considered "high season" because most people vacation in the summer, so the number of passengers traveling by air, train, car, and boat substantially increases. Expenditures for gasoline are highest during the summer months. In the construction sector, the start of residential units occurs toward the end of winter or beginning of spring to avoid potential costs related to inclement weather delays. In the food industry, sales of liquor and alcohol tend to increase in the winter months as do sales of ice cream in the summer months. In the automobile industry, dealers generally report increases in sales of new cars during the fall season. In the entertainment industry, sales of tickets are higher on weekends than on weekdays. In the stock market, the volume of trading is larger at the beginning and at the end of the trading day. In summary, production, consumption, and other economic activities are generally organized according to the calendar (quarters, months, days, hours, and special holidays). These actions appear in the data as a seasonal cycle at the quarterly, monthly, daily, or hourly frequency.

In many economic databases, we find seasonally adjusted time series for which the seasonal cycle has been removed. At the macrolevel, policy makers, institutions, and economic forecasters in general are more concerned with the analysis of the nonseasonal component, which, by definition, has less regularity than the seasonal component. As we saw in Section 7.2, forecasting the nonseasonal component offers a better understanding of where the economy is heading. However, at the microlevel, it does not make sense to remove the seasonal component. Businesses generally are very much interested in forecasting sales every month or every quarter; thus, they need the joint analysis of the seasonal and nonseasonal components in sales. In this section, we learn how to model seasonality by distinguishing deterministic from stochastic seasonality. Within a regression framework, we assign specific effects to each month, quarter, hour, and so on, so that deterministic seasonality can be easily captured in a regression model, and, fortunately in many instances, that is all we need. Stochastic seasonality requires the specification of dynamics in the seasonal component. We will see that MA (Chapter 6) and AR specifications in this chapter have natural extensions to model the seasonal component of a series, which implies that autocorrelation functions again play a key role in the analysis.

7.3.1 Deterministic and Stochastic Seasonal Cycles

Suppose that we collect a quarterly time series $\{y_t\}$, for instance sales, and wish to analyze the seasonal component. We would like to understand whether winter sales are different from summer, spring, or fall sales. We start by constructing four time series dummy variables (Q1, Q2, Q3, Q4) so that Q1 will assign a value 1 to the first quarter sales and 0 otherwise, Q2 will assign 1 to the second quarter sales and 0 otherwise, and so on. Then the format of the time series data set looks like the following table:

obs	SALES ($)	Q1	Q2	Q3	Q4
1999Q4	768726.0	0.000000	0.000000	0.000000	1.000000
2000Q1	696048.0	1.000000	0.000000	0.000000	0.000000
2000Q2	753211.0	0.000000	1.000000	0.000000	0.000000
2000Q3	746875.0	0.000000	0.000000	1.000000	0.000000
2000Q4	792622.0	0.000000	0.000000	0.000000	1.000000
2001Q1	704757.0	1.000000	0.000000	0.000000	0.000000
2001Q2	779011.0	0.000000	1.000000	0.000000	0.000000
2001Q3	756128.0	0.000000	0.000000	1.000000	0.000000
2001Q4	827829.0	0.000000	0.000000	0.000000	1.000000
2002Q1	717302.0	1.000000	0.000000	0.000000	0.000000
2002Q2	790486.0	0.000000	1.000000	0.000000	0.000000
2002Q3	792657.0	0.000000	0.000000	1.000000	0.000000
2002Q4	833877.0	0.000000	0.000000	0.000000	1.000000
2003Q1	741233.0	1.000000	0.000000	0.000000	0.000000
2003Q2	819940.0	0.000000	1.000000	0.000000	0.000000

If every quarter contributes differently to the volume of sales, it is natural to postulate the following regression:

$$Y_t = \beta_1 {*} Q1_t + \beta_2 {*} Q2_t + \beta_3 {*} Q3_t + \beta_4 {*} Q4_t + \varepsilon_t$$

This is a standard regression model (see Chapter 2) with dummy variables as regressors and a customary error term, which we assume to be normally distributed, that is, $\varepsilon_t \rightarrow N(0, \sigma^2)$. What is the meaning of the regression coefficients $\beta_1, \beta_2, \beta_3, \beta_4$?

By taking the conditional expectation, we have:

$$E(Y_t|Q1) = \beta_1, \quad E(Y_t|Q2) = \beta_2, \quad E(Y_t|Q3) = \beta_3, \quad E(Y_t|Q4) = \beta_4$$

Thus, each regression coefficient is interpreted as the expected sales in each quarter. By now, it should be evident why we talk about **deterministic seasonality**: The regressors (dummy variables) are always predictable; we know when we are in winter, spring, summer, or fall quarter.

Let us simulate the following artificial time series model with deterministic seasonality:

$$Y_t = 1{*}Q1_t + 0.5{*}Q2_t + 0.5{*}Q3_t + 3{*}Q4_t + \varepsilon_t$$

where $\varepsilon_t \rightarrow N(0,0.25)$. In this model, we claim that the expected sales in the fourth quarter are three times higher than those in the first quarter and six times higher than those in the second and third quarters. Once you have generated the dummy variables Q1, Q2, Q3, and Q4 as discussed, type the following statement in the command line of EViews and plot the generated time series y_t (see Figure 7.14):

```
y = Q1 + 0.5*Q2 + 0.5*Q3 + 3*Q4 + 0.5*nrnd
```

Observe in Figure 7.14 the seasonal periodicity of the time series; the peaks correspond to sales in Q4; the troughs correspond to sales in Q2 and Q3; and sales in Q1 are between. In this context, a forecast of sales for next quarter is trivial because we know whether next quarter will be winter, spring, summer, or fall. We need only to estimate the regression model and to choose the corresponding $\hat{\beta}_1, \hat{\beta}_2, \hat{\beta}_3, \hat{\beta}_4$ to produce the expected sales next quarter.

In **stochastic seasonality**, the seasonal component is driven by random variables. The following model is an example of a seasonal AR model:

$$Y_t = c + \phi_s Y_{t-s} + \varepsilon_t$$

FIGURE 7.14 Deterministic Seasonality

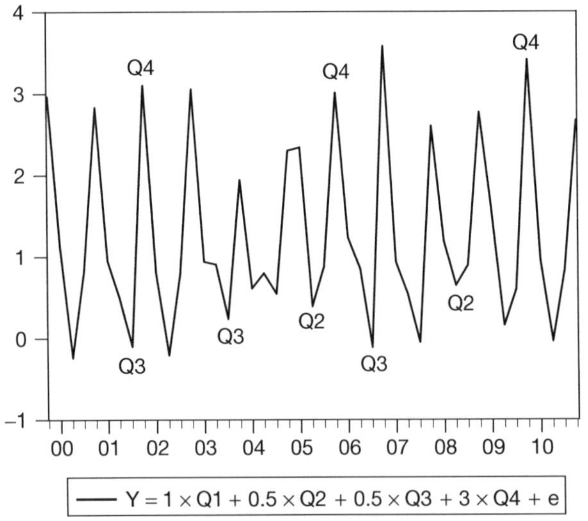

with $\varepsilon_t \rightarrow N(0, \sigma^2)$. Observe that in the right-hand side of the model, we have a random variable Y_{t-s}. The subindex s refers to the frequency of the data. For instance, if we have quarterly data $s = 4$ because the seasonal cycle repeats itself every four observations, for example, today's winter relates to the next winter (four observations apart) and to the winter before. Similarly, for monthly data, $s = 12$; for daily data (five working days), $s = 5$; and so on. Suppose that we work with quarterly data; thus, $s = 4$. By taking conditional expectation in the quarterly model, we have that

$$E(Y_t | I_{t-1}) = c + \phi_4 Y_{t-4}$$

where $I_{t-1} = \{y_{t-1}, y_{t-2}, y_{t-3}, y_{t-4}, \ldots\}$ is the information set up to time $t-1$. This model explains dynamics across seasons. For instance, if today we are in the winter quarter, the expected sales for winter is a function (a proportion) of the winter sales of the previous year (plus some constant), that is, $c + \phi_4 Y_{t-4}$. Note that the autoregressive coefficient ϕ_4 is the same for all seasons.

Let us simulate a seasonal AR model $Y_t = 0.8Y_{t-4} + \varepsilon_t$ with $\varepsilon_t \rightarrow N(0, 0.25)$. In the command line of EViews, type the following commands:

```
smpl @first @first+3
series y=0
smpl @first+4 @last
series y=0.8*y(-4)+0.5*nrnd
```

In Figure 7.15, we plot 84 observations (21 years times 4 quarters) of the time series. Observe the seasonal periodicity of the series: There are four observations between peak to peak (or from trough to trough). In this context, the forecasting rules are the same as those explained in Section 7.2 for nonseasonal AR processes; for instance, the 1-step-ahead optimal forecast is $f_{t-1,1} = E(Y_t | I_{t-1}) = c + \phi_4 Y_{t-4}$ for the preceding model.

FIGURE 7.15
Stochastic Seasonality

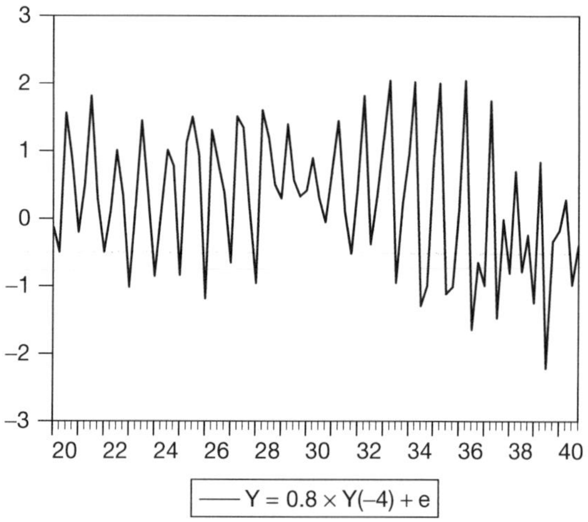

7.3.2 Seasonal ARMA Models

In the previous section, we introduced a seasonal AR(1) process. We can also define seasonal AR models of higher order as well as seasonal MA and seasonal ARMA specifications of any order. However, in the seasonal context, the order of the process needs to be understood in relation to the frequency of the data (the subindex s).

We define a seasonal AR of order p, that is, **S-AR(p)** as the following model:

$$Y_t = c + \phi_s Y_{t-s} + \phi_{2s} Y_{t-2s} + \phi_{3s} Y_{t-3s} + \cdots + \phi_{ps} Y_{t-ps} + \varepsilon_t$$

which, in polynomial form, it is also written as:

$$(1 - \phi_s L^s - \phi_{2s} L^{2s} - \phi_{3s} L^{3s} - \cdots - \phi_{ps} L^{ps}) Y_t = c + \varepsilon_t$$

Thus, an S-AR(1) for quarterly data $s = 4$ is written as

$$Y_t = c + \phi_4 Y_{t-4} + \varepsilon_t$$

and for monthly data $s = 12$ as

$$Y_t = c + \phi_{12} Y_{t-12} + \varepsilon_t$$

An S-AR(2) for quarterly data $s = 4$ is written as

$$Y_t = c + \phi_4 Y_{t-4} + \phi_8 Y_{t-8} + \varepsilon_t$$

and for monthly data $s = 12$ as

$$Y_t = c + \phi_{12} Y_{t-12} + \phi_{24} Y_{t-24} + \varepsilon_t$$

The following EViews program will generate a time series of an S-AR(2):

```
smpl @first @first+7
series y2=0
smpl @first+8 @last
series y2=0.5*y2(-4)+0.3*y2(-8) +0.5*nrnd
```

In Figure 7.16, we plot an S-AR(1) and S-AR(2) for quarterly data and their corresponding autocorrelation functions. Observe the quarterly periodicity in the time series plots, but, more importantly, the shapes of their autocorrelograms, which by now are very familiar to you. For the S-AR(1), the autocorrelation function (ACF) decays smoothly toward zero, but, because this a purely seasonal AR, the significant autocorrelations happen at multiples of the frequency of the data, that is, s, $2s$, $3s$, and so on, and any other autocorrelation coefficient is zero, which is expected. The order of the process is reflected in the number of significant spikes in the partial autocorrelation function (PACF); thus, for an S-AR(1), we expect only one significant spike in the PACF, and this is what we find at displacement $s = 4$. For an S-AR(2), the ACF also decays smoothly toward zero with relevant autocorrelations at displacements s, $2s$, $3s$ . . ., and the PACF exhibits only two significant spikes at displacements $s = 4$ and $s = 8$.

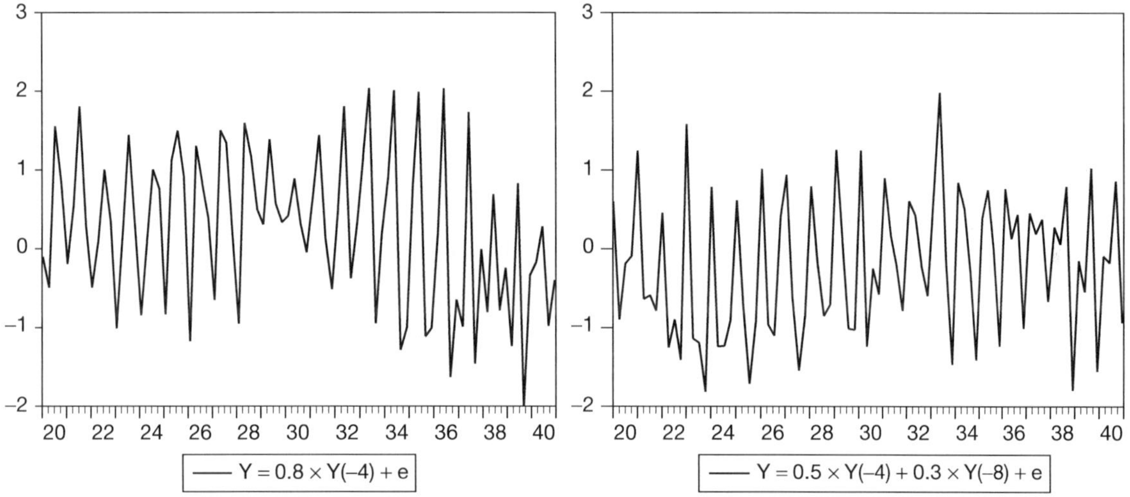

Included observations: 4201

Lag	AC	PAC
1	-0.020	-0.020
2	-0.027	-0.027
3	-0.022	-0.023
4	0.796	0.796
5	-0.007	0.030
6	-0.024	0.004
7	-0.025	-0.009
8	0.641	0.021
9	0.012	0.027
10	-0.017	0.014
11	-0.014	0.036
12	0.515	-0.001
13	0.021	-0.005
14	-0.011	0.004
15	-0.001	0.015
16	0.414	0.002
17	0.025	-0.001
18	-0.004	0.006
19	0.004	-0.007
20	0.337	0.012
21	0.028	0.004

Included observations: 4197

Lag	AC	PAC
1	-0.018	-0.018
2	-0.109	-0.109
3	-0.022	-0.026
4	0.729	0.725
5	-0.003	0.022
6	-0.116	-0.033
7	-0.032	-0.021
8	0.668	0.290
9	0.005	0.010
10	-0.097	0.033
11	-0.035	0.000
12	0.560	0.005
13	0.016	0.008
14	-0.097	-0.005
15	-0.033	0.014
16	0.485	0.002
17	0.021	0.003
18	-0.088	-0.003
19	-0.037	-0.006
20	0.417	0.005
21	0.009	-0.040

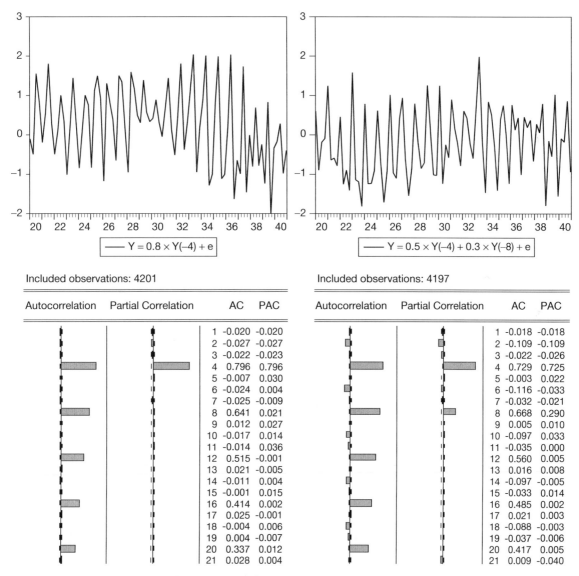

FIGURE 7.16 Seasonal AR(1) and AR(2), Time Series Plots and Autocorrelograms

REAL DATA: Monthly Clothing Sales, January 2003–January 2011

On the U.S. Census Bureau website (http://www.census.gov/econ/currentdata), you can find a wealth of time series both seasonally and nonseasonally adjusted. We have downloaded the time series of monthly clothing sales from January 2003 to January 2010, which is plotted in Figure 7.17. The seasonal cycle is very evident in the time series plot. Sales go dramatically up in the winter months of November and December and go down in January. The autocorrelation functions are dominated by the seasonal cycle. In the ACF, the most significant autocorrelations occur at displacements 12, 24, 36 . . . (all multiples of 12); in the PACF the most significant spike happens at displacement 12. This information indicates that the seasonal component is autoregressive of order 1, that is, S-AR(1). In addition, the seasonal cycle exhibits strong persistence as shown by the magnitude of the PACF spike at displacement 12, which is 0.826.

Stochastic seasonality can also be specified within MA models. We define a seasonal MA of order q, that is, **S-MA(q)** as the following model:

$$Y_t = \mu + \theta_s \varepsilon_{t-s} + \theta_{2s} \varepsilon_{t-2s} + \theta_{3s} \varepsilon_{t-3s} + \cdots + \theta_{qs} \varepsilon_{t-qs} + \varepsilon_t$$

which, in polynomial form, is also written as:

$$Y_t = \mu + (1 + \theta_s L^s + \theta_{2s} L^{2s} + \theta_{3s} L^{3s} + \cdots + \theta_{qs} L^{qs})\varepsilon_t$$

Thus, an S-MA(1) for quarterly data $s = 4$ is written as:

$$Y_t = \mu + \theta_4 \varepsilon_{t-4} + \varepsilon_t$$

and for monthly data $s = 12$ as

$$Y_t = \mu + \theta_{12} \varepsilon_{t-12} + \varepsilon_t$$

An S-MA(2) for quarterly data $s = 4$ is written as

$$Y_t = \mu + \theta_4 \varepsilon_{t-4} + \theta_8 \varepsilon_{t-8} + \varepsilon_t$$

and for monthly data $s = 12$ as

$$Y_t = \mu + \theta_{12} \varepsilon_{t-12} + \theta_{24} \varepsilon_{t-24} + \varepsilon_t$$

The following EViews program generates two time series of an S-MA(1) and an S-MA(2):

```
series e=0.5*nrnd
series y3=2+0.9*e(-4) +e
series y4=2-1*e(-4)+0.25*e(-8)+e
```

In Figure 7.18, we plot an S-MA(1) and S-MA(2) for quarterly data and their corresponding autocorrelation functions. Recall that MA processes are short memory processes and seasonal MAs are not exceptions. Thus, the quarterly periodicity, which is in the data, is not so obvious in the time series plots. However, the autocorrelation functions show strong evidence for a seasonal MA component. Observe that the shapes of the ACF and PACF are the same as those explained in Chapter 6 considering only the autocorrelations at displacements s, $2s$, $3s$, . . ., which are multiples of the frequency of the data. For the S-MA(1), the PACF decays toward zero in an alternating fashion. The order of the process is reflected in the number of significant spikes in the ACF; thus, for

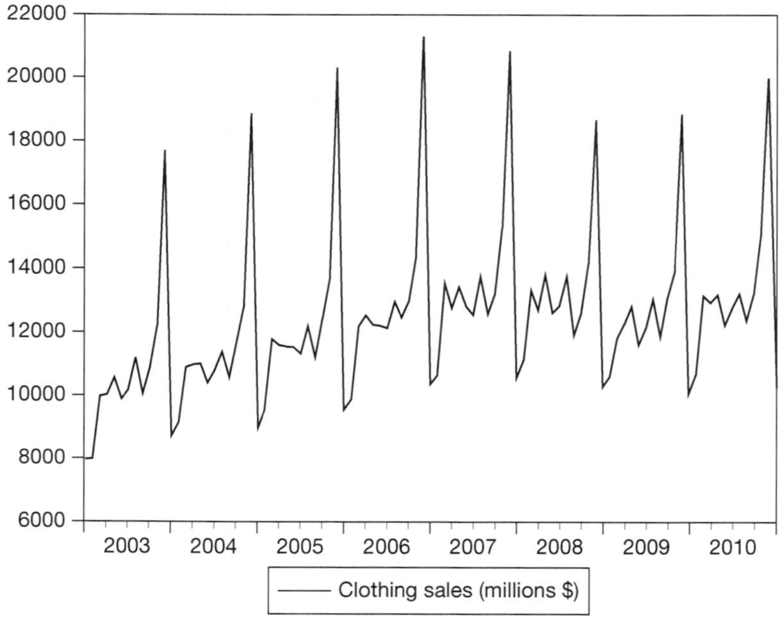

Sample: 2003M01 2011M01
Included observations: 97

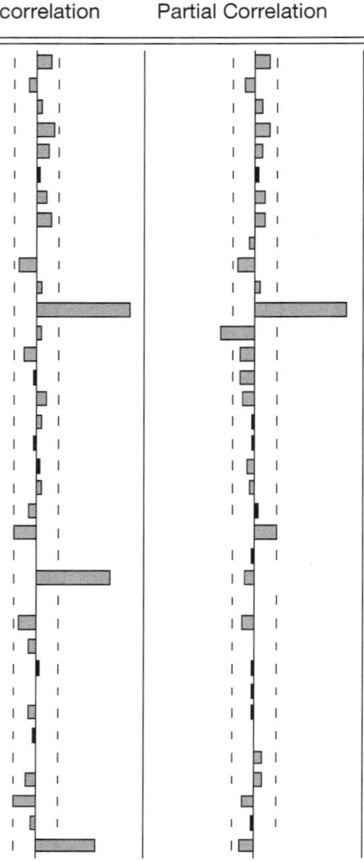

	AC	PAC
1	0.132	0.132
2	-0.069	-0.088
3	0.047	0.070
4	0.157	0.138
5	0.106	0.077
6	0.029	0.026
7	0.095	0.093
8	0.125	0.082
9	-0.001	-0.041
10	-0.150	-0.161
11	0.051	0.051
12	0.826	0.827
13	0.054	-0.375
14	-0.109	-0.132
15	-0.012	-0.119
16	0.088	-0.111
17	0.044	-0.024
18	-0.026	-0.019
19	0.030	-0.066
20	0.055	-0.033
21	-0.059	0.034
22	-0.182	0.197
23	-0.002	-0.024
24	0.672	-0.084
25	0.001	0.006
26	-0.147	-0.112
27	-0.058	-0.004
28	0.031	-0.024
29	0.000	-0.018
30	-0.063	-0.018
31	-0.014	0.004
32	0.011	0.071
33	-0.083	0.059
34	-0.202	-0.096
35	-0.038	-0.011
36	0.536	-0.119

FIGURE 7.17 Monthly Clothing Sales in the United States, Time Series Plot and Autocorrelation Functions (*Source:* http://www.census.gov/econ/currentdata)

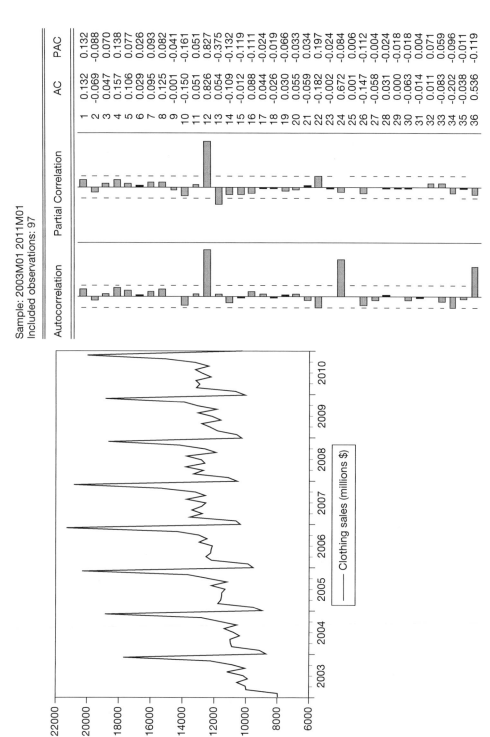

FIGURE 7.18 Seasonal MA(1) and MA(2), Time Series Plots and Autocorrelograms

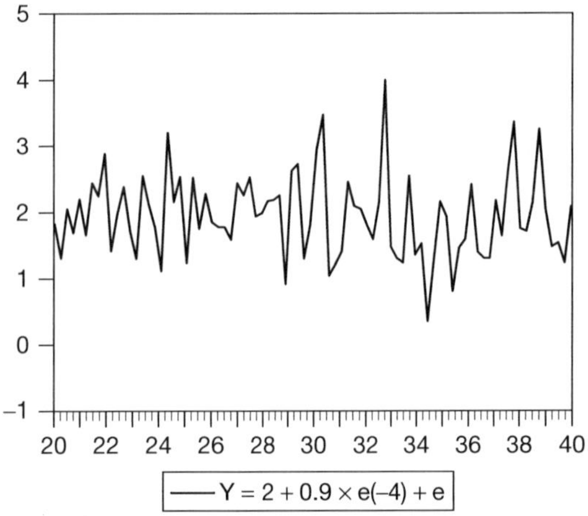

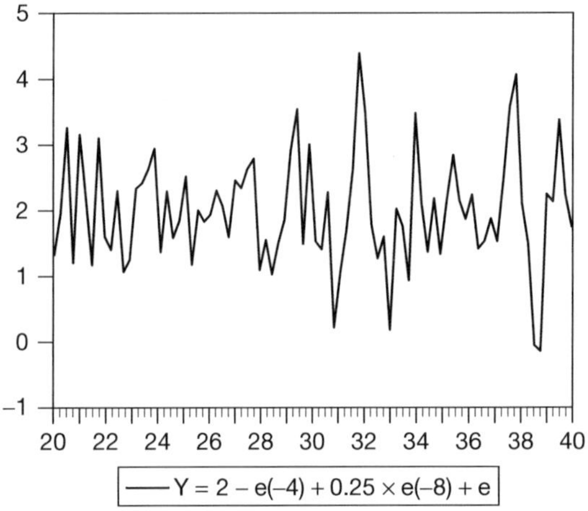

Included observations: 4193

Autocorrelation	Partial Correlation		AC	PAC
		1	-0.035	-0.035
		2	-0.021	-0.023
		3	0.019	0.018
		4	0.490	0.491
		5	-0.038	0.002
		6	0.008	0.028
		7	0.044	0.024
		8	-0.014	-0.331
		9	-0.019	-0.016
		10	-0.003	-0.041
		11	0.026	-0.003
		12	-0.034	0.205
		13	-0.022	-0.014
		14	-0.007	0.027
		15	0.010	0.008
		16	-0.051	-0.202
		17	-0.013	0.004
		18	0.012	-0.006
		19	0.007	0.009
		20	-0.028	0.157
		21	0.008	0.009

Included observations: 4189

Autocorrelation	Partial Correlation		AC	PAC
		1	-0.056	-0.056
		2	-0.023	-0.027
		3	0.047	0.044
		4	-0.613	-0.612
		5	0.026	-0.040
		6	0.047	0.012
		7	-0.016	0.034
		8	0.134	-0.383
		9	-0.005	-0.031
		10	-0.034	0.002
		11	0.011	0.040
		12	-0.000	-0.229
		13	0.006	-0.010
		14	0.013	0.001
		15	-0.012	0.025
		16	-0.016	-0.155
		17	-0.019	-0.034
		18	-0.010	-0.020
		19	0.001	0.003
		20	0.003	-0.117
		21	0.022	-0.020

an S-MA(1), we expect only one significant spike in the ACF, and this is what we find at displacement $s = 4$. For the S-MA(2), the PACF decays smoothly toward zero with relevant autocorrelations at displacements s, $2s$, $3s$, . . ., and the ACF exhibits only two significant spikes at displacements s, $= 4$ and $s = 8$.

In summary, seasonal AR and MA models have the same characteristics as the non-seasonal AR and MA models when we consider that the seasonal cycle is related to the frequency of the data. All concepts explained in Chapter 6 (MA models) and in this chapter (AR models) i.e. point forecast, forecast error, **forecast uncertainty**, and density forecast, apply to S-AR and S-MA. You need to carry only the subindex s carefully.

In addition, the seasonal component may be a mixture of AR and MA dynamics so that we can also define a general S-ARMA(p,q) as:

$$Y_t = c + \phi_s Y_{t-s} + \phi_{2s} Y_{t-2s} + \cdots\cdots + \phi_{ps} Y_{t-ps} + \theta_s \varepsilon_{t-s} + \theta_{2s} \varepsilon_{t-2s} + \theta_{3s} \varepsilon_{t-3s} + \cdots + \theta_{qs} \varepsilon_{t-qs} + \varepsilon_t$$

which will enjoy the combined properties of S-AR and S-MA models.

7.3.3 Combining ARMA and Seasonal ARMA Models

In the previous section, we analyzed time series with only seasonal cycles. However, in practice, time series combine seasonal and nonseasonal cycles. A very common modeling practice is to assume that both cycles interact with each other in a multiplicative fashion. As an example, suppose that we have a quarterly time series and there are a seasonal cycle S-ARMA(1,2) and a nonseasonal cycle ARMA(2,1). Then the multiplicative model is written as

$$(1 - \phi_1 L - \phi_2 L^2)(1 - \phi_4 L^4) Y_t = c + (1 + \theta_4 L^4 + \theta_8 L^8)(1 + \theta_1 L)\varepsilon_t$$

so that the seasonal polynomials multiply the nonseasonal polynomials. The following time series is an example of a multiplicative ARMA and **S-ARMA**.

REAL DATA: Forecasting Changes in U.S. Residential Construction

---

In Figure 7.19, we plot the time series of changes in U.S. residential construction (in millions of dollars) and its autocorrelation functions. The seasonal cycle is evident in the time series plot because construction peaks during the spring months (March, April, and May) and collapses in the winter months (November, December, and January). The ACF shows clearly the 12-month seasonal cycle; however, the PACF is not as clean as those PACFs analyzed in Section 7.3.2, indicating that there may be a nonseasonal component. The PACF shows most significant spikes at displacements 1, 6, and 12. The spike at 1 indicates that the nonseasonal component may be well represented by an AR(1) specification, and the spike at 12 indicates a seasonal cycle as S-AR(1). The significant spike at 6 is the result of the negative autocorrelation when the series goes from a peak to a trough or vice versa (about six months between). Consequently, we propose a model as:

$$(1 - \phi_1 L)(1 - \phi_{12} L^{12}) Y_t = c + \varepsilon_t$$

We proceed to estimate the model in EViews following the same procedure described in Section 7.2. The estimation output is displayed in Table 7.3.

Observe the notation in the EViews output. We write the seasonal component as S-AR(1), but in EViews it is written as SAR(12), which corresponds to the frequency of the data. Both notations are equivalent. We observe that the coefficients ϕ_1 and ϕ_{12} are highly significant. The nonseasonal estimate $\hat{\phi}_1$ is about the same value as the partial autocorrelation coefficient, which is expected in an AR(1) model. The seasonal estimate $\hat{\phi}_{12}$ is rather large, indicating that there is much persistence in the seasonal component. Finally, the construction of a forecast proceeds as in any ARMA model. Observe that the proposed model can be written as an AR(13) specification (with restrictions in the parameters):

$$(1 - \phi_1 L - \phi_{12} L^{12} + \phi_1 \phi_{12} L^{13}) Y_t = c + \varepsilon_t$$

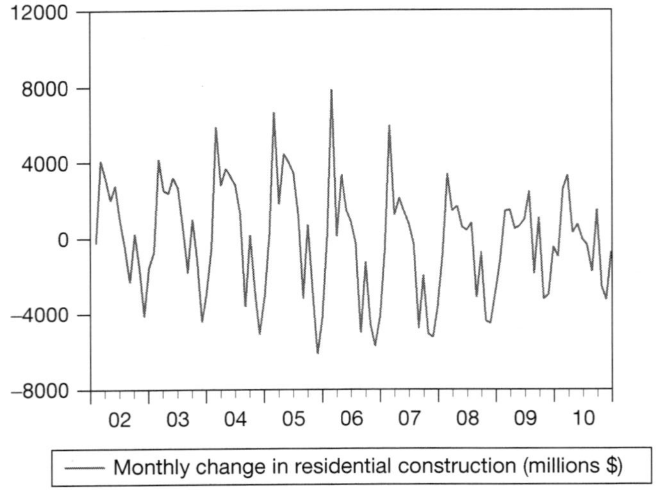

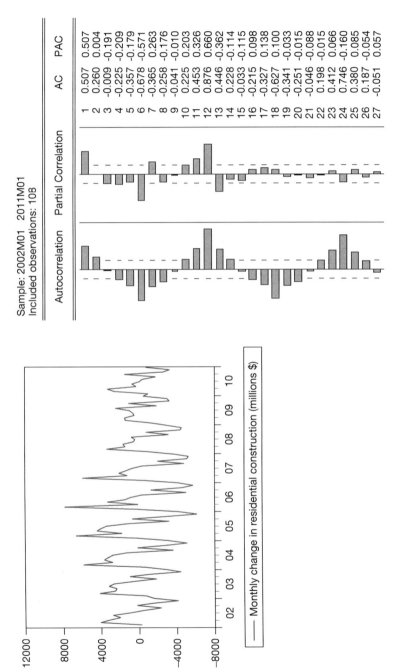

Sample: 2002M01 2011M01
Included observations: 108

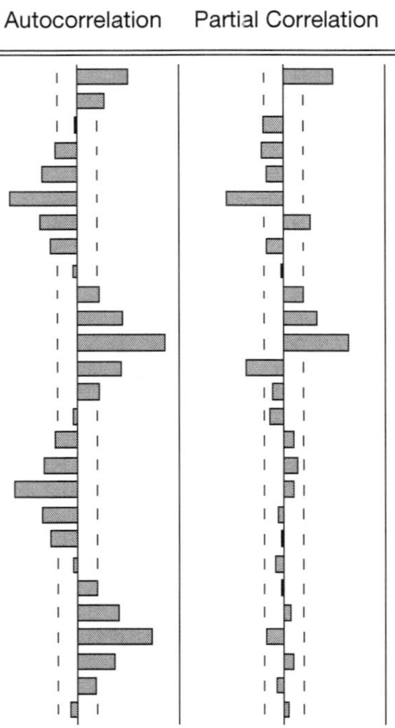

	AC	PAC
1	0.507	0.507
2	0.260	0.004
3	-0.009	-0.191
4	-0.225	-0.209
5	-0.357	-0.179
6	-0.678	-0.571
7	-0.365	0.263
8	-0.258	-0.176
9	-0.041	-0.010
10	0.225	0.203
11	0.453	0.326
12	0.876	0.660
13	0.446	-0.362
14	0.228	-0.114
15	-0.033	-0.115
16	-0.215	0.098
17	-0.327	0.138
18	-0.627	0.100
19	-0.341	-0.033
20	-0.251	-0.015
21	-0.046	-0.088
22	0.198	-0.015
23	0.412	0.066
24	0.746	-0.160
25	0.380	0.085
26	0.187	-0.054
27	-0.051	0.057

FIGURE 7.19 Monthly Changes of Private Residential Construction in U.S. (Millions of Dollars), Time Series Plot and Autocorrelograms

TABLE 7.3 Monthly Changes in Residential Construction, Estimation Results of AR(1) and S-AR(1) Model

Dependent Variable: change CONST
Method: Least Squares
Sample (adjusted): 2003M03 2011M01
Included observations: 95 after adjustments
Convergence achieved after 6 iterations

Variable	Coefficient	Std. Error	t-Statistic	Prob.
C	-593.2408	2399.622	-0.247223	0.8053
AR(1)	0.439971	0.093551	4.703012	0.0000
SAR(12)	0.923569	0.038771	23.82102	0.0000

R-squared	0.894790	Mean dependent var	-128.3158
Adjusted R-squared	0.892502	S.D. dependent var	3036.076
S.E. of regression	995.4326	Akaike info criterion	16.67530
Sum squared resid	91161518	Schwarz criterion	16.75595
Log likelihood	-789.0768	F-statistic	391.2194
Durbin–Watson stat	2.115719	Prob(F-statistic)	0.000000

Thus, by using the estimates from Table 7.3, we construct any forecast by proceeding as in Section 7.2. In Figure 7.20, we plot the multistep forecast from February 2011 to January 2012 with 95% confidence bands (based on normality of the error term). As expected, the forecast captures the seasonal cycle very neatly.

FIGURE 7.20 Monthly Changes in Residential Construction, Multistep Forecast

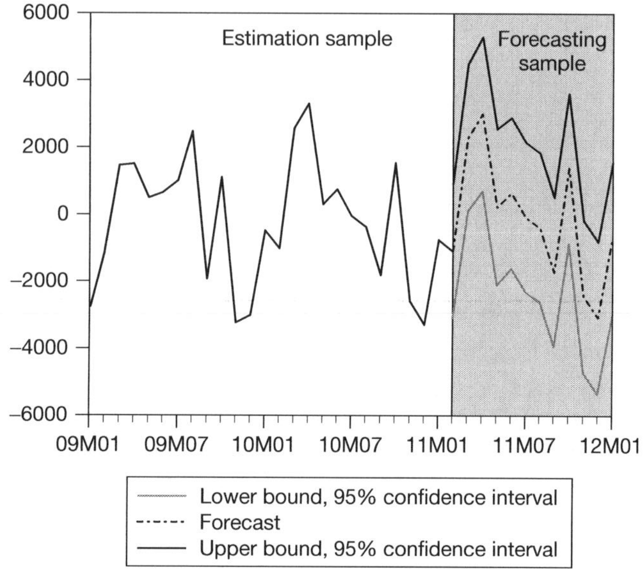

KEY WORDS

autoregressive process AR(1), p. 165
autoregressive process AR(2), p. 165
autoregressive process AR(p), p. 165
chain rule of forecasting, p. 187
density forecast, p. 171
deterministic cycle, p. 162
deterministic seasonality, p. 190
forecast uncertainty, p. 196
multistep forecast, p. 182
optimal forecast, p. 170
persistence, p. 167
S-AR(p), p. 192
S-ARMA, p. 197
seasonal cycle, p. 188
S-MA(q), p. 194
stochastic cycle, p. 163
stochastic seasonality, p. 190

EXERCISES

1. Simulate the following AR(1) processes:

$$Y_t = 1 + 0.7Y_{t-1} + \varepsilon_t$$
$$Y_t = 1 - 0.7Y_{t-1} + \varepsilon_t$$

for $\varepsilon_t \rightarrow N(0, 1)$. Comment on their differences: Contrast their time series and their autocorrelation functions. Comment on the covariance-stationary properties of both processes.

2. Update the time series of Figure 7.3, Unemployed Persons. Calculate the autocorrelation functions and reason the values of the autocorrelation coefficients for different displacements of time. Do you think that an autoregressive process could be a good model to explain the dependence of the series?

3. Update the time series on per capita income growth (California, 1969–2002 in Figure 7.7). Plot the time series. Compute the autocorrelation and partial autocorrelation functions. Which time series model(s) would you entertain? Estimate the model and construct the 1-step-, 2-step-, and 3-step-ahead forecasts, their forecast errors, and the uncertainty associated with the forecasts.

4. Investigate whether personal income in other states follows a similar process to that in Exercise 3.

5. Simulate the following AR(2) processes:

$$Y_t = 1 + 0.3Y_{t-1} + 0.7Y_{t-2} + \varepsilon_t$$
$$Y_t = 1 - 0.3Y_{t-1} - 0.7Y_{t-2} + \varepsilon_t$$

for $\varepsilon_t \rightarrow N(0, 1)$. Comment on their differences: Contrast their time series and their autocorrelation functions. Comment on the covariance-stationary properties of both processes.

6. Download some of the components of the Consumer Price Index (e.g., housing, food, transportation) from the BLS website. Analyze whether the inflation rate for these components may be modeled as an AR(2) process.
7. From Exercise 6, select the time series corresponding to food and gas inflation. Compute the autocorrelation and partial autocorrelation functions. Which time series model(s) would you entertain? Estimate the model and construct the 1-step-, 2-step-, and 3-step-ahead forecasts, their forecast errors, and the uncertainty associated with the forecasts. Which series is more difficult to predict?
8. Compare the general CPI inflation time series with that of the index excluding gas and food. Which inflation rate is more difficult to predict? Calculate the 1-step and 2-step density forecast for each inflation rate.
9. Update the time series on the number of unemployed people looking for part-time work (Figure 7.13). Plot the time series. Compute the autocorrelation and partial autocorrelation functions. Which time series model would you entertain? Estimate the model and construct the 1-step-, 2-step-, and 3-step-ahead forecasts, their forecast errors, and the uncertainty associated with the forecasts.
10. Simulate two AR(3) processes, one with strong persistence and the other with very little persistence. Explain the models that you choose.

CHAPTER 8

Forecasting Practice I

In Chapters 6 and 7, you learned the characteristics of moving average (MA) and autoregressive (AR) processes. The basic tool to choose between an MA or an AR process is the **autocorrelation** function. The different shapes of autocorrelation function (ACF) and partial autocorrelation function (PACF) are very informative to uncover the time dependence in the data. We have also seen that many economic and business time series have ACF and PACF that follow very closely an AR or an MA model. However, in real life, there are many time series for which the selection of an AR or an MA process is not so straightforward. In fact, we will see that the AR and MA process can be combined to give rise to a mixed model that we call autoregressive moving average or ARMA(p, q). If you combine the MA structure (Chapter 6) with the AR structure (Chapter 7) as in

$$Y_t = c + \phi_1 Y_{t-1} + \cdots + \phi_p Y_{t-p} + \varepsilon_t + \theta_1 \varepsilon_{t-1} + \cdots + \theta_q \varepsilon_{t-q}$$

the resulting model is an ARMA process, which will enjoy the combined properties of AR and MA processes. Because the choice among AR, MA, and ARMA models will not be as obvious when we face real time series (as opposed to artificially simulated time series), the forecaster will need to make judgment calls about which model(s) to select. In this chapter, you will learn new tools to evaluate different models, which will be helpful to select or narrow the set of models. This chapter introduces you to the practice of forecasting by putting into perspective all the knowledge that you have accumulated from Chapters 1 through 7. Our final objective is to construct a forecast. We achieve this goal by considering real data (San Diego house price index) and dividing our task into the following three stages:

1. The data: source, definition, descriptive statistics, and autocorrelations.
2. The model: estimation, evaluation, and selection.
3. The forecast: selection of loss function and construction of the forecast.

MODELING THE SAN DIEGO HOUSE PRICE INDEX

8.1 The Data

Our objective is to model the time series of house prices for the Metropolitan Statistical Area (MSA) of San Diego. Several websites provide information about house prices such as Freddie Mac (a mortgage company operating in the secondary market of mortgages) http://www.freddiemac.com, and the website of the Federal Housing Finance Agency (FHFA) http://www.fhfa.gov.

We have selected the quarterly house price index corresponding to the MSA of San Diego from 1975.Q1 to 2008.Q3. In Figure 8.1, we present the time series plot of the index (8.1a) and the corresponding quarterly growth rate (8.1b). The index shows a very dynamic real estate market: a smooth rise in the 1980s, a stagnant period during the recession of the early 1990s, the beginning of an expansion in the mid-1990s, an exponential rise in prices from 1998 to 2006, and, finally, the deflation of the real estate bubble from 2006 to the present. With an overall upward tendency, the index seems to come from a nonstationary process (Chapter 3). To find the stationary transformation we proceed to compute the quarterly growth rate of the index. In the growth rate plot (8.1b),

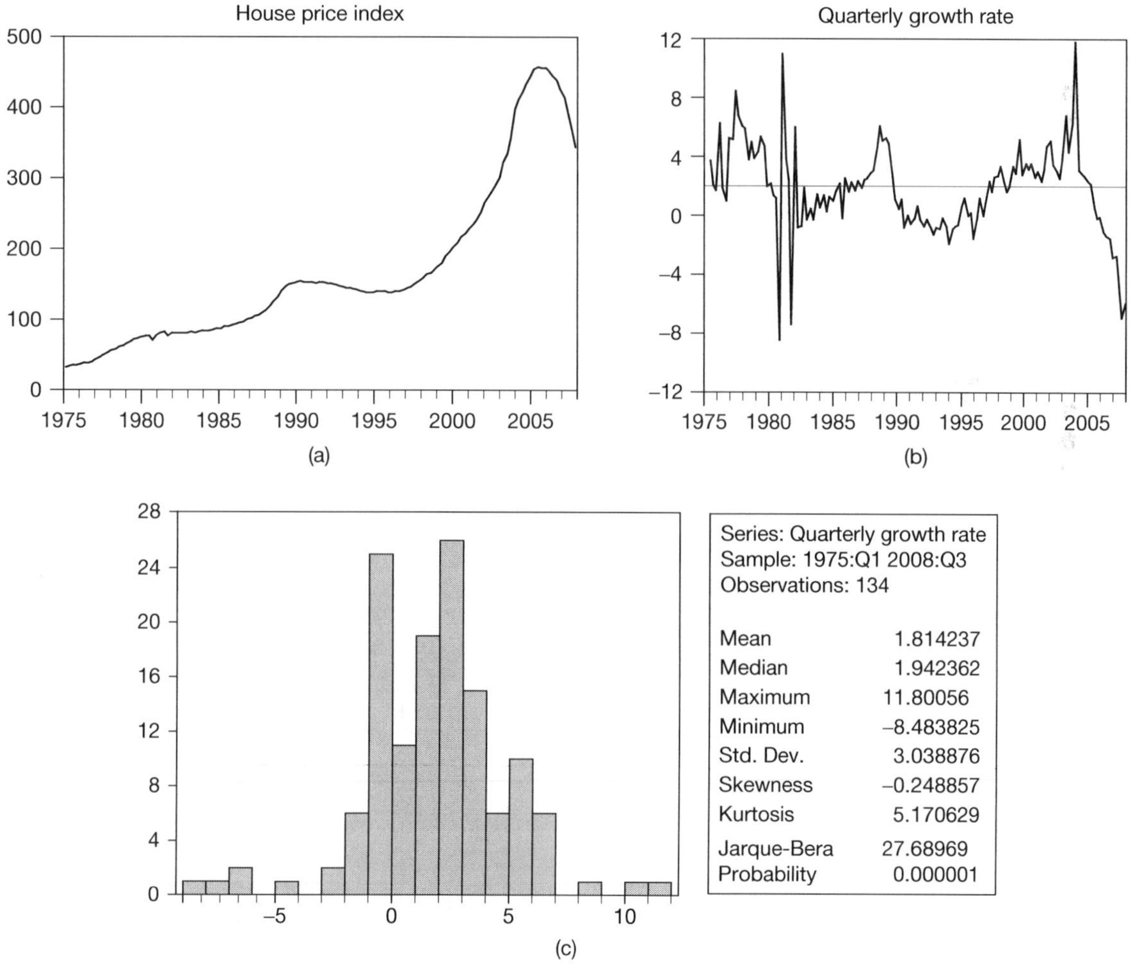

FIGURE 8.1 House Prices in San Diego MSA

we observe that in the second half of the 1970s, the price growth was of similar magnitude as that of the beginning of the 2000s, and in the 1980s, there was negative growth of a similar magnitude to what we have experienced since 2005. In recession years (early 1980s, late 2000s), negative quarterly growth rates reached about –8%. In expansion years (late 1980s, mid-2000s), appreciation rates reached a maximum of about 12% per quarter. For the full sample, the average growth rate has been 1.8% per quarter (horizontal line). See Figure 8.1c for additional descriptive statistics of the growth rate.

Now we proceed to model the growth rate. We calculate the autocorrelation functions presented in Figure 8.2. It is evident that this time series has much dependence. Both functions, ACF and PACF, show large autocorrelation coefficients for many displacements, and the **Q-statistics** (Chapter 4) reveal that we will comfortably reject the null hypothesis of no autocorrelation (observe that the p-values are practically zero). Faced with the information in ACF and PACF, which models could we entertain?

- *Option 1:* If we consider the family of AR processes, we should observe a smooth decay toward zero in the ACF and a limited number of spikes different from zero in the PACF, which will point out the order of the AR process. Figure 8.2 seems to satisfy these requirements although the choice of the cutoff in the PACF is less obvious. We could entertain an AR(2) or AR(4) or even an AR(5).
- *Option 2:* If we consider the family of MA processes, we would like to see a smooth decay toward zero in the PACF and a limited number of spikes different from zero in the ACF. If Figure 8.2 were to describe the dependence of an MA process, we would have observed a quick decay toward zero in the PACF and a substantial number of spikes different from zero in the ACF. With this lens, we could entertain at least an MA(4) or an even higher MA process such as an MA(7).
- *Option 3:* This option is to entertain a combined ARMA model because we could assess some decay toward zero in both the ACF and the PACF and no

FIGURE 8.2 Autocorrelation Functions of San Diego Price Growth

Sample: 1975:Q1 2008:Q4
Included observations: 134

Autocorrelation | Partial Correlation

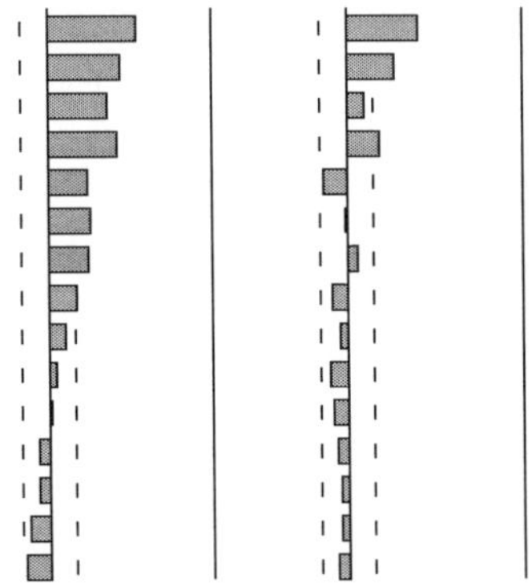

	AC	PAC	Q-Stat	Prob
1	0.487	0.487	32.524	0.000
2	0.486	0.326	65.135	0.000
3	0.401	0.121	87.502	0.000
4	0.464	0.223	117.67	0.000
5	0.257	-0.140	127.02	0.000
6	0.276	0.000	137.85	0.000
7	0.264	0.075	147.86	0.000
8	0.184	-0.092	152.77	0.000
9	0.115	-0.040	154.69	0.000
10	0.049	-0.114	155.04	0.000
11	0.011	-0.090	155.06	0.000
12	-0.064	-0.061	155.67	0.000
13	-0.073	-0.025	156.48	0.000
14	-0.123	-0.041	158.77	0.000
15	-0.156	-0.055	162.48	0.000

clear cutoff in ACF or PACF. We could claim an ARMA(2,2) or an ARMA(2,4) because the first two spikes in the PACF seem to be the most dominant in the partial autocorrelogram—AR(2) component—and to leave the remaining dependence to be picked up by either MA(2) or MA(4) component.

In summary, the shapes of the ACF and PACF seem to point out toward the first option, AR processes, but at this stage we should not fully disregard the possible contribution of an MA component. Remember that ACF and PACF are estimated functions and as such are subject to sampling error, which should be taken into account mainly when the sample size is not very large. The stage where several preliminary models are considered is known as the **identification** stage. Given that our sample is of medium size (134 observations), we start the modeling process by carrying six alternative models: MA(4), AR(3), AR(4), AR(5), ARMA(2,2), and ARMA(2.4).

8.2 Model Selection

At the identification stage, we have selected six models as potential representations of the stochastic process of the growth rate of the house price index. Let us call these models:

Model 1.	MA(4) $Y_t = \mu + \theta_1 \varepsilon_{t-1} + \theta_2\varepsilon_{t-2} + \theta_3\varepsilon_{t-3} + \theta_4\varepsilon_{t-4} + \varepsilon_t$
Model 2.	AR(3) $Y_t = c + \phi_1 Y_{t-1} + \phi_2 Y_{t-2} + \phi_3 Y_{t-3} + \varepsilon_t$
Model 3.	AR(4) $Y_t = c + \phi_1 Y_{t-1} + \phi_2 Y_{t-2} + \phi_3 Y_{t-3} + \phi_4 Y_{t-4} + \varepsilon_t$
Model 4.	AR(5) $Y_t = c + \phi_1 Y_{t-1} + \phi_2 Y_{t-2} + \phi_3 Y_{t-3} + \phi_4 Y_{t-4} + \phi_5 Y_{t-5} + \varepsilon_t$
Model 5.	ARMA(2,2) $Y_t = c + \phi_1 Y_{t-1} + \phi_2 Y_{t-2} + \theta_1\varepsilon_{t-1} + \theta_2\varepsilon_{t-2} + \varepsilon_t$
Model 6.	ARMA(2,4) $Y_t = c + \phi_1 Y_{t-1} + \phi_2 Y_{t-2} + \theta_1\varepsilon_{t-1} + \theta_2\varepsilon_{t-2} + \theta_3\varepsilon_{t-3} + \theta_4\varepsilon_{t-4} + \varepsilon_t$

8.2.1 Estimation: AR, MA, and ARMA Models

At the **estimation** stage, we estimate the parameters of the model based on the time series data. Across models we will obtain the values of the estimators $\hat{\mu}$, $\hat{c}$, $\hat{\phi}_1$, $\hat{\phi}_2$, $\hat{\phi}_3$, $\hat{\phi}_4$, $\hat{\phi}_5$, $\hat{\theta}_1$, $\hat{\theta}_2$, $\hat{\theta}_3$, $\hat{\theta}_4$, and $\hat{\sigma}^2_\varepsilon$. Recall that the symbol ^ means that the estimators are functions of the sample information (time series data). The population parameters do not carry a ^ symbol. We have already explained that AR models can be understood as linear regression models when the regressors are the lagged variables of the stochastic process. Hence, we can estimate the model with ordinary least squares; (reviewed in Chapter 2). The asymptotic or large sample statistical properties (consistency, efficiency, and asymptotic normality) of the least squares estimators in linear time series models are satisfied, and the standard statistics such as the t-ratio and F-test are valid. However, for MA and ARMA models, we cannot implement OLS because the regressors $\varepsilon_{t-1}, \varepsilon_{t-2}, \varepsilon_{t-3}, \ldots$ are not directly observable. The estimation technique for these models is nonlinear least squares, which is beyond the scope of this book.

Fortunately, as we see in the next paragraph, any time series software can estimate these models by specifying the correct commands.

We proceed with the estimation of six proposed specifications. For all models, you will be clicking in EViews (once you have opened your workfile) the following sequence

Object

New Object

Equation

and in Estimation settings select Method LS – Least Squares (NLS and ARMA). In the Equation specification, enter the model that you wish to estimate. For instance, to estimate Model 3, AR(4), write the following command: sdg c AR(1) AR(2) AR(3) AR(4) where 'sdg' is the dependent variable, in this case, "san diego growth," c is the constant, and AR(1), AR(2), AR(3), and AR(4) are the number of lags of the autoregressive model. For Model 1, MA(4), you would write the following command: sdg c MA(1) MA(2) MA(3) MA(4) where MA(1) MA(2) MA(3) MA(4) are the lags of the moving average model. For Model 6, ARMA(2,4), the command would look like sdg c AR(1) AR(2) MA(1) MA(2) MA(3) MA(4). In Table 8.1, we present the estimation output corresponding to these three models. By following similar commands, you could estimate the remaining models.

The output of Table 8.1 is already familiar to us. We reviewed the interpretation of many of these entries in Chapter 2. However, additional information will be very helpful within the context of time series models. We would like to compare the many proposed models along several criteria, and on doing so, we enter into the *evaluation* stage. For every model, we need to answer the following questions:

8.2.2 Is the Process Covariance-Stationary, and Is the Process Invertible?

Finite MA processes are always stationary. Our concern is with the AR processes. Because the proposed AR processes are of high order, to derive the corresponding necessary and sufficient conditions for covariance stationary (presented in Chapter 7) is cumbersome. However, in the estimation output of Table 8.1, we find the necessary information to assess the **covariance-stationarity** property of the process. It suffices to say that whenever the absolute value of the **Inverted AR roots** is strictly less than 1, the process is covariance stationary.[1] This is the case for the AR(4) and the ARMA(2,4) models. Whenever you find complex roots, you need to compute the modulus, for example, in the AR(4) model there are complex roots: $-0.1 \pm .65i$, whose modulus is $(-0.10)^2 + 0.65^2 = 0.432 < 1$.

[1] This topic requires advanced calculus and will not be studied in this book. It suffices to say that, from a mathematical point of view, an autoregressive model is a difference equation and the jargon about *roots* refers to the roots of the characteristic equation associated with the characteristic polynomial of the difference equation.

TABLE 8.1 San Diego House Price Growth, Estimation Output

MA (4)

Dependent Variable: SDG
Method: Least Squares
Sample (adjusted): 1975Q2 2008Q3
Included observations: 134 after adjustments
Convergence achieved after 8 iterations
Backcast: 1974Q2 1975Q1

Variable	Coefficient	Std. Error	t-Statistic	Prob.
C	1.684979	0.503973	3.343391	0.0011
MA(1)	0.353809	0.076941	4.598453	0.0000
MA(2)	0.382798	0.082081	4.663663	0.0000
MA(3)	0.234615	0.083348	2.814876	0.0056
MA(4)	0.464352	0.077820	5.966982	0.0000

R-squared	0.394084	Mean dependent var	1.814237
Adjusted R-squared	0.375296	S.D. dependent var	3.038876
S.E. of regression	2.401874	Akaike info criterion	4.626975
Sum squared resid	744.2007	Schwarz criterion	4.735103
Log likelihood	-305.0073	F-statistic	20.97518
Durbin-Watson stat	1.976946	Prob(F-statistic)	0.000000

Inverted MA Roots	.41+.71i	.41-.71i	-.59-.58i	-.59+.58i

AR (4)

Dependent Variable: SDG
Method: Least Squares
Sample (adjusted): 1976Q2 2008Q3
Included observations: 130 after adjustments
Convergence achieved after 6 iterations

Variable	Coefficient	Std. Error	t-Statistic	Prob.
C	0.106935	2.627275	0.040702	0.9676
AR(1)	0.238943	0.085584	2.791899	0.0061
AR(2)	0.261707	0.088495	2.957323	0.0037
AR(3)	0.111463	0.089509	1.245274	0.2154
AR(4)	0.284998	0.088905	3.205644	0.0017

R-squared	0.428518	Mean dependent var	1.763910
Adjusted R-squared	0.410231	S.D. dependent var	3.055403
S.E. of regression	2.346440	Akaike info criterion	4.581378

(continued)

Sum squared resid	688.2228	Schwarz criterion	4.691668
Log likelihood	-292.7896	F-statistic	23.43241
Durbin-Watson stat	1.898907	Prob(F-statistic)	0.000000
Inverted AR Roots	.96	-.01 -.65i -.01+.65i	-.71

ARMA (2,4)

Dependent Variable: SDG
Method: Least Squares
Sample (adjusted): 1975Q4 2008Q3
Included observations: 132 after adjustments
Convergence achieved after 18 iterations
Backcast: 1974Q4 1975Q3

Variable	Coefficient	Std. Error	t-Statistic	Prob.
C	0.886929	1.639675	0.540918	0.5895
AR(1)	0.297013	0.196977	1.507853	0.1341
AR(2)	0.580522	0.197836	2.934354	0.0040
MA(1)	-0.007620	0.195334	-0.039012	0.9689
MA(2)	-0.338640	0.151912	-2.229184	0.0276
MA(3)	-0.060909	0.095536	-0.637555	0.5249
MA(4)	0.265362	0.098566	2.692235	0.0081

R-squared	0.431114	Mean dependent var	1.797793
Adjusted R-squared	0.403807	S.D. dependent var	3.057434
S.E. of regression	2.360752	Akaike info criterion	4.607410
Sum squared resid	696.6440	Schwarz criterion	4.760286
Log likelihood	-297.0891	F-statistic	15.78793
Durbin-Watson stat	2.025208	Prob(F-statistic)	0.000000

Inverted AR Roots	.92	-.63		
Inverted MA Roots	.59+.38i	.59 -.38i	-.58+.45i	-.58 -.45i

For MA processes we need to check the invertibility property (recall Chapter 6). Although we could also derive necessary and sufficient conditions for the parameters of MA processes, it is easier to check that the absolute value of the **Inverted MA roots** are strictly less than 1 to claim invertibility. In the MA(4) and ARMA(2, 4), we find complex roots, and we need to calculate their modules. For the MA(4) model, we have $0.41 \pm 0.71i$ with modulus $(0.41)^2 + 0.71^2 = 0.672 < 1$ and $-0.59 \pm 0.58i$ with modulus $(-0.59)^2 + 0.58^2 = 0.684 < 1$. For the ARMA(2,4) model, we have $0.59 \pm 0.38i$ with modulus $(0.59)^2 + 0.38^2 = 0.492 < 1$ and $-0.58 \pm 0.45i$ with modulus $(-0.58)^2 + 0.45^2 = 0.539 < 1$. Thus, in both models the invertibility condition is satisfied.

8.2.3 Are the Residuals White Noise?

The model is designed to capture all linear dependence in the time series. It is natural to think that if the model is well specified, the innovation ε_t should not exhibit any linear dependence. As we already know, it should behave as a **white noise** process, which does not have any linear dependence. The innovation of the model is approximated by the residuals. To compute the residual proceed as in the regression framework. The residual is the difference between the observed data and the value estimated by the model. For instance, in the estimated AR(4) model:

$$\begin{aligned}\hat{\varepsilon}_t &= Y_t - \hat{c} - \hat{\phi}_1 Y_{t-1} - \hat{\phi}_2 Y_{t-2} - \hat{\phi}_3 Y_{t-3} - \hat{\phi}_4 Y_{t-4} \\ &= Y_t - 0.011 - 0.238 Y_{t-1} - 0.261 Y_{t-2} - 0.111 Y_{t-3} - 0.284 Y_{t-4}\end{aligned}$$

In this way, you will be forming a time series of $\hat{\varepsilon}_t$. To check whether the white noise property holds, calculate the autocorrelation functions of the residual series. In EViews, after you have estimated the model, the residuals can be obtained by clicking on the following sequence,

Equation
  Procs
    Make Residual Series

and the AC and PAC functions can be obtained by clicking on

Equation
  View
    Residual Tests
      Correlogram-Q stastics

The autocorrelation functions for the estimated MA(4), AR(4), and ARMA(2,4) models are presented in Figure 8.3. Our goal is to test whether the autocorrelation coefficients are equal to zero. In Chapter 3 (Section 3.3), we introduced the Q- statistic (and the p-value of the test) to test hypothesis such as $H_0: \rho_1 = \rho_2 = \cdots\cdots = \rho_k = 0$. Rejecting this hypothesis means that the residuals are not white noise. Failing to reject means that they may be white noise or, at the minimum, we could say that there is not much information to conclude that they are not. We also introduced a single hypothesis test for $H_0: \rho_k = 0$, so that we could check the 95% confidence

FIGURE 8.3 San Diego House Price Growth, Correlograms of the Residuals

MA (4)
Sample: 1975:Q2 2008:Q3
Included observations: 134
Q-stastistic probabilities adjusted for 4 ARMA term(s)

Autocorrelation	Partial Correlation		AC	PAC	*Q*-Stat	Prob
		1	0.004	0.004	0.0022	
		2	0.044	0.044	0.2722	
		3	0.084	0.084	1.2591	
		4	0.046	0.044	1.5514	
		5	0.136	0.131	4.1799	0.041
		6	0.142	0.137	7.0627	0.029
		7	0.125	0.118	9.2956	0.026
		8	0.068	0.048	9.9701	0.041
		9	-0.010	-0.045	9.9835	0.076
		10	-0.009	-0.063	9.9960	0.125
		11	0.024	-0.035	10.081	0.184
		12	-0.031	-0.089	10.224	0.250
		13	-0.016	-0.070	10.262	0.330

AR (4)
Sample: 1976:Q2 2008:Q3
Included observations: 130
Q-stastistic probabilities adjusted for 4 ARMA term(s)

Autocorrelation	Partial Correlation		AC	PAC	*Q*-Stat	Prob
		1	0.043	0.043	0.2433	
		2	0.036	0.034	0.4146	
		3	0.001	-0.002	0.4147	
		4	0.060	0.059	0.9077	
		5	-0.106	-0.111	2.4405	0.118
		6	0.016	0.022	2.4738	0.290
		7	0.156	0.164	5.8619	0.119
		8	0.030	0.010	5.9848	0.200
		9	0.056	0.058	6.4337	0.266
		10	-0.005	-0.025	6.4367	0.376
		11	0.005	-0.016	6.4402	0.489
		12	-0.069	-0.036	7.1398	0.522
		13	-0.025	-0.029	7.2337	0.613

ARMA (2,4)
Sample: 1975:Q4 2008:Q3
Included observations: 132
Q-stastistic probabilities adjusted for 6 ARMA term(s)

Autocorrelation	Partial Correlation		AC	PAC	*Q*-Stat	Prob
		1	-0.019	-0.019	0.0473	
		2	0.014	0.014	0.0742	
		3	0.053	0.054	0.4642	
		4	-0.004	-0.002	0.4666	
		5	-0.061	-0.063	0.9849	
		6	-0.047	-0.052	1.2887	
		7	0.145	0.147	4.2595	0.039
		8	0.048	0.064	4.5857	0.101
		9	0.036	0.038	4.7753	0.189
		10	0.021	-0.002	4.8385	0.304
		11	-0.006	-0.019	4.8438	0.435
		12	-0.048	-0.037	5.1767	0.521
		13	-0.020	-0.001	5.2384	0.631

interval, centered at zero, for *each individual autocorrelation coefficient*. When the AC and PAC spikes are within the 95% confidence interval (dashed lines), they are statistically zero, and when they are outside, the autocorrelations are different from zero.

In Figure 8.3, we observe that for the three models, all spikes in the ACFs and PACFs are within the dashed lines, so statistically speaking, the individual autocorrelation coefficients are zero. However, the Q-statistics tell a different story when the autocorrelations are examined jointly. For the MA(4) model, Q_5, Q_6, Q_7, and Q_8 have p-values lower than 5%, so we reject the null hypothesis of white noise. For the ARMA(2,4) model, only Q_7 has a p-value less than 5%. It is only for the AR(4) model do all Q-statistics have large p-values, meaning that, at the 5% significance level, we cannot reject a joint null hypothesis such as $H_0: \rho_1 = \rho_2 = \rho_3 = \rho_4 = \rho_5 = 0$ for the case of $Q_5 = 2.4405$ (p-value =11.8%). Thus, we conclude that white noise is a reasonable characterization of the residuals of an AR(4) while those from the MA(4) and ARMA(2,4) specifications have some time dependence left, and in this sense, these models are inferior to the AR(4). Pure MA models do not seem to fit the data well; the information that we have analyzed so far points toward some AR structure.

8.2.4 Are the Parameters of the Model Statistically Significant?

The estimation output in Table 8.1 contains the t-ratios and their associated p-values for the null hypothesis involving a single parameter, for instance $H_0{:}\phi_4 = 0$—in the AR(4) model—or $H_0{:}\theta_3 = 0$—in the MA(4) model. We should expect that the parameters of the best specification(s) are statistically different from zero. For instance, in the AR(4) model, the t-ratio for $\phi_4 = 0$ is 3.20 with a p-value smaller than 1%. Thus, we can safely reject the previously mentioned null hypothesis and conclude that the autoregressive parameter ϕ_4 is different from zero.

Reviewing the statistical significance (at the 5% level) of the parameters in the three models, we observe that in the MA(4) all parameters are statistically different from zero, in the AR(4) all but ϕ_3 are significant, and in the ARMA(2,4), only ϕ_1, θ_1, and θ_3 seem to be statistically zero. Thus, we cannot reject any of the three models if we base our selection criteria purely on the significance of the parameters: The MA(4) model comes out as a strong specification as well as the AR(4) and the ARMA(2,4).

8.2.5 Is the Model Explaining a Substantial Variation of the Variable of Interest?

The objective of any statistical model is to explain as much as possible the variation of the variable of interest. Recall that in a linear model, the coefficient of determination (R-squared and adjusted R-squared reviewed in Chapter 2) provides this information. For pure AR models, the R-squared can be interpreted as usual. For instance, for the AR(4), the model explains 41% of the variation of the growth rate in house prices. However, when we deal with MA or ARMA specifications (where some regressors are not directly observable), we prefer to assess the **residual variance**. The estimator of the residual standard deviation $\hat{\sigma}_\varepsilon$ is provided in the lower panels of the estimation output in Table 8.1 (labeled **S.E. of regression**), so that the residual variance is $\hat{\sigma}^2_\varepsilon$.

When comparing the residual variances of several models, we should consider a penalty term (or correction) to account for the number of parameters in the model. Otherwise, we could have smaller residual variances by just increasing the number of regressors (number of lags in our time series models). Recall a similar discussion in Chapter 2 about adjusting or penalizing the R-squared to obtain the adjusted R-squared. The residual variance, adjusted by the number of parameters m, is $\hat{\sigma}_\varepsilon^2 = \sum_t \hat{\varepsilon}_t^2/(T-m)$, so that when m increases, the numerator $\sum_t \hat{\varepsilon}_t^2$ may be smaller, but the denominator T-m will be also smaller counterbalancing the contribution of smaller residuals in the overall ratio.

For the MA(4), the residual variance is 5.769; for the AR(4), 5.505; and for the ARMA(2,4), 5.573. It appears that the AR(4) provides the lowest residual variance followed closely by the ARMA(2,4); in this sense, AR(4) is preferred to the other two specifications. Observe that the ARMA(2,4) has two more parameters than the AR(4) model, but the residual variance is larger, meaning that the two extra parameters do not contribute much in explaining the variability of home prices growth.

8.2.6 Is It Possible to Select One Model Among Many?

All previous questions have helped to narrow the model(s) that are more consistent with the properties of the data. It seems that the AR(4) is the best specification to model the time dependence in house prices, but we cannot yet disregard the ARMA(2,4). In time series analysis we have additional model selection criteria, of which we present the two most popular: the **Akaike information criteria** (AIC) and the **Schwarz information criteria** (SIC). The idea behind AIC and SIC is similar to the (adjusted) R-squared, which in linear models is another selection criterion, and to the residual variance, which we explained in the previous paragraph. Recall that our objective is to find a model that truly extracts the maximum information from the time series and, at the same time, is *parsimonious* enough.[2] We need to balance information versus the number of parameters in the model. With this goal in mind, the formulations of the AIC and SIC include a *penalty term* to capture the trade-off between a large number of lags (large number of parameters) and a potential reduction of the residual variance. If additional lags were needed, the increase in the penalty term would be counterbalanced by the reduction in the residual variance, resulting in a smaller AIC or SIC. Their formulas[3] are

$$AIC = \frac{2m}{T} + \log \frac{\sum_t \hat{\varepsilon}_t^2}{T}$$

[2] The **parsimony principle** dictates that among models with the same explanatory power, the one with the smaller number of parameters is preferred.

[3] You may find slightly different formulas in other books. EViews calculates the AIC and SIC based on the value of the log-likelihood function following the original definition of the criteria. The difference between EViews' calculations and the preceding formulas is only a constant that will not affect model selection.

$$SIC = \frac{m}{T}\log T + \log \frac{\sum_t \hat{\varepsilon}_t^2}{T}$$

where m is the number of estimated parameters and T is the sample size. The penalty terms are $2\,m/T$ and $(m/T)\log T$, which increase whenever the number of estimated parameters m increases. The SIC penalizes more heavily than the AIC because $2\,m/T < (m/T)\log T$ (for samples with $T > 8$ approximately). The preferred model is found by minimizing AIC or SIC with respect to the number of parameters.

The SIC criterion is *consistent*, which means that, as the sample size increases, the probability of selecting the best approximation to the true process generating the data approaches 1. Although AIC is not consistent (it enjoys other optimal properties), it performs well in small samples and should not be disregarded. SIC has a tendency to select more parsimonious models than AIC models. In practice, it is customary to report both criteria; sometimes they agree in the model to be selected and sometimes not. The parsimonious principle should also be considered in the final call.

Going back to the estimation output of Table 8.1, the AR(4) has the smallest AIC and SIC among the three models considered, so it is the preferred model. According to the AIC, the ranking is AR(4), ARMA(2,4), and MA(4) and according to the SIC is AR(4), MA(4), ARMA(2,4), showing the SIC preference for models with fewer parameters.

At the beginning of Section 8.2, we proposed six potential models. Although we have found that the AR(4) model is a preferred model, we could compare it with the remaining specifications (AR(3), AR(5), and ARMA(2,2)) and assess their differences. In Table 8.2, we summarize and evaluate the estimation results for the six proposed specifications. The AR(3) and ARMA(2,2) produce residuals that do not seem to behave as white noise processes. Both have larger residual variances, larger AIC and SIC, than those corresponding to the AR(4) specification so that neither AR(3) nor ARMA(2,2) dominates. However, the AR(5) model may be a contender because it delivers white noise residuals, and it has a slightly smaller residual variance, very similar AIC, and SIC to those of the AR(4) model. The statistical differences between the AR(4) and AR(5) are very small, but given that ϕ_5 is not statistically significant from zero and that the selection of AIC and SIC point toward an AR(4), we could disregard the AR(5) in favor of the more parsimonious AR(4) model.

8.3 The Forecast

Our ultimate objective is to predict the growth rate of house prices in San Diego. Some considerations should be addressed first. Let us ask the following questions:

8.3.1 Who Are the Consumers of Forecasts?

In other words, who will be interested in such forecasts? Any economic agent should be, but the reasons why will differ for different agents. We can point to at least four types of agents who may have a vested interest in this forecast: property owners, real

TABLE 8.2 Summary of Model Estimation and Evaluation

	MA(4)	AR(3)	AR(4)	AR(5)	ARMA(2,2)	ARMA(2,4)
ϕ's (t-ratio) θ's (t-ratio)	$\hat{\theta}_1 = 0.354$ (4.6) $\hat{\theta}_2 = 0.383$ (4.7) $\hat{\theta}_3 = 0.235$ (2.8) $\hat{\theta}_4 = 0.464$ (5.9)	$\hat{\phi}_1 = 0.281$ (3.2) $\hat{\phi}_2 = 0.345$ (3.9) $\hat{\phi}_3 = 0.177$ (1.9)	$\hat{\phi}_1 = 0.238$ (2.8) $\hat{\phi}_2 = 0.261$ (2.9) $\hat{\phi}_3 = 0.111$ (1.2) $\hat{\phi}_4 = 0.284$ (3.2)	$\hat{\phi}_1 = 0.282$ (3.1) $\hat{\phi}_2 = 0.270$ (3.0) $\hat{\phi}_3 = 0.135$ (1.4) $\hat{\phi}_4 = 0.307$ (3.4) $\hat{\phi}_5 = -0.13$ (−1.4)	$\hat{\phi}_1 = 0.134$ (0.6) $\hat{\phi}_2 = 0.777$ (3.5) $\hat{\theta}_1 = 0.137$ (0.5) $\hat{\theta}_2 = -0.415$ (−1.9)	$\hat{\phi}_1 = 0.297$ (1.5) $\hat{\phi}_2 = 0.580$ (2.9) $\hat{\theta}_1 = -0.007$ (−0.04) $\hat{\theta}_2 = -0.338$ (−2.2) $\hat{\theta}_3 = -0.061$ (−0.6) $\hat{\theta}_4 = 0.265$ (2.7)
Covariance-stationary	yes	yes	yes	yes	yes	yes
Invertibility	yes	yes	yes	yes	yes	yes
White noise residuals Q-statistics (p-value)	no $Q_5 = 4.178$ (0.04) $Q_8 = 9.970$ (0.04)	no $Q_4 = 10.722$ (0.0) $Q_8 = 15.099$ (0.01)	yes $Q_5 = 2.440$ (0.1) $Q_8 = 5.984$ (0.2)	yes $Q_6 = 0.704$ (0.4) $Q_8 = 3.968$ (0.2)	no $Q_5 = 7.103$ (0.01) $Q_8 = 11.004$ (0.03)	no $Q_7 = 4.259$ (0.04) $Q_8 = 4.586$ (0.10)
Residual variance $\hat{\sigma}_\varepsilon^2$	5.769	6.003	5.505	5.489	5.784	5.573
Adjusted R-squared	—	0.362	0.410	0.416	—	—
AIC	4.627	4.660	4.581	4.586	4.630	4.607
SIC	4.735	4.747	4.691	4.719	4.739	4.760

estate investors, the government, and mortgage banks. In the U.S. economy, a substantial proportion of households' wealth is the value of their home. A sound wealth management practice requires making decisions on buying and selling, which depends primarily on future prices. Investors decide to invest in housing when they have expectations of potential capital gains; thus, a price forecast will be helpful as a decision tool. In the government, policy makers may be concerned with the effect of a tight or loose monetary policy (i.e., changes in interest rates) on housing prices. Thus, forecasts of home prices under different monetary regimes are helpful. Mortgage banks invest on mortgages, which are risky investments because of the possibility of default by the borrowers. The likelihood of default increases when house prices go down, so a forecast of prices is very important to assess the financial health of these banking institutions.

8.3.2 Is It Possible To Have Different Forecasts from the Same Model?

Economic forecasts are tools in the decision-making process of many agents. Based on incomplete information, decisions are made at the present time about the future. Hence, only when the future is realized can we assess the consequences of such decisions; in economic terms, we evaluate losses or gains. Each agent associates a forecast error (positive or negative) with a loss. The result is a **loss function**, which could be different for different agents. As a result, although we may be analyzing the same time series and agree on the same statistical model, it is possible to have different forecasts because agents may have different loss functions. For instance, a property owner's house price forecast will differ from that of a mortgage bank because the latter may have a more severe loss associated with a forecast error on house prices than the former.

8.3.3 What Is the Most Common Loss Function in Economics and Business?

Although the forecasting profession has recognized for many years the existence of different loss functions, it is customary in practice to provide forecasts based on symmetric loss functions, which assume that the loss of a negative forecast error is the same as the loss of a positive error of the same magnitude. The advantage of symmetry is only mathematical tractability, but there is no economic rationale for such assumption. On the contrary, most of the time, economic agents have asymmetric loss functions; negative forecast errors may have associated more severe losses than positive errors, or vice versa. Let us think about mortgage banks. These institutions are heavily leveraged; that is, they borrow money from capital markets and individual depositors to lend money to individual home buyers. These loans, known as *mortgages,* constitute the assets of the banking institutions. Consider two opposite scenarios: an increase in house prices (positive growth rate) and a decrease in house prices (negative growth rate). When house prices go up, homeowners accumulate equity in their house and have the incentive to keep making their monthly mortgage payments on time. Concurrently, the receipt of these payments will allow the mortgage bank to meet its obligations with its creditors and depositors. In the second scenario when house prices go down, home equity goes down. If homeowners carry large mortgages, they may find that the value of the house is less than the amount of the mortgage. This creates the incentive for homeowners to default. When the bank does not receive the monthly mortgage payments, it will not be able to meet its obligations with its capital providers. The capital providers in turn may not lend any more funds to the bank, potentially ruining its business and jeopardizing its survival. If this behavior is common to many banks, the economy may experience a cascade of bankruptcies with the consequent spillovers in the overall economic system.

The described scenarios are not just an example. The U.S. economy has already experienced two episodes of massive defaults: (1) in the 1980s when many savings and loan institutions, mainly in southern states, went bankrupt because of the extreme drop in house prices; and (2) in 2008, the house bubble bust, and the unprecedented amount of defaults and foreclosures almost caused the collapse of the U.S. financial system and brought the American economy into recession. Can these crises be avoided? As we have explained, decisions on borrowing/lending money are based on the expectations of future house prices. Suppose that the mortgage bank forecasts an appreciation in house prices but the realized growth rate is negative, so there is a negative forecast error (i.e., $e_{t,1} = Y_{t+1} - f_{t,1} < 0$). If, based on the bank's optimistic forecast, it keeps lending money to potential home buyers and borrowing money from capital markets without making sufficient capital provisions, sooner or later it will face unexpected defaults. The loss (defaults on mortgages) associated with a negative forecast error could have terminal consequences for the institution. On the other hand, suppose that the bank forecasts a decline in the growth rate but the realized value is an appreciation in house prices (i.e., $Y_{t+1} > f_{t,1} \rightarrow e_{t,1} > 0$). Given the predicted pessimistic scenario, the bank makes capital provisions to face the expected defaults that are never realized. The loss associated with a positive forecast error is at the most the opportunity cost of the funds in the capital provision fund. By acting conservatively, the bank has foregone potential profits but has not jeopardized its survival. The two scenarios that we have analyzed are extreme but illustrate that the losses of positive forecast errors are substantially less dramatic than the losses of negative errors. The loss function of a mortgage bank should be asymmetric, penalizing negative forecast errors more heavily than positive errors.

In summary:

A forecaster must know prior to producing a forecast the loss function of the agents who will be consuming the forecast.

We proceed with the forecast of the growth rate of house prices in San Diego. In Chapter 4 (Section 4.3.3), we introduced the concept of *optimal forecast* for symmetric loss functions. Recall that an optimal forecast minimizes the expected loss. In this section, we practice the construction of the optimal forecast under symmetric loss, the forecast errors, and the density forecast for the preferred model AR(4). In Chapter 9, we will introduce the notion of optimal forecast under asymmetric loss and construct its corresponding forecast.

With a symmetric quadratic loss function, the forecaster attaches the same penalty to positive and negative forecast errors of equal magnitude. Let us choose a quadratic loss function

$$L = a\,e_{t,h}^2$$

for which only the magnitude, not the sign, of the error matters. We saw in Chapter 4 that for this loss function, the optimal forecast is the *conditional mean* of the process. We proceed to construct a forecast based on the selected AR(4) model following the rules derived in Chapter 7.

Collect the information that we know about the AR(4) model. The estimated model (Table 8.1) is[4]

$$Y_t = 0.011 + 0.2389Y_{t-1} + 0.2617Y_{t-2} + 0.1114Y_{t-3} + 0.2849Y_{t-4} + \hat{\varepsilon}_t$$

$$\hat{\sigma}^2_\varepsilon = 5.505$$

Information set: The time series up to 2008:03. To start the construction of the forecast, we need the last four data points (because we have four lags in the right-hand side of the model),

$t = 2008{:}03$	$Y_{2008:03} = -6.97\%$
$t - 1 = 2008{:}02$	$Y_{2008:02} = -6.93\%$
$t - 2 = 2008{:}01$	$Y_{2008:01} = -4.79\%$
$t - 3 = 2007{:}04$	$Y_{2007:04} = -2.74\%$

Forecasting horizon: We wish to forecast the growth rate for the last quarter of 2008 and the first half of 2009. We construct the 1–, 2–, and 3–periods ahead forecasts, $h = 1, 2, 3$. Recall that

$h = 1$	$f_{t,1} = c + \phi_1 Y_t + \phi_2 Y_{t-1} + \phi_3 Y_{t-2} + \phi_4 Y_{t-3}$	$\sigma^2_{t+1\|t} = \sigma^2_\varepsilon$
$h = 2$	$f_{t,2} = c + \phi_1 f_{t,1} + \phi_2 Y_t + \phi_3 Y_{t-1} + \phi_4 Y_{t-2}$	$\sigma^2_{t+2\|t} = \sigma^2_\varepsilon(1 + \phi_1^2)$
$h = 3$	$f_{t,3} = c + \phi_1 f_{t,2} + \phi_2 f_{t,1} + \phi_3 Y_t + \phi_4 Y_{t-1}$	$\sigma^2_{t+3\|t} = \sigma^2_\varepsilon\{1 + \phi_1^2 + (\phi_1^2 + \phi_2)^2\}$

By straight substitution of the estimated parameters of the model and the four most recent values in the information set, we have:

$h = 2008{:}4$	$f_{t,1} = -4.79\%$	$\sigma^2_{t+1\|t} = 2.35^2 \;\; \hat{\sigma}^2_{t+1\|t} = 2.47^2$
$h = 2009{:}1$	$f_{t,2} = -5.10\%$	$\sigma^2_{t+2\|t} = 2.41^2 \;\; \hat{\sigma}^2_{t+2\|t} = 2.55^2$
$h = 2009{:}2$	$f_{t,3} = -5.21\%$	$\sigma^2_{t+3\|t} = 2.53^2 \;\; \hat{\sigma}^2_{t+3\|t} = 2.67^2$

[4] In the EViews table (Table 8.1) and for the AR(4) model, **C** = 0.1069 corresponds to the estimate of the unconditional mean of the process. Recall that in a covariance-stationary AR(4), $\mu = \dfrac{c}{1 - \phi_1 - \phi_2 - \phi_3 - \phi_4}$; thus, we solve for the constant c and estimate it with the following formula:

$\hat{c} = \hat{\mu}(1 - \hat{\phi}_1 - \hat{\phi}_2 - \hat{\phi}_3 - \hat{\phi}_4) = 0.107(1 - 0.239 - 0.262 - 0.111 - 0.285) = 0.011$

Note that the **forecast uncertainty** increases with the forecasting horizon because the forecast error reflects the accumulation of future innovations. Even though future unpredictable shocks are the main source of uncertainty, we should acknowledge that additional uncertainty is introduced in the forecast because of the parameter estimation. The variance of the forecast, $\sigma^2_{t+h|t}$, was calculated under the assumption that the population parameters are known. In practice, this assumption is not very realistic because in most instances, the parameters of a model need to be estimated, introducing sampling error. This contributes to additional uncertainty and, hence, to a larger variance of the forecast. However, if the variance of the parameters' estimators is small, the uncertainty of the forecast will be driven mainly by future shocks. This is the case for our data: In the preceding table, we denote $\hat{\sigma}^2_{t+h|t}$ as the variance including parameter uncertainty. Observe that its values are only slightly larger than those of $\sigma^2_{t+h|t}$.

If we forecast longer horizons, we observe the convergence of the forecast toward the unconditional moments. In Figure 8.4, we show the multistep forecast for the growth rate up to 2020.Q4. Observe in the shaded area that the point forecast slowly goes back to the unconditional mean of the series (the horizontal line). How fast the forecast reverts to the mean depends on the model's persistence. In the AR(4) model, the persistence is equal to 0.90 ($= \hat{\phi}_1 + \hat{\phi}_2 + \hat{\phi}_3 + \hat{\phi}_4$), a high value, and, not surprisingly, the approach to the unconditional mean takes place over a long period of time.

The upper and lower bands around the forecast are the bounds of a 95% confidence interval, which gives a measure of the uncertainty of the forecast. Note that, at a longer horizon, the bounds are also stabilizing as a consequence of the convergence of the variance of the forecast to the unconditional variance of the process.

FIGURE 8.4 San Diego House Price Growth: Multistep Forecast

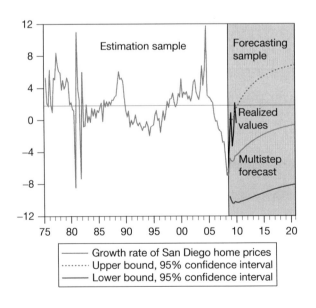

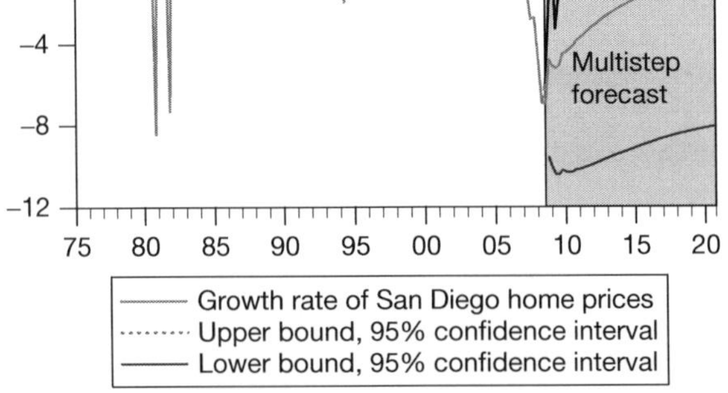

In EViews, you can generate multistep forecasts after estimating your model by clicking on the following sequence:

Equation

Proc

Forecast

In the forecast window, select the dynamic method (this is the **multistep forecast**), enter the forecasting horizon and the names for the forecast series and for the series of the standard errors. You may need to expand the range of your workfile to allow for the forecasting horizon that you wish to analyze.

Let us study in more detail the confidence of a forecast. It is a good forecasting practice to attach probabilities to the point forecast. This is the way to measure its uncertainty. It would be paradoxical to write forecasting reports by just providing a point forecast when the nature of any forecasting exercise is to quantify uncertainty. For decision makers, a probability statement has as much value as the point forecast. At the minimum, we should report confidence intervals, but even better, we should report the **density forecast**, which summarizes all information about the future.

Let us choose a fixed horizon, say $h = 2009{:}2$, for which our point forecast is $f_{t,3} = -5.21\%$ with $\hat{\sigma}^2_{t+3|t} = 2.67^2$. Under the assumption that the shocks εs are normally distributed, we have seen that the density forecast (the conditional density of the variable of interest) is:

$$f(Y_{t+3} \mid I_t) \rightarrow N(\mu_{t+3|t}, \sigma^2_{t+3|t}) = N(-5.21,\ 2.67^2)$$

What does this statement mean? It permits making a statement such as this: In the second quarter of 2009, the probability that San Diego home prices will decline by more than 5.21% is 50% (this forecast will be explained next). Observe that this is a point forecast (−5.21%) on the price growth rate to which we attach a confidence (50% chance). In other words, we could choose either the confidence and find out the point forecast attached to it, or we could choose the point forecast and find out how much confidence is attached to it. We proceed in the following way:

1. We need the **quantiles** of an N(0,1). Find them in the tabulated N(0, 1) at the end of any statistical book, or type the following command in EViews

```
scalar q=@qnorm(p)
```

where p stands for probability and q for quantile. In the following table, we have calculated some quantiles:

p	5%	20%	30%	50%	70%	80%	95%
q	−1.6448	−0.8416	−0.5244	0.0000	0.5244	0.8416	1.6448

For instance, we read an entry of the table as $\Pr(Z \leq -0.5244) = 30\%$, where Z is the N(0, 1) random variable. Graphically, in Figure 8.5, the shaded area is the probability associated with the value −0.5244.

FIGURE 8.5 Standard Normal Probability Density Function

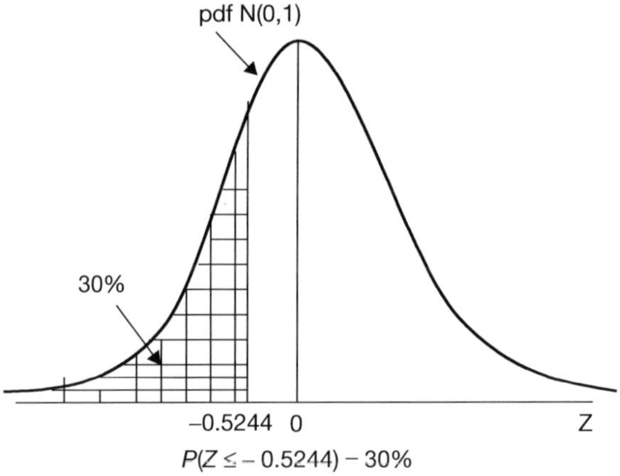

2. We know that Z is a standardized N(0,1) and any normally distributed random variable Y can be standardized as $Z = \frac{Y - \mu}{\sigma}$ so that $Y = \mu + Z\sigma$. In our case, we have that Y_{t+3} is conditionally distributed $N(-5.21, 2.67^2)$. Hence, Y_{t+3} can be written as $Y_{t+3} = -5.21 + Z \times 2.67$. Now, we find out the quantiles of Y_{t+3} by substituting the quantiles of Z in the previous formula. We obtain the following quantiles for Y_{t+3}:

p	5%	20%	30%	50%	70%	80%	95%
q	−9.60	−7.45	−6.61	−5.21	−3.81	−2.96	−0.82

This is the density forecast for the growth of house prices in February 2009. Graphically, in Figure 8.6, we present the density forecast for the growth rate of house prices in February 2009.

FIGURE 8.6 February 2009 Density Forecast for San Diego House Price Growth

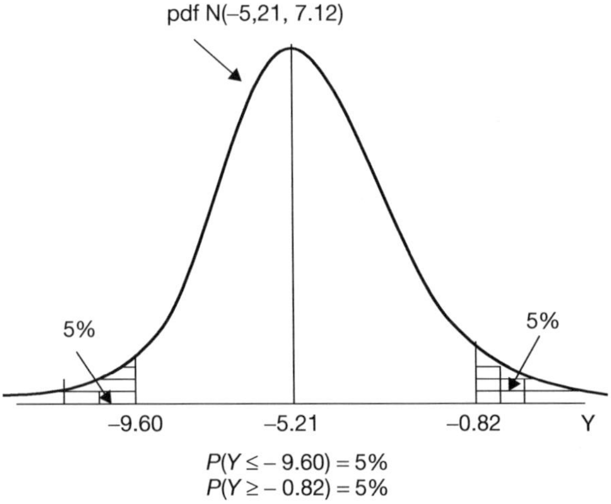

For instance, we could say that in the second quarter of 2009, there is only a 5% probability that home prices will appreciate more than −0.82%. Every forecast of the growth rate has a probability statement attached to it. Figure 8.6 clearly explains our introductory statement: In the second quarter of 2009, the probability that San Diego home prices will decline by more than 5.21% is 50%. The actual decline was 3.27%, above the expected value of the growth rate but well within the values of our density forecast.

8.3.4 Final Comments

We have reached our objective: the construction of a forecast for the quarterly growth rate of home prices in San Diego. Although we have constructed the forecast based on one model, the AR(4), it is good forecasting practice to entertain more than one specification. In the case at hand, we could derive a forecast from each of the six specifications proposed in section 8.2 although we know that some do not fit the data well, and we could inquire about what other factors may help to forecast the evolution of prices. For instance, in addition to the dynamics of the growth rate itself, we could entertain two, nonexclusive, hypotheses: (1) a financial hypothesis that claims mortgage rates drive home prices and (2) a real hypothesis that claims employment/income is the main driver of home prices. Then we may have additional competing model(s) such as

$$Y_t = c + \phi_1 Y_{t-1} + \phi_2 Y_{t-2} + \phi_3 Y_{t-3} + \phi_4 Y_{t-4} + \alpha R_t + \beta U_t + \varepsilon_t$$

where R_t contains past information about mortgage rates (r) (i.e., $R_t = \{\Delta r_{t-1}, \Delta r_{t-2}, \ldots..\}$), and U_t contains past information about employment (emp) (i.e., $U_t = \{\Delta emp_{t-1}, \Delta emp_{t-2}, \ldots..\}$). You will find employment figures at the county level at the Bureau of Labor Statistics website and mortgage rates on conforming 30-year fixed-rate loans at the regional level in the website of Freddie Mac, which conducts primary market mortgage surveys on a weekly basis. By now, you have enough knowledge to estimate and build the forecast from the preceding models. Assuming that you do that, you will have different forecasts coming from different models and must decide which one to choose. How to decide will be discussed in the next chapter where we will learn about the assessment of competing forecasts. No forecasting exercise is complete unless you explore the competition. Assessment of competing forecasts is an out-of-sample exercise: The forecasts are confronted with their realized values, the forecast errors are examined according to the forecaster's loss function, and statistical assessment on the values of the losses will guide the final selection of models and their forecasts.

KEY WORDS

EXERCISES

1. Follow up this chapter's forecasting exercise by computing the multistep forecast, forecast uncertainty, and density forecast based on AR(5) and ARMA(2,4) specifications, which were very similar to the AR(4) model (Table 8.2). Assess the differences between the forecasts based on these two models and the forecast built in Section 8.3.
2. Update the time series of house prices in the San Diego MSA. Does the AR(4) model still hold as the preferred specification? Explain your answer.
3. Download a time series of house prices for the MSA where you live. Conduct a forecasting exercise by explaining your data, model selection, and construction of a multistep forecast.
4. In Section 8.3.4, Final Comments, we propose extensions for the AR(4) model to include mortgage rates $R_t = \{\Delta r_{t-1}, \Delta r_{t-2}, \ldots..\}$ and information in employment (*emp*) $U_t = \{\Delta emp_{t-1}, \Delta emp_{t-2}, \ldots..\}$. Examine the following models:

   i. $Y_t = c + \phi_1 Y_{t-1} + \phi_2 Y_{t-2} + \phi_3 Y_{t-3} + \phi_4 Y_{t-4} + \alpha R_t + \varepsilon_t$
   ii. $Y_t = c + \phi_1 Y_{t-1} + \phi_2 Y_{t-2} + \phi_3 Y_{t-3} + \phi_4 Y_{t-4} + \beta U_t + \varepsilon_t$
   iii. $Y_t = c + \phi_1 Y_{t-1} + \phi_2 Y_{t-2} + \phi_3 Y_{t-3} + \phi_4 Y_{t-4} + \alpha R_t + \beta U_t + \varepsilon_t$

   Estimate and evaluate these three models, and construct the corresponding multistep forecasts. Are the forecasts any different from those provided by the pure AR(4)? Do mortgages rates or/and employment provide additional forecast ability for house price growth?
5. Download the time series of U.S. gross domestic product quarterly growth. Search for the best ARMA model(s), and construct a density forecast.
6. Download the time series of your favorite stock at the daily and monthly frequencies. Compute the time series of returns, and for each frequency, build a density forecast.
7. When the U.S. stock market opens in New York, the European markets have already been in session for several hours. Does the activity in European markets have predictive content for the U.S. market? Download the British stock index (FTSE) and the SP500 index at the daily frequency. Examine whether FTSE returns can help to forecast SP500 returns.
8. Download the monthly time series of the U.S. dollar/euro exchange rate. Could you predict whether the U.S. dollar will appreciate or depreciate next month?

9. In Chapter 7, Section 7.3.3, we proposed an ARMA model with a seasonal component for changes in U.S. residential construction. Construct a density forecast for each month of the next year.

10. Download the time series of monthly sales of new cars. Search for the best ARMA model(s), potentially including a seasonal cycle, and construct a density forecast for each month of the next year.

CHAPTER 9

Forecasting Practice II: Assessment of Forecasts and Combination of Forecasts

In Chapter 8, we examined several ARMA models and, through several statistical criteria, we narrowed the set of models to those that were more consistent with the **in-sample properties** of the data. In this chapter, we continue the evaluation of models, but now we focus on their **out-of-sample properties**. We will evaluate the forecasting ability of each model and, to do so, we need to choose a loss function.

The loss function was introduced in Chapter 4 as one of the forecaster's tools. Now we revisit it again for two important reasons. The first is that the choice of a loss function is linked to the notion of optimality of the forecast. Because uncertainty is inherent in any forecast, the forecaster is bound to commit forecast errors, which are costly. It is logical to expect that the forecaster would like to minimize the costs associated with the forecast errors, and upon doing so, will search for the optimal forecast associated with her loss function. The second reason we bring the loss function again is that in our practice, we confront several models from which we will construct different forecasts. For a given loss function and facing several forecasts, we will wonder which one(s) to choose. Then we would like to evaluate the loss associated with each forecast and to develop a selection criterion. Furthermore, if we have several forecasts, we could ask whether a combination of them would be better (lower loss) than just a forecast from a single model. Hence, this chapter has the title *Assessment of Forecasts and Combination of Forecasts.*

In Chapter 4, we presented different **symmetric loss functions** and **asymmetric loss functions** and introduced the **optimal forecast** for symmetric functions. We have already constructed optimal forecasts for the ARMA models in Chapters 6 and 7 and implemented them in the forecasting exercise of Chapter 8. We also made a strong case for economic agents facing asymmetric loss functions most of the time so that it is natural to ask what the optimal forecast will be in this instance.

Summarizing our task ahead, we have two main objectives to fulfill:

i. Explore further the notion of optimality, in particular the case of asymmetric loss, and learn how to test for optimality.
ii. Evaluate competing forecasts in the light of the loss function chosen by the forecaster, and analyze the advantages of combining several forecasts.

9.1 Optimal Forecast

Let us start by reviewing the notion of optimal forecast introduced in Chapter 4. Suppose that the forecaster has a loss function $L(e)$, that is,

$$L(e_{t,h}) = L(y_{t+h} - f_{t,h})$$

where $f_{t,h}$ is the forecast at time t of the random variable Y_{t+h}, which has a conditional probability density function, say $f(y_{t+h} | I_t)$. Upon choosing $f_{t,h}$, the forecaster would like to minimize the costs associated with potential forecast errors $e_{t,h}$. In particular, she is interested in minimizing the expected loss, or in other words, the average of the loss function

$$E(L(y_{t+h} - f_{t,h})) = \int L(y_{t+h} - f_{t,h}) f(y_{t+h} | I_t) dy \tag{9.1}$$

for Y_{t+h}, being a continuous random variable. Then, we define:

Optimal forecast $f^*_{t,h}$ is the forecast that minimizes the expected loss[1]

$$\min_{f_{t,h}} E\left(L(y_{t+h} - f_{t,h})\right)$$

From (9.1), two components affect the optimal forecast:

1. The conditional probability density function $f(y_{t+h} | I_t)$.
2. The functional form of the loss function $L(y_{t+h} - f_{t,h})$.

As a reminder, let us mention here the graphical representation (Figure 4.6 in Chapter 4) of our search for the optimal forecast $f^*_{t,h}$. In Figure 9.1, observe that the optimal forecast—constructed today—will be an outcome of the random variable Y_{t+h} (some value along the vertical dashed line) at a future time $t + h$. Where to place $f^*_{t,h}$ depends on the functional form of the loss function.

9.1.1 Symmetric and Asymmetric Loss Functions

We have already seen that for a quadratic loss function $L(e_{t,h}) = ae^2_{t,h}$, the optimal forecast is the conditional mean of the random variable Y_{t+h} (Section 4.3.3 in Chapter 4), that is, $f^*_{t,h} = E(Y_{t+h} | I_t) \equiv \mu_{t+h|t}$. If we assume that the conditional density is a normal

[1] The solution to this optimization problem requires some knowledge of calculus. However, the discussion in the text proceeds with no mathematical concepts and focuses only on statistical concepts. In the chapter appendix, the mathematical solution is developed.

FIGURE 9.1
The Forecasting Problem

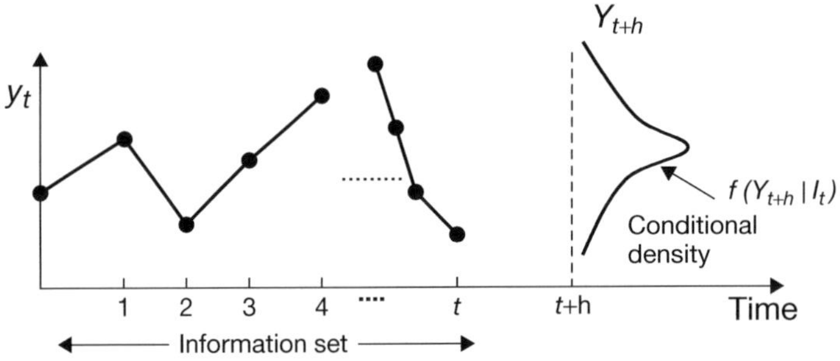

density with conditional mean $\mu_{t+h|t} \equiv E(Y_{t+h} | I_t)$ and conditional variance $\sigma^2_{t+h|t} \equiv \text{Var}(Y_{t+h} | I_t)$, that is, $f(y_{t+h} | I_t) = N(\mu_{t+h|t}, \sigma^2_{t+h|t})$, where will you place $f^*_{t,h}$ in Figure 9.1? (See Figure 4.7 in Chapter 4.)

Now suppose that the forecaster has an asymmetric loss function. Let us choose the linex function, $L(e) = \exp(ae) - ae - 1$, $a \neq 0$ (Chapter 4). What is the optimal forecast in this case? The optimality criterion is the same: We need to minimize the expected loss with respect to $f_{t,h}$. Let us calculate the expected loss:

$$\begin{aligned} E(L(e_{t,h}) | I_t) &= E(\exp(ae_{t,h}) - ae_{t,h} - 1) \\ &= \exp(-af_{t,h})E(\exp(ay_{t+h})) - aE(y_{t+h}) + af_{t,h} - 1 \end{aligned}$$

The expected loss does not look as friendly as in the symmetric case, but nevertheless, you should not lose the perspective of the problem. This is just an average loss that depends on $f_{t,h}$, and the task is to find which $f_{t,h}$ provides the lowest average loss. Following an optimization procedure explained in this chapter appendix, the optimal forecast, under the assumption of normal conditional density for Y_{t+h}, is:

$$f^*_{t,h} = \mu_{t+h|t} + \frac{a}{2}\sigma^2_{t+h|t} \tag{9.2}$$

It is important to understand the differences between the optimal forecast under symmetric loss and that under asymmetric loss (9.2). The symmetric loss produces a forecast that is centered on the conditional mean. The optimal forecast under asymmetric loss contains a correction term that depends on the asymmetry of the loss function (the value of the constant a and the conditional variance of Y_{t+h}). What is the interpretation of the correction term $\frac{a}{2}\sigma^2_{t+h|t}$? Let us assume that $a < 0$ (see Figure 9.2). This is the

FIGURE 9.2
Asymmetric Loss Function: Linex Function

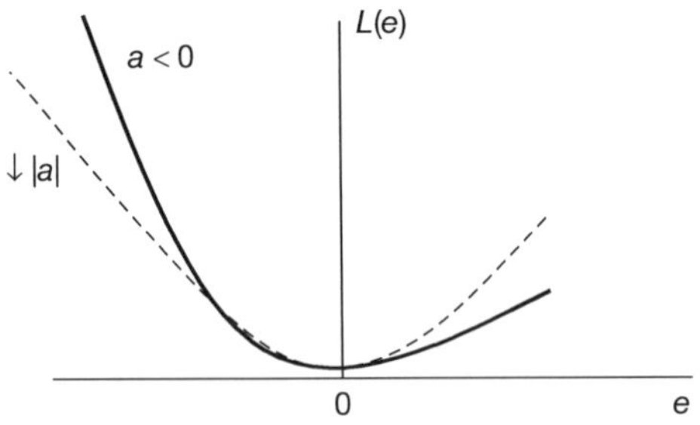

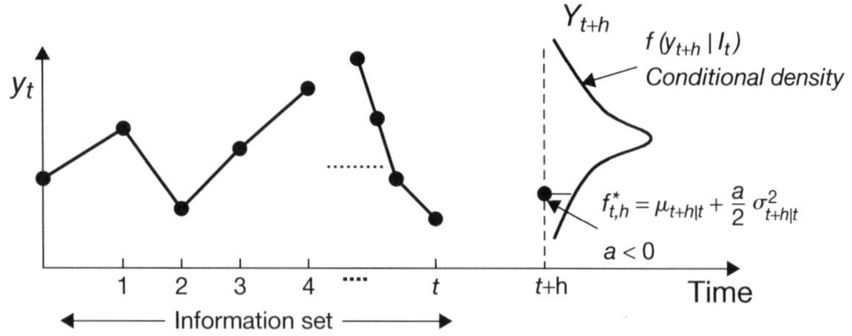

FIGURE 9.3 Optimal Forecast Under Asymmetric Loss Function (Linex Function)

case for which negative forecast errors are more heavily penalized than positive errors. Thus, the forecaster would be interested in avoiding negative errors. Because the forecast error is defined as $e_{t,h} = y_{t+h} - f_{t,h}$, the point forecast $f_{t,h}$ will be pushed down to force an outcome such as $y_{t+h} > f_{t,h}$, and consequently, to increase the likelihood of a positive forecast error. Thus, on average, the forecast error will be positive. The forecaster will push down the point forecast by subtracting the term $\frac{a}{2}\sigma^2_{t+h|t}$, and the optimal point forecast will be located below the conditional mean of Y_{t+h}. Graphically, in Figure 9.3, observe the position of the optimal forecast.

The opposite argument applies when $a > 0$. The forecaster will try to avoid positive forecast errors, and in doing so, the forecast will be pushed above the conditional mean of Y_{t+h}.

REAL DATA: Forecasting Quarterly House Price Index in the San Diego MSA, 1975–2008 Under the Linex Loss Function

Recall our discussion in Chapter 8 on how prevalent asymmetric loss functions are in economics and business. Suppose that a mortgage bank is interested in the forecasting of home prices. For this type of institution, negative forecast errors could be more damaging than positive forecast errors (Section 8.3.3 in Chapter 8). Thus, by acting conservatively, the bank will bias its forecast downward. Let us assume that the forecasters at the bank choose a Linex loss function with $a < 0$ so that negative errors are more penalized than positive errors.

A difference with the quadratic loss function is that we need to know (choose) the magnitude of a, which indicates the steepness of the penalty. The larger (in absolute value) a is, the larger the penalty will be. In practice, the consumer of the forecast (i.e., the mortgage bank) needs to provide this information. Let us assume that $a = -1$ in order to construct the optimal forecast for the growth rate of home prices in San Diego under the Linex function. The forecast calculated under a quadratic loss function (section 8.3 in Chapter 8) will be very helpful because there we computed $\mu_{t+h|t}$ and $\sigma^2_{t+h|t}$. For the asymmetric loss, we just need to calculate the optimal forecast as

$$f^*_{t,h} = \hat{\mu}_{t+h|t} - 0.5\hat{\sigma}^2_{t+h|t}$$

for the forecasting period fourth quarter 2008 (Q4) to second quarter 2009 (Q2):

$h = 2008{:}Q4$	$\hat{\mu}_{t+1\|t} = -4.79\%$	$\hat{\sigma}^2_{t+1\|t} = 2.47^2 = 6.10$	$f^*_{t,1} = -7.84\%$
$h = 2009{:}Q1$	$\hat{\mu}_{t+2\|t} = -5.10\%$	$\hat{\sigma}^2_{t+2\|t} = 2.55^2 = 6.50$	$f^*_{t,2} = -8.35\%$
$h = 2009{:}Q2$	$\hat{\mu}_{t+3\|t} = -5.21\%$	$\hat{\sigma}^2_{t+3\|t} = 2.67^2 = 7.13$	$f^*_{t,3} = -8.77\%$

As expected, the point forecast is lower than the forecast under quadratic loss. The forecaster does not want to be surprised by negative forecast errors and pushes the forecast down.

What Is the Density Forecast Under Asymmetric Loss?

Before we construct the density forecast for home prices, it is important to understand a very important property of the forecast error under an asymmetric loss function. To make the point, analyzing the forecast error for an AR(1) process under a Linex loss function is sufficient.

For $h = 1$, the forecast error is:

$$e_{t,1} = Y_{t+1} - f_{t,1} = c + \phi Y_t + \varepsilon_{t+1} - \mu_{t+1|t} - \frac{a}{2}\sigma^2_{t+1|t} \tag{9.3}$$

$$= c + \phi Y_t + \varepsilon_{t+1} - c - \phi Y_t - \frac{a}{2}\sigma^2_{t+1|t} = \varepsilon_{t+1} - \frac{a}{2}\sigma^2_{t+1|t}$$

For $h = 2$,

$$e_{t,2} = Y_{t+2} - f_{t,2} = c + \phi Y_{t+1} + \varepsilon_{t+2} - \mu_{t+2|t} - \frac{a}{2}\sigma^2_{t+2|t}$$

$$= c + \phi Y_{t+1} + \varepsilon_{t+2} - c - \phi \mu_{t+1|t} - \frac{a}{2}\sigma^2_{t+2|t} = \varepsilon_{t+2} + \phi \varepsilon_{t+1} - \frac{a}{2}\sigma^2_{t+2|t} \tag{9.4}$$

Further horizons can be calculated in the same fashion. These two cases, $h = 1$ and $h = 2$, are informative enough to identify two important issues:

1. Compare these forecast errors with those under a quadratic loss. The difference between the errors from both loss functions is given by the term $(a/2)\sigma^2_{t+h|t}$. This term makes the forecast error under asymmetric loss function biased. What does that mean? If we compute the expected values of (9.3) and (9.4), we have

$$E(e_{t,1}) = E(\varepsilon_{t+1}) - \frac{a}{2}\sigma^2_{t+1|t} = -\frac{a}{2}\sigma^2_{t+1|t}$$

$$E(e_{t,2}) = E(\varepsilon_{t+2}) + \phi E(\varepsilon_{t+1}) - \frac{a}{2}\sigma^2_{t+2|t} = -\frac{a}{2}\sigma^2_{t+2|t}$$

We observe that they are not equal to zero, as it is the case for the forecast errors under quadratic loss function. The expected value will be positive when $a < 0$ and negative when $a > 0$. This strongly agrees with the forecaster's behavior. If the forecaster is avoiding negative forecast errors ($a < 0$), then positive errors will happen with more frequency; hence, the mean of the errors must be biased toward a positive number. The opposite argument will hold when the forecaster is avoiding positive errors.

This issue is important because some forecasting practice uses the unbiasedness of the forecast error (that is, expected value equal to zero) as a test for forecast optimality. However, we have seen that the loss function is important for shaping the forecast error, and optimality of the forecast could hold together with biased forecast errors. Testing for unbiasedness of the forecast error is a correct approach only when the loss function is symmetric. Otherwise, it is perfectly correct to have biased forecast errors with no implication whatsoever for the optimality of the forecast.

2. Is the uncertainty of the forecast under quadratic loss different from that of the forecast under Linex loss? Compute the variances of the forecast errors (9.3) and (9.4) for the AR(1) process under Linex loss, taking into account that now $Ee_{t,h} \neq 0$:

$$\mathrm{var}(e_{t,1}) = E(e_{t,1} - Ee_{t,1})^2 = \mathrm{var}(\varepsilon_{t+1}) = \sigma_\varepsilon^2 = \sigma_{t+1|t}^2 = \mathrm{var}(Y_{t+1} \mid I_t)$$

$$\begin{aligned}\mathrm{var}(e_{t,2}) &= E(e_{t,2} - Ee_{t,2})^2 = E(\varepsilon_{t+2} + \phi\varepsilon_{t+1})^2 \\ &= \sigma_\varepsilon^2(1 + \phi^2) = \sigma_{t+2|t}^2 = \mathrm{var}(Y_{t+2} \mid I_t).\end{aligned}$$

Observe that the term $(a/2)\sigma_{t+h|t}^2$ does not play any role. This term affects the mean value of the forecast error but not its variance. Uncertainty is driven only by the unpredictable future shocks ε s, which obviously are unknown at the present time.

Consequently, the density forecast under Linex loss will not be affected by the asymmetry of the loss function. The density forecast will be the same for symmetric loss functions and asymmetric loss functions; thus, the density forecast for Y_{t+h} is

$$f(Y_{t+h} \mid I_t) \rightarrow N(\mu_{t+h|t}, \sigma_{t+h|t}^2) \tag{9.5}$$

Going back to the data, under Linex loss, the density forecast, for the quarterly growth rate of house prices in 2009:Q2 is $f(Y_{t+3} \mid I_t) \rightarrow N(\mu_{t+3|t}, \sigma_{t+3|t}^2) = N(-5.21, 2.67^2)$, which is the same as the density forecast under quadratic loss (Chapter 8, Figure 8.6). However, given that the point forecast (under Linex loss) is not centered in the mean value of the density, we would like to find the probability associated with it, $f_{t,3}^* = -8.77\%$, which is $\Pr(Y_{n+3} \leq -8.77) = 9.2\%$. Graphically, in Figure 9.4, observe that the forecast of the mortgage bank, which acts conservatively, falls below the expected value of the growth rate; its forecast falls precisely in the lower decile of the density forecast.

9.1.2 Testing the Optimality of the Forecast

We have learned that optimality should be assessed with regard to the loss function chosen by the forecaster. In Chapters 6, 7, and 8, we derived and implemented the optimal forecast under quadratic loss, and in this chapter, we have already learned that under asymmetric loss, the optimal forecast errors are biased, but the uncertainty of the

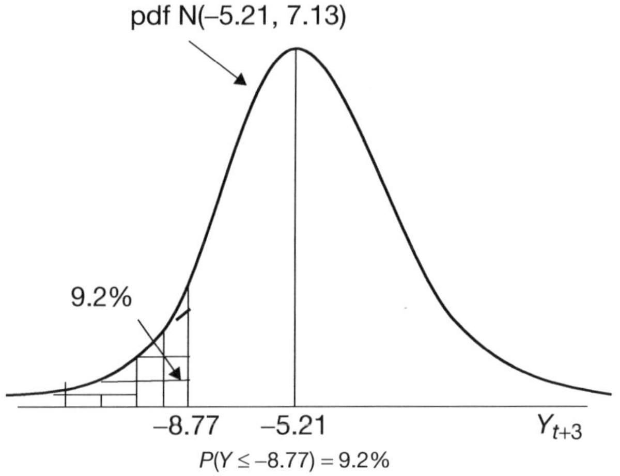

FIGURE 9.4 Density Forecast of Quarterly Growth Rate of House Prices in 2009:Q2, Point Forecast Under Linex Function

forecast and the density forecast are the same as those under quadratic loss. We summarize the results analyzed in Chapter 6, 7, and 8:

1. Under quadratic loss, the optimal forecast at horizon h is the conditional mean of Y_{t+h}:

$$f^*_{t,h} = \mu_{t+h|t}$$

Under asymmetric loss, the optimal forecast at horizon h needs an additional term:

$$f^*_{t,h} = \mu_{t+h|t} + \tau_h$$

where τ_h is a constant for h fixed. If the loss is Linex, we have seen that $\tau_h = \frac{a}{2}\sigma^2_{t+h|t}$.

2. It follows that the mean of the forecast error under quadratic loss is zero, that is, $E(e^*_{t,h}) = 0$; but, under asymmetric loss, the mean is different from zero, for the Linex function $E(e^*_{t,h}) = -\frac{a}{2}\sigma^2_{t+h|t}$.

   The following properties applied for both symmetric and asymmetric loss functions:

3. The uncertainty of the forecast summarized by the variance of the forecast error associated with the optimal forecast, that is, $\sigma^2_{t+h|t} = \text{var}(Y_{t+h} | I_t) = \text{var}(e^*_{t,h})$ is a nondecreasing function of the forecast horizon. Recall the formulas in Chapter 6 and 7 for ARMA models. The forecasting exercises in those chapters and in Chapter 8 also reveal how the variance of the forecast increases as the forecasting horizon increases.
4. The 1-step-ahead forecast errors are uncorrelated, that is, $\text{cov}(e^*_{t,1}, e^*_{t-1,1}) = 0$. Again, by reviewing the formulas in Chapters 6 and 7, we observe that the 1-step-ahead prediction error is the innovation of the model, that is, $e^*_{t,1} = \varepsilon_{t+1}$, which should be white noise if the model captures all linear dependence in the data.

5. The h-step-ahead forecast error for $h > 1$ is autocorrelated, and it follows an MA(h–1) structure. For instance, take the AR(1) process in Chapter 7. We derive the h-step-ahead forecast error as

$$e_{t,h} = Y_{t+h} - f_{t,h} = \varepsilon_{t+h} + \phi\,\varepsilon_{t+h-1} + \phi^2\,\varepsilon_{t+h-2} + \cdots\cdots \phi^{h-1}\varepsilon_{t+1}$$

The right-hand side of the forecast error is an MA(h – 1) model, which implies that the autocorrelation of order h and higher must be zero (recall the autocorrelation functions of MA processes in Chapter 6).

6. The forecast error associated with the optimal forecast must be independent of any information that was in the information set. If the forecast is optimal, it should exploit all information available at the time that the forecast is produced. Recall that the forecast error is a function of unpredictable shocks; thus, it should not have any relation with the information known to the forecaster at the time of the prediction.

   These properties provide the basis of several testing procedures to assess the optimality of the forecast. We examine two testable implications derived from properties 2 and 6, which are based on running simple regressions. These are the test for the mean of the prediction error and the test for informational efficiency. Properties 4 and 5 can be tested by examining the autocorrelation functions of the 1-step-ahead forecast errors and h-step-ahead forecast errors respectively.

In what follows, we maintain the assumption that the **prediction sample** (P observations) is much smaller than the **estimation sample** (R observations) so that the ratio P/R tends to zero. This assumption allows the use of standard distributions for the subsequent tests. In practice, the assumption means that the prediction sample should be no more than 10% of the estimation sample (e.g., if your estimation sample contains 500 observations, use a prediction sample of 50 observations or less).

9.1.2.1 Optimality and the Mean Prediction Error (MPE)

Property 2 speaks to the mean of the forecast error. Under quadratic loss, we know that

$$E(e^*_{t,h}) = 0$$

Based on this expression, we can test the optimality of the forecast by regressing the forecast error on a constant plus some zero-mean error $u_{n+j,h}$, that is,

$$e_{t+j,h} = \alpha + u_{t+j,h} \quad \text{for } j = 0, 1, \ldots . T - h - t$$

and by testing whether the constant is equal to zero. We state the following hypothesis:

$$\begin{aligned} H_0 &: \alpha = 0 \\ H_1 &: \alpha \neq 0 \end{aligned} \tag{9.6}$$

If we reject the null hypothesis, the forecast error will not have a zero mean and optimality under symmetric loss function is rejected. If we fail to reject, there is not enough evidence against optimality. After running the ordinary least squares (OLS) regression, hypothesis (9.6) is easily tested with a standard t-statistic, which asymptotically follows a standard normal distribution

$$t = \frac{\hat{\alpha}}{\hat{\sigma}_{\alpha}} \xrightarrow{A} N(0, 1)$$

where $\hat{\alpha}$ is the OLS estimator and $\hat{\sigma}_{\alpha}$ is the sample standard error of $\hat{\alpha}$. When $h > 1$, the forecast errors $e_{t+j,h}$ are autocorrelated (Property 5); consequently, the variance $\sigma^2_{\hat{\alpha}}$ corresponding to the OLS estimator of α needs to account for serial correlation. We should use an autocorrelation consistent estimator of the variance. EViews provides such an estimator by choosing the robust standard errors in the OLS menu.

Under asymmetric loss function, the mean prediction error will not be zero. We have seen that $E(e^*_{t,h}) = -\frac{a}{2}\sigma^2_{t+h|t}$. If we know the value a, we can run a similar regression of the forecast error on a constant and a zero-mean regression error to test the proper null hypothesis $(H_0 : \alpha = -\frac{a}{2}\sigma^2_{t+h|t})$. Obviously, the difficulty of dealing with asymmetric loss functions is that the parameters of the loss function defining the degree of asymmetry may be unknown. However, this theoretical result alerts us that a zero mean prediction error is a sign of optimality only under a symmetric loss function. If the researcher does not know the loss function, rejecting a zero-mean prediction error does not imply that the forecast is not optimal but that the forecaster may have an asymmetric loss function.

9.1.2.2 Optimality and the Informational Efficiency Test

Property 6 speaks of the lack of correlation of the optimal forecast error with any variable in the information set. Therefore, we should expect that the covariance of the forecast error with the forecast be zero, that is, $E(e^*_{t,h} f_{t,h}) = 0$. To test this optimality property, we run the following regression

$$e_{t+j,h} = \alpha_0 + \alpha_1 f_{t+j,h} + u_{t+j,h} \quad \text{for } j = 0, 1, \ldots . T - h - t$$

and test whether the regression coefficient α_1 is equal to zero,

$$H_0 : \alpha_1 = 0$$
$$H_1 : \alpha_1 \neq 0 \qquad (9.7)$$

Observe that if the loss function is symmetric, the test of efficiency will be also based on the joint hypothesis $H_0 : \alpha_0 = \alpha_1 = 0$, for which an F-test will be the appropriate statistic. If the loss function is asymmetric, the constant α_0 will be different from zero, and the joint hypothesis should be modified accordingly. After running the OLS regression for either a symmetric or an asymmetric loss, the statistic to test the null hypothesis (9.7) is a t-ratio, that is:

$$t_1 = \frac{\hat{\alpha}_1}{\hat{\sigma}_{\alpha_1}} \xrightarrow{A} N(0, 1)$$

where $\hat{\alpha}_1$ is the OLS estimator and $\hat{\sigma}_{\alpha_1}$ is the sample standard error of $\hat{\alpha}_1$. If we reject the null hypothesis, the forecast error is correlated with the information set, and we conclude that the forecast is not efficient on exploiting the available information. Once again, if there is serial correlation in the forecast errors (the case of $h > 1$), the variance should account for the serial correlation. A robust estimator of the variance should be used.

REAL DATA: House Price Growth for California from 1975:Q1 to 2007:Q4 (Optimality Tests)

In this section, we implement the optimality tests of three forecasts for the quarterly growth in house prices in the state of California. You are already familiar with the databases on house prices at the website of Freddie Mac (a mortgage company operating in the secondary market of mortgages), http://www.freddiemac.com. Beginning in 1975, Freddie Mac and Fannie Mae constructed the quarterly Conventional Mortgage Home Price Index (CMHPI) that provides information on the dynamics of house prices in the United States at the MSA, state, and Census Bureau division levels. They also provide a national index defined as a *weighted average* of the nine census division indices. The computation of the indices is based on *conforming* mortgages[2] for single-unit residential houses bought by Freddie Mac or Fannie Mae. The indices are based on a database that has more than 17 million houses, and they are constructed with a methodology based on *repeated transactions*. When the same house is sold (or appraised) in two different occasions, there is a record of the price change. The index is a sophisticated weighted average of all observed growth rates.

From the Freddie Mac website, we have selected the **house price index** corresponding to the state of California from the first quarter of 1975 to fourth quarter 2007 and computed its growth rate. In Figure 9.5, we plot the time series of the quarterly growth rate.

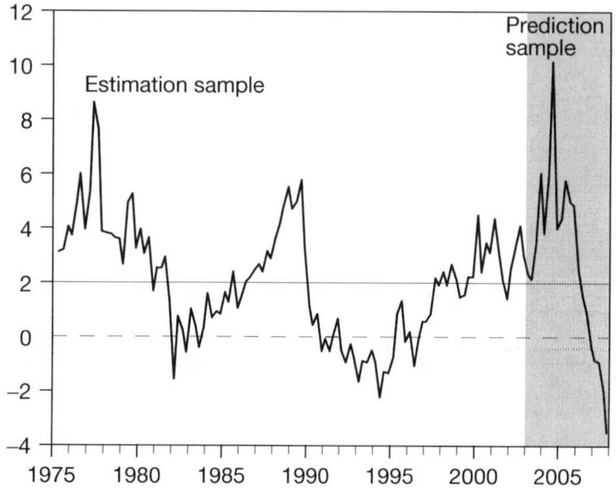

FIGURE 9.5 Quarterly Growth Rate of House Price Index in California

[2] Conforming mortgages are loans than cannot exceed certain limits set by the Federal Housing Finance Board. In 2010, the loan limit was $417,000. The CMHPI does not include homes with mortgages above this limit.

The average growth rate over the estimation sample is 2.02% per quarter (horizontal line). The largest declines in prices occurred during the recession years of the early 1990s with decline rates of more than 2% per quarter and the burst of the housing bubble in 2006 and 2007 with large declines of around 4% (dashed line is 0% growth). On the other side are dramatic appreciation rates during the late 1990s and early 2000s with growth rates of more than 8% per quarter.

Suppose that we are at the end of 2002 and our task is to evaluate the optimality and accuracy of three quarterly forecasts produced by three different time series models. Let us describe the forecasting environment:

- Forecast horizon: 1-step-ahead forecast ($h = 1$); thus, we are interested in the forecast of the price growth for the next quarter.
- Initial information set: From 1975.Q1 to 2002.Q4.
- Fixed sampling scheme with an estimation sample from 1975.Q1 to 2002.Q4 and a prediction sample from 2003.Q1 to 2007.Q4. Recall that in this scheme, the information set is updated as soon as new information arrives. For instance, based on the initial information set, the first forecast will be for 2003.Q1. As time passes and we know the actual growth rate for 2003.Q1, it becomes part of the information set to forecast the growth rate for 2003.Q2.
- We consider three time series models from which the conditional means and conditional variances are provided in Table 9.1.

  The conditional means are quite different across models. In M1, the conditional mean is a function of two of the last three most recent observations (i.e. $\{y_t, y_{t-2}\}$). You recognize this conditional mean as coming from the estimation of an AR(2) process. We have estimated the parameters only once (fixed scheme) with the estimation sample from 1975.Q1 to 2002.Q4. Thus, the parameter estimates will be constant throughout the prediction sample. In M2, the conditional mean is just the most recent observation. This could be interpreted as a naïve forecast with no estimation involved. In M3, the conditional mean is a simple average of the four most recent observations. This could be interpreted as smoothing the series over the last four periods. M3 does not require any estimation.
- We wish to evaluate the optimality of the three forecasts for a given loss function. We consider the symmetric loss (root) MSE function and the asymmetric Linex loss function with $a = 1$. In view of our discussion in Chapter 8 and in hindsight

TABLE 9.1 Three Models to Forecast Quarterly Growth Rate of House Prices in California

	Conditional mean 1975.Q1–2002.Q4	**Conditional variance 1975.Q1–2002.Q4**
Model 1 (M1)	$\mu_{t+1\|t} = 0.21 + 0.74y_t + 0.16y_{t-2}$	$\sigma^2_{t+1\|t} = 1.149$
Model 2 (M2)	$\mu_{t+1\|t} = y_t$	$\sigma^2_{t+1\|t} = 1.239$
Model 3 (M3)	$\mu_{t+1\|t} = \dfrac{y_t + y_{t-1} + y_{t-2} + y_{t-3}}{4}$	$\sigma^2_{t+1\|t} = 1.543$

(given the events of 2008), the choice of $a = 1$ would be considered reckless today. It implies that the forecast would be above the conditional mean of the price growth rate (a somehow optimistic view of the housing market but understandable with the economic lens of 2002). As we have already seen, the optimal forecast under (root) MSE is $f^*_{t,1} = \mu_{t+1|t}$ and under Linex ($a = 1$), $f^*_{t,1} = \mu_{t+1|t} + 0.5\sigma^2_{t+1|t}$.

To implement the optimality tests, let us start by preparing a working table. Table 9.2 contains information on the optimal forecast and forecast error under symmetric loss.

TABLE 9.2 Optimal Forecasts and Forecast Errors Under Symmetric Loss Function (Root-MSE)

Date	Actual	Forecast M1 (Fixed scheme)	Forecast error M1 (Fixed scheme)	Forecast M2	Forecast error M2	Forecast M3	Forecast error M3
2002Q2	3.32						
2002Q3	4.111						
2002Q4	3.002						
2003Q1	2.305	2.933	-0.628	3.002	-0.696	3.239	-0.934
2003Q2	2.154	2.545	-0.391	2.305	-0.152	3.185	-1.031
2003Q3	3.484	2.260	1.224	2.154	1.330	2.893	0.591
2003Q4	6.054	3.129	2.925	3.484	2.570	2.736	3.318
2004Q1	3.825	4.994	-1.170	6.054	-2.229	3.499	0.326
2004Q2	5.950	3.564	2.386	3.825	2.125	3.879	2.071
2004Q3	10.114	5.528	4.586	5.950	4.164	4.828	5.286
2004Q4	3.989	8.240	-4.251	10.114	-6.125	6.486	-2.497
2005Q1	4.344	4.070	0.274	3.989	0.355	5.969	-1.625
2005Q2	5.781	4.983	0.799	4.344	1.437	6.099	-0.318
2005Q3	4.978	5.081	-0.103	5.781	-0.804	6.057	-1.079
2005Q4	4.833	4.546	0.287	4.978	-0.145	4.773	0.060
2006Q1	2.516	4.665	-2.149	4.833	-2.318	4.984	-2.469
2006Q2	1.487	2.835	-1.348	2.516	-1.029	4.527	-3.040
2006Q3	0.912	2.056	-1.144	1.487	-0.575	3.453	-2.541
2006Q4	-0.260	1.271	-1.531	0.912	-1.172	2.437	-2.697
2007Q1	-0.857	0.249	-1.106	-0.260	-0.597	1.164	-2.021
2007Q2	-0.949	-0.280	-0.669	-0.857	-0.091	0.320	-1.269
2007Q3	-1.972	-0.530	-1.441	-0.949	-1.023	-0.288	-1.683
2007Q4	-3.512	-1.376	-2.136	-1.972	-1.540	-1.009	-2.503

Let us review how to construct the forecast columns. As an example, choose Model 1 (M1). We wish to forecast the growth rate for 2003.Q1. The information set is the growth rates until the fourth quarter of 2002.[3]

$$f^*_{2002,2003Q1} = \mu_{2003.Q1|2002} = 0.21 + 0.74 \times 3.002 + 0.16 \times 3.320 = 2.933$$

with a 1-step-ahead forecast error of

$$e_{2002,2003Q1} = y_{2003Q1} - f^*_{2002,2003Q1} = 2.305 - 2.933 = -0.628$$

To compute the 1-step-ahead forecast for 2003.Q2, we proceed in the same way, noting that the information set is updated to include the observation corresponding to 2003.Q1,

$$f^*_{2003Q1,2003Q2} = \mu_{2003.Q2|2003Q1} = 0.21 + 0.74 \times 2.305 + 0.16 \times 4.111 = 2.545$$

The 1-step-ahead forecasts and forecast errors from M2 and M3 are computed in a similar fashion. For M1, which is the only model that involves estimation, we could also use recursive forecasting environments and rolling forecasting environments. In the chapter appendix, we provide the forecasts and forecast errors for M1 under these two other environments. An EViews program to implement the different schemes was provided in Chapter 4, and it is reproduced in the appendix adapted to the data of this section.

Because the optimal forecast with the Linex loss is $f^*_{t,1} = \mu_{t+1|t} + 0.5\sigma^2_{t+1|t}$, we need a new working table, for which we will use the information provided in Table 9.2. In Table 9.3, we present the forecasts and forecast errors from M1, M2, and M3 under Linex with $a = 1$.

Comparing the forecasts of Table 9.3 with those of Table 9.2, observe that the forecasts under Linex ($a = 1$) are more optimistic than those under symmetric loss. This is the case when we add a positive term such as $0.5\sigma^2_{t+1|t}$.

Now we proceed to assess the optimality of the forecasts by running the MPE test and the **informational efficiency test**. The results are displayed in Table 9.4.

In the first panel of Table 9.4 are results of the MPE test. Under symmetric loss, we cannot reject the null hypothesis of the mean prediction error being zero for any of the three forecasts. When the loss is Linex, the average of the forecast errors should be negative given that $a = 1$ and the forecaster avoids positive errors. The tests clearly indicate that the mean prediction error is negative for all forecasts. Hence, the first optimality test is passed by all three forecasts considered. The second panel of Table 9.4 displays the test results for informational efficiency. Observe that the t-statistics are identical for symmetric and asymmetric loss functions. The reason why this happens is that the optimal forecast under linex loss is just the optimal forecast under symmetric loss plus the

[3]The coefficients of the model have been rounded. This is why when you do the algebra, you will obtain 2.96 and not exactly 2.93, which is the number calculated by the computer program using higher precision digits.

TABLE 9.3 Optimal Forecasts and Forecast Errors Under Asymmetric Linex Loss ($a = 1$)

Date	Actual	Forecast M1	Forecast error M1	Forecast M2	Forecast error M2	Forecast M3	Forecast error M3
2003Q1	2.305	3.508	-1.202	3.621	-1.316	4.011	-1.705
2003Q2	2.154	3.119	-0.966	2.925	-0.771	3.956	-1.802
2003Q3	3.484	2.834	0.649	2.773	0.711	3.664	-0.180
2003Q4	6.054	3.703	2.351	4.103	1.951	3.507	2.546
2004Q1	3.825	5.569	-1.744	6.673	-2.848	4.271	-0.446
2004Q2	5.950	4.138	1.812	4.444	1.505	4.650	1.299
2004Q3	10.114	6.102	4.012	6.569	3.545	5.599	4.515
2004Q4	3.989	8.815	-4.826	10.733	-6.745	7.257	-3.268
2005Q1	4.344	4.645	-0.300	4.608	-0.264	6.741	-2.396
2005Q2	5.781	5.557	0.224	4.964	0.818	6.871	-1.089
2005Q3	4.978	5.655	-0.678	6.401	-1.423	6.828	-1.851
2005Q4	4.833	5.120	-0.287	5.597	-0.764	5.544	-0.711
2006Q1	2.516	5.239	-2.723	5.453	-2.937	5.755	-3.240
2006Q2	1.487	3.410	-1.923	3.135	-1.648	5.298	-3.812
2006Q3	0.912	2.631	-1.719	2.106	-1.194	4.225	-3.312
2006Q4	-0.260	1.846	-2.106	1.532	-1.792	3.208	-3.468
2007Q1	-0.857	0.823	-1.680	0.359	-1.217	1.935	-2.792
2007Q2	-0.949	0.294	-1.243	-0.237	-0.711	1.092	-2.040
2007Q3	-1.972	0.044	-2.016	-0.329	-1.643	0.483	-2.455
2007Q4	-3.512	-0.802	-2.711	-1.352	-2.160	-0.238	-3.274

constant $0.5\sigma^2_{t+1|t}$. All three forecasts—from M1, M2, and M3—pass the informational efficiency test because we fail to reject the null hypothesis of no correlation between the forecast error and the forecast at the customary significant level of 5%.

In summary, neither optimality test discriminates among the three forecasts; these seem to be optimal with respect to both symmetric and asymmetric loss functions. However, we should carry out further checks. Property 4 claims that the 1-step-ahead forecast error must be white noise if the forecast is optimal. In Tables 9.2 and 9.3 we have reported the 1-step-ahead forecast errors from all three models. You may want to check the autocorrelation functions of the forecast errors to assess whether they are white noise. Those from models M2 and M3 are not, and in this sense, their forecasts are not optimal as we can exploit the information set further.

TABLE 9.4 Optimality of the Forecast

MPE Test

$$e_{t+j,1} = \alpha + u_{t+j,1}$$

$$t = \frac{\hat{\alpha}}{\hat{\sigma}_{\alpha}} \xrightarrow{A} N(0, 1)$$

	$H_0: \alpha = 0$ $H_1: \alpha \neq 0$ **(*RMSE*)**	$H_0: \alpha \leq 0$ $H_1: \alpha > 0$ **(Linex, a = 1)**
M1	$t = -0.632$	$t = -1.929$
M2	$t = -0.685$	$t = -1.988$
M3	$t = -1.446$	$t = -3.033$

Informational Efficiency Test

$$e_{t+j,1} = \alpha_0 + \alpha_1 f_{t+j,1} + u_{t+j,1}$$

$$t_1 = \frac{\hat{\alpha}_1}{\hat{\sigma}_{\alpha_1}} \xrightarrow{A} N(0, 1)$$

	$H_0: \alpha_1 = 0$ $H_1: \alpha_1 \neq 0$ **(*RMSE*)**	$H_0: \alpha_1 = 0$ $H_1: \alpha_1 \neq 0$ **(Linex, a = 1)**
M1	$t_1 = 0.496$	$t_1 = 0.496$
M2	$t_1 = -0.817$	$t_1 = -0.817$
M3	$t_1 = 0.608$	$t_1 = 0.608$

9.2 Assessment of Forecasts

By now we are familiar with the idea that no unique model fully describes the statistical characteristics of a time series. After all, models are stylized representations of economic and business phenomena. In practice, forecasters entertain several time series models to explain the behavior of the variable of interest and collect competing forecasts. Thus, the question becomes how to assess which forecast(s) are the best. In section 9.1 we introduced optimality tests that rely basically on the properties of the forecast error. In this section, we bring the value of the loss function to the forefront. We have constructed an optimal forecast, which by construction minimizes the average loss, but different models will produce different values of the optimal forecast, different forecast errors, and consequently different values of the loss function. It is logical to think that among competing forecasts, those that produce a lower loss should be preferred. Let us proceed by first explaining a descriptive and simple evaluation procedure, and then we introduce a test to assess how statistically different the competing forecasts are.

9.2.1 Descriptive Evaluation of the Average Loss

In Chapter 4, we introduced the **forecasting environments—recursive, rolling**, and **fixed**—and for each, we showed how to generate the forecast errors. Tables 9.2 and 9.3 also provided some practice. Suppose that the initial information set contains observations to time t and that the forecast horizon is h. After constructing the forecasts, we collect the out-of-sample forecast errors $\{e_{t,h}, e_{t+1,h}, \ldots\ldots e_{t+j,h}, \ldots\ldots e_{T-h,h}\}$and we calculate the *sample* mean loss. Some popular sample averages are:

- ***Mean squared error (MSE)***

$$\bar{L} = \frac{\sum_{j=0}^{T-h-t} e^2_{t+j,h}}{T-h-t+1} \equiv MSE$$

which is the sample average loss corresponding to a symmetric quadratic loss function. It is also customary to report the root mean squared error (i.e., $RMSE = \sqrt{MSE}$).

- ***Mean absolute error (MAE)***

$$\bar{L} = \frac{\sum_{j=0}^{T-h-t} |e_{t+j,h}|}{T-h-t+1} \equiv MAE$$

which is the sample average loss corresponding to an absolute value loss function.

- ***Mean absolute percentage error (MAPE)***

$$\bar{L} = \frac{\sum_{j=0}^{T-h-t} \left|\frac{e_{t+j,h}}{y_{t+j+h}}\right|}{T-h-t+1} \equiv MAPE$$

which is the mean absolute error reported in percentage terms over the realized values.

Similarly for any other loss function that we wish to entertain, we could construct the sample average loss. For instance, we have already analyzed the Linex loss function for which the sample average loss is:

$$\bar{L} = \frac{\sum_{j=0}^{T-h-t} (\exp(ae_{t+j,h}) - ae_{t+j,h} - 1)}{T-h-t+1}$$

Although the sample averages *MSE, MAE,* and *MAPE* are very popular and easy to calculate, the only loss function that is really important is the one the forecaster chooses so that she will evaluate competing forecasts according to that loss.

When we have several competing forecasts, which one performs the best? Suppose that we have J forecasts. The selection procedure is very simple:

1. Select a loss function. Calculate the forecast for every model considered, the forecast error, and the corresponding sample average loss.
2. Rank the J forecasts according to the value of their sample average loss.
3. Select the model and forecast that produce the lowest average loss.

For instance, suppose that the forecaster has a quadratic loss and we have two models i and k from which we obtain a sequence of forecasts $\{f^{(i)}_{t+j,h}\}$ and $\{f^{(k)}_{t+j,h}\}$ with their corresponding sequences of forecast errors $\{e^{(i)}_{t+j,h}\}$ and $\{e^{(k)}_{t+j,h}\}$. Forecast i is preferred to forecast k if its mean squared error loss is smaller than the corresponding to forecast k ($MSE^{(i)} < MSE^{(k)}$).

9.2.2 Statistical Evaluation of the Average Loss

Ranking the sample average loss produced by different forecasts is a simple and quick procedure to choose the best forecast. However, recall that the loss function depends on a random variable and that in practice we work with sample information, so we need to consider sampling variation in our assessment of forecasts. With this objective, we seek a statistical measure to assess the difference in the average losses. For instance, suppose that two average losses are close to each other. Should we disregard one of the forecasts in favor of the other, or should we consider both forecasts to be equally accurate? On the contrary, if the difference in the average losses is large, should we *always* choose the forecast with the lowest loss? The answer will depend on the variability of the average loss. How "small" or "large" the loss difference is will be measured statistically.

Suppose that for a given loss function we have two competing models i and k from which we obtain a sequence of forecasts $\{f^{(i)}_{t+j,h}\}$ and $\{f^{(k)}_{t+j,h}\}$ with their corresponding forecast errors $\{e^{(i)}_{t+j,h}\}$ and $\{e^{(k)}_{t+j,h}\}$ for $j = 0, 1, \ldots T - h - t$. *We say that, on average, forecast* i *is as good as forecast* k *if they generate the same expected loss.* This is the hypothesis to test.

9.2.2.1 Test of Unconditional Predictive Ability[4]

The null hypothesis of **equal predictive ability** is written in terms of the unconditional expectation of the loss difference, that is,

$$H_0: E(L(e^{(i)}_{t,h})) = E(L(e^{(k)}_{t,h})) \quad \Rightarrow \quad E(L(e^{(i)}_{t,h}) - L(e^{(k)}_{t,h})) = E(\Delta L_{t,h}) = 0$$

This null says that, on average, both forecasts are equally accurate over the entire prediction sample because the average loss is the same for both forecasts.

Let us proceed with the construction of the statistical test for the null hypothesis of equal unconditional predictive ability. We build the test within the framework of a regression model. Observe the following regression

$$\Delta L_{t+j,h} = \beta_0 + \varepsilon_{t+j} \quad \text{for } j = 0, 1, 2 \ldots . T-t-h$$

[4] As in section 9.1.2, we keep the assumption that $(P/R) \rightarrow 0$.

where ε_{t+j} is a zero-mean regression error. Taking expectations, we obtain

$$E(\Delta L_{t+j,h}) = \beta_0$$

Hence, if both forecasts deliver the same expected loss, the coefficient β_0 must be zero. Then it follows that the null hypothesis to test is

$$H_0: \beta_0 = 0 \tag{9.8}$$

which is equivalent to $H_0: E(\Delta L_{t+j,h}) = 0$.

Once we have estimated the regression model by OLS, we need only to construct a standard t-statistic for the null hypothesis (9.8). That is,

$$t = \frac{\hat{\beta}_0}{\hat{\sigma}_{\hat{\beta}_0}} \xrightarrow{A} N(0, 1)$$

where $\hat{\beta}_0$ is the OLS estimator and $\hat{\sigma}_{\hat{\beta}_0}$ is the sample standard error of $\hat{\beta}_0$. Asymptotically, the t-statistic follows a standard normal distribution. A word of caution: It is very likely that $\Delta L_{t+j,h}$ will be autocorrelated, particularly when $h > 1$. In this case, the variance of the OLS estimator, $\sigma^2_{\hat{\beta}_0}$, should account for serial correlation. We should use a robust estimator of the variance $\hat{\sigma}_{\hat{\beta}_0}$. EViews provides such an estimator. Finally, we will reject the null hypothesis of equal unconditional predictive ability whenever $|t| > z_{\alpha/2}$, where $z_{\alpha/2}$ is the critical value of $N(0, 1)$ for the chosen α-significance level.

To conclude this section, let us go back to our introductory remarks on assessing the difference in the loss functions. Now you can see the role of uncertainty by checking the denominator of the t-statistic, which considers the sample variability of the loss. A large difference in the average losses may be insignificant if the variance of $\Delta L_{t+j,h}$ is large. If much uncertainty exists, such a large loss difference may not be statistically significant and both forecasts could be equally accurate. On the contrary, if we encounter a small loss difference but the variance of $\Delta L_{t+j,h}$ is also small so that there is not much uncertainty, the small loss difference can be statistically significant, and one forecast will be deemed superior to the other.

REAL DATA: House Price Growth for California from 1975:Q1 to 2007:Q4 (Predictive Ability Test)

With the information provided in Tables 9.2 and 9.3, we proceed to compute the value of the loss functions over the prediction sample. In Table 9.5, we present a working table with the computation of the quadratic loss for the two models M1 and M3. Similar tables could be prepared for the remaining models and loss functions. The last column of Table 9.5, Quadratic **loss differential** refers to the difference between the losses produced by the two models M3 and M1, that is, $\Delta L_{t+j,1}$ for $j = 0, 1, 2 \ldots . T - t - 1$. When the difference is positive, the loss produced by M3 is larger than the loss produced by M1; consequently, M1 is the preferred model. On the contrary, when the difference is negative, M3 is preferred to M1. In Figure 9.6, we plot the quadratic loss differential over the prediction sample. If both models have equivalent predictive ability, we should

TABLE 9.5 Quadratic Loss Differential

Date	Forecast error M1 (fixed scheme)	Quadratic loss M1 (fixed scheme)	Forecast error M3	Quadratic loss M3	Quadratic loss differential (M3–M1)
2003Q1	-0.628	0.394	-0.934	0.872	0.478
2003Q2	-0.391	0.153	-1.031	1.063	0.909
2003Q3	1.224	1.497	0.591	0.349	-1.148
2003Q4	2.925	8.555	3.318	11.007	2.452
2004Q1	-1.170	1.368	0.326	0.106	-1.262
2004Q2	2.386	5.692	2.071	4.288	-1.404
2004Q3	4.586	21.030	5.286	27.940	6.909
2004Q4	-4.251	18.075	-2.497	6.234	-11.841
2005Q1	0.274	0.075	-1.625	2.641	2.566
2005Q2	0.799	0.638	-0.318	0.101	-0.537
2005Q3	-0.103	0.011	-1.079	1.165	1.154
2005Q4	0.287	0.082	0.060	0.004	-0.079
2006Q1	-2.149	4.618	-2.469	6.094	1.476
2006Q2	-1.348	1.818	-3.040	9.243	7.425
2006Q3	-1.144	1.309	-2.541	6.458	5.149
2006Q4	-1.531	2.345	-2.697	7.274	4.928
2007Q1	-1.106	1.223	-2.021	4.083	2.860
2007Q2	-0.669	0.447	-1.269	1.610	1.163
2007Q3	-1.441	2.077	-1.683	2.834	0.756
2007Q4	-2.136	4.564	-2.503	6.265	1.701
Average	-0.279	3.799	-0.703	4.981	**1.183**
Square root		1.949		2.232	

expect an *average* loss differential of zero. The sample average loss differential is 1.183. Because the average is positive, a priori we may claim that M1 is preferred to M3 overall. But is this number statistically significant from zero? This is the question that the test of predictive ability answers.

Observe that in Figure 9.6, M1 has a better performance overall the prediction sample with a large exception in 2004.Q4.

Similar tables to Table 9.5 could be prepared for every model and every loss function. In Table 9.6, we summarize the sample average loss for each model and each loss function for the prediction period 2003.Q1 to 2007.Q4.

We observe that for the symmetric loss function RMSE, M1 is the preferred model because it delivers the smallest loss (value in bold), followed by M2 and then M3. For MAE, MAPE, and the asymmetric Linex functions, M2 is the preferred forecast followed by M1 and M3. This disagreement between symmetric and asymmetric loss functions stresses how important is for the forecaster to choose the loss function *a priori*. Ultimately,

FIGURE 9.6 Quadratic Loss Differential

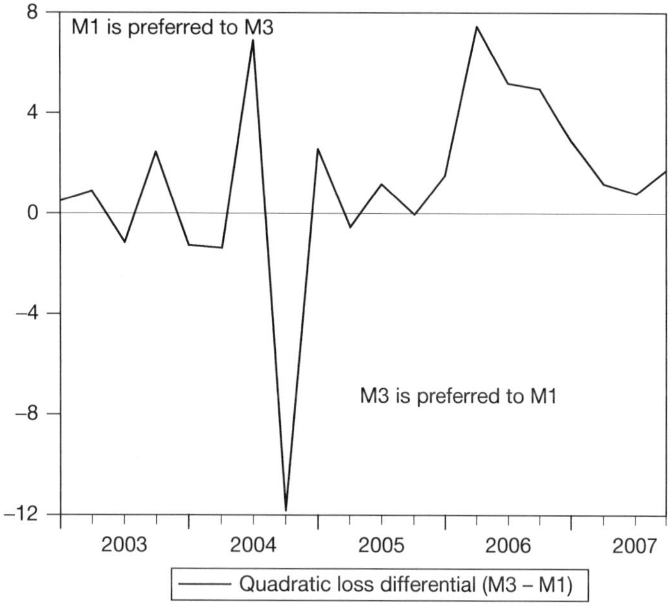

the choice of a loss function drives the selection of the best forecast. However, Table 9.6 is a descriptive picture. The question is whether the differences among models are significant enough to reject some in favor of some others. This is what we answer in Table 9.7 where we implement the statistical test of equal predictive ability.

TABLE 9.6 Descriptive Evaluation of the Average Loss

	RMSE	*MAE*	*MAPE* (%)	**Linex (a = 1)**
M1	**1.949**	1.527	80.174	3.807
M2	2.098	**1.524**	**65.443**	**2.672**
M3	2.232	1.868	126.430	6.031

TABLE 9.7 Statistical Evaluation of the Average Loss

Test of Unconditional Predictive Ability

$$\Delta L_{t+j,1} = \beta_0 + \varepsilon_{t+j}$$
$$H_0 : \beta_0 = 0$$
$$H_1 : \beta_0 < 0$$

	***MSE* (M1 – M2)**	***MAE* (M2 – M1)**	***MAPE* (%) (M2 – M1)**	**Linex (a = 1) (M2 – M1)**
$t = \dfrac{\hat{\beta}_0}{\hat{\sigma}_{\hat{\beta}_0}} \xrightarrow{A} N(0,1)$	$t = -0.56$ p-value = 29%	$t = -0.025$ p-value = 49%	$t = -1.640$ p-value = 5.8%	$t = -1.110$ p-value = 14%

The pair-wise comparisons are between the two models with the lowest loss; that is, we will compare M1 and M2 for the MSE symmetric loss function and between M2 and M1 for MAE, MAPE, and Linex functions. After running the OLS regression, we construct the t-statistics. These are not large enough to reject the null of equal predictive ability. Hence, the M1 forecast is statistically equivalent to the M2 forecast. Observe that the p-values are large, with the exception of the MAPE function for which the p-value is around 5%. In this case, we have marginal statistical evidence for M2 to be preferred to M1 in the overall prediction sample.

In summary, although the optimality tests of Section 9.1 conclude that the three forecasts (M1, M2, and M3) are equivalent, the test of predictive ability is more discriminatory, indicating a preference for the M1 or M2 forecasts. Again, although we used different loss functions, the preferred forecast is dictated by the loss function chosen a priori by the forecaster. Thus, comparing forecasts across loss functions does not make sense; instead, we fix first the loss function and then choose the best forecast among those coming from competing models.

9.3 Combination of Forecasts

The optimality tests and the forecasting ability test help us to discriminate further among competing forecasts, but, as we saw in section 9.1, it is possible that several forecasts are statistically equivalent although they may come from different models. It is natural to ask whether a **combination of forecasts** can do better than any individual forecast. An important argument in favor of combining forecast is that, borrowing language from portfolio theory, it achieves **diversification gains**. This term means that the combined forecast will deliver a smaller expected loss than that of any other individual forecast. This may be the case when different forecasts are based on different information sets, some of which may not be publicly available. In this case, the combined forecast indirectly pools many sources of information, and it should provide a lower loss. Other more statistical reasons favor the combination of forecasts. Given that in most instances we are not able to find a unique model that is *best* all the time, it is very likely that some models will be misspecified in certain periods of time. For instance, some models may work better in high volatility times than in calmer times; some models may adjust faster than others to regime changes caused by new institutional rules or new policies; or it may be that the best model changes over the time span of the series. In these instances, combining forecasts from all models may offer some protection against unknown sources of misspecification.

There are several approaches on how to combine of forecasts. We present only linear combinations of individual forecasts although it is possible to devise nonlinear schemes. First, we introduce simple linear combinations that are very easy to implement, and then we present combinations based on estimating optimal weights, for which, once more, the choice of a loss function is important.

9.3.1 Simple Linear Combinations

Suppose that we have n forecasts $\{f_{t,h}^{(1)}, f_{t,h}^{(2)}, \ldots, f_{t,h}^{(n)}\}$ with their corresponding forecast errors $\{e_{t,h}^{(1)}, e_{t,h}^{(2)}, \ldots\ldots, e_{t,h}^{(n)}\}$. A linear combination of forecasts $f_{t,h}^{c}$ is given by

$$f^c_{t,h} = \omega_1 f^{(1)}_{t,h} + \omega_2 f^{(2)}_{t,h} + \cdots + \omega_n f^{(n)}_{t,h}$$

where ω_i is the weight assigned to forecast $f^{(i)}_{t,h}$. A priori, there is no reason that the weights need to add to 1 or be strictly positive (negative weights can also be useful to the forecaster) although this is the common approach when thinking about weights.

When the weights are equal (i.e., $\omega_i = 1/n$), we have an equal-weighted forecast that is the arithmetic average of the individual forecasts. In this case, the combination is convex ($0 \leq \omega_i \leq 1$), guaranteeing that the combined forecast falls within the range of values of the individual forecasts and the sum of weights is equal to 1.

Alternatively, the forecaster may wish to weight some forecasts more heavily than others. Those forecasts with a lower MSE may be assigned a larger weight than those with larger MSE. In this case, we could weight each individual forecast by the inverse of its MSE, that is,

$$\omega_i = \frac{1/MSE_i}{\sum_{j=1}^{n}(1/MSE_j)}$$

These weights are strictly positive and also sum to 1.

With these two simple schemes, no estimation is involved, the combined forecasts are very easy to implement, and empirically these combinations, in particular the equal-weight combined forecast, perform very well.

9.3.2 Optimal Linear Combinations

Optimality in this instance refers to the choice of weights that minimize the forecaster's expected loss. Suppose that the forecaster has a quadratic loss function, that is, $E(e^2_{t,h})$, and consider a combination of two **unbiased forecasts** such that $f^c_{t,h} = \omega f^{(1)}_{t,h} + (1-\omega) f^{(2)}_{t,h}$. The problem is to find the optimal weight ω such that the average loss is minimized.

Let us construct the forecast error associated with the combined forecast:

$$e^c_{t,h} = y_{t+h} - f^c_{t,h} = \omega(y_{t+h} - f^{(1)}_{t,h}) + (1-\omega)(y_{t+h} - f^{(2)}_{t,h}) = \omega e^{(1)}_{t,h} + (1-\omega) e^{(2)}_{t,h},$$

and let $\text{var}(e^{(1)}_{t,h}) \equiv \sigma^2_1$, $\text{var}(e^{(2)}_{t,h}) \equiv \sigma^2_2$ be the variances of the forecast errors, which also may be correlated with correlation coefficient $\rho_{12} = \sigma_{12}/(\sigma_1\sigma_2)$.

Now the simplest optimization problem is minimizing the expected quadratic loss with respect to a single variable ω:

$$\min_\omega E(e^2_{t,h}) = \min_\omega E(y_{t+h} - f^c_{t,h})^2$$
$$= \min_\omega E(\omega e^{(1)}_{t,h} + (1-\omega) e^{(2)}_{t,h})^2 = \min_\omega (\omega^2\sigma^2_1 + (1-\omega)^2\sigma^2_2 + 2\omega(1-\omega)\sigma_{12})$$

The solution to this problem[5] is

$$\omega^* = \frac{\sigma^2_2 - \sigma_{12}}{\sigma^2_1 + \sigma^2_2 - 2\sigma_{12}}$$

[5] This is an easy calculus problem. Find the first order condition by taking the first derivative of the expected loss with respect to ω, make it equal to zero, and solve for ω.

$$1 - \omega^* = \frac{\sigma_1^2 - \sigma_{12}}{\sigma_1^2 + \sigma_2^2 - 2\sigma_{12}}$$

Suppose that $f_{t,h}^{(2)}$ has a lower forecast error variance than $f_{t,h}^{(1)}$ (i.e., $\sigma_1^2 > \sigma_2^2$), the formula of the optimal weight says that the weight assigned to $f_{t,h}^{(2)}$ is larger than that assigned to $f_{t,h}^{(1)}$; thus, the more precise (lower variance) the forecast is, the larger its weight will be in the combined forecast. By inserting ω^* in the loss function $E(e_{t,h}^2)$, we find the minimum value of the expected loss as

$$E(e_{t,h}^2(\omega^*)) \equiv \sigma_c^2(\omega^*) = \frac{\sigma_1^2\sigma_2^2(1 - \rho_{12}^2)}{\sigma_1^2 + \sigma_2^2 - 2\rho_{12}\sigma_1\sigma_2}$$

It can be proven that this value is lower than (or at most equal to) the smallest of the forecast error variances, that is, $\sigma_c^2(\omega^*) \leq \min(\sigma_1^2, \sigma_2^2)$, and by this property, the combined forecast offers diversification gains.

Observe that given the formulas for optimal weights, the equal-weighted forecast in Section 9.3.1 is not optimal. Only in the case of equal variances (i.e., $\sigma_1^2 = \sigma_2^2$) will we have $\omega^* = 1 - \omega^*$, and the equal-weight forecast will be optimal.

It is also possible to estimate the weights by regressing the realized values on the individual forecasts as in

$$y_{t+h} = \omega_0 + \omega_1 f_{t,h}^{(1)} + \omega_2 f_{t,h}^{(2)} + \cdots + \omega_n f_{t,h}^{(n)} + \varepsilon_{t+h}$$

Applying OLS, we obtain estimates of $\hat{\omega}_i$ s, which may be positive or negative and may not total 1 although it is possible to run a constrained linear regression imposing non-negative weights that add to 1. If the individual forecasts are unbiased, the constant in the regression will be zero (i.e., $\omega_0 = 0$), and if they are not, the constant will pick up the bias assuming that this is not time-varying.

REAL DATA: House Price Growth for California from 1975:Q1 to 2007:Q4 (Combination of Forecasts)

We implement the four combination schemes with the forecasts derived from models M1, M2, and M3 (under symmetric loss MSE, Table 9.2). See Table 9.8 for the results.

TABLE 9.8 Combination of Forecasts—Weights and MSEs

	1/*n*	**1/*MSE***	**Optimal ω^* (for M1 and M2 only)**	**OLS weight**
M1 (MSE = 3.799)	1/3	0.38	1.23	4.79
M2 (MSE = 4.399)	1/3	0.33	−0.23	−2.56
M3 (MSE = 4.981)	1/3	0.29	—	−0.71
MSE of combined forecast	3.985	3.963	3.695	**3.244**

The equal-weighted forecast assigns 1/3 weight to each individual forecast and delivers an average loss of 3.985. The MSE-inversely weighted forecast assigns similar weights as the equal-weighted scheme with slightly higher weight to M1 forecast (38%) and delivers an average loss of 3.963. In neither case do we obtain any diversification gains because their MSEs are slightly higher than that of the M1 forecast. Why is that? Because both schemes constrain the weights to be strictly positive, even bad forecasts may have a substantial weight, thus they will not contribute to the reduction of the loss. Furthermore, the forecasts of the three models are heavily correlated with correlation coefficients of about 0.9 so that there is much overlap among the individual forecasts but not much new information in the combination. However, the optimal combination schemes tell a different story. When we run the OLS regression, we observe that the MSE of the combined forecast is reduced to 3.244 with some weights being negative and some positive. The OLS scheme weights the M1 forecast very heavily at the expense of the M2 and M3 forecasts, which are negatively penalized. Now the diversification gains are obvious because the MSE of the combined forecast is substantially smaller (3.244) than the minimum of the three individual MSEs (3.799). The same story is true when we obtain the optimal weights for M1 and M2 forecasts, which are the models chosen by the predictive ability test. In this case, the average loss is 3.695, smaller than that of the M1 forecast. This gain is obtained because the M1 forecast is positively weighted by 123% at the expense of negatively weighting (–23%) the M2 forecast.

In summary, although it is very likely that in our forecasting practice we will not find a unique model as the best model to characterize a time series, combining forecasts from different models may turn out to be to the forecaster's advantage. It will be possible to find a combined forecast that provides a smaller expected loss than that of any other individual forecast.

KEY WORDS

asymmetric loss function, p. 224

combination of forecasts, p. 244

diversification gains, p. 244

equal predictive ability, p. 240

estimation sample, p. 231

fixed forecasting environment, p. 239

house price index, p. 233

informational efficiency test, p. 236

in-sample properties, p. 224

loss differential, p. 241

mean prediction error test, p.

optimal forecast, p. 224

out-of-sample properties, p. 224

prediction sample, p. 231

recursive forecasting environment, p. 239

rolling forecasting environment, p. 239

symmetric loss function, p. 224

unbiased forecast, p. 245

APPENDIX

9.A.1 Optimal Forecast

- ***under quadratic loss function***

$$E(L(e_{t,h})\,|\,I_t) = aE(e_{t,h}^2) = aE(y_{t+h} - f_{t,h})^2 = aE(y_{t+h}^2 - 2f_{t,h}y_{t+h} + f_{t,h}^2)$$
$$= a(E(y_{t+h}^2) - 2f_{t,h}E(y_{t+h}) + f_{t,h}^2)$$

The first order condition of the minimization problem is:

$$\frac{\partial E(L(e_{t,h}\,|\,I_t)}{\partial f_{t,h}} = -2aE(y_{t+h}) + 2af_{t,h} = 0 \Rightarrow f_{t,h}^* = E(y_{t+h}\,|\,I_t)$$

- ***under a Linex loss function***

$$E(L(e_{t,h})\,|\,I_t) = E(\exp(ae_{t,h})) - aE(e_{t,h}) - 1$$
$$= \exp(-af_{t,h})E(\exp(ay_{t+h})) - aE(y_{t+h}) + af_{t,h} - 1$$

The first order condition of the minimization problem is:

$$\frac{\partial E(L(e_{t,h}\,|\,I_t)}{\partial f_{t,h}} = -a\exp(-af_{t,h})E(\exp(ay_{t+h})) + a = 0$$

Assuming normality of Y_{t+h}, it is possible to calculate the following expectation:

$$E(\exp(ay_{t+h})) = \exp\left(a\mu_{t+h|t} + \frac{a^2\sigma_{t+h|t}^2}{2}\right)$$

$$\Rightarrow f_{t,h}^* = \frac{\log E(\exp(ay_{t+h}))}{a} = \mu_{t+h|t} + \frac{a\,\sigma_{t+h|t}^2}{2}$$

9.A.2 Optimal Forecast and Forecast Errors from Model M1 Under Symmetric Loss Function with Recursive and Rolling Schemes (Continuation of Table 9.2)

		Recursive scheme		*Rolling scheme*	
Date	**Actual growth**	**Forecast M1**	**Forecast error M1**	**Forecast M1**	**Forecast error M1**
2002Q2	3.32				
2002Q3	4.111				
2002Q4	3.002				
2003Q1	2.305	2.933	-2.933	2.933	-2.933
2003Q2	2.154	2.536	-2.536	2.536	-2.536
2003Q3	3.484	2.246	-2.246	2.246	-2.246

(continued)

		Recursive scheme		*Rolling scheme*	
Date	**Actual growth**	**Forecast M1**	**Forecast error M1**	**Forecast M1**	**Forecast error M1**
2003Q4	6.054	3.129	-3.129	3.128	-3.128
2004Q1	3.825	5.089	-5.089	5.052	-5.052
2004Q2	5.950	3.578	-3.578	3.523	-3.523
2004Q3	10.114	5.598	-5.598	5.562	-5.562
2004Q4	3.989	8.514	-8.514	8.512	-8.512
2005Q1	4.344	4.339	-4.339	4.102	-4.102
2005Q2	5.781	5.650	-5.650	5.294	-5.294
2005Q3	4.978	4.976	-4.976	4.898	-4.898
2005Q4	4.833	4.557	-4.557	4.489	-4.489
2006Q1	2.516	4.849	-4.849	4.816	-4.816
2006Q2	1.487	3.098	-3.098	3.069	-3.069
2006Q3	0.912	2.346	-2.346	2.314	-2.314
2006Q4	-0.260	1.396	-1.396	1.373	-1.373
2007Q1	-0.857	0.364	-0.364	0.326	-0.326
2007Q2	-0.949	-0.187	0.187	-0.207	0.207
2007Q3	-1.972	-0.512	0.512	-0.523	0.523
2007Q4	-3.512	-1.377	1.377	-1.381	1.381

9.A.3 EViews Computer Program To Implement the Fixed, Rolling, and Recursive Schemes Adapted to the Data and Models of House Price Growth in California in Sections 9.1 and 9.2

```
'Alternative Forecasting Schemes

load c:\EViews3\112_S08\ca_hp.wf1

'Fixed Scheme
smpl 1975q2 2002q4
coef(3) prms1
ls g = prms1(1) + prms1(2)*g(-1)+prms1(3)*g(-3)

vector(20) frcst1
for !i = 1 to 20
    frcst1(!i) = prms1(1) + prms1(2)*g(111+!i)+prms1(3)*g(109+!i)
next

'Recursive Scheme
vector(20) frcst2
```

```
for !i = 1 to 20
        smpl 1975q2 2002q4+(!i-1)
        coef(3) prms2
        ls g = prms2(1) + prms2(2)*g(-1)+prms2(3)*g(-3)
    frcst2(!i) = prms2(1) + prms2(2)*g(111+!i)+prms2(3)*g(109+!i)
next

'Rolling Scheme
vector(20) frcst3
for !i = 1 to 20
        smpl 1975q2+(!i) 2002q4+(!i-1)
        coef(3) prms3
        ls g = prms3(1) + prms3(2)*g(-1)+prms3(3)*g(-3)
    frcst3(!i) = prms3(1) + prms3(2)*g(111+!i)+prms3(3)*g(109+!i)
next

'Model II
vector(20) frcst4
for !i = 1 to 20
    frcst4(!i) = g(111+!i)
next

'Model III
vector(20) frcst5
for !i = 1 to 20
    frcst5(!i) = (g(111+!i)+g(110+!i)+g(109+!i)+g(108+!i))/4
next
```

EXERCISES

The exercises of Chapter 9 are based on the results you have obtained in the exercises of Chapter 8. You primarily need forecasts, forecast errors, and forecast error variances.

From Exercises 1 and 2 (Chapter 8): Quarterly House Price Index in San Diego Metropolitan Statistical Area (MSA). We already have forecasting results for three models: AR(4), AR(5), and ARMA(2,4), under the MSE loss function.

1. For the AR(4), AR(5), and ARMA(2,4), construct the optimal forecast, forecast errors, and density forecast under Linex loss function.
2. Using a fixed scheme, prepare two tables similar to Table 9.2 and 9.3, one for symmetric loss and the other for asymmetric loss for AR(4), AR(5), and ARMA(2,4).
3. Implement the forecast optimality tests (MPE and informational efficiency tests) for each model. Write your conclusions. Could you discard any model at this stage?
4. Implement a descriptive evaluation of average loss delivered by the forecasts of the three models under symmetric loss and under asymmetric loss.
5. Under MSE loss function, choose which model among the three has the lowest loss. Consider an alternative and simpler forecast that is calculated by averaging the last six observations (simple smoothing technique that does not require estimation). By implementing the test of unconditional predictability, explain which forecast is preferred.
6. Under MSE loss function, combine the three forecasts. Calculate the MSE loss for the combined forecast by implementing the equal-weighted forecast, the MSE-inversely weighted forecast, and the OLS-weighted forecast. Are there any diversification gains for any of these combined forecasts?
7. Under an MSE loss function, assess all your results from the previous exercises 1 to 6, and choose the overall best model of the three models AR(4), AR(5), and ARMA(2,4). For this model, compute the 1-step-ahead forecast and corresponding forecast errors under a recursive scheme and under a rolling scheme. With this information, compare the forecasts under the three schemes (fixed, recursive, and rolling) and comment on their similarities and differences.

   From Exercise 5 (Chapter 8), U.S. GDP quarterly growth. You have already selected the best ARMA model. Go back to your results and choose the best two models. Complete the following for both models:
8. Under the MSE loss function, implement the forecast optimality tests (MPE and informational efficiency tests) and comment on your findings.
9. Under the MSE loss function, choose the best model of the two. Calculate an alternative forecast such as $f_{t,1} = (y_t + y_{t-3})/2$. Compare this smoothed forecast with that of your best model by implementing the test of unconditional predictability. Which forecast is preferred? Explain your answer.
10. Under the MSE loss function, combine the two forecasts. Calculate the MSE loss for the combined forecast by implementing the equal-weighted forecast, the MSE-inversely weighted forecast, the optimal weight forecast, and the OLS-weighted forecast. Are there any diversification gains for any of these combined forecasts?

A PAUSE

WHERE ARE WE AND WHERE ARE WE GOING?

Before starting with Chapter 5, we paused to summarize our learning from Chapter 1 to Chapter 4. Now that we have finished five additional chapters, Chapter 5 to Chapter 9, it is again a good time to stop and take stock of *what we have learned* and sketch the route ahead. We could sum up our knowledge in just one sentence: We have learned how to model and forecast *linear dependence* when the data are *stationary* by building on the foundational blocks of Chapters 1 to 4. Thus, it seems natural to ask what else we need to know when the data are *nonstationary* or/and the dependence is *nonlinear*. But before we decipher these cryptic words, let us summarize the six main ideas that we have learned in the last five chapters:

1. Although not absolutely necessary to embark on model building, we ask the question "*where does time dependence come from?*" (Chapter 5). Dependence is not an artificial property of the data but, to the contrary, it is a natural consequence of real actions on the part of the many agents in the economic system. The behavior of consumers and producers, rules governing markets and institutions, financial characteristics of assets, and so on are all behind the generation of economic and business data such as prices, inflation, interest rates, returns, wages, and so on.
2. The simplest form of time dependence is linear. The information on linear dependence is contained in the autocorrelations functions, which are the key tools for discovering the best linear model(s) that fit the time series data. The many shapes of the autocorrelation functions translate into different *ARMA models* (Chapters 6 and 7). The objective is to build the optimal forecast based on these models. For moving average (MA) processes (Chapter 6), it is important that the process is invertible to guarantee that present information depends on past information. For autoregressive (AR) processes (Chapter 7), we are concerned about the restrictions on the parameters of the model so that covariance-stationarity holds. Finite MA processes are always stationary, and AR processes are always invertible. When stationarity and invertibility hold, we have three very important properties of ARMA models: (1) they are mean-reverting processes so that the data may fluctuate but, sooner or later, the process reverts to its unconditional mean, (2) they are short memory processes so that information in the far and very far past is irrelevant to produce a forecast

today, and (3) their multistep forecast converges to the unconditional mean of the process when the forecast horizon is far into the future. We may understand (3) as a consequence of (1) and (2). Because of these properties, ARMA specifications are well suited to model short/medium-term features of the data; for instance, business cycles are well represented by ARMA models. A forthcoming question is: How are the long-term features of the data modeled?

3. ARMA models are foundational models in the sense that any stationary stochastic process with complex dynamics can be approximated by a linear model. The *Wold decomposition* (Chapter 6) guarantees this approximation. Thus, any model-building strategy should entertain the best ARMA model(s) to which other nonlinear refinements may be added. A forthcoming question is: How do we detect and model nonlinear features in the data?
4. The *practice of forecasting* is full of judgment calls. Because all models are approximations and stylized representations of the data, it is rare to find that just one model fits the data best. We have seen that in the practice of forecasting, we entertain several models (Chapter 8), but all models should be subject to statistical hurdles. For forecasting purposes, it is important to specify the correct lag structure and to have white noise residuals, but, in practice, we will face issues of borderline statistical significance and, in these cases, it is best to carry more than a few models to the next stage in the modeling and forecasting exercise.
5. Facing many models, we need to have evaluation criteria in place. *In-sample evaluation* (Chapter 8) refers to a battery of tests aiming to ensure that the proposed specification(s) match the properties of the time series data. *Out-of-sample evaluation* (Chapter 9) focuses on the properties of the forecasts provided by the selected models and, for the most part, out-of-sample testing depends on the loss function of the forecaster. Optimality tests and predictive ability tests are meaningful only with regard to the chosen loss function.
6. A *combined forecast* (Chapter 9) may afford a lower loss than that of any other individual forecast. Diversification gains are a powerful incentive whenever we face a variety of forecasts, which may come from a diversity of sources.

Where Are We Going from Here?

In the forthcoming chapters, as natural extensions of the ideas that we have already developed, we will explore three main topics: (1) modeling of long-term features of a time series, (2) multivariate modeling or joint analysis of several time series, and (3) combining short and long-term features of the data in a multivariate context.

We will start by relaxing the stationarity property, which is behind the main ideas summarized in the earlier points (2) and (3). In many economic and business time series, we observe growth over time; it is easy to detect a persistent upward tendency over the long term. Think about the U.S. gross domestic product (GDP) from the beginning of the

20th century. In these cases, it is difficult to maintain even the simplest assumption of a constant unconditional mean: If there is long term growth, the average of the time series also must be changing over time. In Chapter 3, we encountered some nonstationary time series, but we proceeded to transform them (i.e., taking first differences of the logarithm of the original data) as a mean to achieve stationary. But on transforming the data, we change the meaning of the time series. For instance, it is not the same exercise to model the U.S. GDP *level* or to model U.S. GDP *growth.* In Chapter 10, we will learn how to deal with nonstationary time series; we will introduce the concept of *trend* as a long-term feature of the data, and we will learn how to *statistically* discriminate between a stationary and a nonstationary process.

Up to here, we have been concerned with the modeling of linear dependence of just one time series, but our economic models taught us that economic variables interact with each other. We could study the time series of consumption in isolation, but consumption is highly dependent on the level of income, which in turn has its own dynamics. Then in our modeling strategy, it makes sense to analyze both time series jointly. In Chapter 11, we will introduce a system called *vector autoregression (VAR)* that will model the joint dynamics of several time series and will allow dynamic interactions among them. Many concepts that we have learned in a univariate context will translate easily into a multivariate setting.

Pedagogically, we have introduced first the analysis of models with short-term features followed by models that capture long-term characteristics, but when we study a time series or a system of time series, both short and long features are jointly present. In Chapter 12, we will learn how to integrate our knowledge about short- and long-term dynamics. We will learn new concepts such as cointegration among different time series and the building of error correction models (ECM). Intellectually, Chapter 12 will give us the opportunity to synthesize all our understanding of linear dependence, stationarity and nonstationary, short- and long-term dynamics, and how all is combined to produce a forecast.

Finally, a note: The forthcoming Chapters 10, 11, and Chapter 12 will add new models to our time series library, and as we did with the ARMA models (Chapters 6 and 7), they will need to be evaluated with the same techniques that we learned in Chapters 8 and 9. Thus, keep in mind these chapters for the forthcoming exercises.

That's all, folks (for now)!

CHAPTER 10

Forecasting the Long Term: Deterministic and Stochastic Trends

The analysis of ARMA models that we studied in Chapters 6 and 7 relies on the assumption that the data are covariance stationary. We have seen that short/medium-term features of the data such as economic cycles are well characterized by the dynamics of ARMA models. The main objective of this chapter is to relax the assumption of stationarity and learn how to analyze *nonstationary data*. We will study some stochastic processes that are well suited to represent the *long-term* features of economic and business time series. Intuitively, a long-term feature in a time series is a smooth and persistent upward (or downward) tendency in the data for long periods of time; in this case, we say that there is *a trend*. For instance, we observe that the national output of developed economies has an upward trend; in the short term, the economy goes through expansions and recessions (cycles), but in the long term, there is economic growth (trend) either because of technological progress or population growth, or both. If our objective is to study trends, we have to give up the stationarity assumption. Recall that the weakest form of stationarity requires a constant unconditional mean; thus, a trend as a smooth evolution through time must be incompatible with a constant mean.

Examine the four time series plots in Figure 10.1. There is a variety of information: In 10.1a, we present the quarterly U.S. national output from 1993:Q3 to 2002:Q2; in 10.1b, the index of annual total hours worked in three Organization for Economic Cooperation and Development (OECD) countries from 1970 to 2002; in 10.1c, graduate enrollment in the sciences and engineering in U.S. universities from 1975 to 2001; and in 10.1d, the U.S. population from 1790 to 2000. The information contained in these plots is diverse, but there is a common feature that runs through all of them. There is a trend in every plot; however, the shape is different.

In Figure 10.1a, indexes of U.S. output, productivity, and worked hours have an upward linear trend though with different slopes. The output index has a larger slope than the productivity and hours indexes. Because the three indexes have a starting value of 100 in 1990:Q3, it is very easy to calculate the growth rate over any time horizon. For instance, output grew 45% smoothly from 1990:3Q to 2002:2Q. How much did productivity and the number of worked hours grow in the

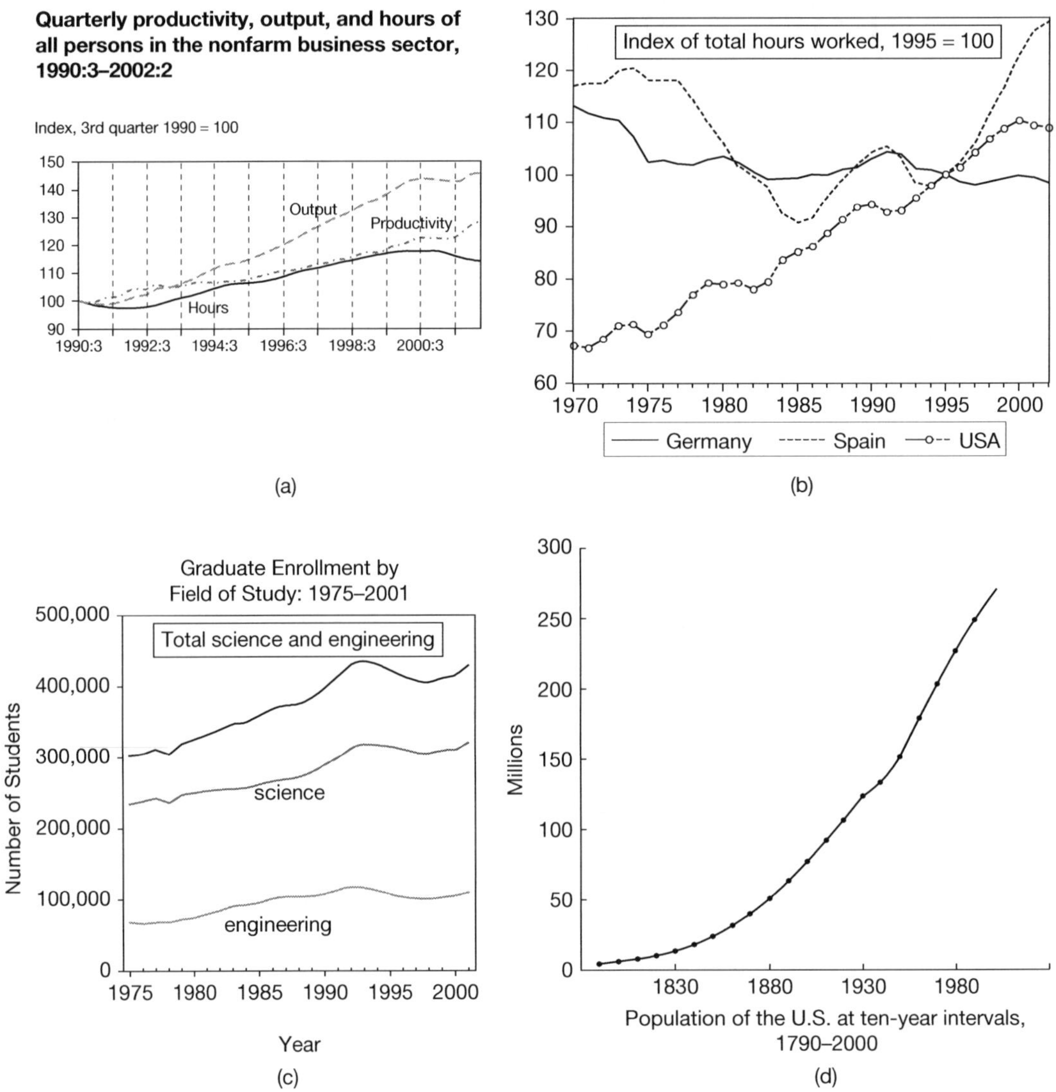

FIGURE 10.1 Economic Time Series with Trends

Note: Labour productivity is output per hour worked

Sources: (a) Bureau of Labor Statistic, September 5, 2002; (b) OECD Productivity Database; (c) National Science Foundation.

same period? Why is output growth equal to the sum of the growth of productivity and the growth of hours worked? Remember that *productivity* is defined as output per unit of labor.

In Figure 10.1b, we detect a somewhat downward tendency in the index of total hours worked in Germany, but a clear upward tendency in United States, and a somewhat mixed tendency in Spain. What can we say about the trend in each country? Would a linear trend be a good representation for these time series? Do we really have a trend in the Spanish series?

In Figure 10.1c, the number of graduate students in science and engineering in the United States exhibits an upward trend, but we detect a hump in 1993. The trend may not be linear. What functional form should we choose for the trend in this time series?

Finally, in Figure 10.1d, there is an obvious upward trend in the U.S. population. It has steadily increased at an accelerated pace. The growth rate in any decade is higher than that of the previous one. This behavior cannot be represented by a linear trend; maybe an exponential or quadratic trend would be more appropriate.

All of the preceding questions are the subject of this chapter. The two main objectives of this chapter are to:

1. Understand deterministic and stochastic trends; we will construct models that produce these trends and analyze their properties and forecasts.
2. Design statistical procedures to detect deterministic and stochastic trends in the data.

In Figure 10.1, trends are characterized by a persistent upward or downward tendency, generally smooth, that may evolve over time in a linear or nonlinear fashion. Most of the macroeconomic aggregates such as GNP, consumption, income, price indexes, and so on exhibit a trend. How does a trend come about? To keep the persistent movement in mainly one direction, information must accumulate from one period to the next. For instance, think about the population plot in Figure 10.1d. From one period to the next, population increases because the number of births exceeds the number of deaths and/or because the number of immigrants exceeds the number of emigrants. We are adding, that is, accumulating a positive number of people in every period. Thus, we define

A trend is a relatively smooth, mostly unidirectional, pattern in the data that arises from the accumulation of information over time.

The accumulation could be deterministic or stochastic, so we will distinguish between deterministic or stochastic trends. Their analysis is performed in the following sections.

10.1 Deterministic Trends

The simplest model with a **deterministic trend** is

$$Y_t = \beta_0 + \beta_1 t + \varepsilon_t \qquad \text{for } t = 1, 2, 3, \ldots \tag{10.1}$$

The trend is a line, that is, $\beta_0 + \beta_1 t$ with β_0 as intercept and β_1 as slope. Economic and business time series data do not fall perfectly into a line; we always encounter some degree of uncertainty and, because of that, we add an unpredictable term, a white noise error ε_t. The trend is generated by accumulating time t deterministically. For instance, if $t = 3 = 1 + 1 + 1$, we have accumulated three time periods at the rate of β_1 units per period (growth rate) so that $Y_3 = \beta_0 + \beta_1(1 + 1 + 1) + \varepsilon_3 = \beta_0 + 3\beta_1 + \varepsilon_3$.

Simulate a time series with a deterministic linear trend as in (10.1) by typing in the Genr window of your EViews workfile a command of the following type:

```
y=1+0.5*@trend(1)+nrnd
```

In this example, $\beta_0 = 1$ and $\beta_1 = 0.5$, and the trend, which increases by one unit at the time ($t = 1, 2, 3 \ldots.$), is created by the command @trend(1). The command nrnd adds a white noise error that is normally distributed with zero mean and unit variance. In Figure 10.2, we plot the resulting time series (solid line), which exhibits a smooth upward tendency. The linear trend $1 + 0.5t$ is the dashed line. The contribution of the white noise error term makes the time series move above and below the linear trend.

The analysis of deterministic trends focuses on three aspects: (1) trend shapes, (2) stationarity properties, and (3) construction of optimal forecasts.

10.1.1 Trend Shapes

In Figure 10.1, we saw that trends can have different shapes. In this section, we focus on different functional forms of deterministic trends. Because trends represent growth, it is also of interest to calculate the growth rate of the variable of interest for different functional forms of the deterministic trend. In Figure 10.3, we plot four trend specifications: **linear**, **quadratic**, **exponential**, and **logistic** type. For simplicity, we have omitted the stochastic term ε_t.

FIGURE 10.2 Time Series with Linear Deterministic Trend

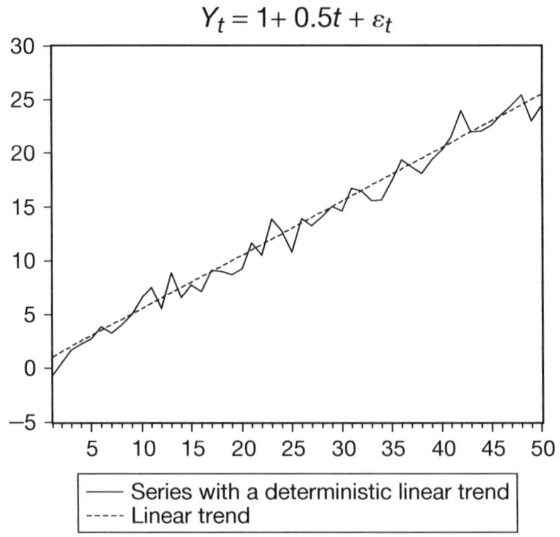

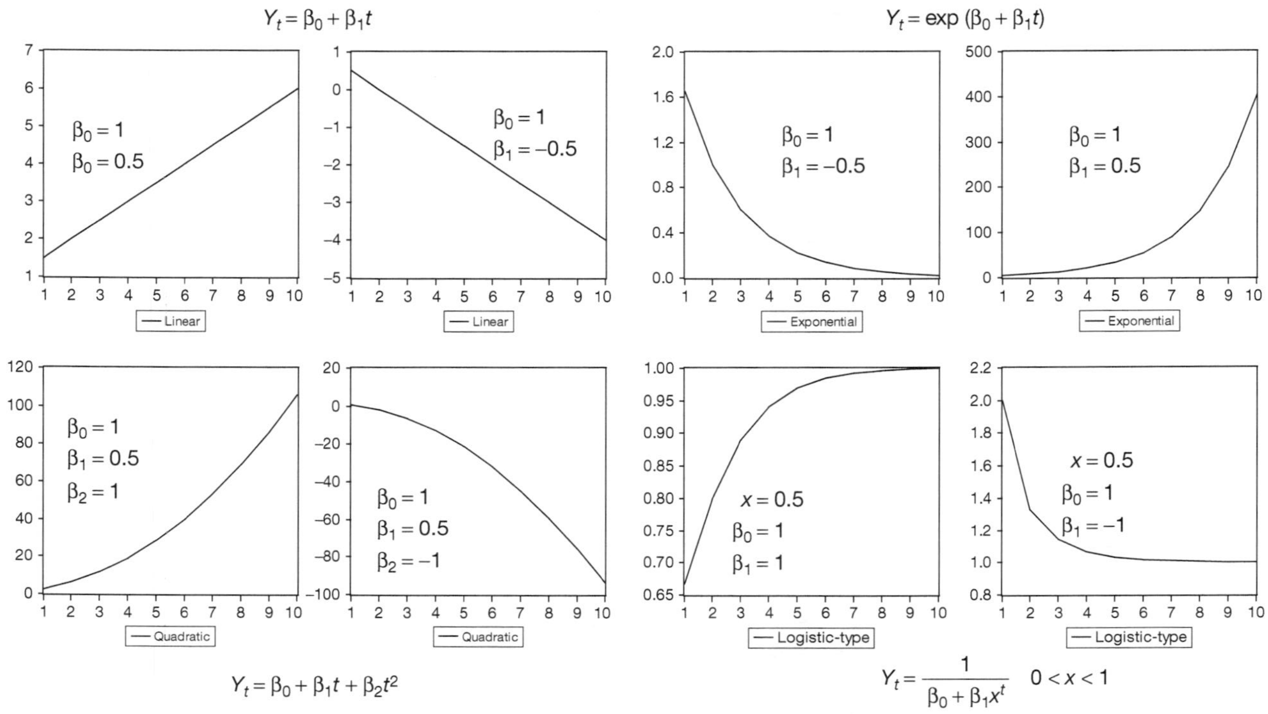

FIGURE 10.3 Common Deterministic Trends

The growth rate is defined as the change in Y_t per unit of time, that is, how much we expect Y_t to move from one period to the next. If you are familiar with calculus, the growth rate is the first derivative of the trend function with respect to time, and we write dY_t/dt in which the notation d means derivative. If you are not familiar with calculus, think of dY_t/dt as an approximation to the ratio $\Delta Y_t/\Delta t$, that is, $\frac{dY_t}{dt} \approx \frac{\Delta Y_t}{\Delta t}$. This is an approximation because the definition of *derivative* refers to changes in Y_t for very small—infinitesimal—changes in time. Because in our analysis we deal with discrete time, the change in time is always one unit, $\Delta t = 1$. In the next paragraphs, see how the approximation works.

For linear trends, the growth rate is constant; for quadratic trends, exponential trends, and logistic-type trends, the growth rate will depend on time t. For instance, let us look in more detail at the plot of the linear and quadratic trends in Figure 10.4. In the linear trend, moving from period 3 to period 4, the change in the variable is the same as the change in moving from period 7 to period 8. The growth rate is 0.5 units per period, which is the slope β_1 of the linear trend. However, in the quadratic trend, moving from period 4 to period 5, there is a change of 9.5 units, and moving from period 7 to period 8, the change is 15.5 units; the growth rate will keep increasing when time increases. Note the difference between the computation of the derivative and the discrete change, ΔY_t. Computing $\frac{dY_t}{dt}$ at time $t = 4$, we have a growth rate of 8.5, that is, $\frac{dY_t}{dt} = 0.5 + 2 \times 4 = 8.5$, which is relatively close to the discrete change $\Delta Y_t = 9.5$. It is customary to report the growth rate calculated according to the derivative $\frac{dY_t}{dt}$.

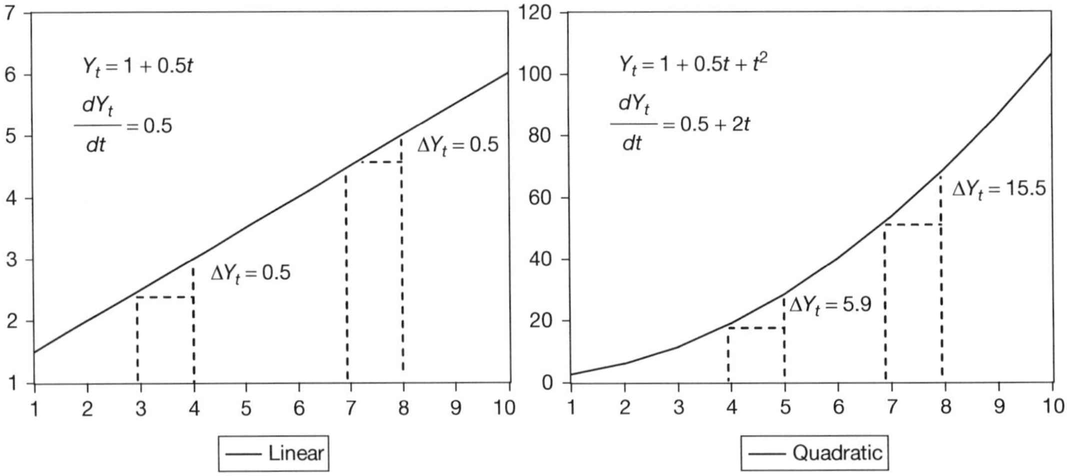

FIGURE 10.4 Growth Rate with Linear and Quadratic Deterministic Trends

The growth rates calculated from exponential trends and logistic-type trends also depend on the time period. For the exponential trend $Y_t = \exp(\beta_0 + \beta_1 t)$, the growth rate is $\frac{dY_t}{dt} = \beta_1 Y_t$, which depends on Y_t. Note that the exponential trend can be linearized by taking logs in both sides of the model, that is, $\log Y_t = \beta_0 + \beta_1 t$. Now in the log-model, the trend becomes linear in t and the parameter β_1 is the growth rate of Y_t in relative terms (percentage terms when multiplied by 100) (i.e., $\beta_1 = 100 \times dY_t / Y_t$), which is a constant regardless of the time period we consider.

10.1.2 Trend Stationarity

The time series plots of Figure 10.1 and Figure 10.2 are incompatible with the property of mean-stationarity (review the concept in Chapter 3). Recall that a process is first-order weakly stationarity (mean stationarity) when the unconditional mean is constant over time. Thus, if a deterministic trend is an evolutionary pattern over time, the mean of a process with a deterministic trend cannot be constant but must vary with time.

Let us choose a process with a linear trend and compute the first (mean) and second (variance and autocovariances) unconditional moments:

$$Y_t = \beta_0 + \beta_1 t + \varepsilon_t$$

Note that there is nothing random about t, $t = 1, 2, 3 \ldots$ It must be very easy to take expectations in such a model because the only random behavior comes from ε_t, which is assumed to be a white noise process $N(0, \sigma_\varepsilon^2)$. The parameters β_0 and β_1 are also constant; thus, by taking expectations we have:

Unconditional mean

$$E(Y_t) = E(\beta_0 + \beta_1 t + \varepsilon_t) = \beta_0 + \beta_1 t + E(\varepsilon_t) = \beta_0 + \beta_1 t \equiv \mu_t$$

Unconditional variance

$$\sigma_Y^2 = E(Y_t - \mu_t)^2 = E(Y_t - \beta_0 - \beta_1 t)^2 = E(\varepsilon_t)^2 = \sigma_\varepsilon^2 \equiv \gamma_0$$

Autocovariance of order k

$$\gamma_k \equiv E(Y_t - \mu_t)(Y_{t-k} - \mu_{t-k}) = E(Y_t - \beta_0 - \beta_1 t)(Y_{t-k} - \beta_0 - \beta_1 (t-k))$$
$$= E(\varepsilon_t \varepsilon_{t-k}) = 0$$

Autocorrelation of order k

$$\rho_k = \frac{\gamma_k}{\gamma_0} = \frac{0}{\sigma_\varepsilon^2} = 0$$

We observe that although the unconditional mean μ_t is time varying (we have attached the subindex t to our notation), the unconditional variance is not, and the autocovariance and autocorrelation functions do not depend on time. Remember the properties of a covariance stationary process. Because the unconditional mean is not constant over time, the process is not mean stationary. However, because the variance and autocovariances satisfy the requirement for weakly stationarity, we say that a process with a deterministic linear trend is *trend-stationary*.[1]

In general, we say that:

Processes with deterministic trends are trend-stationary

10.1.3 Optimal Forecast

Let us proceed as we did with the ARMA models in Chapters 6 and 7. Assume that the forecaster has a quadratic loss function so that the optimal forecast is the conditional mean and recall that $f_{t,h} = \mu_{t+h|t} = E(Y_{t+h}|I_t)$ for $h = 1, 2, \ldots . s$. Let us choose a process with a deterministic linear trend

$$Y_t = \beta_0 + \beta_1 t + \varepsilon_t$$

The information set runs to time t, and we are interested in a forecasting horizon $h = 1$. The value of the process at the future time $t + 1$ is

$$Y_{t+1} = \beta_0 + \beta_1(t + 1) + \varepsilon_{t+1}$$

What is the optimal point forecast $f_{t,1}$?

$$f_{t,1} = \mu_{t+1|t} = E(Y_{t+1}|I_t) = E(\beta_0 + \beta_1(t + 1) + \varepsilon_{t+1}|I_t) = \beta_0 + \beta_1(t + 1)$$

What is the one-period ahead forecast error $e_{t,1}$?

The difference between the realized value Y_{t+1} and the forecast value $f_{t,1}$,

$$e_{t,1} = Y_{t+1} - f_{t,1} = \beta_0 + \beta_1(t + 1) + \varepsilon_{t+1} - \beta_0 - \beta_1(t + 1) = \varepsilon_{t+1}$$

What is the uncertainty associated with the forecast?

It is the variance of the forecast error,

$$\sigma^2_{t+1|t} = \text{var}(Y_{t+1}|I_t) = E(Y_{t+1} - f_{t,1}|I_t)^2 = E(e^2_{t,1}) = E(\varepsilon^2_{t+1}) = \sigma^2_\varepsilon$$

What is the density forecast?

It is the conditional probability density function of the process at the future date $t + 1$. Recall that we have assumed a normally distributed white noise; thus,

$$f(Y_{t+1}|I_t) \rightarrow N(\mu_{t+1|t}, \sigma^2_{t+1|t}) = N(\beta_0 + \beta_1(t + 1), \sigma^2_\varepsilon)$$

---

[1]The term **trend-stationary** may seem a contradiction because we have said that a trend is not compatible with stationarity. However, *trend-stationary* should be understood as a combination of two words: *trend,* referring to the mean of the process that has a deterministic trend, and *stationary,* referring to the remaining moments that do not depend on time; thus, they satisfy the properties of a stationary process.

It is straightforward to compute the forecast at any other horizon. In general, for $h = s$, we find

$$f_{t,s} = \beta_0 + \beta_1(t + s)$$
$$e_{t,s} = \varepsilon_{t+s}$$
$$\sigma^2_{t+s|t} = \sigma^2_\varepsilon$$
$$f(Y_{t+s|t} \mid I_t) \rightarrow N(\beta_0 + \beta_1(t + s), \sigma^2_\varepsilon)$$

Observe that the uncertainty of the forecast is the same regardless of the forecasting horizon because we have assumed that ε_t is a white noise process. In general, the trend models can also accommodate further linear dependence (any ARMA specification) in ε_t. The following modeling exercise illustrates such a possibility.

REAL DATA: Modeling and Forecasting the U.S. Outstanding Mortgage Debt

In Figure 10.5, we present the quarterly time series of the U.S. outstanding debt from Households Home Mortgages. Note that this is a stock variable. The series runs from 1992:Q1 to 2004:Q1 and is seasonally adjusted. You will find estimates of mortgage debt in the flow of funds accounts of the Federal Reserve Board http://www.federalreserve.gov. The striking feature of this time series is the enormous growth of residential debt during this 13-year period, which was mainly triggered by the price appreciation of homes and by the growth of the population and the number of households. The outstanding debt went from 2.7 trillion dollars in 1992:Q1 to almost 7 trillions in 2004:Q1, which represents a growth rate of 155.5%! Would this growth be maintained beyond 2004? Let us produce a forecast based on the univariate time series.

FIGURE 10.5 Home Mortgage Outstanding Debt (Billions of Dollars)

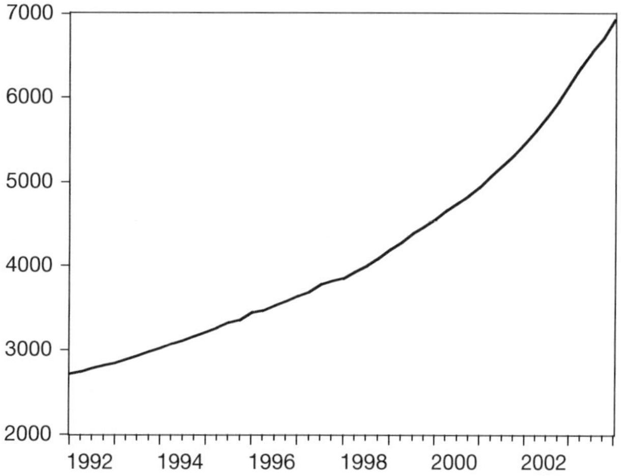

The time series plot clearly exhibits a trend. Compare Figure 10.5 with the plots in Figure 10.3. Do you find similarities? Just by inspection, we say that the trend does not seem to be linear. The plots in Figure 10.3 that match more closely the plot in Figure 10.5 seem to be the exponential and the quadratic plots.

How do we find the best trend model? Implementing the modeling methodology that we described in detail in Chapter 8, we will focus on the estimation of several models and the construction of the forecast.

To identify the trend model that fits the data best, we will proceed with the estimation of several models. Criteria such as the adjusted R-squared (in linear models), the (AIC) and (SIC) will be instrumental to select the best model(s). **Linear trends, quadratic trends**, and, in general, any **polynomial trends** are linear models (linear with respect to the parameters βs). These are linear regression models in which the regressors are powers of the time trend so that they can be estimated by ordinary least squares (reviewed in Chapter 2). The exponential trend models require a more sophisticated estimation procedure called *nonlinear least squares*[2] because they are nonlinear with respect to the parameters βs. Note that the exponential trends can be linearized by applying a *log* transformation. In this case, the model becomes linear in the parameters, and it can be estimated by ordinary least squares. However, the dependent variable will not be Y_t but $log\ Y_t$. This is important because the R-squared and the adjusted R-squared of two models with different dependent variables, such as Y_t and $log\ Y_t$, cannot be compared.

We proceed with least squares estimation of several trend specifications, and we present the estimation output of the preferred model. In Table 10.1, there are two panels separated by a thick horizontal line. In the first panel, all specifications have the same dependent variable, Y_t, whereas in the second panel, the dependent variable is log Y_t. This means that the adjusted R-squared, AIC, and SIC are comparable across models of the same panel but not across panels. Note that the adjusted R-squared is not reported for the exponential trends because these are nonlinear models.

It is clear from the first panel of Table 10.1 that a linear trend is the least desirable of the models; its adjusted R-squared is the lowest, and the AIC and the SIC are the highest. Among the models of the first panel, a polynomial trend of order 4 is the preferred model because the AIC and SIC are the lowest. The adjusted R-squared is almost identical across models. In the second panel, the SIC selects a logarithmic transformation with a polynomial trend of order 5 and the AIC a polynomial trend of order 6, although there is not much difference with that of order 5. In summary, there are two preferred models that we could use to construct the forecast.

In Table 10.2, we present the estimation output corresponding to a polynomial trend of order 4. The estimated trend is

$$\hat{Y}_t = 2668.57 + 31.63t + 1.06t^2 - 0.03t^3 + 0.0007t^4$$

---

[2] We will not enter into the technical details of a nonlinear least squares procedure, but the basic idea is the same as that of ordinary least squares: The nonlinear estimator is the result of minimizing the sum of squared residuals.

TABLE 10.1 Deterministic Trend Specifications

Trend model	Adjusted R-squared	AIC	SIC
$Y_t = \beta_0 + \beta_1 t$	0.9358	14.292	14.369
$Y_t = \beta_0 + \beta_1 t + \beta_2 t^2$	0.9945	11.847	11.963
$Y_t = \beta_0 + \beta_1 t + \beta_2 t^2 + \beta_3 t^3$	0.9994	9.520	9.674
$Y_t = \beta_0 + \beta_1 t + \beta_2 t^2 + \beta_3 t^3 + \beta_4 t^4$	0.9997	**8.827**	**9.020**
$Y_t = \beta_0 + \beta_1 t + \beta_2 t^2 + \beta_3 t^3 + \beta_4 t^4 + \beta_5 t^5$	0.9997	8.861	9.093
$Y_t = \beta_0 \exp(\beta_1 t + \beta_2 t^2)$		10.382	10.498
$Y_t = \beta_0 \exp(\beta_1 t + \beta_2 t^2 + \beta_3 t^3)$		9.933	10.087
$Y_t = \beta_0 \exp(\beta_1 t + \beta_2 t^2 + \beta_3 t^3 + \beta_4 t^4)$		9.114	9.307
$Y_t = \beta_0 \exp(\beta_1 t + \beta_2 t^2 + \beta_3 t^3 + \beta_4 t^4 + \beta_5 t^5)$		8.855	9.087
$\log Y_t = \beta_0 + \beta_1 t + \beta_2 t^2$	0.9986	-6.343	-6.227
$\log Y_t = \beta_0 + \beta_1 t + \beta_2 t^2 + \beta_3 t^3$	0.9997	-7.874	-7.719
$\log Y_t = \beta_0 + \beta_1 t + \beta_2 t^2 + \beta_3 t^3 + \beta_4 t^4$	0.9997	-7.906	-7.713
$\log Y_t = \beta_0 + \beta_1 t + \beta_2 t^2 + \beta_3 t^3 + \beta_4 t^4 + \beta_5 t^5$	0.9997	-7.974	**-7.743**
$\log Y_t = \beta_0 + \beta_1 t + \beta_2 t^2 + \beta_3 t^3 + \beta_4 t^4 + \beta_5 t^5 + \beta_6 t^6$	0.9997	**-7.977**	-7.707

Observe that the trend is dominated by the linear term t and the quadratic term t^2. The contribution of t^4 is the smallest, albeit one of the most statistically significant (check its t-ratio and p-value). The growth rate calculated from the model is

$$\frac{d\hat{Y}_t}{dt} = 31.63 + 2.13t - 0.09t^2 + 0.003t^3$$

which is not constant but depends on the time period. For instance, in 1993:Q1, $t = 5$ and the quarterly growth was

$$\frac{d\hat{Y}_t}{dt} = 31.63 + 2.13 \times 5 - 0.09 \times 5^2 + 0.003 \times 5^3 = 40.40 \text{ billions of dollars}$$

In 2000:Q1, $t = 33$, and the quarterly growth was

$$\frac{d\hat{Y}_t}{dt} = 31.63 + 2.13 \times 33 - 0.09 \times 33^2 + 0.003 \times 33^3 = 111.72 \text{ billions of dollars}$$

The fit is almost perfect because the R-squared is 0.999. In the bottom plot accompanying Table 10.2, we cannot distinguish very well between the actual and the fitted values because the residuals are very tiny compared to the values of the dependent variable.

TABLE 10.2 Least Squares Estimation of a Polynomial Trend

Dependent Variable: DEBT
Method: Least Squares
Sample: 1992:1 2004:1
Included observations: 49

Variable	Coefficient	Std. Error	t–Statistic	Prob.
C	2668.571	15.45319	172.6874	0.0000
TRND	31.63280	4.190147	7.549329	0.0000
TRND^2	1.065196	0.335967	3.170541	0.0028
TRND^3	-0.032256	0.010048	-3.210235	0.0025
TRND^4	0.000688	9.97E-05	6.897960	0.0000

R-squared	0.999765	Mean dependent var	4184.486
Adjusted R-squared	0.999743	S.D. dependent var	1188.904
S.E. of regression	19.04364	Akaike info criterion	8.827795
Sum squared resid	15957.05	Schwarz criterion	9.020838
Log likelihood	-211.2810	F-statistic	46759.77
Durbin-Watson stat	0.731080	Prob(F-statistic)	0.000000

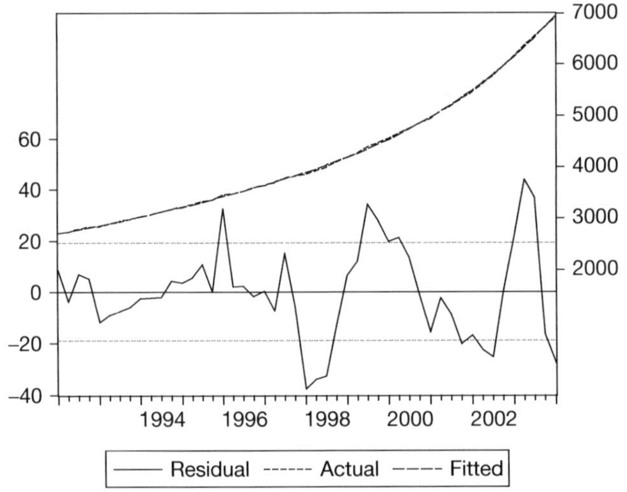

Based on the estimated model and information up to 2004:Q1 ($t=49$), we compute the forecast of outstanding debt 11 periods ahead, that is, in 2006:Q4 ($t+s=60$). The forecast is

$$\begin{aligned} f_{49,11} &= 2668.57 + 31.63 \times 60 + 1.06 \times 60^2 - 0.03 \times 60^3 + 0.0007 \times 60^4 \\ &= 10{,}350.40 \text{ billions} \end{aligned}$$

FIGURE 10.6 Forecast of Outstanding Mortgage Debt Based on Table 10.2

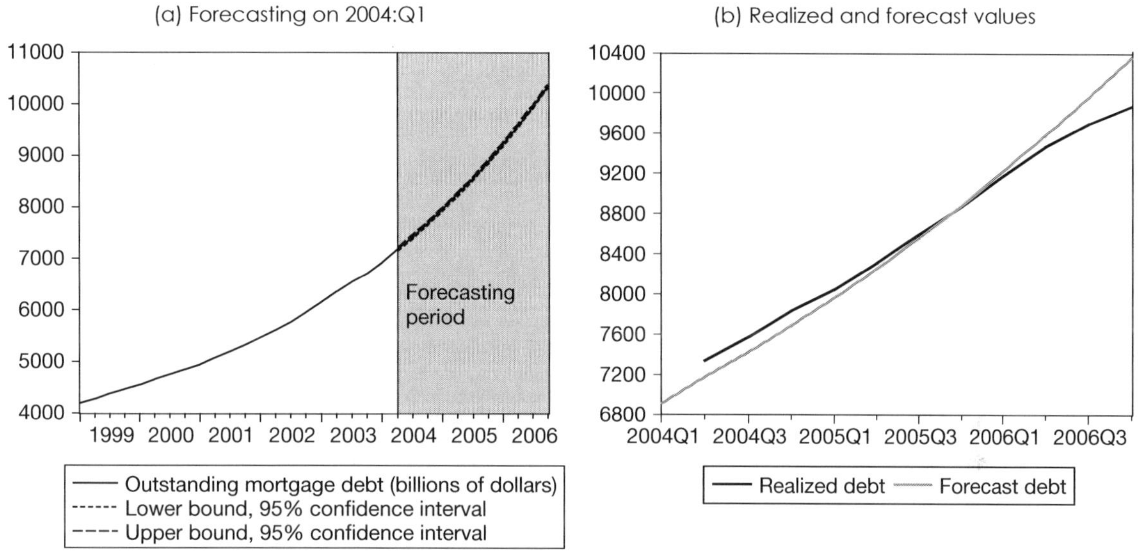

which represents a 50% increase with respect to the debt amount in 2004:Q1. The variance of the forecast is $\hat{\sigma}^2_{60|49} = \sigma^2_{\hat{\varepsilon}} = 19.04^2$ (see standard error (s.e.) of the regression in Table 10.2). Similarly, we can compute the forecast for any other future time. In Figure 10.6(a), we present the forecasts from 2004:Q2 to 2006:Q4 with the 95% confidence bands, which as expected are extremely narrow because the residual standard error is very small.

The deterministic trend model that we have estimated has assumed that the error term ε_t is a white noise process

$$Y_t = 2668.57 + 31.63t + 1.06t^2 - 0.03t^3 + 0.0007t^4 + \hat{\varepsilon}_t$$

Do we have enough information to verify this assumption? Examine the bottom plot of residuals in Table 10.2. A preliminary assessment shows that the residuals are persistent; they remain above or below zero for several periods of time in a row. This is not what it would be expected from a white noise process. It is necessary to run the autocorrelation functions for the residuals, which are presented in Figure 10.7, to assess whether they are white noise. The shape of these autocorrelograms must be familiar to you; it looks like an autoregressive process of order 2. Thus, the white noise assumption is not satisfied, and we can identify an AR(2) model for the error term such as $\varepsilon_t = \phi_1\varepsilon_{t-1} + \phi_2\varepsilon_{t-2} + v_t$, where v_t is now a white noise process.

We finish this modeling exercise presenting in Table 10.3 the estimation of an extended model that combines long-term information—a polynomial trend of order 4—with short-term information—an AR(2). Examine the following estimation output and compare with that of Table 10.2.

FIGURE 10.7 Correlograms of the Residuals of the Fourth-Order Polynomial Trend Model

Sample: 1992:1 2004:1
Included observations: 49

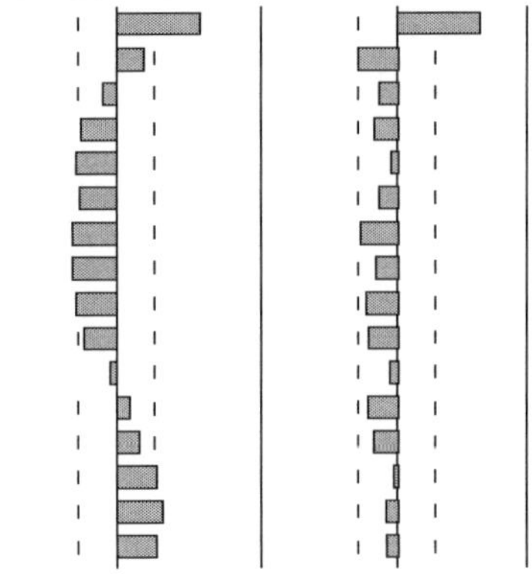

Autocorrelation	Partial Correlation		AC	PAC	Q-Stat	Prob
		1	0.608	0.608	19.270	0.000
		2	0.197	-0.276	21.323	0.000
		3	-0.084	-0.118	21.706	0.000
		4	-0.268	-0.169	25.680	0.000
		5	-0.300	-0.042	30.796	0.000
		6	-0.274	-0.116	35.174	0.000
		7	-0.323	-0.270	41.366	0.000
		8	-0.326	-0.152	47.862	0.000
		9	-0.304	-0.223	53.620	0.000
		10	-0.244	-0.210	57.425	0.000
		11	-0.049	-0.045	57.583	0.000
		12	0.096	-0.204	58.210	0.000
		13	0.177	-0.161	60.393	0.000
		14	0.296	-0.004	66.666	0.000
		15	0.338	-0.063	75.081	0.000
		16	0.298	-0.064	81.792	0.000

TABLE 10.3 Least Squares Estimation of Trend and AR Model

Dependent Variable: DEBT
Method: Least Squares
Sample(adjusted): 1992:3 2004:1
Included observations: 47 after adjusting endpoints
Estimation settings: tol = 0.00010, derivs = accurate mixed (linear)
Convergence achieved after 8 iterations

Variable	Coefficient	Std. Error	t-Statistic	Prob.
C	2661.391	50.60255	52.59402	0.0000
TRND	33.90561	11.62180	2.917415	0.0058
TRND^2	0.870626	0.831794	1.046684	0.3015
TRND^3	-0.026140	0.023088	-1.132204	0.2643
TRND^4	0.000625	0.000217	2.874052	0.0065
AR(1)	0.826760	0.152925	5.406303	0.0000
AR(2)	-0.281622	0.161740	-1.741197	0.0893

R-squared	0.999863	Mean dependent var	4246.766
Adjusted R-squared	0.999842	S.D. dependent var	1173.817
S.E. of regression	14.73993	Akaike info criterion	8.355601
Sum squared resid	8690.616	Schwarz criterion	8.631155
Log likelihood	-189.3566	F-statistic	48613.50
Durbin-Watson stat	2.070406	Prob(F-statistic)	0.000000
Inverted AR Roots	.41-.33i	.41+.33i	

(continued)

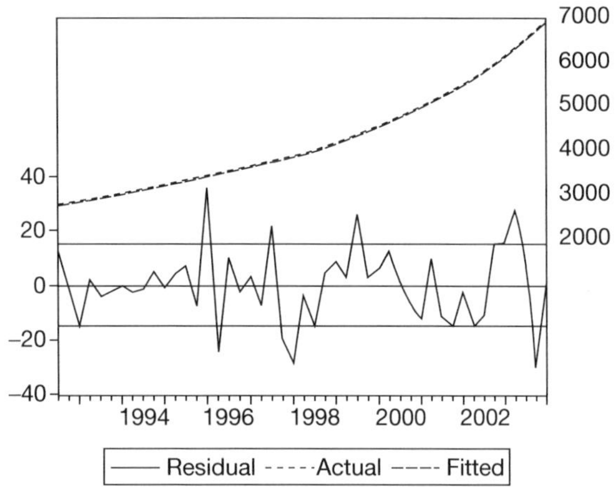

This new model is preferred because the autoregressive parameters are highly significant; AIC and SIC and the residual variance are smaller than those in Table 10.2; now the residuals do not seem to have any autocorrelation left. A forecast based on the results of Table 10.3 is left as an exercise. You will need to combine your knowledge of forecasting with deterministic trends and with AR processes (Chapter 7).

Finally, a note of caution: The danger of fitting a deterministic trend to the data is that the trend may break, rendering the forecast useless. It is important to update your data set as soon as new data are available and to question any deterministic component of the model. In this specific case, we question the functional form of the trend. This is a situation that you will face constantly in the practice of forecasting: New data will come, and it will give you an opportunity to revise or update your forecasts. New data releases may also have revisions of the previous data, and it is likely that the old data will be slightly different from those in the most recently released version. As a point in case, in Figure 10.6(b), we compare the realized values of outstanding mortgage debt from 2004:Q2 to 2006:Q4 with the forecasts for the same period. The forecast is quite good until 2006:Q2, but, from that time on, we observe that the growth rate of debt has decreased. This is the result of the softening of the residential home market that started toward the end of 2006. Given the rise in foreclosures and credit defaults, we anticipate that outstanding debt will stabilize or may diminish in the forthcoming years. This is a call for revising the model; it is very likely that a break in the trend has occurred. With the information that we had on 2004:Q1, a model with a polynomial trend of order 4 worked well but, as the new data revealed, from 2006:Q2, the model produced larger debt predictions than those observed. The economic landscape has changed, and the model should adapt to the new dynamics. It is left as an exercise to update these data and assess whether the four-order polynomial trend is now granted or has had a break and the entire model should be revaluated.

10.2 Stochastic Trends

The analysis of **stochastic trends** focuses on three aspects: (1) trend shapes, (2) stationarity properties, and (3) construction of optimal forecasts. Within each of the three subsections, we will compare deterministic with stochastic trends to understand their differences and similarities. Chapter 7 on autoregressive processes will be very useful to follow the material of this section.

10.2.1 Trend Shapes

A stochastic trend is the result of the accumulation over time of random shocks or innovations in the following fashion:

$$Y_t = \sum_{j=0}^{t-1} \varepsilon_{t-j} = \varepsilon_t + \varepsilon_{t-1} + \varepsilon_{t-2} + \cdots + \varepsilon_1$$

with ε_{t-j} a white noise error assumed to be $N(0, \sigma_\varepsilon^2)$. We call the trend *stochastic* because ε_{t-j} s are random variables. Note that each ε_{t-j} has the same weight in the sum.

Now let us write an autoregressive process AR(1) with persistence parameter $\phi = 1$, that is,

$$Y_t = Y_{t-1} + \varepsilon_t$$

The index t refers to any time period, so the process can also be written as $Y_{t-1} = Y_{t-2} + \varepsilon_{t-1}$ or $Y_{t-2} = Y_{t-3} + \varepsilon_{t-2}$, and so on; what matters is the time ordering. Let us rewrite the AR(1) using *backward substitution.* In the process $Y_t = Y_{t-1} + \varepsilon_t$, substitute Y_{t-1} according to $Y_{t-1} = Y_{t-2} + \varepsilon_{t-1}$ and Y_{t-2} according to $Y_{t-2} = Y_{t-3} + \varepsilon_{t-2}$, and keep substituting backward until you reach the beginning of time. Then we have

$$\begin{aligned} Y_t &= Y_{t-1} + \varepsilon_t \\ &= Y_{t-2} + \varepsilon_{t-1} + \varepsilon_t \\ &= Y_{t-3} + \varepsilon_{t-2} + \varepsilon_{t-1} + \varepsilon_t \\ &= Y_{t-4} + \varepsilon_{t-3} + \varepsilon_{t-2} + \varepsilon_{t-1} + \varepsilon_t = \cdots \\ &= Y_0 + \varepsilon_1 + \varepsilon_2 + \varepsilon_3 + \cdots + \varepsilon_t \end{aligned}$$

What do you observe? Y_t is the result of the accumulation of all past innovations from the beginning of time until time t. We assume that the beginning of the process Y_0 is a constant, in particular $Y_0 = 0$, and state that:

An AR(1) with $\phi = 1$ has a stochastic trend

We also call the AR(1) with $\phi = 1$ a *random walk* or a ***unit root*** *process.* We distinguish between

1. **Random walk without drift** such as $Y_t = Y_{t-1} + \varepsilon_t$.
2. **Random walk with drift** such as $Y_t = c + Y_{t-1} + \varepsilon_t$, where c is a drift.

What will happen when in a random walk with drift we substitute backward the process itself? Note that we can write $Y_{t-1} = c + Y_{t-2} + \varepsilon_{t-1}$ or $Y_{t-2} = c + Y_{t-3} + \varepsilon_{t-2}$ or $Y_{t-3} = c + Y_{t-4} + \varepsilon_{t-3}$, and so on. Then

$$\begin{aligned} Y_t &= c + Y_{t-1} + \varepsilon_t = c + c + Y_{t-2} + \varepsilon_{t-1} + \varepsilon_t \\ &= c + c + c + Y_{t-3} + \varepsilon_{t-2} + \varepsilon_{t-1} + \varepsilon_t = \cdots \\ &= ct + Y_0 + \varepsilon_1 + \varepsilon_2 + \cdots + \varepsilon_t = ct + Y_0 + \sum_{j=0}^{t-1} \varepsilon_{t-j} \end{aligned}$$

We see that, in addition to the accumulation of past innovations, the drift has created a deterministic time trend ct. In EViews, simulate a random walk without a drift by writing the following statements:

```
smpl @first @first
series y=0
smpl @first+1 @last
series y=y(-1) +nrnd
```

and a random walk with drift with the following statements:

```
smpl @first @first
series y=0
smpl @first+1 @last
series y=0.5+ y(-1) +nrnd
```

In this example, the drift is $c = 0.5$, and the innovation is $N(0, 1)$.

In Figure 10.8, we present two simulated time series of 500 observations each from a random walk without drift and from a random walk with drift ($c = 0.5$). In both cases, the innovation is distributed $N(0, 4)$. Observe the effect of the drift. The random walk with drift exhibits a more dramatic upward tendency than the random walk without drift. A common feature to both plots is the persistence of the process. In the first plot, 10.8a the process remains below zero throughout the 500 observations; in the second plot 10.8b, the process remains above the deterministic trend through most of the 500 observations.

In other words, there is not reverting behavior toward a constant value (10.8a) or toward a deterministic trend (10.8b). As we saw in Chapter 3, this is a characteristic of nonstationary processes. Recall from Chapter 7 that an AR(1) with $\phi = 1$ is a nonstationary process. In the next subsection 10.2.2, we will study the first and second moments of these processes to analyze where the **nonstationarity** comes from.

You may wonder whether the stochastic trend or unit root behavior is associated only with a nonstationary AR(1). Can we find a stochastic trend in an AR(2) and in any other higher order autoregressive processes? Yes. In fact, you have already encountered a nonstationary AR(2) with a unit root. Go back to Chapter 7 and check the simulated time series 4. It represents a sample from the AR(2) process $Y_t = 1 + 0.5Y_{t-1} + 0.5Y_{t-2} + \varepsilon_t$. In this case, the necessary conditions for covariance stationarity are satisfied, but the sufficient condition $\phi_1 + \phi_2 < 1$ is not. In this particular case, we have

FIGURE 10.8 Random Walk Without Drift and with Drift

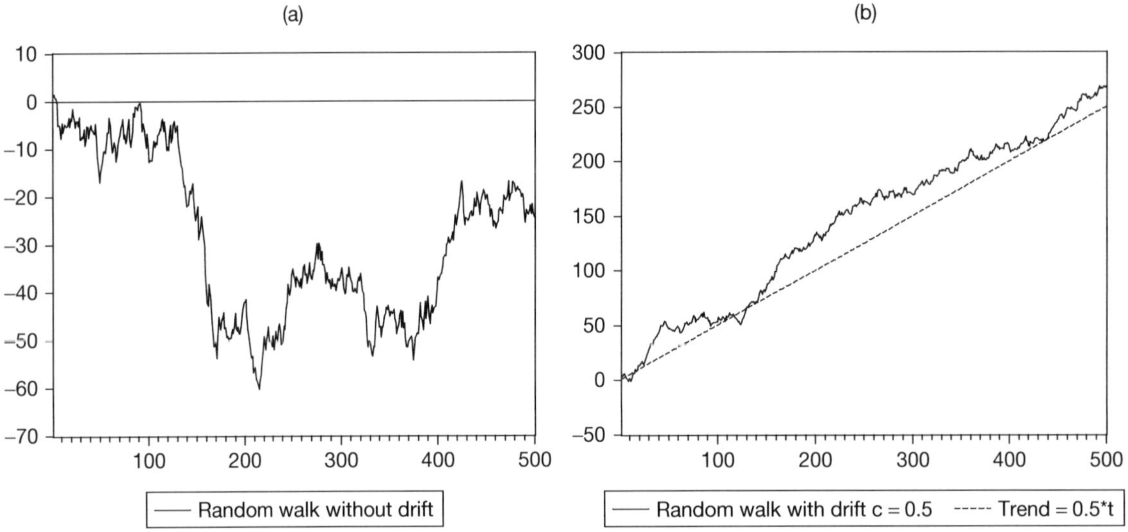

$\phi_1 + \phi_2 = 0.5 + 0.5 = 1$ (exactly 1) that indicates that there is a stochastic trend. In general, for any higher order AR(p) processes, the estimation output in EViews provides the values of the inverted AR roots. It suffices to say that if any of the inverted AR roots is equal to 1, the process has a unit root and it is nonstationary.

10.2.2 Stationarity Properties

Let us analyze the first and second moments of a random walk and, in doing so, we will understand the plots in Figure 10.8. We will focus exclusively on the AR(1) process, but the same arguments can be extended to unit roots in higher AR processes albeit with more elaborate algebraic derivations. To follow the next lines, you need to remember that ε_t is a white noise process $N(0, \sigma_\varepsilon^2)$; that is,

$$E(\varepsilon_t) = 0, \; E(\varepsilon_t)^2 = \sigma_\varepsilon^2, \text{ and } E(\varepsilon_{t-i}\varepsilon_{t-j}) = 0 \quad i \neq j$$

Random walk without drift ($Y_0 = 0$):

$$Y_t = Y_{t-1} + \varepsilon_t = \varepsilon_t + \varepsilon_{t-1} + \varepsilon_{t-2} + \cdots + \varepsilon_1$$

Unconditional mean

$$\mu \equiv E(Y_t) = E(\varepsilon_t + \varepsilon_{t-1} + \cdots + \varepsilon_1) = 0$$

Unconditional variance

$$\sigma_Y^2 = E(Y_t - \mu)^2 = E(\varepsilon_t + \varepsilon_{t-1} + \cdots + \varepsilon_1)^2 = t\sigma_\varepsilon^2$$

Autocovariance of order k

$$\begin{aligned}\gamma_{t,t-k} &\equiv E(Y_t - \mu)(Y_{t-k} - \mu) \\ &= E(\varepsilon_t + \varepsilon_{t-1} + \cdots + \varepsilon_{t-k} + \cdots + \varepsilon_1)(\varepsilon_{t-k} + \varepsilon_{t-k-1} + \cdots + \varepsilon_1) \\ &= (t-k)\sigma_\varepsilon^2\end{aligned}$$

Autocorrelation of order k

$$\rho_{t,t-k} = \frac{\gamma_{t,t-k}}{\sigma_{Y_t}\sigma_{Y_{t-k}}} = \frac{(t-k)\sigma_\varepsilon^2}{\sqrt{t\sigma_\varepsilon^2}\sqrt{(t-k)\sigma_\varepsilon^2}} = \sqrt{\frac{t-k}{t}} \to 1 \quad \text{for } t \text{ large}$$

In a random walk without drift, the mean is a constant and equal to zero but the variance and the autocovariances depend on time, and these are increasing functions of time. This property violates the conditions for weakly stationarity (Chapter 3). Go back to Figure 10.8 and examine the plot 8a. The horizontal line is set at zero, which is the unconditional mean of the process, but the time series seems to go far from this line over time. That is because the variance is an increasing function of time: Every time that the process moves forward, the random variable Y_t becomes more dispersed, increasing the probability of getting large observations and, by that, it becomes more difficult for the process to go back to its mean. Will the process ever revert to the mean? It may but it will take infinitely many periods.

The autocorrelation function of a random walk is very characteristic. The autocorrelations are asymptotically 1 regardless of the distance k. For a given time series, you will not observe sample autocorrelations exactly equal to 1 although they will be very close to it; you should observe a very slow decay in the autocorrelation function. This is a sign of the high persistence that characterizes this type of processes (remember that $\phi = 1$) because the shocks never die. In Figure 10.9, we present the sample autocorrelation functions of the time series in Figure 10.8.

Random walk with drift ($Y_0 = 0$):

$$Y_t = c + Y_{t-1} + \varepsilon_t = ct + \varepsilon_t + \varepsilon_{t-1} + \varepsilon_{t-2} + \cdots + \varepsilon_1$$

Unconditional mean

$$\mu_t \equiv E(Y_t) = E(ct + \varepsilon_t + \varepsilon_{t-1} + \cdots + \varepsilon_1) = ct$$

Unconditional variance

$$\sigma_Y^2 = E(Y_t - \mu_t)^2 = E(Y_t - ct)^2 = E(\varepsilon_t + \varepsilon_{t-1} + \cdots + \varepsilon_1)^2 = t\sigma_\varepsilon^2$$

Autocovariance of order k

$$\gamma_{t,t-k} \equiv E(Y_t - \mu_t)(Y_{t-k} - \mu_{t-k}) = E(\varepsilon_t + \varepsilon_{t-1} + \cdots + \varepsilon_{t-k} + \cdots + \varepsilon_1)$$
$$(\varepsilon_{t-k} + \varepsilon_{t-k-1} + \cdots + \varepsilon_1) = (t-k)\sigma_\varepsilon^2$$

Autocorrelation of order k

$$\rho_{t,t-k} = \frac{\gamma_{t,t-k}}{\sigma_{Y_t}\sigma_{Y_{t-k}}} = \frac{(t-k)\sigma_\varepsilon^2}{\sqrt{t\sigma_\varepsilon^2}\sqrt{(t-k)\sigma_\varepsilon^2}} = \sqrt{\frac{t-k}{t}} \to 1 \quad \text{for } t \text{ large}$$

In a random walk with drift, the mean, variance, and autocovariances are all increasing functions of time. Hence, the process is not covariance stationary. It has the same characteristics as those of the random walk without drift. Note that the only difference with a random walk without drift is that the mean is a deterministic linear trend to which the process may revert in an infinite number of periods. Check the plot 10.8b. The simulated time series is persistently above the linear trend and may cross the trend at some point in the infinite future.

FIGURE 10.9
Autocorrelograms of Random Walks

(a) Random Walk Without Drift (Figure 10.8a)

Sample: 2 500
Included observations: 499

Autocorrelation Partial Correlation

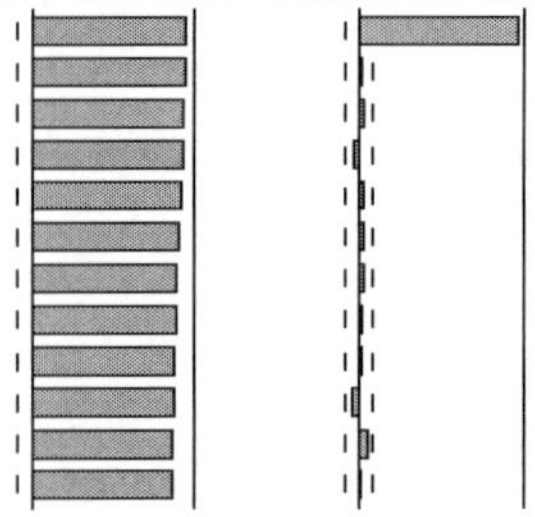

	AC	PAC	Q-Stat	Prob
1	0.990	0.990	492.08	0.000
2	0.980	-0.014	975.14	0.000
3	0.970	0.020	1449.7	0.000
4	0.960	-0.029	1915.4	0.000
5	0.951	0.024	2372.9	0.000
6	0.942	0.027	2822.8	0.000
7	0.934	0.023	3265.7	0.000
8	0.925	0.004	3701.7	0.000
9	0.917	0.001	4131.1	0.000
10	0.909	-0.036	4553.2	0.000
11	0.901	0.042	4968.9	0.000
12	0.893	0.009	5378.5	0.000

(b) Random Walk with Drift (Figure 10.8b)

Sample: 2 500
Included observations: 499

Autocorrelation Partial Correlation

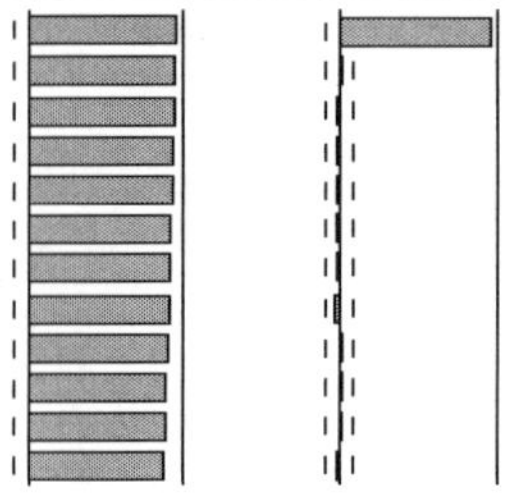

	AC	PAC	Q-Stat	Prob
1	0.993	0.993	495.20	0.000
2	0.986	0.000	984.67	0.000
3	0.980	-0.006	1468.4	0.000
4	0.973	-0.004	1946.4	0.000
5	0.966	-0.014	2418.6	0.000
6	0.959	-0.014	2884.9	0.000
7	0.952	-0.011	3345.1	0.000
8	0.944	-0.019	3799.2	0.000
9	0.937	0.015	4247.4	0.000
10	0.930	0.000	4689.7	0.000
11	0.923	0.006	5126.4	0.000
12	0.916	-0.004	5557.3	0.000

After this analysis, we learned that a trend-stationary process has very different properties than those of a unit root process. However, you may wonder, why should we care about the distinction between a trend-stationary process and a unit root process? After all, the simulated time series that we have presented in this and in the previous sections look somewhat similar. Not surprisingly, the main and very important reason is that the forecast of a trend-stationary process is very different from that of a unit root process. Thus, the next question is: When do we know that a time series has a unit root? Going back to Figure 10.1, could you tell which series are trend stationary and which ones have a unit root? The construction of the forecast depends on the answer to this question.

10.2.2.1 Testing for Unit Root

Deciding whether a time series has a unit root (stochastic trend) or is trend stationary (deterministic trend) presents some statistical difficulties that can be resolved only with more advanced mathematical methods than those required in this book. However, in this subsection, we provide an introductory explanation as to why the standard z-ratio is not appropriate to test for unit root, and we will introduce an alternative statistical procedure.

Let us bring an AR(1) model $Y_t = \phi Y_{t-1} + \varepsilon_t$, which is also a regression model with no intercept and regressor $X_t = Y_{t-1}$. We proceed with the least squares estimation of the model to obtain the OLS estimator $\hat{\phi}$ and calculate its variance, which is $\sigma^2_{\hat{\phi}} \equiv \text{var}(\hat{\phi}) = \frac{1-\phi^2}{T}$.[3] Because the AR(1) with $\phi = 1$ is the model with a unit root ($Y_t = Y_{t-1} + \varepsilon_t$), it seems natural to test this hypothesis $H_0: \phi = 1$. However, under the null $\phi = 1$, the variance of the estimator, $\sigma^2_{\hat{\phi}} \equiv \text{var}(\hat{\phi}) = \frac{1-\phi^2}{T}$, becomes zero, and the z-ratio $\frac{\hat{\phi}-1}{\sigma_{\hat{\phi}}}$ to test the previously mentioned hypothesis will be undetermined. How then can we test for unit root? Fortunately, we will be able to use a (pseudo) z-ratio, but we will need to modify its asymptotic distribution as we will see next.

Under the null hypothesis of unit root, the z-ratio is not normally distributed. In more technical terms, it can be proven that the ratio has a nonstandard density function known as the **Dickey-Fuller distribution**, which does not have a tractable mathematical expression and it needs to be tabulated by simulation techniques. The shape of this nonstandard distribution is asymmetric and skewed to the left, very different from the symmetric and bell-shaped normal density function (see Table 10.4 for a stylized plot of the distribution).

The statistical procedure to test for unit root is in essence a test of nonstationarity versus stationary of the stochastic process. Recall that the AR(1) process is stationary when $|\phi| < 1$. Then the hypothesis to test is written as

$$H_0: \phi = 1 \text{ (nonstationarity)}$$
$$H_1: \phi < 1 \text{ (stationarity)}$$

thus the alternative hypothesis is a one-sided hypothesis.

In Table 10.4, we present the critical values of the Dickey-Fuller distribution for a critical region of 5%, and a graphical example on how to read the rejection and acceptance regions of the Dickey-Fuller density. The critical values of the distribution have been tabulated for three cases depending on the model that is estimated under the alternative hypothesis. In cases I and II, the null hypothesis is a random walk without drift and in case III, a random walk with drift. In case I, the alternative hypothesis is a stationary AR(1) (i.e. $\phi < 1$) with zero mean; in case II, a stationary AR(1) with a nonzero mean; and in case III, a stationary AR(1) with a deterministic linear trend. Observe that the critical values depend on the case you choose so that in practice, it matters whether we estimate a model with an intercept or/and a deterministic trend.

---

[3] $\sigma^2_{\hat{\phi}} \equiv \text{var}(\hat{\phi}) = \frac{\sigma^2_\varepsilon}{\sum_{t=1}^{T} Y^2_{t-1}} = \frac{\sigma^2_\varepsilon}{\frac{\sum_{t=1}^{T} Y^2_{t-1}}{T} T} \approx \frac{\sigma^2_\varepsilon}{\frac{\sigma^2_\varepsilon}{1-\phi^2} T} = \frac{1-\phi^2}{T}$

TABLE 10.4 Dickey-Fuller Critical Values for a 5% Critical Region

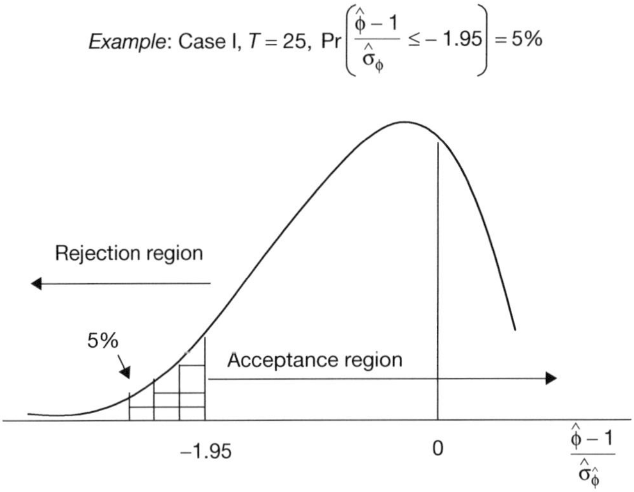

	Case I	Case II	Case III
Sample size T	$H_0: Y_t = Y_{t-1} + \varepsilon_t$ $H_1: Y_t = \phi Y_{t-1} + \varepsilon_t$	$H_0: Y_t = Y_{t-1} + \varepsilon_t$ $H_1: Y_t = c + \phi Y_{t-1} + \varepsilon_t$	$H_0: Y_t = c + Y_{t-1} + \varepsilon_t$ $H_1: Y_t = c + \alpha t + \phi Y_{t-1} + \varepsilon_t$
25	−1.95	−3.00	−3.60
50	−1.95	−2.93	−3.50
100	−1.95	−2.89	−3.45
250	−1.95	−2.88	−3.43
500	−1.95	−2.87	−3.42
∞	−1.95	−2.86	−3.41

How do we use this information in the practice of forecasting? Should we estimate an AR(1) with or without intercept, with or without a deterministic trend? The guiding principle should be to estimate a model that is compatible with the data under the null and under the alternative hypotheses. Let us take Case I: If we were to reject the null in favor of the alternative, we would say that the data must be reverting toward a zero mean because the model under the alternative is a stationary AR(1) with zero unconditional mean. In Case II, by rejecting the null in favor of the alternative, we would say that the data come from a stationary AR(1) with a nonzero unconditional mean (the constant is different from zero); thus, we should observe in the time series a reverting behavior toward a nonzero constant. In Case III, under the null and under the alternative, we hypothesize that there is a trend although we do not know whether the trend is stochastic (under the null) or deterministic (under the alternative). If we reject the null, we would be accepting the model under the alternative, which is a stationary AR(1) with a deterministic trend; thus, the time series must exhibit a trending behavior.

To illustrate these choices, let us go back to Figure 10.8. Suppose that we are given these two time series and need to decide whether there is a unit root. Which case should we choose? Because we have simulated the data, the choice of Case I, II, or III is trivial: we would run Case I for the time series 10.8a and Case III for the time series 10.8b. However, let us pretend that we do not know this information. Plot 10.8a does not exhibit any upward or downward tendency; thus, Case III must be excluded. To choose between Case I and Case II is more difficult because if there is a reverting behavior toward the mean, it seems to be toward a nonzero mean (even though we know that the series was simulated with no intercept). Then Case II is a better candidate than case I. Plot 10.8b clearly exhibits an upward trend; thus, Case III is the best candidate. Let us look at the results of the least-squares regressions in Table 10.5 and carry out the unit root testing procedure.

TABLE 10.5 Unit Root Testing Procedure

	OLS-Estimated model (standard error of $\hat{\phi}$)	**Ratio: $\frac{\hat{\phi}-1}{\hat{\sigma}_{\hat{\phi}}}$**	**Dickey-Fuller critical value at 5% level (Table 10.4)**	**Decision**
Fig 10.8a				
Case I $H_0: Y_t = Y_{t-1} + \varepsilon_t$ $H_1: Y_t = \phi Y_{t-1} + \varepsilon_t$	$Y_t = 0.9988 Y_{t-1} + \hat{\varepsilon}_t$ (0.0025)	$\frac{0.9988-1}{0.0025} = -0.4341$	−1.95	−1.95 < −0.43 fail to reject $H_0 \Rightarrow$ unit root
Case II $H_0: Y_t = Y_{t-1} + \varepsilon_t$ $H_1: Y_t = c + \phi Y_{t-1} + \varepsilon_t$	$Y_t = -0.325 +$ $+ 0.9905 Y_{t-1} + \hat{\varepsilon}_t$ (0.0051)	$\frac{0.9905-1}{0.0051} = -1.8530$	−2.87	−2.87 < −1.85 fail to reject $H_0 \Rightarrow$ unit root
Fig. 10.8b				
Case III $H_0: Y_t = c + Y_{t-1} + \varepsilon_t$ $H_1: Y_t = c + \alpha t + \phi Y_{t-1} + \varepsilon_t$	$Y_t = 0.9167 + 0.0082t +$ $+ 0.9830 Y_{t-1} + \hat{\varepsilon}_t$ (0.0077)	$\frac{0.9830-1}{0.0077} = -2.1853$	−3.42	−3.42 < −2.18 fail to reject $H_0 \Rightarrow$ unit root

For both time series, we cannot reject the null hypothesis of unit root at the 5% significance level because the value of the ratio $\frac{\hat{\phi}-1}{\hat{\sigma}_{\hat{\phi}}}$ falls into the acceptance region of the Dickey-Fuller distribution. When we fail to reject the unit root, we choose for the time series in Figure 10.8a a random walk with no drift, $Y_t = Y_{t-1} + \varepsilon_t$, which is the model under the null hypothesis; for the time series in Figure 10.8b, our model will be a random walk with drift, $Y_t = c + Y_{t-1} + \varepsilon_t$, which is the model under the null. At this stage, we have accomplished our task: We know how to discriminate a stochastic trend from a deterministic trend.

To finish this section, three important remarks are necessary:

1. For ease of exposition, we have assumed all along that the error term ε_t is white noise, but it may have more interesting dynamics; it may be an ARMA process of some order. In this case, the Dickey-Fuller distribution still holds and the critical values of Table 10.4 are unchanged. We need only to adjust the OLS regression to incorporate the dynamics of the error term. We will see how to do that in the forthcoming 'Real Data' section.
2. Once we fail to reject the first unit root, it is possible to ask whether there are additional unit roots in the model. We have concluded that if we have a unit root, the model is $Y_t = Y_{t-1} + \varepsilon_t$, which equivalently can be written as $\Delta Y_t = Y_t - Y_{t-1} = \varepsilon_t$. However, if there were additional unit roots, the first difference of the series ΔY_t would also be nonstationary. In this case, before settling into a final model, we need to check for additional unit roots running the Dickey-Fuller test on the successive differences of the series (i.e., ΔY_t, $\Delta^2 Y_t$, $\Delta^3 Y_t$ and so on) until we reject the unit root in favor of a stationary model.
3. Given the two previous remarks, let us add some additional jargon. When there is one unit root, the process is also called *integrated of order* 1, and we write I(1) so that ΔY_t becomes stationary; when there are two unit roots, the process is said to be integrated of order 2, I(2), so that $\Delta^2 Y_t$ is stationary; when there are three unit roots, the process is said to be integrated of order 3, I(3), so that $\Delta^3 Y_t$ is stationary; and so on. Hence, the most general representation of a process with linear dependence comes with the name ARIMA(p,d,q) processes, which is written as

$$\Phi_p(L)\Delta^d Y_t = \theta_q(L)\varepsilon_t$$

When $d = 0$, the process does not have a unit root; thus, Y_t is stationary, and we will model its dependence by searching for the best ARMA(p,q) model for Y_t. When $d = 1$, there is a unit root; thus, ΔY_t will be stationary, and we will model its time dependence by searching for the best ARMA (p,q) model for ΔY_t and so forth. For economic and business data, we rarely have time series with more than one unit root, but it is a good practice to check for additional unit roots. In summary, all techniques that we have learned in Chapters 6 to 9 will apply to a unit root process once we settle the number of unit roots. This is why testing for unit root is so important in the practice of forecasting.

10.2.3 Optimal Forecast

Because the properties of a random walk with drift and one without drift differ only in the behavior of the mean, the forecast of each process will also differ in the behavior of the conditional mean. Assume that the forecaster has a quadratic loss function so that the optimal forecast is a conditional mean; recall that $f_{t,h} = \mu_{t+h|t} = E(Y_{t+h} | I_t)$ for $h = 1, 2, \ldots s$. The information set runs up to time t and we are interested in two forecasting horizons, $h = 1$ and $h = 2$.

The value of the processes at the future times $t + 1$ and $t + 2$ are

	$t+1$	$t+2$
Random walk without drift (RW)	$Y_{t+1} = Y_t + \varepsilon_{t+1}$	$Y_{t+2} = Y_t + \varepsilon_{t+1} + \varepsilon_{t+2}$
Random walk with drift (RW-D)	$Y_{t+1} = c + Y_t + \varepsilon_{t+1}$	$Y_{t+2} = 2c + Y_t + \varepsilon_{t+1} + \varepsilon_{t+2}$

What are the optimal point forecasts $f_{t,1}$ and $f_{t,2}$?

RW	$f_{t,1} = \mu_{t+1\|t} = E(Y_{t+1} \| I_t) = E(Y_t + \varepsilon_{t+1} \| I_t) = Y_t$ $f_{t,2} = \mu_{t+2\|t} = E(Y_{t+2} \| I_t) = E(Y_t + \varepsilon_{t+1} + \varepsilon_{t+2} \| I_t) = Y_t$
RW-D	$f_{t,1} = \mu_{t+1\|t} = E(Y_{t+1} \| I_t) = E(c + Y_t + \varepsilon_{t+1} \| I_t) = c + Y_t$ $f_{t,2} = \mu_{t+2\|t} = E(Y_{t+2} \| I_t) = E(2c + Y_t + \varepsilon_{t+1} + \varepsilon_{t+2} \| I_t) = 2c + Y_t$

What are the 1-period and 2-period-ahead forecast errors $e_{t,1}$ and $e_{t,2}$?

The difference between the realized values Y_{t+1} and Y_{t+2} and their respective forecast values $f_{t,1}$, $f_{t,2}$

RW	$e_{t,1} = Y_{t+1} - f_{t,1} = Y_t + \varepsilon_{t+1} - Y_t = \varepsilon_{t+1}$ $e_{t,2} = Y_{t+2} - f_{t,2} = Y_t + \varepsilon_{t+1} + \varepsilon_{t+2} - Y_t = \varepsilon_{t+2} + \varepsilon_{t+1}$
RW-D	Convince yourself that the forecast errors are the same as those of RW.

What is the uncertainty associated with the forecast?

The variance of the forecast error. For both processes, the RW and the RW-D,

$\sigma^2_{t+1|t} = \text{var}(Y_{t+1} | I_t) = E(Y_{t+1} - f_{t,1} | I_t)^2 = E(e^2_{t,1}) = E(\varepsilon^2_{t+1}) = \sigma^2_\varepsilon$

$\sigma^2_{t+2|t} = \text{var}(Y_{t+2} | I_t) = E(Y_{t+2} - f_{t,2} | I_t)^2 = E(e^2_{t,2}) = E(\varepsilon_{t+2} + \varepsilon_{t+1})^2 = 2\sigma^2_\varepsilon$

What is the density forecast?

The conditional probability density function of the process at the future dates $t + 1$ and $t + 2$. Recall that we have assumed a normally distributed white noise.

RW	$f(Y_{t+1} \mid I_t) \rightarrow N(\mu_{t+1\|t}, \sigma^2_{t+1\|t}) = N(Y_t, \sigma^2_\varepsilon)$ $f(Y_{t+2} \mid I_t) \rightarrow N(\mu_{t+2\|t}, \sigma^2_{t+2\|t}) = N(Y_t, 2\sigma^2_\varepsilon)$
RW-D	$f(Y_{t+1} \mid I_t) \rightarrow N(\mu_{t+1\|t}, \sigma^2_{t+1\|t}) = N(c + Y_t, \sigma^2_\varepsilon)$ $f(Y_{t+2} \mid I_t) \rightarrow N(\mu_{t+2\|t}, \sigma^2_{t+2\|t}) = N(2c + Y_t, 2\sigma^2_\varepsilon)$

In general, for $h = s$, we write

Point forecast

$$\text{RW} \quad f_{t,s} = Y_t$$
$$\text{RW-D} \quad f_{t,s} = sc + Y_t$$

Forecast error and variance of the forecast

RW and RW-D

$$e_{t,s} = \varepsilon_{t+s} + \cdots + \varepsilon_{t+2} + \varepsilon_{t+1}$$
$$\sigma^2_{t+s|t} = s\sigma^2_\varepsilon$$

Density forecast

$$\text{RW} \quad f(Y_{t+s|t} \mid I_t) \rightarrow N(Y_t, s\sigma^2_\varepsilon)$$
$$\text{RW-D} \quad f(Y_{t+s|t} \mid I_t) \rightarrow N(sc + Y_t, s\sigma^2_\varepsilon)$$

In summary, the main characteristics of a forecast based on a random walk model are:

- When there is no drift, the point forecast is constant for any forecasting horizon and is equal to the most recent value of the process in the information set. When there is a drift, the point forecast is a line with slope c and intercept Y_t.
- The uncertainty of the forecast is the sum of *equally weighted* future innovations.
- The variance of the forecast is a linear function of the forecasting horizon with slope σ^2_ε.

In Figure 10.10, we summarize the forecasts properties of random walks and trend-stationary processes. The figure is self-explanatory. In the random walk without drift, the forecast is constant over the forecast horizon while in the random walk with drift, the forecast is a line, which starts at Y_t and has a slope equal to the drift c. Compare this line with the forecast from a trend-stationary model. The dotted lines represent the uncertainty of the point forecast; for every forecasting horizon, the dotted lines contain 1 standard deviation interval forecast, that is, $f_{t,s} \pm \sqrt{s}\,\sigma_\varepsilon$ for both random walks and $f_{t,s} \pm \sigma_\varepsilon$ for the trend-stationary model. The uncertainty of the random walk forecasts increases with the forecast horizon while that from a trend-stationary process remains constant for any horizon.

REAL DATA: Modeling and Forecasting the Index of Total Hours Worked in Spain and the United States

In the introductory section of this chapter, Figure 10.1b, we presented time series plots of the index of total hours worked in the United States, Spain, and Germany. These time series are very important for the measurement of *productivity,* which is defined as produced output per unit of labor. There are different measures of labor. The 1993 System of National Accounts favors the total hours worked as the preferred aggregate measure of labor input. You will find labor and other economic statistics in the OECD Productivity Database http://www.oecd.org. The time series in Figure 10.1b is an index with base 1995. We cannot read directly out of the plot the number of hours, but we can read the growth rate in a given period. For instance, in Spain, the index in 1995 was 100 and in 2002, 129.35, an increase of 29.35% in the number of total hours worked during these six years. In United States, the index in 1995 was 100 and in 2002, 108.86, for an increase

FIGURE 10.10 Differences in the Forecasts of Random Walk and Trend-Stationary Processes

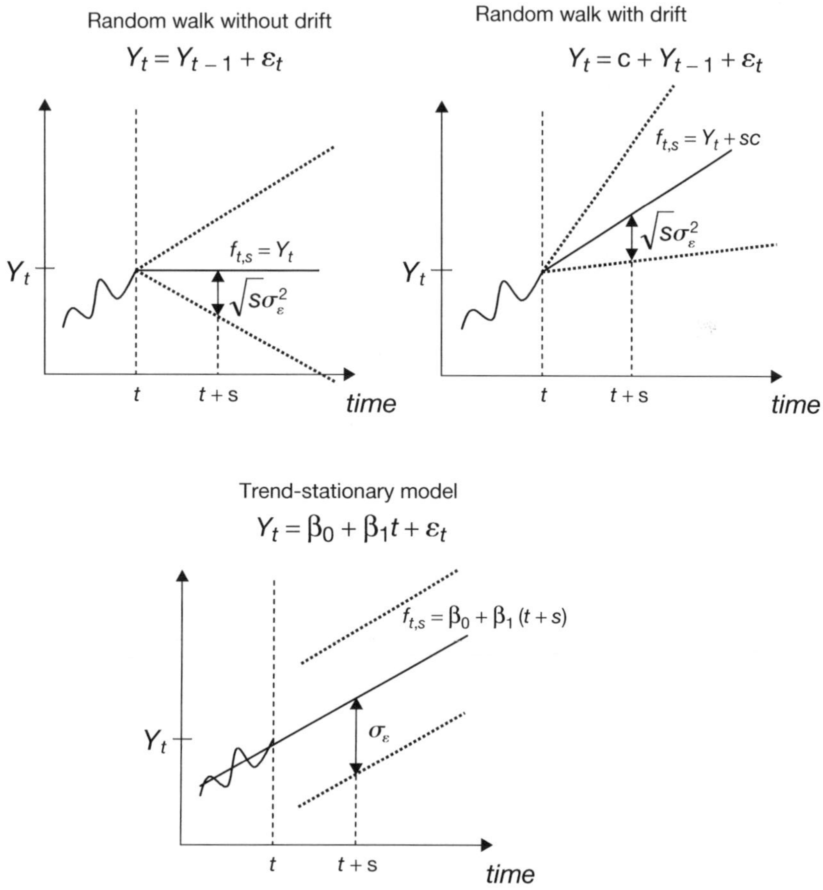

FIGURE 10.11 Index of Total Hours Worked in United States and Spain

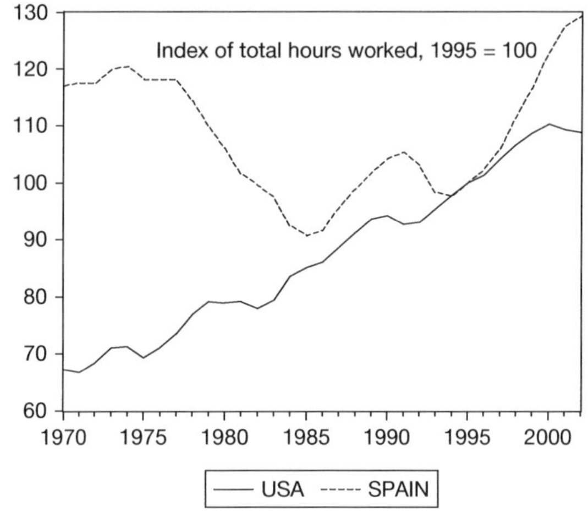

of 8.86%. This large difference between the two countries is mainly due to the many reforms that have taken place in the Spanish labor markets, allowing for more flexible contracts and hiring of part-time workers. Let us bring the time series plots of the index for Spain and United States (Figure 10.11). The series runs from 1970 to 2002. Compare the U.S. index with the Spanish index. Can we say that the Spaniards are working more hours than the Americans? Not necessarily; an index does not provide the number of hours. We need information on how many hours correspond to an index equal to 100 to convert the index to hours worked. It is important to understand the interpretation of these time series plots before engaging in the forecasting exercise.

The forecasting of the index is important to forecast productivity growth. From a first inspection of the plots, the first question that arises is the possibility of a trend. An upward tendency is more obvious in the United States than in Spain, but by now, we are familiar with the behavior of stochastic and deterministic trends and should not disregard a potential trend in the Spanish series. But at this point, we do not know whether the trend should be deterministic or stochastic. It is important to discriminate between a deterministic trend and a stochastic trend because the type of time dependence is very different, and consequently, the properties of their respective forecasts are also different (Figure 10.10). As a practical rule, it would be beneficial to run unit root tests as a first diagnostic before embarking on modeling exercises such as those presented in Chapter 8.

We proceed to answer the question of potential trends in the data. Let us start with the Spanish series. Because we do not see an obvious trend, the testing for unit root should start with case II. This is the hypothesis that we wish to test

$H_0: Y_t = Y_{t-1} + \varepsilon_t$	(unit root without drift)
$H_1: Y_t = c + \phi Y_{t-1} + \varepsilon_t$	(stationary AR(1) with nonzero mean)

Recall that ε_t is assumed to be a white noise process and it will be necessary to check whether this assumption is plausible for the index for Spain. The EViews software provides a nice shortcut to testing for unit root. In your workfile, click the series that you wish to analyze and go to

View

Unit Root Test

You will be prompted with a series of choices. For the Spanish series, we will click on the following:

Test type:	Augmented Dickey-Fuller (*Augmented* will be explained shortly)
Test for unit root in:	Level (no transformation of the series is needed)
Include in test equation:	Intercept (under H_1 there is an intercept)
Lagged differences:	0 (under H_1 there are no lagged differences)

These choices correspond to the model that we wish to estimate under the alternative hypothesis. The EViews output is presented in Table 10.6.

TABLE 10.6 Augmented Dickey-Fuller Unit Root Test on Spain

ADF Test Statistic	0.140798	1% Critical Value*	-3.6496
		5% Critical Value	-2.9558
		10% Critical Value	-2.6164

*MacKinnon critical values for rejection of hypothesis of a unit root.

Augmented Dickey-Fuller Test Equation
Dependent Variable: D(SPAIN)
Method: Least Squares
Sample(adjusted): 1971 2002
Included observations: 32 after adjusting endpoints

Variable	Coefficient	Std. Error	t-Statistic	Prob.
SPAIN(-1)	0.008178	0.058084	0.140798	0.8890
C	-0.494473	6.272498	-0.078832	0.9377

R-squared	0.000660	Mean dependent var	0.384840
Adjusted R-squared	-0.032651	S.D. dependant var	3.254600
S.E. of regression	3.307307	Akaike info criterion	5.290607
Sum squared resid	328.1483	Schwarz criterion	5.382215
Log likelihood	-82.64971	F-statistic	0.019824
Durbin-Waston stat	0.437263	Prob(F-statistic)	0.888970

Let us understand this information. Start with the lower panel that is the output of a linear regression model. What model has been estimated? Read the dependent variable line. It says **D(SPAIN)**, which means a first difference of the original series, that is, **D(SPAIN)** = $\text{Spain}_t - \text{Spain}_{t-1} = \Delta\text{Spain}_t$. The dependent variable is run against a constant and a lag of the original series, Spain_{t-1}. In summary, the model that has been estimated for a generic time series, Y_t, is the following

$$\Delta Y_t = c + \beta Y_{t-1} + \varepsilon_t$$

Is this model the same as the model that we have under the alternative hypothesis

$$H_1 : Y_t = c + \phi Y_{t-1} + \varepsilon_t?$$

Yes, but it is reparametrized. If we subtract Y_{t-1} from the left- and right-hand sides of the model in the alternative hypothesis, we have

$$Y_t - Y_{t-1} = c + \phi Y_{t-1} - Y_{t-1} + \varepsilon_t = c + (\phi - 1)Y_{t-1} + \varepsilon_t$$

implying that

$$\Delta Y_t = c + \beta Y_{t-1} + \varepsilon_t \qquad \beta \equiv (\phi - 1)$$

To perform the test for unit root in this reparametrized model, we proceed as usual because the ratio $\frac{\hat{\phi} - 1}{\hat{\sigma}_{\hat{\phi}}}$ is not affected, that is, $\frac{\hat{\phi} - 1}{\hat{\sigma}_{\hat{\phi}}} = \frac{\hat{\beta}}{\hat{\sigma}_{\hat{\beta}}}$. We read from the computer output the value of the ratio $\frac{\hat{\beta}}{\hat{\sigma}_{\hat{\beta}}} = \frac{0.0081}{0.0580} = 0.1407$ (ADF statistic), which we compare with the 5% critical value of the Dickey-Fuller distribution, that is $0.1407 > -2.9558$. Because 0.1407 falls in the acceptance region of the distribution (see the picture in Table 10.4), we fail to reject the null hypothesis of unit root.

Let us understand the meaning of the word *augmented.* In the implementation of the test, we have assumed that the error ε_t is a white noise process. We could check this assumption by calculating the autocorrelation functions of the residuals of the regression $\Delta Y_t = c + \beta Y_{t-1} + \varepsilon_t$. What do you see in the autocorrelograms in Figure 10.12?

First, the residuals are not white noise. There is a clear pattern in the autocorrelation (AC) function, and there is at least one spike statistically different from zero in the partial correlation (PAC) function. The Q-statistics very clearly reject the hypothesis of no correlation in the residuals. Because the assumption of white noise is not satisfied, we cannot trust the value of the **Augmented Dickey-Fuller statistic** (ADF). We need to correct the problem of autocorrelation. One solution is to augment the Dickey-Fuller regression with further lags, that is,

$$\Delta Y_t = c + \beta Y_{t-1} + \alpha_1 \Delta Y_{t-1} + \alpha_2 \Delta Y_{t-2} + \alpha_3 \Delta Y_{t-3} + \cdots + \varepsilon_t$$

Including lagged differences $\Delta Y_{t-1}, \Delta Y_{t-2}, \Delta Y_{t-3}, \ldots$ helps to clean up the residuals and to approximate their behavior to that of a white noise process.

FIGURE 10.12 Correlogram of Residuals

Correlogram of Residuals

Sample: 1971 2002
Included observations: 32

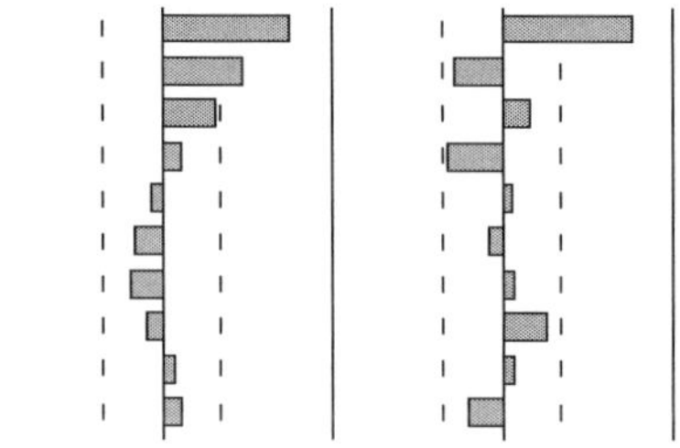

	AC	PAC	Q-Stat	Prob
1	0.779	0.779	21.279	0.000
2	0.487	-0.303	29.881	0.000
3	0.315	0.160	33.613	0.000
4	0.115	-0.340	34.125	0.000
5	-0.067	0.041	34.303	0.000
6	-0.156	-0.076	35.324	0.000
7	-0.182	0.058	36.761	0.000
8	-0.086	0.265	37.097	0.000
9	0.073	0.065	37.350	0.000
10	0.107	-0.202	37.921	0.000

Let us proceed with the Spanish index and add one lagged difference. In Table 10.7, we present the estimation output and the autocorrelograms of the residuals corresponding to the augmented model $\Delta Y_t = c + \beta Y_{t-1} + \alpha_1 \Delta Y_{t-1} + \varepsilon_t$.

Note that **D(SPAIN(-1))** = $\text{Spain}_{t-1} - \text{Spain}_{t-2} = \Delta\text{Spain}_{t-1}$; this is a one-lagged difference that is very statistically significant; its p-value is practically zero (the t-ratios for the augmented terms are distributed asymptotically normal, so the corresponding p-values are valid probabilities). A note of warning: When reading the statistical significance of the estimates of the coefficients corresponding to **SPAIN(-1)** and **C**, remember that their distribution is nonstandard, so disregard the p-values provided by the computer output.

With augmentation, the residuals are clean of autocorrelation; now they clearly seem to behave as a white noise process (the p-values associated to the Q-statistics are very high, indicating that the autocorrelations are zero). Thus, this is the model to test for unit root.

In practice, the choice of number of lags in the augmented Dickey-Fuller depends on the autocorrelation of the residuals. As we did in Tables 10.6 and 10.7, first run the simple Dickey-Fuller test, retrieve the residuals, and compute their autocorrelation functions. Observe the ACF functions, judge whether there is significant autocorrelation, and choose the number of lags accordingly. Finally, run the augmented Dickey-Fuller test. The objective is to obtain residuals as close as possible to a white noise process. Alternatively, the number of lags can also be chosen by minimizing AIC or SIC.

In Table 10.7 read the value of the ADF statistic and compare it with the 5% critical value: ADF $= -2.1536 > -2.9591$. What do we conclude? We cannot reject the presence of a unit root in the data, implying that $\beta \equiv \phi - 1 = 0 \rightarrow \phi = 1$. Consequently, there is a unit root in Y_t. It is possible that we may have more than one unit root. To check for this, it is advisable to keep running successive unit root tests on the successive differences of the series, that is ΔY_t, $\Delta^2 Y_t$, $\Delta^3 Y_t$, and so on, proceeding in a similar fashion as in Table 10.7. For the series at hand, there is only one unit root, so we say that Y_t is

TABLE 10.7 Augmented Dickey-Fuller Unit Root Test on SPAIN

ADF Test Statistic	-2.153659	1% Critical Value*	-3.6576
		5% Critical Value	-2.9591
		10% Critical Value	-2.6181

*MacKinnon critical values for rejection of hypothesis of a unit root.

Augmented Dickey-Fuller Test Equation
Dependent Variable: D(SPAIN)
Method: Least Squares
Sample(adjusted): 1972 2002
Included observations: 31 after adjusting endpoints

Variable	Coefficient	Std. Error	t-Statistic	Prob.
SPAIN(-1)	-0.079919	0.037109	-2.153659	0.0400
D(SPAIN(-1))	0.864257	0.115315	7.494743	0.0000
C	8.661998	3.982150	2.175206	0.0382

R-squared	0.667569	Mean dependent var	0.384577
Adjusted R-squared	0.643824	S.D. dependent var	3.308399
S.E. of regression	1.974467	Akaike info criterion	4.290240
Sum squared resid	109.1586	Schwarz criterion	4.429013
Log likelihood	-63.49872	F-statistic	28.11405
Durbin-Watson stat	1.737471	Prob(F-statistic)	0.000000

Correlogram of Residuals

Sample: 1972 2002
Included observations: 31

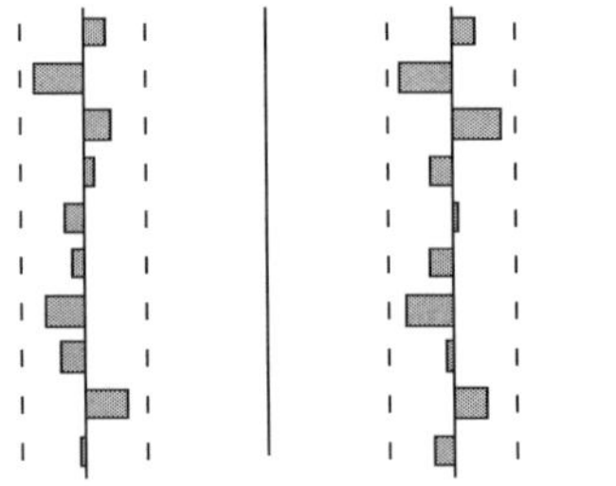

Autocorrelation	Partial Correlation		AC	PAC	Q-Stat	Prob
		1	0.129	0.129	0.5661	0.452
		2	-0.272	-0.293	3.1666	0.205
		3	0.148	0.257	3.9699	0.265
		4	0.060	-0.119	4.1085	0.392
		5	-0.114	0.022	4.6232	0.464
		6	-0.070	-0.115	4.8221	0.567
		7	-0.221	-0.260	6.9045	0.439
		8	-0.128	-0.044	7.6381	0.470
		9	0.239	0.188	10.284	0.328
		10	-0.022	-0.112	10.308	0.414

integrated of order 1, that is, I(1), and consequently, ΔY_t is integrated of order zero I(0), which means that the first difference of the series is stationary. A concise statement about the model for Y_t is to say that it follows an ARIMA(1,1,0)

$$\Delta Y_t = \alpha_1 \Delta Y_{t-1} + \varepsilon_t \quad \text{(model in first differences, ARMA(1, 0) for } \Delta Y_t\text{)}$$

or equivalently

$$Y_t = Y_{t-1} + \alpha_1 \Delta Y_{t-1} + \varepsilon_t \quad \text{(model in levels } Y_t\text{, random walk without drift)}$$

The forecast will be based on such a model. The estimation output of the AR(1) model in first differences is presented in Table 10.8.

Remember that our ultimate goal is to forecast the index itself. To this end, first we estimate the model in first differences (Table 10.8), and secondly, we will combine our expertise on forecasting stationary AR processes and unit root processes.

It is very helpful to consider the following recursive relations between the levels and the first differences of a process. Recall the optimal forecast under quadratic loss. Consider an information set I_t containing information up to time t, and a forecasting horizon of s periods into the future. Let us call $f^*_{t,s}$ the forecast for the level of the series, that is, $f^*_{t,s} = E(Y_{t+s} | I_t)$ and $f_{t,s} = E(\Delta Y_{t+s} | I_t)$ the forecast for the first difference of the series. Then, we write

$$f_{t,s} = E(\Delta Y_{t+s} | I_t) = E(Y_{t+s} - Y_{t+s-1} | I_t) = E(Y_{t+s} | I_t) - E(Y_{t+s-1} | I_t) = f^*_{t,s} - f^*_{t,s-1}$$

and, from this equality, we can establish the first recursive relation

$$\textbf{(R1)} \quad f^*_{t,s} = f_{t,s} + f^*_{t,s-1} \quad \text{with } f^*_{t,0} = Y_t$$

In a similar fashion, we derive the relation between forecast errors for the level and for the first differences of the series. By writing $e^*_{t,s} = Y_{t+s} - E\,(Y_{t+s} | I_t)$, we have

$$\begin{aligned} e_{t,s} &= \Delta Y_{t+s} - E(\Delta Y_{t+s} | I_t) = (Y_{t+s} - Y_{t+s-1}) - (E(Y_{t+s} | I_t) - E(Y_{t+s-1} | I_t)) \\ &= (Y_{t+s} - E(Y_{t+s} | I_t)) - (Y_{t+s-1} - E(Y_{t+s-1} | I_t)) = e^*_{t,s} - e^*_{t,s-1} \end{aligned}$$

TABLE 10.8 Least Squares Estimation of $\Delta Y_t = \alpha_1 \Delta Y_{t-1} + \varepsilon_t$

Dependent Variable: D(SPAIN)
Method: Least Squares
Sample(adjusted): 1972 2002
Included observations: 31 after adjusting endpoints
Convergence achieved after 2 iterations

Variable	Coefficient	Std. Error	t-Statistic	Prob.
AR(1)	0.789202	0.113642	6.944641	0.0000

R-squared	0.611151	Mean dependent var	0 384577
Adjusted R-squared	0.611151	S.D. dependent var	3.308399
S.E. of regression	2.063043	Akaike info criterion	4.317967
Sum squared resid	127.6844	Schwarz criterion	4.364225
Log likelihood	-65.92849	Durbin-Watson stat	1.532094
Inverted AR Roots	.79		

TABLE 10.9 Four-Step-Ahead Forecast of Index of Total Hours Worked in Spain

$t = 2002$	$\Delta Y_{2002} = 1.88$		$Y_{2002} = 129.35$	
Forecasting horizon	$f_{2002,s} = \phi^s \Delta Y_{2002}$	$\sigma_{t+s\|2002}$	$f^*_{2002,s} = f_{2002,s} + f^*_{2002,s-1}$	$\sigma^*_{t+s\|2002}$
$s=1$ 2003	1.48	2.07	130.83	2.07
$s=2$ 2004	1.17	2.64	132.01	4.25
$s=3$ 2005	0.92	2.93	132.93	6.56
$s=4$ 2006	0.73	3.10	133.66	8.90

establishing the second recursive relation

$$\textbf{(R2)} \quad e^*_{t,s} = e_{t,s} + e^*_{t,s-1} \quad \text{with } e^*_{t,0} = 0$$

To eventually forecast the level of the series, first we construct the forecast $f_{t,s}$ from the model in first differences, which in the case of the Spanish index is a stationary AR(1) process, and then we will use the **R1** and **R2** recursive relations to produce the forecast $f^*_{t,s}$ of the level. In Table 10.9 and Figure 10.13, we present the forecasting results of the index of total hours worked in Spain 4 years ahead.

To construct confidence intervals for the forecast, we need to calculate the variance of the forecast, that is, $\sigma^2_{t+s|2002}$. The recursive relation **R2** is very useful. For instance, for $s = 1$,

FIGURE 10.13 Forecast of Index of Total Hours Worked in Spain with 95% Confidence Bands

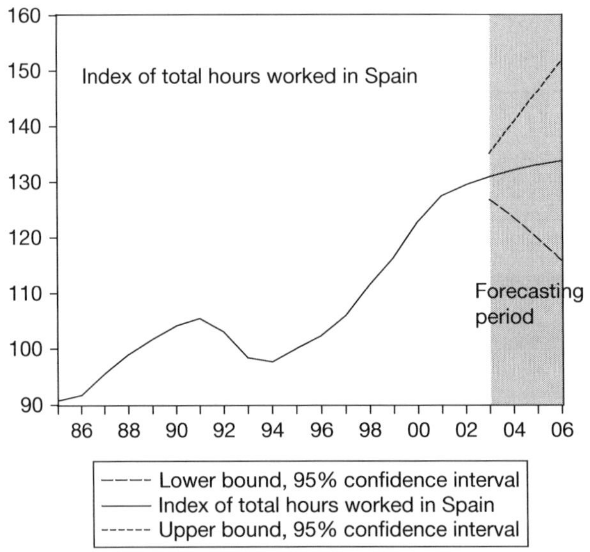

$$e^*_{t,1} = e_{t,1} = \varepsilon_{t+1}$$

which implies that $\sigma^2_{t+1|t} = \sigma^2_\varepsilon$. For $s = 2$,

$$e^*_{t,2} = e_{t,2} + e^*_{t,1} = \varepsilon_{t+2} + \phi\varepsilon_{t+1} + \varepsilon_{t+1} = \varepsilon_{t+2} + (\phi + 1)\varepsilon_{t+1}$$

implying that $\sigma^2_{t+2|t} = \sigma^2_\varepsilon(1 + (\phi + 1)^2)$, and so forth. In Figure 10.13, we present the lower and upper bands of a 95% confidence interval under the assumption that ε_t is normally distributed.

REAL DATA: U.S. Index of Total Hours Worked

The analysis of the U.S. index will proceed in the same fashion. In Table 10.10, we present the output corresponding to the testing for unit root. Because we have an obvious upward tendency, it seems sensible to start with case III.

TABLE 10.10 Augmented Dickey-Fuller Unit Root Test on the United States

ADF Test Statistic	-3.990533	1% Critical Value*	-4.2826
		5% Critical Value	-3.5614
		10% Critical Value	-3.2138

*MacKinnon critical values for rejection of hypothesis of a unit root.

Augmented Dickey-Fuller Test Equation
Dependent Variable: D(USA)
Method: Least Squares
Sample(adjusted): 1972 2002
Included observations: 31 after adjusting endpoints

Variable	Coefficient	Std. Error	t-Statistic	Prob.
USA(-1)	-0.517706	0.129733	-3.990533	0.0005
D(USA(-1))	0.560822	0.155317	3.610828	0.0012
C	33.11862	8.048930	4.114661	0.0003
@TREND(1970)	0.743516	0.190148	3.910203	0.0006

R-squared	0.441795	Mean dependent var	1.362174
Adjusted R-squared	0.379772	S.D. dependent var	1.515655
S.E. of regression	1.193648	Akaike info criterion	3.311820
Sum squared resid	38.46948	Schwarz criterion	3.496850
Log likelihood	-47.33320	F-statistic	7.123095
Durbin-Watson stat	1.667691	Prob(F-statistic)	0.001126

This is the hypothesis that we wish to test:

$H_0: Y_t = c + Y_{t-1} + \varepsilon_t$	(unit root with drift)
$H_1: Y_t = c + \alpha t + \phi Y_{t-1} + \varepsilon_t$	(stationary AR(1) with deterministic linear trend)

We also need to guarantee that the residual from the estimated model under the alternative hypothesis is a white noise process; thus, it may be necessary to include some lagged differences as for the index for Spain. Looking at the computer output, could you tell which model has been estimated? Do we have a unit root?

Note that there is a similar reparameterization of the model as in the case of the Spanish index. The estimated model in Table 10.10 is

$$\Delta Y_t = c + \alpha t + \beta Y_{t-1} + \alpha_1 \Delta Y_{t-1} + \varepsilon_t$$

and the ADF statistic is −3.99, which is less than the 5% critical value of −3.56. Hence, we reject the unit root and conclude that the time series comes from a stationary process with a deterministic linear trend. Observe that the 1% critical value is −4.28. If we were to compare the ADF statistic with this critical value $-3.99 > -4.28$, we would fail to reject the null of unit root. Thus, the evidence for unit root is borderline. In these cases,

TABLE 10.11 Least Squares Estimation of Index of Total Hours Worked in United States

Dependent Variable: USA
Method: Least Squares
Sample(adjusted): 1972 2002
Included observations: 31 after adjusting endpoints
Convergence achieved after 3 iterations

Variable	Coefficient	Std. Error	t-Statistic	Prob.
C	64.18975	0.892726	71.90305	0.0000
@TREND(1970)	1.436174	0.046881	30.63453	0.0000
AR(1)	1.043117	0.162677	6.412190	0.0000
AR(2)	-0.560822	0.155317	-3.610828	0.0012

R-squared	0.992864	Mean dependent var	88.59333
Adjusted R-squared	0.992071	S.D. dependent var	13.40497
S.E. of regression	1.193648	Akaike info criterion	3.311820
Sum squared resid	38.46948	Schwarz criterion	3.496850
Log likelihood	-47.33320	F-statistic	1252.185
Durbin-Watson stat	1.667691	Prob(F-statistic)	0.000000
Inverted AR Roots	.52+.54i	.52-.54i	

we would recommend building the forecast under both scenarios, with and without unit root, and assess the goodness of the forecasts by the evaluation criteria presented in Chapter 9.

Following our results by testing at the 5% critical level, we have rejected the unit root and conclude that the upward trend is due to a deterministic linear trend. From this point on, our task is to find the best ARMA model for Y_t incorporating a deterministic trend. Run a regression such as $Y_t = c + \alpha t + v_t$. Examine the ACFs of the residual $\hat{v}_t$ and find the best ARMA model to model the autocorrelations. In Table 10.11, we present the estimation output of such a model for the U.S. index of hours worked: $Y_t = c + \alpha t + \phi_1 Y_{t-1} + \phi_2 Y_{t-2} + \varepsilon_t$.

We leave as an exercise the construction of the forecast of the U.S. index for 2006. You need to combine your expertise on forecasting with AR(2) processes and with deterministic trend models. Some additional information for your forecasting exercise: the values of the U.S. index, $Y_{2002} = 108.86$ and $Y_{2001} = 109.35$.

KEY WORDS

augmented Dickey-Fuller statistic, p. 284
deterministic trend, p. 257
Dickey-Fuller distribution, p. 275
exponential trend, p. 258
linear trend, p. 264
logistic trend, p. 258
nonstationarity, p. 271
polynomial trend, p. 264
quadratic trend, p. 264
random walk with drift, p. 270
random walk without drift, p. 270
stochastic trend, p. 270
trend-stationarity, p. 262
unit root, p. 270

EXERCISES

1. Assume a deterministic trend model where the trend is a polynomial of order 3, that is, $Y_t = \beta_0 + \beta_1 t + \beta_2 t^2 + \beta_3 t^3 + \varepsilon_t$. Experiment with different values of the parameters $\beta_1, \beta_2, \beta_3$ to generate upward or downward trends or no trend at all. You are free to choose the distributional properties of the error term. Plot the generated series.
2. Consider an exponential and a logistic-type trend and reason why the growth rate generated by these trends depends on time. (You may follow a similar argument as in the quadratic case of Section 10.1.1).
3. Choose a model with a cubic polynomial trend and a model with an exponential trend. For both models, compute the first and second unconditional moments (mean, variance, and autocovariances). Are these processes covariance stationary? Why or why not?

4. Compute the point forecast, the forecast error, its variance, and the density forecast of a process with a linear deterministic trend for $h = 2$, 3, and 4.
5. Download the most recent data on outstanding mortgage debt and proceed with the search for a model with deterministic trends. Do you find any trend? With the new data, can you justify the polynomial trend of order 4 in Section 10.1? How different is the new model from the model in Section 10.1? Comment on the trend shape (long-term feature) and the potential autocorrelation once you account for the trend (short-term feature). Construct a short-term and a long-term forecast based on the new model. Split your sample into estimation and forecasting samples so that you will be able to evaluate your forecasts.
6. Simulate a random walk with and without drift for a sample of 10,000 observations. Observe when each process reverts to or/and crosses its unconditional mean. If they do not cross their means, keep on increasing the sample size until you find a cross. How large is your sample? Compute their unconditional first and second moments and their autocorrelation functions. Comment on your results.
7. For the time series that you have generated in Exercise 10.6, implement the augmented Dickey-Fuller tests for unit root. Explain your choices and your results. For the updated data set in Exercise 10.5, test for unit root. What do you find? Can you reject the unit root? Comment on your findings and explain your preferences on the deterministic trend versus the stochastic trend in this data set.
8. Update the time series on the index of total hours worked in Spain. Test for unit root. Propose a model for the series. How is this model different from the model in Section 10.2? Construct a short- and long-term forecast based on your model.
9. Based on the results of Table 10.11, construct the 1, 2, 3, and 4-step-ahead forecasts of the index of total hours worked in United States.
10. Update the time series on index of total hours worked in United States. Test for unit root. Propose a model for the series. How is this model different from the model in section 10.2? Construct a short- and long-term forecast based on your model.

CHAPTER 11

Forecasting with a System of Equations: Vector Autoregression

Previously, we have been engaged in modeling and forecasting a single stochastic process. Our objective has been to understand the time dependence of the series in order to guide us in the search for the best ARIMA model(s), and based on the model(s), we constructed an optimal forecast. We analyzed many individual time series such as house prices, consumer price index, returns, interest rates, total hours worked, outstanding mortgage debt, and so on. However, as economists, we build economic models—simplified representations of the economy—with many economic variables interacting with each other. We think about consumption depending on the level of income or investment decisions as a function of interest rates, money supply influencing inflation, or exchange rates linking production of two or more countries. How are these interactions modeled from an econometric and forecasting perspective? This is the question that we will answer in this chapter.

We will consider several time series—for example, consumption and income—jointly, and we will analyze not only the time dependence in each series but also the interdependence between consumption and income over time. In this way, we will create a system of equations, one equation for each variable, with much richer dynamics than those contained in each univariate process. Each equation will contain information about not only the history of the variable of interest but also the history of the other variables in the system. Having now a multivariate information set, for instance, past information in consumption and in income, we may be able to construct a better forecast for each variable in the system.

We will propose a system of equations known as a **vector autoregression** (VAR). As the name indicates, the dynamics will be modeled as autoregressive representations. Although a system of equations is a more complex specification than a single equation, the econometric analysis of such a system is not much more complicated than that of a single equation. This is very good news because the tools that we have already in place will be enough to undertake estimating, testing, and forecasting a VAR system. Ordinary least squares (OLS) regression is the key for estimation and testing. Optimal forecast techniques developed for autoregressive (AR) processes are also applicable to VAR. We will encounter some new concepts, such as Granger-causality and impulse-response functions, that will enhance our knowledge of dynamic relationships and time dependence in general.

11.1 What Is Vector Autoregression (VAR)?

Suppose that we have two stochastic processes $\{Y_t\}$ and $\{X_t\}$. Let us assume that both processes are covariance-stationary. A vector autoregression of order p, VAR(p), is defined as a system of two regression equations where the regressors are the lagged values of $\{Y_t\}$ and $\{X_t\}$:

$$Y_t = c_1 + \alpha_{11}Y_{t-1} + \alpha_{12}Y_{t-2} + \cdots + \alpha_{1p}Y_{t-p} + \beta_{11}X_{t-1} + \beta_{12}X_{t-2} + \cdots \beta_{1p}X_{t-p} + \varepsilon_{1t}$$
$$X_t = c_2 + \alpha_{21}Y_{t-1} + \alpha_{22}Y_{t-2} + \cdots + \alpha_{2p}Y_{t-p} + \beta_{21}X_{t-1} + \beta_{22}X_{t-2} + \cdots \beta_{2p}X_{t-p} + \varepsilon_{2t}$$

The error terms ε_{1t} and ε_{2t} are assumed to be normal random variables with the following properties $\varepsilon_{1t} \rightarrow N(0, \sigma_1^2)$ and $\varepsilon_{2t} \rightarrow N(0, \sigma_2^2)$, and both errors can be correlated, that is, $\text{cov}(\varepsilon_{1t}, \varepsilon_{2t}) \neq 0$.

The characteristics of a VAR system are:

1. The autoregressive specification is evident as only lagged values of $\{Y_t\}$ and $\{X_t\}$ are considered in the right-hand side of each equation. We do not entertain any moving average (MA) terms (i.e., lagged values of ε_{1t} and ε_{2t}).
2. All equations in the system enjoy the same regressors, that is, $\{Y_{t-1}, Y_{t-2}, \ldots Y_{t-p}, X_{t-1}, X_{t-2} \ldots . X_{t-p}\}$, so that it is possible for the past history of $\{X_t\}$ to affect the present value of $\{Y_t\}$, and vice versa, the past history of $\{Y_t\}$ may affect the present value of $\{X_t\}$.
3. The order of the system is the largest number of lags p, which is common to all equations. Accordingly, the system will be denoted as VAR(p).
4. Although we have considered only two processes, $\{Y_t\}$ and $\{X_t\}$, a general VAR may entertain as many variables as desired. For instance, for three processes $\{Y_t\}$, $\{X_t\}$, and $\{Z_t\}$, we will have three equations, each with the same regressors: $\{Y_{t-1}, Y_{t-2}, \ldots Y_{t-p}, X_{t-1}, X_{t-2} \ldots . X_{t-p}, Z_{t-1}, Z_{t-2}, \ldots . Z_{t-p}\}$.
5. The number of parameters increases very quickly with the number of lags and/or the number of variables in the system. For instance in a system of two variables, going from a VAR(p) to a VAR($p + 1$) means increasing the number of parameters by four (two new parameters per equation: 2×2). In a system of three variables, it means increasing the number of parameters by nine (three new parameters per equation: 3×3). In general, the number of parameters will increase by n^2, where n is the number of equations or, equivalently, the number of variables in the system. Thus, a VAR system can become overparameterized rather quickly, and we will need a large sample size to be able to estimate such a large number of parameters.

11.2 Estimation of VAR

The estimation of the parameters of a VAR system requires the choice of the number of lags, but to choose the number of lags, we need to estimate the system. This is a circular problem! Our approach to modeling a VAR is slightly different from that of modeling a univariate process. Recall that we use the information in the autocorrelation functions to entertain different (ARMA) specifications for a single time series. In VAR, the autocorrelation functions are also useful but because we would also need cross-correlations at different leads and lags, among all the variables in the system, the identification problem will become more difficult. Thus, we prefer to identify the number of lags by estimation and by the use of information criteria. We will proceed by choosing several values of the order $p = 1, 2, 3 \ldots$ and estimating a VAR(p) for each value of p. We will record the values of AIC and SIC for each VAR(p) and we will select the VAR(p^*) such as p^* minimizes the AIC or/and the SIC.[1]

The good news is that the estimation of a VAR is a simple task. As far as each equation has the same regressors, $\{Y_{t-1}, Y_{t-2}, \ldots Y_{t-p}, X_{t-1}, X_{t-2} \ldots X_{t-p}\}$, we will estimate the regression coefficients $\{c_1, \alpha_{11}, \alpha_{12} \ldots \alpha_{1p}, \beta_{11}, \beta_{12}, \ldots \beta_{1p}\}$ and $c_2, \alpha_{21}, \alpha_{22} \ldots \alpha_{2p}, \beta_{21}, \beta_{22}, \ldots \beta_{2p}$ by performing an OLS regression for each equation. The OLS estimation and testing results reviewed in Chapter 2 are applicable to each equation of the VAR system. Let us practice VAR estimation by analyzing the following data set.

REAL DATA: Quarterly House Price Index in Los Angeles and Riverside Metropolitan Statistical Areas, 1975:Q2–2010:Q2

From a familiar website, Freddie Mac, http://www.freddiemac.com, we download the time series of the quarterly **house price index** for two MSAs in Southern California, Los Angeles and Riverside, which are about 60 miles apart.

Why do we think that a VAR system is the right approach to forecast prices in both locations? The regional economies of Los Angeles and Riverside are linked by thousands of people who commute daily in both directions. Los Angeles, being a large metropolitan area, attracts many businesses in the manufacturing, entertainment, health, education, and services industries. Riverside County and its surroundings have a smaller economy and benefits greatly from the economic activity in Los Angeles area. As the population expands, the demand for housing in Los Angeles bids up real estate prices, producing an exodus from there to the inland area of Riverside where real estate is cheaper and the land is abundant. Thus, the Riverside economy is highly dependent on the economy of Los Angeles. If we want to forecast Riverside house prices, it seems natural to take into account the activity in Los Angeles. Will we be able to observe this link between the real estate sectors in Riverside and Los Angeles in the data? In Figure 11.1,

[1] We also select the optimal lag by implementing a log-likelihood ratio test, which measures the distance between the (log) determinants of the residual variance-covariance matrices of a VAR(p) and a VAR($p+1$). This test is more advanced because it requires understanding matrix algebra. The basic idea is testing order p against order $p+1$; If we reject p, we move to estimate a system of higher order VAR($p+1$) and entertain again successive tests such as $p+1$ against $p+2$, $p+2$ against $p+3$, and so on until we fail to reject the null hypothesis.

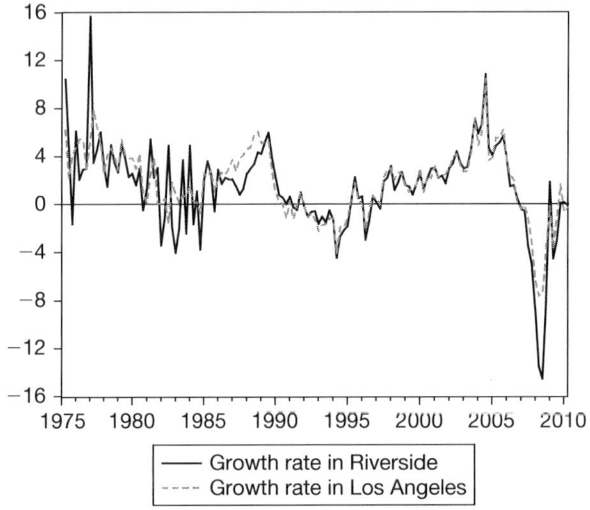

FIGURE 11.1 House Price Growth in Riverside and Los Angeles MSAs

we plot both time series. Although the burst of the housing market bubble has been more dramatic in Riverside (−14.6% decline in 2008:Q3) than in Los Angeles (−7.5 decline in 2008:Q3), we observe that both time series tend to move together with a correlation coefficient of 0.84, which is very high.

A VAR system seems a good starting point to analyze the joint dynamics of house prices in Los Angeles and Riverside. In EViews, open your workfile, and select the following sequence:

Object

New Object

VAR

In the **VAR Specification** screen, select Unrestricted VAR (VAR Type), enter the name of the variables (Endogenous Variables) in the system, the number of lags (Lag Intervals for Endogenous), and the estimation sample. For our data, we select an estimation sample up to 2009:Q2, and we reserve the last four observations, 2009:Q3 to 2010:Q2, for forecasting evaluation. The estimation output is presented in Table 11.1.

The endogenous variables are the house price growth in Los Angeles (GLA) and in Riverside (GRiv). The estimated system is a VAR(1) with six parameters to estimate (plus the variances and covariance of the error terms) such as

$$Y_t = c_1 + \alpha_{11} Y_{t-1} + \beta_{11} X_{t-1} + \varepsilon_{1t}$$
$$X_t = c_2 + \alpha_{21} Y_{t-1} + \beta_{21} X_{t-1} + \varepsilon_{2t}$$

In Table 11.1, after the sample information at the top, there are three main panels. In the first, we read the regression estimates, standard errors, and t-statistics for each

TABLE 11.1 Vector Autoregression Estimates

Vector Autoregression Estimates
Sample (adjusted): 1975Q3 2009Q2
Included observations: 136 after adjustments
Standard errors in ( ) & t-statistics in [ ]

	GLA	GRiv
GLA(−1)	0.788974	0.894338
	(0.08831)	(0.13684)
	[8.93417]	[6.53548]
GRiv(−1)	0.046362	0.053929
	(0.06811)	(0.10555)
	[0.68067]	[0.51094]
C	0.255229	-0.359998
	(0.16840)	(0.26095)
	[1.51564]	[-1.37959]
R-squared	0.698351	0.554138
Adj. R-squared	0.693815	0.547433
Sum sq. resids	341.0861	819.0215
S.E. equation	1.601423	2.481543
F-statistic	153.9552	82.64933
Log likelihood	-255.5003	-315.0666
Akaike AIC	3.801475	4.677450
Schwarz SC	3.865724	4.741700
Mean dependent	1.814859	1.410004
S.D. dependent	2.894106	3.688762
Determinant resid covariance (dof adj.)		10.11450
Determinant resid covariance		9.673198
Log likelihood		-540.2677
Akaike information criterion		8.033348
Schwarz criterion		8.161848

equation in the system. These have been obtained by performing OLS estimation in each equation. The second panel contains all regression statistics and information criteria for each individual equation, and the third panel gives some statistics for the full system from which we are mainly interested in the AIC and SIC. The interpretation of all these statistics proceeds as in any OLS regression model. We note the strong statistical significant (large *t*-ratios) of the regressor GLA(-1) and the high Adjusted *R*-squared (69% and 55%) in both equations. In particular, our hypothesis that the real estate market in Riverside is very dependent on the Los Angeles market is confirmed: On average, 1% growth in Los Angeles translates into 0.9% growth in Riverside. On the contrary, the Los Angeles market does not seem to be affected by the Riverside market.

A pending question is whether one lag is sufficient or we need more lags to model the dynamics of the system. The SIC and AIC will be very helpful because we will choose the **lag length** by minimizing these criteria as we did in the univariate case. In EViews, after estimating the VAR system, select the sequence

View

Lag Structure

Lag Length Criteria

A table, like Table 11.2, will show the values of many information criteria as a function of the number of lags in the VAR. The optimal lag is denoted by an asterisk. Focusing on the AIC and SIC (boxed values in Table 11.2), we observe that both criteria agree on choosing one lag as the optimal length of the VAR system.[2]

TABLE 11.2 Lag Order Selaction in VAR

VAR Lag Order Selection Criteria
Endogenous variables: GLA GRiv
Exogenous variables: C
Sample: 1975Q1 2009Q2
Included observations: 129

Lag	LogL	LR	FPE	AIC	SC	HQ
0	-569.9297	NA	24.32180	8.867127	8.911465	8.885142
1	-487.7585	160.5205	7.238637*	7.655170*	7.788185*	7.709217*
2	-487.2043	1.065406	7.636332	7.708594	7.930285	7.798671
3	-481.6932	10.42418*	7.460515	7.685165	7.995532	7.811274
4	-477.4558	7.883524	7.434896	7.681485	8.080528	7.843624
5	-476.7097	1.364911	7.822540	7.731933	8.219653	7.930104
6	-472.1276	8.240713	7.756466	7.722908	8.299304	7.957109
7	-470.3528	3.136797	8.034679	7.757408	8.422480	8.027640
8	-469.6694	1.186753	8.466835	7.808827	8.562576	8.115091

*indicates lag order selected by the criterion
LR: sequential modified LR test statistic (each test at 5% level)
FPE: Final prediction error
AIC: Akaike information criterion
SC: Schewarz information criterion
HQ: Hannan-Quinn information criterion

[2] There is a small discrepancy between the values of AIC and SIC in Tables 11.1 and 11.2 that is due to the different number of observations used in both tables.

11.3 Granger Causality

The main idea behind any VAR system is that a multivariate information set could be more helpful than a univariate set in forecasting the variables of interest. But we could ask which among the many variables in the information set are most useful to forecast others. The definition of **Granger-causality** seeks to answer this question.

Suppose that, for a process of interest $\{Y_t\}$, we have a multivariate information set:

$$I_t = \{y_0, y_1, y_2, \ldots .y_t, x_0, x_1, x_2, \ldots .x_t, z_0, z_1, z_2, \ldots ..z_t\}$$

We are interested in whether the information provided by the time series corresponding to the processes $\{X_t\}$ and $\{Z_t\}$ are helpful to forecast future values of $\{Y_t\}$.

If the processes $\{X_t\}$ and $\{Z_t\}$ *do not help to predict* $\{Y_t\}$, *we say that* $\{X_t\}$ and $\{Z_t\}$ *do not Granger-cause the process* $\{Y_t\}$.

How do we operationalize this concept? Recall the forecast error $e_{t,h} = y_{t+h} - f_{t,h}$. As we already know, small forecast errors mean better predictions. Suppose that we construct two alternative forecasts: one is based on a univariate information set, and the other is based on a multivariate set, that is,

$$f_{t,h}^{(1)} = g(y_0, y_1, \ldots ..y_t)$$
$$f_{t,h}^{(2)} = g(y_0, y_1, \ldots ..y_t, x_0, x_1, \ldots x_t, z_0, z_1, \ldots ..z_t)$$

For each forecast, we compute their corresponding forecast errors, that is,

$$e_{(1)t,h} = y_{t+h} - f_{t,h}^{(1)}$$
$$e_{(2)t,h} = y_{t+h} - f_{t,h}^{(2)}$$

and we evaluate them on the basis of a loss function. Suppose that we choose a mean-squared error loss function. Then we can compare the value of both loss functions:

$$MSE^{(1)} = \frac{\sum_{j=0}^{N} e_{(1)t+j,h}^2}{N+1} \quad \text{and} \quad MSE^{(2)} = \frac{\sum_{j=0}^{N} e_{(2)t+j,h}^2}{N+1}$$

- If $MSE^{(1)} = MSE^{(2)}$, then $\{X_t\}$ and $\{Z_t\}$ do not Granger-cause the process $\{Y_t\}$. In this case, the multivariate information set that includes past values $\{x_0, x_1, \ldots x_t, z_0, z_1, \ldots z_t\}$ is not informative for the prediction of $\{Y_t\}$.
- If $MSE^{(1)} > MSE^{(2)}$, then $\{X_t\}$ and $\{Z_t\}$ Granger-cause the process $\{Y_t\}$. This means that the past values $\{x_0, x_1, \ldots x_t, z_0, z_1, \ldots z_t\}$ help to forecast $\{Y_t\}$. On average, the forecast errors are smaller when more information is included in the information set; consequently, the mean squared error loss is smaller.

To test for Granger-causality, we will only need familiar regression techniques. If the $g(.)$ function is linear in the information set, we can write a regression model for y_t as

$$y_t = \alpha_0 + \alpha_1 y_{t-1} + \cdots + \alpha_p y_{t-p} + \beta_1 x_{t-1} + \cdots + \beta_p x_{t-p} + \gamma_1 z_{t-1} + \cdots + \gamma_p z_{t-p} + \varepsilon_t$$

The regressors are the lagged values: $\{y_{t-1} \ldots y_{t-p}, x_{t-1}, \ldots x_{t-p}, z_{t-1}, \ldots z_{t-p}\}$. After estimating the regression coefficients $\{\alpha_0, \alpha_1, \ldots \ldots \alpha_p, \beta_1 \ldots \ldots \beta_p, \gamma_1 \ldots \ldots \gamma_p\}$ by OLS, we formulate the following null hypothesis:

$$H_0: \beta_1 = \cdots = \beta_p = \gamma_1 = \cdots = \gamma_p = 0$$
$$H_1: \text{any } \beta \text{ or } \gamma \neq 0$$

Under the classical assumptions of a linear regression model, this null hypothesis can be tested with an F-statistic. Under the null hypothesis, the regression model becomes:

$$y_t = \alpha_0 + \alpha_1 y_{t-1} + \cdots + \alpha_p y_{t-p} + u_t$$

If this model is true, then the information in $\{x_{t-1}, \ldots x_{t-p}, z_{t-1}, \ldots z_{t-p}\}$ is not helpful in explaining y_t. Thus, they will not have any predictive content to forecast y_{t+h}. We say that $\{x_{t-1}, \ldots x_{t-p}, z_{t-1}, \ldots z_{t-p}\}$ do not Granger-cause y_t. A test for the above null hypothesis is called a Granger-causality test.

In general, to construct the F-statistic, implement the following steps:

1. Run the regression model under the null: $y_t = \alpha_0 + \alpha_1 y_{t-1} + \cdots + \alpha_p y_{t-p} + u_t$ (univariate information set). Retrieve the residuals. Construct the sum of squared residuals, that is, $SSR_0 = \sum_{t=1}^{T} \hat{u}_t^2$.
2. Run the extended regression model based on the multivariate information set:

$$y_t = \alpha_0 + \alpha_1 y_{t-1} + \cdots + \alpha_p y_{t-p} + \beta_1 x_{t-1} + \cdots$$
$$+ \beta_p x_{t-p} + \gamma_1 z_{t-1} + \cdots + \gamma_p z_{t-p} + \varepsilon_t$$

   and retrieve the residuals. Construct the sum of squared residuals, that is, $SSR_1 = \sum_{t=1}^{T} \hat{\varepsilon}_t^2$.
3. Construct the F-statistic:

$$F = \frac{(SSR_0 - SSR_1)/k_0}{SSR_1/k_1}$$

   where k_0 is the number of restrictions under the null and k_1 is the number of degrees of freedom for the unrestricted model. Because the regressors are lagged dependent variables, the F-test is valid only asymptotically, and it will be better to implement an equivalent asymptotic chi-squared test:

$$F^* = \frac{T(SSR_0 - SSR_1)}{SSR_1}$$

   which, for large samples, it is just $F^* = k_0 F$.
4. For a given critical region, the null hypothesis should be rejected when F^* is greater than the critical value of a chi-square probability distribution with k_0 degrees of freedom. By rejecting the null hypothesis, we say that $\{x_{t-1}, \ldots \ldots x_{t-p}, z_{t-1}, \ldots \ldots z_{t-p}\}$ Granger-causes y_t.

Going back to our data on house prices in Riverside and Los Angeles, we could ask two questions:

"Is the Riverside market Granger-causing the Los Angeles real estate market?" and "Is the Los Angeles market Granger-causing the Riverside market?" Given the VAR(1) system estimated in Table 11.1,

$$Y_t = c_1 + \alpha_{11}Y_{t-1} + \beta_{11}X_{t-1} + \varepsilon_{1t}$$
$$X_t = c_2 + \alpha_{21}Y_{t-1} + \beta_{21}X_{t-1} + \varepsilon_{2t}$$

the null hypotheses to entertain are $H_0{:}\beta_{11} = 0$ in the first equation, that is, X does not Granger-cause Y; and $H_0 : \alpha_{21} = 0$ in the second equation, that is, Y does not Granger-cause X. Now we need only to implement the four steps described earlier. The restricted models (models under the null) will be $Y_t = c_1 + \alpha_{11}Y_{t-1} + \varepsilon_{1t}$ and $X_t = c_2 + \beta_{21}X_{t-1} + \varepsilon_{2t}$, respectively. After OLS estimation of these models, we calculate the sum of squared residuals of the restricted and unrestricted models, we construct the test F^*, and we compare its value with the critical value of a chi-square with 1 degree of freedom (this is the number of restrictions under the null hypothesis). The results are presented in Table 11.3.

In the first equation, we are testing the effect of the Riverside market (GRiv) on the Los Angeles market (GLA), and we obtain a very small value of the chi-squared test $F^* = 0.46$, with p-value equal to 49%. Thus, we fail to reject the null, and we conclude that the Riverside market does not Granger-cause the Los Angeles market, in other words, the Riverside market does not have predictive ability for the Los Angeles market. On the other hand, when we examine the second equation in which we are testing the effect of the Los Angeles market on the Riverside market, the value of the chi-squared test is very large $F^* = 42.71$ with a p-value of 0%, which means that we reject the null hypothesis very strongly (we reject that Los Angeles does not Granger-cause

TABLE 11.3 Testing for Granger-Causality in VAR

VAR Granger Causality/Block Exogeneity Wald Tests Sample: 1975Q1 2009Q2 Included observations: 136			
Dependent variable: GLA			
Excluded	Chi-sq	df	Prob.
GRiv	0.463310	1	0.4961
All	0.463310	1	0.4961
Dependent variable: GRiv			
Excluded	Chi-sq	df	Prob.
GLA	42.71250	1	0.0000
All	42.71250	1	0.0000

Riverside). Thus, we conclude that the Los Angeles market has predictive ability for the Riverside market. This is additional evidence for our original hypothesis that the real estate sector in Riverside depends highly on the Los Angeles sector.

11.4 Impulse-Response Functions

An advantage of estimating a VAR system is that we are able to track how shocks to one variable are transmitted to the other variables in the system. Consider the VAR(1) system that models the interdependence over time between the real estate sectors in Los Angeles and Riverside. Suppose that there is a shock to Los Angeles economy. For instance, a reduction in the federal defense budget will affect the many businesses in the area that work directly or indirectly for the Department of Defense. Some business will close, others will reduce the number of employees, and still others may be merged with other companies. How is the shock transmitted to the Riverside economy? If the layoffs are large, some people who live in Riverside and commute daily to Los Angeles are likely to lose their jobs. The lack of income may affect their mortgage payments, and their home eventually may be foreclosed. A large number of foreclosures will bring the price of other homes down, and eventually the real estate in Riverside will suffer as much as the Los Angeles market. How do we measure this effect statistically? Observe the estimated VAR(1) where the first equation represents the dynamics of the Los Angeles real estate market and the second equation, the Riverside market.

$$Y_t = c_1 + \alpha_{11} Y_{t-1} + \beta_{11} X_{t-1} + \varepsilon_{1t}$$
$$X_t = c_2 + \alpha_{21} Y_{t-1} + \beta_{21} X_{t-1} + \varepsilon_{2t}$$

The shock to the Los Angeles market comes through the error term ε_{1t}. An increase in ε_{1t} translates immediately into a change in Y_t. In turn, through the second equation, the change in Y_t affects the Riverside market in the next period (X_{t+1}), which in turn will affect the Los Angeles market in the following period (Y_{t+2}), and so on.

To illustrate the transmission of the shock throughout the system, let us assume that at $t=0$, the values of the variables are $Y_0 = X_0 = 0$. Suppose that, at time $t=1$, there is a shock to Y of magnitude 1 (i.e., $\varepsilon_{11} = 1$) but there is no shock to X ($\varepsilon_{21} = 0$). Furthermore, we assume that there are no more shocks to the system in the forthcoming periods. In addition, and for mathematical tractability, let us assume that the constant terms are equal to zero, that is, $c_1 = c_2 = 0$. Then let us observe how the system reacts at time $1, 2, 3, \ldots$:

$$t=1 \qquad Y_1 = \varepsilon_{11} = 1$$
$$X_1 = 0$$
$$t=2 \qquad Y_2 = \alpha_{11} Y_1 + \beta_{11} X_1 + \varepsilon_{12} = \alpha_{11}$$
$$X_2 = \alpha_{21} Y_1 + \beta_{21} X_1 + \varepsilon_{22} = \alpha_{21}$$
$$t=3 \qquad Y_3 = \alpha_{11} Y_2 + \beta_{11} X_2 + \varepsilon_{13} = \alpha_{11}^2 + \beta_{11}\alpha_{21}$$
$$X_3 = \alpha_{21} Y_2 + \beta_{21} X_2 + \varepsilon_{23} = \alpha_{21}\alpha_{11} + \beta_{21}\alpha_{21}$$

We could keep on going for $t=4, 5, 6\ldots$ by repeated substitution of past values of the variables into the present system. The stationarity property of the system ensures that the shock eventually will die out. How strong and how long is the response of Y and X to the shock? As you can see, it will depend on the estimates of the parameters of the VAR.

The **impulse-response** *function* is precisely the statistical tool that informs about the persistence and magnitude of the shocks. The "impulse" is the shock and the "response" is the change that we observe in the variables of the VAR system over time. Formally, the impulse-response function is defined as

$$\frac{\partial Y_{t+s}}{\partial \varepsilon_{1t}} \simeq \frac{\Delta Y_{t+s}}{\Delta \varepsilon_{1t}}$$

$$\frac{\partial X_{t+s}}{\partial \varepsilon_{1t}} \simeq \frac{\Delta X_{t+s}}{\Delta \varepsilon_{1t}}$$

and

$$\frac{\partial Y_{t+s}}{\partial \varepsilon_{2t}} \simeq \frac{\Delta Y_{t+s}}{\Delta \varepsilon_{2t}}$$

$$\frac{\partial X_{t+s}}{\partial \varepsilon_{2t}} \simeq \frac{\Delta X_{t+s}}{\Delta \varepsilon_{2t}}$$

for $s = 0, 1, 2, 3, \ldots$.

In a bivariate system, we have four responses because for every impulse ε_1 and ε_2, we have to account for the responses of Y and X. A shock to the Los Angeles area may not only affect the Los Angeles market but also may be transmitted to the Riverside market; likewise, a shock to the Riverside area may affect not only the Riverside market but also may be transmitted to the Los Angeles market.

It is customary to think of the impulse in terms of units of standard deviations, -**standardized innovation**- so that when we write $\varepsilon_{11} = 1$, we mean $\varepsilon_{11}/\sigma_1 = 1$, which says that the impulse is equal to 1 standard deviation. However, we face a technical problem when the error terms ε_1 and ε_2 are correlated because an impulse in ε_1 has a contemporary reaction in ε_2 when their covariance is not zero. Then our previously mentioned assumption regarding an impulse of magnitude 1 (i.e. $\varepsilon_{11} = 1$) but no shock to X (i.e., $\varepsilon_{21} = 0$) will not be satisfied. The solution to this problem requires advanced knowledge of matrix algebra, which is beyond the scope of this book. Suffice it to say that the original errors terms ε_1 and ε_2 are transformed, say u_1 and u_2, in such a way that the covariance of u_1 and u_2 will be zero. Then the impulse is not just 1 standard deviation of ε_1 and ε_2 but also 1 standard deviation of u_1 and u_2.[3] From a practical point of view, the implication of this transformation is that in some instances, the ordering of the variables in the VAR system matters for the analysis of the impulse-response functions. In general, the choice of the ordering of the variables should be informed by prior knowledge on the transmission of shocks. It is also advisable to change the ordering of

[3] A standard transformation is based on the Cholesky decomposition of the variance-covariance matrix of the error terms.

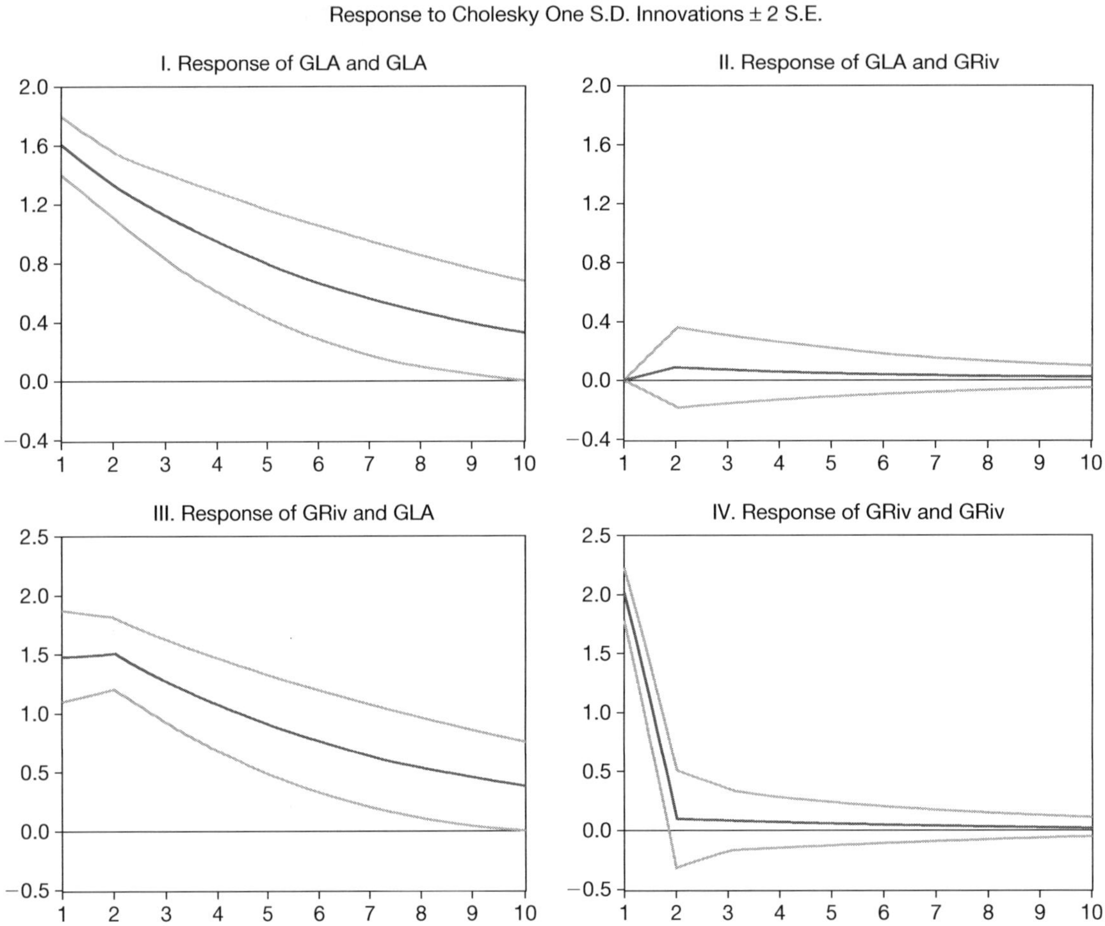

FIGURE 11.2 Impulse-Response Functions for Riverside and Los Angeles House Markets

the variables and to observe how much the impulse response functions change. In our study case, we choose the ordering (GLA, GRiv), which implies that a shock in the Riverside housing market does not have any *contemporaneous* effect in the Los Angeles market (the effect may be coming in future periods) while a shock in the Los Angeles market contemporaneously impacts both the Riverside and the Los Angeles markets (this is a consequence of the Cholesky decomposition when the covariance between the errors is not zero). Fortunately, for forecasting purposes, the ordering of the variables in the VAR system does not matter.

In Figure 11.2, we show the four impulse response functions for the order (GLA, GRiv). In each graph, there are 95% confidence bands (light grey lines) around the value of the response, which help to evaluate the statistical significance of the response. If the bands include zero, we consider the response statistically zero. It is interesting to observe that a shock to the Los Angeles market lives for about 10 quarters in both markets, Los Angeles and Riverside, while a shock in Riverside is much shorter-lived; in fact, a shock in Riverside does not have any effect over time in Los Angeles and is absorbed in not more than 2 quarters by the Riverside market. In summary, the Los Angeles market clearly dominates the dynamics and the variability of home prices in both markets.

11.5 Forecasting with VAR

Because every equation in the VAR system obeys an autoregressive specification, the construction of the forecast follows the same rules that we have seen for the forecast of a univariate process in Chapter 7. The main insight is that the forecast will be constructed in a recursive fashion. The only complication is that for each forecasting horizon, we need to forecast two (or more) variables. To keep the algebra at the simplest level, let us work with a VAR(1) for two variables:

$$
\begin{aligned}
Y_t &= c_1 + a_{11}Y_{t-1} + \beta_{11}X_{t-1} + \varepsilon_{1t} \\
X_t &= c_2 + a_{21}Y_{t-1} + \beta_{21}X_{t-1} + \varepsilon_{2t}
\end{aligned}
$$

with normally distributed error terms ε_{1t} and ε_{2t}, that is, $\varepsilon_{1t} \rightarrow N(0, \sigma_1^2), \varepsilon_{2t} \rightarrow N(0, \sigma_2^2)$, and $\text{cov}(\varepsilon_{1t}, \varepsilon_{2t}) \neq 0$.

Our objective is to forecast the values of the series X_{t+h} and Y_{t+h}. Assume that the forecaster has a quadratic loss function so that the optimal forecast is a conditional mean; recall that $f_{t,h} = \mu_{t+h|t} = E(Y_{t+h}|I_t)$ for $h = 1, 2, \ldots s$. The information set runs up to time *t*, and we are interested in two forecasting horizons, $h = 1$ and $h = 2$.

The value of the system at the future time $t + 1$ is

$$
\begin{aligned}
Y_{t+1} &= c_1 + \alpha_{11}Y_t + \beta_{11}X_t + \varepsilon_{1,t+1} \\
X_{t+1} &= c_2 + \alpha_{21}Y_t + \beta_{21}X_t + \varepsilon_{2,t+1}
\end{aligned}
$$

and $t + 2$ is

$$
\begin{aligned}
Y_{t+2} &= c_1 + \alpha_{11}Y_{t+1} + \beta_{11}X_t + \varepsilon_{1,t+2} \\
X_{t+2} &= c_2 + \alpha_{21}Y_{t+1} + \beta_{21}X_t + \varepsilon_{2,t+2}
\end{aligned}
$$

i. *What Are the Optimal Point Forecasts $f_{t,1}$ and $f_{t,2}$?*

$$
\begin{aligned}
f_{t,1}^Y = \mu_{t+1|t}^Y = E(Y_{t+1}|I_t) &= E(c_1 + \alpha_{11}Y_t + \beta_{11}X_t + \varepsilon_{1,t+1}|I_t) \\
&= c_1 + \alpha_{11}Y_t + \beta_{11}X_t \\
f_{t,1}^X = \mu_{t+1|t}^X = E(X_{t+1}|I_t) &= E(c_2 + \alpha_{21}Y_t + \beta_{21}X_t + \varepsilon_{2,t+1}|I_t) \\
&= c_2 + \alpha_{21}Y_t + \beta_{21}X_t
\end{aligned}
$$

$$f_{t,2}^{Y} = \mu_{t+2|t}^{Y} = E(Y_{t+2} | I_t) = E(c_1 + \alpha_{11} Y_{t+1} + \beta_{11} X_{t+1} + \varepsilon_{1,t+2} | I_t)$$
$$= c_1 + \alpha_{11} f_{t,1}^{Y} + \beta_{11} f_{t,1}^{X}$$
$$f_{t,2}^{X} = \mu_{t+2|t}^{X} = E(X_{t+2} | I_t) = E(c_2 + \alpha_{21} Y_{t+1} + \beta_{21} X_{t+1} + \varepsilon_{2,t+2} | I_t)$$
$$= c_2 + \alpha_{21} f_{t,1}^{Y} + \beta_{21} f_{t,1}^{X}$$

Observe the recursive nature of the forecast, which is already familiar to us from the forecast of a univariate AR process. For forecasting horizon $t+2$, the forecast depends on the forecast of the previous period. Following this recursive approach, we could calculate the forecast for any other horizon.

ii. *What Are the One-Period and Two-Period Ahead Forecast Errors $e_{t,1}$ and $e_{t,2}$?*
The difference between the realized values (X_{t+1}, Y_{t+1}), (X_{t+2}, Y_{t+2}), and their respective forecast values $f_{t,1}$, $f_{t,2}$:

$$e_{t,1}^{Y} = Y_{t+1} - f_{t,1}^{Y} = c_1 + \alpha_{11} Y_t + \beta_{11} X_t + \varepsilon_{1,t+1} - c_1 - \alpha_{11} Y_t - \beta_{11} X_t = \varepsilon_{1,t+1}$$

$$e_{t,1}^{X} = X_{t+1} - f_{t,1}^{Y} = c_2 + \alpha_{21} Y_t + \beta_{21} X_t + \varepsilon_{2,t+1} - c_2 - \alpha_{21} Y_t - \beta_{21} X_t = \varepsilon_{2,t+1}$$

and

$$e_{t,2}^{Y} = Y_{t+2} - f_{t,2}^{Y} = c_1 + \alpha_{11} Y_{t+1} + \beta_{11} X_{t+1} + \varepsilon_{1,t+2} - c_1 - \alpha_{11} f_{t,1}^{Y} - \beta_{11} f_{t,1}^{X}$$
$$= \alpha_{11} e_{t,1}^{Y} + \beta_{11} e_{t,1}^{X} + \varepsilon_{1,t+2}$$
$$e_{t,2}^{X} = X_{t+2} - f_{t,2}^{X} = c_2 + \alpha_{21} Y_{t+1} + \beta_{21} X_{t+1} + \varepsilon_{2,t+2} - c_2 - \alpha_{21} f_{t,1}^{Y} - \beta_{21} f_{t,1}^{X}$$
$$= \alpha_{21} e_{t,1}^{Y} + \beta_{21} e_{t,1}^{X} + \varepsilon_{2,t+2}$$

Observe that the forecast errors are also calculated recursively.

iii. *What Is the Uncertainty Associated with the Forecast?*
The variance of the forecast error

$$\sigma_{Y,t+1|t}^{2} = \text{var}(Y_{t+1} | I_t) = E(Y_{t+1} - f_{t,1}^{Y} | I_t)^2 = E(e_{t,1}^{Y})^2 = E(\varepsilon_{1,t+1}^{2}) = \sigma_{\varepsilon_1}^{2}$$
$$\sigma_{X,t+1|t}^{2} = \text{var}(X_{t+1} | I_t) = E(X_{t+1} - f_{t,1}^{X} | I_t)^2 = E(e_{t,1}^{X})^2 = E(\varepsilon_{2,t+1}^{2}) = \sigma_{\varepsilon_2}^{2}$$

and

$$\sigma_{Y,t+2|t}^{2} = \text{var}(Y_{t+2} | I_t) = E(Y_{t+2} - f_{t,2}^{Y} | I_t)^2 = E(e_{t,2}^{Y})^2$$
$$= \sigma_{\varepsilon_1}^{2}(1 + \alpha_{11}^{2}) + \sigma_{\varepsilon_2}^{2}\beta_{11}^{2} + 2\alpha_{11}\beta_{11}\text{cov}(\varepsilon_1, \varepsilon_2)$$
$$\sigma_{X,t+2|t}^{2} = \text{var}(X_{t+2} | I_t) = E(X_{t+2} - f_{t,2}^{X} | I_t)^2 = E(e_{t,2}^{X})^2$$
$$= \sigma_{\varepsilon_1}^{2}\alpha_{21}^{2} + \sigma_{\varepsilon_2}^{2}(1 + \beta_{21}^{2}) + 2\alpha_{21}\beta_{21}\text{cov}(\varepsilon_1, \varepsilon_2)$$

Observe that the covariance terms appear because the error terms of the two equations may be contemporaneously correlated.

iv. *What Is the Density Forecast?*
The conditional probability density function of the system at the future date $t+1$. Recall that we have assumed normally distributed white noises. Because we deal with a system, we have the marginal density forecast of each variable and the joint bivariate density forecast. Here we just report the 1-period-ahead marginal density forecast for each variable:

$$f(Y_{t+1} \mid I_t) \rightarrow N(\mu^Y_{t+1|t}, \sigma^2_{Y,t+1|t})$$
$$f(X_{t+1} \mid I_t) \rightarrow N(\mu^X_{t+1|t}, \sigma^2_{X,t+1|t})$$

If the VAR model includes higher order dynamics, the algebra becomes more complicated, but the principles for constructing the forecasts remain the same. Point forecasts and forecast errors obey recursive relations, so the forecast at long horizons are functions of the forecasts at shorter horizons.

REAL DATA: Forecasting Quarterly House Price Growth in Los Angeles and Riverside MSAs, 2009:Q3–2011:Q4

We finish this section by constructing the multistep forecast for house price growth in Los Angeles (Y_t) and Riverside (X_t) based on the VAR(1) system estimated in the previous sections.

The information set runs to 2009:Q2, and we will build the forecast from 2009:Q3 to 2011:Q4 ($h = 1, 2 \ldots 10$). Because the VAR contains one lag, we need the following values of the information set to start the recursive relation: $Y_{2009:Q2} = -3.689$ and $X_{2009:Q2} = -4.550$.

For $t+1 =$ 2009:Q3:

$$f^Y_{t,1} = 0.255 + 0.788 \times (-3.689) + 0.046 \times (-4.550)$$
$$f^X_{t,1} = -0.359 + 0.894 \times (-3.689) + 0.053 \times (-4.550)$$

with forecast errors $e^Y_{t,1} = \varepsilon_{1,t+1}$ and $e^X_{t,1} = \varepsilon_{2,t+1}$.

For $t+2 =$ 2009:Q4:

$$f^Y_{t,2} = 0.255 + 0.788 \times f^Y_{t,1} + 0.046 \times f^X_{t,1}$$
$$f^X_{t,2} = -0.359 + 0.894 \times f^Y_{t,1} + 0.053 \times f^X_{t,1}$$

with forecast errors $e^Y_{t,2} = 0.788 e^Y_{t,1} + 0.046 e^X_{t,1} + \varepsilon_{1,t+2}$ and $e^X_{t,2} = 0.894 e^Y_{t,1} + 0.053 e^X_{t,1} + \varepsilon_{2,t+2}$.

For additional horizons, we will proceed in a similar fashion by using the recursive relation. In EViews, the multistep forecast is calculated by clicking the following sequence in the VAR estimation window:

Proc

Make Model

Solve Model

In the Model Solution (Basic Options) window, select "Deterministic" (in the simulation type) and "Dynamic solution" (in Dynamics) and choose the forecasting sample in the "Solution sample."

In Figure 11.3, we present the forecasts up to 2011:Q4.

For most of the forecasting horizon, the point forecast of the price growth remains negative for both areas although it seems that Los Angeles could experience positive rates by the last half of 2011. However, the 95% confidence bands are quite

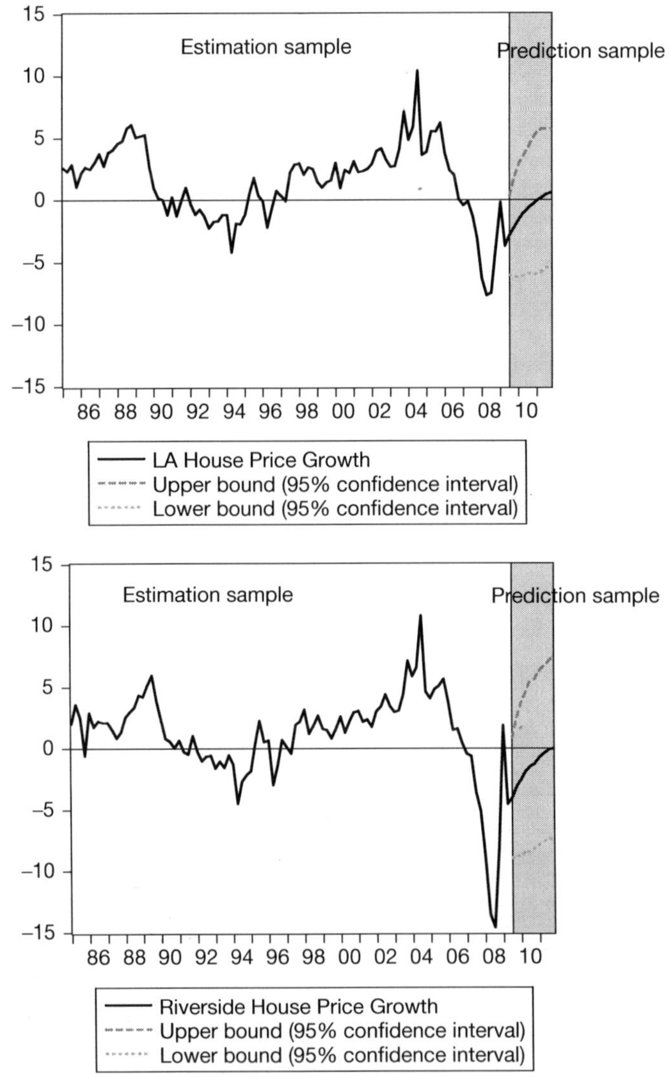

FIGURE 11.3 Forecasts of House Price Growth in Riverside and Los Angeles

wide, which means that there is much uncertainty in both markets; in particular, the Riverside market seems to be sluggish and more uncertain than the Los Angeles market.

KEY WORDS

EXERCISES

From the Freddie Mac website, download the house prices of two MSAs in the *same geographical area or county* and calculate the price growth. Let us call them MSA1 and MSA2. You may want to choose the MSAs in the area where you live. Split your sample into estimation and prediction samples (leave at least 20 observations in your prediction sample).

1. Describe your samples. Estimate a VAR for price growth in MSA1 and MSA2. Choose the lag structure optimally. Comment on the estimation results.
2. Assess whether there is Granger-causality between both series. Construct the appropriate statistical tests, choose the size of the test, and explain your decision.
3. Calculate the impulse-response functions. Explain the four functions and discuss your findings. Do you have any prior knowledge about the economies of both MSAs? Comment on whether the ordering of the series matters for your results.
4. Construct the 1-step-ahead forecast. Because you have reserved some of your observations (prediction sample), evaluate how good the 1-step-ahead forecasts are by implementing a test of unconditional predictability (Chapter 9). Compare the 1-step-ahead forecasts from the VAR model with those that you would obtain from the best univariate model that you could find for each series.
5. Construct several multistep forecasts with a 95% confidence band. Discuss your results. Then pick either MSA1 or MSA2 and download house prices of another *very distant* MSA, say MSA3. For instance, if you have an MSA in the west coast, choose an additional MSA in the east coast. Calculate the growth rates, and, as before, split the sample into two segments, estimation and prediction.
6. Describe your new sample. Estimate a bivariate VAR for the price growth for MSA1 (or MSA2) and MSA3. Choose the lag structure optimally. Comment on

the estimation results. Assess whether there is Granger-causality between both series. Construct the appropriate statistical tests, choose the size of the test, and explain your decision.

7. Calculate the impulse-response functions. Explain the four functions and discuss your findings. Comment on whether the ordering of the series matters for your results.
8. Construct the 1-step-ahead forecast. Because you have reserved some of your observations (prediction sample), evaluate how good the 1-step-ahead forecasts are by implementing a test of unconditional predictability. Construct several multistep forecasts and with a 95% confidence band. Discuss your results.
9. Now gather the three series of house price growth for the three MSAs and estimate the best trivariate VAR model. Construct the 1-step-ahead forecasts based on this larger VAR, and compare the forecasts with those that you obtained in Exercises 11.4 and 11.8. Comment on your results.
10. Suppose that you need to explain your findings to your supervisor. Write a professional forecast report on house prices in MSA1, MSA2, and MSA3.

CHAPTER 12

Forecasting the Long Term and the Short Term Jointly

In this book, we have introduced first the analysis of models that capture short-term features (stationary data) followed by models that capture long-term characteristics (non stationary data), but when we study a time series, or a system of time series, both short and long features are jointly present. In this chapter we will learn how to integrate our knowledge of short- and long-term dynamics in time series data. This is the chapter where we will synthesize all our understanding of linear dependence. We will work with stationarity data (Chapters 6, 7, and 8) and nonstationary data (Chapter 10), with univariate and multivariate models (Chapter 11), and we will learn how all this is combined to eventually produce a forecast.

To motivate the forthcoming ideas, we will start by analyzing the interplay between economic models and forecasting models, and the relations between long- and short-term information. Macroeconomic models describe, in a stylized form, how economic activity takes place and the forces that are in play to push the economic variables toward a **long-term equilibrium** or steady state. Because of that, economic models could be very useful to design better forecasting models. However, we need to translate economic notions of *equilibrium* into statistical concepts that when implemented are relevant to the production of a forecast. We introduce the general setup of this chapter by contrasting the thinking of an economist with the thinking of a forecaster.

Let us start with the reasoning of an economist. Consider a simple economy that is in equilibrium: The demand for goods and services is equal to their supply. Producers manufacture the amount of goods and services desired by consumers. Let us call the level of production Y and the level of demand C. We say that the economy is in equilibrium when $Y = C$. In Figure 12.1, this is the 45 degree line.

In equilibrium, there is no incentive to increase production further than Y because there will be no demand for it or to increase consumption further than C because there will not be enough production to satisfy the demand. In equilibrium, we observe that the growth of production is equal to the growth of demand such that $Y = C$ holds indefinitely. This is also called the **steady state** of the economy. In your economics and business courses, you must have built more sophisticated macroeconomic models that consider a larger demand side coming not only from consumers but also from investors, government, and the external sector. For our purposes, suffice it to assume that all demand is concentrated in C. Assume that there is some external event, for instance, some natural disaster that reduces the level of production, so that $Y < C$ (below the 45 degree line). The economy is thrown

FIGURE 12.1
The Economist's Reality

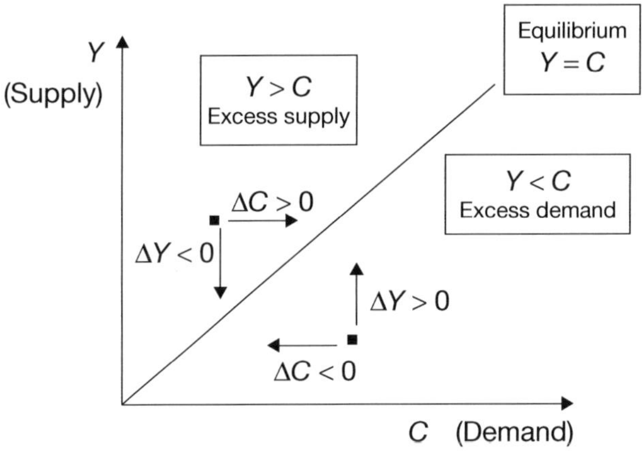

out of the equilibrium path. Would it be possible to achieve equilibrium again? If there are corrective forces in the economy, a new equilibrium will be achieved. In our case, the excess demand will be corrected either by decreasing consumption or increasing production or a combination of both. The economist will think that in the short term, increasing prices will partly correct the excess demand, and when new production processes are restored, a gradual increase in future production will take place. Thus, equilibrium will be reinstated by a combination of supply ($\Delta Y > 0$) and demand ($\Delta C < 0$) forces. However, these changes will not happen overnight but will take place over several periods of time and *in the short term*, the economy will be in disequilibrium. Similar arguments can be made if the disequilibrium is an excess supply, $Y > C$ (above the 45 degree line). In this case, producers will reduce prices in order to sell their present overproduction and they will lower their future production. Consumers observing lower prices will have the incentive to consume more. In the short run, a reduction in production ($\Delta Y < 0$) and an increase in consumption ($\Delta C > 0$) will remove the excess supply, pushing the economy back to *the long term* equilibrium path $Y = C$.

What is the forecaster's view? Our ultimate interest is to produce a forecast of production or/and demand. Our first step is to collect data on production and demand. For instance, the forecaster will face some time series as those in Figure 12.2. These are the quarterly real gross domestic product (GDP) and consumption expenditure for the U.S. economy from 1947:Q1 to 2004:Q2, which you will find at http://www.bea.gov.

REAL DATA: U.S. Real Gross Domestic Product and Real Consumption 1947–2004

What is the similarity of Figure 12.2 with Figure 12.1? At first sight, there is no similarity between the two plots. Figure 12.1 is a stylized plot of production versus consumption and Figure 12.2 is a time series plot. However, we could plot the time series of production against the time series of consumption. This scatter plot is in Figure 12.3.

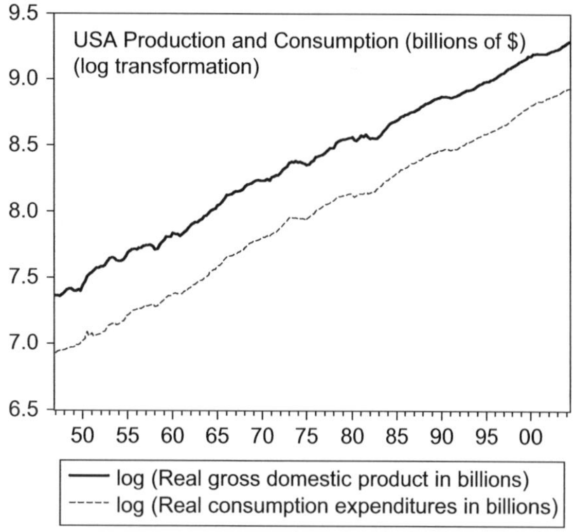

FIGURE 12.2 The Forecaster's Reality

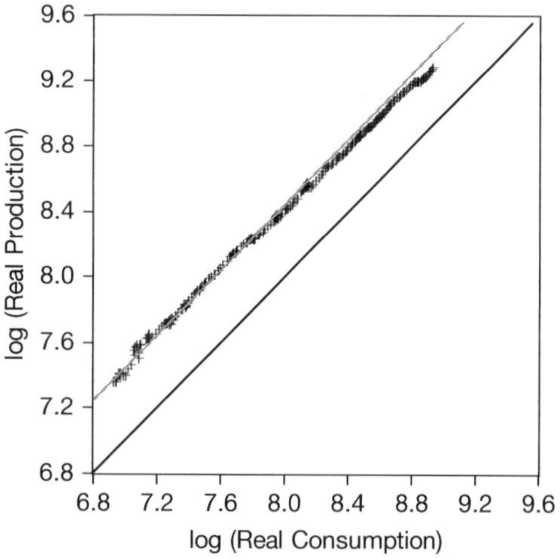

FIGURE 12.3 Production Versus Consumption

Figure 12.3 is much closer to Figure 12.1. The black solid line is the 45 degree line (slope equal to 1) and the data points are more or less aligned on the light grey line, which is parallel to the 45 degree line. The fact that the data are above the 45 degree line is not worrisome at all because in the demand side, we have considered only consumption. The important feature is the slope of the data. Notice that we have plotted the log of production and the log of consumption. The 45 degree line is where $\log Y = \log C$, implying that the growth rate of production is equal to the growth rate of consumption, that is,

$$\text{slope} = \frac{\frac{\Delta Y}{Y}}{\frac{\Delta C}{C}} = 1 \rightarrow \frac{\Delta Y}{Y} = \frac{\Delta C}{C}$$

FIGURE 12.4
Deviation from Equilibrium: $z_t \equiv \log Y_t - \log C_t$

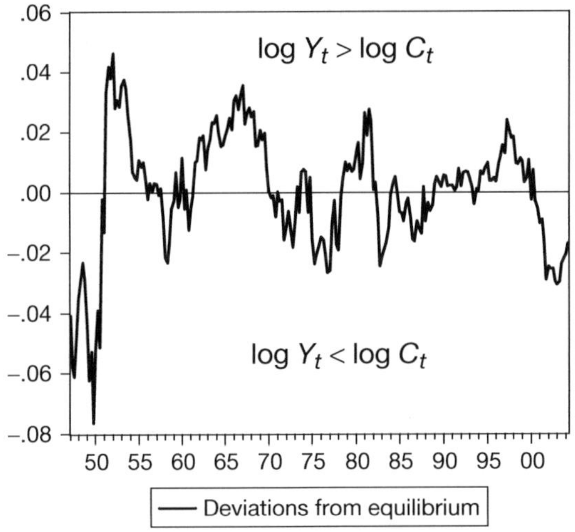

This is the long-term equilibrium or steady state of the economy: equal growth rates over time. We can understand the similarity with Figure 12.1. In that figure, the equilibrium is $Y = C$, which implies that there is equal growth, that is, $\Delta Y = \Delta C$ (the log transformation implies equal growth *rates*).

In Figure 12.3, although the data are very close to the light grey line (with slope equal to 1), observe that the data points are sometimes below and sometimes above the light grey line. This means that in some periods, production grows at a faster (or slower) rate than consumption; thus, the economy is in disequilibrium. Let us clarify this behavior by making the following interesting plot. Let us construct the time series difference $z_t \equiv logY_t - logC_t$ (minus deterministic components) and plot it[1] as in Figure 12.4.

If $\log Y_t - \log C_t = 0$, then $\frac{\Delta Y_t}{Y_t} = \frac{\Delta C_t}{C_t}$ and the economy is in equilibrium at time t.

If $\log Y_t - \log C_t > 0$, then $\frac{\Delta Y_t}{Y_t} > \frac{\Delta C_t}{C_t}$ and production grows faster than consumption.

If $\log Y_t - \log C_t < 0$, then $\frac{\Delta Y_t}{Y_t} < \frac{\Delta C_t}{C_t}$ and production grows slower than consumption. In the last two instances, the economy is in disequilibrium.

Figures 12.2, 12.3, and 12.4 are the forecaster's tools for understanding how the economist thinks. These three figures support the economist's reasoning, but they are

---

[1] Because the light grey line has a nonzero intercept, properly speaking, the difference $\log Y_t - \log C_t$ should account for a constant and/or any other deterministic component. In Figure 12.4, $z_t = \log Y_t - \log C_t - 0.475 + 0.0004t$. However, ignoring the deterministic components does not affect our arguments.

even more informative because they provide quantifiable information on the dynamics of the economy, which will be used to produce forecasts. For instance, we could say that, for the U.S. economy, the data seem to support the existence of a long-term equilibrium with episodes of disequilibrium that are rather long and persistent. At this point, we do not have enough tools to appreciate the joint dynamics of production and consumption, but we know that they are moving in the right direction because we observe that the disequilibria tend to be corrected.

In the following sections, we will learn (1) how to verify the existence of a long-term equilibrium (i.e., how to obtain the light grey line in Figure 12.3); (2) how to quantify the short-term dynamics, that is, the movements in the variables (i.e., $\Delta \log Y_t, \Delta \log C_t$) that correct the disequilibria in Figure 12.4; and (3) how to construct a forecast based on (1) and (2).

12.1 Finding a Long-Term Equilibrium Relationship

With the time series of production and consumption (Figure 12.2), the forecaster's objective is to analyze whether the data support the long-term equilibrium predicted by the economist. Why is this important for forecasting? If the objective is to forecast production, we could proceed as in the previous section, searching for a univariate model that fits the data best and use it as the basis of our forecast. However, if we know that there is an equilibrium relation that links the movements of consumption and production (the economist's argument), we can expand our modeling strategy to include consumption and incorporate its dynamics into the construction of the forecast for production, and vice versa, we could incorporate the dynamics of production to forecast consumption.

How can we find the long-term equilibrium relation? In Figure 12.3, we plotted $\log Y_t$ against $\log C_t$ and we have observed that the data points are scattered around the light grey line $\log Y = \alpha_0 + \alpha \log C$. Given our discussion at the beginning of the chapter, this line is the equilibrium relation whenever $\alpha = 1$. However, a priori, we do not know the values of the intercept and the slope of this line. Thus, our task is to estimate α_0 and α. This setting is very familiar to us because we can understand the problem as a regression model (Chapter 2). If we regress $\log Y_t$ on $\log C_t$, we have a linear regression model as

$$\log Y_t = \alpha_0 + \alpha \log C_t + z_t$$

where z_t is the error term of the regression. If $\alpha = 1$, we can interpret the error of the regression as follows. When $z_t = 0$, the data point falls on the line, that is, $\log Y_t = \alpha_0 + \log C_t$ (equilibrium); when $z_t > 0$, the data point is above the line, that is, $\log Y_t > \alpha_0 + \log C_t$ (disequilibrium); and when $z_t < 0$, the data point is below the line, that is, $\log Y_t < \alpha_0 + \log C_t$ (disequilibrium).

However, this regression framework is not as straightforward as it seems because of the nature of the time series that we are analyzing. Go back to Figure 12.2 and observe that both series, consumption and production, have an upward trend, that could be deterministic or stochastic. We could run a **unit root** test to decide on the nature of the trend. Because a trend is very obvious in both series, we run a unit root test for case III (Chapter 10) and proceed to estimate a model with a time trend and a constant. The full set of results is provided in Table 12.1. LGDP stands for $\log Y$ and LCONS for $\log C$. The Dickey-Fuller regression has been augmented by one lag of the first differences of log production and by two lags of the first differences of log consumption. Then the ADF statistic is compared with the 5% critical value (arrows), and because the value of the ADF test falls within the acceptance region of the test for both series, we conclude that a unit root cannot be rejected.

In summary, we have a regression $\log Y_t = \alpha_0 + \alpha \log C_t + z_t$ that has a dependent variable $\log Y_t$ and a regressor $\log C_t$ that are nonstationary processes. How common are these processes in economic data? Unit roots are omnipresent in economics and business time series data. Most of the macroeconomic aggregates such as gross national product (GNP), consumption, price indexes, interest rates, stock prices, exchange rates, and so on have a unit root. This is somehow expected because all these macroeconomic variables, although measuring different aspects of the economy, are intimately related. Think for a moment about the workings of an economic system. A compact description of an economy could be the following. Firms engage in production processes that employ labor and capital to produce goods and services, which are consumed by the people who, at the same time, supply labor as employees and capital as shareholders. Capital investments are determined by interest rates. Stock prices reflect information about the prospects of the firms. Excess demand or/and excess supply of goods determines the price level. Through trade, open economies affect exchange rates, which in turn may affect the price level and interest rates. In a word, the interdependence among the macroeconomic aggregates makes their corresponding time series to share common statistical properties.

Recall that in the classical linear regression model, the dependent and the explanatory variables are required to be stationary with constant means and variances. Thus, regressions with unit root processes such as

$$\log Y_t = \alpha_0 + \alpha \log C_t + z_t$$

violate this requirement with consequences for the interpretation and statistical analysis of the model.

Examining the preceding equation, two very important questions arise:

i. What are the properties of z_t? Is this also a nonstationary process?
ii. How can the intercept and the slope of the regression be estimated?

Both questions are related to the concept of equilibrium that we are looking for. If the preceding linear regression is in fact a long-term equilibrium relation, $\log Y_t$ and $\log C_t$ are tied to each other in such a way that one cannot wander indefinitely far apart from the other. For instance, if $\log Y_t$ moves up, we expect $\log C_t$ to move up too (see Figure 12.1 and follow the economist's reality). In this case, z_t, which is a linear

TABLE 12.1 Testing for Unit Root in Production and Consumption

Augmented Dickey-Fuller unit root test on LGDP			
ADF test statistic	-2.843711	1% Critical value*	-4.0013
		5% Critical value	-3.4307
		10% Critical value	-3.1387

*MacKinnon critical values for rejection of hypothesis of a unit root.

Augmented Dickey-Fuller test equation
Dependent variable: D(LGDP)
Method: Least squares
Sample(adjusted): 1947:Q3–2004:Q2
Included observations: 228 after adjusting endpoints

Variable	Coefficient	Std. Error	t-Statistic	Prob.
LGDP(-1)	-0.043454	0.015281	-2.843711	0.0049
D(LGDP(-1))	0.348971	0.062228	5.607964	0.0000
C	0.328285	0.113106	2.902463	0.0041
@TREND(1947:1)	0.000354	0.000128	2.769354	0.0061

R-squared	0.145037	Mean dependent var	0.008450
Adjusted R-squared	0.133587	S.D. dependent var	0.010025
S.E. of regression	0.009332	Akaike information criterion	-6.493411
Sum squared resid	0.019506	Schwarz criterion	-6.433247
Log likelihood	744.2489	F-statistic	12.66658
Durbin-Watson stat	2.086753	Prob(F-statistic)	0.000000

Augmented Dickey-Fuller unit root test on LCONS			
ADF Test Statistic	-2.493565	1% Critical Value*	-4.0015
		5% Critical Value	-3.4307
		10% Critical Value	-3.1387

*MacKinnon critical values for rejection of hypothesis of a unit root.

Augmented Dickey-Fuller Test Equation
Dependent Variable: D(LCONS)
Method: Least Squares
Sample(adjusted): 1947:4 2004:2
Included observations: 227 after adjusting endpoints

(continued)

TABLE 12.1 Testing for Unit Root in Production and Consumption (*continued*)

Variable	Coefficient	Std. Error	t-Statistic	Prob.
LCONS(-1)	-0.039022	0.015649	-2.493565	0.0134
D(LCONS(-1))	0.034437	0.064008	0.538001	0.5911
D(LCONS(-2))	0.298994	0.063944	4.675910	0.0000
C	0.276544	0.108304	2.553418	0.0113
@TREND(1947:1)	0.000341	0.000138	2.468731	0.0143

R-squared	0.104383	Mean dependent var	0.008757
Adjusted R-squared	0.088245	S.D. dependent var	0.008482
S.E. of regression	0.008099	Akaike info criterion	-6.772317
Sum squared resid	0.014563	Schwarz criterion	-6.696877
Log likelihood	773.6579	F-statistic	6.468433
Durbin-Watson stat	2.009563	Prob(F-statistic)	0.000061

combination of $\log Y_t$ and $\log C_t$ (i.e., $z_t = \log Y_t - \alpha_0 - \log C_t$), must be a stationary process because the two nonstationary processes are reacting to each other's movements and not letting the difference $\log Y_t - \log C_t$ drift away. We have reached a very important concept: **cointegration**.

> **For any two unit root processes, say Y_t and X_t, we say that they are cointegrated if there is a linear combination Z_t of these two processes (i.e., $Z_t = Y_t - \alpha_0 - \alpha\, X_t$) that is stationary.**

Cointegration is the statistical notion that corresponds to the economic notion of equilibrium. For every t, the **cointegrating relation** $Y_t = \alpha_0 + \alpha X_t + z_t$ indicates whether there is equilibrium ($z_t = 0$) or disequilibrium ($z_t > 0$ or $z_t < 0$). The process z_t is called the **disequilibrium error** that measures how far the system Y_t, X_t is from the equilibrium path. Figure 12.4 exhibits the disequilibrium error corresponding to the long-term equilibrium between production and consumption.

From the statistical point of view, it must be the case that if z_t is a stationary process, the stochastic trend that is present in both Y_t and X_t processes must have been removed. Because z_t is a linear combination of Y_t and X_t (i.e. $z_t = Y_t - \alpha_0 - \alpha X_t$), the only possibility for the trend to disappear is that Y_t and X_t share the same stochastic trend, which must be canceled out when Y_t and X_t are combined as in z_t. Thus, the stochastic trend that runs throughout these variables is a manifestation of common information: We say that *cointegrated variables share a common stochastic trend.* In our analysis of production and consumption, their common stochastic trend is very likely related to technological progress and population growth.

Testing for cointegration is equivalent to testing for long-term equilibrium among variables. From the definition of cointegration, it seems that an appropriate test is to evaluate the potential **nonstationarity** of z_t. We formulate the hypothesis as

$$H_0: \text{noncointegration } (z_t \text{ has a unit root})$$
$$H_1: \text{cointegration } (z_t \text{ is stationary})$$

If we reject the null hypothesis, z_t is stationary, and consequently, Y_t and X_t are cointegrated, which is equivalent to say, that there is a long-term equilibrium between Y_t and X_t.

The following procedure provides a good strategy to test for the existence of a long-term equilibrium:

1. Test for unit root in Y_t and X_t.
2. If there is a unit root in both Y_t and X_t, run the regression $Y_t = \alpha_0 + \alpha\, X_t + z_t$; estimation by least squares produces a superconsistent[2] estimator of the slope and a consistent estimator of the intercept, although their asymptotic distributions are not standard. This is due to the nonstationarity of the Y_t and X_t processes.
3. Compute the residuals of the OLS regression, that is, $\hat{z}_t = Y_t - \hat{\alpha}_0 - \hat{\alpha}\, X_t$.
4. Run an augmented Dickey-Fuller test on $\hat{z}_t$; if there is not a unit root (rejection of the null hypothesis), the residual is stationary and there is cointegration: there exists long-term equilibrium. Although an ADF statistic is constructed in the usual way, we should be aware that the test is performed on the time series $\hat{z}_t$ that has been generated through estimation in step 3 (as opposed to real data). This means that further uncertainty is added to the statistical procedure and the usual ADF critical values will not be appropriate to test for unit root. A new set of critical values needs to be tabulated to take into account the uncertainty introduced by the residual. Table 12.2 provides 5% critical values for the model

$$Y_t = \alpha_0 + \alpha\, X_t + z_t$$
$$\Delta \hat{z}_t = \gamma\, \hat{z}_{t-1} + \varepsilon_t$$

Let us implement this procedure to test for cointegration between production and consumption. We have already run the first step by conducting unit root tests and we have concluded that both series are nonstationary. Step 2 consists of running a regression as

$$\log Y_t = \alpha_0 + \alpha \log C_t + z_t$$

The estimation results and the calculation of residuals (step 3) are:

$$\log Y_t = 0.84 + 0.95 \log C_t + \hat{z}_t$$
$$\hat{z}_t = \log Y_t - 0.84 - 0.95 \log C_t$$

---

[2] *Superconsistency* is an asymptotic (large sample) property of the estimator that guarantees that there is convergence of the estimator to a population parameter. The prefix *super* means that the convergence rate is faster than that of estimators based on stationary processes.

TABLE 12.2 Critical Values to Test for Cointegration[3]

Sample size T	**5% critical values of ADF test** $= \dfrac{\hat{\gamma}}{\hat{\sigma}_{\hat{\gamma}}}$ **for** H_0: noncointegration (z_t has a unit root) H_1: cointegration (z_t is stationary)
25	−3.5907
50	−3.4606
100	−3.3982
250	−3.3617
500	−3.3496

Table 12.3 provides the estimation in more detail. The black rectangle collects the only useful information. This is not a classical regression model; recall that we are dealing with nonstationary processes and the least-squares estimators do not have standard distributions like the normal or the Student-t. However, given that the estimators are consistent, the residuals are also consistent; they are good approximations to the population errors.

TABLE 12.3 Estimation of the Cointegrating Relation

Dependent Variable: LGDP
Method: Least squares
Sample: 1947:Q1 2004:Q2
Included observations: 230

Variable	Coefficient	Std. Error	t-Statistic	Prob.
C	0.836611	0.018185	46.00562	0.0000
LCONS	0.947909	0.002282	415.3304	0.0000

R-squared	0.998680	Mean dependent var	8.368959
Adjusted R-squared	0.998674	S.D. dependent var	0.556685
S.E. of regression	0.020270	Akaike info criterion	4.950726
Sum squared resid	0.093676	Schwarz criterion	-4.920830
Log likelihood	571.3335	F-statistic	172499.4
Durbin-Watson stat	0.181269	Prob (F-statistic)	0.000000

[3]The following critical values have been obtained from the following equation (MacKinnon's response surface): $-3.3377 - 5.967/T - 8.98/T^2$ where T is the sample size. As is indicated in the text, these critical values are valid only when the cointegration equation has two variables, Y and X, and includes a constant.

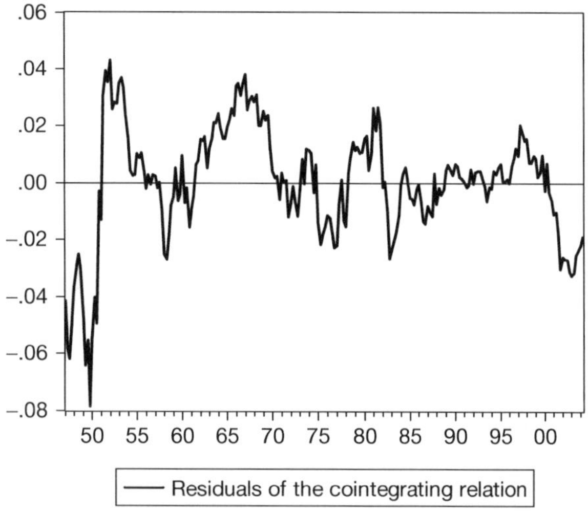

FIGURE 12.5 Residuals $\hat{z}_t$ of the Cointegrating Relation

The time series plot of residuals $\hat{z}_t$ is presented in Figure 12.5. Compare it with Figure 12.4. The figures are virtually identical.

Finally, in step 4, we run an ADF test on the residuals of the potential cointegrating relation. The test results are provided in Table 12.4.

Note that we have included four lags of the first differences of the residuals. The ADF test is equal to −3.5081, but we have crossed out the critical values provided by the EViews software. These critical values are good only when the test is performed on real data. Recall that the residuals are generated data. Thus, we go to the 5% critical values provided in step 4 (Table 12.2). Our sample size is 225, and the 5% critical value is close to −3.3617. Compare this critical value with that in Table 12.4, which is −1.9411; we see that it is substantially larger in magnitude, indicating the uncertainty brought up by generated data as opposed to real data. Now because $-3.5081 < -3.3617$, we reject the null hypothesis of unit root, which means that we reject noncointegration. Hence, the residuals are stationary and there is a long-term equilibrium between log(production) and log(consumption).

The forecaster has found in the data an equilibrium given by $\log Y = 0.84 + 0.95$ log. This is practically the equilibrium postulated by the economist. Furthermore, the residual of the cointegrating relation is the disequilibrium error, which will play a very important role in the next section where we will study the development of a model for the short-term dynamics of production and consumption.

A final note: Sometimes the long-term equilibrium is known or it is given by economic theory; in this case, we can directly impose the equilibrium restriction and proceed to test for cointegration. For instance, if we follow the economist's reality, the long-term equilibrium between production and consumption should be $\log Y_t = \alpha_0 + \log C_t$ so that in equilibrium both consumption and production grow at the same rate. This is as much as saying that in the cointegration relation, we need $\alpha = 1$. We can proceed to impose this

TABLE 12.4 Testing the Stationarity of the Residuals

Augmented Dickey-Fuller Unit Root Test on Z

ADF Test Statistic	-3.508121	1% Critical Value*	-2.5747
		5% Critical Value	-1.9411
		10% Critical Value	-1.6164

*MacKinnon critical values for rejection of hypothesis of a unit root.

Augmented Dickey-Fuller test equation
Dependent variable: D(Z)
Method: Least squares
Sample(adjusted): 1948:2–2004:2
Included observations: 225 after adjusting endpoints

Variable	Coefficient	Std. Error	t-Statistic	Prob.
Z(-1)	-0.106201	0.030273	-3.508121	0.0005
D(Z(-1))	-0.076846	0.064500	-1.191406	0.2348
D(Z(-2))	0.225750	0.063838	3.536289	0.0005
D(Z(-3))	0.143224	0.065098	2.200142	0.0288
D(Z(-4))	-0.156098	0.064713	-2.412158	0.0167

R-squared	0.148810	Mean dependent var	7.70E-05
Adjusted R-squared	0.133334	S.D. dependent var	0.008545
S.E. of regression	0.007955	Akaike info criterion	-6.808042
Sum squared resid	0.013922	Schwarz criterion	-6.732129
Log likelihood	770.9048	Durbin-Watson stat	1.992696

restriction and calculate the difference $z_t = \log Y_t - \log C_t$ so that the test for cointegration is performed directly on z_t, which is not generated data any longer but observable data. In this case, we do not need new critical values as those in Table 12.2 and we will use the critical values of the ADF test directly to evaluate whether z_t is stationary (there is cointegration) or has a unit root (there is not cointegration and the proposed long run equilibrium does not exist).

12.2 Quantifying Short-Term Dynamics: Vector Error Correction Model

At this point, the forecaster has confirmed that there is equilibrium between two variables. Analyzing the disequilibrium error (Figure 12.4 for the case of production and consumption), we observe that the economy is most of the time in disequilibrium (sometimes there is excess supply, $\log Y_t > \log C_t$; and sometimes there is excess

FIGURE 12.6
Short-Term Dynamics

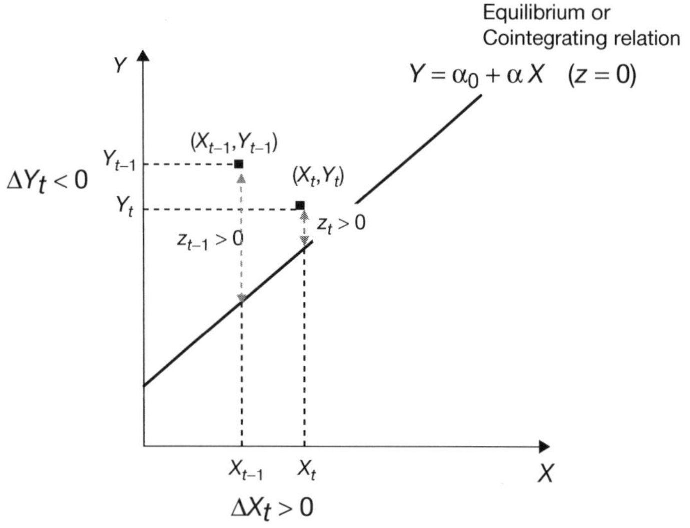

demand, $\log Y_t < \log C_t$). However, the disequilibria are corrected because the variables are attracted to the equilibrium path. This is the cointegrating relation. In this section, our objective is to quantify the short-term movements that correct the disequilibrium and move the variables toward the cointegrating relation.

Let us examine Figure 12.6. Consider two processes Y_t and X_t that are cointegrated. The cointegrating relation is $Y = \alpha_0 + \alpha X$. Assume that the system is at time $t-1$ and the value of the processes is given by the point (X_{t-1}, Y_{t-1}). At this point, the system is out of equilibrium by as much as $z_{t-1} > 0$. The question is how will the system move from $t-1$ to t.

Because the cointegrating relation exercises a gravitational pull, it is expected that the system will try to correct the disequilibrium of the previous period and will move toward the equilibrium path. Suppose that the system moves to a new point (X_t, Y_t). To reach this point, X has increased $\Delta X_t > 0$, and Y has decreased $\Delta Y_t < 0$, but in doing so, we observe that there is still a disequilibrium, z_t, although of smaller magnitude ($z_{t-1} > z_t$). From one period to the next, the system, has partially corrected itself. If there is no other shock, the system will keep correcting the disequilibrium error until it reaches the equilibrium path, and once there, it will not have any incentive to move out. Given this argument, it seems sensible to write the short-term dynamics, in the simplest way, as in the following model:

$$\Delta X_t = \gamma_1 z_{t-1} + \varepsilon_{1,t}$$

$$\Delta Y_t = \gamma_2 z_{t-1} + \varepsilon_{2,t}$$

The coefficients γ_1 and γ_2, known as the **adjustment coefficients**, indicate how much of the previous disequilibrium error is corrected on moving from $t-1$ to t. The error terms $\varepsilon_{1,t}$ and $\varepsilon_{2,t}$ represent idiosyncratic uncertainty; these are the innovations that cannot be predicted (white noise processes), and they can shock the system anytime (remember that X_t and Y_t are stochastic processes). We will assume that $\varepsilon_{1,t}$ and $\varepsilon_{2,t}$ are normally distributed, $N(0, \sigma^2_{\varepsilon_1})$ and $N(0, \sigma^2_{\varepsilon_2})$, and they may be contemporaneously correlated with each other so that cov $(\varepsilon_{1,t}, \varepsilon_{2,t}) \neq 0$. This model is known as *a* **vector error correction model (VEC)**. Guess where the name comes from!

The VEC model can be expanded to acknowledge two potential features: (1) that the variables ΔY_t and ΔX_t may be autocorrelated so that there is temporal dependence that needs to be modeled, and (2) that ΔY_t and ΔX_t may be cross-correlated so that past values of ΔY_t affect ΔX_t, and, vice versa, past values of ΔX_t affect ΔY_t. Taking into account (1) and (2), we can write a general vector error correction model as

$$\Delta X_t = c_1 + \gamma_1 z_{t-1} + \beta_{11}\Delta X_{t-1} + \beta_{12}\Delta X_{t-2} + \cdots + \phi_{11}\Delta Y_{t-1} + \phi_{12}\Delta Y_{t-2} + \cdots\cdots + \varepsilon_{1,t}$$
$$\Delta Y_t = c_2 + \gamma_2 z_{t-1} + \beta_{21}\Delta X_{t-1} + \beta_{22}\Delta X_{t-2} + \cdots + \phi_{21}\Delta Y_{t-1} + \phi_{22}\Delta Y_{t-2} + \cdots\cdots + \varepsilon_{2,t}$$

This system is very similar to a VAR model (Chapter 11) with an extra term that is the error correction term z_{t-1}.

The characteristics of this VEC model are:

1. It is a *bivariate system* because we model two stochastic processes jointly.
2. Each equation has an *autoregressive structure* with the same regressors and the same number of lags, similar to the VAR models that we saw in Chapter 11.
3. All the variables in the left- and right-hand sides are *stationary*; recall that the disequilibrium error z_{t-1} is stationary because the variables are cointegrated, and the first differences of a unit root process, ΔY_t and ΔX_t, are also stationary.
4. An error correction model must have at least one *adjustment coefficient different from zero*, $\gamma_1 \neq 0$ or (and) $\gamma_2 \neq 0$; otherwise, the variables are not cointegrated.

The estimation of an error correction model is very simple. Ordinary least squares is as much as we need. Once we choose the number of lags to be included in the model, we run least squares equation by equation. Model selection criteria such as (AIC) and (SIC) (Chapter 8) will help to select the optimal number of lags. The disequilibrium error has already been estimated when we tested for cointegration so that we need only to plug $\hat{z}_{t-1}$ in each equation of the model.

Let us estimate the error correction model for production and consumption. Remember that we have already estimated the disequilibrium error:

$$\log Y_t = 0.84 + 0.95 \log C_t + \hat{z}_t$$
$$\hat{z}_t = \log Y_t - 0.84 - 0.95 \log C_t$$

We plug in the estimated disequilibrium error $\hat{z}_{t-1}$ in each equation of the EC model, and in order to choose the number of lags, we run several models with different lags. The results are displayed in Table 12.5. We will select the model for which the AIC and SIC have the smallest values.

The AIC selects either two or three lags, but the SIC selects a more parsimonious specification, either one or three lags. The equation for consumption seems to require

TABLE 12.5 Choice of Number of Lags in VEC

Number of lags	AIC		SIC	
	$\Delta \log Y_t$	$\Delta \log C_t$	$\Delta \log Y_t$	$\Delta \log C_t$
1	–6.54	–6.73	**–6.49**	–6.67
2	**–6.57**	–6.75	–6.48	–6.66
3	–6.56	**–6.81**	–6.43	**–6.69**
4	–6.55	–6.80	–6.39	–6.65
5	–6.53	–6.79	–6.34	–6.60

more lags than the equation for production. Three specifications (one lag, two lags, and three lags) of the EC model may be run; select the one for which the residuals $\hat{\varepsilon}_{1,t}$ and $\hat{\varepsilon}_{2,t}$ seem to be closer to white noise processes. The final model that we have selected has two lags. The estimation results are presented in Table 12.6.

Writing these results in equation form, we have

$$\Delta \log Y_t = .003 - 0.11\, z_{t-1} + 0.15 \Delta \log Y_{t-1} + 0.04 \Delta \log Y_{t-2} + 0.27 \Delta \log C_{t-1} + 0.17 \Delta \log C_{t-2} + \hat{\varepsilon}_{2,t}$$

$$\Delta \log C_t = .006 - 0.005\, z_{t-1} + 0.14 \Delta \log Y_{t-1} - 0.07 \Delta \log Y_{t-2} - 0.06 \Delta \log C_{t-1} + 0.27 \Delta \log C_{t-2} + \hat{\varepsilon}_{1,t}$$

These are classical regressions, and the estimators have standard distributions; asymptotically, the OLS estimators are normally distributed so that we can use t-ratios and F-statistics to test any hypothesis about the coefficients of the model. Hence, the interpretation of the estimation output runs in the usual fashion as we did for VAR systems. Observe that the adjustment coefficient is only statistically significant in the production equation. This means that the movements in production mainly carry the system toward equilibrium. In every period, 11% of the disequilibrium error is corrected. In addition, note that the dynamics of production are relevant in the consumption equation and, vice versa, the dynamics of consumption are important in the production equation. This dependence as well as the effect of the error correction term will be exploited in the construction of the forecast for production and consumption.

The link between cointegration and error correction models is stated in a very important theorem known as the *Granger representation theorem.* A simplified version of the theorem is as follows:

Consider two stochastic processes, Y_t and X_t, *both characterized as unit root processes, that is,* ***I(1)***. *If* Y_t and X_t *are cointegrated, then*

1. *There exists a linear combination of* Y_t and X_t *such as* $z_t = Y_t - \alpha_0 - \alpha X_t$ *that is a stationary process, that is,* ***I(0)***.
2. *There exists an error correction representation as*

$$\Delta X_t = c_1 + \gamma_1 z_{t-1} + \beta_{11} \Delta X_{t-1} + \beta_{12} \Delta X_{t-2} + \cdots + \phi_{11} \Delta Y_{t-1} + \phi_{12} \Delta Y_{t-2} + \cdots + \varepsilon_{1,t}$$

TABLE 12.6 Estimation of VEC

Dependent variable: D(LGDP)
Method: Least Squares
Sample(adjusted): 1947:Q4–2004:Q2
Included observations: 227 after adjusting endpoints

Variable	Coefficient	Std. Error	t-Statistic	Prob.
C	0.003048	0.001053	2.893813	0.0042
Z(-1)	-0.112269	0.031380	-3.577739	0.0004
D(LGDP(-1))	0.150254	0.079990	1.878402	0.0616
D(LGDP(-2))	0.043939	0.075205	0.584260	0.5596
D(LCONS(-1))	0.273711	0.090891	3.011415	0.0029
D(LCONS(-2))	0.166686	0.090854	1.834661	0.0679

R-squared	0.217937	Mean dependent var	0.008489
Adjusted R-squared	0.200243	S.D. dependent var	0.010030
S.E. of regression	0.008970	Akaike info criterion	-6.563852
Sum squared resid	0.017781	Schwarz criterion	-6.473325
Log likelihood	750.9972	F-statistic	12.31716
Durbin-Watson stat	1.970518	Prob (F-statistic)	0.000000

Dependent variable: D(LCONS)
Method: Least squares
Sample(adjusted): 1947:Q4–2004:Q2
Included observations: 227 after adjusting endpoints

Variable	Coefficient	Std. Error	t-Statistic	Prob.
C	0.006345	0.000956	6.637523	0.0000
Z(-1)	-0.004944	0.028479	-0.173603	0.8623
D(LGDP(-1))	0.143919	0.072594	1.982505	0.0487
D(LGDP(-2))	-0.074316	0.068251	-1.088863	0.2774
D(LCONS(-1))	-0.064761	0.082488	-0.785101	0.4332
D(LCONS(-2))	0.271938	0.082454	3.298067	0.0011

R-squared	0.099334	Mean dependent var	0.008757
Adjusted R-squared	0.078957	S.D. dependent var	0.08482
S.E. of regression	0.008140	Akaike info criterion	-6.757885
Sum squared resid	0.014645	Schwarz criterion	-6.667357
Log likelihood	773.0199	F-statistic	4.874789
Durbin-Watson stat	2.037702	Prob(F-statistic)	0.000299

$$\Delta Y_t = c_2 + \gamma_2 z_{t-1} + \beta_{21}\Delta X_{t-1} + \beta_{22}\Delta X_{t-2} + \cdots + \phi_{21}\Delta Y_{t-1} + \phi_{22}\Delta Y_{t-2} + \cdots + \varepsilon_{2,t}$$

with $\gamma_1 \neq 0$ or (and) $\gamma_2 \neq 0$.

It is also true that if there is a VEC model for ΔY_t and ΔX_t, then the processes Y_t and X_t must be cointegrated.

12.3 Constructing the Forecast

The VEC model is a system of autoregressive processes. In Chapters 7 and 11, we studied univariate and multivariate (VAR) autoregressive processes, respectively. In both instances, we calculated their respective forecasts in a recursive fashion. In this section, we will follow a similar approach because the VEC is a special case of a VAR system. In order to keep the algebra at the simplest level, let us choose the simplest VEC model:

$$\Delta X_t = \gamma_1 z_{t-1} + \varepsilon_{1,t}$$
$$\Delta Y_t = \gamma_2 z_{t-1} + \varepsilon_{2,t}$$
$$\text{with } z_{t-1} = Y_{t-1} - \alpha_0 - \alpha X_{t-1}$$

Our objective is to forecast either the changes in Y_t and X_t (i.e., ΔY_t and ΔX_t), or to forecast the level of Y_t and X_t. But both objectives are related because if we were to forecast ΔY_t and ΔX_t, we would need z_{t-1}, which in turn depends on the levels of Y_{t-1} and X_{t-1}. Let us focus on the forecast of the levels of the nonstationary series X_{t+h} and Y_{t+h}.

Because the VEC model is in first differences (stationary form), it is helpful to convert it to levels. We need only to substitute $\Delta X_t = X_t - X_{t-1}$, $\Delta Y_t = Y_t - Y_{t-1}$, and the disequilibrium error z_{t-1} in the VEC model to obtain a system such as

$$X_t - X_{t-1} = \gamma_1 (Y_{t-1} - \alpha_0 - \alpha X_{t-1}) + \varepsilon_{1,t}$$
$$Y_t - Y_{t-1} = \gamma_2 (Y_{t-1} - \alpha_0 - \alpha X_{t-1}) + \varepsilon_{2,t}$$

Rearranging terms, we write

$$X_t = \gamma_1 Y_{t-1} + (1 - \gamma_1 \alpha) X_{t-1} - \gamma_1 \alpha_0 + \varepsilon_{1,t}$$
$$Y_t = (1 + \gamma_2) Y_{t-1} - \gamma_2 \alpha X_{t-1} - \gamma_2 \alpha_0 + \varepsilon_{2,t}$$

Now the system is in levels, this is known as a **restricted vector autoregressive system** because the coefficients are restricted by the cointegration property of the variables. We will base the construction of the forecast on this system.

Assume that the forecaster has a quadratic loss function so that the optimal forecast is a conditional mean; recall that $f_{t,h} = \mu_{t+h|t} = E(Y_{t+h} | I_t)$ for $h = 1, 2, \ldots s$. The information set runs up to time t and we are interested in two forecasting horizons, $h = 1$ and $h = 2$.

The value of the system at the future time $t + 1$ is

$$X_{t+1} = \gamma_1 Y_t + (1 - \gamma_1 \alpha) X_t - \gamma_1 \alpha_0 + \varepsilon_{1,t+1}$$
$$Y_{t+1} = (1 + \gamma_2) Y_t - \gamma_2 \alpha X_t - \gamma_2 \alpha_0 + \varepsilon_{2,t+1},$$

and at time $t+2$ is

$$X_{t+2} = \gamma_1 Y_{t+1} + (1-\gamma_1\alpha)X_{t+1} - \gamma_1\alpha_0 + \varepsilon_{1,t+2}$$
$$Y_{t+2} = (1+\gamma_2)Y_{t+1} - \gamma_2\alpha X_{t+1} - \gamma_2\alpha_0 + \varepsilon_{2,t+2}$$

What are the optimal point forecasts $f_{t,1}$ and $f_{t,2}$?

$$\begin{cases} f_{t,1}^X = \mu_{t+1|t}^X = E(X_{t+1}|I_t) = E(\gamma_1 Y_t + (1-\gamma_1\alpha)X_t - \gamma_1\alpha_0 + \varepsilon_{1,t+1}|I_t) \\ \qquad = \gamma_1 Y_t + (1-\gamma_1\alpha)X_t - \gamma_1\alpha_0 \\ f_{t,1}^Y = \mu_{t+1|t}^Y = E(Y_{t+1}|I_t) = E((1+\gamma_2)Y_t - \gamma_2\alpha X_t - \gamma_2\alpha_0 + \varepsilon_{2,t+1}|I_t) \\ \qquad = (1+\gamma_2)Y_t - \gamma_2\alpha X_t - \gamma_2\alpha_0 \end{cases}$$

$$\begin{cases} f_{t,2}^X = \mu_{t+2|t}^X = E(X_{t+2}|I_t) = E(\gamma_1 Y_{t+1} + (1-\gamma_1\alpha)X_{t+1} - \gamma_1\alpha_0 + \varepsilon_{1,t+2}|I_t) \\ \qquad = \gamma_1 f_{t,1}^Y + (1-\gamma_1\alpha)f_{t,1}^X - \gamma_1\alpha_0 \\ f_{t,2}^Y = \mu_{t+2|t}^Y = E(Y_{t+2}|I_t) = E((1+\gamma_2)Y_{t+1} - \gamma_2\alpha X_{t+1} - \gamma_2\alpha_0 + \varepsilon_{2,t+2}|I_t) \\ \qquad = (1+\gamma_2)f_{t,1}^Y - \gamma_2\alpha f_{t,1}^X - \gamma_2\alpha_0 \end{cases}$$

Observe the recursive nature of the forecast, which is already familiar to us. For forecasting horizon $t+2$, the forecast depends on the forecast of the previous period. Following the same recursion, we could calculate the forecast for any other horizon.

What are the 1-period- and 2-period-ahead forecast errors$e_{t,1}$ and $e_{t,1}$?
The difference between the realized values (X_{t+1}, Y_{t+1}) and (X_{t+2}, Y_{t+2}) and their respective forecast values$f_{t,1}$, $f_{t,2}$

$$\begin{cases} e_{t,1}^X = X_{t+1} - f_{t,1}^X = \gamma_1 Y_t + (1-\gamma_1\alpha)X_t - \gamma_1\alpha_0 + \varepsilon_{1,t+1} \\ \qquad - \gamma_1 Y_t - (1-\gamma_1\alpha)X_t + \gamma_1\alpha_0 = \varepsilon_{1,t+1} \\ e_{t,1}^Y = Y_{t+1} - f_{t,1}^Y = (1+\gamma_2)Y_t - \gamma_2\alpha X_t - \gamma_2\alpha_0 + \varepsilon_{2,t+1} \\ \qquad - (1+\gamma_2)Y_t + \gamma_2\alpha X_t + \gamma_2\alpha_0 = \varepsilon_{2,t+1} \end{cases}$$

$$\begin{cases} e_{t,2}^X = X_{t+2} - f_{t,2}^X = \gamma_1 Y_{t+1} + (1-\gamma_1\alpha)X_{t+1} - \gamma_1\alpha_0 + \varepsilon_{1,t+2} \\ \qquad - \gamma_1 f_{t,1}^Y - (1-\gamma_1\alpha)f_{t,1}^X + \gamma_1\alpha_0 \\ \qquad = \gamma_1 e_{t,1}^Y + (1-\gamma_1\alpha)e_{t,1}^X + \varepsilon_{1,t+2} \\ e_{t,2}^Y = Y_{t+2} - f_{t,2}^Y = (1+\gamma_2)Y_t - \gamma_2\alpha X_t - \gamma_2\alpha_0 + \varepsilon_{2,t+2} \\ \qquad - (1+\gamma_2)f_{t,1}^Y + \gamma_2\alpha f_{t,1}^X + \gamma_2\alpha_0 \\ \qquad = (1+\gamma_2)e_{t,1}^Y - \gamma_2\alpha e_{t,1}^X + \varepsilon_{2,t+2} \end{cases}$$

Observe that the forecast errors are also calculated recursively.

What is the uncertainty associated with the forecast?
The variance of the forecast error.

$$\begin{cases} \sigma_{X,t+1|t}^2 = \mathrm{var}(X_{t+1}|I_t) = E(X_{t+1} - f_{t,1}^X|I_t)^2 = E(e_{t,1}^X)^2 = E(\varepsilon_{1,t+1}^2) = \sigma_{\varepsilon_1}^2 \\ \sigma_{Y,t+1|t}^2 = \mathrm{var}(Y_{t+1}|I_t) = E(Y_{t+1} - f_{t,1}^Y|I_t)^2 = E(e_{t,1}^Y)^2 = E(\varepsilon_{2,t+1}^2) = \sigma_{\varepsilon_2}^2 \end{cases}$$

$$\begin{cases} \sigma^2_{X,t+2|t} = \text{var}(X_{t+2} \mid I_t) = E(X_{t+2} - f^X_{t,2} \mid I_t)^2 = E(e^X_{t,2})^2 \\ \qquad = \sigma^2_{\varepsilon_1}(1 + (1 - \gamma_1\alpha)^2) + \gamma_1^2\sigma^2_{\varepsilon_2} + 2(1 - \gamma_1\alpha)\gamma_1\text{cov}(\varepsilon_1, \varepsilon_2) \\ \sigma^2_{Y,t+2|t} = \text{var}(Y_{t+2} \mid I_t) = E(Y_{t+2} - f^Y_{t,2} \mid I_t)^2 = E(e^Y_{t,2})^2 \\ \qquad = \sigma^2_{\varepsilon_2}(1 + (1 + \gamma_2)^2) + \gamma_2^2\alpha^2\sigma^2_{\varepsilon_1} - 2(1 + \gamma_2)\gamma_2\alpha\,\text{cov}(\varepsilon_1, \varepsilon_2) \end{cases}$$

Observe that the covariance terms show up because the error terms of the two equations can be contemporaneously correlated.

What is the density forecast?
It is the conditional probability density function of the system at the future date t+1. Recall that we have assumed normally distributed white noises. Because we deal with a system, we have the marginal density of each variable and the joint bivariate density. Here we report only the 1-period-ahead marginal density forecast for each variable

$$f(X_{t+1} \mid I_t) \rightarrow N(\mu^X_{t+1|t}, \sigma^2_{X,\,t+1|t})$$
$$f(Y_{t+1} \mid I_t) \rightarrow N(\mu^Y_{t+1|t}, \sigma^2_{Y,\,t+1|t})$$

If the VEC model includes additional dynamics, the algebra becomes more complicated, but the principles to construct the forecast for the levels of the variables remain the same. Point forecasts and forecast errors obey recursive relations. Because the variables X_t and Y_t are nonstationary, their forecasts must have the same characteristics as those of unit root processes, which we studied in Chapter 10. For any horizon, their forecasts will be a function of the most recent values in the information set, that is (X_t, Y_t), and the uncertainty of the forecasts will increase with the forecasting horizon.

REAL DATA: Forecasting the U.S. Real Gross Domestic Product and Real Consumption Expenditures 2004.Q3–2008.Q4

Let us construct the forecast for production and consumption based on the VEC model estimated in the previous section:

$$\begin{aligned} \Delta\log Y_t &= .003 - 0.11\,z_{t-1} + 0.15\Delta\log Y_{t-1} + 0.04\Delta\log Y_{t-2} + 0.27\Delta\log C_{t-1} \\ &\quad + 0.17\Delta\log C_{t-2} + \hat{\varepsilon}_{2,t} \\ \Delta\log C_t &= .006 - 0.005\,z_{t-1} + 0.14\Delta\log Y_{t-1} - 0.07\Delta\log Y_{t-2} - 0.06\Delta\log C_{t-1} \\ &\quad + 0.27\Delta\log C_{t-2} + \hat{\varepsilon}_{1,t} \end{aligned}$$

with $\hat{z}_{t-1} = \log Y_{t-1} - 0.84 - 0.95\,\log C_{t-1}$.
Converting the VEC model to a model in levels, we have

$$\begin{aligned} \log Y_t &= 0.11 + 1.03\log Y_{t-1} - 0.10\log Y_{t-2} - 0.04\log Y_{t-3} + 0.38\log C_{t-1} \\ &\quad - 0.11\log C_{t-2} - 0.17\log C_{t-3} + \hat{\varepsilon}_{2,t} \end{aligned}$$

$$\log C_t = 0.01 + 0.14\log Y_{t-1} - 0.22\log Y_{t-2} + 0.07\log Y_{t-3} + 0.94\log C_{t-1} + 0.34\log C_{t-2} - 0.27\log C_{t-3} + \hat{\varepsilon}_{1,t}$$

with

$$\text{var}(\hat{\varepsilon}_{2,t}) = 0.0000802, \text{var}(\hat{\varepsilon}_{1,t}) = 0.0000665, \text{ and } \text{cov}(\hat{\varepsilon}_{2,t}, \hat{\varepsilon}_{1,t}) = 0.0000426.$$

Let us consider an information set up to $t = 2004$: Q2. Because the autoregressive system contains three lags, we need the following values of the information set in order to start the recursive relation:

$$\begin{aligned} \log Y_{2004.Q2} &= 9.2846 & & \log C_{2004.Q2} = 8.9323 \\ \log Y_{2004.Q1} &= 9.2777 & \text{and} \quad & \log C_{2004.Q1} = 8.9283 \\ \log Y_{2003.Q4} &= 9.2667 & & \log C_{2003.Q4} = 8.9182 \end{aligned}$$

For $t + 1 = 2004$: Q3:

$$\begin{aligned} f_{t,1}^{Y} &= 0.11 + 1.03 \times 9.2846 - 0.10 \times 9.2777 - 0.04 \times 9.2667 + 0.38 \times 8.9323 \\ &\quad - 0.11 \times 8.9283 - 0.17 \times 8.9182 \\ f_{t,1}^{C} &= 0.01 + 0.14 \times 9.2846 - 0.22 \times 9.2777 + 0.07 \times 9.2667 + 0.94 \times 8.9323 \\ &\quad + 0.34 \times 8.9283 - 0.27 \times 8.9182 \end{aligned}$$

with forecast errors $e_{t,1}^{Y} = \varepsilon_{2,t+1}$ and $e_{t,1}^{C} = \varepsilon_{1,t+1}$.

For $t + 2 = 2004$: Q4:

$$\begin{aligned} f_{t,2}^{Y} &= 0.11 + 1.03 \times f_{t,1}^{Y} - 0.10 \times 9.2846 - 0.04 \times 9.2777 + 0.38 \times f_{t,1}^{C} \\ &\quad - 0.11 \times 8.9323 - 0.17 \times 8.9283 \\ f_{t,2}^{C} &= 0.01 + 0.14 \times f_{t,1}^{Y} - 0.22 \times 9.2846 + 0.07 \times 9.2777 + 0.94 \times f_{t,1}^{C} \\ &\quad + 0.34 \times 8.9323 - 0.27 \times 8.9283 \end{aligned}$$

with errors $e_{t,2}^{Y} = \varepsilon_{2,t+2} + 1.03 \times e_{t,1}^{Y} + 0.38 \times e_{t,1}^{C}$ and $e_{t,2}^{C} = \varepsilon_{1,t+2} + 0.14 \times e_{t,1}^{Y} + 0.94 \times e_{t,1}^{C}$.

We could proceed in similar fashion for further horizons. In Figure 12.7, we present the multistep forecast for production and consumption up to 2008: Q4. Observe that the forecast is dominated by the drift of the random walk and that the forecast uncertainty is an ever increasing function of the forecasting horizon (recall Figure 10.10 in Chapter 10).

Once the forecasts of the levels of production and consumption have been calculated, we calculate the forecasts of their growth rates very easily. The growth rate can be approximated by the first differences of the log transformation, that is, $\frac{\Delta Y}{Y} \approx \log Y_t - \log Y_{t-1}$. In Table 12.7, we calculated the quarterly growth rates up to 2005: Q2.

TABLE 12.7 Multistep Forecast for Consumption and Production Growth Rates

Forecasting horizon h	$f_{t,h}^{C}$	$f_{t,h}^{Y}$	Consumption growth rate	Production growth rate
2004.Q2	8.932305	9.284650		
$h = 1$, 2004.Q3	8.941044	9.292789	0.87%	0.81%
$h = 2$, 2004.Q4	8.948264	9.301228	0.72%	0.84%
$h = 3$, 2005.Q1	8.956830	9.309969	0.85%	0.87%
$h = 4$, 2005.Q2	8.964910	9.318798	0.80%	0.88%

FIGURE 12.7 Multistep Forecast for Consumption and Production

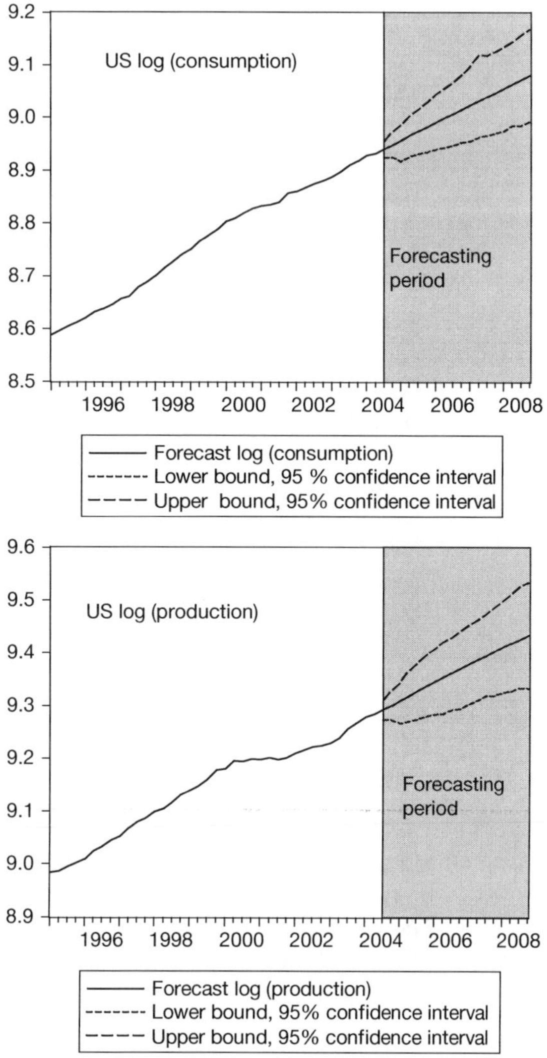

KEY WORDS

adjustment coefficient, p. 323
cointegrating relation, p. 318
cointegration, p. 318
disequilibrium error, p. 318
I(1) and I(0), p. 325
long-term equilibrium, p. 311
nonstationarity, p. 319
restricted vector autoregressive system, p. 327
steady state, p. 311
unit root, p. 316
vector error correction model, p. 324

EXERCISES

1. Update the data set on U.S. production and consumption. Following the reasoning of an economist, the cointegrating relation should be $\log Y_t = \alpha_0 + \log C_t + z_t$. How would you confirm that this in fact is a cointegrating equation? What is the disequilibrium error? Is it stationary? If it is, find the best vector error correction model. Construct the 1-year-ahead forecast for production and consumption.
2. With the updated data set from Exercise 1, find the cointegrating relation between production and consumption by implementing the test for cointegration. Is it different from the cointegrating relation in Exercise 1? If it is, go ahead and find the best vector error correction model, construct the 1-year-ahead forecast, and compare your results with those from Exercise 1.
3. Recall the purchasing power parity (PPP) theories from your international economics course. PPP says that the same good sold in any two countries should have the same price in both countries once it is adjusted by the exchange rate (and net of transportation costs). Choose any two countries, say the United States and Germany. Let P_t be the Consumer Price Index (CPI) in the United States and P_t^* the CPI for Germany. If e_t is the exchange rate between Germany and the United States (dollars per euro), then PPP claims that $P_t = P_t^* \,.\, e_t$. Downloaded the three time series: CPIs for both countries and the dollar/euro exchange rate. Convert the German CPI to dollars, that is, $P_t^* \,.\, e_t$. Analyze the difference $P_t - P_t^* \,.\, e_t$. Is this a cointegrating relation? If it is, PPP holds, albeit in a weaker form.
4. The Fisher equation relates real interest rates to nominal interest rates. Let r_t be the real interest rate, i_t the nominal interest rate, and π_t^e the expected rate of inflation. The Fisher equation states that $r_t = i - \pi_t^e$. Because expected inflation is not observable today, we will use the realized inflation. Download the U.S. CPI and construct the inflation series. Is inflation stationary? Download the U.S. 3-month Treasury bill rates. Is the Treasury Bill rate stationary? Construct the difference $r_t = i - \pi_t^e$. Is it stationary? Is it a cointegrating relation?

5. The difference between long- and short-term interest rates is known as the *spread* or the *slope of the yield curve*. Download monthly short-term rates (3-month Treasury bills) and long-term rates (10-year Treasury bonds). Are short- and long-term rates stationary? Construct the spread. Is it stationary? Is it a cointegrating relation?
6. With the data from Exercise 5, build a forecasting model to forecast the 1, 2, . . . and 6-step-ahead forecasts of long- and short-term interest rates.
7. In Chapter 11 (VAR systems), we analyzed the dynamics of house prices in two different locations, Riverside and Los Angeles, California. It would be interesting to investigate whether there is long-term equilibrium for house prices in both locations. If there is, the forecasting model(s) may be different from those in Chapter 11. Go ahead and analyze whether house prices in Riverside and Los Angeles are cointegrated. If they are, find the best forecasting model, construct the 1-, 2-, and 3-step-ahead forecasts, and comment on the differences you may find with the previous forecasts.
8. Foreign companies trade in American stock markets by issuing American depository receipts (ADR). Consider the stock price of a company trading in the stock exchange of its own country and the price of the corresponding ADR, which is traded in the U.S. stock exchange. What relation should you expect between ADRs and the national stock prices? Download the stock prices of a company that has ADRs and analyze the stationary properties of both series (national prices and ADRs). Are they cointegrated? Will you be able to forecast stock prices?
9. In the construction of the CPI , the *housing component* is defined as the cost of shelter or rent. Download the rent index and the owner's equivalent rent of primary residence (OER) for any city of your choice. Are they stationary? Download the house prices for the same city or Metropolitan Statistical Area. What is the statistical relation between rents and house prices? Are they cointegrated? Do rents help to forecast house prices?
10. The present value theory of stock prices says that the stock price should be equal to the discounted stream of its future dividends. Choose any stock you like. Download the stock prices and dividends. What is the statistical relation between dividends and stock prices? Are they cointegrated? Will you be able to forecast stock prices?

A PAUSE

WHERE ARE WE AND WHERE ARE WE GOING?

Before starting with the final module of this textbook, let us pause to summarize what we have learned and make a case for the chapters ahead, which will add a higher level of complexity to the idea of dependence. In Chapters 5 to Chapter 9, we learned how to model and forecast *linear dependence* when the data are *stationary* by building on the foundational blocks of Chapters 1 and 4 (see previous "A Pause" sections before Chapter 5 and before Chapter 10). In the last three chapters (Chapters 10 to 12), we extended our methodology in two directions: first, we analyzed *nonstationary* data and second, we expanded the *univariate* analysis to a *multivariate* framework in which we have analyzed the dynamics of two or more time series jointly. The following is a summary of the main five ideas contained in the last three chapters:

1. We relaxed the assumption of stationarity in Chapter 10 by introducing models with *deterministic trends* and models with *stochastic trends*, also known as *unit root process*. Trends are long-term features of the data. Unit root processes are very prevalent in economic and business data. We should be careful when we model deterministic trends because they may be subject to breaks in the data.
2. We stressed how important it is to statistically discriminate between a trend-stationary and a nonstationary process because the optimal forecast of a deterministic trend process is very different from that of a stochastic trend process (see Figure 10.10). The statistical tests for unit roots, such as the *Dickey-Fuller* and Augmented Dickey Fuller tests (testing nonstationarity versus stationary), follow nonstandard distributions, which means that the critical values of the distribution of the tests need to be tabulated by simulation. If we were to use the standard critical values based on a normal density, we would be rejecting a unit root process more often than we should.
3. In Chapter 11, we introduced a multivariate system called *vector autoregression* (VAR) that allows for joint dynamics of two or more time series. The main reason for analyzing a VAR system is that a VAR-based forecast may improve upon the univariate forecast. A key idea is *Granger-causality* that measures whether predictability of a given variable may be improved by adding dynamic information of other related variables. Although a VAR model is still an ad hoc representation of the economy, it is a very appealing mechanism to economists that are used to thinking in terms of economic models.

4. An additional use of a VAR system is in the economic policy field. *Impulse-response* functions measure the propagation of shocks to the economic system over time so that policy instruments could be ranked in terms of their effectiveness and speed (e.g. the debate between fiscal versus monetary policies).
5. By introducing two key ideas in Chapter 12, we synthesized all our understanding of linear dependence, stationarity and nonstationary, short- and long-term dynamics, and how all is combined to produce a forecast. *Cointegration* reconciles the economic notion of "equilibrium" or "steady state" with the forecasting notion of common stochastic trends running through several time series. An *error correction model* links short-term dynamics with long-term dynamics. The *Granger Representation Theorem* is the key result that formalizes all these statistical connections.

On closing this summary, we must say that all the dependence analyzed in the last 12 chapters of this textbook focuses on the *conditional mean* of a stochastic process.

Where Are We Going from Here?

By now we have accumulated an extensive forecasting jargon. We started by analyzing concepts such as *linear dependence, stationary* data, *univariate* modeling, and *conditional mean.* We followed up with *nonstationary* data and *multivariate* modeling. If we were to play a game of matching words, it is easy to see that we would be missing two words to complete the picture: *nonlinear dependence* and *conditional variance*. This is exactly where we are going in Chapters 13 to 16.

Chapters 13, 14, and 15 will deal with the modeling of the conditional variance of a stochastic process. As we have said, the objective of any forecasting exercise is to characterize a random variable some periods ahead. Up to now, we have analyzed all the potential dynamics in the conditional mean of the future random variable, and it seems natural to ask whether higher moments, like the variance, have dynamics on their own. In Chapter 13 we will make a case for the conditional variance being a time-varying moment. As such, questions about time-dependence and how to model it will emerge. At first, we will propose simple specifications for the conditional variance that are not properly speaking "models" but smoothing algorithms. Nevertheless, smoothing is very appealing because it is a low-cost approach that is easy to implement, does not require estimation, and provides valuable information to detect patterns in volatility. In Chapter 14, we properly model the dynamics in conditional variance by exploiting the dependence patterns in the autocorrelograms of the *squared* variable of interest. The chapter will focus mostly on the ARCH (autoregressive conditional heteroscedasticity) family, but we will also include some introduction to the notion of *realized volatility*. In Chapter 15, our objective is to put into practice the modeling and forecasting of conditional variance. We will survey four financial applications, which are very useful in the world of finance: risk management, portfolio allocation, asset pricing, and option pricing.

Finally, in Chapter 16, we offer a glimpse of nonlinear models. Nonlinearity is often present in economic data. For instance, the dynamics of the economy in recession may be different from those in expansion, or financial prices may behave differently in times of high or low volatility. Thus, we will start by making a case for the relevance of nonlinearities in economic and business data, and again the question of how to model nonlinear dependence arises. We will offer an introduction to several specifications. Most of these models require estimation and testing techniques that go beyond the scope of this textbook. Nevertheless, we seek a more descriptive than statistical approach of what these models can achieve. There are some instances in which ordinary least squares will suffice to deliver standard inference results, and those will be explained in more detail. We will end the chapter by underscoring the complexity of the multistep forecast from a nonlinear specification. All in all, this chapter is a summary of the challenges that lie ahead were you to "dig deeper" in the field of economic forecasting!

How To Organize Your Reading of the Forthcoming Chapters?

As we mentioned, Chapters 13 to 16 deal with more complex and technical issues of dependence in economic data. These are very interesting forecasting topics with a strong demand within the private industry, government agencies, and academia. Depending on your background, you may choose among the following routes designed to help you to navigate these last four chapters:

Route 1 (introductory)

Chapter 13 (all sections)
Chapter 15: Section 15.1.1 (Value-at-Risk) and 15.1.2 (Expected Shortfall)
Chapter 16: Section 16.1 (Introduction to Nonlinear Dependence)

Route 2 (intermediate)

Chapter 13 (all sections)
Chapter 14: Section 14.1 (ARCH Family)
Chapter 15: Section 15.1 (Risk Management) and 15.3 (Asset Pricing)
Chapter 16: Section 16.1 (Introduction to Nonlinear Dependence), Section 16.2.2 (Smooth Transition Models), and Section 16.3 (Forecasting with Nonlinear Models)

Route 3 (advanced)

Chapters 13, 14, 15, and 16 (all sections)

That's all folks!

MODULE III

MODELING MORE COMPLEX DEPENDENCE

CHAPTER 13

Forecasting Volatility I

13.1 Motivation

To this point, we have modeled a stochastic process $\{Y_t\}$ by discovering the linear time dependence contained in its autocorrelation functions. Once a model was in place, the next step was the construction of a forecast. We have defined the h-step optimal forecast[1] as the conditional expectation of the process based on the information set I_t, that is,

$$f_{t,h} \equiv \mu_{t+h|t} \equiv E(Y_{t+h} | I_t).$$

Thus, our focus has been centered around the understanding of the first conditional moment, the conditional mean, of the random variable Y_{t+h}. We have made statements such as by next quarter, house prices will increase 1%, or it is expected that next year gross national product (GNP) will contract by 0.5%; in these cases, we meant that *the conditional mean* of house price growth is expected to be 1%, or that the conditional mean of GNP growth is expected to be −0.5%.

13.1.1 The World is Concerned About Uncertainty

Reading the economic and business press, it is very likely that you will find statements related not only to average price increases or average GNP growth but also to price volatility, or output volatility, or asset risk, or market uncertainty, just to mention a few.

[1] Assuming a quadratic loss function.

The following statements (italics added) highlight the importance of volatility in the lives of economic agents:

1. "As *interest rate volatility* nearly disappeared in recent times, home mortgage rates decline appreciably, making the American Dream of homeownership more affordable."[2]
2. "Volatility can wreak havoc on economies. Sudden, *sharp ups and downs in business activity* can make it difficult for consumers to plan their spending, workers to feel secure in their jobs and companies to determine their future investments. Because of their impact on expectations and business and consumer confidence, swings in the economy can become self-reinforcing. *Volatility* can also spill over into real and financial asset markets, where *severe price movements* can produce seemingly arbitrary redistributions of wealth. It's good news, then, that the US economy has become much more stable."[3]
3. "Illiquid assets become *very risky in volatile times*," as the preference for liquid assets creates an environment in which "the negative effect of volatility is reflected more strongly on (the suddenly shunned) illiquid assets."[4]
4. "The choice of exchange rate regime has important implications in terms of *output volatility*."[5]
5. "Some of the complex and often illiquid financial products hedge funds have helped foster are difficult to value, raising concern that potential losses might remain hidden for a considerable time and lead to *market uncertainty* and unpleasant surprises for investors."[6]

The authors of these statements are preoccupied not just with the level of interest rates but with the *volatility* of interest rates (1); not just with asset prices but also with the likelihood of *severe price movements* (2); not just with different categories of assets but also with those that are *very risky* (3); not just with exchange rate systems but also with their effects on *output volatility* (4); not just with the products created by hedge funds but also with the increase of *market uncertainty* that they may bring (5).

From an econometric modeling and forecasting perspective, all this means that we need to go beyond modeling the conditional mean and start exploring other characteristics of the stochastic process under study. Just from the preceding statements, we see that a common and pressing topic is emerging: **volatility**, **severe price movements**, **risk**, and **uncertainty**. All these terms, with more or less subtlety, point to measures of dispersion and/or quantile measures of the random variable of interest.

---

[2]"The Dangers of Complacency about Risk: A Conversation with Harvey Rosenblum," *Southwest Economy*, Federal Reserve Bank of Dallas, March/April 2008.

[3]E.F. Koenig and N. Ball, "The 'Great Moderation' in Output and Employment Volatility: An Update," *Economic Letter, Insights from the Federal Reserve Bank of Dallas*, 2007.

[4]"Illiquidity Raises Investment Risk" (summary of the paper by Dimitri Vayanos, "Flight to Quality, Flight to Liquidity, and the Pricing of Risk"), *The NBER Digest*, June 2004.

[5]"Flexible Exchange Rates Reduce Economic Volatility" (summary of the paper by Sebastian Edwards and Eduardo Levy Yeyati "Flexible Exchange Rates as Shock Absorbers"), *The NBER Digest*, January 2004.

[6]J.W. Gunther and A. Zhang, "Hedge Fund Investors More Rational Than Rash," *Economic Letter, Insights from the Federal Reserve Bank of Dallas*, 2007.

13.1.2 Volatility Within the Context of Our Forecasting Problem

Let us recall from Chapter 1 the following Figure 13.1 that graphically describes the forecasting problem.

Our ultimate goal is the characterization of a future (h-step ahead) random variable, Y_{t+h}, given the information that we know up to today t. Let us briefly summarize what we have learned. Previously, we have mainly focused on the *point forecast* $f_{t,h}$, which under a quadratic loss function, is the conditional expectation, that is,

$$f_{t,h} \equiv \mu_{t+h|t} \equiv E(Y_{t+h} | I_t)$$

The uncertainty of the forecast has been defined as the variance of the forecast error, that is,

$$\sigma^2_{t+h|t} \equiv \text{var}(Y_{t+h} | I_t) = E(Y_{t+h} - f_{t,h} | I_t)^2$$

and, for an *assumed* density function and confidence level, we constructed the *interval forecast*. For instance, under normality, a 95% confidence interval looks like this:

$$\mu_{t+h|t} \pm 1.96\sigma_{t+h|t} = (\mu_{t+h|t} - 1.96\sigma_{t+h|t}, \mu_{t+h|t} + 1.96\sigma_{t+h|t})$$

Because of the assumption of normality, we have also constructed the *density forecast* as $N(\mu_{t+h|t}, \sigma^2_{t+h|t})$.

Now, review the MA, AR, and ARMA models that we have studied in Chapters 6, 7, and 8 and check their forecasts. The optimal forecast depends on the information set. However, the variance of the forecast error does not depend on the information set because we have *assumed* that it is constant over time. To illustrate this point, let us choose a simple AR(1) model $Y_t = \phi Y_{t-1} + \varepsilon_t$ and a forecast horizon $h = 1$. The optimal 1-step-ahead forecast is

$$f_{t,1} \equiv \mu_{t+1|t} \equiv E(Y_{t+1} | I_t) = \phi Y_t$$

FIGURE 13.1
The Forecasting Problem

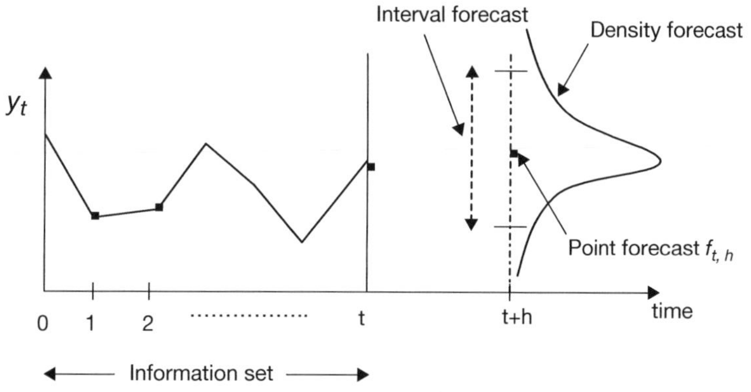

Thus, when the information set changes, the forecast, which depends on Y_t, will change. It is time varying. If we wish to compute a forecasting interval, we need the variance of the 1-step-ahead forecast error, which for the case of AR(1) is

$$\sigma^2_{t+1|t} \equiv \text{var}(Y_{t+1} \mid I_t) = E(Y_{t+1} - \phi Y_t \mid I_t)^2 = E(\varepsilon^2_{t+1}) = \sigma^2_\varepsilon$$

Even though our notation $\sigma^2_{t+1|t} \equiv \text{var}(Y_{t+1} \mid I_t)$ indicates that the conditional variance also depends on the information set, eventually the conditional variance becomes a constant, that is, $\sigma^2_{t+1|t} \equiv \text{var}(Y_{t+1} \mid I_t) = \sigma^2_\varepsilon$ because the innovation ε_t is *assumed* to have constant variance. In addition, the 95% confidence forecasting interval, $\phi Y_t \pm 1.96\sigma_\varepsilon$, has a time-invariant term, that is, $1.96\sigma_\varepsilon$, which does not depend on the information set. The range of the forecasting interval is the same for all 1-step-ahead forecasts, which means that the range of the forecasting interval is also time invariant. If we bring the assumption of normality, the 1-step-ahead density forecast will be $N(\phi Y_t, \sigma^2_\varepsilon)$, which also has a constant variance.

In summary, up to now the forecasting exercise has exclusively focused on the modeling of the conditional mean of the stochastic process $\{Y_t\}$ and any other conditional moment (like the variance) and the conditional density functional form (for instance normality) have been assumed constant over time.

13.1.3 Setting the Objective

If the world is concerned about uncertainty, focusing only on the conditional mean of Y_{t+h} will not be very helpful. We need additional modeling techniques for other conditional moments. Ideally, we would like to fully characterize the random variable Y_{t+h} by producing the h-step-ahead density forecast. We would like to make statements such as given current information, the probability of a drop of 20% in the SP500 index in the next 5 days is 5%; that is, $P_t(Y_{t+5} \leq -20\%) = 5\%$, where $P_t(.)$ stands for the time-varying probability of the event conditional on the information up to time t. This type of statement is possible only when the density forecast is available. Unfortunately, to produce a truly time-varying density forecast is a difficult task unless we rely on a restrictive set of assumptions as we have seen in the AR(1) example. Alternatively, we could characterize the random variable Y_{t+h} by focusing on partial aspects such as **conditional dispersion** (variance, standard deviation, **range**, interquartile range), conditional asymmetry (third moments, skewness coefficient), conditional tail behavior (fourth moment, kurtosis coefficient), and so on.

The objective of this chapter is to go beyond the conditional mean and analyze *volatility.* There is an intuitive understanding of what volatility is. Very often in the business press we read the word *volatility* associated with *uncertainty* and/or *risk.* See, for instance, the statements of the opening section. But there are some differences among these words.

Let us start with the most general. We will use the word *uncertainty* to mean that, at the present time, we look into the future by acknowledging that there is a set of many possible events to which we can assign only some probability of occurrence. From your introductory statistics courses, you are guessing that a representation of uncertainty is the probability density function of a random variable. And you are right! However, uncertainty is a much more general word because we acknowledge that the future also consists of events completely unknown to us today so that it is impossible to assign probabilities to something that is completely unknown.

The word *risk* is attached to a potential loss. Suppose that at the present time, you make a decision to hold a portfolio long in stocks; if the prices of the stocks go down, you will suffer a loss. You could quantify your risk now by assessing the probability of a down movement in the stock price, and based on that, you may consider buying insurance or increasing your capital reserves. On the other hand, if your portfolio is short in stocks, a down movement will be beneficial to you. By shorting stocks, your risk is in the upward movements and, as before, you could assess the probability of a move upward to make the appropriate decision to cushion your loss. Thus, the quantification of risk also entails some knowledge of the probability distribution function. You may be more concerned with the probability of extreme values or values far away from the mean—those in the upper and lower tails of the distribution—than with the values in the central area of the distribution.

The word *volatility* is more specific and aims to measure the dispersion of a random variable. Sometimes we use the word *volatility* to indistinctly refer to the variance of a random variable $\sigma^2 = E(Y - \mu_Y)^2$ or the standard deviation $\sigma = \sqrt{\sigma^2}$. There are many other measures of dispersion, for instance, the absolute deviation $E|Y - \mu_Y|$, the range $Y_{max} - Y_{min}$, and the interquartile range $Y_{.75} - Y_{.25}$. All these measures capture the uncertainty of a random variable to a certain degree, and they are very relevant in the assessment of risk associated with decision making.

In this chapter, we focus on the analysis of the variance. In the same spirit as in the modeling of the conditional mean $\mu_{t+1|t} \equiv E(Y_{t+1} | I_t)$, now our target is the modeling of the conditional variance $\sigma^2_{t+1|t} \equiv \text{var}(Y_{t+1} | I_t)$. Section 13.2 will show that we need to relax the assumption of constant conditional variance because in practice, many economic and business time series exhibit episodes of very high, high, and low volatility, which means that volatility changes over time. Thus, an assumption such as $\sigma^2_{t+1|t} \equiv \text{var}(Y_{t+1} | I_t) = \sigma^2_\varepsilon$ will not be enough to model the dynamics of the time series and will not be helpful for the construction of forecasting intervals such as $f_{t,h} \pm k\sigma_{t+h|t}$. Furthermore, if we discover how volatility depends on the information set, we will be able to model it, as we did with the conditional mean, and eventually to forecast it.

13.2 Time-Varying Dispersion: Empirical Evidence

The following figures provide some evidence that, in fact, volatility is time varying. In Figure 13.2, we observe the quarterly GDP growth (annualized) from 1959 to 2007. In the time series plot, the horizontal volatility bands enclose 95% of the observations in a given period of time. Between 1959 and 1983, the average GDP growth was 3.6% and a 95% interval was $3.6 \pm 8.9 = (-5.3, 12.5)$. Between 1984 and 1995, the same

FIGURE 13.2 U.S. Real GDP Growth with Volatility Bands

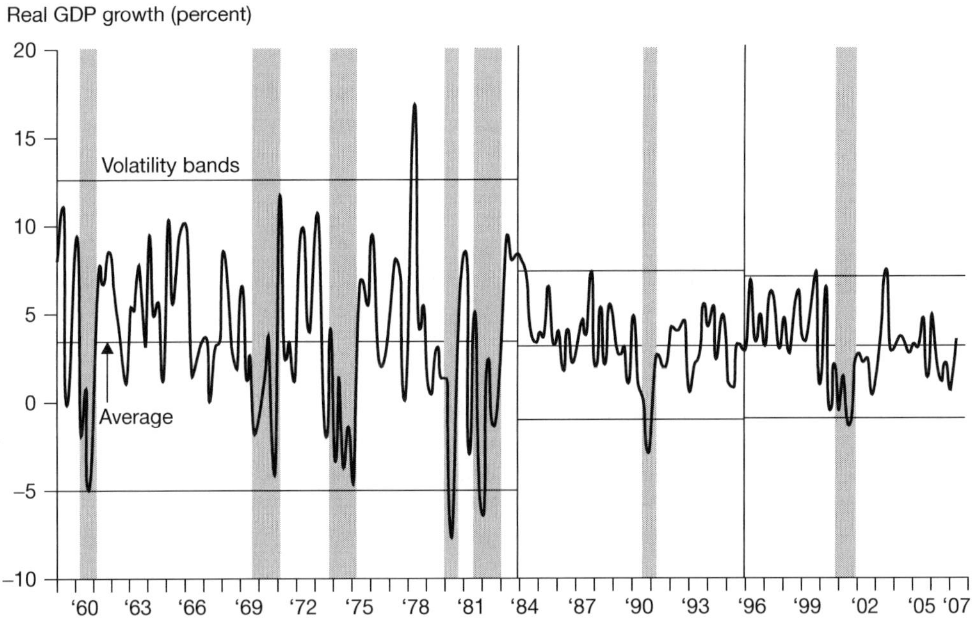

Note: Shaded areas denote recessions.

Source: U.S. Real GDP Growth with Volatility Bands." From Koenig and Ball, "The 'Great Moderation' in Output and Employment Volatility: An Update", Economic Letter, Insights from the Federal Reserve Bank of Dallas, 2, 9.," © October 2007, in *From Koenig, E.F. and N. Ball, "The 'Great Moderation' in Output and Employment Volatility: An Update", Economic Letter, Insights from the Federal Reserve Bank of Dallas, 2, 9. October 2007, Chart 1.,* http://dallasfed.org/research/eclett/2007/el0709.pdf

interval was (−1.1, 7.5); and between 1996 and 2007 (−1.0, 7.2). There is a big decline in volatility in the 1980s that has continued into the 2000s. The standard deviation of GDP growth was 4.47% from 1959 to 1983; 2.14% from 1984 to 1995; and 2.04% from 1996 to 2007.

In Figure 13.3, we have the monthly time series plot of the volatility of Consumer Price Index inflation (the smooth line). This volatility was much higher during the 1980s than in the 1990s and 2000s. Price stability brought down the inflation risk perceived by investors, which translated in lower premium for bonds (the ragged line).

In Figure 13.4, we observe the *median* global inflation rate (solid line), which dropped from 15% in 1980 to around 5% in 2005. For our purposes, the interesting feature is that the dispersion of the world inflation rate measured by the interquartile range (the shaded area) has been changing over time. There was a small range from 1950 to about 1980. However, in the 1980s and 1990s, the interquartile interval expanded considerably, ranging from 2% to more than 30% in the mid-1990s.

FIGURE 13.3 Volatility of Consumer Price Index Inflation

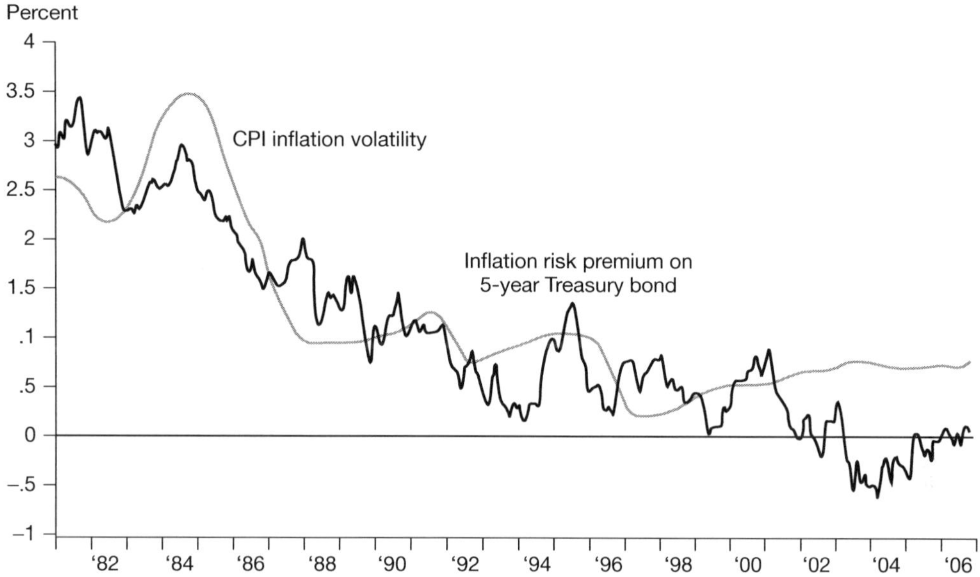

Source: Volatility of Consumer Price Index Inflation. From Wu, "Globalization's Effect on Interest Rates and the Yield Curve", Economic Letter, Insights from the Federal Reserve Bank of Dallas, 1, 9.," © Sept 2006, in *From Wu, "Globalization's Effect on Interest Rates and the Yield Curve", Economic Letter, Insights from the Federal Reserve Bank of Dallas, 1, 9; Chart 9,* http://dallasfed.org/research/eclett/2006/el0609.pdf

FIGURE 13.4 Global Inflation Rate

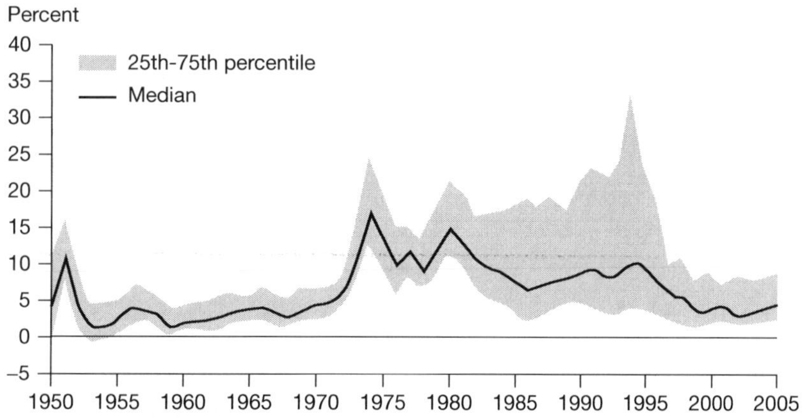

Source: Global Inflation Rate. From Wynne and Kersting, Openness and Inflation", Staff Papers, Federal Reserve Bank of Dallas, 2 (April 2007), Figure 1.," http://dallasfed.org/research/staff/2007/staff0702.pdf

FIGURE 13.5 Monthly Returns of the SP500 Index

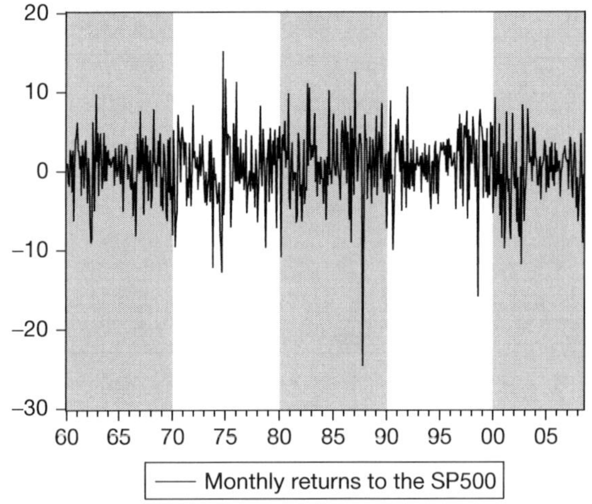

In Figure 13.5, we plot the monthly returns of the SP500 index from January 1960 to July 2008. It is apparent that the 1960s were calmer times than the 1980s. While in the 1960s the returns oscillated approximately between 10% and −10%, in the 1980s, the market was highly volatile, exhibiting large negative returns (−24.5% in October 1987). The measures of dispersion in Table 13.1—sample standard deviation, the range, and the interquartile range—summarize these facts. For each row, the entry in boldface, italic type is the largest (or the smallest) number.

The most volatile decade was the 1980s; it has the largest standard deviation, the largest monthly drop in returns, and the largest range. In contrast, the 1960s and 2000s were calmer times according to the previously mentioned measures.

TABLE 13.1 Summary of the Dispersion in the Monthly Returns to the SP500

	1960–1969	1970–1979	1980–1989	1990–1999	2000–2008 (July)
Sample standard deviation	3.45%	4.59%	***4.79%***	3.88%	4.05%
Maximum **Minimum**	9.67% –8.99%	***15.10%*** –12.71%	12.38% ***–24.54%***	10.58% –15.76%	9.23% –11.65%
Range	18.66	27.81	***36.92***	26.34	20.88
Interquartile interval	(–1.62, 2.69)	(***–2.21***, 3.56)	(–1.42, ***3.96***)	(–1.00, 3.80)	(–2.03, 2.10)
Interquartile range	4.31	***5.77***	5.38	4.80	4.13

The preceding figures make a strong case in favor of time-varying volatilities. The problem now is to figure out whether, within this time variation, there is enough time dependence so that we can build a model to capture the dynamics of volatility. If this is the case, then we could also build a forecast for volatility, which while being a worthy task in itself, will also be very useful for decision making under uncertainty. For instance, we would like to say that, if today we are in a highly volatile market, the expected return of a given financial asset will be between –15% and 15% with 95% probability; on the contrary, if today we are in a low volatility market, the expected return will be between –1% and 1% with 95% probability. In these two situations, the confidence interval attached to our forecast is very different, and for those engaged in the business of risk management, these forecasts may have different consequences. In high volatility times, the possibility of large losses in our portfolio may require extra insurance, which may not be all that necessary in low volatility times.

13.3 Is There Time Dependence in Volatility?

Suppose that we are studying the stochastic process $\{Y_t\}$. We have measured time dependence in the conditional mean by examining the autocorrelation functions of the original process $\{Y_t\}$. Now we would like to measure time dependence in the conditional variance. Because we are dealing with second moments, it is logical to analyze the autocorrelation functions of the process $\{(Y_t - \mu)^2\}$. But there are other measures of dispersion that we can also analyze, such as the absolute deviation $|Y_t - \mu|$ or the difference between the highest and the lowest values $(Y_t^{HI} - Y_t^{LO})$. By examining the autocorrelation functions of these new transformed processes, $\{|Y_t - \mu|\}$ and $\{(Y_t^{HI} - Y_t^{LO})\}$, we will investigate whether there is time dependence in volatility. Let us use the data, perform some of these transformations, and observe their autocorrelation functions.

We will analyze the SP500 index (weekly observations from January 1998 to July 2008), the yen/U.S. dollar exchange rate (daily data from December 1987 to July 2008), and the 10-year Treasury constant maturity rates (daily data from March 2000 to July 2008). Their corresponding time series plots are presented in Figure 13.6. Observe that the three series exhibit a high degree of persistence so that we may question whether they are nonstationary. We could conduct a unit root test like those explained in Chapter 10. See the results in Table 13.2.

In none of the three cases can we reject the null hypothesis of unit root test. The *p*-values are larger than the customary 5% level. Thus, the data are nonstationary, and we proceed to take the first difference of each series (in logs), which are the returns. We proceed with the analysis of returns by looking at different transformations and examining their time dependence properties.

Let us start with the weekly returns to the SP500 index from January 1998 to July 2008, and call them $\{r_t\}$. In Figure 13.7, we picture r_t, r_t^2, $|r_t|$, and $r_t^{HI} - r_t^{LO}$

FIGURE 13.6
Time Series of SP500 Index, Yen/Dollar Exchange Rate, and 10-Year Treasury Note Yield

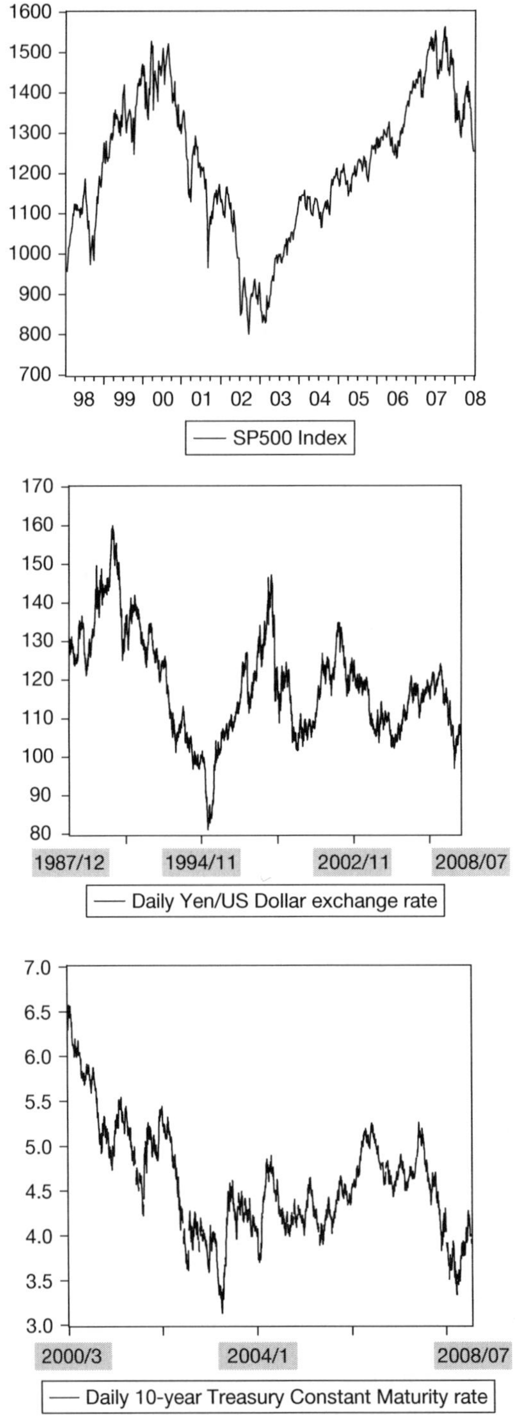

TABLE 13.2 Unit Root Testing: Value of the Dickey-Fuller Test

SP500 Index	Yen/Dollar exchange rate	10-year Treasury Note
−2.07	−2.69	−2.09
p-value = 0.25	p-value = 0.08	p-value = 0.24

with their corresponding autocorrelation functions. The time series of returns r_t does not have any autocorrelation; its autocorrelograms seem to point to a white noise process. However, the transformations r_t^2, $|r_t|$, and $r_t^{HI} - r_t^{LO}$ all have positive autocorrelations that resemble those of autoregressive processes. Although the autocorrelations of r_t^2 and $|r_t|$ are small in magnitude, they are statistically different from zero. Observe that the p-values corresponding to the Q-statistics are zero, rejecting very strongly the null hypothesis of zero autocorrelation. The largest autocorrelation coefficients are found in the time series $r_t^{HI} - r_t^{LO}$, followed by those of $|r_t|$, and r_t^2. These findings are good news because it means that we could propose models for higher moments than the mean that will capture the time dependence of any of these series.

In Figure 13.8, we plot the time series of returns to the yen/U.S. dollar exchange rate from December 15, 1987, to July 10, 2008. We also plot the squared and absolute returns and calculate their autocorrelation functions. A pattern similar to that of the SP500 returns emerges. The raw returns do not exhibit any autocorrelation and they resemble a white noise process, but the squared and absolute returns do have significant autocorrelation resembling that of autoregressive processes. Observe that the autocorrelation of squared returns exhibits somehow less persistence than that of the absolute returns.

Similarly, in Figure 13.9, we plot the daily returns to the 10-year Treasury note from March 20, 2000, to July 8, 2008. We observe similar behavior: very little autocorrelation in the raw returns but a positive autocorrelation in the squared and absolute returns.

In conclusion, volatility is not only time varying but also exhibits a time dependence that is amenable to modeling. Therefore, we need to determine what models we could propose to capture time dependence.

Finally, let us look at the unconditional density function of the returns of the three just mentioned series. The clusters of activitiy and the high-volatility times that we find in the returns to the SP500, to the exchange rate, and to the Treasury notes, contribute to the tails of the density function. In Figure 13.10, we plot the histograms of the three time series of returns and the histograms of volatility approximated by the absolute returns. The series of returns are not normally distributed, mainly because of leptokurtosis or fat-tail behavior. The coefficient of kurtosis is much larger than 3. The histograms are approximately symmetric because the coefficient of skewness is small. On the contrary, the histograms of volatility are highly skewed to the right with a large coefficient of skewness of about 2.

Sample: 1/12/1998 7/07/2008
Included observations: 547

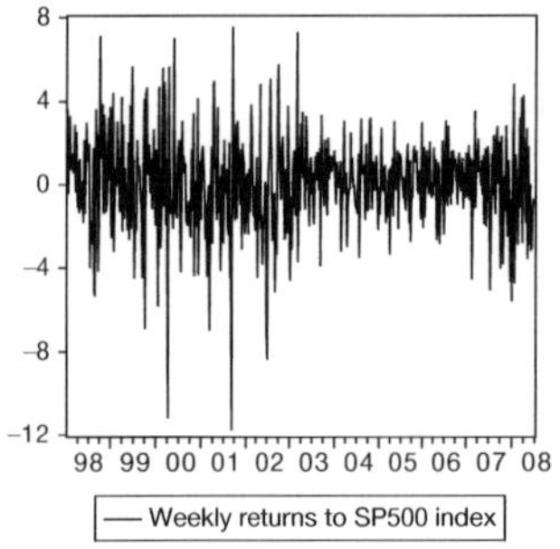

Autocorrection	Partial Correlation		AC	PAC	Q-Stat	Prob
		1	-0.077	-0.077	3.2986	0.069
		2	0.040	0.035	4.1955	0.123
		3	-0.024	-0.019	4.5169	0.211
		4	-0.039	-0.044	5.3473	0.253
		5	0.001	-0.003	5.3481	0.375
		6	0.048	0.051	6.6214	0.357
		7	-0.112	-0.107	13.568	0.059
		8	-0.009	-0.031	13.610	0.093
		9	-0.047	-0.039	14.823	0.096
		10	0.087	0.083	19.066	0.039
		11	0.058	0.065	20.964	0.034
		12	0.009	0.006	21.011	0.050

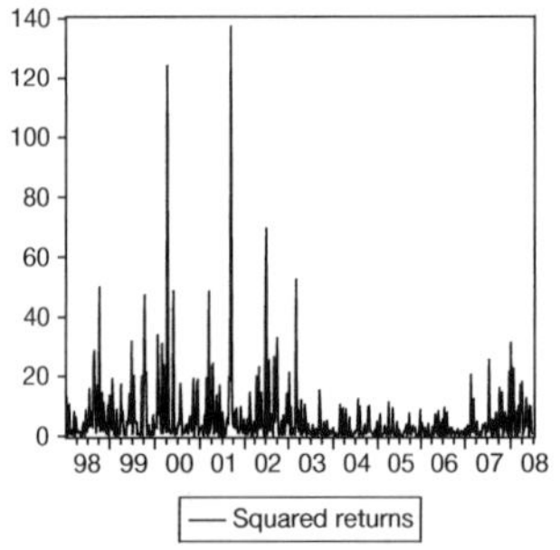

Autocorrelation	Partial Correlation		AC	PAC	Q-Stat	Prob
		1	0.236	0.236	30 605	0.000
		2	0.058	0.002	32.441	0.000
		3	0.083	0.073	36.282	0.000
		4	0.065	0.030	38.590	0.000
		5	0.041	0.017	39.525	0.000
		6	0.062	0.045	41.644	0.000
		7	0.072	0.044	44.538	0.000
		8	0.002	-0.032	44.541	0.000
		9	0.031	0.030	45.083	0.000
		10	0.057	0.035	46.911	0.000
		11	0.068	0.045	49.486	0.000
		12	0.054	0.023	51.110	0.000

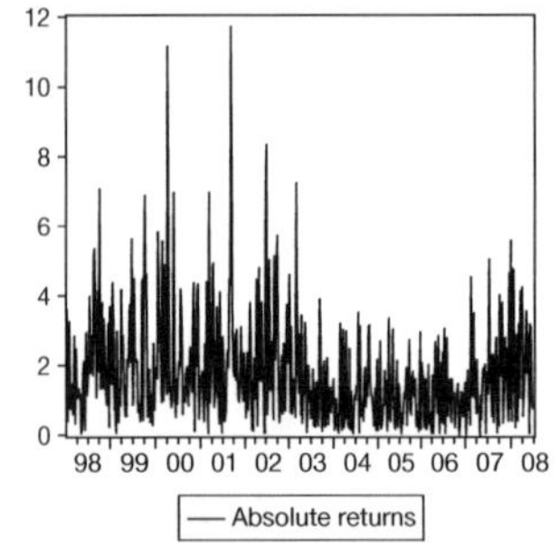

Autocorrelation	Partial Correlation		AC	PAC	Q-Stat	Prob
		1	0.187	0.187	19.217	0.000
		2	0.109	0.077	25.738	0.000
		3	0.153	0.125	38.715	0.000
		4	0.138	0.088	49.233	0.000
		5	0.120	0.067	57.270	0.000
		6	0.071	0.011	60.066	0.000
		7	0.085	0.037	64.116	0.000
		8	0.067	0.012	66.581	0.000
		9	0.078	0.036	69.985	0.000
		10	0.111	0 068	76.830	0.000
		11	0.109	0 058	83.446	0.000
		12	0.098	0.042	88.885	0.000

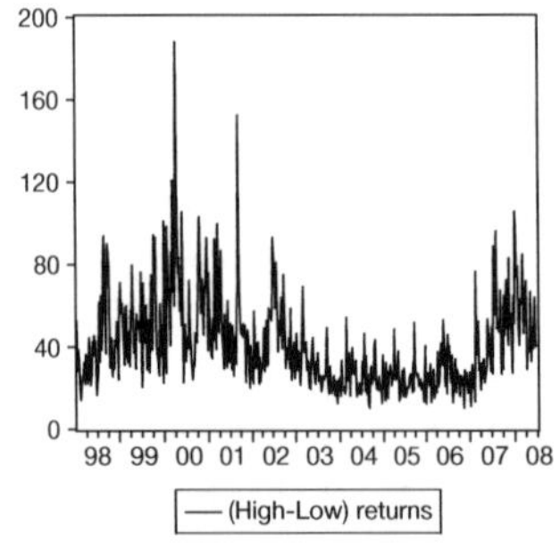

Autocorrelation	Partial Correlation		AC	PAC	Q-Stat	Prob
		1	0.589	0.589	190.89	0.000
		2	0.525	0.273	342.84	0.000
		3	0.510	0.206	486.51	0.000
		4	0.454	0.079	600.44	0.000
		5	0.451	0.111	713.29	0.000
		6	0.388	-0.006	796.94	0.000
		7	0.381	0.053	877.81	0.000
		8	0.364	0.031	951.46	0.000
		9	0.324	-0.003	1010.2	0.000
		10	0.383	0.137	1092.0	0.000
		11	0.328	-0.011	1152.5	0.000
		12	0.304	-0.007	1204.3	0.000

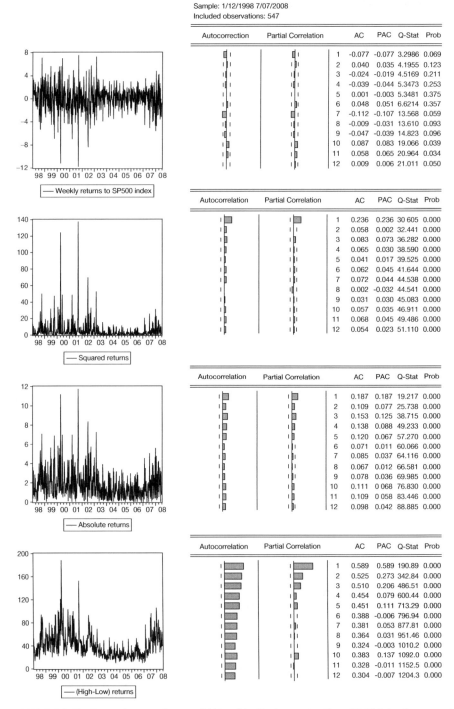

FIGURE 13.7 Transformations of Weekly Returns to the SP500 Index and Their Autocorrelations

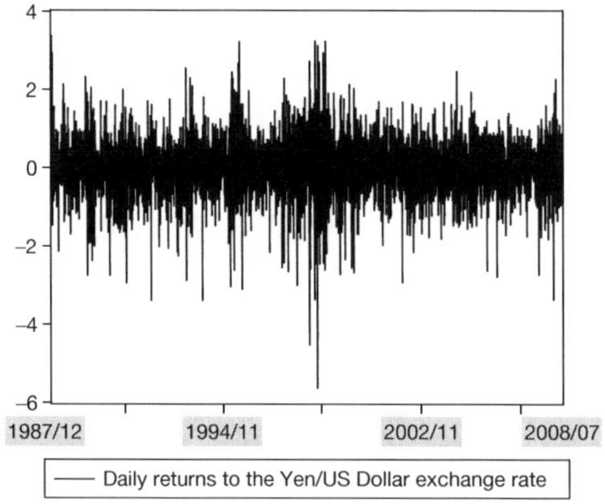

Sample: 4251 9414
Included observations: 5164

Autocorrelation	Partial Correlation		AC	PAC	Q-Stat	Prob
		1	0.020	0.020	2.1653	0.141
		2	0.008	0.008	2.5119	0.285
		3	-0.027	-0.028	6.3895	0.094
		4	-0.001	0.000	6.3949	0.172
		5	0.004	0.005	6.4908	0.261
		6	-0.017	-0.018	7.9488	0.242
		7	0.018	0.019	9.6769	0.208
		8	-0.000	-0.001	9.6778	0.288
		9	0.004	0.003	9.7815	0.368
		10	0.032	0.033	15.050	0.130
		11	-0.008	-0.009	15.373	0.166
		12	0.016	0.015	16.641	0.164

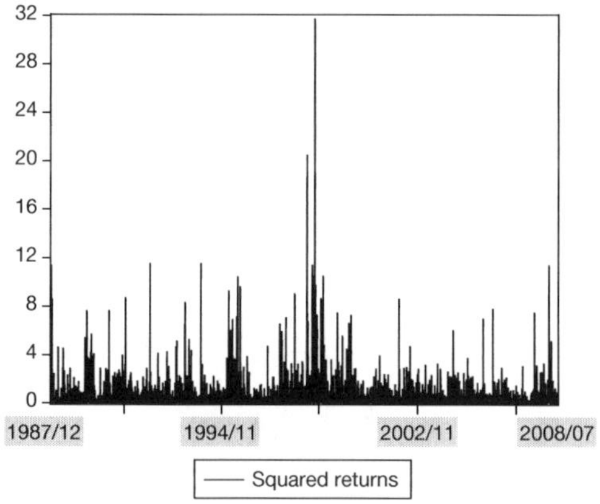

Sample: 4251 9414
Included observations: 5164

Autocorrelation	Partial Correlation		AC	PAC	Q-Stat	Prob
		1	0.198	0.198	201.84	0.000
		2	0.113	0.077	268.31	0.000
		3	0.088	0.054	307.91	0.000
		4	0.069	0.037	332.92	0.000
		5	0.103	0.076	387.32	0.000
		6	0.090	0.049	428.94	0.000
		7	0.090	0.049	470.50	0.000
		8	0.094	0.051	515.75	0.000
		9	0.089	0.044	556.38	0.000
		10	0.032	-0.019	561.60	0.000
		11	0.071	0.041	587.55	0.000
		12	0.041	-0.001	596.28	0.000

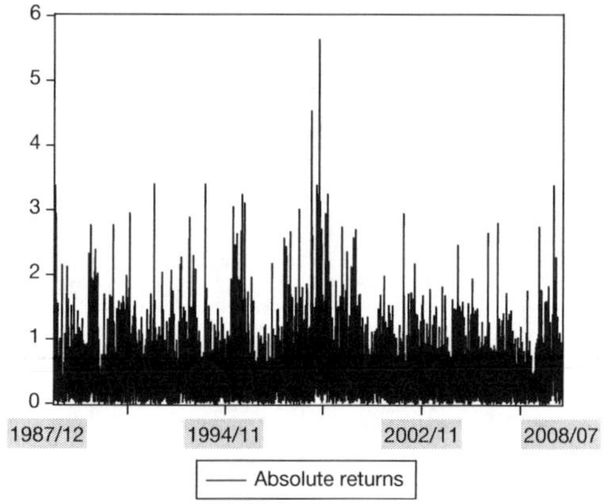

Sample: 4251 9414
Included observations: 5164

Autocorrelation	Partial Correlation		AC	PAC	Q-Stat	Prob
		1	0.122	0.122	76.904	0.000
		2	0.107	0.093	135.78	0.000
		3	0.102	0.081	189.60	0.000
		4	0.104	0.077	245.41	0.000
		5	0.111	0.079	309.65	0.000
		6	0.100	0.061	361.14	0.000
		7	0.104	0.063	417.35	0.000
		8	0.087	0.040	456.12	0.000
		9	0.104	0.058	511.96	0.000
		10	0.067	0.015	535.09	0.000
		11	0.088	0.040	575.23	0.000
		12	0.065	0.013	596.87	0.000

FIGURE 13.8 Transformations of Daily Returns to Yen/Dollar Exchange Rate and Their Autocorrelations

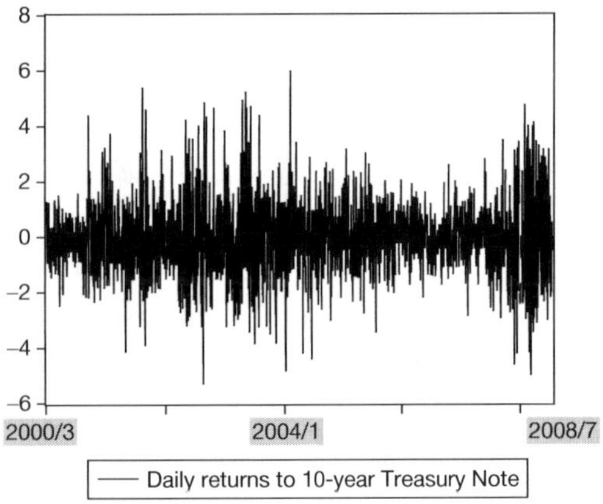

Sample: 10000 12136
Included observations: 1960

Autocorrelation	Partial Correlation		AC	PAC	Q-Stat	Prob
		1	0.004	0.004	0.0262	0.872
		2	-0.062	-0.062	7.5887	0.022
		3	-0.020	-0.020	8.3849	0.039
		4	0.003	0.001	8.3979	0.078
		5	0.040	0.038	11.518	0.042
		6	0.025	0.024	12.710	0.048
		7	0.056	0.061	18.905	0.008
		8	-0.008	-0.004	19.031	0.015
		9	-0.035	-0.027	21.463	0.011
		10	-0.027	-0.028	22.902	0.011
		11	0.013	0.006	23.217	0.016
		12	0.037	0.027	25.850	0.011

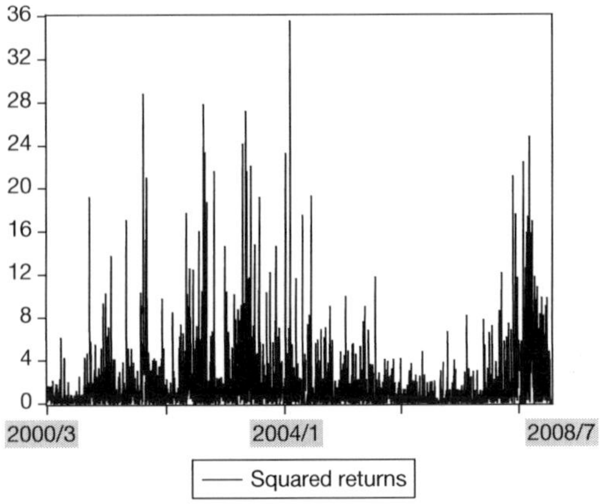

Sample: 10000 12136
Included observations: 1960

Autocorrelation	Partial Correlation		AC	PAC	Q-Stat	Prob
		1	0.089	0.089	15.563	0.000
		2	0.096	0.089	33.691	0.000
		3	0.067	0.052	42.535	0.000
		4	0.121	0.105	71.317	0.000
		5	0.186	0.163	139.06	0.000
		6	0.109	0.069	162.55	0.000
		7	0.111	0.068	186.85	0.000
		8	0.090	0.045	202.79	0.000
		9	0.126	0.072	234.20	0.000
		10	0.154	0.093	280.80	0.000
		11	0.129	0.067	313.52	0.000
		12	0.128	0.066	345.92	0.000

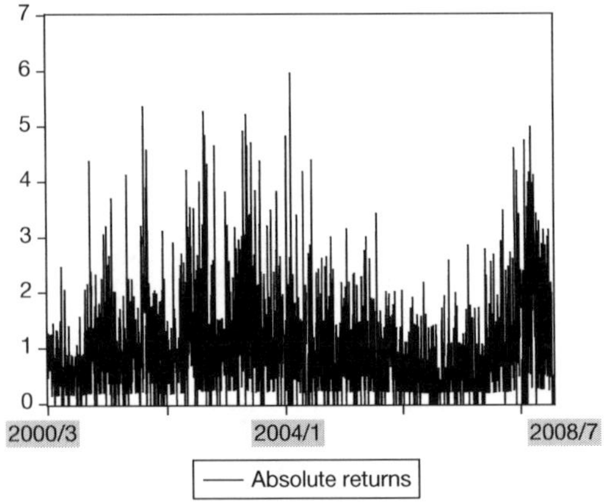

Sample: 10000 12136
Included observations: 1960

Autocorrelation	Partial Correlation		AC	PAC	Q-Stat	Prob
		1	0.107	0.107	22.671	0.000
		2	0.131	0.121	56.344	0.000
		3	0.103	0.079	77.035	0.000
		4	0.128	0.099	109.23	0.000
		5	0.178	0.143	171.22	0.000
		6	0.132	0.082	205.62	0.000
		7	0.118	0.058	232.99	0.000
		8	0.126	0.067	264.32	0.000
		9	0.144	0.080	305.40	0.000
		10	0.177	0.107	367.31	0.000
		11	0.138	0.060	404.70	0.000
		12	0.142	0.063	444.49	0.000

FIGURE 13.9 Transformations of Daily Returns to the 10-Year Treasury Notes and Their Autocorrelations

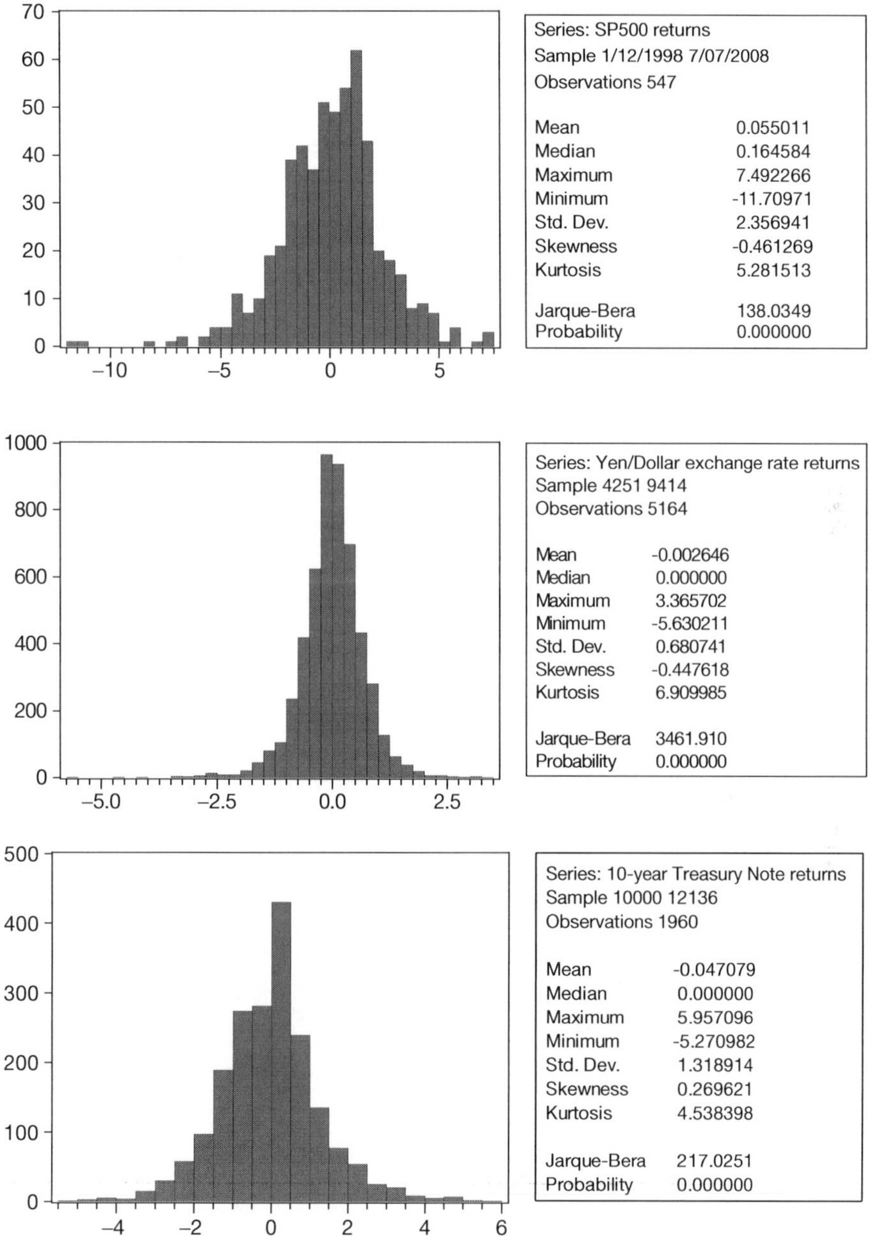

FIGURE 13.10 Unconditional Histograms of SP500, Exchange Rate, and 10-Year Treasury Returns

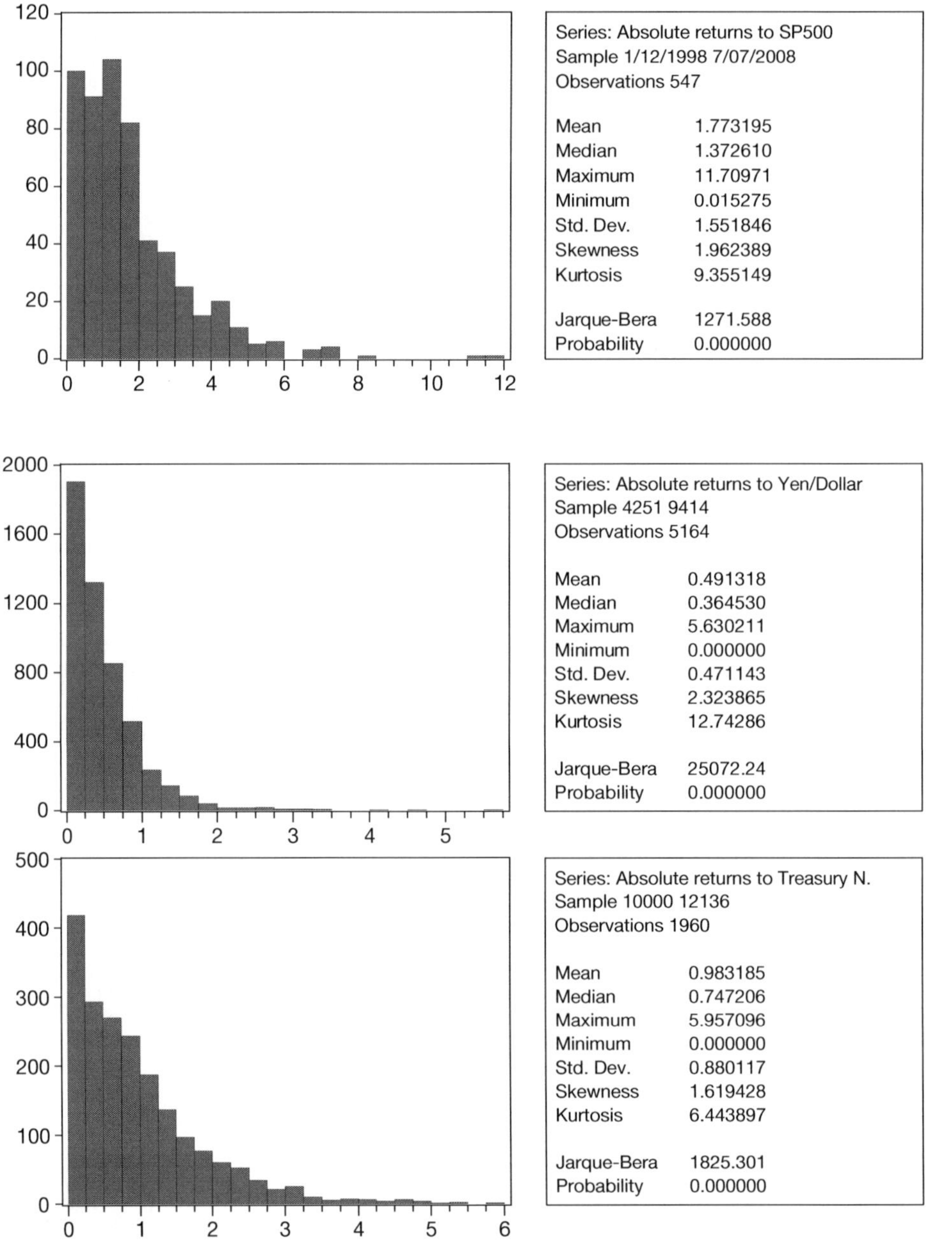
Series: Absolute returns to SP500
Sample 1/12/1998 7/07/2008
Observations 547
Mean 1.773195
Median 1.372610
Maximum 11.70971
Minimum 0.015275
Std. Dev. 1.551846
Skewness 1.962389
Kurtosis 9.355149
Jarque-Bera 1271.588
Probability 0.000000
Series: Absolute returns to Yen/Dollar
Sample 4251 9414
Observations 5164
Mean 0.491318
Median 0.364530
Maximum 5.630211
Minimum 0.000000
Std. Dev. 0.471143
Skewness 2.323865
Kurtosis 12.74286
Jarque-Bera 25072.24
Probability 0.000000
Series: Absolute returns to Treasury N.
Sample 10000 12136
Observations 1960
Mean 0.983185
Median 0.747206
Maximum 5.957096
Minimum 0.000000
Std. Dev. 0.880117
Skewness 1.619428
Kurtosis 6.443897
Jarque-Bera 1825.301
Probability 0.000000

FIGURE 13.10 *(continued)*

In summary, when volatiliy is time varying, it is also time dependent. In addition, time-varying volatiltiy makes the probability density function of the original process non-normal because of the thickness of the tails. The probability density function of time-varying volatility is positively skewed.

13.4 What Have We Learned So Far?

Let us summarize the main points of our discussion.

- Uncertainty can be measured in many ways. We have focused on several measures of dispersion, which broadly speaking, we refer to as "volatility."
- Volatility is not only time varying but also time dependent, which prompts us to think about econometric models that could capture these dynamics.
- We have examined several economic and financial time series and concluded that they share several statistical properties:

1. *Nonstationarity.* Stock prices, exchange rates, interest rates, and in general, any speculative prices have stochastic trends: unit root behavior is difficult to reject.
2. *Returns are calculated as the first difference of the log of prices.* This is the stationary transformation of speculative prices.
3. *Returns are uncorrelated.* From the autocorrelation functions, we conclude that they look like white noise processes.
4. *Returns have time-varying volatility, and large (small) movements tend to be followed by large (small) movements.* Thus, there are clusters of activity. Consequently, returns are not independent processes because we find dependence in their second moments (volatility).
5. *Returns are not normally distributed because they have fat tails.* They are leptokurtic with kurtosis coefficient larger than 3.
6. *Volatility can be estimated by several measures such as squared returns, absolute returns, or high-low range returns.* The auto correlograms of these measures point to autoregressive processes. In general, we find more persistence in absolute returns and in high-low range than in squared returns.
7. *The unconditional distribution of volatility is skewed to the right.*

13.5 Simple Specifications for the Conditional Variance

By following the notation related to returns, let us consider a general stochastic process $\{r_t\}$. Now our objective is to estimate and forecast the conditional volatility of this process. We start with two simple specifications that are very easy to implement because they will not require any estimation technique. In the following chapter, we will construct models that are more complex and require estimation and testing techniques.

For the stochastic process $\{r_t\}$, we define the conditional variance at time t, that is, $\sigma^2_{t|t-1}$, as the expectation of the squared deviations from the mean of the process, conditioning on the information up to time $t-1$:

$$\sigma^2_{t|t-1} = \left[E(r_t - \mu_{t|t-1})^2 \,|\, I_{t-1}\right]$$

As we have seen with the conditional mean, the modeling problem for the conditional variance consists of specifying the dependence of the conditional variance on the information set. In this section, we will analyze the following two models that are data-driven specifications:

1. **Rolling window average** or moving average (MA).
2. **Exponentially weighted moving average** (EWMA) or RiskMetrics model.

Both are considered smoothing algorithms because they are basically moving averages of past observations. We will implement MA and EWMA for the SP500 index returns. The implementation for the yen/dollar exchange rate and the 10-year Treasury notes is left as an exercise.

13.5.1 Rolling Window Volatility

The simplest estimator of the conditional variance at time t, conditioning on the information up to time $t-1$, is an average of the squared returns (in deviation from the mean) over the last n periods:

$$\hat{\sigma}^2_{t|t-1} = \frac{1}{n}\sum_{i=1}^{n}(r_{t-i} - \mu)^2$$

In this case the information set is the collection of the past n returns $I_{t-1} = \{r_{t-1}, r_{t-2}, \ldots\ldots r_{t-n}\}$. Note that to obtain the time series of volatility estimates, we roll the sample window. For instance, the estimator at time t runs from observation r_{t-1} to observation r_{t-n} with a total of n observations in the sum; now we roll the window one observation at a time so that the estimator at time $t+1$ will add the observation r_t and drop the observation r_{t-n} with a total again of n observations in the sum; the estimator at time $t+2$ will add the observation r_{t+1} and drop the observation r_{t-n-1} with a total again of n observations; and so on. The estimator can also be considered as a moving average where all the components of the moving sum have the same weight $1/n$.

The question is how to choose n. Although there is no rule to choose the optimal number of elements, a large number will produce a smoother and less noisy estimator as there are more components in the average. The 1-step-ahead forecast based on this estimator is simply the current estimate. With information up to time t, the 1-step-ahead forecast is

$$\hat{\sigma}^2_{t+1|t} = \frac{1}{n}\sum_{i=1}^{n}(r_{t+1-i} - \mu)^2$$

We can generate the time series of 1-step-ahead volatility forecast by typing the following command in the **Genr** function of an EViews workfile:

```
vol_ma = 0.25*(r2(−1)+r2(−2)+r2(−3)+r2(−4))
```

FIGURE 13.11 Rolling Window Volatility Forecast

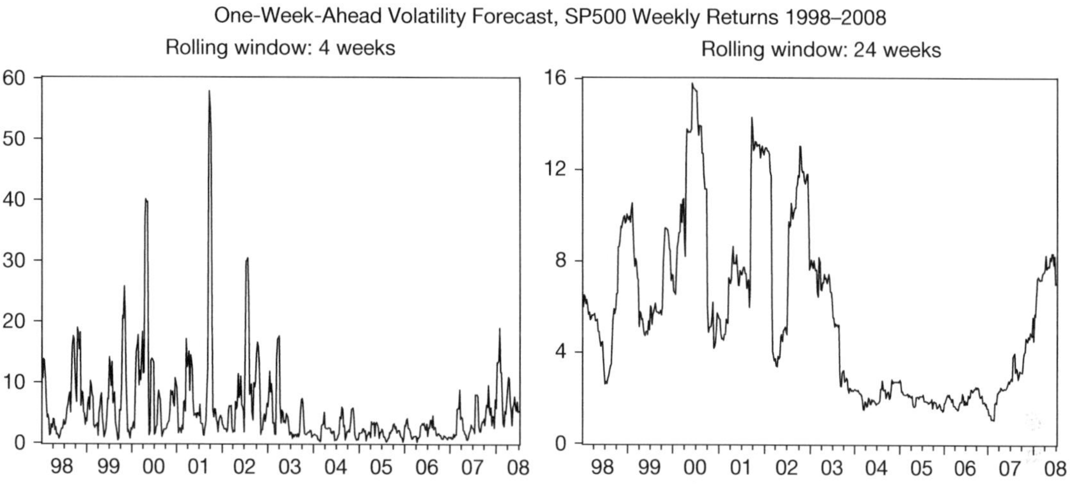

In this command, we are assuming that the mean is zero and that the rolling window is 4 weeks. The **r2** notation means "squared returns" that you need to obtain before you type the command (Genr r2=r*r).

In Figure 13.11, we plot the 1-week-ahead volatility forecast for the SP500 weekly returns. Observe the effect of a small rolling window (4 weeks) versus a larger window (24 weeks). The overall message is the same in both plots: the market was highly volatile from 2000 to 2002 and much less so from 2003 to 2006. In 2007 and 2008, volatility started to increase as the economic conditions related to the subprime market of mortgages in the United States deteriorated greatly. As expected, the 24-week window forecast is smoother and smaller in magnitude than the 4-week window forecast.

Given that the MA volatility estimator is not, properly speaking, derived from a model explaining the dynamics of $\{r_t\}$, we are severely constrained when we need to produce the multistep volatility forecast $\hat{\sigma}^2_{t+h|t}$. In this instance, the most we can do is to equate $\hat{\sigma}^2_{t+h|t} = \hat{\sigma}^2_{t+1|t}$.

13.5.2 Exponentially Weighted Moving Average (EWMA) Volatility

If instead of equally weighting past squared realizations (that is, weight $= 1/n$) we assign more weight to the most recent realizations than to those in the far past, we can define another estimator of the conditional variance as:

$$\hat{\sigma}^2_{t|t-1} = (1-\lambda)\sum_{i=1}^{t-1} \lambda^{i-1}(r_{t-i}-\mu)^2 \quad \text{for } \lambda \in (0,1)$$

so that the r_{t-1} observation has a weight of 1, r_{t-2} a weight of λ, r_{t-3} a weight of λ^2, r_{t-4} a weight of λ^3, and so on. This weighting scheme is called *exponential weighting* or *exponential smoothing*. Observe that the information set consists of all previous realizations $I_{t-1} = \{r_{t-1}, r_{t-2}, \ldots, r_{t-i}, \ldots, r_1\}$, but because $\lambda > 1$, the observations in the far past have an almost negligible effect in the current estimator of the conditional variance. This estimator is very popular within the risk management professionals. The technical document of RiskMetrics (JP Morgan, 1996) uses the EWMA estimator with a value of $\lambda \in [0.94, 0.97]$ for financial time series.

When the sample size is large, the previous estimator is well approximated by the following recursive expression, which is very easy to implement once we choose the value of λ:

$$\hat{\sigma}^2_{t|t-1} = \lambda \hat{\sigma}^2_{t-1|t-2} + (1-\lambda)(r_{t-1} - \mu)^2$$

This expression is a weighted average that assigns a weight of λ to the previous estimator of the conditional variance $\hat{\sigma}^2_{t-1|t-2}$ and a weight of $1 - \lambda$ to the most recent realization in the information set, that is, $(r_{t-1} - \mu)^2$.

As in the case of the rolling window estimator, the 1-step-ahead volatility forecast is the current estimate. With information up to time *t*, the forecast is equal to

$$\hat{\sigma}^2_{t+1|t} = \lambda \hat{\sigma}^2_{t|t-1} + (1-\lambda)(r_t - \mu)^2$$

We can generate the time series of the 1-step-ahead volatility forecast by typing the following program in the command window of your EViews workfile:

```
smpl 1/11/1960 1/11/1960
series vol_ewma=4.18
smpl 1/18/1960 @last
series vol_ewma= 0.94*vol_ewma(-1)+0.06*r2(-1)
```

We set the mean to zero and initialize the recursion by plugging in the value of the unconditional variance, which for the SP500 weekly returns is 4.18 (our sample started in January 11, 1960). The r2 notation means "squared returns" that we need to obtain before typing the command. We have chosen $\lambda = 0.94$. As a result, we obtain the 1-week-ahead volatility forecasts for the SP500 returns, which are plotted in Figure 13.12. Compare this figure with 13.12 to assess the differences between the EWMA and MA estimators. The time series profile between both figures is very similar, but the EWMA forecast is much smoother than the MA(24) forecast, and both are similar in magnitude. This is not very surprising because, by construction, EWMA considers a very large number of elements in the average.

In summary, the MA and EWMA specifications are not properly speaking "models" because their construction does not involve an analysis of the intrinsic time dependence of the conditional variance. We have not used the information about the dependence structure observed in the autocorrelograms of Figures 13.7, 13.8, and 13.9. The MA and EWMA specifications should be understood as smoothing mechanisms because they average (weighted or unweighted) past squared returns. These volatility estimators are

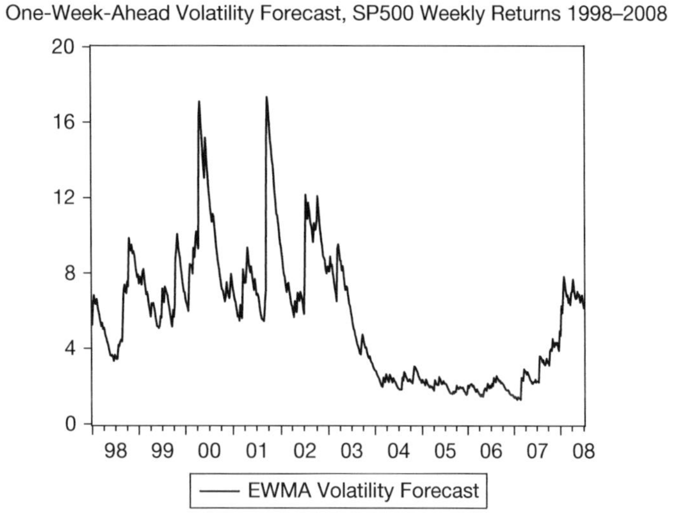

FIGURE 13.12
EWMA Volatility Forecast

appealing because of their simplicity: they are low cost, are easy to implement, do not require any estimation technology, and are very valuable for detecting trends in volatility.

KEY WORDS

conditional dispersion, p. 340
exponentially weighted moving average, p. 354
risk, p. 338
rolling window average, p. 354
severe price movement, p. 338
range, p. 340
uncertainty, p. 338
volatility, p. 338

EXERCISES

1. Choose any newspaper or business magazines and search for an article(s) or commentary that refers to risky, uncertain, or volatile environments. Interpret the article from the point of view of an economist and a forecaster.
2. Update the time series in Section 13.2 and comment on the volatility of recent times compared to that of past times.
3. Update the time series in Section 13.3 and for each of the three series, compute a 1-step-ahead volatility forecast by implementing MA and EWMA.
4. Based on the forecasts from Exercise 3, construct a 95% interval forecast for the returns of each of the three series. Assume that the 1-step-ahead forecast of the return is zero and that the returns are conditionally normal distributed.

5. Download the time series of U.S. CPI and GDP. Construct the inflation rate and GDP growth. For each, calculate the unconditional mean, compute the 1-step-ahead volatility forecast by implementing MA and EWMA, and construct the corresponding 95% interval forecast.
6. For the inflation rate and GDP growth from Exercise 5, find the best ARMA model for the conditional mean. Let us write this model as $Y_t = \mu_{t|t-1} + \varepsilon_t$ where $\mu_{t|t-1}$, the conditional mean, is the ARMA that you have found. Then, the conditional variance is $\sigma^2_{t|t-1} = [E(Y_t - \mu_{t|t-1})^2 | I_{t-1}] = [E(\varepsilon_t)^2 | I_{t-1}]$. Given this expression, retrieve the residuals $\hat{\varepsilon}_t$ and construct the 1-step-ahead volatility forecast by implementing MA and EWMA. Construct the corresponding 95% interval forecast for inflation and GDP growth, and compare these intervals with those from Exercise 5.
7. How volatile are house prices? Download house prices for several MSAs. Calculate their growth rate and compute their 1-step-ahead volatility forecast by implementing MA and EWMA. Which MSAs are more volatile?
8. Download a stock index at different frequencies: daily, weekly, and monthly. For each frequency, compute the 1-step-ahead volatility forecast by implementing MA and EWMA. Compare the volatility forecast across frequencies.
9. Download the daily stock prices of several stocks that belong to the index that you downloaded in Exercise 8. Calculate their returns and compute their 1-step-ahead volatility forecast by implementing MA and EWMA. Are they more or less volatile than the index?
10. For the time series that you worked with in Exercises 6, 7, 8, and 9, compute the autocorrelograms of the squared variables, the absolute value of the variables, and the range (whenever possible) of the variables. For which series do you find more time dependence? Explain.

CHAPTER 14

Forecasting Volatility II

In Chapter 13, we saw that the **conditional variance** of several economic variables is time-varying, that is, $\sigma^2_{t+h|t} \equiv \text{var}(Y_{t+h} \mid I_t)$. From a forecasting perspective, this is very important because when we construct forecast intervals, such as $f_{t,h} \pm k\sigma_{t+h|t}$, the time-varying standard deviation of the process will make the interval forecast either wider or narrower. We have also introduced two simple specifications of time-varying volatility, the moving average (MA) and exponentially weighted moving average (EWMA), which by being moving averages of past *squared* returns are very easy to compute. These are useful smoothing mechanisms to produce a quick estimator of volatility. However, they have limitations. MA and EWMA are not models in the sense that they are not designed to capture the intrinsic time dependence in volatility, and because of this, the most that they can offer, from a forecasting perspective, is the 1-step-ahead forecast of volatility.

If we want to exploit the inherent time dependence in volatility, a good starting point is to use the information contained in the autocorrelation functions of the *squared* variable of interest. The use of the autocorrelation functions has been our practice to propose different models for the conditional mean, and now we extend it to suggest different specifications for the conditional variance.

In Chapter 13, we saw the autocorrelograms of weekly squared returns to the **SP500 index**, daily squared returns to the yen/U.S. dollar exchange rate, and to the 10-year Treasury note (Figures 13.8, 13.9, and 13.10), which are reproduced here in Figure 14.1.

A common characteristic for the three autocorrelograms is that all show positive autocorrelation coefficients, and although the coefficients seem to be small in magnitude, they are statistically different from zero as the Q-statistics and their corresponding p-values (basically 0% probability) indicate. In addition, the autocorrelation functions show a slow decay toward zero, indicating that the squared returns may be amenable to be modeled as autoregressive processes.

In this chapter, our objective is to analyze different models for the conditional variance that will capture the time dependence that we observe in the autocorrelation functions such as those in Figure 14.1.

First, in Section 14.1—The ARCH Family—we focus on autoregressive processes for the conditional variance. As we did for the conditional mean, we introduce the modeling of the conditional variance by generating time series with similar dependence to that of Figure 14.1; we will analyze what the series looks like and, accordingly, we propose specifications that capture the dynamics of the data. Once a model is in place, we will construct the optimal forecast of volatility. In Section 14.2—Realized volatility—, we introduce the notion of realized volatility, which has a more complex

FIGURE 14.1 Autocorrelograms of the Squared Returns

SP500 index (weekly data)

Sample: 1/12/1998 7/07/2008
Included observations: 547

Autocorrelation	Partial Correlation		AC	PAC	Q-Stat	Prob
		1	0.236	0.236	30.605	0.000
		2	0.058	0.002	32.441	0.000
		3	0.083	0.073	36.282	0.000
		4	0.065	0.030	38.590	0.000
		5	0.041	0.017	39.525	0.000
		6	0.062	0.045	41.644	0.000
		7	0.072	0.044	44.538	0.000
		8	0.002	-0.032	44.541	0.000
		9	0.031	0.030	45.083	0.000
		10	0.057	0.035	46.911	0.000
		11	0.068	0.045	49.486	0.000
		12	0.054	0.023	51.110	0.000

Yen/US Dollor exchange rate (daily data)

Sample: 4251 9414
Included observations: 5164

Autocorrelation	Partial Correlation		AC	PAC	Q-Stat	Prob
		1	0.198	0.198	201.84	0.000
		2	0.113	0.077	268.31	0.000
		3	0.088	0.054	307.91	0.000
		4	0.069	0.037	332.32	0.000
		5	0.103	0.076	387.32	0.000
		6	0.090	0.049	428.94	0.000
		7	0.090	0.049	470.50	0.000
		8	0.094	0.051	515.75	0.000
		9	0.089	0.044	556.38	0.000
		10	0.032	-0.019	561.60	0.000
		11	0.071	0.041	587.55	0.000
		12	0.041	-0.001	596.28	0.000

10-year Treasury Note (daily data)

Sample: 10000 12136
Included observations: 1960

Autocorrelation	Partial Correlation		AC	PAC	Q-Stat	Prob
		1	0.089	0.089	15.563	0.000
		2	0.096	0.089	33.691	0.000
		3	0.067	0.052	42.535	0.000
		4	0.121	0.105	71.317	0.000
		5	0.186	0.163	139.06	0.000
		6	0.109	0.069	162.55	0.000
		7	0.111	0.068	186.85	0.000
		8	0.090	0.045	202.79	0.000
		9	0.126	0.072	234.20	0.000
		10	0.154	0.093	280.80	0.000
		11	0.129	0.067	313.52	0.000
		12	0.128	0.066	345.92	0.000

mathematical treatment, but from a practical point of view, it is much easier to implement than the models in Section 14.1 if we have access to **high-frequency data** (data sampled at very small time intervals).

14.1 The ARCH Family

By following the notation related to returns, let us consider a general stochastic process $\{r_t\}$. Our main objective is to estimate and forecast the volatility of this process.

We characterize the process $\{r_t\}$ as

$$r_t = \mu_{t|t-1} + \varepsilon_t$$

where $\mu_{t|t-1}$ is the conditional mean, which is a function of the information set containing all relevant information up to time t–1. We can think of any AR or MA or ARMA specification as we have analyzed in the previous chapters. The innovation ε_t is a white noise process, which by definition is uncorrelated. For an information set containing information up to time t–1, we define the conditional variance at time t, that is $\sigma^2_{t|t-1}$, as the expectation of the squared process in deviation from its mean:

$$\sigma^2_{t|t-1} = [E(r_t - \mu_{t|t-1})^2 \,|\, I_{t-1}] = [E\varepsilon_t^2 \,|\, I_{t-1}]$$

If the conditional mean $\mu_{t|t-1}$ is zero, then the conditional variance reduces to $\sigma^2_{t|t-1} = E(r_t^2 \,|\, I_{t-1})$. In Chapter 13, we have learned that financial returns behave like white noise processes (Figures 13.8, 13.9, and 13.10), thus assuming $\mu_{t|t-1} = 0$ is not a very stringent assumption, at least within the class of linear models.

To proceed with the modeling of the conditional variance, we emphasize three important points:

1. The error term ε_t is conditionally heteroscedastic because the conditional variance is time varying. We assume that the error term is multiplicative as in $\varepsilon_t = \sigma_{t|t-1} z_t$ where z_t is an independent innovation with zero mean and unit variance. Thus, the **heteroscedasticity** of ε_t is just driven by $\sigma_{t|t-1}$. The assumptions in z_t are consistent with the definition of the conditional variance: by taking the conditional expectation of ε_t^2, we have that

$$E\varepsilon_t^2 \,|\, I_{t-1} = E[\sigma^2_{t|t-1} z_t^2 \,|\, I_{t-1}] = \sigma^2_{t|t-1} E[z_t^2 \,|\, I_{t-1}] = \sigma^2_{t|t-1}$$

   where the second equality follows because $\sigma_{t|t-1}$ is a function of the information set so that it can come out of the expectation operator, and the third equality follows because z_t is assumed to be independent over time; thus, it does not depend on the information set, $E[z_t^2 \,|\, I_{t-1}] = E[z_t^2] = 1$.
2. Although the conditional variance of ε_t is time varying, the *unconditional* variance is constant. This is analogous to the results that we have already seen in the modeling of the conditional mean where the conditional mean is a function of the information set but the unconditional mean is a constant. We see that the unconditional variance of the innovation ε_t is a constant, σ^2_ε, by taking unconditional expectations as $E[E\varepsilon_t^2 \,|\, I_{t-1}] = E\varepsilon_t^2 = \sigma^2_\varepsilon$.
3. Within this characterization (points 1 and 2) of the process $\{r_t\}$, the conditional variance is predetermined as of time t–1. This is to say that because all information up to time t–1 is known, the conditional variance of the process is also known.

Now the interesting question becomes how $\sigma^2_{t|t-1}$ depends on the information set. Let us start by defining the **autoregressive conditional heteroscedasticity (ARCH)** models, in which the conditional variance is assumed to follow an autoregressive process. This is consistent with the information that we have encountered in the autocorrelograms of Figure 14.1. We propose a model with an error term that is conditionally heteroscedastic (see point 1),

$$r_t = \mu_{t|t-1} + \varepsilon_t$$

where $\varepsilon_t = \sigma_{t|t-1} z_t$, and z_t is an independent and identically distributed innovation with $E(z_t) = 0$ and $Var(z_t) = 1$, and $\sigma^2_{t|t-1}$ follows an ARCH process of order p, ARCH(p):

$$\begin{aligned}\sigma^2_{t|t-1} &\equiv E(r_t - \mu_{t|t-1})^2 \,|\, I_{t-1} = E(\varepsilon^2_t \,|\, I_{t-1}) \\ &= \omega + \alpha_1 \varepsilon^2_{t-1} + \alpha_2 \varepsilon^2_{t-2} + \cdots\cdots \alpha_p \varepsilon^2_{t-p}\end{aligned}$$

It is easy to see the autoregressive nature of this specification: In the left-hand side, the dependent variable is ε^2_t, and in the right-hand side, the regressors are p autoregressive terms $\varepsilon^2_{t-1}, \varepsilon^2_{t-2} \ldots\ldots \varepsilon^2_{t-p}$. The important feature of this specification is that the conditional variance of r_t is a function of the magnitude of the previous surprises ε_{t-i} for $i = 1, 2 \ldots. p$. Because ε_{t-i} is squared, the sign of the surprise is irrelevant; only the magnitude matters. This specification makes sense if we think that "surprises" are the source of uncertainty, which is at the heart of volatility. Because ARCH(p) is a parametric specification, our task is to estimate the values of the parameters α_is to obtain the estimates of the conditional variances. To guarantee that the conditional variance is positive, we need to impose the following conditions on the parameters: $\omega > 0$, $\alpha_i \geq 0 \; \forall i$.

Note that the modeling exercise of a process with conditional heteroscedasticity becomes slightly more complicated because we will need to model the conditional mean $\mu_{t|t-1}$ and the conditional variance $\sigma^2_{t|t-1}$ of the process. For the conditional mean, we may entertain any AR, MA, ARMA, or (ARIMA) specifications as we learned in the previous chapters of this textbook. For the conditional variance, we focus mainly on autoregressive representations such as ARCH models. In this chapter, we assume that there are not dynamics in the conditional mean; this is to say, $\mu_{t|t-1}$ is constant over time, and we focus exclusively on the modeling and forecast of the conditional variance of the process.

Let us proceed by simulating several ARCH processes. We can understand the main properties of ARCH processes by focusing primarily on an ARCH(1). An easy but less detailed extension, ARCH(p), will follow, and finally we complete the family by defining and analyzing a more general process known as a *GARCH(1,1) process*—generalized autoregressive conditional heteroscedasticity (GARCH). For these models, we answer the following questions:

- What does a time series of a (G)ARCH process look like?
- What do the corresponding autocorrelation functions look like?
- What is the optimal forecast?

14.1.1 ARCH(1)

Let us start with the first question and simulate a low order, ARCH(1), process. We specify an equation for the conditional mean and an equation for the conditional variance:

$$\begin{aligned} r_t &= \mu_{t|t-1} + \varepsilon_t = \mu_{t|t-1} + \sigma_{t|t-1} z_t \\ \sigma^2_{t|t-1} &= \omega + \alpha \varepsilon^2_{t-1}\end{aligned}$$

We say then that the process $\{r_t\}$ follows an ARCH(1) specification. We set the conditional mean to a constant value $\mu_{t|t-1} = 2$ to focus just on the dynamics of the conditional variance, and we assume that the innovation z_t is normally distributed $z_t \rightarrow N(0, 1)$ and is independent and identically distributed.

The following program in EViews simulates a time series with 1,000 observations for the return process r_t and for the conditional variance $\sigma^2_{t|t-1}$:

```
smpl @first @last
'define series: normal innovation (z),variance (vr), error (e), return (r)

series z= nrnd
series vr
series e
series r

'initialize the series to start the recursion, the vr starts at the unconditional
'variance value of 4

vr(1)=4
e(1) = @sqrt(vr(1))*z(1)
r(1)= 2+e(1)

'start the recursion from 2 to the number of observations you wish to generate
'we have set omega = 2 and alpha = 0.5

for !i=2 to 1000
vr(!i)=2+0.5*e(!i-1)*e(!i-1)
e(!i) = @sqrt(vr(!i))*z(!i)
r(!i) = 2+e(!i)
next
```

14.1.1.1 What Does a Time Series of an ARCH(1) Process Look Like?

We have simulated three ARCH(1) processes with three different values of $\alpha = 0.3$, 0.6, and 0.9 (see Figure 14.2). In all three cases, we set $\omega = 2$. The first column is the simulated time series r_t, and the second column is the corresponding conditional standard deviation $\sigma_{t|t-1}$.

Observe that when α becomes larger (other things being equal) the time series of returns (left column) becomes more volatile: Many more outbursts of activity occur, and the magnitude of the returns (either positive or negative sign) increases. This behavior is also reflected in the time series of conditional volatilities (right column); for instance, when $\alpha = 0.3$, the maximum spike in volatility is about 6%, but when $\alpha = 0.9$, the largest spikes are well above 40%.

What do we learn about the properties of the process $\{r_t\}$ if there is conditionally heteroscedasticity of the ARCH type? The lessons are in Table 14.1, which we describe next.

The *unconditional* mean and variance of $\{r_t\}$ are *constant*. In Table 14.1 (Panel A), we read that the unconditional mean is about 2, which is the value that we have set in the simulation. In Figure 14.2, we see that the time series of the returns (left column) wanders around this central value.

TABLE 14.1 Descriptive Statistics of ARCH(1) Process and Standardized Process

Panel A

Descriptive Statistics of an ARCH(1) process (returns)
Sample: 1 1000

	$\alpha = 0.3$	$\alpha = 0.6$	$\alpha = 0.9$
Mean	1.975935	1.947474	1.881775
Median	1.930632	1.924136	1.906267
Maximum	11.78598	24.60907	55.02234
Minimum	-4.482281	-17.69567	-49.36718
Std. Dev.	1.766631	2.611512	4.810237
Skewness	0.208300	-0.065491	-0.863349
Kurtosis	4.847531	19.48612	56.65335
Jarque-Bera	149.4553	11325.38	120069.3
Probability	0.000000	0.000000	0.000000

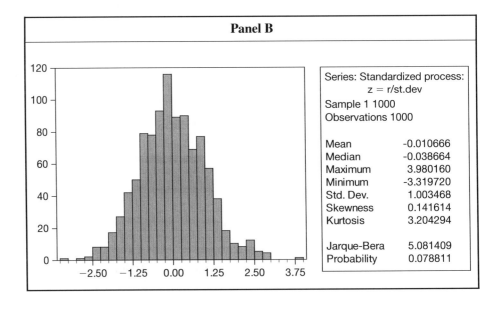

Panel B

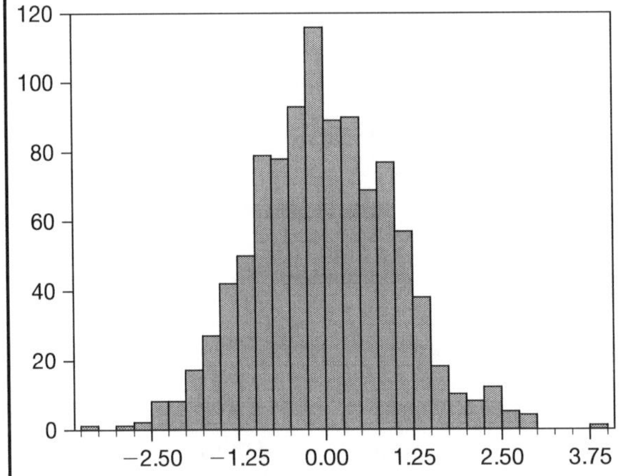

Series: Standardized process: z = r/st.dev
Sample 1 1000
Observations 1000

Mean	-0.010666
Median	-0.038664
Maximum	3.980160
Minimum	-3.319720
Std. Dev.	1.003468
Skewness	0.141614
Kurtosis	3.204294
Jarque-Bera	5.081409
Probability	0.078811

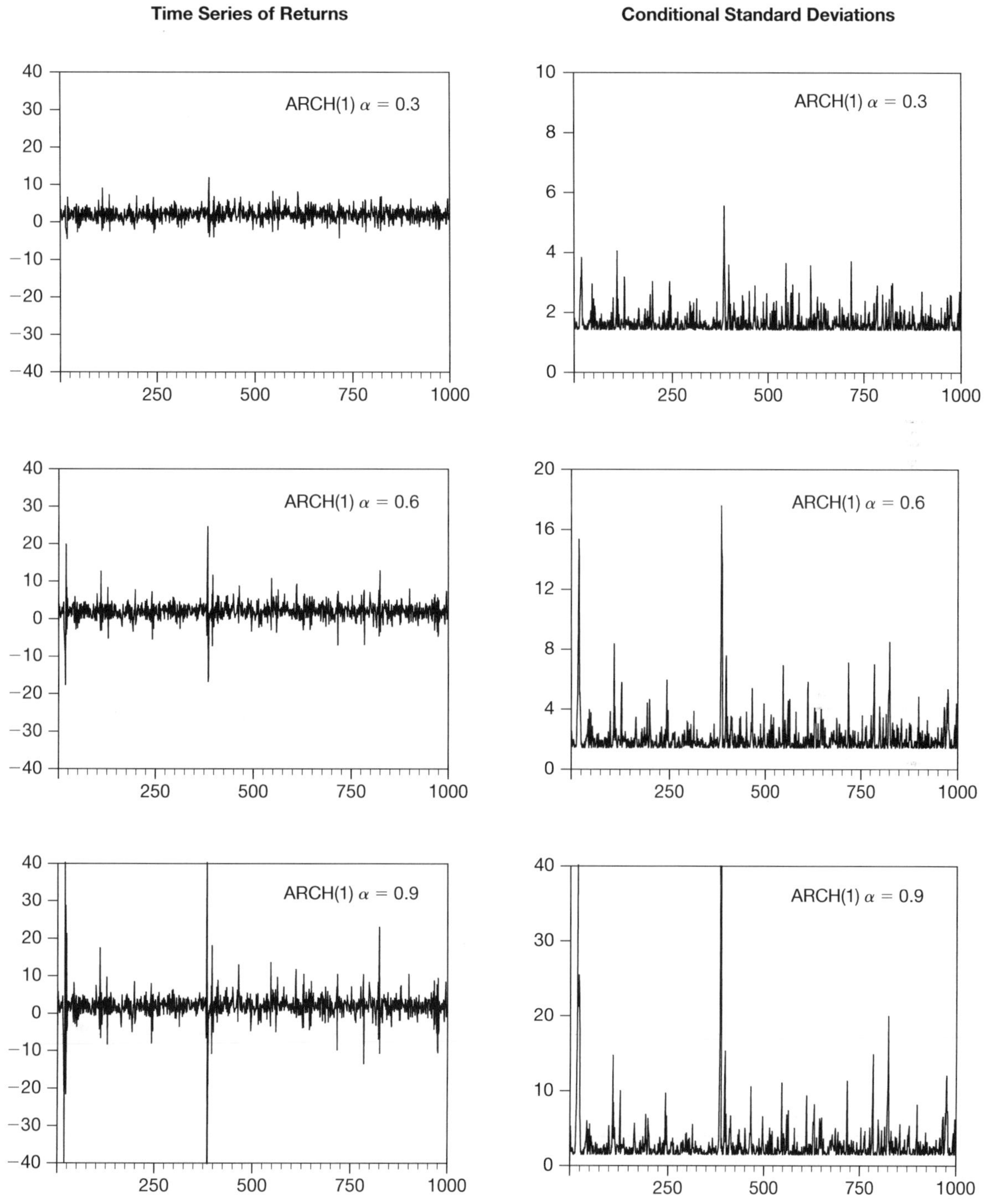

FIGURE 14.2 Simulated ARCH(1) Processes

The unconditional variance of $\{r_t\}$ is a function of the parameters in the conditional variance. Other things being equal, the unconditional variance (and standard deviation) increases with high values of α. In Panel A, the standard deviations are 1.77 (when $\alpha = 0.3$), 2.61 (when $\alpha = 0.6$), and 4.81 (when $\alpha = 0.9$).

The *unconditional* distribution of r_t *is not normal*. By checking Panel A we see that, though the skewness is close to zero, the kurtosis is much higher than 3, and the Jarque-Bera test rejects normality very strongly (p-values of the test are zero). This means that the process $\{r_t\}$ contains very large observations that contribute to the fatness of the tails of the unconditional distribution, hence the large kurtosis coefficient (see Figure 14.2). These large values are the result of the heteroscedasticity of the process so that the kurtosis increases for high values of the parameter α, other things being equal.

Now, let us check Panel B in Table 14.1. This panel describes the unconditional moments and histogram of the process z_t. From the equation for the conditional mean, $r_t = \mu + \sigma_{t|t-1} z_t$, we solve for z_t so that $\frac{r_t - \mu_{t|t-1}}{\sigma_{t|t-1}} = z_t$. We call z_t the *standardized process*. Remember that in our simulated time series, we assumed $z_t \rightarrow N(0, 1)$. Then once the conditional mean and the conditional standard deviation are estimated, we can construct the estimated standardized $\hat{z}_t$. If the dynamics of the conditional mean and variance are correctly specified, we should expect that $\hat{z}_t$ *be a standard normal random variable*. Because in Table 14.1 we simulated the process, we are sure that $\hat{z}_t$ will be normally distributed; however, when we use real data, this assumption needs to be tested. Observe that the skewness in Panel B is basically zero and that the kurtosis is around 3, and the Jarque-Bera test does not reject normality. In addition the estimated mean of $\hat{z}_t$ is around zero and the variance around 1, as we expected.

14.1.1.2 What Do the Corresponding Autocorrelation Functions Look Like?

Let us choose one of the simulated time series, say ARCH(1) with $\alpha = 0.3$. In Figure 14.3 we plot the autocorrelograms of r_t, r_t^2, $r_t/\sigma_{t|t-1}$, and $r_t^2/\sigma_{t|t-1}^2$.

In Panel A of Figure 14.3, we observe that the series r_t is uncorrelated; the simulated process does not have any dynamics in the conditional mean, therefore the autocorrelations functions should be zero. In contrast, the series r_t^2 is autocorrelated with the autocorrelation functions indicating an autoregressive process. These are the dynamics implied by the ARCH(1) model. Once we model the conditional variance as an ARCH(1), the standardized time series $r_t/\sigma_{t|t-1}$ and $r_t^2/\sigma_{t|t-1}^2$ should not have any autocorrelation left. What we find in Panel B is that the autocorrelation functions are clean, indicating that the ARCH(1) model is adequate to capture all dynamics of the process $\{r_t\}$.

With real data (Figure 14.1), we saw the autocorrelation functions of the weekly squared returns to the SP500 index. Observe that they have a similar profile to those of the simulated ARCH(1) process in Figure 14.3 Panel A, which makes this specification a candidate for modeling the dynamics of the conditional variance of the weekly SP500 returns.

FIGURE 14.3 Autocorrelation Functions of ARCH(1) Process

$$r_t = 2 + \varepsilon_t$$
$$\sigma^2_{t|t-1} = 2 + 0.3\varepsilon^2_{t-1}$$

Panel A

Times series r_t

Sample: 1 1000
Included observations: 1000

Lag	AC	PAC
1	-0.090	-0.090
2	-0.062	-0.071
3	0.071	0.059
4	0.050	0.059
5	-0.033	-0.015
6	0.020	0.018
7	0.011	0.004
8	-0.054	-0.051
9	0.009	0.001
10	-0.000	-0.009
11	0.001	0.008
12	0.036	0.042

Times series r_t^2

Sample: 1 1000
Included observations: 1000

Lag	AC	PAC
1	0.450	0.450
2	0.177	-0.032
3	0.063	-0.007
4	0.009	-0.015
5	-0.040	-0.044
6	-0.037	0.001
7	-0.030	-0.009
8	-0.040	-0.026
9	-0.033	-0.005
10	0.004	0.029
11	0.015	0.003
12	0.084	0.090

Panel B

Times series $r_t / \sigma_{t|t-1}$

Sample: 1 1000
Included observations: 1000

Lag	AC	PAC
1	-0.072	-0.072
2	-0.034	-0.039
3	0.079	0.074
4	0.050	0.061
5	-0.027	-0.014
6	0.024	0.018
7	-0.005	-0.012
8	-0.059	-0.060
9	0.013	0.003
10	-0.011	-0.015
11	-0.002	0.008
12	0.046	0.051

Times series $r_t^2 / \sigma^2_{t|t-1}$

Sample: 1 1000
Included observations: 1000

Lag	AC	PAC
1	0.067	0.067
2	-0.012	-0.017
3	0.018	0.020
4	0.007	0.004
5	-0.048	-0.049
6	-0.008	-0.001
7	0.033	0.032
8	-0.033	-0.036
9	-0.037	-0.031
10	0.012	0.012
11	-0.052	-0.055
12	0.018	0.031

14.1.1.3 What Is the Optimal Forecast Corresponding to an ARCH(1) Process?

With a quadratic loss function, that is, a mean squared error loss, and with an information set up to time t, the 1-step-ahead **variance forecast** is

$$\sigma^2_{t+1|t} = \omega + \alpha\varepsilon^2_t,$$

which is just an updating of the equation for the conditional variance. When the forecasting horizon is more than one-step $h > 1$, we need to use a recursive procedure.

Let us consider $h = 2$. Given that the information goes up to time t, the innovation ε_{t+1} is unknown at time t, and the most we can do is to ask for the conditional expectation of the squared innovation. Thus, the two-step-ahead forecast is:

$$\sigma^2_{t+2|t} = \omega + \alpha E(\varepsilon^2_{t+1} \,|\, I_t) = \omega + \alpha\sigma^2_{t+1|t}$$

Reasoning along the same lines, the three-step-ahead forecast is:

$$\sigma^2_{t+3|t} = \omega + \alpha E(\varepsilon^2_{t+2} \,|\, I_t) = \omega + \alpha\sigma^2_{t+2|t} = \omega(1 + \alpha) + \alpha^2\sigma^2_{t+1|t}$$

where the last equality follows from substituting the previous expression for $\sigma^2_{t+2|t}$.

For any $h > 1$, using backward substitution we find that the h-step-ahead forecast of the conditional variance is

$$\sigma^2_{t+h|t} = \omega(1 + \alpha + \alpha^2 + \alpha^3 + \ldots\ldots + \alpha^{h-2}) + \alpha^{h-1}\sigma^2_{t+1|t}$$

$$\underset{\text{h}\rightarrow\text{large}}{=} \frac{\omega}{1-\alpha} + \alpha^{h-1}\sigma^2_{t+1|t},$$

where the last equality follows by taking into account the sum of a geometric progression with $\alpha < 1$, which is equal to $1/(1 - \alpha) = 1 + \alpha + \alpha^2 + \alpha^3 + \cdots\cdots$. In addition, the forecast converges to a constant when the forecast horizon is large, i.e. $\sigma^2_{t+h|t} = \dfrac{\omega}{1-\alpha}$ for $h \to \infty$. This constant is the unconditional variance of the process (see Appendix A1 to show that $\sigma^2 = \omega/(1 - \alpha)$). Because $\alpha < 1$, the decay toward the unconditional variance is slow when α is large, and fast when α is small. This is analogous to the result that we saw when forecasting the conditional mean: As the forecast horizon increases, the memory of the model is lost, and the forecast converges to the unconditional mean.

14.1.2 ARCH(p)

An ARCH(p) is a generalization of the ARCH model that we analyzed in the previous section. The specification of the ARCH(p) process is

$$r_t = \mu_{t|t-1} + \varepsilon_t = \mu_{t|t-1} + \sigma_{t|t-1}z_t$$
$$\sigma^2_{t|t-1} = \omega + \alpha_1\varepsilon^2_{t-1} + \alpha_2\varepsilon^2_{t-2} + \cdots + \alpha_p\varepsilon^2_{t-p}$$

for $\omega > 0$, $\alpha_i \geq 0$ $i = 1, 2 \ldots p$.

The properties of the ARCH(1) extend to ARCH(p) processes with small modifications. The essential features that characterize ARCH processes remain the same. By now you have enough tools to simulate time series with ARCH effects. Choose any values for the parameters ω, and α_is with the restriction $\alpha_1 + \alpha_2 + \cdots + \alpha_p < 1$, which ensures the existence of the unconditional variance. You may want to start with a low p and increase it gradually. This is how you will proceed:

1. Modify the EViews program to allow for more autoregressive terms.
2. Plot the simulated series r_t and the conditional standard deviation or conditional variance. Check the effect of the ARCH terms on the time series of returns.
3. Look at the unconditional moments (mean and variance) of the simulated series r_t and check that they are in agreement with the population values that you have chosen in the simulation.
4. Understand the level of kurtosis and the non-normality of the time series r_t as a function of the ARCH parameters.
5. Read the autocorrelation function of the simulated time series r_t and the squared observations r_t^2 and check that the standardized series $r_t/\sigma_{t|t-1}$ and $r_t^2/\sigma_{t|t-1}^2$ have clean autocorrelograms.
6. Construct the optimal forecast $\sigma_{t+h|t}^2$ for several forecasting horizons.

Let us explore some real data. We saw that the weekly returns to the SP500 index may have some ARCH effects. Now instead of studying the weekly frequency, we analyze the daily frequency of returns. The overall profile of the daily returns is not very different from the weekly returns. It should not be, but when we analyze the autocorrelograms of *squared* daily returns, we find a striking difference because the daily data seem to have more persistence in the squared daily returns. In Figure 14.4, we plot the daily returns and their corresponding autocorrelograms of the *squared* returns.

The partial autocorrelation function of squared returns has many more significant spikes than that of the ARCH(1) process, and it prompts us to think that the autoregressive structure in the squared returns should be longer. Therefore, we could entertain an ARCH(8) or ARCH(9) for these data. At this point, we would like to estimate these

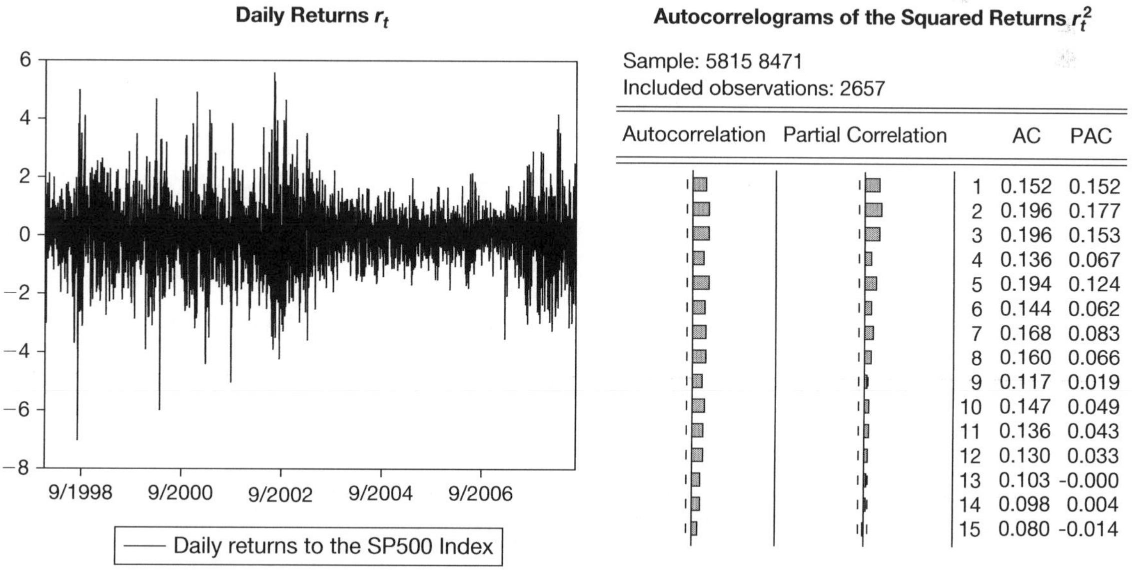

FIGURE 14.4 Daily SP500 Returns and Autocorrelations of Squared Returns

specifications, but because we have not yet discussed estimation of ARCH models, we are going to simulate the following ARCH(9) and calculate its autocorrelation functions:

$$r_t = 0.037 + \varepsilon_t$$
$$\sigma^2_{t|t-1} = 0.27 + 0.03\varepsilon^2_{t-1} + 0.15\varepsilon^2_{t-2} + 0.10\varepsilon^2_{t-3} + 0.10\varepsilon^2_{t-4} +$$
$$+ 0.08\varepsilon^2_{t-5} + 0.06\varepsilon^2_{t-6} + 0.09\varepsilon^2_{t-7} + 0.14\varepsilon^2_{t-8} + 0.08\varepsilon^2_{t-9}$$

Note that the sum of the α coefficients is very high, that is, $\alpha_1 + \alpha_2 + \cdots + \alpha_9 \approx 0.83$. This sum is also known as the *persistence in variance*. When the persistence is high, the conditional variance will tend to be high (or low) for many consecutive days. By simulating this process, we will obtain a time series with an autocorrelation function of squared returns very similar to those in Figure 14.4. In fact, the previously mentioned ARCH(9) model is the result of estimating the conditional variance of the SP500 daily returns. We deal with the estimation of these processes in forthcoming sections.

For now, we may be concerned that this model is highly parameterized, there are many parameters to estimate and we may wonder, in the spirit of parsimony, whether we can find a more parsimonious representation of a high order ARCH process. The answer is the subject of the next section.

14.1.3 GARCH(1,1)

A low order **generalized autoregressive conditional heteroscedasticity (GARCH)** is the GARCH(1,1), which has the following specification:

- An equation describing the dynamics of the conditional mean with an error term that is heteroscedastic

$$r_t = \mu_{t|t-1} + \varepsilon_t = \mu_{t|t-1} + \sigma_{t|t-1} z_t$$

  that is, $\varepsilon_t = \sigma_{t|t-1} z_t$, where $z_t \rightarrow N(0, 1)$ is an independent and identically distributed innovation (this is the same equation that we saw in the ARCH process).
- An equation describing the conditional variance

$$\sigma^2_{t|t-1} = \omega + \alpha\varepsilon^2_{t-1} + \beta\sigma^2_{t-1|t-2}$$

  with non-negative parameters $\omega > 0$, $\alpha \geq 0$, and $\beta \geq 0$.

The main difference with the ARCH specification is that the conditional variance at time t depends not only on the past innovation ε_{t-1} but also on the most recent level of volatility $\sigma_{t-1|t-2}$. For instance, if $\beta = 0.80$, we say that 80% of yesterday's variance carries over to today's variance. The order (1,1) means that we consider only the most recent lagged shock ε_{t-1} and the most recent lagged variance $\sigma^2_{t-1|t-2}$. It is possible to entertain higher order processes such as a GARCH(2,2) or GARCH(2,1), but these specifications are not that common with financial and economic data.

The main advantage of introducing the term $\sigma^2_{t-1|t-2}$ is that we obtain a specification that is more parsimonious (less number of parameters) than an ARCH process of large order. With a GARCH (1,1) model, we have three parameters (ω, α, β) to estimate while with an ARCH(9), as in the example of the previous section, we had 10 parameters to estimate. To understand this equivalence, we could use backward substitution in the GARCH(1,1) conditional variance equation as follows:

$$\begin{aligned}
\sigma^2_{t|t-1} &= \omega + \alpha\varepsilon^2_{t-1} + \beta\sigma^2_{t-1|t-2} = \\
&= \omega + \alpha\varepsilon^2_{t-1} + \beta(\omega + \alpha\varepsilon^2_{t-2} + \beta\sigma^2_{t-2|t-3}) = \\
&= \omega(1+\beta) + \alpha(\varepsilon^2_{t-1} + \beta\varepsilon^2_{t-2}) + \beta^2\sigma^2_{t-2|t-3} = \\
&= \omega(1+\beta+\beta^2) + \alpha(\varepsilon^2_{t-1} + \beta\varepsilon^2_{t-2} + \beta^2\varepsilon^2_{t-3}) + \beta^3\sigma^2_{t-3|t-4} = \\
&= \ldots\ldots\ldots\ldots\ldots\ldots\ldots\ldots \\
&= \omega/(1-\beta) + \alpha\sum_{i=1}^{\infty}\beta^{i-1}\varepsilon^2_{t-i}
\end{aligned}$$

As a result we learn that

1. A GARCH(1,1) process is equivalent to an ARCH process of infinite order, that is, ARCH(∞), with exponentially decreasing weights $\{\alpha, \alpha\beta, \alpha\beta^2, \ldots \alpha\beta^{i-1}, \ldots\}$ on the past innovations $\{\varepsilon_{t-1}, \varepsilon_{t-2}, \varepsilon_{t-3}, \ldots . \varepsilon_{t-i}, \ldots\}$, respectively.
2. The persistence of the GARCH(1,1) process (how permanent are the shocks ε_{t-i}s in variance) is the sum of all weights $\alpha + \alpha\beta + \alpha\beta^2 + \cdots\cdots + \alpha\beta^{i-1} + \cdots = \alpha/(1-\beta)$
3. When the persistence is equal to 1, that is, $\dfrac{\alpha}{1-\beta} = 1$, then $\alpha + \beta = 1$. This particular process is called an **integrated GARCH (IGARCH)** process, that is, IGARCH(1,1), borrowing the name from the integrated processes in mean or unit root processes that we studied in Chapter 10. An interesting feature of an IGARCH process is that the unconditional variance of the process, that is, $\sigma^2_\varepsilon = \dfrac{\omega}{1-\alpha-\beta}$ (see Appendix A1), does not exist. Because in the IGARCH(1,1) $\alpha + \beta = 1$, the denominator of σ^2_ε becomes zero and the unconditional variance of the error term explodes.

14.1.3.1 What Does a Time Series of GARCH(1,1) Process Look Like?

Let us simulate two GARCH(1,1) processes to assess the contribution of the α and β parameters. As in the ARCH(1) process, we set the conditional mean to a constant value, say $\mu_{t|t-1} = 2$, to focus just on the dynamics of the conditional variance, and we assume that the innovation z_t is normally distributed $z_t \rightarrow N(0, 1)$. We also set $\omega = 2$:

$$\begin{aligned}
r_t &= 2 + \varepsilon_t \\
\sigma^2_{t|t-1} &= 2 + \alpha\varepsilon^2_{t-1} + \beta\sigma^2_{t-1|t-2}
\end{aligned}$$

We simulate a time series with 2,500 observations for the return process r_t and for the conditional variance $\sigma^2_{t|t-1}$ in two instances:

1. Low persistence process: $\alpha = 0.4$, $\beta = 0.4$; the persistence is $\alpha/(1-\beta) = 0.67$.
2. High persistence process: $\alpha = 0.1$, $\beta = 0.88$; the persistence is $\alpha/(1-\beta) = 0.83$.

In both cases $\alpha + \beta < 1$, which ensures the existence of the unconditional variance. We modify slightly the EViews program to account for the GARCH term.
For process 1:

```
smpl @first @last
'define series: normal innovation (z),variance (vr), error (e), return (r)

series z= nrnd
series vr
series e
series r

'initialize the series to start the recursion, the vr starts at the unconditional
'variance value of 20

vr(1)=2/(1-0.4-0.4)
e(1) = @sqrt(vr(1))*z(1)
r(1)= 2+e(1)

'start the recursion from 2 to the number of observations you wish to generate
'we have set omega = 2 , alpha = 0.4, beta=0.4

for !i=2 to 2500
vr(!i)=2+0.4*e(!i-1)*e(!i-1)+0.4*vr(!i-1)
e(!i) = @sqrt(vr(!i))*z(!i)
r(!i) = 2+e(!i)
next
```

In Figure 14.5, we plot the simulated time series r_t and the corresponding conditional standard deviation $\sigma_{t|t-1}$ for the two GARCH(1,1) processes. In both processes, the unconditional mean of the process is 2, but the unconditional variance is larger in the high persistence process than in the low persistence process because the variance is a function of the sum $\alpha + \beta$. This is obvious from the plots. By calculating the population unconditional variance $\sigma^2_\varepsilon = \dfrac{\omega}{1-\alpha-\beta}$, we have that in the low persistence process, $\sigma^2_\varepsilon = 10$, and in the high persistence process, $\sigma^2_\varepsilon = 100$. In addition, the conditional standard deviations tend to be not larger in the high persistence process than in the low persistence process. The magnitude depends on the values of the parameters α and β.

FIGURE 14.5 Low and High Persistence GARCH(1,1) Processes

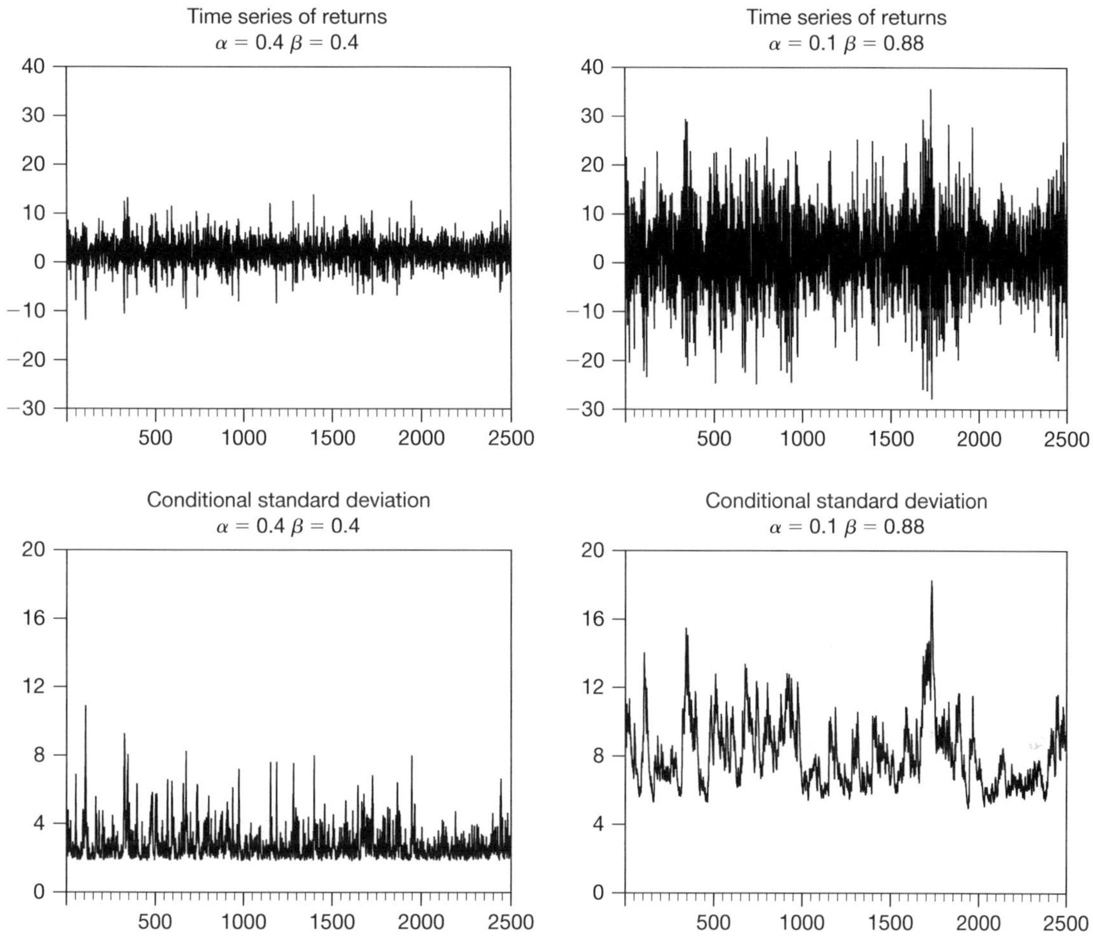

The plots of the conditional standard deviations also show the persistence of the process. For a high persistence process, once the volatility is high (low), it tends to remain high (low). In the high persistence process, 88% of the past volatility is transferred to the current volatility while in the low persistence process, it is only 40%. Thus, in a high persistence process, high (low) volatility is followed by high (low) volatility over longer periods of time than in a low persistence process.

In Table 14.2 we present the unconditional moments of the time series r_t for both processes. It is in agreement with the values of the parameters that we have chosen in the simulation: The unconditional mean is about 2, the unconditional variance is around 100 and 10 for the high persistence process and the low persistence process, respectively; the skewness is around zero (as expected for any symmetric density such as the normal), and the kurtosis is much higher than 3.

TABLE 14.2 Descriptive Statistics of Low and High Persistence GARCH(1,1) Processes

Descriptive Statistics of a GARCH(1,1) process (returns) Sample: 1 20000		
	$\alpha = 0.4$, $\beta = 0.4$	$\alpha = 0.1$, $\beta = 0.88$
Mean	1.992061	2.019090
Median	1.998115	1.993319
Maximum	67.24605	84.91548
Minimum	-46.49060	-80.57394
Std. Dev.	3.281838	9.920762
Skewness	0.160152	0.116894
Kurtosis	26.86840	5.859899
Jarque-Bera	474835.8	6861.400
Probability	0.000000	0.000000

14.1.3.2 What Do the Corresponding Autocorrelation Functions Look Like?

In Figure 14.6, we plot the autocorrelograms of the squared time series r_t^2 for the low and high persistence cases (1) and (2) respectively. The autocorrelation function profiles correspond to those from autoregressive processes. The degree of persistence in variance is also evident in the speed of the decay toward zero. The decay is faster in the low persistence process than in the high persistence process. In process (1), the autocorrelations are basically zero after 8 periods, while in process (2) the decay is very slow; even at the 14 lag there is substantial autocorrelation. Process (1) could be well approximated by an ARCH(3) while in process (2) we would need a higher order ARCH, that is, ARCH(5) or ARCH(9).

Going back to real data, review Figure 14.4, daily returns to the SP500 index, and compare the autocorrelation functions of the series of squared returns r_t^2 to those in Figure 14.6. Which process, low persistence (1) or high persistence (2), is closer to the autocorrelation function of the squared SP500 returns? No doubt, it is process (2). Remember that we estimated an ARCH(9) with a persistence of 0.83. Now we will see that a GARCH(1,1) offers a more parsimonious representation of the conditional variance of the SP500 daily returns than an ARCH(9) does.

In your EViews workfile, click on the following sequence

Object

New Object

Equation

FIGURE 14.6 Autocorrelation Functions of Low and High Persistence GARCH(1,1) Processes

$$r_t = 2 + \varepsilon_t$$
$$\sigma^2_{t|t-1} = 2 + \alpha\varepsilon^2_{t-1} + \beta\sigma^2_{t-1|t-2}$$

Time series r_t^2

(1) $\alpha = 0.4$, $\beta = 0.4$ (low persistence)

Sample: 1 20000
Included observations: 20000

	AC	PAC
1	0.470	0.470
2	0.383	0.208
3	0.376	0.182
4	0.249	-0.022
5	0.167	-0.046
6	0.139	-0.006
7	0.113	0.019
8	0.089	0.018
9	0.086	0.024
10	0.048	-0.029
11	0.034	-0.014
12	0.026	-0.006
13	0.015	0.002
14	0.019	0.017

Time series r_t^2

(2) $\alpha = 0.1$, $\beta = 0.88$ (high persistence)

Sample: 1 20000
Included observations: 20000

	AC	PAC
1	0.263	0.263
2	0.301	0.249
3	0.249	0.143
4	0.254	0.129
5	0.209	0.065
6	0.255	0.119
7	0.277	0.139
8	0.248	0.079
9	0.260	0.085
10	0.215	0.025
11	0.199	0.009
12	0.212	0.041
13	0.233	0.064
14	0.245	0.073

To estimate a GARCH(1,1) write the following commands in the specification window:

- In the mean equation: r c (the dependent variable is the return r and you want just a constant c in the conditional mean).
- In the variance equation select ARCH 1; GARCH 1.
- In the estimation settings choose ARCH.

In the rest of the options, leave the program defaults.

The estimation output is reported in Table 14.3. We go into more detail about the estimation technique of these models in the following sections. At the moment, pay attention to the estimates of the GARCH(1,1) model.

This is the estimated model (pick up the marked values):

$$r_t = 0.036 + \hat{\varepsilon}_t$$
$$\hat{\sigma}^2_{t|t-1} = 0.010 + 0.066\hat{\varepsilon}^2_{t-1} + 0.927\hat{\sigma}^2_{t-1|t-2}$$

With these estimated values of α and β, the estimated persistence is about $.90 = \dfrac{0.066}{1 - 0.927}$, very close to the persistence (0.83) of the ARCH(9) model. The advantage is that we have summarized the dynamics of the conditional variance with two parameters in the GARCH(1,1) specification versus nine parameters in the ARCH(9). A quick specification test is to check the autocorrelations of the standardized squared residuals, $\hat{\varepsilon}^2_t/\hat{\sigma}^2_{t|t-1}$. If these autocorrelations are zero, it means that the

TABLE 14.3 SP500 Daily Returns: Estimation of a GARCH(1,1) Model

Dependent Variable: R
Method: ML - ARCH (BHHH) - Normal distribution
Sample: 5815 8471
Included observations: 2657
Convergence achieved after 10 iterations
Bollerslev-Wooldrige robust standard errors & covariance
Variance backcast: ON
GARCH = C(2) + C(3)*RESID(-1)^2 + C(4)*GARCH(-1)

	Coefficient	Std. Error	z-Statistic	Prob.
C	0.036267	0.017439	2.079665	0.0376
	Variance Equation			
C	0.010421	0.005245	1.987099	0.0469
RESID(-1)^2	0.065649	0.011338	5.790038	0.0000
GARCH(-1)	0.927400	0.011045	83.96233	0.0000

R-squared	-0.000534	Mean dependent var	0.009761
Adjusted R-squared	-0.001666	S.D. dependent var	1.146761
S.E. of regression	1.147716	Akaike info criterion	2.888638
Sum squared resid	3494.671	Schwarz criterion	2.897498
Log likelihood	-3833.556	Durbin-Watson stat	2.079139

FIGURE 14.7 Autocorrelation Function of the Standardized Squared Residuals $\hat{\varepsilon}_t^2/\hat{\sigma}_{t|t-1}^2$ from GARCH(1,1) for SP500 Daily Returns

Sample: 5815 8471
Included observations: 2657

Autocorrelation	Partial Correlation		AC	PAC	Q-Stat	Prob
		1	-0.031	-0.031	2.5244	0.112
		2	0.033	0.032	5.4669	0.065
		3	0.007	0.009	5.6164	0.132
		4	0.005	0.005	5.6914	0.223
		5	0.006	0.005	5.7756	0.329
		6	-0.016	-0.016	6.4731	0.372
		7	0.000	-0.001	6.4731	0.486
		8	0.023	0.024	7.8948	0.444
		9	0.001	0.002	7.8965	0.545
		10	0.024	0.023	9.4796	0.487
		11	0.009	0.010	9.7071	0.557
		12	-0.010	-0.012	9.9971	0.616
		13	0.002	0.000	10.011	0.693
		14	-0.004	-0.003	10.063	0.758

dynamics in the mean and in the variance are correctly specified. This is the case for the SP500 returns. The autocorrelation function of $\hat{\varepsilon}_t^2/\hat{\sigma}_{t|t-1}^2$ is practically zero (see Figure 14.7), so that a GARCH(1,1) is a good model for the conditional variance of the SP500 returns.

14.1.3.3 What Is the Optimal Forecast Corresponding to a GARCH(1,1) Process?

As in the ARCH processes, we assume a quadratic loss function, that is, a mean squared error loss. With an information set up to time t, the 1-step-ahead variance forecast is

$$\sigma^2_{t+1|t} = \omega + \alpha\varepsilon^2_t + \beta\sigma^2_{t|t-1}$$

which is just an updating of the equation for the conditional variance. When the forecasting horizon is more than 1-step-ahead $h > 1$, we need to use a recursive procedure.

Let us consider $h = 2$. With information up to time t, the 2-step-ahead forecast is

$$\sigma^2_{t+2|t} = \omega + \alpha E(\varepsilon^2_{t+1} \,|\, I_t) + \beta\sigma^2_{t+1|t} = \omega + (\alpha + \beta)\sigma^2_{t+1|t}$$

and the 3-step-ahead forecast is:

$$\begin{aligned}\sigma^2_{t+3|t} &= \omega + \alpha E(\varepsilon^2_{t+2} \,|\, I_t) + \beta\sigma^2_{t+2|t} = \omega + (\alpha + \beta)\sigma^2_{t+2|t} = \\ &= \omega(1 + \alpha + \beta) + (\alpha + \beta)^2\sigma^2_{t+1|t},\end{aligned}$$

where the last equality follows from substituting the expression for $\sigma^2_{t+2|t}$.

Thus, by using backward substitution, for any $h > 1$ we find that the h-step-ahead forecast of the conditional variance is

$$\sigma^2_{t+h|t} = \omega(1 + (\alpha + \beta) + (\alpha + \beta)^2 + \cdots + (\alpha + \beta)^{h-2}) + (\alpha + \beta)^{h-1}\sigma^2_{t+1|t}$$

If the forecast horizon is very large, and for $\alpha + \beta < 1$, the effect of $\sigma^2_{t+1|t}$ becomes negligible, and the h-step-ahead forecast becomes

$$\sigma^2_{t+h|t} = \omega(1 + (\alpha + \beta) + (\alpha + \beta)^2 + (\alpha + \beta)^3 + \cdots) \rightarrow \frac{\omega}{1 - (\alpha + \beta)} \equiv \sigma^2$$

In other words, for $\alpha + \beta < 1$, the forecast converges to the unconditional variance of the process, that is, $\sigma^2_{t+h|t} = \sigma^2$ for $h \rightarrow \infty$.

If $\alpha + \beta = 1$—that is, IGARCH(1,1)—the forecast is different because the sum of the geometric progression in $\alpha + \beta$ is not finite. In this process

$$\begin{aligned}\sigma^2_{t+h|t} &= \omega(1 + (\alpha + \beta) + (\alpha + \beta)^2 + (\alpha + \beta)^3 + \cdots) + (\alpha + \beta)^{h-1}\sigma^2_{t+1|t} = \\ &= (h - 1)\omega + \sigma^2_{t+1|t}\end{aligned}$$

which says that the h-step-ahead forecast of the conditional variance is a linear function of the forecast horizon.

In summary, with the exception of the IGARCH process, the forecast of the conditional variance of a GARCH process enjoys similar properties to those of an ARCH process.

14.1.4 Estimation Issues for the ARCH Family

Although it is possible to estimate an ARCH model by running an ordinary least squares (OLS) regression of ε_t^2 on $\varepsilon_{t-1}^2, \varepsilon_{t-2}^2, \varepsilon_{t-3}^2 \ldots\ldots$, this is not the most efficient estimation technique. The preferred estimation method is maximum likelihood estimation (MLE).[1] This technique consists of maximizing the likelihood of occurrence of a sample of observations (time series sample) with respect to the parameters of the model. Let $\theta = \{\mu, \omega, \alpha \ldots\ldots\}$ be a vector of parameters—for instance, those in a ARCH(1) process—and $\{r_T, r_{T-1}, \ldots\ldots r_2, r_1\}$ the time series at hand. The likelihood of the time series is summarized by the joint density function of all the random variables in the stochastic process, say $f(r_T, r_{T-1}, \ldots\ldots r_2, r_1)$. Then, the *maximum (log)-likelihood estimator* $\hat{\theta}$ is obtained by maximizing the likelihood of obtaining the actual time series sample, that is,

$$\max_{\theta} \ \log f(r_T, r_{T-1}, \ldots\ldots r_2, r_1; \theta)$$

For most part, this mathematical problem does not have a closed form solution for the parameters of a (G)ARCH model. However, there are numerical techniques to obtain the maximum. Although MLE is the subject of more advanced textbooks, the program EViews provides maximum likelihood routines to estimate models such as those in the (G)ARCH family with just a couple of clicks.

We have already encountered the estimation of a GARCH(1,1) process for the daily SP500 returns in Table14.3. Let us reconsider this table and the estimation results of an ARCH(9) for the same data. Our purpose is to understand the information provided by the EViews program and contrast one model versus the other. Any other software will provide similar output.

In Table 14.4, we present the computer output for each model. Each table has four panels. In the upper panel, you read the dependent variable R; the estimation method is maximum likelihood, ML, under the assumption of conditional normality, and the numerical procedure to obtain the maximum is (BHHH) (for more information, you should check the EViews manual). The Bollerslev-Wooldridge robust standard errors is an option that you should choose most of the time. Recall that we have assumed conditional normality. This is an assumption and in some instances, it may be wrong. However, statistical theory proves that the MLE under normality is still asymptotically consistent even in those cases in which normality is the incorrect assumption; this theory is known as *quasi-maximum-likelihood* (QMLE). This is not so for the standard errors of the estimators, which are incorrect if normality is a false assumption. In this case, we can proceed to "robustize" the standard error against departures of normality. This is the option provided in the EViews output.

In the second panel of the computer output in Table 14.4, you find the estimates of the parameters in the mean; in both models, ARCH(9) and GARCH(1,1), we have a constant only in the mean equation. In the third panel, you see the parameter estimates of the conditional variance. Next to the coefficients, you read the robust standard error, the asymptotic t-ratio (z-statistic), and the p-value corresponding to

[1] See Appendix A2 for a detailed explanation of MLE for (G)ARCH processes.

TABLE 14.4 Maximum Likelihood Estimation of ARCH and GARCH Processes

SP500 daily returns—ARCH(9)

Dependent Variable: R
Method: ML - ARCH (BHHH) - Normal distribution
Sample: 5815 8471
Included observations: 2657
Convergence achieved after 16 iterations
Bollerslev-Wooldrige robust standard errors & covariance
Variance backcast: ON
GARCH = C(2) + C(3)*RESID(-1)^2 + C(4)*RESID(-2)^2 + C(5)*RESID(-3)^2 + C(6)*RESID(-4)^2 + C(7)*RESID(-5)^2 + C(8)*RESID(-6)^2 + C(9)*RESID(-7)^2 + C(10)*RESID(-8)^2 + C(11)*RESID(-9)^2

	Coefficient	Std. Error	z-Statistic	Prob.
C	0.037003	0.018214	2.031594	0.0422
Variance Equation				
C	0.271763	0.040891	6.645982	0.0000
RESID(-1)^2	0.029949	0.028081	1.066510	0.2862
RESID(-2)^2	0.149370	0.044623	3.347391	0.0008
RESID(-3)^2	0.095260	0.026377	3.611510	0.0003
RESID(-4)^2	0.101684	0.027620	3.681607	0.0002
RESID(-5)^2	0.082439	0.023397	3.523482	0.0004
RESID(-6)^2	0.060298	0.021251	2.837387	0.0045
RESID(-7)^2	0.090927	0.030511	2.980119	0.0029
RESID(-8)^2	0.142659	0.029601	4.819476	0.0000
RESID(-9)^2	0.082659	0.023815	3.470870	0.0005

R-squared	-0.000565	Mean dependent var	0.009761
Adjusted R-squared	-0.004346	S.D. dependent var	1.146761
S.E. of regression	1.149251	Akaike info criterion	2.910013
Sum squared resid	3494.776	Schwarz criterion	2.934377
Log likelihood	-3854.952	Durbin-Watson stat	2.079077

SP500 daily returns—GARCH(1,1)

Dependent Variable: R
Method: ML - ARCH (BHHH) - Normal distribution
Sample: 5815 8471
Included observations: 2657
Convergence achieved after 10 iterations
Bollerslev-Wooldrige robust standard errors & covariance

(continued)

Variance backcast: ON
GARCH = C(2) + C(3)*RESID(-1)^2 + C(4)*GARCH(-1)

	Coefficient	Std. Error	z-Statistic	Prob.
C	0.036267	0.017439	2.079665	0.0376
	Variance Equation			
C	0.010421	0.005245	1.987099	0.0469
RESID(−1)^2	0.065649	0.011338	5.790038	0.0000
GARCH(−1)	0.927400	0.011045	83.96233	0.0000

R-squared	-0.000534	Mean dependent var	0.009761
Adjusted R-squared	-0.001666	S.D. dependent var	1.146761
S.E. of regression	1.147716	Akaike info criterion	2.888638
Sum squared resid	3494.671	Schwarz criterion	2.897498
Log likelihood	-3833.556	Durbin-Watson stat	2.079139

the *t*-ratio for the null hypothesis of the parameter value equal to zero. This is the standard computer output that you have already encountered in the estimation of ARMA models in previous chapters. You could assess that all the coefficients are statistically different from zero at the 5% level (with the exception of α_1 in the ARCH(9) model). Both models seem to be good representations of the dynamics of the SP500 daily returns.

In the last and fourth panel of the computer output in Table 14.4 you read very standard statistics to assess the fit of the models. These statistics refer for most part to the fit of the mean equation. You may be surprised to find an R-squared that is negative—impossible! This is just a numerical glitch, and you should read a zero value here. However, remember that the adjusted R-squared may be negative. Finally, there is an entry in the last row of the tables that says **Log likelihood**. This is an important number because is the maximum value of the log-likelihood function. Compare both values for the ARCH(9) and GARCH(1,1) models. The value of the log-likelihood function for the GARCH(1,1) process is higher than that of the ARCH(9), indicating that the GARCH(1,1) model is preferred to the ARCH(9). Although this is an informal comparison, it is valuable information.

14.2 Realized Volatility

Conceptually, volatility is a latent variable: It is not observable, which means that we do not have databases from which to grab data on volatility. Within the ARCH family, we construct the conditional variance of a process by building a model, which depends on some information set. **Realized volatility** is an alternative measurement of price variability that relies on high-frequency data (data collected at very fine intervals of time such as every minute or every few seconds) and that has the advantage of being model free. In contrast to the ARCH family, we do not entertain any model but simply we will construct a measure, called *realized volatility,* from the raw (high-frequency) data itself.

In the ARCH family, we consider observations sampled at discrete intervals such as days, weeks, months, etc. so that the (G)ARCH models are defined in a **discrete time** environment. However, within the day, time flows continuously. If we think that information also flows continuously over time, then the dynamics of prices must also be continuous functions of time. Although the mathematical treatment of **continuous time models** is complex, we think of them as limiting representations of discrete time models when the time interval tends to zero. For instance, suppose that we have a discrete interval, say one day $[t-1, t]$ from Monday opening bell to Monday closing bell, and we partition the day in very small intervals of Δ length (see Figure 14.8).

Observe the time series of (log) prices over the interval $[t-1, t]$, $\{p(t-1), p(t-1+\Delta), p(t-1+2\Delta), \ldots\ldots p(t)\}$. Note that the notation has changed slightly from p_t to $p(t)$ to indicate that time t moves in a continuous fashion. Corresponding to the time series of prices, we construct the time series of returns as usual, that is, as the difference of the log-prices, $\{r(t-1+\Delta), r(t-1+2\Delta), r(t-1+3\Delta), \ldots\ldots\}$, where $r(t-1+i\Delta) = p(t-1+i\Delta) - p(t-1+(i-1)\Delta)$. When, the interval length becomes smaller and smaller such that $\Delta \to 0$, we will have *instantaneous* prices $p(t)$ and *instantaneous* returns $r(t)$. This is the meaning of continuous time observations. Accordingly, for this continuous time process $p(t)$, we can define an instantaneous mean or drift, $\mu(t)$, and an instantaneous or spot volatility, $\sigma(t)$, as the fundamental moments that drive the dynamics of continuous time prices.

Suppose now that we are interested in the *daily* variance of the daily return process, $r(t) = p(t) - p(t-1)$, where prices are in continuous time. If $\sigma^2(t)$ is the *instantaneous* variance, we could accumulate $\sigma^2(s)$ over every instant s contained in the one-day interval $[t-1, t]$ to obtain the daily variance. Technically, we write

$$IV \equiv \int_{t-1}^{t} \sigma^2(s)ds$$

where the integral $\int_{t-1}^{t}$ represents the continuous sum of the instantaneous variances. This measure IV is known as the **integrated variance** over the day. Note that IV is not observable because the instantaneous variances are not observable. However, it is possible to construct an estimator of IV so that this measurement becomes operational.

FIGURE 14.8
Partition of One Trading Day in Time Intervals of Δ Length

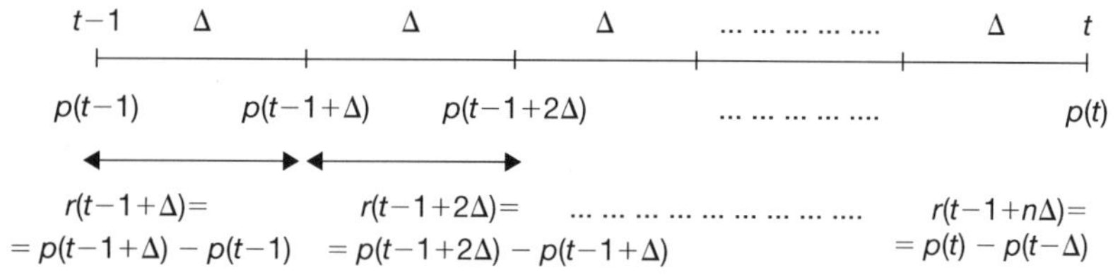

This estimator is known as the *realized variance* and it is calculated as the sum of the intraday squared returns (see the intraday return in Figure 14.8):

$$RV(t, \Delta) = r^2(t-1+\Delta) + r^2(t-1+2\Delta) + r^2(t-1+3\Delta) + \cdots\cdots + r^2(t-1+n\Delta)$$

$$RV(t, \Delta) = \sum_{i=1}^{n} r^2(t-1+i\Delta)$$

Observe that Δ is a discrete partition of the day, for example, 1-minute blocks or 5-minute blocks. When the partition becomes finer and finer, that is, $\Delta \rightarrow 0$, we move toward continuous time, and $RV(t,\Delta)$ approaches the integrated variance. If we have observations of intraday returns (high-frequency data), it is very easy to construct $RV(t, \Delta)$. Note that $RV(t, \Delta)$ is not a model for the daily variance but is just a measurement.

Let us construct $RV(t, \Delta)$ for the SP500 index. We have collected intraday data from January 3, 1994, to May 30, 2003. The data are sampled at the 5-minute frequency ($\Delta = 5$ min), and observations prior to 9 AM or after 3 PM have been eliminated. Thus, in one day we have 73 observations. To construct the realized variance, we prepare the data as in Table 14.5, where for illustration purposes we have chosen just one day, May 30, 2003.

TABLE 14.5 Construction of Realized Volatility Measure

Day	Time	SP500 index	5-min. return(%)	Squared return
20030530	900	954.75	—	—
20030530	905	956.20	0.151757	0.023030
20030530	910	958.29	0.218335	0.047670
20030530	915	959.89	0.166825	0.027831
20030530	920	960.38	0.051034	0.002605
20030530	925	960.71	0.034355	0.001180
20030530	930	961.82	0.115473	0.013334
20030530	935	961.70	-0.012477	0.000156
20030530	940	962.51	0.084190	0.007088
20030530	945	963.65	0.118370	0.014012
20030530	950	963.91	0.026977	0.000728
20030530	955	963.54	-0.038393	0.001474
20030530	1000	962.44	-0.114228	0.013048
20030530	1005	962.66	0.022856	0.000522
20030530	1010	963.15	0.050888	0.002590
20030530	1015	962.86	-0.030114	0.000907
20030530	1020	961.39	-0.152787	0.023344

(continued)

Day	Time	SP500 index	5-min. return(%)	Squared return
20030530	1025	961.18	-0.021846	0.000477
20030530	1030	961.51	0.034327	0.001178
20030530	1035	962.71	0.124726	0.015557
20030530	1040	962.47	-0.024933	0.000622
20030530	1045	962.29	-0.018704	0.000350
20030530	1050	962.40	0.011430	0.000131
20030530	1055	963.44	0.108005	0.011665
20030530	1100	963.38	-0.006228	3.88E-05
20030530	1105	962.84	-0.056068	0.003144
20030530	1110	962.05	-0.082083	0.006738
20030530	1115	962.52	0.048842	0.002386
20030530	1120	962.60	0.008311	6.91E-05
20030530	1125	961.88	-0.074825	0.005599
20030530	1130	961.49	-0.040554	0.001645
20030530	1135	962.68	0.123690	0.015299
20030530	1140	963.10	0.043619	0.001903
20030530	1145	963.62	0.053978	0.002914
20030530	1150	963.37	-0.025947	0.000673
20030530	1155	962.44	-0.096583	0.009328
20030530	1200	961.76	-0.070679	0.004995
20030530	1205	962.15	0.040542	0.001644
20030530	1210	962.25	0.010393	0.000108
20030530	1215	962.76	0.052987	0.002808
20030530	1220	962.97	0.021810	0.000476
20030530	1225	962.82	-0.015578	0.000243
20030530	1230	962.65	-0.017658	0.000312
20030530	1235	961.08	-0.163225	0.026642
20030530	1240	961.75	0.069689	0.004857
20030530	1245	961.05	-0.072810	0.005301
20030530	1250	960.16	-0.092650	0.008584
20030530	1255	960.86	0.072878	0.005311
20030530	1300	960.83	-0.003122	9.75E-06
20030530	1305	962.00	0.121696	0.014810

(continued)

Day	Time	SP500 index	5-min. return(%)	Squared return
20030530	1310	962.08	0.008316	6.92E-05
20030530	1315	962.45	0.038451	0.001478
20030530	1320	962.37	-0.008312	6.91E-05
20030530	1325	962.45	0.008312	6.91E-05
20030530	1330	962.99	0.056091	0.003146
20030530	1335	963.51	0.053984	0.002914
20030530	1340	964.74	0.127577	0.016276
20030530	1345	963.12	-0.168062	0.028245
20030530	1350	962.71	-0.042579	0.001813
20030530	1355	962.44	-0.028050	0.000787
20030530	1400	962.55	0.011429	0.000131
20030530	1405	961.54	-0.104985	0.011022
20030530	1410	961.57	0.003120	9.73E-06
20030530	1415	961.52	-0.005200	2.70E-05
20030530	1420	961.84	0.033275	0.001107
20030530	1425	962.69	0.088333	0.007803
20030530	1430	963.23	0.056077	0.003145
20030530	1435	963.53	0.031140	0.000970
20030530	1440	963.28	-0.025950	0.000673
20030530	1445	964.26	0.101684	0.010340
20030530	1450	963.49	-0.079886	0.006382
20030530	1455	962.94	-0.057100	0.003260
20030530	1500	963.08	0.014538	0.000211
				RV = 0.435278

The first column is the day; the entry 20030530 means May 30, 2003. The second column is the time written as a four-digit number; that is, 1355 reads as 13:55. The third column is the 5-min. SP500 index, the fourth column is the 5-min. return, and the fifth column is the *square* of the 5-min. return. The realized variance (RV) for the day May 30, 2003, is the sum of all the numbers in the fifth column and is equal to 0.435278, which correspond to a daily realized volatility of 0.6597% ($\sqrt{0.4352}$). By proceeding in the same fashion, we calculate the realized variance for each day in the sample to finally obtain a time series of daily realized variances. In Figure 14.9, we plot the *daily realized variance* for the SP500 index returns and its autocorrelograms.

The advantage of realized volatility is that we can model it with familiar techniques. By analyzing its autocorrelation function, we could propose some ARMA model. In Figure 14.9, we observe that there is high persistence in RV as the

FIGURE 14.9 Daily Realized Variance of the SP500 Index Returns and its Autocorrelation Functions

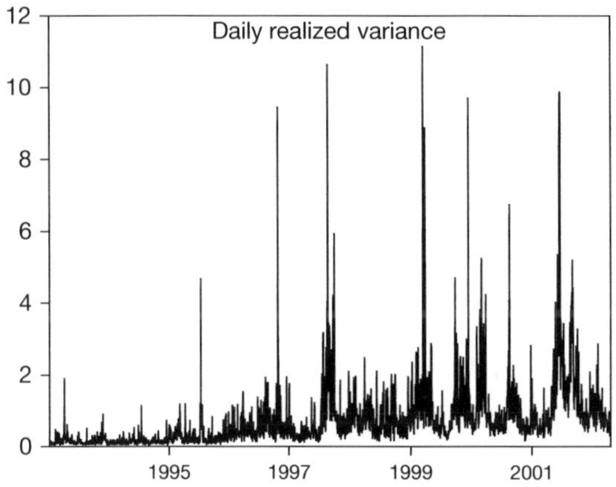

Sample: 1 2325
Included observations: 2325

Autocorrelation	Partial Correlation		AC	PAC
		1	0.664	0.664
		2	0.558	0.210
		3	0.492	0.112
		4	0.457	0.098
		5	0.437	0.087
		6	0.444	0.115
		7	0.466	0.133
		8	0.464	0.080
		9	0.418	-0.015
		10	0.395	0.020
		11	0.375	0.017
		12	0.352	0.000
		13	0.354	0.036
		14	0.348	0.013
		15	0.352	0.031

autocorrelation function decays very slowly toward zero; however, a unit root is rejected very strongly at the customary significance levels. The profile of the autocorrelograms seems to indicate that we will need a high order AR process to capture all linear dependence. An AR(8) seems to be a good model. The estimation results are presented in Table 14.6. As expected, most coefficients are highly significant and, most importantly, the autocorrelation of the residuals are whitened out, indicating that the AR(8) is a good model. The forecasting exercise now is straightforward. The guidelines that we studied in Chapters 7 and 8 on modeling and evaluating AR models apply. The AR(8) model is a standard AR process, and we need a recursive procedure to obtain the h-step-ahead forecast for $h > 1$. The only additional consideration when dealing with RV is that its probability density function is non-normal; it is heavily skewed to the right. This should be taken into account if we were to construct a density forecast for the variance.

However, by taking logs, the transformed log-realized variance seems to be distributed almost normally. Observe the histograms of the realized variance and the logarithmic realized variance of the SP500 returns in Figure 14.10. For these data, the logarithmic realized variance is closer to a normal density function than the realized variance, though there seems to be a bit of asymmetry to the left.

In summary, in Chapters 13 and 14, we have analyzed five different specifications to construct or estimate the conditional variance of a process. Some are purely data filters or smoothing mechanisms, such as the MA and EWMA, which do not require any estimation; some are parametric models, such as the ARCH and GARCH processes, which require estimation and testing; and some are nonparametric measures such as the realized variance, which are very easy to implement but require high-frequency data. There are many other models for the conditional variance in the econometric literature, but, in essence, they are variants of the specifications that we have analyzed in these chapters.

TABLE 14.6 Model Estimation for Realized Variance and Autocorrelations of the Residuals of the Model

Dependent Variable: RV
Method: Least Squares
Sample (adjusted): 9 2325
Included observations: 2317 after adjustments
Convergence achieved after 3 iterations

Variable	Coefficient	Std. Error	t-Statistic	Prob.
C	0.711977	0.099070	7.186622	0.0000
AR(1)	0.445480	0.020750	21.46895	0.0000
AR(2)	0.115790	0.022639	5.114754	0.0000
AR(3)	0.038028	0.022749	1.671618	0.0947
AR(4)	0.031595	0.022761	1.388122	0.1652
AR(5)	0.012130	0.022764	0.532867	0.5942
AR(6)	0.042751	0.022751	1.879081	0.0604
AR(7)	0.096943	0.022641	4.281793	0.0000
AR(8)	0.079860	0.020750	3.848777	0.0001

R-squared	0.500127	Mean dependent var	0.707774
Adjusted R-squared	0.498394	S.D. dependent var	0.925269
S.E. of regression	0.655314	Akaike info criterion	1.996472
Sum squared resid	991.1389	Schwarz criterion	2.018799
Log likelihood	-2303.913	F-statistic	288.6468
Durbin-Watson stat	1.997589	Prob(F-statistic)	0.000000

Inverted AR Roots	.95	.57-.55i	.57+.55i	-.04-.71i
	-.04+.71i	-.48+.43i	-.48-.43i	-.63

Sample: 9 2325
Included observations: 2317
Q-statistic probabilities adjusted for 8 ARMA term(s)

Autocorrelation	Partial Correlation		AC	PAC	Q-Stat	Prob
		1	0.001	0.001	0.0031	
		2	0.000	0.000	0.0033	
		3	-0.002	-0.002	0.0165	
		4	-0.003	-0.003	0.0431	
		5	-0.005	-0.005	0.1067	
		6	-0.008	-0.008	0.2441	
		7	-0.009	-0.009	0.4402	
		8	-0.008	-0.008	0.5868	
		9	-0.037	-0.037	3.7464	0.053
		10	-0.014	-0.014	4.1855	0.123
		11	-0.008	-0.008	4.3411	0.227
		12	-0.036	-0.037	7.3711	0.118
		13	0.002	0.001	7.3768	0.194
		14	-0.009	-0.010	7.5766	0.271
		15	0.010	0.009	7.8266	0.348
		16	0.011	0.009	8.0897	0.425

FIGURE 14.10 Descriptive Statistics of Realized and Log-Realized Variances

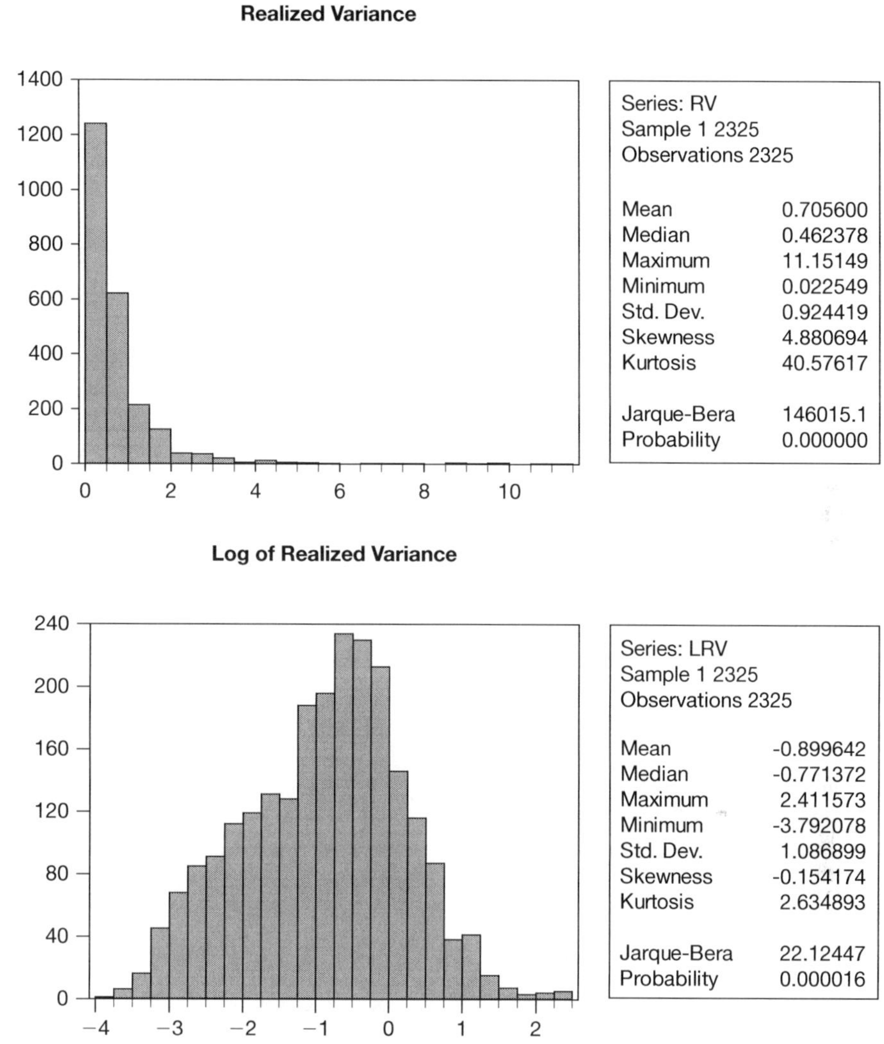

To finish this chapter, it is interesting to compare the daily conditional variances corresponding to the daily SP500 returns estimated by the previous five methods in addition to the **index of volatility (VIX)** provided by the Chicago Board Options Exchange (CBOE). This is reported in Figure 14.11. The scales are comparable across graphs except for the VIX. The profiles are very similar across the six time series plots, indicating a high volatile period from 1998 to 2002 in contrast to low volatility times from 2003 to the beginning of 2007. The magnitude of the conditional variance tends to be larger and more ragged in ARCH(9) and RV estimates, and, not surprisingly, MA, EWMA, and GARCH(1,1) specifications provide the smoothest estimates.

See Table 14.7 for the calculation of the contemporaneous correlation among the six series. The smallest correlation coefficient is between RV and the other five

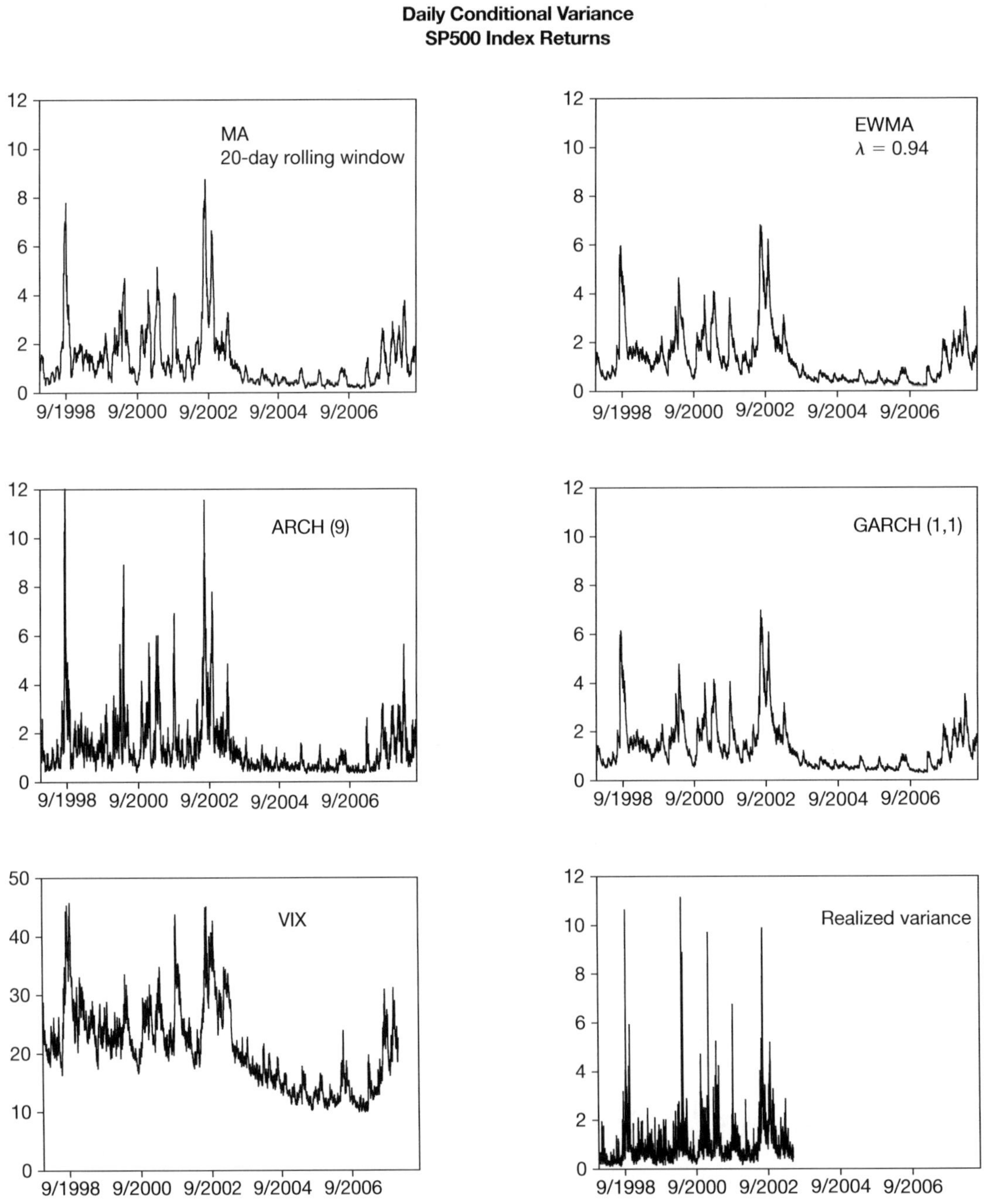

FIGURE 14.11
Six Specifications for the Daily SP500 Index Conditional Variances

TABLE 14.7 Correlation Among Six Different Models of the Daily SP500 Conditional Variance

Pairwise Correlation Matrix						
	MA	**EWMA**	**ARCH(9)**	**GARCH(1,1)**	**VIX**	**RV**
MA	1.000000	0.964857	0.835871	0.968584	0.761634	0.529553
EWMA	0.964857	1.000000	0.859502	0.996350	0.817245	0.559920
ARCH(9)	0.835871	0.859502	1.000000	0.886868	0.685414	0.462368
GARCH(1,1)	0.968584	0.996350	0.886868	1.000000	0.807793	0.563200
VIX	0.761634	0.817245	0.685414	0.807793	1.000000	0.464296
RV	0.529553	0.559920	0.462368	0.563200	0.464296	1.000000

estimates but nevertheless is substantial, around 0.50. The rest of the correlations are very high between 0.7 and 0.99, indicating the high similarity among the estimates. In particular, observe that EWMA and GARCH(1,1) estimates are almost identical and their correlation coefficient is almost 1. Both models have the strongest correlation with the VIX index, which is constructed from option market prices. This is good news because implementing EWMA is an easy task, and we can obtain a 1-step-ahead variance forecast very quickly.

Finally, given that we have alternative representations for conditional variances, a fair question is which one(s) is (are) best? The evaluation of volatility models is more complicated than that of the models for the conditional mean because, as we mentioned, volatility is nonobservable. However, we could run simple in-sample tests to assess whether the model is correctly specified. For (G)ARCH models, we should always check that the autocorrelations of the **standardized residuals** $\frac{r_t - \hat{\mu}_{t|t-1}}{\hat{\sigma}_{t|t-1}}$ and functions of them, such as the squared standardized residuals $\frac{(r_t - \hat{\mu}_{t|t-1})^2}{\hat{\sigma}^2_{t|t-1}}$, are statistically zero. This means that all linear dependence in the mean and in the variance has been correctly modeled and there is nothing left in the standardized residuals. In Sections 14.1.2 and 14.1.3, we have checked the autocorrelograms of the standardized residuals coming from an ARCH(9) and GARCH(1,1), and they seem to be white noise, confirming that these two specifications are good enough to capture the dynamics of variances. In contrast, the evaluation of models for the realized variance is straightforward because, as we saw, we follow the evaluation techniques that we learned for ARMA models. Overall, how good or bad a volatility model is depends eventually on the economic function of the user. What is the model needed for: to evaluate risk, to price securities, to formulate economic policy, and so on? These are meaningful "loss functions" that should guide the choice of the model. In the next chapter, we present several economic applications for which volatility forecasts are paramount.

KEY WORDS

APPENDIX

A1 Unconditional Mean and Unconditional Variance of (G)ARCH Processes

For any ARCH or GARCH processes, the unconditional mean of the process is obtained by taking the unconditional expectation in the equation for the conditional mean $r_t = \mu + \varepsilon_t = \mu + \sigma_{t|t-1} z_t$, so that we obtain

$$E(r_t) = \mu + E(\varepsilon_t) = \mu.$$

This result follows because $E(\varepsilon_t) = E(\sigma_{t|t-1} z_t) = E[E_{t-1}\sigma_{t|t-1} z_t] = E[\sigma_{t|t-1} E_{t-1} z_t] = 0$. We have used an important property of the expectation: For a given information set, the unconditional expectation of a random variable can be written as the unconditional expectation of the conditional expectation, where the conditioning is the information set, that is, $E[E_{t-1}(.)] = E(.)$. Because the conditional expectation $E_{t-1}(.)$ is taken with respect to the information up to time $t-1$, the conditional standard deviation $\sigma_{t|t-1}$ is not a random variable because at time $t-1$, all information is known. This is why $\sigma_{t|t-1}$ comes out of the conditional expectation operator in the third equality. From here, z_t is an independent random variable (it does not depend on the information set) with zero mean, and the final result follows.

To obtain the unconditional variance of the process, we proceed by analyzing different variance equations. Remember that the conditional variance is defined as

$$\sigma^2_{t|t-1} = E_{t-1}(r_t - \mu)^2 = E_{t-1}\varepsilon_t^2$$

and the unconditional variance is defined as

$$\sigma^2 = E(r_t - \mu)^2 = E(\varepsilon_t^2) \text{ for all } t.$$

ARCH(1): $\sigma^2_{t|t-1} = \omega + \alpha\,\varepsilon^2_{t-1}$

By taking unconditional expectations in this equation, we obtain

$$E\sigma^2_{t|t-1} = \omega + \alpha E(\varepsilon^2_{t-1}),$$

and, by applying the property of the expectation we have $E\sigma^2_{t|t-1} = E[E_{t-1}(\varepsilon^2_t)] = E(\varepsilon^2_t) = \sigma^2$. In addition, because the last equality holds for any t, that is, $E(\varepsilon^2_{t-1}) = \sigma^2$, we obtain that $\sigma^2 = \omega + \alpha\sigma^2$, and solving for the unconditional variance, we finally obtain $\sigma^2 = \dfrac{\omega}{1-\alpha}$.

ARCH(p): $\sigma^2_{t\,|t-1} = \omega + \alpha_1\varepsilon^2_{t-1} + \alpha_2\varepsilon^2_{t-2} + \cdots\cdots\cdots\cdots \alpha_p\varepsilon^2_{t-p}$

By proceeding as in the ARCH(1) process, we obtain that

$$\sigma^2 = \omega/(1 - \alpha_1 - \alpha_2 - \cdots\cdots \alpha_p).$$

GARCH(1,1): $\sigma^2_{t\,|\,t-1} = \omega + \alpha\,\varepsilon^2_{t-1} + \beta\,\sigma^2_{t-1|t-2}$
By taking unconditional expectations in this equation, we obtain

$$E\sigma^2_{t\,|t-1} = \omega + \alpha E\varepsilon^2_{t-1} + \beta E\sigma^2_{t-1|t-2},$$

We proceed as in the ARCH process: $E\sigma^2_{t|t-1} = E[E_{t-1}(\varepsilon^2_t)] = E(\varepsilon^2_t) = \sigma^2$; $E(\varepsilon^2_{t-1}) = \sigma^2$ and $E\sigma^2_{t-1|t-2} = E[E_{t-2}(\varepsilon^2_{t-1})] = E(\varepsilon^2_{t-1}) = \sigma^2$. Thus, the unconditional variance is $\sigma^2 = \omega/(1 - \alpha - \beta)$.

A2 Maximum Likelihood Estimation of (G)ARCH Processes

In time series, we construct the likelihood function of a sample by using a fundamental theorem of probability that relates a multivariate density to the conditional and marginal density functions. For two random variables, say X and Y, their joint bivariate probability density function $f(y, x)$ can be written as $f(y, x) = f(y\,|\,x)f(x)$ where $f(y\,|\,x)$ is the conditional density of Y given X, and $f(x)$ is the marginal density function of X.

How do we use this theorem with time series data? Let us assume that our sample has three observations $\{y_3, y_2, y_1\}$. We have three random variables, which may be time dependent, with a joint density function $f(y_3, y_2, y_1)$. The conditional density of Y_3 given past information $\{y_2, y_1\}$ is $f(y_3\,|\,y_2, y_1)$, so that $f(y_3, y_2, y_1) = f(y_3\,|\,y_2, y_1)f(y_2, y_1)$. But $f(y_2, y_1)$ can be decomposed further; by the same logic, $f(y_2, y_1) = f(y_2\,|\,y_1)f(y_1)$. Then

$$f(y_3, y_2, y_1) = f(y_3\,|\,y_2, y_1)f(y_2, y_1) = f(y_3\,|\,y_2, y_1)f(y_2\,|\,y_1)f(y_1)$$

Generalizing to a sample of T observations $\{y_T, y_{T-1}, \ldots\ldots\ldots y_3, y_2, y_1\}$, we write the joint density function of this sample as a product of the conditional density functions (and the marginal of the first random variable):

$$f(y_T, y_{T-1}, \ldots.\, y_2, y_1) = \prod_{t=2}^{T} f(y_t\,|\,I_{t-1})f(y_1)$$

where the information set is $I_{t-1} = \{y_{t-1}, y_{t-2}, \ldots\ldots y_1\}$.

By taking logs, we have $\log f(y_T, y_{T-1}, \ldots\ldots y_2, y_1) = \sum_{t=2}^{T} \log f(y_t | I_{t-1}) + \log f(y_1)$

If the sample is large, the effect of the first observation is negligible so that we can omit $f(y_1)$ from the previous expression. Alternatively, we could also condition on the first observation y_1 to write that

$$\log f(y_T, y_{T-1}, \ldots\ldots y_2 | y_1) = \sum_{t=2}^{T} \log f(y_t | I_{t-1})$$

Now let us recall any of the (G)ARCH models, for instance ARCH(1),

$$\begin{aligned} r_t &= \mu_{t|t-1} + \varepsilon_t = \mu_{t|t-1} + \sigma_{t|t-1} z_t \\ \sigma^2_{t|t-1} &= \omega + \alpha \varepsilon^2_{t-1} \end{aligned}$$

and recall that we have assumed that $z_t = \dfrac{r_t - \mu_{t|t-1}}{\sigma_{t|t-1}} = \dfrac{\varepsilon_t}{\sigma_{t|t-1}}$ is normally distributed. This assumption is equivalent to write that ε_t is also *conditionally* normally distributed $\varepsilon_t | I_{t-1} \rightarrow N(0, \sigma^2_{t|t-1})$ or that $r_t | I_{t-1} \rightarrow N(\mu_{t|t-1}, \sigma^2_{t|t-1})$.

Then the *maximum (log)-likelihood estimation* technique consists of obtaining the values of the parameters of the model, $\theta = \{\mu, \omega, \alpha\}$ such that the likelihood of occurrence of the sample $\{r_T, r_{T-1}, \ldots\ldots r_2, r_1\}$ is maximized. The likelihood of the sample is summarized by the joint density function of all random variables in the stochastic process; thus, we summarize this method by writing

$$\max_{\theta} \log f(r_T, r_{T-1}, \ldots\ldots r_2 | r_1; \theta) = \max_{\theta} \sum_{t=2}^{T} \log f(r_t | I_{t-1})$$

In addition, we already know what the conditional density of the returns is; that is,

$$f(r_t | I_{t-1}) = \frac{1}{\sqrt{2\pi\sigma^2_{t|t-1}}} \exp\left(-\frac{(r_t - \mu_{t|t-1})^2}{2\sigma^2_{t|t-1}} \right)$$

and by substituting it in the log-likelihood function, we have that

$$\max_{\theta} \log f(r_T, r_{T-1}, \ldots\ldots r_2 | r_1; \theta)$$

$$= \max_{\theta} \left[-(T-1)/2 \log 2\pi - \frac{1}{2} \log \sigma^2_{t|t-1} - \frac{1}{2} \sum_{t=2}^{T} \left(\frac{(r_t - \mu_{t|t-1})^2}{\sigma^2_{t|t-1}} \right) \right].$$

EXERCISES

1. Simulate an ARCH(4) process with high persistence in variance. Plot the time series and the conditional variances. Plot the histograms of the original time series and of the standardized time series. Comment on their differences. Compute the autocorrelograms of the original time series, the square of the series, the standardized series, and the square of the standardized series. Comment on their differences.
2. Simulate two GARCH(1,1) processes, one with low persistence and the other with high persistence in variance. For each process, plot the time series and the conditional variances. Plot the histograms of the original time series and of the standardized time series. Comment on their differences. Compute the autocorrelograms of the original time series, the square of the series, the standardized series, and the square of the standardized series. Comment on their differences.
3. Update the time series of the SP500 index in Section 14.1 and comment on the volatility of recent times compared to that of past times. Compute the autocorrelation functions of returns and squared returns. Find the best ARCH process to model the volatility of the index. Could you find an equivalent more parsimonious GARCH process?
4. Based on your findings from Exercise 3, calculate the one and two-step ahead volatility forecasts. Construct a 95% interval forecast for the SP500 returns. Assume that the returns are conditionally normal distributed.
5. In Exercise 5 of Chapter 13, you downloaded the time series of US CPI and GDP and constructed the inflation rate and GDP growth. For each, calculate the unconditional mean, and compute the 1-step-ahead volatility forecast by implementing the best (G)ARCH model, and construct the corresponding 95% interval forecast.
6. In Exercise 6 of Chapter 13, you found the best ARMA models for the conditional mean of the inflation rate and GDP growth. For each series, let us write this model as $Y_t = \mu_{t|t-1} + \varepsilon_t$ where $\mu_{t|t-1}$, the conditional mean, is the ARMA that you have found. Then, the conditional variance is $\sigma^2_{t\,|t-1} = [E(Y_t - \mu_{t|t-1})^2 \,|\, I_{t-1}] = [E(\varepsilon_t)^2 \,|\, I_{t-1}]$. Given this expression, retrieve the residuals $\hat{\varepsilon}_t$ and construct the 1-step-ahead volatility forecast by implementing the best (G)ARCH model. Construct the corresponding 95% interval forecast for inflation and GDP growth, and compare these intervals with those from Exercise 5.
7. Following with Exercise 7 of Chapter 13: How volatile are house prices? You have downloaded house prices for several MSAs and calculated their growth rate. Compute their 1-step-ahead volatility forecast by implementing the best (G)ARCH process. Which MSAs are more volatile? Compare the GARCH volatilities with those from the MA and EWMA. Are they highly correlated?

8. Following with Exercise 8 of Chapter 13: you have downloaded a stock index at different frequencies, daily, weekly, and monthly. For each frequency, compute the 1-step-ahead volatility forecast by implementing the best (G)ARCH model and compare it to that of MA and EWMA.

9. Following with Exercise 9 of Chapter 13: you have downloaded the daily stock prices of several stocks that belong to the index in Exercise 8. Compute the 1-step-ahead volatility forecast of stock returns by implementing the best (G)ARCH model and compare it to those of MA and EWMA. Are they more or less volatile than the index?

10. In Section 14.2 we have constructed the daily realized volatility measurement for the SP500 index returns. Suppose that we would like to construct the monthly realized volatility of the SP500 index returns by aggregating daily squared returns. Construct such a measure, and compare it with the monthly volatility from the best GARCH process and with the monthly volatility provided by MA and EWMA.

CHAPTER 15

Financial Applications of Time-Varying Volatility

Introduction

In Chapters 13 and 14, we learned that volatility is time varying and that we can construct models that explain the time dependence in variance. In this chapter, our objective is to practice the modeling and forecasting of time-varying conditional variances. The areas of finance and investments provide a natural field to showcase the relevance of conditional variances for modeling and forecasting returns and risk relations. In this chapter, we analyze four applications: **risk management**, **portfolio allocation**, **asset pricing**, and **option pricing**.

Investors and financial institutions allocate capital among different assets that may present different risk profiles. Some assets are considered less risky than others because their payoffs are more certain than others. For instance, money market accounts, Treasury bills, and bonds are safer assets than stocks. With any fixed income product, you enter into a contractual obligation that specifies your payoffs over the life of an asset. Although the payoffs may be fixed, the price of the bond still moves up and down, and unless you keep the bond to maturity, you bear the risk that the principal will shrink over time. In contrast, a stock is a participation in the business of a company; fundamentally, the price of a stock reflects the company's future outlook, and it faces the uncertainty of the particular business and of the economy in general. The stock may or may not pay a dividend. Thus, investors decide what to invest in by assessing not only the future return but also the associated risk of the investment. This is *decision making under uncertainty.* In the previous chapters, we learned how to measure this uncertainty by focusing on the modeling of the conditional variance, and now we are ready to apply our knowledge to very relevant economic questions.

15.1 Risk Management

In **risk management**, the main issue involves the assessment of losses in a probabilistic fashion. Although there are different approaches to risk evaluation, all offer complementary views of risk. We will analyze the following two measures: value-at-risk and expected shortfall.

15.1.1 Value-at-Risk (VaR)

Suppose that you are managing a portfolio of assets and you have a long position, that is, you are a buyer of assets. A negative scenario for your portfolio is when the prices of the assets go down, and a positive scenario is when the prices go up. Then it is easy to calculate the potential *maximum* loss: If all assets in your portfolio become worthless, you will have a 100% capital loss. However, a more difficult but more interesting issue refers to the probability of such an event. It is hoped that this probability is negligible! Moving away from the extreme scenario of a 100% capital loss, we find it of interest to assess what is the probability of, for instance, a 40%, 30%, or 10% loss. Equivalently, we may want to investigate how much capital would be lost if a low-probability but negative event were to happen. These are the fundamental questions behind *value-at-risk* (VaR).

VaR calculations are very prominent among the banking and nonbanking financial institutions. U.S. banking and thrift institutions need to maintain minimum capital requirements, which regulatory agents monitor periodically. These institutions follow the normative of the Basle Accord, originated in 1989, that endorses the VaR methodology to assess and monitor market risk capital requirements. Regulators primarily require the institution to calculate the 1% VaR (99% confidence level) for a 10-day horizon, and to hold enough capital to cover the potential losses assessed by the VaR measure.

The definition of **value-at-risk (VaR)** is straightforward. You may have already guessed that we are talking about the quantiles of a random variable. Formally speaking, for a random variable r_t (e.g., portfolio return), we define the α-VaR, called $r_t^{VaR(\alpha)}$, as the value of r_t such that the probability of obtaining an equal or smaller value than r_t is $\alpha\%$. Thus, we write

$$P(r_t \leq r_t^{VaR(\alpha)}) = \alpha$$

Because $P(r_t \leq r_t^{VaR(\alpha)})$ is the cumulative distribution function F of the random variable r_t, we can also write that

$$F(r_t^{VaR(\alpha)}) = \alpha$$

so that, solving for $r_t^{VaR(\alpha)}$ we have that

$$r_t^{VaR(\alpha)} = F^{-1}(\alpha)$$

which is also known as the α-quantile of r_t.

Graphically, in Figure 15.1, we draw the probability density function of r_t, and we find the value $r_t^{VaR(\alpha)}$ that satisfies $P(r_t \leq r_t^{VaR(\alpha)}) = \alpha$.

FIGURE 15.1
α-Value-at-Risk

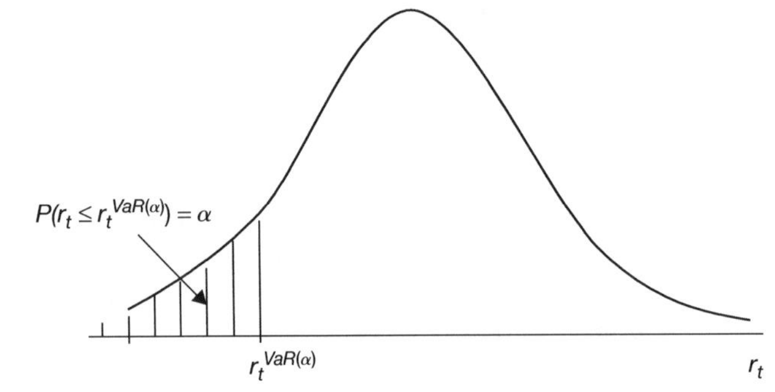

Now suppose that $\{r_t\}$ is the stochastic process of returns to a portfolio of assets that has the following familiar representation analyzed in Chapter 14:

$$r_t = \mu_{t|t-1} + \sigma_{t|t-1} z_t$$

where $z_t \rightarrow N(0,1)$ is an identical and independently distributed normal variate, and $\mu_{t|t-1}$ and $\sigma_{t|t-1}$ are the conditional mean and conditional standard deviation, respectively. We would like to calculate the VaR $r_t^{VaR(\alpha)}$ of this portfolio. By standardizing the random variable r_t and applying the definition of VaR, we write

$$P\left(\frac{r_t - \mu_{t|t-1}}{\sigma_{t|t-1}} \leq \frac{r_t^{VaR(\alpha)} - \mu_{t|t-1}}{\sigma_{t|t-1}}\right) = \alpha$$

but the standardized random variable r_t is a standard normal variable, that is, $\frac{r_t - \mu_{t|t-1}}{\sigma_{t|t-1}} = z_t$.

If we choose probability α, say $\alpha = 5\%$, we can easily find the value of r_t that corresponds to a 5% probability in the left tail, which is $P(z_t \leq -1.645) = 5\%$. Then it must be the case that

$$\frac{r_t^{VaR(\alpha)} - \mu_{t|t-1}}{\sigma_{t|t-1}} = -1.645$$

and, solving for the 5% VaR, we have

$$r_t^{VaR(\alpha)} = \mu_{t|t-1} - 1.645\sigma_{t|t-1}$$

If $\alpha = 1\%$, then $P(z_t \leq -2.33) = 1\%$, and $r_t^{VaR(\alpha)} = \mu_{t|t-1} - 2.33\sigma_{t|t-1}$. Thus, the constant that multiplies the conditional standard deviation depends on the distributional assumption on z_t. Observe that $r_t^{VaR(\alpha)}$ is also a *conditional* measure because it depends on the same information set as the conditional mean and the conditional standard deviation. A forecast for $r_t^{VaR(\alpha)}$ depends on the forecast of the conditional mean and of the conditional standard deviation. This is where our knowledge of time series modeling of the conditional mean and variance needs to be applied.

Let us take advantage of our modeling of the SP500 daily returns in Chapter 14 and calculate the 5% and 1% VaRs. In Table 14.3 (Chapter 14), we estimated a GARCH(1,1) process. From this model, we use the 1-step-ahead conditional standard deviation to calculate the 1-step-ahead VaR. We set the conditional mean to zero because the estimated value is basically zero. Then for the SP500 daily returns, the 5% VaR is

$$r_{t+1|t}^{VaR(.05)} = -1.645\sigma_{t+1|t}$$

and the 1% VaR is

$$r_{t+1|t}^{VaR(.01)} = -2.33\sigma_{t+1|t}$$

In Figure 15.2, the light grey line is the conditional 1% VaR. Let us take any of the values of the 1-day-ahead forecast of the conditional standard deviation. For instance, on April 2, 2008, the 1-day-ahead conditional standard deviation is $\sigma_{t+1|t} = 1.78$, so that the 1-day-ahead 1% VaR is –4.16% (-2.33×1.78). If on April 2, we have a portfolio of \$100,000, there is 1% chance that we could lose at least \$4,160 on April 3. Observe that, over the time series plot, there are some violations of the 1% boundary; these are

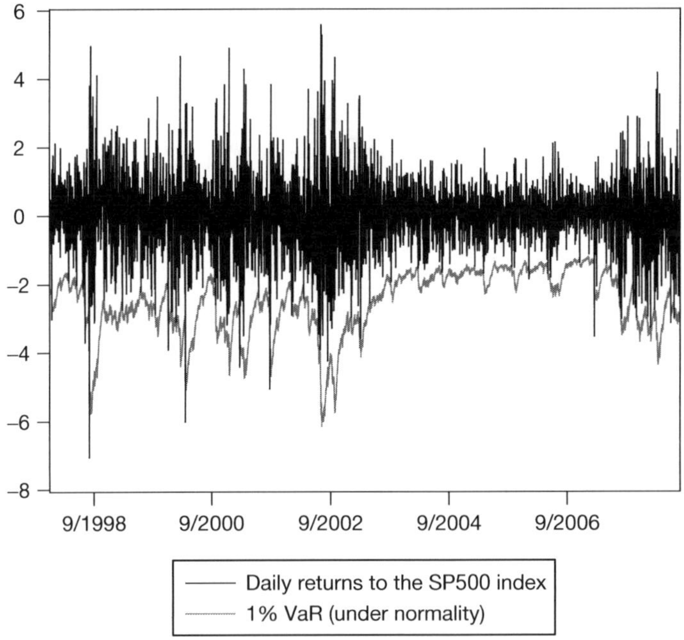

FIGURE 15.2 SP500 Daily Returns and Their Conditional 1% VaR Under Conditional Normality

the days in which the actual returns are larger in magnitude than the VaR. Theoretically, with a sample of 2657 observations, we should expect, on average, 1% of the observations (about 26 or 27) to be higher (in magnitude) than the 1% VaR. The actual number of violations is 37, which is slightly higher. Recall that the setting of the VaR boundary relies critically on the normality assumption of the innovation z_t. We can propose many other densities, and on doing so, the VaR boundary changes.

Within the autoregressive conditional heteroscedasticity (ARCH) family of models, it is common to assume a conditional Student-*t* density for the innovation z_t because this density has fatter tails than the normal; thus, it can accommodate any excess kurtosis that it is not captured by a normal conditional density.[1] If we were to choose the Student-*t* with 9 degrees of freedom—this is the estimated value when we run a GARCH(1,1) with Student-*t* for the SP500 daily returns—the 1% critical value is −2.821, which is larger in magnitude than the 1% critical value under normality. In addition, to compute the 1% VaR under Student-*t* we have to consider that the variance of a Student-*t* random variable is a function of the degrees of freedom ν: $\sigma^2_{Student-t} = \frac{\nu}{\nu - 2}$. At the same time, recall that $\frac{r_t - \mu_{t|t-1}}{\sigma_{t|t-1}}$ has variance equal to 1. Then, if we assume a Student-*t*, we need to standardize the t_ν random variable as

[1] In EViews, you are able to estimate (G)ARCH models with different conditional densities.

$\frac{t_\nu}{\sqrt{\frac{\nu}{\nu-2}}}$ so that $r_t = \mu_{t|t-1} + \sigma_{t|t-1} t_\nu / \left(\sqrt{\nu/(\nu-2)}\right)$. Consequently, the 1% VaR under Student-t is calculated as

$$r_{t+1|t}^{VaR(.01)} = \mu_{t+1|t} - 2.821\sqrt{\frac{\nu-2}{\nu}}\sigma_{t+1|t}$$

In Figure 15.3, we plot the conditional 1% VaR under Student-t (assuming that the conditional mean is zero). For April 2, 2008, the 1-day-ahead VaR is –4.44%, and we compare it with the value under normality (–4.16%). The 1% VaR is larger in magnitude because of the fat-tail property of the Student-t. The number of violations now is 22 (compared with the 37 violations under normality), which is closer to the theoretical value of 26.

Regulators usually require the calculation of VaR for a 10-day horizon. This is accomplished by using the rule of "square root to time" to extend the daily VaR forecasts to horizons with multiple trading days. If we are interested in a 10-day horizon, we multiply the daily forecast by $\sqrt{10}$. Thus, on April 2, 2008, the 10-day-ahead 1% VaR under normality will be –13.15% ($\sqrt{10} \times -4.16$). For example, if on April 2 we have a portfolio of \$100,000, there is 1% chance that 10 days later, on April 12, we could face a loss of at least \$13,150. Under Student-t ($\nu = 9$), the 10-day-ahead 1% VaR will be –14.04%, which means that we could lose at least \$14,040 in our \$100,000 portfolio.

FIGURE 15.3
SP500 Daily Returns and Their Conditional 1% VaR Under Conditional Student-t

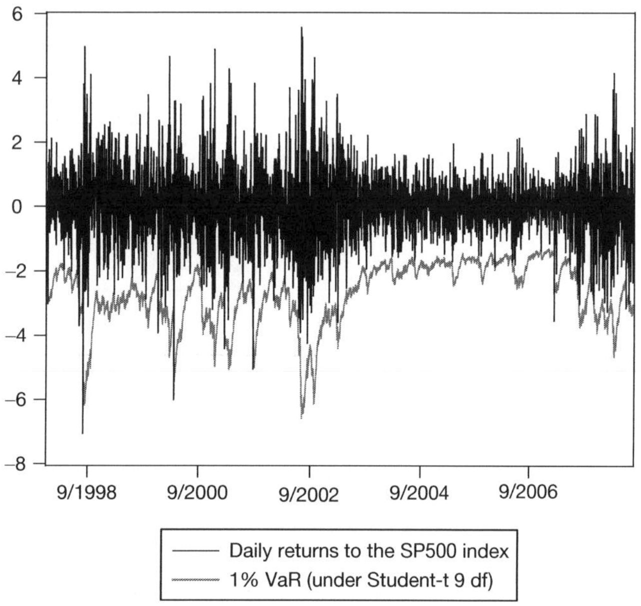

15.1.2 Expected Shortfall (ES)

Note that the VaR is the minimum loss that we should expect with $\alpha\%$ probability, which means that the losses could be higher. Then it is of interest to have a measure of the *average loss* within the observations contained in the $\alpha\%$ region.

Suppose that we consider just the observations in the $\alpha\%$ lower tail of the probability density function of r_t, and we compute their average. Then we are calculating the expected value of r_t for only those values of r_t such as $r_t < r_t^{VaR(\alpha)}$, which is written as

$$ES(\alpha) \equiv E(r_t \,|\, r_t < r_t^{VaR(\alpha)})$$

This measure is called the **expected shortfall (ES)**, which is graphically described in Figure 15.4.

Let us consider the standard normal density. The formula to compute the expected shortfall for a standard normal random variable z is[2]

$$ES \equiv E(z \,|\, z < z_\alpha) = \frac{\frac{1}{\sqrt{2\pi}} \exp\left(-\frac{z_\alpha^2}{2}\right)}{\alpha}$$

which requires only the value of z_α. Then for $\alpha = 5\% \rightarrow z_\alpha = -1.645$, and $ES_z = -2.0622$; and for $\alpha = 1\% \rightarrow z_\alpha = -2.33$, and $ES_z = -2.6426$. With the expected shortfall values corresponding to a standard normal random variable, we can readily calculate the expected shortfall for any other normal random variable. For instance, the expected shortfall associated with the 1% VaR for the random variable r_t is

$$\frac{r_t^{ES(\alpha)} - \mu_{t|t-1}}{\sigma_{t|t-1}} = -2.6426 \quad \Rightarrow r_{t+1|t}^{ES(\alpha)} = \mu_{t+1|t} - 2.6426\sigma_{t+1|t}$$

FIGURE 15.4 Expected Shortfall for α-VaR

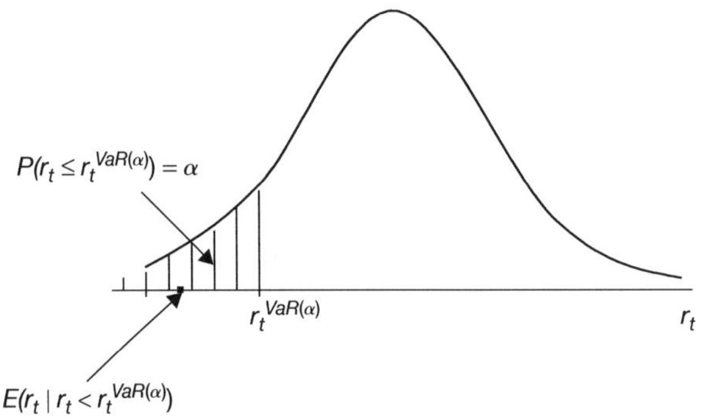

[2]We need to calculate the following integral $ES \equiv E(z \,|\, z < z_\alpha) = \frac{\int_{-\infty}^{z_\alpha} z \frac{1}{\sqrt{2\pi}} \exp\left(-\frac{z^2}{2}\right) dz}{\alpha}$. The numerator of this ratio is just the formula to calculate the average of a standard normal random variable but restricted to those values between $-\infty$ and z_α. The denominator is the area for the $\alpha\%$-probability tail, which is $\alpha\%$ itself.

Following with the SP500 daily returns, for April 2, 2008, the 1% VaR was –4.16% (under conditional normality). The corresponding expected shortfall for the 1% VaR is then –4.72%, which is the average of the values of r_t within the interval $(-\infty, -4.16)$. The expected shortfall is calculated as $r_{t+1|t}^{ES(1\%)} = -2.6426 \times 1.78$ (assuming that the conditional mean is practically zero). This means that, if on April 2 we have a portfolio of \$100,000, there is 1% chance that on April 3 we could have an average loss of \$4,720.

15.2 Portfolio Allocation

Suppose that we want to allocate some capital between two risky assets but we also wish to minimize our risk exposure. The question is how much money we should invest in each asset. This is the problem of portfolio allocation. Let us call r_1 the return to asset 1 and r_2 the return to asset 2. The portfolio return is a weighted average of both returns

$$r_p = w_1 r_1 + w_2 r_2$$

where w_1 and w_2 are the weights corresponding to asset 1 and 2, respectively. Let μ_1, μ_2 and σ_1^2, σ_2^2 be their respective means and variances. To simplify the calculations, we assume that both assets are uncorrelated so that their covariance is zero.[3] Then the mean and variance of this portfolio are

$$\mu_p = w_1\mu_1 + w_2\mu_2$$
$$\sigma_p^2 = w_1^2\sigma_1^2 + w_2^2\sigma_2^2$$

The problem is to find the weights w_1 and w_2. Given that we wish to minimize our risk exposure, we set up an optimization problem that consists of minimizing the portfolio variance σ_p^2 with respect to the weights w_1 and w_2 subject to a fixed desired portfolio return $\bar{\mu}_p$:

$$\min_{w_1,w_2} \sigma_p^2 = w_1^2\sigma_1^2 + w_2^2\sigma_2^2$$
$$s.t.\ \bar{\mu}_p = w_1\mu_1 + w_2\mu_2$$

The solution is (see the appendix to this chapter for the derivation of the following formulas):

$$w_1^* = \frac{\mu_1/\sigma_1^2}{\dfrac{\mu_1^2}{\sigma_1^2} + \dfrac{\mu_2^2}{\sigma_2^2}}\bar{\mu}_p \qquad w_2^* = \frac{\mu_2/\sigma_2^2}{\dfrac{\mu_1^2}{\sigma_1^2} + \dfrac{\mu_2^2}{\sigma_2^2}}\bar{\mu}_p$$

Observe that the **optimal weights** are proportional to the ratio mean/variance of each asset so that the larger the ratio the more capital is allocated to the asset. The ratio mean/variance can be interpreted as a risk-corrected return, which considers the

[3] If the covariance is different from zero ($\sigma_{12} \neq 0$), the variance of the portfolio needs to be modified as $\sigma_p^2 = w_1^2\sigma_1^2 + w_2^2\sigma_2^2 + 2w_1w_2\sigma_{12}$. Although the optimal weights have more complicated formulas, the logic of the problem remains the same.

trade-off between profitability and risk. Suppose that an asset has a high return but is very risky. If we divide the return by the variance (as a measure of risk), we convert the return to units of risk (i.e., return per unit of variance), so a high return may be in fact lower when it is risk adjusted; on the contrary, a low return may be in fact higher when its variance is very small.

A dynamic investor will be modifying the weights of her or his portfolio according to the dynamics of the assets. This means that the preceding problem can be cast in a conditional framework. Today at time t, we would like to find the optimal weights for tomorrow's portfolio by processing all information that we have at this moment. This means that the weights are time varying because they are functions of time-varying means and variances, that is,

$$w_{1t}^* = \frac{\mu_{1,t+1|t}/\sigma^2_{1,t+1|t}}{\dfrac{\mu^2_{1,t+1|t}}{\sigma^2_{1,t+1|t}} + \dfrac{\mu^2_{2,t+1|t}}{\sigma^2_{2,t+1|t}}}\overline{\mu}_p \qquad w_{2t}^* = \frac{\mu_{2,t+1|t}/\sigma^2_{2,t+1|t}}{\dfrac{\mu^2_{1,t+1|t}}{\sigma^2_{1,t+1|t}} + \dfrac{\mu^2_{2,t+1|t}}{\sigma^2_{2,t+1|t}}}\overline{\mu}_p$$

Let us put these results into action. We choose two stocks, Apple (AAPL) in the computer industry, and Freeport-McMoRan Copper (FCX) in the mining industry. The sample consists of daily prices from January 2, 1998, to August 8, 2008, for a total of 2,667 observations. We compute the daily returns. To be consistent with our assumptions, these two stocks should be uncorrelated. In fact, the correlation coefficient of their returns is 0.09, which is practically zero. The next step is to build a model for their conditional means and conditional variances. We have checked the autocorrelation functions of the series of returns, and they seem to be white noise; thus, we do not find any linear dynamics of the ARMA type. We proceed to set the conditional means equal to the unconditional means (i.e., $\mu_{t+1|t} = \mu$). The daily average return is $\mu = 0.13\%$ for APPL and $\mu = 0.07\%$ for FCX. The autocorrelation functions of their squared returns exhibit significant correlation. Thus, for both assets, we have fitted a GARCH(1,1) processes. Based on the GARCH model, we have calculated the 1-step-ahead conditional variances $\sigma^2_{t+1|t}$.

Finally, let us assume that our goal is to obtain a daily return of 0.10 % $\overline{\mu}_p = 0.10$. Observe that the desired return is the equal-weighted average of both returns ($0.10 = 0.5 \times (0.13 + 0.07)$). This is to say, if we were to put half of the money in AAPL and the other half in FCX, we would obtain an average return of 0.10% over the sample period. However, our goal is also to minimize the variance of the portfolio. Because we cannot ignore the risk of each stock, we need the conditional variances of the assets. Using the preceding formulas for optimal weights, we compute the daily weights, which are plotted in Figure 15.5.

Observe that the sum of the weights does not have to equal 1. In the optimization problem, we did not impose this restriction. This is why sometimes FCX has a weight larger than one rendering the sum higher than 1. For instance, on October 2, 2000, FCX weight is 1.36 and AAPL weight is 0.03, almost zero. What does this mean? After all, if we have \$100, we will not be able to allocate more than that amount to any or both stocks. Because we do not have the sum restriction, we allow for the possibility of

FIGURE 15.5 Optimal Weights for AAPL and FCX for $\overline{\mu}_p = 0.10$

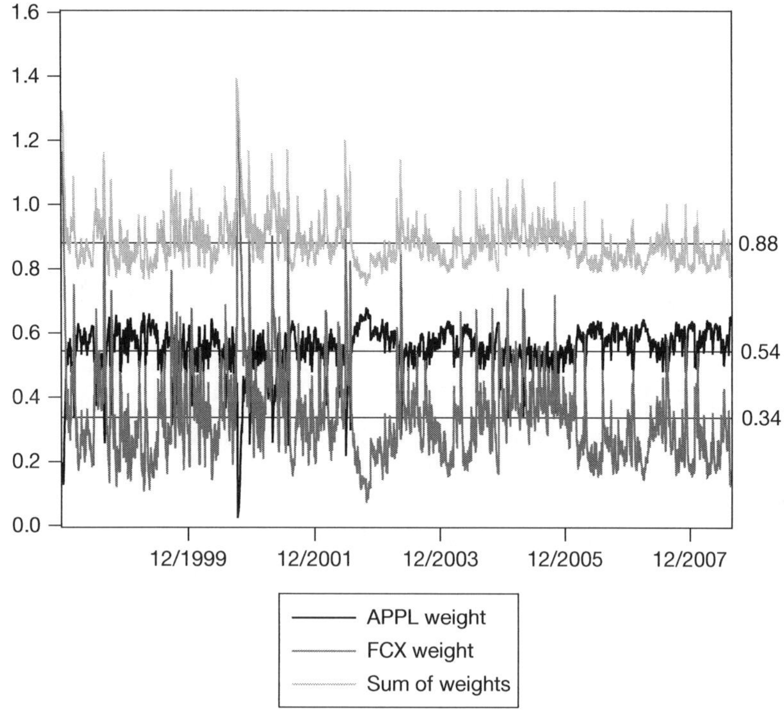

borrowing and lending at the risk-free rate. Thus, for a total weight of 1.39, we need to supplement the actual capital by borrowing an additional 39%. On the contrary, on August 8, 2008, the FCX weight is 0.12 and APPL's 0.65 for a sum of 0.77, which means that we will be lending 23% of our capital. A descriptive summary of the weights is presented in Table 15.1. On average, weight for FCX is 0.34 and for AAPL 0.54. For both stocks, on average we are deploying 88% of our capital and lending 12%.

TABLE 15.1 Descriptive Statistics of Optimal Weights for AAPL and FCX

Sample: 1 2667		
	AAPL weights	FCX weights
Mean	0.544335	0.337121
Median	0.557106	0.311801
Maximum	0.677203	1.363401
Minimum	0.026716	0.073685
Std. Dev.	0.076174	0.151029
Skewness	-2.018902	2.018902
Kurtosis	10.50023	10.50023

15.3 Asset Pricing

Modern finance theory claims that expected asset returns must be a function of risk. Investors demand a higher return if they are to buy risky assets. The classical **capital asset pricing model (CAPM)** and the **arbitrage pricing theory (APT)** state that there is a *linear* relationship between expected returns and risk. The CAPM model defines risk as the covariance of the asset return with the market portfolio return, that is, $\frac{cov(r_i, r_m)}{var(r_m)}$, and it claims that the expected return of an asset is given by the following relation:

$$E(r_i) = r_f + \frac{cov(r_i, r_m)}{var(r_m)}(E(r_m) - r_f)$$

where r_f is the risk-free rate, r_i is the return to asset i, and r_m is the return to the market portfolio. The ratio $\frac{\text{cov}(r_i, r_m)}{\text{var}(r_m)}$ is also known as systematic risk, which cannot be diversified away. In the finance parlance, this ratio is also called the **beta (β) of an asset**,

$$\beta_i \equiv \frac{\text{cov}(r_i, r_m)}{\text{var}(r_m)} = \frac{\sigma_{im}}{\sigma_m^2}$$

The β is the expected change in the asset return when a marginal change occurs in the market portfolio return. A $\beta > 1$ classifies the asset as risky because a 1% movement in the market return translates into a change larger than 1% in the asset return. This means that the asset is greatly exposed to the overall risk of the economy, which is summarized by the market portfolio. On the contrary, a $\beta < 1$ indicates that the asset return does not fully mimic movements in the market.

The APT theory claims that there are more risk factors than the market risk and allows for a richer, yet linear, relationship between other factors and the asset return.

Although the classical asset pricing theories were developed to explain the cross-sectional variation of asset returns, there are also time series versions that cast CAPM and APT in a conditional framework. A conditional CAPM model exploits the information set so that the *conditional* expected return of the asset is a linear function of its *conditional* β. Then the *conditional* CAPM is written as

$$E(r_{i,t}|I_{t-1}) = r_f + \frac{\text{cov}(r_{i,t}, r_{m,t}|I_{t-1})}{\text{var}(r_{m,t}|I_{t-1})}(E(r_{m,t}|I_{t-1}) - r_f)$$

which makes β time varying because it is a function of time-varying covariance and variance:

$$\beta_{i,t} \equiv \frac{\text{cov}(r_{i,t}, r_{m,t}|I_{t-1})}{\text{var}(r_{m,t}|I_{t-1})} = \frac{\sigma_{im,t|t-1}}{\sigma_{m,t|t-1}^2}$$

How risky are AAPL and FCX? We compute their respective βs. It is possible to estimate a time-varying covariance along the same lines as the modeling of time-varying variances. However, doing so requires more complex models because we need to extend the univariate approach to a multivariate setting. Alternatively, a simpler way to go about the estimation of a time-varying covariance is to recall the formula of the correlation coefficient and solve for the covariance i.e., $\sigma_{im} = \rho_{im}\sigma_i\sigma_m$, where ρ_{im} is the correlation coefficient between asset i and the market. Let us assume that ρ_{im} is constant over time. Then substituting the covariance into the β formula, the conditional beta is equal to

$$\beta_{i,t} = \rho_{im}\frac{\sigma_{i,t|t-1}}{\sigma_{m,t|t-1}}$$

To implement this formula, we need only to estimate the conditional standard deviations of the asset and the market return and their correlation coefficient. In Section 15.2, we estimated a GARCH(1,1) model for the conditional variances of AAPL and FCX. We approximate the market portfolio by the SP500 index because this index includes the largest U.S. corporations. In Chapter 14, we also estimated a GARCH(1,1) model for the SP500 returns (Table 14.3). Finally, the correlation coefficient of AAPL with the SP500 returns is 0.45 and that of FCX is 0.28. With all this information, we calculate the conditional beta $\beta_{i,t}$ using the preceding formula. In Figure 15.6 we present the time-varying conditional betas for both assets. Clearly, AAPL is riskier than FCX. While the AAPL average beta is 1.48, the average beta of FCX is 0.83. AAPL's beta is also more volatile with the largest betas occurring over the tech bubble period from 1999 to 2001.

FIGURE 15.6 Conditional Betas for AAPL and FCX

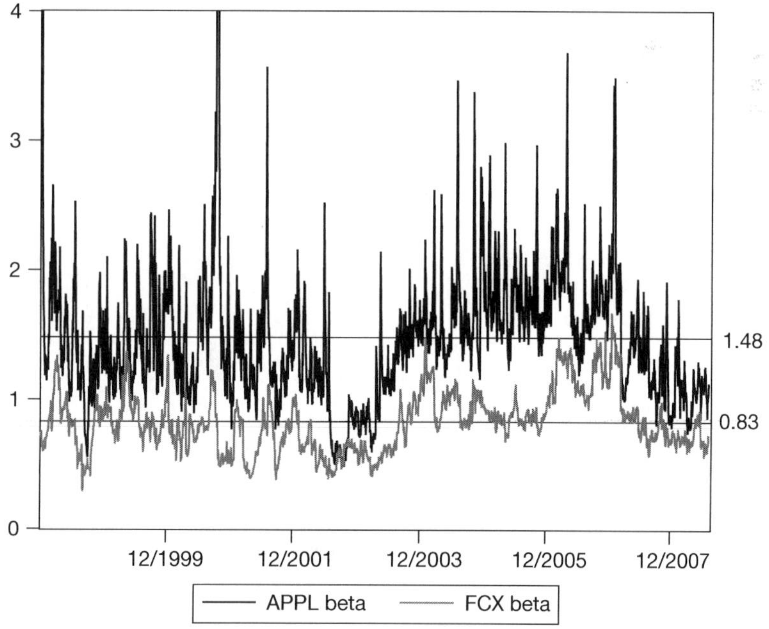

15.4 Option Pricing

An *option* is an asset whose payoff is attached to a primitive asset such as a stock, bond, or interest rate, etc. Options are also known as *derivatives* because they derive their value from the value of a primitive asset. Options are complex instruments and their pricing requires advanced mathematical statistics. Nevertheless, our objective is to highlight the importance of modeling the variance of the primitive asset. We do so by focusing on the simplest instrument, the European call option.

Suppose that the primitive asset is a stock with today's price S. A **call option (C)** on the stock confers to the option buyer the right to buy the stock at a predetermined future date (expiration date) and at a predetermined price, which is called the *strike price* (K). For instance, today's price of one share of the stock is $S = 50$. If you buy a call option today, you enter into a contractual agreement that, for example, gives you the "right to buy 1 share of stock one month from today at a price of 45." The question is how much you will pay for this call option. If today's price is $S = 50$, nobody will sell you the option for less than \$5 (5 = 50 – 45). Why? Suppose that you do find a seller willing to accept C = 3. Then you buy the option, immediately exercise your right to buy the stock at 45 for a total cost of \$48 (45+3), and immediately sell the stock at 50 with a net gain of \$2. Your gain is the seller's loss! Do you think that you are likely to find many sellers willing to take C = 3? We doubt it! So then, what is the price of the call? At the moment, we have a lower bound (\$5), which depends on today's stock price and the strike price agreed upon in the contract. But the contract expires in a month and the stock price over this month is not going to be fixed; to the contrary, it will move up and down. We have already seen very interesting dynamics of stock returns and how crucial is to understand volatility dynamics. Time to expiration and stock volatility both must be additional determinants of the call option price. Now let us go forward and understand what will happen at the expiration date. If the stock price at expiration is $S_T =$ \$50 (the option is in the money, that is, $S_T > K$), the buyer of the call will exercise her or his right to buy the stock for a profit of \$5. If the stock at expiration is \$40 (the option is out of the money, that is, $S_T < K$), the option will expire worthless. It is not sensible for the buyer to exercise her or his right because she or he can buy the stock at a lower price of \$40 instead of \$45. At expiration, the call price is

$$C_T = \max\{S_T - K, 0\}$$

But again, what is the price of the call option *today*? In an implicit fashion, we can say that today's call price C_t must be a function of today's stock price S_t, the strike price K, time to expiration T, the stock volatility σ^2, and the risk-free interest rate r_f (you may borrow some money to buy the stock), so that the price of the call is written as a function of all these determinants, that is,

$$C_t = C(S_t, K, T, \sigma^2, r_f)$$

A seminal solution was proposed by Black and Scholes. The famous **Black-Scholes (BS) formula** is

$$C_t = S_t N(d_1) - K \exp(-r_f T)\, N(d_2)$$

$$d_1 \equiv \frac{\log(S_t / K \exp(-r_f T))}{\sigma\sqrt{T}} + \sigma\sqrt{T}/2$$

$$d_2 \equiv d_1 - \sigma\sqrt{T}$$

where $N(.)$ is the cumulative normal distribution function. Although the formula may seem intimidating, there is some intuition to it. Observe that $N(d_1)$ and $N(d_2)$ are probabilities that weight the stock S_t and the present value of the strike price $K \exp(-r_f T)$, respectively. Assuming some dynamics for the stock price, the call price is obtained by calculating today the *probabilistic* present value of the difference $S_T - K$.

The BS formula assumes that the variance of the stock returns is constant over the life of the option and that stock returns are normally distributed. These two assumptions are very restrictive in the light of our findings on time-varying variances and the consequences for the unconditional density function of stock returns (Chapter 14). There are many option pricing formulas (some explicit, some implicit) that take care of more complex assumptions on the stochastic process of stock returns. Nevertheless, we will use the BS formula as an approximation to the actual price of the option.

Let us implement our knowledge of time-varying volatility to calculate the BS call option price and compare it with its actual price. We will use options on the SP500 index (symbol SPX; you can find them in http://www.cboe.com).

This is the information that we need:

Today's date: August 11, 2008
SP500 index price: $S_t = 1305.32$
Option characteristics: Call option with $K = 1295$ and expiration date August 16, 2008, so that $T = 5$ days
Short-term risk-free interest rate: $r_f = 2\%$ (this is the federal funds rate; you may use any other short-term Treasury bill rate)

We would like to know what C_t, the price of this call option today, August 11, is.

As you may have noticed, we are missing the information on the variance of the index σ^2. Because the BS formula requires that the variance should be constant over the life of the option, we can approximate this assumption by implementing one of two approaches:

1. Forecast the daily conditional variances of the SP500 daily returns over the life of the option; so we will forecast the variance on August 12 (1-step ahead),

August 13 (2-steps-ahead), August 14 (3-steps-ahead), August 15 (4-steps-ahead), and August 16 (5-steps ahead), and find the average over these five days to expiration; or

2. Work with the frequency of the data that corresponds to the expiration time; for the SP500 index data, we need a five-day frequency, which is one week in trading time. Thus, we need to move from daily returns to weekly returns (the trading week is five days). With weekly data, the 1-step-ahead forecast is one week, so we will be forecasting the variance from today, August 11, to August 16, which is the expiration date of the option. This is equivalent to having a constant variance over the expiration interval.

We implement both approaches. First, we estimate a GARCH(1,1) for daily data from January 4, 2008, to August 11, 2008, and for weekly data from January 10, 2008, to August 11, 2008. This is the content of Table 15.2. Now we have the information that we need to compute the forecasts of the variance.

Daily Variance Forecasts

The 1-step-ahead variance forecast is obtained by plugging the required values in $\sigma^2_{t+1|t} = \omega + \alpha\varepsilon^2_t + \beta\sigma^2_{t|t-1}$. Read the parameter estimates from Table 15.2 and, because the mean is practically zero, plug in $\varepsilon^2_t = r^2_t = (0.6918\%)^2$ and $\sigma^2_{t|t-1} = 2.3522$ (these values are in the corresponding EViews workfile). For the 2-, 3-, 4-, and 5-steps-ahead forecasts, use the forecast formula that we already know (Chapter 14),

$$\sigma^2_{t+h|t} = \omega(1+(\alpha+\beta)+(\alpha+\beta)^2 + \cdots\cdots + (\alpha+\beta)^{h-2}) + (\alpha+\beta)^{h-1}\sigma^2_{t+1|t}$$

and start the recursion. These are the forecasts:

12-Aug	2.218063
13-Aug	2.209897
14-Aug	2.201801
15-Aug	2.193772
16-Aug	2.185812
Average	2.201869

Weekly Variance Forecast

We need only the 1-step-ahead forecast because 1 step is the five-day week. As before, plug in the required parameter estimates (Table 15.2) in $\sigma^2_{t+1|t} = \omega + \alpha\varepsilon^2_t + \beta\sigma^2_{t|t-1}$ together with $\varepsilon^2_t = r^2_t = (2.8171\%)^2$ and $\sigma^2_{t|t-1} = 5.2479$. Then the 1-step-ahead variance forecast for August 16 is $\sigma^2_{t+1|t} = 5.3627$.

Now we proceed to use the BS formula to find the price of the call option. You can do the calculation on any calculator or run the following script in EViews, which

TABLE 15.2 SP500 Index Volatility at the Daily and Weekly Frequencies

(1) Daily Returns. Variance Estimation

Dependent Variable: R
Method: ML – ARCH (Marquardt) – Normal distribution
Sample (adjusted): 1/04/2000 8/11/2008
Included observations: 2163 after adjustments
Convergence achieved after 24 iterations
Variance backcast: ON
GARCH = C(2) + C(3)*RESID(-1)^2 + C(4)*GARCH(-1)

	Coefficient	Std. Error	z-Statistic	Prob.
C	0.029222	0.019244	1.518502	0.1289
Variance Equation				
C	0.010455	0.002006	5.213235	0.0000
RESID(-1)^2	0.066657	0.008584	7.765606	0.0000
GARCH(-1)	0.924948	0.009172	100.8432	0.0000

R-squared	-0.000911	Mean dependent var	-0.005026
Adjusted R-squared	-0.002302	S.D. dependent var	1.134728
S.E. of regression	1.136034	Akaike info criterion	2.832690
Sum squared resid	2786.346	Schwarz criterion	2.843192
Log likelihood	-3059.554	Durbin-Watson stat	2.093706

(2) Weekly Returns. Variance Estimation

Dependent Variable: R
Method: ML – ARCH (Marquardt) – Normal distribution
Sample (adjusted): 1/10/2000 8/8/2008
Included observations: 447 after adjustments
Convergence achieved after 17 iterations
Variance backcast: ON
GARCH = C(2) + C(3)*RESID(-1)^2 + C(4)*GARCH(-1)

	Coefficient	Std. Error	z-Statistic	Prob.
C	0.077725	0.096341	0.806773	0.4198
Variance Equation				
C	0.045423	0.025833	1.758329	0.0787
RESID(-1)^2	0.047095	0.014756	3.191489	0.0014
GARCH(-1)	0.942009	0.016859	55.87414	0.0000

R-squared	-0.001932	Mean dependent var	-0.023744
Adjusted R-squared	-0.008717	S.D. dependent var	2.311257
S.E. of regression	2.321308	Akaike info criterion	4.367593
Sum squared resid	2387.094	Schwarz criterion	4.404305
Log likelihood	-972.1571	Durbin-Watson stat	2.136488

is the example for the weekly SP500 data (pay attention to the units of all the inputs):

```
vector (9) S
S(1)=1305.32                                              'current price of the stock
S(2)=1295                                                 'strike price
S(3)=0.02/52                                              'annual risk-free rate converted to weekly rate
S(4)=1                                                    'time to expiration (one week)
S(5)=5.3416/10000                                         'weekly unconditional variance
'S(5)= 5.3627/10000                                       'weekly one-step-ahead conditional variance
S(6)=@sqrt(S(5)*S(4))
S(7)=(log(S(1)/S(2))+ S(4)*(S(3)+S(5)/2))/S(6)            'd1
S(8)=S(7)-S(6)                                            'd2
S(9)=S(1)*@cnorm(S(7))-S(2)*exp(-S(3)*S(4))*@cnorm(S(8))  'BS formula
```

See Table 15.3 for the results for the option price under four scenarios: the first two correspond to the approaches (1) and (2) that we just discussed; the other two correspond to the case when we do not model volatility and use the unconditional variances of the asset returns (estimates in Table 15.2). The BS prices should be compared with the actual price of the option on August 11, 2008. It is also known that the BS formula tends to overprice options at the money and in the money, which means that the BS price is higher than the actual price for options with a strike price lower than the actual price of the stock. This is exactly what we see in Table 15.3. There is a major overpricing when we use the average of the daily variance forecasts: the BS call price is \$23.07, and the actual price is between \$16.40 and \$18.40. This method tends to overestimate the variance and, consequently, the option price over the expiration period. The best approximation happens when we model the variance with weekly data. In this example, the unconditional variance of weekly returns is very similar to

TABLE 15.3 Black-Scholes Call Option Pricing

Actual Price on August 11, 2008 $C_{bid} = 16.40$, $C_{ask} = 18.40$

	Daily Returns	**Weekly Returns**
Conditional Variance	Average variance forecast = 2.2018	$\sigma^2_{t+1\|t} = 5.3627$
BS Option Price	$C_t = 23.0687$	$C_t = 18.1851$
Unconditional Variance	$\sigma^2 = (1.1347)^2 = 1.2875$	$\sigma^2 = (2.3112)^2 = 5.3416$
BS Option Price	$C_t = 19.1791$	$C_t = 18.1629$

the 1-step-ahead conditional variance so that the price of the option is also similar. The BS price calculated by either modeling the weekly conditional variance ($C_t = 18.18$) or using the weekly unconditional variance ($C_t = 18.16$) delivers a very close approximation to the actual price of the call calculated as the average between the bid and ask price (i.e., $C_t = 17.40$).

KEY WORDS

asset pricing, p. 395
beta (β) of an asset, p. 404
Black-Scholes (BS) formula, p. 407
call option (C), p. 406
capital asset pricing model (CAPM), p. 403
expected shortfall (ES), p. 400
optimal weights, p. 401
option pricing, p. 395
portfolio allocation, p. 395
risk management, p. 395
value-at-risk (VaR), p. 396

APPENDIX

The following is the solution to the optimization problem of **portfolio allocation**:

$$\min_{w_1,w_2} \sigma_p^2 = w_1^2\sigma_1^2 + w_2^2\sigma_2^2$$
$$s.t.\ \overline{\mu}_p = w_1\mu_1 + w_2\mu_2$$

This is a constrained optimization problem. Form the Lagrange equation, find the first-order conditions and make them equal to zero, and solve the system of three equations with three unknowns, which has a unique solution.

$$\ell = w_1^2\sigma_1^2 + w_2^2\sigma_2^2 + \lambda(\overline{\mu}_p - w_1\mu_1 - w_2\mu_2)$$
$$\frac{\partial \ell}{\partial w_1} = 2w_1\sigma_1^2 - \lambda\mu_1 = 0$$
$$\frac{\partial \ell}{\partial w_2} = 2w_2\sigma_2^2 - \lambda\mu_2 = 0$$
$$\frac{\partial \ell}{\partial \lambda} = \overline{\mu}_p - w_1\mu_1 - w_2\mu_2 = 0$$

The optimal weights are the solution to this system of equations:

$$w_1^* = \frac{\mu_1/\sigma_1^2}{\dfrac{\mu_1^2}{\sigma_1^2} + \dfrac{\mu_2^2}{\sigma_2^2}}\overline{\mu}_p \qquad w_2^* = \frac{\mu_2/\sigma_2^2}{\dfrac{\mu_1^2}{\sigma_1^2} + \dfrac{\mu_2^2}{\sigma_2^2}}\overline{\mu}_p$$

EXERCISES

1. Update the data set in Section 15.1.1. Find the 1% VaR under normality (Figure 15.2) and under Student-t (Figure 15.3). What is the expected shortfall for the 1% VaR under normality?
2. Download the prices of your favorite stock and compute the 1% and 5% VaR under the assumptions of conditional normality of stock returns and Student-t with degrees of freedom 5, 6, and 7.
3. For the same data as in Exercise 2, compute the expected shortfall for the 1% and 5% VaR and conditionally normal returns.
4. Choose two uncorrelated stocks and form an equal-weighted portfolio by establishing a long position in stock 1 and a short position in stock 2. Find the conditional 1% and 5% VaR of this portfolio.
5. For the same data as in Exercise 4, compute the expected shortfall for the 1% and 5% VaR and conditionally normal returns.
6. Update the data set of Section 15.2 and compute the optimal weights as in Figure 15.5 and the conditional betas as in Figure 15.6.
7. Form a portfolio of your three favorite stocks in three different industries (for instance, technology, financial, and oil). Suppose that you wish to allocate your capital among the three stocks but you wish to minimize risk. Find the optimal weights assuming that you wish a daily return of 0.15%.
8. Find the conditional beta for the three stocks of Exercise 7. Which stock is the riskiest?
9. Compute the Black-Scholes price of three (in-the-money, at-the-money, and out-of-the-money) call options on the SP500 index by using the *unconditional* variance of the SP500 returns. How good is the approximation?
10. Compute the Black-Scholes price of three (in-the-money, at-the-money, and out-of-the-money) call options on the SP500 index by modeling the *conditional* variance of the SP500 returns. How good is the approximation? Compare your results with those in Exercise 9.

CHAPTER 16

Forecasting with Nonlinear Models: An Introduction

This chapter offers an introduction to modeling and forecasting with nonlinear models. Because the complexity of the analysis requires techniques beyond the scope of this textbook, the exposition is limited to those instances in which ordinary least squares (OLS) estimation suffices, and testing can be carried out with standard statistics. When OLS is feasible, the analysis is statistical, and when more advanced estimation and testing techniques are required, the analysis is descriptive. The overall objective is to open new questions that motivate further reading in the field of forecasting.

Introduction

Our objective in the preceding chapters has been to understand *linear* dependence in a time series. We learned a set of tools to identify the degree of dependence, mainly through the autocorrelograms and partial autocorrelograms of a time series. We proposed time series models that summarize the *linear* dependence found in the autocorrelograms, and based on these models, we constructed optimal forecasts.

Notice that we emphasize the word *linear* to make the point that the idea of dependence is a much wider concept. Thus, if we speak of a linear dependence, should we expect something like nonlinear dependence? The answer is yes; the present observation may depend on the past observations in a nonlinear fashion, and if so, we will face new questions concerning modeling and forecasting of nonlinear time series. For instance, can we identify nonlinearity? Which nonlinear model should we choose? What is the forecast based on a nonlinear model? Are nonlinear models superior to linear models? Nonlinear dependence is the subject of this chapter.

16.1 Nonlinear Dependence

16.1.1 What Is It?

To answer this question, we proceed by defining linearity so that anything else that does not satisfy the definition of linearity will be considered nonlinear. Consider a stochastic process $\{Y_t\}$ and an information set

$$I_{t-1} = \{Y_{t-1}, Y_{t-2}, \ldots, X_{t-1}, X_{t-2}, \ldots\}$$

where $\{Y_{t-1}, Y_{t-2}, \ldots\}$ is the past history of the process $\{Y_t\}$, and $\{X_{t-1}, X_{t-2}, \ldots\}$ is the history of any other relevant variables that explain the process $\{Y_t\}$.

We say that the process $\{Y_t\}$ is *linear in mean* if the conditional mean of the process is a linear function of the information set, that is,

$$E(Y_t|I_{t-1}) = \phi_1 Y_{t-1} + \phi_2 Y_{t-2} + \cdots + \beta_1 X_{t-1} + \beta_2 X_{t-2} + \cdots$$

Under this definition, all the AR(p), MA(q), ARMA(p, q), and ARIMA(p, d, q) models that we have studied are linear models. Notice that the definition focuses on the conditional mean and nothing is said about the conditional variance. We could also write an analogous definition for linearity in conditional variance that would include the volatility models that we studied in Chapters 13 and 14. However, we focus exclusively on the linear/nonlinear specification of the conditional mean so that if a process $\{Y_t\}$ has a linear conditional mean and conditional heteroscedasticity of some type (as in Chapters 13 and 14), the process will be deemed linear.

Then, in contrast, a nonlinear process is characterized by a conditional mean that is a nonlinear function of the information set. Because there are many nonlinear functional forms, it is not possible to define **nonlinearity**; thus, the approach taken to the definition of nonlinearity is justified.

As an introduction, let us work with an example of a nonlinear model. Suppose that for some stochastic process $\{Y_t\}$ there is a threshold value that determines different dynamics when the process is above or below the threshold, for instance:

$$Y_t = \begin{cases} \phi_{11} Y_{t-1} + \varepsilon_t & \text{if } Y_{t-1} > 0 \\ \phi_{12} Y_{t-1} + \varepsilon_t & \text{if } Y_{t-1} \leq 0 \end{cases}$$

for $\phi_{11} \neq \phi_{12}$ and $\varepsilon_t \rightarrow N(0, \sigma^2)$. When $Y_{t-1} > 0$, the process behaves like an AR(1) with persistence parameter ϕ_{11}, and when, $Y_{t-1} \leq 0$ the process is still AR(1) but with different persistence, ϕ_{12}. The threshold value is 0, which determines two different regimes. This is an example of a nonlinear specification that is called *self-exciting threshold autoregressive* (SETAR) model. Although the process is linear in each regime, unconditionally the process $\{Y_t\}$ exhibits nonlinear dynamics because it is a mixture of two processes. An equivalent way of writing this model is

$$Y_t = \phi_{11} Y_{t-1} I(Y_{t-1} > 0) + \phi_{12} Y_{t-1} I(Y_{t-1} \leq 0) + \varepsilon_t$$

where $I(Y_{t-1} > 0) = 1$, and $I(Y_{t-1} \leq 0) = 1$ is an indicator function that takes the value 1 when the condition inside the indicator is met and zero otherwise. With this representation, it is easy to see that the previous definition of linearity is not satisfied; hence, the model is nonlinear. Thus, we will write a nonlinear process as

$$Y_t = g(I_{t-1};\theta) + \varepsilon_t$$

where the function $g(.)$ is a nonlinear function of the information set I_{t-1}, and θ is a set of parameters within the function.

Let us simulate the SETAR model with parameters $\phi_{11} = 0.9$ and $\phi_{12} = 0.3$ in order to learn various aspects of nonlinear processes. The estimation of this model will be presented in Section 16.2. In EViews, write the following program:

```
'define series: normal innovation (e) with standard deviation 0.25, and the time series (y)
series e=0.25*nrnd
series y
'initialize the series to start the recursion
y(1)=e(1)
'start the recursion from 2 to the number of observations you wish to generate for !i=2 to 1000
'regime 1 with persistence parameter 0.9
     if y(!i-1) > 0 then
     y(!i)=0.9*y(!i-1) + e(!i)
'regime 2 with persistence parameter 0.3
     else
     y(!i)=0.3*y(!i-1) + e(!i)
     endif
next
```

See Figure 16.1 for a simulated time series of 600 observations from the SETAR process.

Notice the presence of the two regimes. When the observations are positive (negative), there is high (low) persistence in the process, so that observations in positive (negative) territory remain there for a long (short) time span. This is a reflection of the magnitude of the persistence parameter $\phi_{11} = 0.9$ versus $\phi_{12} = 0.3$.

The nonlinearity of the process becomes evident when we plot Y_t versus Y_{t-1} (see Figure 16.2). There are two regression lines with different slopes corresponding to the two regimes, which depend on whether $Y_{t-1} > 0$ or $Y_{t-1} \leq 0$. In addition, a histogram of the time series also reveals that the process is a mixture of processes. Even though the innovation ε_t is normally distributed within each regime, the process Y_t is non-normal because we observe substantial positive skewness (Figure 16.3) in the density. This is the result of mixing two probability density functions.

Now suppose that we are given a time series of the SETAR process and without entertaining the possibility of a nonlinear model, we calculate the autocorrelation functions (Figure 16.4). What should we expect?

FIGURE 16.1
Time Series of a SETAR Process with Two Regimes and Threshold Zero

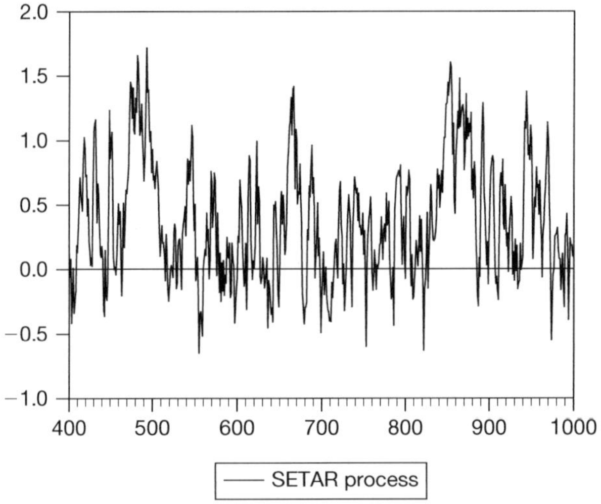

FIGURE 16.2
SETAR Process in a Regression Framework

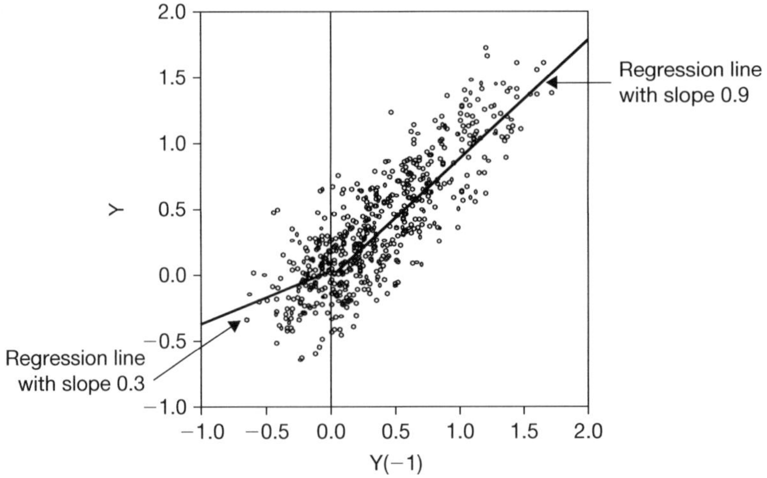

FIGURE 16.3
Unconditional Histogram of the SETAR Time Series

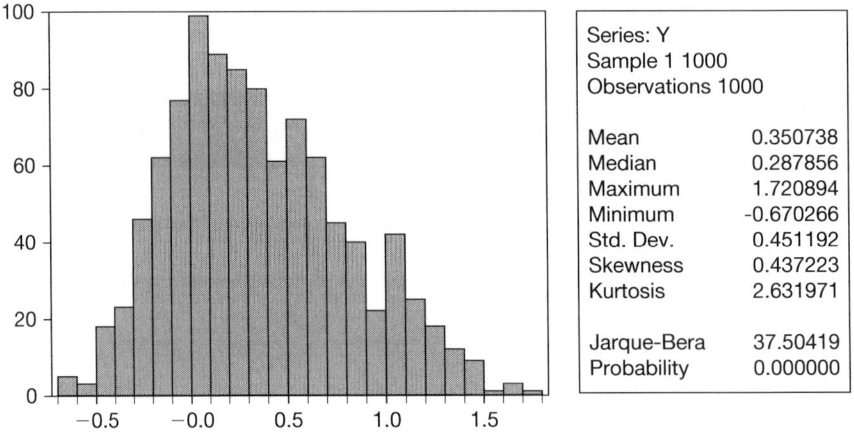

FIGURE 16.4
Autocorrelograms of a SETAR Process

Sample: 1 1000
Included observations: 1000

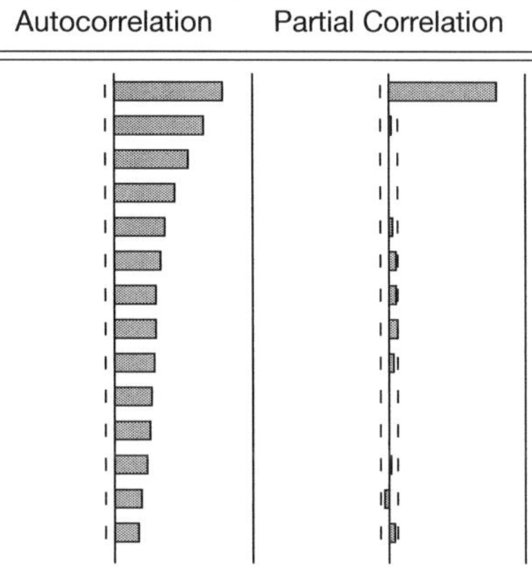

	AC	PAC
1	0.823	0.823
2	0.680	0.007
3	0.560	-0.005
4	0.461	-0.001
5	0.389	0.030
6	0.346	0.054
7	0.321	0.051
8	0.314	0.059
9	0.309	0.033
10	0.294	-0.003
11	0.274	-0.001
12	0.250	0.000
13	0.213	-0.036
14	0.196	0.043

It is evident that the autocorrelograms point toward an AR(1) process with high persistence $\phi \cong 0.8$. Because we have simulated the SETAR process, we know that this linear AR(1) is a misspecified model. However, the linear model is picking up features of both regimes. There is high persistence, which is coming from the prevalence in the series of regime 1. When the process is in regime 1, the linear AR(1) could be a good approximation. The contribution of regime 2 to the linear model consists of damping the persistence of regime 1. If we were in regime 2, the linear AR would be a bad specification because it would indicate much more persistence than is needed. Nevertheless, in the absence of knowing what the true model is (as happens in all empirical work), we should consider linear specifications as alternatives among many other nonlinear specifications. In this sense, the linear specification is an approximation to the true nonlinear specification.

16.1.2 Is There Any Evidence of Nonlinear Dynamics in the Data?

You may be wondering that, if we need to study nonlinear processes, there must be plenty of evidence in favor of these models in economic and business data. We present three examples. In Figure 16.5, we show the time series of U.S. industrial production (yearly changes) from 1955 to 2008 The shaded areas are the recessions dated by the NBER.

Upon examining the time series plot, we could make a case for recessions behaving differently from expansions. When the economy goes into recession, it does so rather abruptly; the contraction is sharp but short; in contrast, the recovery is slower and the expansions are longer. This indicates that it is possible to entertain at least two regimes in industrial production with an expansion regime exhibiting a higher persistence than a recession regime, and, by that, a nonlinear model is a possibility.

In Figure 16.6, we present the yearly interest rate on a 3-month Treasury Bill from 1955 to 2008. Observe that in the early 1980s, the rates were extremely high, well above 10%. Some authors claim[1] that the short-term interest rate is a mixture of two

[1] Pfann, G.A., P.C. Schotman, and R. Tscherning (1996), "Nonlinear interest rate dynamics and implications for the term structure", *Journal of Econometrics*, 74, 149–176.

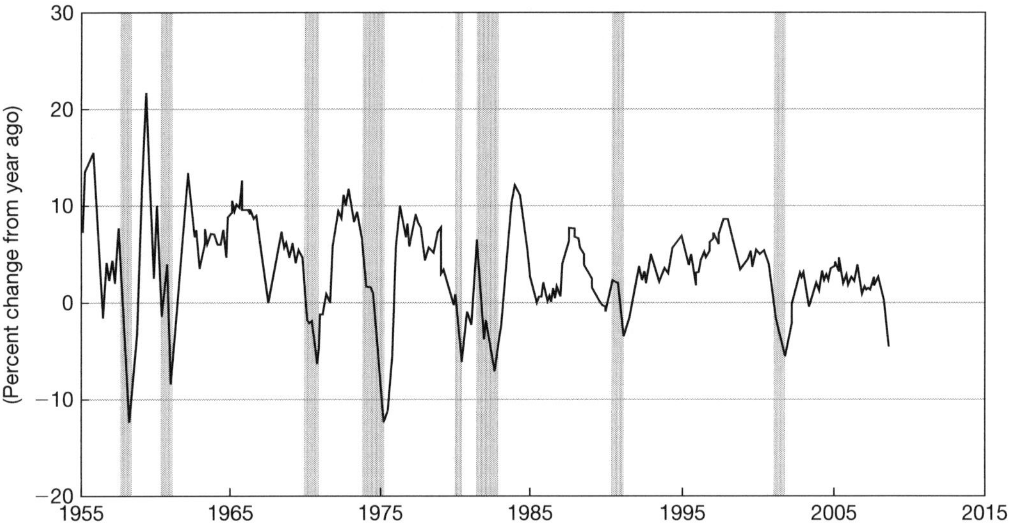

Note: Shaded areas indicate U.S. recessions as determined by the NBER.

Source: Board of Governors of the Federal Reserve System. Federal Reserve Bank of St. Louis: research.stlouisfed.org

FIGURE 16.5 U.S. Industrial Production Index (Year-to-Year Changes)

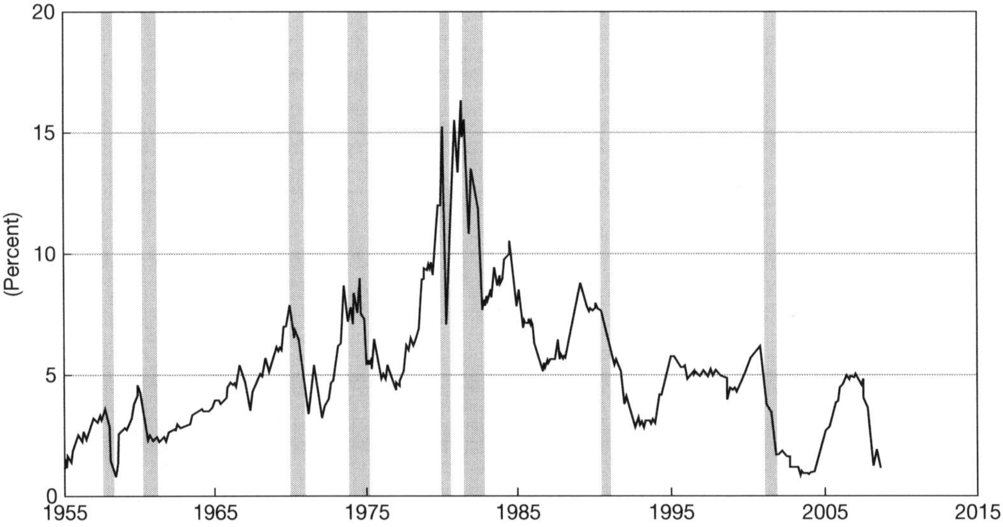

Note: Shared areas indicate U.S. recessions as determined by the NBER.

Source: Board of Governors of the Federal Reserve System. Federal Reserve Bank of St. Louis: research.stlouisfed.org

FIGURE 16.6 3-Month Treasury Bill Rates

processes: a nonstationary process (random walk) when the rates remain low and a stationary process when the rates are very high. In Figure 16.6, we could observe that when the rates are higher than approximately 9%, the series has a much lower persistence than when the rates are below 9%. Once again, the possibility of two regimes should be entertained.

The U.S. gross national product (GNP) time series has also been consistently modeled as a nonlinear process with several regimes. Some authors propose two regimes and some others, three and four regimes. Figure 16.7 is a stylized representation of the U.S. business cycle[2] that considers three/four regimes: rapid linear contractions, aggressive short-lived convex early expansions, and moderate/slow relatively long concave late expansions.

16.1.3 Nonlinearity, Correlation, and Dependence

We have mentioned repeatedly that model forecasting consists of exploiting the historical dependence of the stochastic process, which is summarized by a time series model. For linear processes, the time dependence is detected by the autocorrelation functions, which give rise to AR, MA, and (ARMA) type models. Notice that the autocorrelation functions inform only about *linear* dependence and, as a consequence, a forecast based on a linear model exploits only linear dependence. The autocorrelation functions do not offer any information about nonlinear dependence and, unfortunately, we do not have for nonlinear models such neat tools as the autocorrelation function (ACF) and partial autocorrelation function (PACF) to discover the type of nonlinearity. We rely mainly on statistical testing and on forecasting performance to entertain a particular nonlinear specification.

FIGURE 16.7
U.S. GNP Business Cycle with Four Regimes (Stylized Business Cycle)

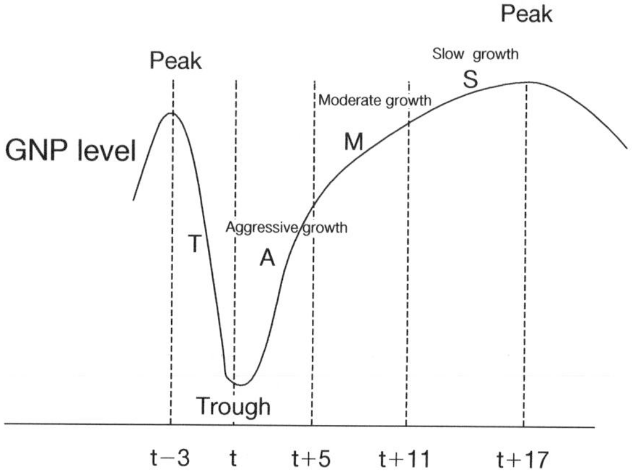

[2] Dahl, C.M. and G. González-Rivera (2003), "Identifying non-linear components by random fields in the US GNP growth. Implications for the shape of the business cycle", Studies in Nonlinear Dynamics and Econometrics, vol. 7(1), article 2.

From a modeling point of view and given a time series, we will analyze linear and nonlinear specifications. Because we do not know what the true model is, we should consider linear models as approximations to nonlinear models. Suppose that the best linear model that we can entertain is a white noise process. Should we say that the time series at hand is nonforecastable? If the true model is a white noise process, the answer is yes. However, a priori, the absence of linear dependence should not be understood as lack of predictability because there may be a nonlinear model that fits the data so that the dependence is nonlinear, and a forecast could be built based on the nonlinear model.

In summary, uncorrelatedness does not imply independence and it does not imply lack of predictability. The following example illustrates that an uncorrelated process may be forecastable. A nonlinear model known as a *bilinear* process is specified as follows:

$$Y_t = \phi Y_{t-2}\varepsilon_{t-1} + \varepsilon_t$$

Generate a time series of this process by writing the following program in EViews:

```
'define series: normal innovation (e) with standard deviation 0.25, and the time series (yb)
series e=0.25*nrnd
series yb

'initialize the series to star+the recursion
yb(1)=e(1)
yb(2)=e(2)

'start the recursion from 3 to the number of observations you wish to generate for !i=3 to 1000
'bilinear process with φ=0.6
yb(!i)=0.6*e(!i-1)*yb(!i-2)+e(!i)

next
```

The autocorrelation functions of this time series are pictured in Figure 16.8. All the autocorrelations are zero, indicating that the best linear model for this series is a white noise process. However, the true specification is bilinear and, based on that, we could construct a forecast as a function of the information set, that is, the 1-step-ahead forecast looks like $f_{t,1} = \phi Y_{t-1}\varepsilon_t$.

16.1.4 What Have We Learned So Far?

This is a summary of the ideas that we should have in mind as we proceed with our discussion:

- Nonlinearity in mean is present when the conditional mean of the stochastic process is a nonlinear function of the information set. Thus, nonlinear specifications are many and they could be very complex.

FIGURE 16.8 Autocorrelations of a Bilinear Process

Sample: 1 1000
Included observations: 1000

Autocorrelation	Partial Correlation		AC	PAC	Q-Stat	Prob
		1	0.034	0.034	1.1366	0.286
		2	0.018	0.017	1.4596	0.482
		3	-0.012	-0.013	1.5982	0.660
		4	-0.025	-0.024	2.2061	0.698
		5	-0.046	-0.044	4.3064	0.506
		6	-0.021	-0.017	4.7424	0.577
		7	-0.008	-0.006	4.8037	0.684
		8	0.018	0.018	5.1443	0.742
		9	0.049	0.046	7.5809	0.577
		10	0.037	0.031	8.9973	0.532
		11	0.037	0.032	10.368	0.498
		12	0.057	0.055	13.652	0.323
		13	-0.044	-0.045	15.616	0.270

- Within this context, linear models can be understood as approximations to nonlinear specifications. This underscores very much the importance of the Wold decomposition (for stationary processes) (Chapter 6), and the importance of understanding linear dynamics. From a modeling and forecasting perspective, linear models will be the benchmark against any nonlinear specification should be measured up.
- The absence of linear autocorrelation does not imply that the process is not predictable because we could construct forecasts based on nonlinear specifications.
- Identification tools such as ACF and PCFs are nonexistent for nonlinear models. The choice of the best or more adequate nonlinear specification among many is guided by statistical testing and by assessing the forecasting performance of the proposed models.
- Because the statistical implementation of nonlinear models is complex and we sometimes lack the appropriate statistical inference, **linearity testing** should be an important stage in our modeling strategy when possible.

16.2 Nonlinear Models: An Introduction

In this section we introduce three nonlinear specifications that are most popular within economic and business data. These are:

- Threshold models.
- Smooth transition models.
- Markov-switching models.

For the most part, these models require estimation and testing techniques that go beyond the scope of this textbook. However, our objective is more descriptive than statistical as we intend to:

1. Highlight the economic relevance of these models.
2. Analyze a few instances in which ordinary least squares suffices to deliver standard inference results.
3. Show the complexity of the multistep forecast with nonlinear models.

On doing so, an agenda of new topics to explore elsewhere will emerge for those inclined to "dig deeper" in the field of economic forecasting.

16.2.1 Threshold Autoregressive Models (TAR)

In Section 16.1.1, we introduced a SETAR model, which is an example of a threshold model. In general, **threshold autoregressive** models can be understood as piecewise linear autoregressions with the following specification:

$$Y_t = \begin{cases} \phi_{10} + \sum_{j=1}^{p} \phi_{1j} Y_{t-j} + \varepsilon_{1t} & \text{if } x_t < c_1 \\ \phi_{20} + \sum_{j=1}^{p} \phi_{2j} Y_{t-j} + \varepsilon_{2t} & \text{if } c_1 \le x_t < c_2 \\ \cdots\cdots\cdots\cdots & \\ \phi_{r0} + \sum_{j=1}^{p} \phi_{rj} Y_{t-j} + \varepsilon_{rt} & \text{if } c_{r-1} \le x_t < c_r \end{cases}$$

The model contains r regimes, and in each one, the process is a linear autoregressive process of order p. The variable x_t is the threshold variable, which can be any Y_{t-j} or any other exogenous variable. When the threshold variable is any of the lagged dependent variable Y_{t-j}s, the process is called *self-exciting threshold autoregressive*. There are r thresholds $c_1, c_2, \ldots . c_r$, and the innovation ε_{it} is assumed to be independently and identically distributed (i.i.d.) $N(0, \sigma_i^2)$. For most economic data, the number of regimes is between two and three and the dynamics in each regime are usually of low order. In section 16.1.1, we have seen a SETAR(1) model where $Y_{t-p} = Y_{t-1}$, $x_t = Y_{t-1}$, and $c_1 = 0$, $c_2 = +\infty$, that is,

$$Y_t = \begin{cases} \phi_{11} Y_{t-1} + \varepsilon_t & \text{if } Y_{t-1} > 0 \\ \phi_{12} Y_{t-1} + \varepsilon_t & \text{if } Y_{t-1} \le 0 \end{cases}$$

Before we proceed with the estimation of TAR models, we need to specify how many regimes to entertain, the autoregressive lag in each regime, the threshold variable, and the threshold values. A priori, we do not have any identification tool that can help with these choices, so we need to rely on estimation and testing. The threshold values $c_1, c_2, \ldots . c_r$ could be also endogenous, and as such, they need to be estimated. In this case, the statistical inference is nonstandard, and we require advance econometric techniques to estimate the model. However, when the threshold value is known, we can use least squares or maximum likelihood estimation; in addition, if the process is stationary, standard statistical inference applies. Let us work with a SETAR(1) to illustrate that the estimation of the model can be accomplished by least squares. Write SETAR(1) as

$$Y_t = \phi_{11} Y_{t-1} I(Y_{t-1} > 0) + \phi_{12} Y_{t-1} I(Y_{t-1} \leq 0) + \varepsilon_t$$

and notice that the indicator functions, $I(Y_{t-1} > 0)$ and $I(Y_{t-1} \leq 0)$, can be interpreted as dummy variables taking the values 1 or 0, depending on whether or not the condition is satisfied. Furthermore, we can also write $I(Y_{t-1} \leq 0) = 1 - I(Y_{t-1} > 0)$, and rewrite the model as

$$Y_t = \phi_{11} Y_{t-1} I(Y_{t-1} > 0) + \phi_{12} Y_{t-1}[1 - I(Y_{t-1} > 0)] + \varepsilon_t$$
$$Y_t = \phi_{12} Y_{t-1} + (\phi_{11} - \phi_{12}) Y_{t-1} I(Y_{t-1} > 0) + \varepsilon_t$$
$$Y_t = \phi_{12} Y_{t-1} + \phi Y_{t-1} I(Y_{t-1} > 0) + \varepsilon_t$$

where $\phi \equiv \phi_{11} - \phi_{12}$. Now we have a regression model that it is easy to work with. After we construct the dummy variable $I(Y_{t-1} > 0)$, we regress Y_t on Y_{t-1} and $Y_{t-1} I(Y_{t-1} > 0)$ estimating the parameters ϕ_{12} and ϕ by ordinary least squares (OLS). When Y_t is covariance stationary, hypothesis testing in any of the parameters of the model can be performed with the usual t-tests and F-tests, which have standard distributions.

In this setting, a test for linearity follows immediately. The regression model will become linear when $\phi = 0$, which is equivalent to say that the two piecewise linear regressions have the same slope, that is, $\phi_{11} = \phi_{12}$. Thus, a standard t-statistic for the null hypothesis $H_0 : \phi = 0$ versus the alternative $H_1 : \phi \neq 0$ will suffice to test for linearity versus nonlinearity.

REAL DATA: U.S. Treasury Bills

Recall the time series of yearly interest rates on the 3-month Treasury Bill (Figure 16.6). In our discussion, we proposed two different regimes depending on whether the rates are high or low. Let us consider two specifications: a linear model, which is equivalent to hypothesize just one regime, and a SETAR model with two regimes (nonlinear process). We will work with monthly rates from 1934 January to 2008 September. The time series plot is in Figure 16.9. The series can be downloaded from http://research.stlouisfed.org.

Upon analyzing the time series plot, the most prominent feature is very high interest rates (in double digits) during the historical period 1979–1982, reaching a maximum of 16% in May 1981. On the other extreme, we observe very low rates in the 1930s, 1940s, 2001–2004, and 2008 with rates in the neighborhood of 1 and 2%. Furthermore, it seems that the time series is more persistent for low interest rates than for high rates. Given these observations, it is reasonable to think that the dynamics for high versus low interest rates may be different, and in this case, we may want to consider a nonlinear model.

However, before we engage in nonlinear modeling, we should also entertain the possibility of a linear model, which is equivalent to claim that there is only one regime. If we move only within the class of linear models and with the profile of the time series (high persistence), we should assess whether or not this is a unit root process. An augmented

FIGURE 16.9
3-Month Treasury Bill Interest Rates (Monthly Data)

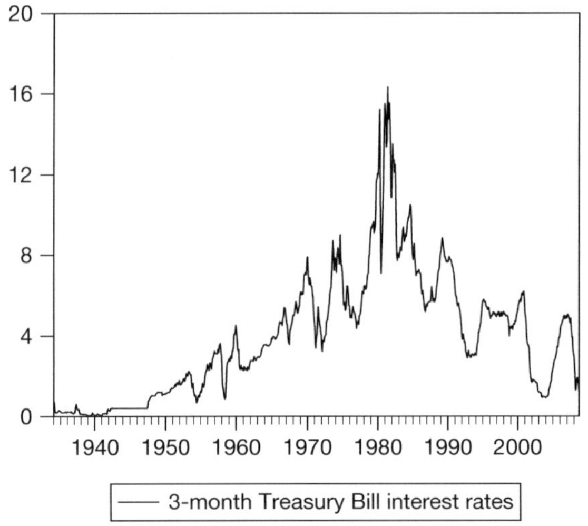

Dickey-Fuller test for unit root reveals that we cannot reject the unit root (Table 16.1). The p-value of the test is 0.1765, which is larger than the conventional 5% significance level.

Thus, if we were to accept just one regime, the linear model would be a random walk with some additional autocorrelation.

However, as discussed, it is plausible that there may be more than one regime and that some regimes may be stationary (low persistence) and some others may not (very high persistence). To capture this possibility, we entertain the following nonlinear model, a two-regime SETAR model

$$\Delta r_t = \begin{cases} c_1 + \phi_{11} r_{t-1} + \phi_{12}\Delta r_{t-1} + \phi_{13}\Delta r_{t-2} + \cdots\cdots + \varepsilon_t & \text{if } r_{t-1} > 8.5 \\ c_2 + \phi_{21} r_{t-1} + \phi_{22}\Delta r_{t-1} + \phi_{23}\Delta r_{t-2} + \cdots\cdots + \varepsilon_t & \text{if } r_{t-1} \le 8.5 \end{cases}$$

that discriminates between high interest rates, those above 8.5%, and low interest rates, those below 8.5%. Observe that the proposed model also allows for stationary

TABLE 16.1 Augmented Dickey-Fuller Unit Root Test for 3-Month Treasury Bill Rates

Null Hypothesis: T3 has a unit root			
Exogenous: Constant			
Lag Length: 13 (Automatic based on SIC, MAXLAG = 20)			
		t-Statistic	Prob.*
Augmented Dickey-Fuller test statistic		-2.287025	0.1765
Test critical values:	1% level	-3.437533	
	5% level	-2.864600	
	10% level	-2.568453	

*MacKinnon (1996) one-sided p-values.

and nonstationary regimes. We include in the right-hand side of the model the level of the series, r_{t-1}, with several lags of the first differences, $\Delta r_{t-1}, \Delta r_{t-2}, \ldots\ldots$ This regression is similar to the regression we write when we wish to test for unit root. If $\phi_{11} = 0$, the upper regime will be nonstationary (a unit root process), and if $\phi_{21} = 0$, the lower regime will also have a unit root. However, when these parameters ϕ_{11} and ϕ_{21} are different from zero, the regimes will be stationary.

To estimate this model, we proceed to build a dummy variable D that discriminates between the two regimes

$$D \equiv I(r_{t-1} > 8.5\%) = \begin{cases} 1 & \text{if } r_{t-1} > 8.5\% \\ 0 & \text{if } r_{t-1} < 8.5\% \end{cases}$$

and rewrite the SETAR model as

$$\Delta r_t = (c_1 + \phi_{11} r_{t-1} + \phi_{12} \Delta r_{t-1} + \phi_{13} \Delta r_{t-2} + \ldots\ldots) \times D + (c_2 + \phi_{21} r_{t-1} \\ + \phi_{22} \Delta r_{t-1} + \phi_{23} \Delta r_{t-2} + \ldots.)(1 - D) + \varepsilon_t$$

or equivalently,

$$\Delta r_t = c_2 + (c_1 - c_2)D + \phi_{21} r_{t-1} + (\phi_{11} - \phi_{21}) r_{t-1} D + \phi_{22} \Delta r_{t-1} \\ + \phi_{23} \Delta r_{t-2} + (\phi_{12} - \phi_{22}) \Delta r_{t-1} D + (\phi_{13} - \phi_{23}) \Delta r_{t-2} D \ldots. + \varepsilon_t$$

Because the threshold is fixed, this model is a regression model that will be estimated by OLS. We need only to regress Δr_t on a constant, the dummy D, the levels r_{t-1} and $r_{t-1}D$, and the lags of the first differences $\Delta r_{t-1}, \Delta r_{t-2}, \ldots\ldots$ and the interaction terms $\Delta r_{t-1}D, \Delta r_{t-2}D, \ldots\ldots.$ The estimation output of this two-regime SETAR model is provided in Table 16.2.

With these estimation results, the estimated SETAR model becomes:

$$\Delta r_t = \begin{cases} 1.029 - 0.099 r_{t-1} + 0.441 \Delta r_{t-1} - 0.261 \Delta r_{t-2} + \hat{\varepsilon}_t & \text{if } r_{t-1} > 8.5 \\ 0.008 - 0.0001 r_{t-1} + 0.391 \Delta r_{t-1} - 0.122 \Delta r_{t-2} + \hat{\varepsilon}_t & \text{if } r_{t-1} \leq 8.5 \end{cases}$$

Comparing both regimes, we observe that the estimates of ϕ_{11} and ϕ_{21} are very different. The lower regime ($r_{t-1} \leq 8.5\%$) seems to be nonstationary because $\hat{\phi}_{21} = -0.0001$ is basically zero, but the upper regime ($r_{t-1} > 8.5\%$) seems to be stationary because $\hat{\phi}_{11} \approx -0.10$ is different from zero. This is evidence for nonlinearity, although a formal test would involve the asymptotic distribution of the t-ratios in the preceding regression. Because the threshold variable r_{t-1} seems to be unconditionally (regardless of regimes) nonstationary (Table 16.1), the asymptotic distribution of the t-ratios in Table 16.2 will follow nonstandard distributions for which critical values must be obtained by simulation. Nevertheless, and in the absence of the proper critical values, we still observe that the t-ratio associated with the variable T3(-1)*D is very large, about –4.92, suggesting that ϕ_{11} is likely to be different from zero. In addition, the t-ratio associated with the variable T3(-1) is basically zero, about –0.03, strongly suggesting that ϕ_{21} is likely to be zero. Overall, the evidence points to two regimes in interest rates with very different dynamics.

TABLE 16.2 OLS Estimation of a Two-Regime SETAR Model for 3-Month Treasury Bill

Dependent Variable: DT3
Method: Least Squares
Sample (adjusted): 1934M04 2008M09
Included observations: 894 after adjustments

Variable	Coefficient	Std. Error	t-Statistic	Prob.
C	0.007931	0.020883	0.379779	0.7042
D	1.022221	0.217054	4.709531	0.0000
T3(-1)	-0.000147	0.005086	-0.028914	0.9769
T3(-1)*D	-0.099166	0.020153	-4.920634	0.0000
DT3(-1)	0.391347	0.055726	7.022722	0.0000
DT3(-2)	-0.122577	0.043348	-2.827742	0.0048
DT3(-1)*D	0.050344	0.068522	0.734715	0.4627
DT3(-2)*D	-0.139051	0.066895	-2.078649	0.0379

R-squared	0.184175	Mean dependent var	0.000996
Adjusted R-squared	0.177729	S.D. dependent var	0.386187
S.E. of regression	0.350191	Akaike info criterion	0.748232
Sum squared resid	108.6534	Schwarz criterion	0.791146
Log likelihood	-326.4596	F-statistic	28.57380
Durbin-Watson stat	1.990387	Prob(F-statistic)	0.000000

Given this discussion, it is of interest to point out the conditions under which OLS estimation and standard statistical inference can be performed for a general TAR specification such as

$$Y_t = \begin{cases} \phi_{10} + \sum_{j=1}^{p} \phi_{1j} Y_{t-j} + \varepsilon_{1t} & \text{if } x_t < c_1 \\ \phi_{20} + \sum_{j=1}^{p} \phi_{2j} Y_{t-j} + \varepsilon_{2t} & \text{if } c_1 \le x_t < c_2 \\ \cdots\cdots\cdots\cdots & \\ \phi_{r0} + \sum_{j=1}^{p} \phi_{rj} Y_{t-j} + \varepsilon_{rt} & \text{if } c_{r-1} \le x_t < c_r \end{cases}$$

The following are sufficient conditions for classical asymptotic OLS results to hold:

1. When the thresholds $c_1, c_2, \ldots . c_r$ are known.
2. The threshold variable X_t is stationary.

3. The overall TAR is stationary, which means that either all the regimes are stationary or, if some regimes contain a unit root, the nonstationary regimes must be dominated by the stationary regimes,[3] then OLS estimation can be performed, and t-ratios and F-tests will enjoy standard asymptotic distributions.

16.2.2 Smooth Transition Models

The TAR model assumes that moving from one regime to the next happens abruptly. It does because the indicator function $I(Y_{t-1}>0)$ in $Y_t=\phi_{12}Y_{t-1}+\phi Y_{t-1}I(Y_{t-1}>0)+\varepsilon_t$ is a step function taking the value either 1 or 0. At a macroeconomic level, we should expect smoother changes between regimes because economic decisions tend to percolate slowly through the economic system. For these cases, we would like to model a **smooth transition** from one regime to another instead of discrete jumps from zero to one or vice versa. To capture this type of transition, we propose the smooth transition autoregressive (STAR) model, which has the following representation:

$$Y_t = c_0 + \phi_{01}Y_{t-1} + \phi_{02}Y_{t-2} + \cdots\cdots + \phi_{0p}Y_{t-p} + (c_1 + \phi_{11}Y_{t-1} + \phi_{12}Y_{t-2} + \ldots\ldots \phi_{1p}Y_{t-p})\, G(s_t, \gamma, c) + \varepsilon_t$$

where $\varepsilon_t \to N(0, \sigma^2)$, and $G(s_t, \gamma, c)$ is now the transition function that is a continuous and bounded function of the transition variable s_t. In autoregressive models, the transition variable is usually one of the lagged variables $s_t = y_{t-d}$, $d > 0$. The parameter γ is the slope parameter or the speed of the transition, and the constant c is a location or threshold parameter.

Notice the difference between a TAR model and a STAR model. We maintain the autoregressive representation in the different regimes. However, in the TAR model, the number of regimes is finite and discrete, but in the STAR model, the number of regimes is continuous because it is driven by the values of the continuous transition function $G(s_t, \gamma, c)$.

The function $G(s_t, \gamma, c)$ can have different shapes. We refer to two of the most popular in economics and business: the logistic function and the exponential function. The simplest functional forms are:

$$\text{Logistic function: } G(s_t, \gamma, c) = \frac{1}{1 + \exp\{-\gamma(s_t - c)\}} \qquad \gamma > 0$$

and

$$\text{Exponential function: } G(s_t, \gamma, c) = 1 - \exp\{-\gamma(s_t - c)^2\} \qquad \gamma > 0$$

When $G(s_t, \gamma, c)$ is the logistic function, the model is logistic smooth transition autoregressive (LSTAR) and when it is the exponential, the model is exponential smooth transition autoregressive (ESTAR). Let us draw these two functions to understand which characteristics of the time series we are modeling. See Figure 16.10 for both functions.

---

[3] This condition is more technical. In a threshold model with two regimes and one lag such as $Y_t(\phi_{11}\, Y_{t-1}I(Y_{t-1} > 0) + \phi_{12}Y_{t-1}I(Y_{t-1} \leq 0) + \varepsilon_t$, overall TAR stationarity requires that $E(\phi_{11}I(Y_{t-1} > 0) + \phi_{12}I(Y_{t-1} \leq 0))^2 < 1$. See González and Gonzalo (1997), 'Threshold Unit Root Models', Working Paper 97–50, Universidad Carlos III de Madrid.

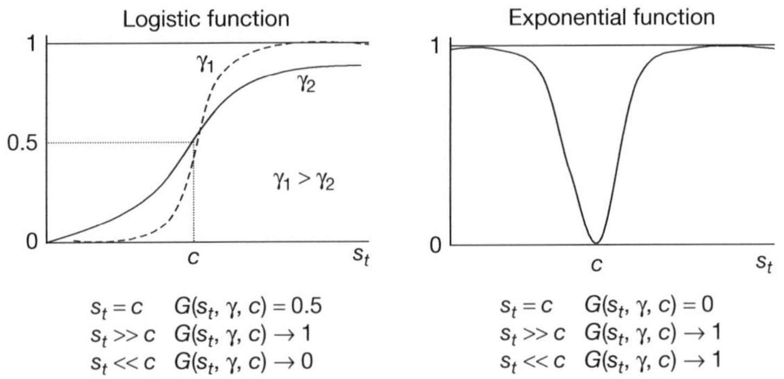

FIGURE 16.10 Logistic and Exponential Transition Functions

The LSTAR model is appropriate when we claim two extreme distinctive regimes in the data (0 and 1), which happen when the values of the transition variable s_t are far from the threshold c. Between these two extremes are some intermediate regimes around the value c. How smoothly the transition occurs between the continuum of regimes depends on the slope parameter γ. Notice that if the parameter γ is very large, the logistic function becomes very steep—it is almost a step function—and the LSTAR model is undistinguishable from a TAR model. The ESTAR model is adequate when extreme regime 1 occurs for values of the transition variable far from the threshold and when extreme regime 0 occurs for values of the transition variable around the threshold. Again the transition between regimes is guided by the parameter γ. However, if γ is very large, the ESTAR model has just one regime because it practically collapses to a linear model (the transition function is equal to 1 for all values of the transition variable). Which function to choose is part of the modeling exercise and depends on the data characteristics.

16.2.2.1 Testing for Linearity Against a STAR Model

Because the estimation of a STAR model is not straightforward, it is advisable to test for linearity first. If linearity is rejected, we can proceed with the specification of a nonlinear STAR model. Let us work with a simple model to understand some of the issues of estimation and testing in the STAR environment. Suppose that we have a STAR(1) model such as

$$Y_t = \phi_0 Y_{t-1} + \phi_1 Y_{t-1} G(s_t, \gamma, c) + \varepsilon_t$$

Testing for linearity requires testing the null hypothesis $H_0 : \phi_1 = 0$. Under the null, the model becomes a linear AR(1). The problem is that, under the null hypothesis, the parameters γ and c are not identified. This is to say, the potential contribution of the transition function to the model is also lost; thus, any values of γ and c will deliver the same likelihood of the data. The solution to this problem is not straightforward because it requires the construction of tests that do not have standard asymptotic distributions. However, a solution that requires only an auxiliary OLS regression is available. It involves the linearization of the transition function G around $\gamma = 0$ by a Taylor's expansion. For a given transition variable s_t and a value c, a Taylor's expansion of $G(\gamma)$ around $\gamma = 0$ is as follows

$$G(\gamma) = G(0) + G'(0)\gamma + \frac{1}{2!}G''(0)\gamma^2 + \frac{1}{3!}G'''(0)\gamma^3 + \cdots\cdots + R$$

where $G'(0)$, $G''(0)$, $G'''(0)$ are the first, second, and third derivatives of the function with respect to γ evaluated at zero, and R is a remainder term. For the logistic function (the exponential case is left as an exercise), the required derivatives are

$$G(0) = 1/2$$
$$G'(0) = (s_t - c)/4$$
$$G''(0) = 0$$
$$G'''(0) = -(s_t - c)^3/8$$

By plugging the Taylor's expansion in the STAR(1) model

$$Y_t = \phi_0 Y_{t-1} + \phi_1 Y_{t-1} G(s_t, \gamma, c) + \varepsilon_t$$

we form an auxiliary regression (disregarding the remainder term) such as:

$$Y_t = \beta_0 + \beta_1 Y_{t-1} + \beta_2 Y_{t-1} s_t + \beta_3 Y_{t-1} s_t^2 + \beta_4 Y_{t-1} s_t^3 + w_t$$

where the new regression coefficients $\beta_0, \beta_1, \beta_2, \beta_3, \beta_4$ subsume the original parameters $\phi_0, \phi_1, \gamma, c$ and any other constants in the expansion. Once the regression model has been estimated by OLS, the null hypothesis of linearity can be rephrased as $H_0: \beta_2 = \beta_3 = \beta_4 = 0$, which can be tested with an F-statistic. In fact, the null hypothesis claims that there is no effect due to the transition variable; consequently, the transition function does not play any role in the model. Notice that the degrees of freedom of the new test have increased substantially. In the original test, we had only one parameter in the null hypothesis, $H_0: \phi_1 = 0$, but in the F-statistic, we now have three parameters under the null. If we do not have many observations in our sample and the linear model has a substantial number of regressors, the auxiliary regression may not be a feasible device because, as we have seen, we need to consider all interactions of the whole set of regressors, $Y_{t-1}, Y_{t-2}, Y_{t-3}, \ldots\ldots$ with the different powers of the transition variable, $s_t, s_t^2, s_t^3, \ldots$ and by doing that, we consume many degrees of freedom. We then implement these ideas with the following analysis of the time series of U.S. industrial production growth (IPG).

REAL DATA: U.S. Industrial Production

We collect data on quarterly growth rates of U.S. Industrial Production Index from 1962:Q1 to 2008:Q3. In Figure 16.11, we picture the time series with the shaded areas corresponding to the NBER dated recessions.

The most prominent feature of this plot is the deep recessions in the mid-1970s and beginning of the 1980s. Given these data, it is natural to ask whether the dynamics of recessions are different from those of expansions. Graphically, we observe that recessions are much shorter than expansions and that there is a quick rebound from recession into expansion. This asymmetry hints that the choice of a nonlinear model could be appropriate to model the dynamics of IPG.

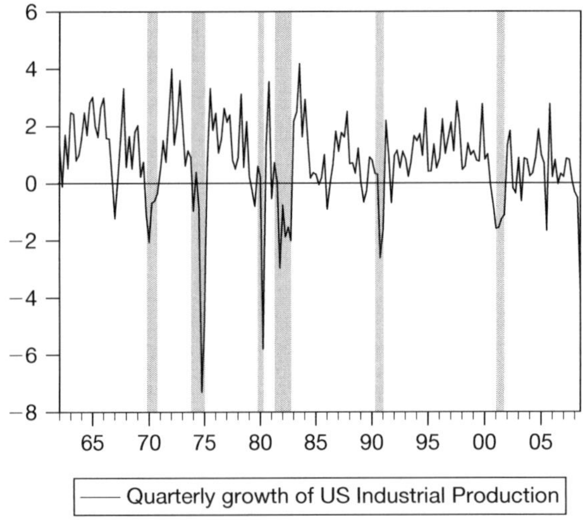

FIGURE 16.11 U.S. Industrial Production (Quarterly Growth Rates)

First, we should ask for the best linear model that fits the data. Using the tools that we already have, we find that an AR(8) seems to be adequate for explaining the autocorrelation present in the data. The estimation output of the linear model is presented in Table 16.3. The statistically significant lags are 1 and 8, which means that the linear

TABLE 16.3 The Best Linear Model for U.S. Industrial Production Growth

Dependent Variable: IPG
Method: Least Squares
Sample (adjusted): 1964Q1 2008Q3
Included observations: 179 after adjustments
Convergence achieved after 3 iterations

Variable	Coefficient	Std. Error	t-Statistic	Prob.
C	0.699270	0.140845	4.964823	0.0000
AR(1)	0.440961	0.067847	6.499381	0.0000
AR(8)	-0.185786	0.067524	-2.751421	0.0066

R-squared	0.236243	Mean dependent var	0.697882
Adjusted R-squared	0.227564	S.D. dependent var	1.595064
S.E. of regression	1.401876	Akaike info criterion	3.530117
Sum squared resid	345.8850	Schwarz criterion	3.583537
Log likelihood	-312.9455	F-statistic	27.21986
Durbin-Watson stat	1.896603	Prob(F-statistic)	0.000000

Inverted AR Roots	.82 + .30i	.82 - .30i	.37 + .73i	.37 - .73i
	-.26 + .74i	-.26 - .74i	-.70 - .31i	-.70 + .31i

dynamics of the series are driven by the immediate short run (the previous quarter), and by a longer run (up to 8 past quarters).

The residuals are white noise, so that there is not autocorrelation left to model. The inverted roots, all being complex and with modulus less than 1, indicate that there are four cycles of different length and intensity in the data and that the process is covariance stationary.

Now before we embark in the construction of a nonlinear model, it is sensible to test for linearity. We choose the family of STAR models to test against. To implement the linearity test, we need to choose the transition variable. Given the estimation in Table 16.3, we may want to entertain two possible transition variables, either Y_{t-1} or Y_{t-8}, although any other lagged variable in between may be an option. The threshold value $c = 0$ is plausible because we wish to distinguish positive from negative growth rates.

Suppose that we choose the transition variable to be $s_t = Y_{t-1}$. The linearity test involves estimating the auxiliary regression:

$$Y_t = \beta_0 + \beta_1 Y_{t-1} + \beta_2 Y_{t-8} + \beta_{21} Y_{t-1} s_t + \beta_{22} Y_{t-8} s_t + \beta_{31} Y_{t-1} s_t^2 + \beta_{32} Y_{t-8} s_t^2 + \beta_{41} Y_{t-1} s_t^3 + \beta_{42} Y_{t-8} s_t^3 + w_t$$

in which we substitute $s_t = Y_{t-1}$ to finally run the following regression:

$$Y_t = \beta_0 + \beta_1 Y_{t-1} + \beta_2 Y_{t-8} + \beta_{21} Y_{t-1}^2 + \beta_{22} Y_{t-8} Y_{t-1} + \beta_{31} Y_{t-1}^3 + \beta_{32} Y_{t-8} Y_{t-1}^2 + \beta_{41} Y_{t-1}^4 + \beta_{42} Y_{t-8} Y_{t-1}^3 + w_t$$

The linearity test is an F-test for the null hypothesis

$$H_0 : \beta_{21} = \beta_{22} = \beta_{31} = \beta_{32} = \beta_{41} = \beta_{42} = 0$$

which is an assessment of the contribution of the transition variable $s_t = Y_{t-1}$ and its successive powers s_t^2, s_t^3 in addition to their interactions with the regressors of the linear model Y_{t-1} and Y_{t-8}. If we reject the null hypothesis, we conclude that the model is nonlinear; if we fail to reject the null, the model is linear. The implementation of this test in EViews is straightforward because it only requires running an OLS estimation, and then, once in the Equation window, click View, select Coefficient Tests, and select Wald-Coefficient Restrictions.

In Table 16.4 we show the estimation results of the auxiliary regression when the transition variable is Y_{t-1}, and in Table 16.5, when the transition variable is Y_{t-8}. In both tables, we also show the corresponding F-statistics for testing the null hypothesis of linearity.

Comparing the test results in both tables, we observe that both F-tests reach the same conclusion and in both cases, we very strongly reject linearity in favor of a nonlinear STAR model. The p-values of both tests are much smaller than 1% so that we could choose either Y_{t-1} or Y_{t-8} as a transition variable. For the next modeling step, we work with Y_{t-1} as the transition variable, but it is advisable also to try Y_{t-8} and make sure that the final conclusions are robust to the choice of the transition variable.

Finally at this stage, we should gather evidence either for the logistic or the **exponential transition function**. It can be proven that we have evidence for the LSTAR

TABLE 16.4 Testing for Linearity

Auxiliary Regression with Transition Variable Y_{t-1}

F**-test (Wald test)** $H_0: \beta_{21} = \beta_{22} = \beta_{31} = \beta_{32} = \beta_{41} = \beta_{42} = 0$

Dependent Variable: IPG
Method: Least Squares
Sample (adjusted): 1964Q1 2008Q3
Included observations: 179 after adjustments

Variable	Coefficient	Std. Error	t-Statistic	Prob.
C	0.251543	0.169940	1.480180	0.1407
IPG(-1)	0.716780	0.128954	5.558403	0.0000
IPG(-8)	0.183551	0.083730	-2.192175	0.0297
IPG(-1)*IPG(-1)	0.139389	0.072274	1.928626	0.0554
IPG(-8)*IPG(-1)	0.104347	0.079483	1.312812	0.1910
IPG(-1)*IPG(-1)*IPG(-1)	-0.047910	0.012051	-3.975704	0.0001
IPG(-8)*IPG(-1)*IPG(-1)	-0.036457	0.022931	-1.589826	0.1137
IPG(-1)*IPG(-1)*IPG(-1)*IPG(-1)	-0.006986	0.004195	-1.665417	0.0977
IPG(-8)*IPG(-1)*IPG(-1)*IPG(-1)	-0.000265	0.007292	-0.036295	0.9711

R-squared	0.330539	Mean dependent var	0.697882
Adjusted R-squared	0.299035	S.D. dependent var	1.595064
S.E. of regression	1.335446	Akaike info criterion	3.465380
Sum squared resid	303.1809	Schwarz criterion	3.625639
Log likelihood	-301.1515	F-statistic	10.49194
Durbin-Watson stat	1.974439	Prob(F-statistic)	0.000000

Wald Test:
Equation: Untitled

Test Statistic	Value	df	Probability
F-statistic	3.990851	(6, 170)	0.0009
Chi-square	23.94511	6	0.0005

Null Hypothesis Summary:

Normalized Restriction (= 0)	Value	Std. Err.
C(4)	0.139389	0.072274
C(5)	0.104347	0.079483
C(6)	-0.047910	0.012051
C(7)	-0.036457	0.022931
C(8)	-0.006986	0.004195
C(9)	-0.000265	0.007292

Restrictions are linear in coefficients.

TABLE 16.5 Testing for Linearity

Auxiliary Regression with Transition Variable Y_{t-8}

F-test (Wald test) $H_0: \beta_{21} = \beta_{22} = \beta_{31} = \beta_{32} = \beta_{41} = \beta_{42} = 0$

Dependent Variable: IPG
Method: Least Squares
Sample (adjusted): 1964Q1 2008Q3
Included observations: 179 after adjustments

Variable	Coefficient	Std. Error	t-Statistic	Prob.
C	0.808812	0.159965	5.056190	0.0000
IPG(-1)	0.250007	0.088321	2.830671	0.0052
IPG(-8)	-0.113910	0.147573	-0.771892	0.4413
IPG(-1)*IPG(-8)	0.089816	0.091154	0.985315	0.3259
IPG(-8)*IPG(-8)	-0.099897	0.061995	-1.611362	0.1090
IPG(-1)*IPG(-8)*IPG(-8)	0.047105	0.020878	2.256139	0.0253
IPG(-8)*IPG(-8)*IPG(-8)	-0.011953	0.011150	-1.072021	0.2852
IPG(-1)*IPG(-8)*IPG(-8)*IPG(-8)	-0.000971	0.006793	-0.142999	0.8865
IPG(-8)*IPG(-8)*IPG(-8)*IPG(-8)	-0.000821	0.002495	-0.329117	0.7425

R-squared	0.334975	Mean dependent var	0.697882
Adjusted R-squared	0.303679	S.D. dependent var	1.595064
S.E. of regression	1.331015	Akaike info criterion	3.458732
Sum squared resid	301.1721	Schwarz criterion	3.618991
Log likelihood	-300.5565	F-statistic	10.70366
Durbin-Watson stat	1.828603	Prob(F-statistic)	0.000000

Wald Test:
Equation: Untitled

Test Statistic	Value	df	Probability
F-statistic	4.206454	(6, 170)	0.0006
Chi-square	25.23873	6	0.0003

Null Hypothesis Summary:

Normalized Restriction (= 0)	Value	Std. Err.
C(4)	0.089816	0.091154
C(5)	-0.099897	0.061995
C(6)	0.047105	0.020878
C(7)	-0.011953	0.011150
C(8)	-0.000971	0.006793
C(9)	-0.000821	0.002495

Restrictions are linear in coefficients.

model when, in the auxiliary regression, the statistical significance of the terms that interact with the transition variable s_t and s_t^3 (odd powers of the transition variable) is high. When the transition function is exponential, the odd powers of the transition variable are statistically insignificant. In Table 16.4, we perform an F-test for $H_0: \beta_{41} = \beta_{42} = 0$, which assesses the significance of terms with s_t^3. The p-value of this test is 2.2% so that we reject the null hypothesis at the customary 5% level and conclude that the logistic function is appropriate to model the data.

With statistical evidence on nonlinearities and a **logistic transition function** in the data, we proceed with the estimation of the following model:

$$Y_t = c_0 + \phi_{01} Y_{t-1} + \phi_{02} Y_{t-8} + (c_1 + \phi_{11} Y_{t-1} + \phi_{12} Y_{t-8}) G(Y_{t-1}, \gamma, 0) + \varepsilon_t$$

$$G(Y_{t-1}, \gamma, 0) = \frac{1}{1 + \exp\{-\gamma\, Y_{t-1}\}}, \quad \gamma > 0$$

If γ is known, the estimation of the model is very straightforward because OLS suffices to obtain the estimates of the parameters. When γ is unknown, the estimation requires nonlinear techniques that are beyond the scope of this book. Nevertheless, we proceed by searching for γ with a grid procedure. Let us assume that $\gamma \in (\underline{\gamma}, \overline{\gamma})$. For each value in this interval, we perform an OLS regression for the proposed model (this is a regression conditioning in a predetermined value of γ). Let us note the sum of squared residuals (SSR) in each conditional regression. The optimal γ would be the value that delivers the smallest SSR among all the conditional regression models. This is the result:

γ	0.5	1	2	2.5	3	4	5	10
SSR	330.95	326.29	322.73	322.51	322.74	323.79	325.07	330.13

A $\gamma = 2.5$ delivers the smallest SSR. We plot the corresponding logistic transition function in two ways. First, we plot the function itself (left panel of Figure 16.12) and then the time series of the values of the function (right panel Figure 16.12). We observe that the logistic function is very steep, reaching the upper regime ($G = 1$) when the growth rate is larger than 2% (expansion cycle) and the lower regime ($G = 0$) when the rate is smaller than −2% (recession cycle). The intermediate regimes are located between −2% and 2% growth rates. The time series plot of the logistic function provides an additional message: The economy tends to aggressively rebound from the lower regime so that recessions are much shorter than expansions. Notice that the logistic function indicates that in 2008:Q3, the very beginning of the global financial crisis of 2008–2010, the economy had already entered into a recessionary cycle.

The estimation of the model, conditioning of a value of $\gamma = 2.5$, is presented in Table 16.6.

The notation $G(-1, 2.5)$ means the logistic function

$$G(Y_{t-1}, 2.5, 0) = \frac{1}{1 + \exp\{-2.5 \times Y_{t-1}\}}.$$

Note that the nonlinear model provides a better fit than the linear one because the modeling of the nonlinearity is able to reduce the residual variance. In the linear model

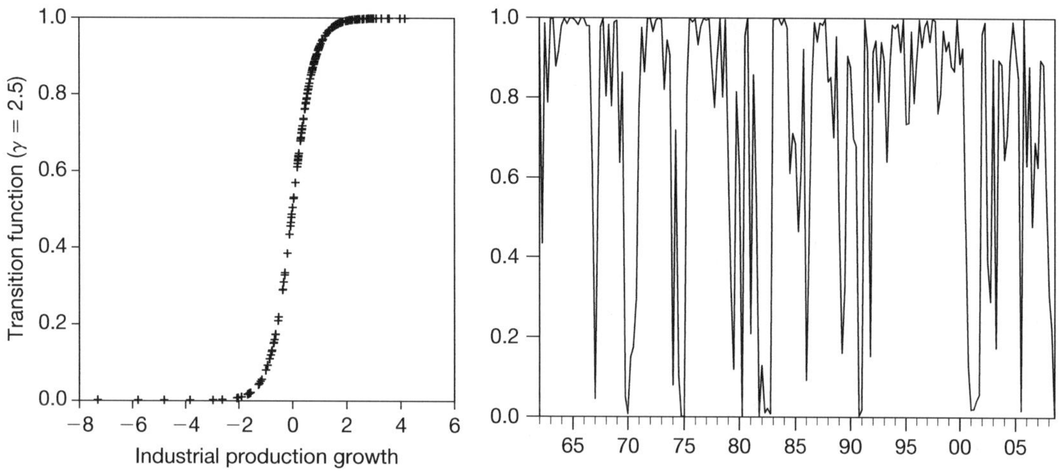

FIGURE 16.12 Logistic Transition Function for U.S. Industrial Production Growth

(Table 16.3), the residual variance is 1.97; in the nonlinear model (Table 16.6), it is reduced to 1.86, which indicates a better fitting.

To interpret the results in Table 16.6, we calculate the dynamics in the extreme upper ($G = 1$) and lower ($G = 0$) regimes. The dynamics of the intermediate regimes

TABLE 16.6 Estimation of Logistic Smooth Transition Autoregressive Model

Dependent Variable: IPG
Method: Least Squares
Sample (adjusted): 1964Q1 2008Q3
Included observations: 179 after adjustments

Variable	Coefficient	Std. Error	t-Statistic	Prob.
C	-0.505909	0.391892	-1.290939	0.1984
IPG(-1)	0.002398	0.156247	0.015347	0.9878
IPG(-8)	-0.379683	0.155987	-2.434063	0.0159
G(-1,2.5)	1.628712	0.610019	2.669939	0.0083
G(-1,2.5)*IPG(-1)	0.189926	0.180711	1.050991	0.2947
G(-1, 2.5)*IPG(-8)	0.259353	0.193100	1.343104	0.1810

R-squared	0.287843	Mean dependent var	0.697882
Adjusted R-squared	0.267260	S.D. dependent var	1.595064
S.E. of regression	1.365378	Akaike info criterion	3.493685
Sum squared resid	322.5167	Schwarz criterion	3.600525
Log likelihood	-306.6848	F-statistic	13.98480
Durbin-Watson stat	1.917068	Prob(F-statistic)	0.000000

are bounded between these two and can be calculated in a similar fashion for different values of the function G.

The autoregressive process in the lower regime is ($G = 0$ in the regression model):

$$Y_t = -0.50 - 0.38Y_{t-8} + \varepsilon_t$$

We have removed the coefficient corresponding to Y_{t-1} because it is statistically zero. The unconditional mean in the lower regime is $\mu_L = -0.50/(1 + 0.38) = -0.36\%$.

The autoregressive process in the upper regime is ($G = 1$ in the regression model):

$$\begin{aligned} Y_t &= (-0.50 + 1.62) + 0.19Y_{t-1} + (-0.38 + 0.26)Y_{t-8} + \varepsilon_t \\ &= 1.12 + 0.19Y_{t-1} - 0.12Y_{t-8} + \varepsilon_t \end{aligned}$$

The unconditional mean in the upper regime is

$$\mu_U = 1.12/(1 - 0.19 + 0.12) = 1.20\%.$$

Note that the mean of the lower (upper) regime is negative (positive) as expected because we are dealing with negative (positive) growth rates. In addition, by analyzing the roots of the characteristic equation of both processes, we can extract information about the stationarity of the processes. For industrial production, the processes in both the upper and lower regimes are stationary. Check that all roots are complex so that both processes generate cycles. In the upper regime, the roots are such that the longest period of an expansionary cycle is about 17 quarters (4.25 years) while in the lower regime, the recessionary cycle is shorter, between 1 and 1.5 years.[4]

16.2.3 Markov Regime-Switching Models: A Descriptive Introduction

A common feature to threshold and smooth transition models is that the threshold and the transition variables guiding the change from one regime to another is an observable variable, sometimes exogenous to the model and sometimes a predetermined or lagged endogenous variable. In some instances, it is not easy to specify the transition variable because there is no acceptable proxy to represent the complexity of the situation or because the proxy cannot be easily quantified or is of a qualitative nature. We can think of changes in government policies such as a new fiscal or monetary environment that affects the level of output of the economy, a financial crisis that may cause waves of panic, and irrational exuberance that may cause waves of euphoria in the financial markets. In these cases, we need models that allow for different regimes and some switching variable, which cannot be measured satisfactorily but should be accounted for in some fashion. **Markov switching models** allow for different regimes guided by a latent

[4] A complex root is represented as $a \pm bi$. The modulus is $m = \sqrt{a^2 + b^2}$. The period of a cycle is calculated as $d = 360/\theta$ where θ is the angle obtained from $\cos(\theta) = a/m$.

variable (nonobservable), called the *state variable.* Suppose that we have two states; for instance, state 1 is expansion and state 2 is recession. Although we will not be able to observe a specific meaningful value of the state variables 1 and 2, it is possible to calculate the conditional probabilities of states 1 and 2 based on an information set as well as the best prediction for the value of the process of interest. Markov switching models offer this possibility.

16.2.3.1 A Simple Specification of a 2-State Markov Switching Process

The simplest model consists of two states or regimes represented by the state variable s_t taking the value $s_t = 1$, for example, in an expansion state, and $s_t = 2$ in a recession state. Suppose that the outcome of the random variable Y_t, for example, GDP, depends on the state of the economy so that Y_t is normally distributed $N(\mu_1, \sigma^2)$ when $s_t = 1$ and $N(\mu_2, \sigma^2)$ when $s_t = 2$. We write the model for Y_t as

$$Y_t = \mu_{s_t} + \varepsilon_t; \qquad \varepsilon_t \rightarrow N(0, \sigma^2)$$

or equivalently

$$\begin{aligned} Y_t|_{s_t=1} &= \mu_1 + \varepsilon_{1t} \quad \text{or} \quad Y_t|_{s_t=1} \rightarrow N(\mu_1, \sigma^2) \\ Y_t|_{s_t=2} &= \mu_2 + \varepsilon_{2t} \quad \text{or} \quad Y_t|_{s_t=2} \rightarrow N(\mu_2, \sigma^2) \end{aligned}$$

so that the constant μ_{s_t} is state dependent; that is, in state 1, the mean is μ_1, and in state 2 is μ_2 (the variance could also be state dependent). Shifting from one regime to the next takes place according to the following transition mechanism. We define the transition probabilities between states as $P(s_t = j | s_{t-1} = i) = p_{ij}$, which says that if yesterday we were in state i, the probability of switching to state j today is p_{ij}. This setup is described as a *2-state* **Markov chain** with transition probabilities p_{ij} for $i, j = 1, 2$. Because there are two states, we have four possible actions: $(i, j) = (1, 1), (1, 2), (2, 1)$ and $(2, 2)$ with their corresponding transition probabilities, which can be collected in a transition matrix as

$$P = \begin{bmatrix} p_{11} & p_{21} \\ p_{12} & p_{22} \end{bmatrix}$$

so that each column in this matrix must total 1, that is, $p_{i1} + p_{i2} = 1$ for $i = 1, 2$.

Let us simulate the simplest model to learn some features of a time series with a Markov switching mechanism. This is the 2-state Markov switching model to simulate:

$$\begin{aligned} Y_t|_{s_t=1} &= 1 + \varepsilon_{1t} \quad \varepsilon_{1t} \rightarrow N(0, 1) \\ Y_t|_{s_t=2} &= -1 + \varepsilon_{2t} \quad \varepsilon_{2t} \rightarrow N(0, 1) \end{aligned} \quad \text{and} \quad P = \begin{bmatrix} p_{11} & p_{21} \\ p_{12} & p_{22} \end{bmatrix} = \begin{bmatrix} 0.7 & 0.1 \\ 0.3 & 0.9 \end{bmatrix}$$

This process will jump from state 1with a positive mean of 1 to state 2 with a negative mean of -1. The transition probability matrix says that state 2 will be more persistent than state 1 because once the process is in state 2, the probability of staying in state 2 is very high, 0.9. If the process is in state 1, the probability of staying is 0.7, and the probability of jumping to state 2 is 0.3. If the process is in state 2, the probability of jumping to state 1 is 0.1. In both states, the error term is assumed to be i.i.d. $N(0, 1)$.

The following program in EViews will generate a time series of the Markov process $\{Y_t\}$.

```
series ym              'this is the time series to be generated
series s1              'state 1: a binomial variable taking value 1 when the
                       state is on and 0 when is off
series s2              'state 2: a binomial variable taking value 1 when the
                       state is on and 0 when is off
series e               'innovation in both states
e=nrnd                 'normal(0,1) innovation
s1(1)=@rbinom(1,0.7)   'initializing state 1 as a draw from a binomial with
                       probability 0.7
'generating 500 observations of the time series
for !i=1 to 500
   if s1(!i)=1 then                'model in state 1
           ym(!i)=1+e(!i)
           s1(!i+1)=@rbinom(1,0.7)
   else                            'model in state 2
           ym(!i)=-1+e(!i)
           s2(!i+1)=@rbinom(1,0.9)
   endif

   if s2(!i+1)=0 then s1(!i+1)=1
   endif
next
```

We plot 500 realizations of the Markov simulated time series in Figure 16.13. The horizontal line is the unconditional mean of the process, which is negative. This is not a surprise because we have already mentioned that state 2, with a negative mean, is more persistent than state 1. The time series tends to linger longer in the negative area than in the positive. This is the result of the assumed values for the probabilities in the transition matrix.

Because we have simulated the series, we know the conditional mean of the process in each state, that is, $E(Y_t|s_t = 1) = 1$ and $E(Y_t|s_t = 2) = -1$. Unconditionally, (regardless of the state), the mean of the process depends on the *unconditional* probabilities of each state, also known as *ergodic probabilities*. Let us call the unconditional probabilities π_j for $j = 1,2$. Then the unconditional mean of the process is

$$E(Y_t) = \pi_1 E(Y_t|s_t = 1) + \pi_2 E(Y_t|s_t = 2) = \pi_1 \times 1 + \pi_2 \times (-1)$$

which is the sum of the weighted conditional means of the process in each state with the weight given by the probability of occurrence of each state.

FIGURE 16.13
A Time Series of a 2-State Markov Switching Process

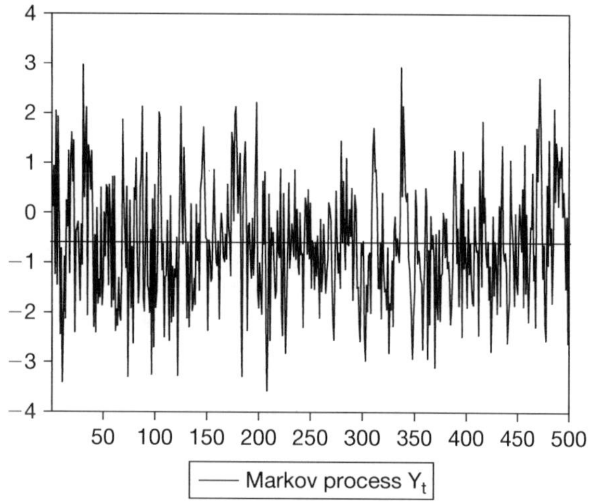

The ergodic probabilities must depend on the transition probabilities.[5] For a 2-state Markov chain, the formulas are as follows:

$$\pi_1 \equiv P(s_t = 1) = \frac{1 - p_{22}}{2 - p_{11} - p_{22}}$$
$$\pi_2 \equiv P(s_t = 2) = 1 - \pi_1$$

For the simulated Markov process, we calculate that $\pi_1 = 0.25$ and $\pi_2 = 0.75$, which means that state 2 has more weight than state 1 in the mixture. Then, the unconditional mean of the process is $E(Y_t) = -0.50$, which corresponds approximately to the solid horizontal line in Figure 16.13.

More generally, the unconditional density of Y_t must capture features from both densities in state 1 and state 2. The ergodic probabilities again play an important role as weighting factors for the densities in both states. The unconditional density of Y_t is a **mixture of densities** in each state, that is

$$f(y_t) = \pi_1 \times N(\mu_1, \sigma_1^2) + \pi_2 \times N(\mu_2, \sigma_2^2)$$

For the simulated Markov process in Figure 16.13, the unconditional density of the process is $f(y_t) = 0.25 \times N(1, 1) + 0.75 \times N(-1, 1)$. In Figure 16.14, we plot the components of the mixture $N(1, 1)$(state 1) and $N(-1, 1)$ (state 2); and the smoothed histogram of the simulated time series Y_t.

We observe that the mixture is clearly dominated by state 2 because the ergodic probability of state 2 is much higher than that of state 1 (0.75 versus 0.25). The realizations in the lower tail of the mixture density are clearly generated by the latent state 2

[5]We need some results from matrix algebra to calculate the ergodic probabilities. We solve for π in the following eigenvalue/eigenvector problem: $\pi = P\pi$. This is also read as: π is the eigenvector of P associated with the unit eigenvalue.

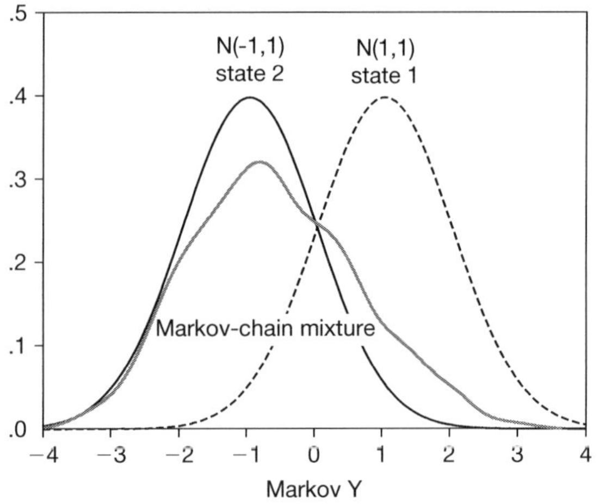

FIGURE 16.14 Unconditional Density of a 2-State Markov Regime-Switching Process and the Densities in Each State

while those observations in the uppermost tail are likely generated by state 1. Those realizations around zero may come from either state.

Markov switching models can become more complex by adding more dynamics in the conditional mean of each state. For instance, we could specify an AR process in each state with the switching taking place through different constants in each state, as in

$$\begin{aligned} Y_t|_{s_t=1} &= c_1 + \phi_1 Y_{t-1} + \phi_2 Y_{t-2} + \varepsilon_t \\ Y_t|_{s_t=2} &= c_2 + \phi_1 Y_{t-1} + \phi_2 Y_{t-2} + \varepsilon_t \end{aligned} \quad \text{with} \quad P = \begin{bmatrix} p_{11} & p_{21} \\ p_{12} & p_{22} \end{bmatrix}, \quad \varepsilon_t \rightarrow N(0, \sigma^2)$$

The complexity arises because we need to estimate two unobservable processes: the Markov chain (number of states and transition probability matrix) and the stochastic process itself within each state. In these instances, additional econometric knowledge beyond OLS estimation is required.

16.3 Forecasting with Nonlinear Models

The notions of optimal forecast and associated loss functions introduced in Chapters 4 and 9 remain valid for forecasting with nonlinear models. Recall that for a quadratic loss function, the optimal forecast is the conditional expectation of the process conditioning on the available information until today, that is,

$$f_{t,h} = \mu_{t+h|t} = E(Y_{t+h}|I_t)$$

16.3.1 One-Step-Ahead Forecast

When $h = 1$, the optimal forecast based on a nonlinear model is easy to calculate analytically by following the same rules that we learned for linear models. We are looking for the forecast of the process at $t + 1$, Y_{t+1}. We proceed by redating the model at $t + 1$

and taking conditional expectations based on an information set that runs up to time t, I_t. Let us recall some of the nonlinear models of the previous section. In all, we will assume that the innovation is i.i.d $\varepsilon_t \rightarrow N(0, \sigma^2)$. For instance,

SETAR(1)

$$Y_t = \begin{cases} \phi_{11} Y_{t-1} + \varepsilon_t & \text{if } Y_{t-1} > 0 \\ \phi_{12} Y_{t-1} + \varepsilon_t & \text{if } Y_{t-1} \leq 0 \end{cases}$$

Redate the model at time $t+1$:

$$Y_{t+1} = \begin{cases} \phi_{11} Y_t + \varepsilon_{t+1} & \text{if } Y_t > 0 \\ \phi_{12} Y_t + \varepsilon_{t+1} & \text{if } Y_t \leq 0 \end{cases}$$

we observe that at time t, we know exactly whether Y_t is positive or negative, and on taking conditional expectation, we obtain the 1-step-ahead forecast:

$$f_{t,1} = \mu_{t+1|t} = E(Y_{t+1} | I_t) = \phi_{11} Y_t I(Y_t > 0) + \phi_{12} Y_t I(Y_t \leq 0)$$

where $I(Y_t > 0)$ and $I(Y_t \leq 0)$ are indicators that take the value 1 when the condition in parenthesis is satisfied and zero otherwise. It should not be confused with I_t, which denotes the information set. Thus, the 1-step-ahead forecast takes the value $\phi_{11} Y_t$ or $\phi_{12} Y_t$, depending on the sign of the threshold variable Y_t.

STAR(1)

$$Y_t = \phi_{01} Y_{t-1} + \phi_{11} Y_{t-1} G(Y_{t-1}, \gamma, c) + \varepsilon_t$$

Following the same procedure, the 1-step-ahead forecast from this model is

$$f_{t,1} = \mu_{t+1|t} = E(Y_{t+1} | I_t) = \phi_{01} Y_t + \phi_{11} Y_t G(Y_t, \gamma, c)$$

16.3.2 Multistep-Ahead Forecast

When $h > 1$, forecasting with nonlinear models becomes more complex because of the difficulty in computing the conditional mean. To understand this point, let us write a general low-order nonlinear model as

$$Y_t = g(Y_{t-1}; \theta) + \varepsilon_t$$

where $g(Y_{t-1}; \theta)$ is a nonlinear function like the SETAR(1) or STAR(1) models. We saw that when the forecasting horizon is 1 step, calculating the 1-step ahead forecast is straightforward because the argument inside the function belongs to the information set, that is,

$$f_{t,1} = \mu_{t+1|t} = E(Y_{t+1} | I_t) = g(Y_t; \theta)$$

If $h = 2$, the process written at the future date $t+2$ is

$$Y_{t+2} = g(Y_{t+1}; \theta) + \varepsilon_{t+2}$$

and by taking conditional expectation, we have

$$f_{t,2} = \mu_{t+2|t} = E(Y_{t+2} | I_t) = E(g(Y_{t+1};\theta) | I_t)$$

Note that Y_{t+1} does not belong to the information set I_t because it contains information only to time t; be aware that $E(g(Y_{t+1};\theta) | I_t) \neq g(E(Y_{t+1} | I_t);\theta)$. Furthermore, substituting Y_{t+1} in the expectation, we have that

$$f_{t,2} = E(Y_{t+2} | I_t) = E(g(g(Y_t;\theta) + \varepsilon_{t+1};\theta) | I_t)$$

with $Y_t \in I_t$, but $\varepsilon_{t+1} \notin I_t$. Then the only solution is to calculate the conditional expectation $E(g(g(Y_t;\theta) + \varepsilon_{t+1};\theta) | I_t)$ by using analytical or numerical methods. Analytical methods involve solving some integrals that can be tedious and difficult. Numerical methods are easy to implement and are very common for calculating long horizon forecasts.

An easy but inefficient forecast is what it is called the skeleton forecast. This solution avoids calculating the difficult conditional expectation at the expense of producing a biased forecast. For instance, in $Y_{t+2} = g(Y_{t+1};\theta) + \varepsilon_{t+2}$, Y_{t+1} is substituted by its forecast such the 2-step-ahead forecast becomes

$$\tilde{f}_{t,2} = g(f_{t,1};\theta)$$

Longer horizon forecasts can be calculated in the same fashion by implementing a recursive procedure.

To illustrative these points, let us work with a STAR(1) model,

$$Y_t = \begin{cases} \phi_{11} Y_{t-1} + \varepsilon_t & \text{if } Y_{t-1} > 0 \\ \phi_{12} Y_{t-1} + \varepsilon_t & \text{if } Y_{t-1} \leq 0 \end{cases}$$

which we write in a more compact form as

$$Y_t = \phi_{11} Y_{t-1} I(Y_{t-1} > 0) + \phi_{12} Y_{t-1} I(Y_{t-1} \leq 0) + \varepsilon_t$$

Suppose that at time t, $Y_t > 0$. Then, the 1-step-ahead forecast is

$$f_{t,1} = \phi_{11} Y_t$$

Let us compute the 2-step-ahed forecast. At time $t + 2$, the process must satisfy

$$Y_{t+2} = \phi_{11} Y_{t+1} I(Y_{t+1} > 0) + \phi_{12} Y_{t+1} I(Y_{t+1} \leq 0) + \varepsilon_{t+2}$$

The **skeleton forecast** is

$$\tilde{f}_{t,2} = g(f_{t,1};\theta) = \phi_{11} f_{t,1} I(f_{t,1} > 0) + \phi_{12} f_{t,1} I(f_{t,1} \leq 0)$$

if it happens that $\phi_{11} > 0$, then $f_{t,1} = \phi_{11} Y_t > 0$ and $\tilde{f}_{t,2} = g(f_{t,1};\theta) = \phi_{11}^2 Y_t$.

The **analytical forecast** is obtained by solving the appropriate integrals. Under the stated assumptions, that is, $Y_t > 0$, the process at $t + 1$ will be given by

$$Y_{t+1} = \phi_{11} Y_t I(Y_t > 0) + \phi_{12} Y_t I(Y_t \leq 0) + \varepsilon_{t+1} = \phi_{11} Y_t + \varepsilon_{t+1}$$

which we will substitute in Y_{t+2},

$$\begin{aligned} Y_{t+2} &= \phi_{11}Y_{t+1}I(Y_{t+1}>0) + \phi_{12}Y_{t+1}I(Y_{t+1}\leq 0) + \varepsilon_{t+2} \\ &= \phi_{11}[\phi_{11}Y_t + \varepsilon_{t+1}]I(\phi_{11}Y_t + \varepsilon_{t+1} > 0) + \phi_{12}[\phi_{11}Y_t + \varepsilon_{t+1}]I(\phi_{11}Y_t + \varepsilon_{t+1} \leq 0) + \varepsilon_{t+2} \end{aligned}$$

Now we need to take a conditional expectation with respect to an information set containing information up to t,

$$\begin{aligned} f_{t,2} &= \mu_{t+2|t} = E(Y_{t+2}\,|\,I_t) \\ &= \phi_{11}^2 Y_t E[I(\phi_{11}Y_t + \varepsilon_{t+1} > 0)\,|\,I_t] + \phi_{11}E[\varepsilon_{t+1}I(\phi_{11}Y_t + \varepsilon_{t+1} > 0)\,|\,I_t] + \\ &\quad + \phi_{12}\phi_{11}Y_t E[I(\phi_{11}Y_t + \varepsilon_{t+1} \leq 0)\,|\,I_t] + \phi_{12}E[\varepsilon_{t+1}I(\phi_{11}Y_t + \varepsilon_{t+1} \leq 0)\,|\,I_t] \end{aligned}$$

Observe that the expectations depend on the distributional assumption on the random variable ε_{t+1}. The calculation of the conditional expectations is provided in the Appendix to this chapter, assuming that the innovation is i.i.d. and $\varepsilon_t \rightarrow N(0, \sigma^2)$. By comparing the skeleton forecast $\tilde{f}_{t,2} = \phi_{11}^2 Y_t$ with the analytical forecast $f_{t,2}$, it is easy to see why the skeleton forecast is biased.

The **numerical forecast** is a helpful alternative to the analytical forecast because it is easy to implement. Our goal is to approximate the conditional expectations by their sample estimates. A popular numerical method is Monte-Carlo simulation that consists of drawing realizations of the innovation ε_{t+1} from the assumed density. Because we assumed that $\varepsilon_t \rightarrow N(0, \sigma^2)$, we need to use the normal random number generator and generate as many observations as we desire. Let us call $\varepsilon_{t+1}^{(i)}$ the observation that we obtain in replication (i). The number of replications needs to be large to ensure that the sample average converges to the population integral. We want to approximate $f_{t,2} = \mu_{t+2|t} = E(Y_{t+2}\,|\,I_t)$. Then, for every $\varepsilon_{t+1}^{(i)}$, we compute $Y_{t+2}^{(i)}$ as in

$$Y_{t+2}^{(i)} = \phi_{11}[\phi_{11}Y_t + \varepsilon_{t+1}^{(i)}]I(\phi_{11}Y_t + \varepsilon_{t+1}^{(i)} > 0) + \phi_{12}[\phi_{11}Y_t + \varepsilon_{t+1}^{(i)}]I(\phi_{11}Y_t + \varepsilon_{t+1}^{(i)} \leq 0)$$

The Monte Carlo forecast is then computed by averaging all $Y_{t+2}^{(i)}$s across replications; that is,

$$f_{t,2}^{MC} = \frac{\sum_{i=1}^{N} Y_{t+2}^{(i)}}{N}$$

where N is the number of replications.

In summary, we learned that economic and business data have nonlinear features that can be captured by relatively simple nonlinear models. Estimation and testing with nonlinear models are not always trivial matters. Thus, testing for linearity when possible should be the first step in our modeling strategy. Only when linearity is rejected should a nonlinear model be entertained. Analytical multistep forecasts based on nonlinear models are difficult to obtain; this is the reason we implement numerical methods in practice. Nevertheless, the forecasting performance of a nonlinear model is not always superior to that of a linear model for several reasons. Among them is the frequency of the nonlinear feature in the forecasting sample. If the forecast sample is short and the nonlinear feature is not very frequent, it is very likely that the linear forecast will outperform the nonlinear forecast. Consequently, even if linearity is rejected, we should entertain a linear forecast at least as a benchmark against which to compare the improvement of a nonlinear forecast. In addition, we can always combine the linear with the nonlinear forecasts, resulting in a new combined forecast. We may think of attaching different weights depending on more or less sophisticated schemes. In any case, an important lesson is that forecasts based on linear models still play a prominent role even in a nonlinear world.

KEY WORDS

analytical forecast, p. 442
exponential transition function, p. 431
linearity testing, p. 421
logistic transition function, p. 434
Markov chain, p. 437
Markov switching model, p. 436
mixture of densities, p. 439
nonlinearity, p. 414
numerical forecast, p. 443
skeleton forecast, p. 442
smooth transition, p. 427
threshold autoregressive, p. 422

APPENDIX

Conditional Expectations for a 2-Step-Ahead Forecast from STAR(1)

Assuming that the innovation is i.i.d. $\varepsilon_t \rightarrow N(0, \sigma^2)$, the conditional expectations are calculated by solving the following integrals:

$$E[I(\phi_{11}Y_t + \varepsilon_{t+1} > 0) \mid I_t] = E[I(\varepsilon_{t+1} > -\phi_{11}Y_t) \mid I_t]$$

$$= \int_{-\phi_{11}Y_t}^{\infty} f(\varepsilon_{t+1}) d\varepsilon_{t+1} = 1 - \Phi\left(-\frac{\phi_{11}Y_t}{\sigma}\right)$$

$$E[\varepsilon_{t+1} I(\phi_{11}Y_t + \varepsilon_{t+1} > 0) \mid I_t] = E[\varepsilon_{t+1} I(\varepsilon_{t+1} > -\phi_{11}Y_t) \mid I_t]$$

$$= \int_{-\phi_{11}Y_t}^{\infty} \varepsilon_{t+1} f(\varepsilon_{t+1}) d\varepsilon_{t+1} = \sigma\, \phi\left(-\frac{\phi_{11}Y_t}{\sigma}\right)$$

$$E[I(\phi_{11}Y_t + \varepsilon_{t+1} \leq 0) \,|\, I_t] = E[I(\varepsilon_{t+1} \leq -\phi_{11}Y_t) \,|\, I_t]$$

$$= \int_{-\infty}^{-\phi_{11}Y_t} f(\varepsilon_{t+1}) d\varepsilon_{t+1} = \Phi\left(-\frac{\phi_{11}Y_t}{\sigma}\right)$$

$$E[\varepsilon_{t+1} I(\phi_{11}Y_t + \varepsilon_{t+1} \leq 0) \,|\, I_t] = E[\varepsilon_{t+1} I(\varepsilon_{t+1} \leq -\phi_{11}Y_t) \,|\, I_t]$$

$$= \int_{-\infty}^{-\phi_{11}Y_t} \varepsilon_{t+1} f(\varepsilon_{t+1}) d\varepsilon_{t+1} = -\sigma\,\phi\left(-\frac{\phi_{11}Y_t}{\sigma}\right)$$

where $\Phi\left(-\frac{\phi_{11}Y_t}{\sigma}\right)$ is the cumulative distribution function of a standard normal random variable evaluated at $\left(-\frac{\phi_{11}Y_t}{\sigma}\right)$, and $\phi\left(-\frac{\phi_{11}Y_t}{\sigma}\right)$ is the standard normal density function evaluated at the same point.

EXERCISES

1. Download the U.S. GDP time series and comment on the dynamics of growth rates in recessions versus expansions. Follow the NBER dating of recessions from 1955 to date. Describe how long recessions and expansions last and any other features that describe the U.S. business cycle.
2. Update the time series on Industrial Production (Figure 16.5) and 3-month Treasury Bills (Figure 16.6). Comment on the possibility of entertaining models with nonlinear features.
3. Revisit the SETAR model for the 3-month Treasury Bills in Section 16.2.1 using the updated time series from Exercise 2. Does the SETAR model proposed in Section 16.2.1 hold? Change the value of the threshold from 8.5% to 8%, 7.5% and 7%. In these new models, is it still possible to find two regimes, stationary and nonstationary? Are any of these models better than the model with the 8.5% threshold? Comment on your findings.
4. If investors expect that inflation will run high in the future, they will demand higher interest rates in their bonds investments. Thus, nominal interest rates must react to changes in inflation expectations. To test the relation between bond yields and inflation, download the time series on interest rates for the 10-year Treasury notes and the Consumer Price Index. Find the best linear dynamic model for interest rates changes as a function of CPI changes (inflation) potentially including past information on interest rates and CPI changes. Do you find evidence for our claim?

5. Suppose that we suspect that there is a threshold for inflation beyond which bond yields are becoming more responsive to changes in inflation. Specify a 2-regime TAR model for interest rates when the threshold variable is yesterday's inflation. Experiment with different threshold values. Do you find evidence for a TAR model? If so, is this model better than the linear model you found in Exercise 4? Explain.
6. Revisit the LSTAR model for U.S. industrial production in Section 16.2.2 using the updated time series from Exercise 2. Find the best linear model, implement a linearity test, and if linearity is rejected, find the best LSTAR model. How different is the revised model from the LSTAR model proposed in Section 16.2.1?
7. Find the best dynamic linear model for the time series of U.S. GDP growth rates in Exercise 1. Entertain a nonlinear model that captures your findings in Exercise 1. First, implement a linearity test against a STAR model. If linearity is rejected, find the best STAR model. Interpret the dynamics in the upper, lower, and intermediate regimes.
8. Comment on the shape and features of the transition function in Exercise 7. Plot the function itself and the time series of the values of the transition function. If this function is very steep, it may be a SETAR model that is very similar to the STAR model that you propose in Exercise 7. Verify this claim.
9. Calculate a sequence of 1-step-ahead forecasts for GDP growth rates based on the linear model (Exercise 7), the STAR model (Exercise 7), and the SETAR model (Exercise 8). Evaluate the forecasting performance of each model. Which model(s) is(are) best?
10. Calculate the 2-step-ahead forecast for GDP growth rates based on the STAR model (Exercise 7) by implementing a numerical forecast.

Appendix A
Review of Probability and Statistics

Review of Basic Statistics

In this Appendix, we will review foundational statistics, which are necessary for understanding econometric models and forecasting methods. The primary aim is to refresh concepts that you have already learned in your introductory statistics course.

1 Population and Sample

Suppose that for policy reasons, we wish to analyze the level of income of the residents in Southern California (SoCal). For instance, we may need to forecast the income tax revenue in the region and among many variables, we may be interested in learning the mean level of household income, or the median, or how many households are below the poverty threshold, or how many households are in the highest bracket of income. We can proceed in two ways. We could interview every single household in SoCal and ask for their level of income so that we collect information on each and every household in the region, or we could draw a subset of the population in SoCal and ask for the level of income collecting a subset of information. In the first case, we have **population information** and in the second, **sample information**. Ideally, we would like to have information on the full population, but in reality, this could will be very expensive because we would need a huge amount of resources for data collection. Because of this constraint, we are forced to work with sample information. Since our ultimate goal is to analyze a population; we could ask whether it is possible to draw any conclusions about an entire population when we have access to only a subset of information. This is the fundamental question for statisticians and econometricians. Fortunately, the answer is yes. Statistical inference provides the necessary tools to infer the properties of the population based on sample information.

Let us call Y the random variable "household income." Suppose that we choose a random sample of 100 households in SoCal and we denote these as $\{Y_1, Y_2, \ldots . Y_{100}\}$. For each Y we have a numerical realization or outcome so that our sample information is denoted as $\{y_1, y_2, \ldots \ldots y_{100}\}$. For instance, $y_3 = \$30{,}000$ means that the randomly selected household number 3 has an annual income of \$30,000 a year. This random variable is continuous in the sense that the potential values of each random variable are infinite.—for instance, $y_i = \$30{,}210$ \$25,153.50, or \$11,234.65, and so on (the outcomes are all in the real line). There are also discrete random variables for which the outcomes are associated with only non-negative integers, for instance, the "number of cars in a household" can be $y_i = 0$, 1, or 3, and so on. A word about notation: We will be using uppercase letters to denote the random variable and lowercase to denote a particular numerical value or outcome of the random variable.

Now that we have collected the information, how can we summarize all possible outcomes of Y? We characterize a random variable Y by

- The cumulative distribution function (**CDF**) and the probability density function (**PDF**); and/or
- The moments of Y such as the mean, variance, skewness, kurtosis, etc.

The first route is the most complete because having the CDF or PDF, we can calculate any moment, but there will be instances in which we will be interested in some partial features of Y so that calculating some moments will be sufficient.

2 Cumulative Distribution Function (CDF) and Probability Density Function (PDF)

If the random variable is discrete the PDF provides the probability associated with each outcome. For instance, suppose that we throw a die into the air and record the possible outcomes. This random variable Y has six possible outcomes {1, 2, 3, 4, 5, 6}, and each outcome has an equal probability of occurrence, $P(Y=1)=P(Y=2)=\cdots\cdots=P(Y=6)=1/6$.

We define the PDF of a discrete random variable as the function that assigns to each outcome y_i (for $i=1, 2, \ldots k$) a probability p_i

$$f(y_i) = P(Y = y_i) \equiv p_i \quad \text{for } i = 1, 2 \ldots . k \tag{A.1}$$

Recall that probabilities are always positive or zero, $0 \leq p_i \leq 1$ and that they should total 1, $\sum_i^k p_i = 1$.

The CDF provides answers to questions such as what the probability is that on throwing a die we get at most a 3. In this case, we are considering just three possible outcomes {1, 2, 3}, and the probability that we are concerned about is $P(Y \leq 3) = P(Y = 1) + P(Y = 2) + P(Y = 3) = 1/6 + 1/6 + 1/6 = 1/2$. The CDF (accumulates) the probabilities (PDF) of single events y_j such that $y_j \leq y$,

$$\begin{aligned} F(y) \equiv P(Y \leq y) &= P(Y = y_1) + P(Y = y_2) + \cdots\ P(Y = y_j) \\ &= f(y_1) + f(y_2) + \cdots\ f(y_j) \end{aligned} \tag{A.2}$$

In Figure A.1, we plot the CDF and the PDF for the outcomes corresponding to our experiment of throwing the die into the air.

If the random variable is continuous, the CDF is defined in a similar fashion considering that now the outcomes are numbers y in the real line.

$$F(y) = P(Y \leq y) \tag{A.3}$$

For instance, we can ask what the probability is that a household in SoCal has a level of income of at most \$30,000. The answer is $F(30{,}000) \equiv P(Y \leq 30{,}000)$. However, to obtain this probability, we need the "addition" of probabilities over all levels of income below \$30,000. Thus, we need the definition of PDF for continuous random variables, which is slightly more complicated than the PDF of discrete random variables. The PDF of a continuous variable is a continuous function $f(y)$, and the *area* under $f(y)$ will provide

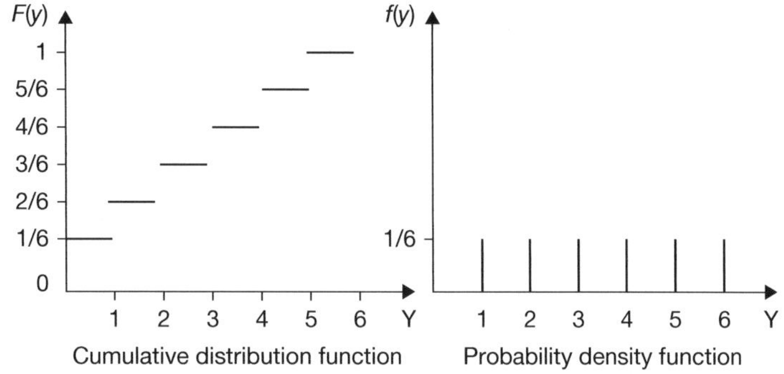

FIGURE A.1
CDF and PDF of a Discrete Random Variable

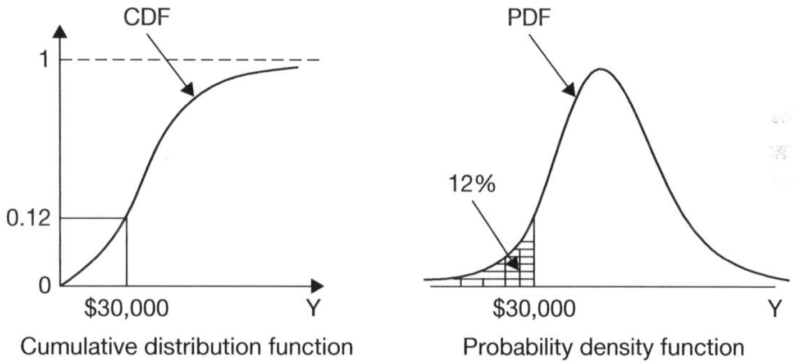

FIGURE A.2
CDF and PDF of a Continuous Random Variable

the probability for a range of outcomes. In Figure A.2, we plot the CDF and the PDF of a continuous random variable, which you should compare with those in Figure A.1. Notice that in the example of Figure A.2, the probability $P(Y \leq 30{,}000) = 0.12$, which is the area under the PDF.

3 Moments of a Random Variable

A random variable can also be characterized by its which **moments**. These are measures based on the probability density function of the random variable. We will review three types of measures: measures of centrality, measures of dispersion, and measures of shape.

3.1 Measures of Centrality

For a random variable Y, a measure of centrality is the **mean** or **expected value**, which is also known as the *first moment* of Y. The mean is an average of all possible values of Y and as such, it measures the center of the distribution of Y.

For a discrete random variable, the expected value is defined as

$$E(Y) = y_1 p_1 + y_2 p_2 + \cdots \cdot y_k p_k = \sum_{i=1}^{k} y_i p_i = \sum_{i=1}^{k} y_i f(y_i) \tag{A.4}$$

Each value of Y is weighted by its corresponding probability, which is $p_i = f(y_i)$. For instance, the expected value of the random value that takes values on $\{1, 2, 3, 4, 5, 6\}$, all with equal probability of 1/6, is $E(Y) = (1 \times 1/6) + (2 \times 1/6) + (3 \times 1/6) + (4 \times 1/6) + (5 \times 1/6) + (6 \times 1/6) = 3.5$.

For a continuous random variable, the expected value is defined as

$$E(Y) = \int_{-\infty}^{+\infty} yf(y)dy, \tag{A.5}$$

which requires some knowledge of calculus because the definition involves an integral. Nevertheless, this expression has similarities with the expected value of a discrete random variable: The summation sign Σ is "similar" to the integral $\int$, and each value y is weighted by its probability $f(y)$. In summary, for both types of random variables, the expected value is a weighted average of all possible values of Y.

The expected value is one of the most important concepts in statistics. The operator E has very useful properties. We should review three rules:

1. The expectation of a constant c is the constant itself: $E(c) = c$.
2. For any constants a and b, the expectation of a linear combination such as $aY + b$ is $E(aY + b) = aE(Y) + b$.
3. The expectation of a linear combination of random variables $Y_1, Y_2, \ldots. Y_k$ is the sum of the expectations. For any constants $c_1, c_2, \ldots\ldots c_k$, $E(c_1Y_1 + c_2Y_2 + \cdots\cdot c_kY_k) = c_1E(Y_1) + c_2E(Y_2) + \cdots\cdot c_kE(Y_k)$.

The expected value is also known as the *population mean* and is also denoted with Greek letters as $\mu_Y = E(Y)$. We will distinguish between population moments and sample moments. In real life, we work with sample information, and we need to compute sample statistics, which will be "approximations" to population statistics. For a random sample of n observations $(y_1, y_2, y_3, \ldots\ldots y_n\}$, the *sample mean* $\bar{y}_n$ is defined as

$$\bar{y}_n = \frac{\sum_{i=1}^{n} y_i}{n} \tag{A.6}$$

The subscript n in $\bar{y}_n$ means that we work with a finite sample of n observations, and the bar $^{-}$ in $\bar{y}_n$ means that this is a sample moment. When we write population moments, we will use the expectation operator E, and when we write sample moments, we will use bars $^{-}$ or hats.

How are $E(Y)$ and $\bar{y}_n$ related? Both are measures of centrality: $E(Y)$ is the population mean and $\bar{y}_n$ is the sample mean, which is an estimator or an approximation to the population mean. It can be proven that $E(\bar{y}_n) = E(Y)$, and in this sense, we say that the sample mean $\bar{y}_n$ is an *unbiased* estimator of the population mean $E(Y)$.

Another measure of centrality is the *median* y_m. This is the value of Y for which one half of the observations is below y_m and the other half is above it. Using the CDF of Y, we write that $F(y_m) = P(Y \leq y_m) = 0.50$. If the PDF is symmetric around μ_Y, then the median and the mean are identical.

3.2 Measures of Dispersion

For a random variable Y, the *variance* $Var(Y)$ measures how far (on average) the values of Y are from its mean μ_Y. It is defined as the expected value of the squared deviations of Y from μ_Y

$$Var(Y) = E(Y - \mu_Y)^2 \tag{A.7}$$

The variance $Var(Y)$ is also denoted as σ_Y^2, and it is also known as the *second central moment* of Y. The variance of a random variable is always a positive number. The variance of a constant is zero. The variance of a linear combination such as $aY + b$, for any constants a and b, is $Var(aY + b) = a^2 Var(Y)$. Using the properties of the expectation operator E, we write the variance as

$$\sigma_Y^2 \equiv Var(Y) = E(Y - \mu_Y)^2 = E(Y^2 - 2Y\mu_Y + \mu_Y^2) = E(Y^2) - \mu_Y^2. \tag{A.8}$$

Notice that the units of the variance are different from those of the mean because the variance requires the square of the values of Y. For instance, if the values are measured in dollars, then the variance is in squared dollars. To have a measure of dispersion with the same units as the mean, we define the *standard deviation* σ_y of Y as the square root of the variance

$$\sigma_Y = \sqrt{Var(Y)} \tag{A.9}$$

The corresponding sample moments are the sample variance $\hat{\sigma}^2$ and the sample standard deviation $\hat{\sigma}$. For a random sample of n observations $\{y_1, y_2, \ldots y_n\}$, the **sample variance** $\hat{\sigma}_n^2$ and the *sample standard deviation* $\hat{\sigma}_n$ are defined as

$$\hat{\sigma}_n^2 = \frac{\sum_{i=1}^{n} (y_i - \bar{y}_n)^2}{n - 1} \tag{A.10}$$

$$\hat{\sigma}_n = \sqrt{\hat{\sigma}_n^2} \tag{A.11}$$

It can be proven that the sample variance is an unbiased estimator of the population variance: $E(\hat{\sigma}_n^2) = \sigma_Y^2$.

3.3 Measures of Shape

If the probability density function of a random variable Y is symmetric around its expected value, then the third central moment, that is, $E(Y - \mu_Y)^3$, is equal to zero. We define a measure of **skewness** as

$$sk = \frac{E(Y - \mu_Y)^3}{\sigma_Y^3} \tag{A.12}$$

Positive values of sk indicate that the distribution is skewed to the right and negative values indicate that the distribution is skewed to the left. The denominator σ_Y^3 in sk scales the random variable such that the measure of skewness is unit free.

FIGURE A.3
Moments of a Random Variable

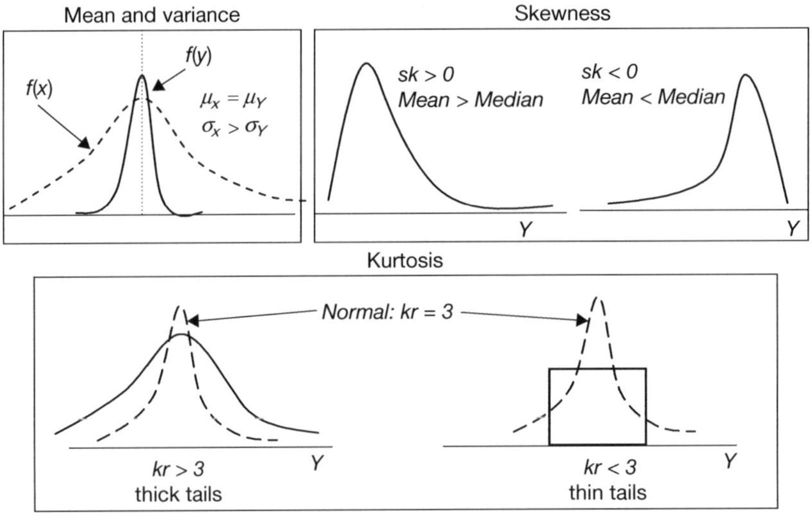

The fourth central moment, that is, $E(Y-\mu_Y)^4$, provides information about the "thickness" of the tails of the distribution. The measure of **kurtosis** is defined as

$$kr = \frac{E(Y-\mu_Y)^4}{\sigma_Y^4} \tag{A.13}$$

Kurtosis is always positive, and because it is scaled by σ_Y^4, it is also a unit-free measure. The higher the value of kr is, the "thicker" the tails of the distribution are. We measure kurtosis in relation to the kurtosis of a normal distribution, which we will review in the next section. For a normal PDF, $kr = 3$. If $kr > 3$, we say that there is leptokurtosis or "fat tails." This means that there is more probability in the tails than in the normal density. If $kr < 3$, we say that the distribution has "thin tails" (i.e., less probability in the tails than in the normal case).

In Figure A.3, we plot several stylized probability density functions with different shapes.

4 Common Probability Density Functions

We review four common probability density functions that we will use extensively in the textbook. These are the normal, the chi-square, the student-t, and the F distributions.

4.1 The Normal Distribution

Many random variables in economics and business are very well characterized by a **normal probability density** function. We say that a random variable Y is normally distributed, that is, $Y \rightarrow N(\mu, \sigma^2)$ if and only if the PDF has the following functional form

$$f(y) = \frac{1}{\sqrt{2\pi}\sigma}\exp\left(-\frac{(y-\mu)^2}{2\sigma^2}\right) \mathit{for} -\infty < y < \infty \tag{A.14}$$

If we plot $f(y)$, we obtain the well-known bell-shaped function. We also refer to the normal density as the *Gaussian density*. This density is centered in the mean μ, and it is symmetrically distributed around μ. Because of symmetry, the coefficient of skewness is $sk = 0$. The variance is σ^2, and the coefficient of kurtosis is $kr = 3$.

If we wish to find the probability of any event, we need to find the area under the curve $f(y)$ by calculating an integral. For instance, if $Y \rightarrow N(1, 4)$ and we are interested in the probability of $0.5 \leq Y \leq 1.5$, we need to find $P(0.5 \leq Y \leq 1.5) = \int_{0.5}^{1.5} f(y)dy$. Fortunately, we do not need to compute this type of integral because it has already been tabulated. However, the statistical tables that you will use are just for the $N(0, 1)$. This is not a problem because any normal random variable Y can be standardized to a $N(0, 1)$ by subtracting its mean and dividing by its standard deviation:

$$Z = \frac{Y - \mu}{\sigma} \rightarrow N(0, 1) \tag{A.15}$$

It is customary to write the PDF of standard normal as $\phi(z)$ and the CDF as $\Phi(z) = P(Z \leq z)$. The values that you will find in the tables are the probabilities $\Phi(z) = P(Z \leq z)$. Then, in our example, we will proceed as follows

$$\begin{aligned} P(0.5 \leq Y \leq 1.5) &= P\left(\frac{0.5 - 1}{2} \leq \frac{Y - 1}{2} \leq \frac{1.5 - 1}{2}\right) \\ &= P(-0.25 \leq Z \leq 0.25) = \Phi(0.25) - \Phi(-0.25) \\ &= 0.5987 - 0.4013 = 0.1974 \end{aligned} \tag{A.16}$$

Alternatively, suppose that you are interested in finding the value y such that the probability of an event as large as y is 95%. You are asking: What is the value of y such that $P(Y \leq y) = 0.95$? In this case, you know the probability but you do not know the value of the random variable Y. You can also use the tables to find such a value. Let us follow with our example where $Y \rightarrow N(1, 4)$.

$$P\left(\frac{Y - 1}{2} \leq \frac{y - 1}{2}\right) = P(Z \leq z) = 0.95 \tag{A.17}$$

From the tables corresponding to the standard normal $N(0, 1)$, we find that $z = 1.65$ approximately. Then, $1.65 = \frac{y-1}{2}$, and solving for y, we obtain that $y = 4.3$. We illustrate these examples in Figure A.4.

4.2 The Chi-Square Distribution

The chi-square distribution is based on random variables that are standard $N(0, 1)$. The **chi-square distribution** with ν degrees of freedom is defined as the sum of ν independent standard normal random variables:

$$\chi^2_\nu = \sum_{i=1}^{\nu} Z_i^2 \tag{A.18}$$

where $Z_i \rightarrow N(0, 1)$. The degrees of freedom correspond to the number of elements in the sum. Because Z is squared, the new random variable χ^2_ν is strictly positive. The shape is asymmetric and skewed to the right, so the coefficient of skewness is positive. There are also tables that provide the probability of a chi-square outcome so that we do not need to compute elaborated integrals. You need to state the degrees of freedom and read directly from the tables. For instance, for $\nu = 4$, we find that $P(\chi_4^2 \geq 7.78) = 10\%$. In Figure A.4, we plot the chi-square density for different degrees of freedom. The larger the degrees of freedom, the less skewed the density becomes.

4.3 The Student-*t* Distribution

The Student-*t* distribution is based on the standard normal and chi-square distributions. The **Student-*t* distribution** with ν degrees of freedom is defined as the ratio of a standard normal random variable to the squared root of a chi-square random variable:

$$t_\nu = \frac{Z}{\sqrt{\frac{\chi_\nu^2}{\nu}}} \tag{A.19}$$

where Z and χ_ν^2 are independent random variables. The degrees of freedom of the Student-*t* are the same as those of the chi-square random variable in the denominator. The Student-*t* is a symmetric density around zero. Because of symmetry, the skewness coefficient is equal to zero. The main difference with the normal density is that there is more probability mass in the tails. The Student-*t* has "fat tails," which are a function of the degrees of freedom. The lower the degrees of freedom are, the fatter the tails become, making the kurtosis coefficient larger than 3. As the degrees of freedom increase, the Student-*t* converges toward the standard normal. We also have tables in which we can read the probability of Student-*t* outcomes. For instance, for $\nu = 10$, we find that $P(t_{10} \geq 2.228) = 2.5\%$. In Figure A.4, we plot the Student-t density for different degrees of freedom.

4.4 The *F*-Distribution

The **F-distribution** is the ratio of two independent chi-square distributions:

$$F_{\nu_1,\nu_2} = \frac{\chi_{\nu_1}^2/\nu_1}{\chi_{\nu_2}^2/\nu_2} \tag{A.20}$$

Because this is a ratio of two strictly positive random variables, the *F*-distribution is also strictly positive. It is also a positively skewed density. We also read the probability of an *F*-distributed random variable from tables. You need to state the degrees of freedom of the chi-squared densities in the numerator and in the denominator. For instance for ν_1=6, ν_2=14, we find that $P(F_{6,14} \geq 2.85) = 5\%$. In Figure A.4, we plot the *F* density for different degrees of freedom.

4.5 Some Examples

In Figure A.5, we present the probability density function and some descriptive statistics of three random variables: returns to the SP500 index, U.S. GDP growth, and U.S. income distribution.

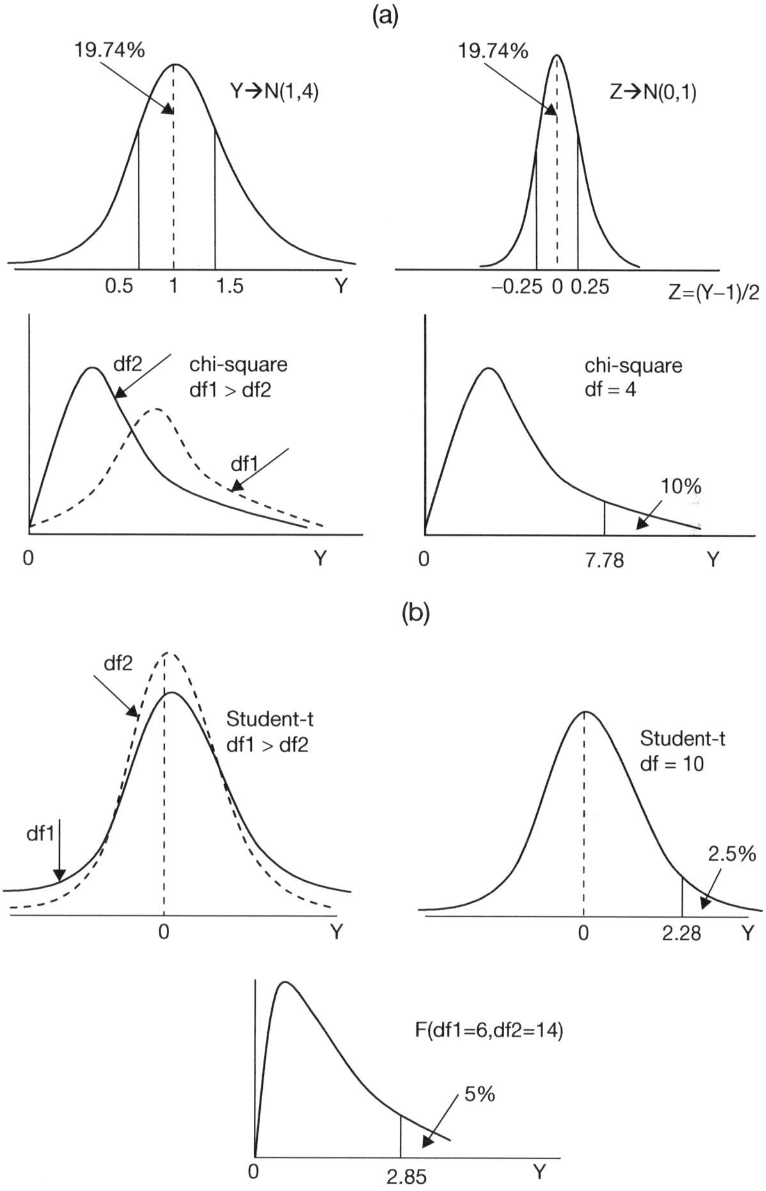

FIGURE A.4
Normal and Chi-Square Distributions and Student-*t* and *F*-Distributions

4.5.1 Example 1

The SP500 index returns (^GSPC is the symbol for the index) can be downloaded from http://www.finance.yahoo.com. In Figure A.5, we present the weekly returns from January 4, 1960, to November 16, 2009, for a total of 2,601 observations. The weekly return is the percentage gain (or loss) that you would obtain if you were to buy the SP500 index and sell it one week later. The graph in the right side of Figure A.05 is a histogram that is a frequency

FIGURE A.5 SP500 Index : Weekly Returns; USA Gross Domestic Product : Quarterly Growth; 2005 USA Income Distribution

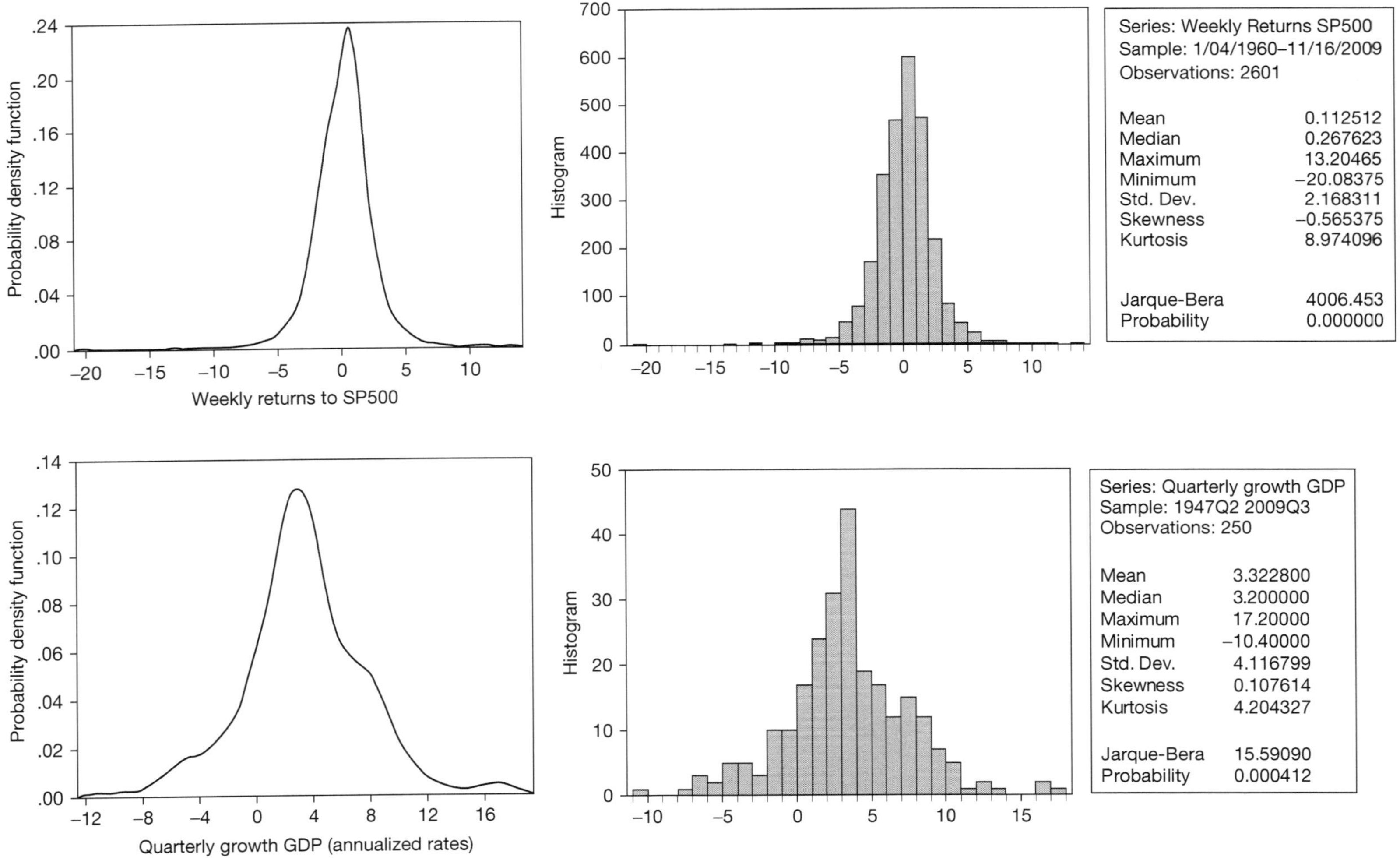

FIGURE A.5 Continued

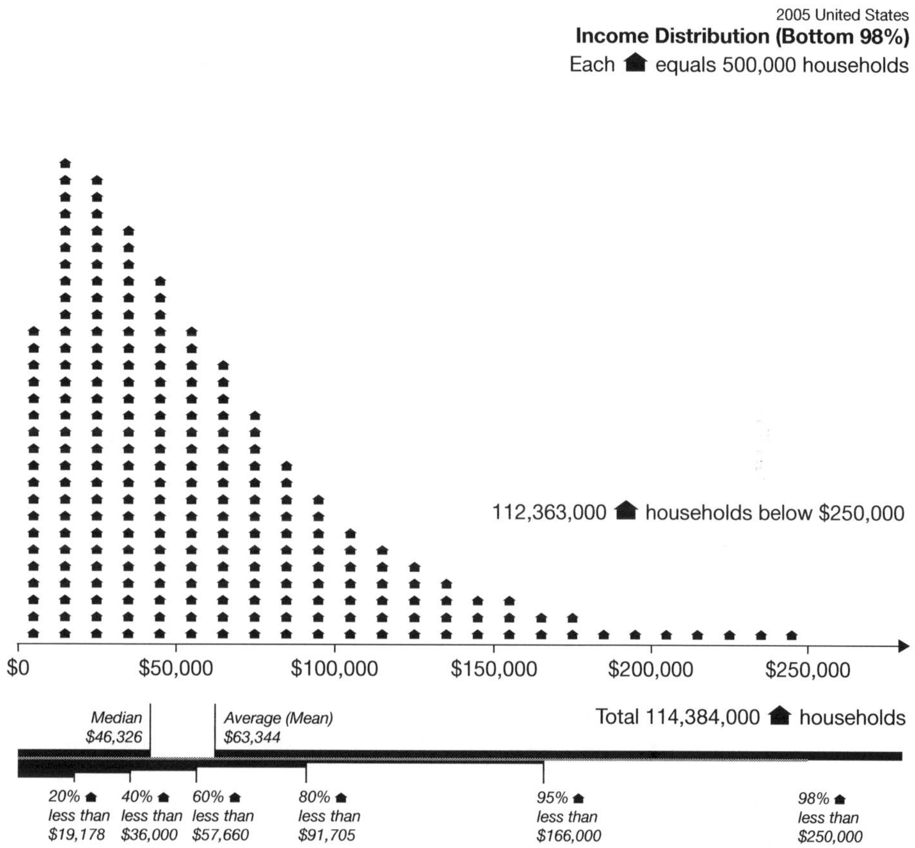

Source: "2005 USA Income Distribution." From VisualizingEconomics.com by Catherine Mulbrandon, http://visualizingeconomics.com/2006/11/05/2005-us-income-distribution/

distribution. When we smooth the histogram, we obtain an estimation of the PDF, which is the graph on the right of the figure. From the table, we can read that the average weekly return is 0.11%, the median 0.27%, and the standard deviation 2.17%. Overall, the density is very peaked, centered approximately in zero, and the tails are quite fat with a coefficient of kurtosis of 8.97, which is much larger than 3 (the value for the normal density). There is some mild negative skewness triggered by an extremely negative return of −20%, which happened on October 6, 2008, in the midst of the great panic in financial markets. Because the kurtosis is very large and the skewness is very small, we can say that the density is closer to a Student-t than to the normal. In the table, you can also read the Jarque-Bera statistic *JB*. This statistic is based on the kurtosis coefficient *kr* and the skewness coefficient *sk*:

$$JB = \frac{n}{6}\left(sk^2 + \frac{(kr-3)^2}{4} \right) \tag{A.21}$$

with n being the number of observations. With the JB statistic, we construct a test for normality. The null hypothesis is H_0: normal density, and the alternative H_1: non-normal density. Under normality, $JB = 0$ because $sk = 0$ and $kr = 3$. For a particular sample, rarely we will get exactly zero and 3, thus, we need to statistically measure the deviations from these benchmark numbers. The JB test is distributed as a chi-square with 2 degrees of freedom: $JB \rightarrow \chi^2_2$. For a chosen significance level, say $\alpha = 5\%$, we will find the critical value of the chi-square for which the probability in the upper tail is 5%. This value is $\chi^2_{2,(5\%)} = 5.991$. Then we will reject normality whenever $JB > 5.991$. For the SP500 returns, the $JB = 4006.45 > .5.99$. Then we reject normality very strongly, confirming our conjecture that weekly returns are not normally distributed.

4.5.2 Example 2

The next random variable is quarterly U.S. GDP growth. You can download these data from the Bureau of Economic Analysis of the U.S. Department of Commerce, http://www.bea.gov. The data run from 1947.Q2 to 2009.Q3. From the table, we read that the mean growth rate is 3.32% (annualized rate), the median is 3.20%, and the standard deviation is 4.12%. The PDF is mildly skewed to the right with a coefficient of skewness of 0.11, and the tails are slightly fat with a coefficient of kurtosis of 4.20. We also reject normality because the JB test is larger ($JB = 15.59$) than the critical value of the $\chi^2_{2,(5\%)} = 5.991$.

In EViews, you can replicate the results related to the SP500 returns or/and U.S. GDP growth by following these instructions:

1. Import the data into a workfile.
2. Click the variable of interest and choose **View/Descriptive Statistics**, and you will see a histogram and a table with a collection of descriptive statistics.
3. Click on **View/Distribution/Kernel Density Graph** to generate the PDF.

4.5.3 Example 3

The third example deals with the 2005 U.S. income distribution. We download this graph directly from http://www.visualizingeconomics.com. The most striking feature of this density with respect to those above is the large tail to the right. The distribution is greatly skewed to the right, meaning that high levels of income are concentrated in only a few households: only 5% of U.S. households enjoy incomes of more than \$166,000 a year. The mean household income is \$63,344, and the median income is \$46,326. It is obvious that the PDF is not normal. The shape of its PDF of income distribution is more consistent with that of a chi-square or of an F-distribution.

5 Measures of Association: Covariance and Correlation

The moments that we have seen in the previous sections refer to only one random variable. We call these *univariate moments*. In economics and business, we rarely analyze one random variable at a time. Very often we are interested in finding relations between variables. For instance, we would like to know how income and consumption are related to each other, or how the stock market and the real economy interact with each other. A measure of association between two random variables Y and X is the **covariance** that is defined as

$$\sigma_{YX} \equiv cov(Y, X) = E(Y - \mu_Y)(X - \mu_X) \tag{A.22}$$

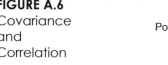

FIGURE A.6
Covariance and Correlation

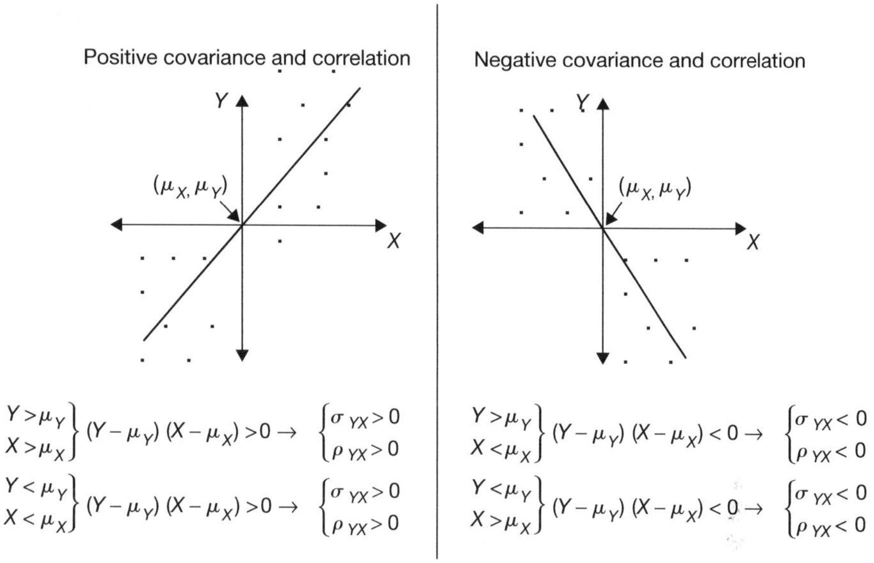

which, by using the properties of expectation, we also write as $\sigma_{YX} = E(YX) - \mu_Y\mu_X$. This measure could be positive, negative, or zero. When $\sigma_{YX} > 0$, the cross-product $(Y-\mu_Y)(X-\mu_X) > 0$ on average, which means that Y and X tend to be above (below) their respective means, $Y > \mu_Y$ and $X > \mu_X$, ($Y < \mu_Y$ and $X < \mu_X$); thus, Y and X tend to move in the same direction. When $\sigma_{YX} < 0$, the cross-product $(Y-\mu_Y)(X-\mu_X) < 0$ on average, which means that Y tends to be above (below) its mean and X tends to be below (above) its mean, $Y > \mu_Y$ and $X < \mu_X$, ($Y < \mu_Y$ and $X > \mu_X$); thus, Y and X tend to move in opposite directions. In Figure A.6, we draw two plots; in the left side, Y and X move in the same direction so that their covariance is positive, and in the right side, Y and X move in opposite direction so that their covariance is negative.

The covariance measures only *linear* dependence. There may be a nonlinear relation between Y and X, for instance a quadratic relation as in Figure A.7, (i.e., $Y = a + bX^2$), but

FIGURE A.7
Examples of Uncorrelated Variables

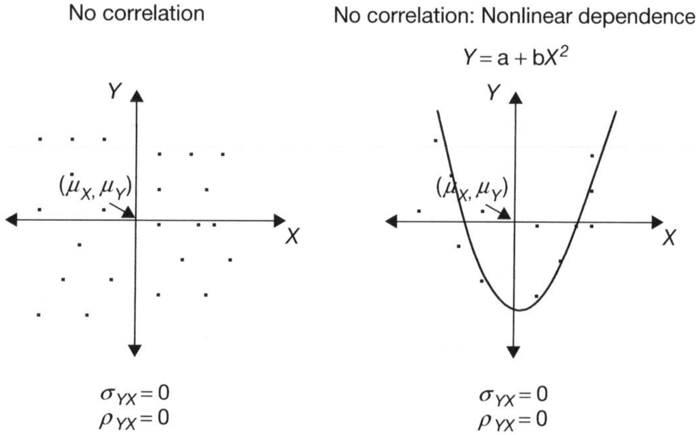

the covariance will be zero because sometimes Y and X move in the same direction and sometimes in opposite directions; thus, on average, no direction prevails. Then we can state that only when Y and X are independent does $\sigma_{YX} = 0$; however, the opposite is not true; that is, the covariance may be equal to zero and the random variables may still be dependent, albeit in a nonlinear fashion.

For random samples of n observations, $\{y_1, y_2, \ldots y_n\}$ and $\{x_1, x_2, \ldots x_n\}$, the *sample* covariance $\hat{\sigma}_{YX}$ is calculated as

$$\hat{\sigma}_{YX} = \frac{\sum_{i=1}^{n}(y_i - \bar{y}_n)(x_i - \bar{x}_n)}{n-1} \tag{A.23}$$

where $\bar{y}_n$ and $\bar{x}_n$ are the **sample averages** of Y and X, respectively. The **correlation coefficient** is another measure of linear dependence between two random variables. It is based on the notion of covariance and variances and is defined as

$$\rho_{YX} = \frac{\sigma_{YX}}{\sigma_Y \sigma_X} \tag{A.24}$$

The sign of ρ_{YX} is the same as that of the covariance. The advantage over the covariance is that ρ_{YX} is easy to interpret because it does not have units and is bounded $-1 \leq \rho_{YX} \leq 1$, so that when the dependence is the strongest, $\rho_{YX} = 1$ or $\rho_{YX} = -1$. In other words, it gives a metric to assess the degree of dependence.

Three important rules are related to variances and covariances:

1. The variance of a constant c is zero: $Var(c) = 0$.
2. For any constants a and b, the variance of a linear combination such as $aY + b$ is $Var(aY + b) = a^2 Var(Y)$.
3. The variance of a linear combination of random variables $Y_1, Y_2, \ldots . Y_k$ involves not only the variance of each random variable but also the covariances: for any constants $c_1, c_2, \ldots \ldots c_k$,

$$Var(c_1Y_1 + c_2Y_2 + \cdots\cdot c_kY_k) = \sum_{i=1}^{k} c_i^2 Var(Y_i) + 2\sum_{i=1}^{k-1}\sum_{j>i}^{k} c_i c_j cov(Y_i, Y_j) \tag{A.25}$$

For instance, when we have two variables, $Var(c_1Y_1 + c_2Y_2) = c_1^2 Var(Y_1) + c_2^2 Var(Y_2) + 2c_1c_2 cov(Y_1, Y_2)$. If the random variables are uncorrelated, then their covariances are zero and the variance reduces to $Var(c_1Y_1 + c_2Y_2 + \ldots . c_kY_k) = \sum_{i=1}^{k} c_i^2 Var(Y_i)$.

As an example, we calculate the correlations between the quarterly U.S. GDP growth and the growth of personal consumption, domestic investment, and government expenditures. In Figure A.8 we plot these data.

In all three plots, we observe that the correlation is positive; thus, GDP growth moves in the same direction as consumption, investment, and government expenditures growth. However the correlation is the strongest between GDP and investment growth, $\rho_{YX} = 0.77$, and it is the weakest between GDP and government expenditures growth, $\rho_{YX} = 0.16$. Observe that the higher the correlation, the tighter the alignment of the observations around a line.

FIGURE A.8 Examples of Correlated Variables

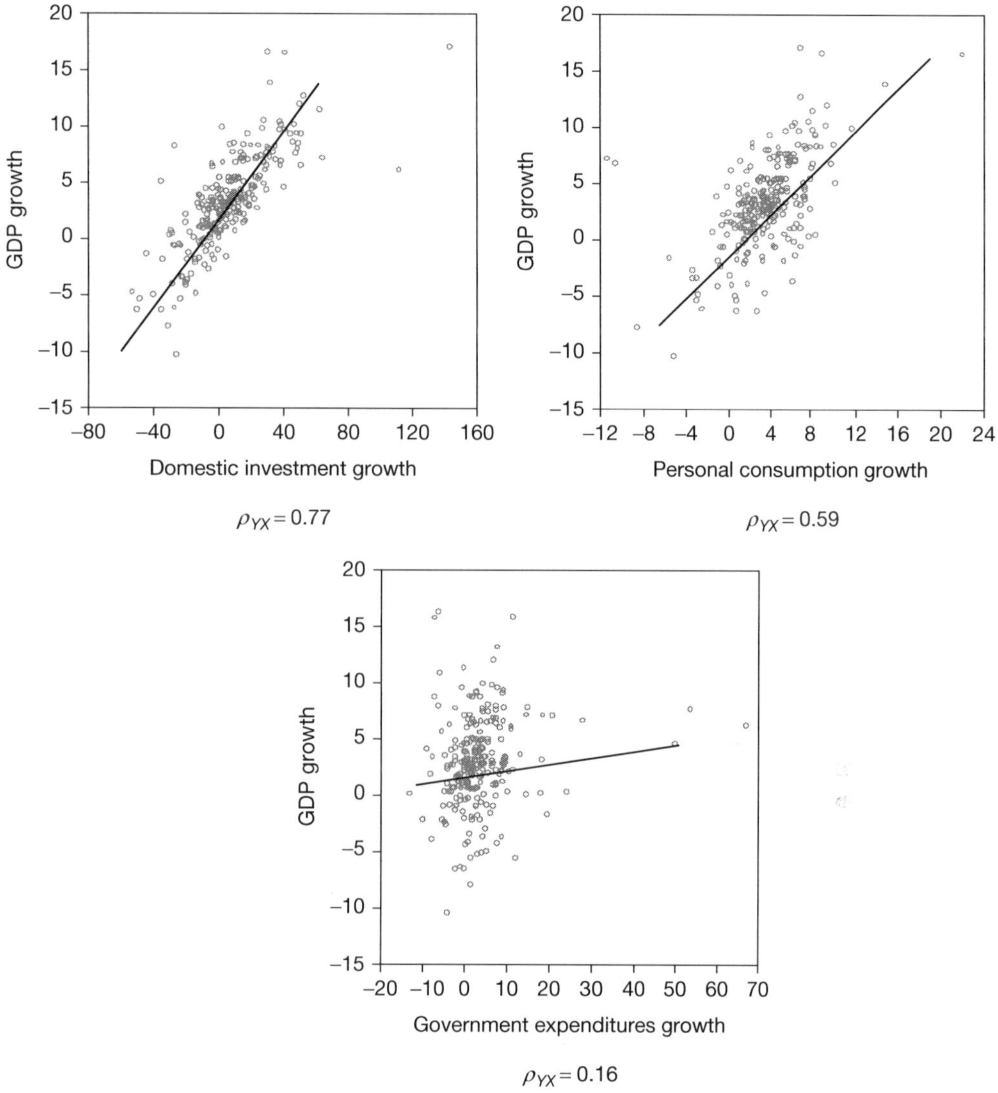

KEY WORDS

CDF, p. 448
chi-square distribution, p. 453
correlation coefficient, p. 460
covariance, p. 458
expected value, p. 449
F-distribution, p. 454
kurtosis, p. 452
mean value, p. 449

moment, p. 449

normal probability density, p. 452

PDF, p. 448

population information, p. 447

sample average, p. 460

sample information, p. 447

sample variance, p. 451

skewness, p. 451

Student-t probability distribution, p. 454

EXERCISES

1. Suppose that we survey 100 people in your neighborhood and we asked how many cars they own. The possible outcomes are {Y} = {0, 1, 2, 3}. The results of the survey are tabulated as

numbers of cars	0	1	2	3
numbers of people	10	50	35	5

a. Compute and plot the frequency distribution. Plot the cumulative distribution function of this random variable.
b. What is the probability of having at least one car? What is the probability of having more than two cars?
c. What is the expected number of cars?
d. What is the variance of this random variable?

2. Consider a continuous random variable Y. If $Y \rightarrow N(2, 9)$, compute the following
a. $P(Y \leq 6)$ and $P(Y \leq 1.5)$ and $P(1.5 \leq Y \leq 6)$.
b. $P(Y \geq 9)$ and $P(Y \geq 0)$ and $P(0 \leq Y \leq 9)$.
c. What is the value of y such that $P(Y \geq y) = 0.10$? Find two values y_1 and y_2 such that $P(y1 \leq Y \leq y_2) = 0.30$.

3. Using the appropriate tables, find the following:
a. $P(3 \leq \chi_6^2 \leq 5)$.
b. $P(t_7 \geq 2.3)$.
c. $P(F_{2,10} \leq 3.75)$
d. What is the t such that $P(t_6 \geq t)=0.20$?

4. You have already downloaded some of the time series described in Chapter 1. Take the series of unemployed persons from the FRED database and the number of people in poverty from the U.S. Census Bureau. Respond to the following for both series:
a. Compute the descriptive statistics: mean, median, variance, standard deviation, skewness, and kurtosis.
b. Examine the histograms. By analyzing the JB statistic, are these random variables normally distributed?
c. From those distributions reviewed in the chapter, which one may better describe these random variables?
d. Compute the correlation between both series and comment on your findings.

Appendix B
Statistical Tables

TABLE I Normal Curve Areas

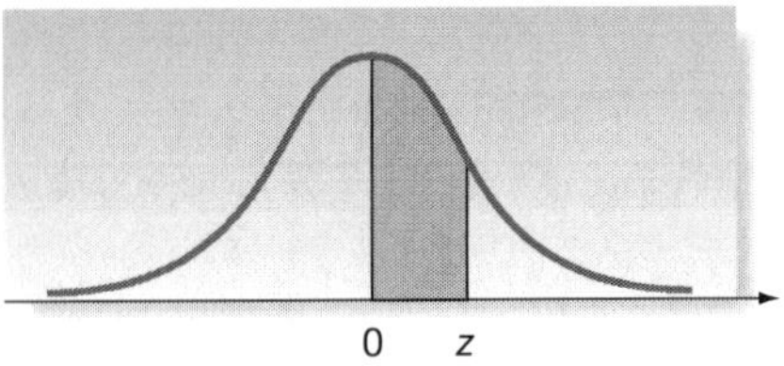

z	.00	.01	.02	.03	.04	.05	.06	.07	.08	.09
.0	.0000	.0040	.0080	.0120	.0160	.0199	.0239	.0279	.0319	.0359
.1	.0398	.0438	.0478	.0517	.0557	.0596	.0636	.0675	.0714	.0753
.2	.0793	.0832	.0871	.0910	.0948	.0987	.1026	.1064	.1103	.1141
.3	.1179	.1217	.1255	.1293	.1331	.1368	.1406	.1443	.1480	.1517
.4	.1554	.1591	.1628	.1664	.1700	.1736	.1772	.1808	.1844	.1879
.5	.1915	.1950	.1985	.2019	.2054	.2088	.2123	.2157	.2190	.2224
.6	.2257	.2291	.2324	.2357	.2389	.2422	.2454	.2486	.2517	.2549
.7	.2580	.2611	.2642	.2673	.2704	.2734	.2764	.2794	.2823	.2852
.8	.2881	.2910	.2939	.2967	.2995	.3023	.3051	.3078	.3106	.3133
.9	.3159	.3186	.3212	.3238	.3264	.3289	.3315	.3340	.3365	.3389
1.0	.3413	.3438	.3461	.3485	.3508	.3531	.3554	.3577	.3599	.3621
1.1	.3643	.3665	.3686	.3708	.3729	.3749	.3770	.3790	.3810	.3830
1.2	.3849	.3869	.3888	.3907	.3925	.3944	.3962	.3980	.3997	.4015
1.3	.4032	.4049	.4066	.4082	.4099	.4115	.4131	.4147	.4162	.4177
1.4	.4192	.4207	.4222	.4236	.4251	.4265	.4279	.4292	.4306	.4319
1.5	.4332	.4345	.4357	.4370	.4382	.4394	.4406	.4418	.4429	.4441
1.6	.4452	.4463	.4474	.4484	.4495	.4505	.4515	.4525	.4535	.4545
1.7	.4554	.4564	.4573	.4582	.4591	.4599	.4608	.4616	.4625	.4633
1.8	.4641	.4649	.4656	.4664	.4671	.4678	.4686	.4693	.4699	.4706
1.9	.4713	.4719	.4726	.4732	.4738	.4744	.4750	.4756	.4761	.4767
2.0	.4772	.4778	.4783	.4788	.4793	.4798	.4803	.4808	.4812	.4817
2.1	.4821	.4826	.4830	.4834	.4838	.4842	.4846	.4850	.4854	.4857
2.2	.4861	.4864	.4868	.4871	.4875	.4878	.4881	.4884	.4887	.4890
2.3	.4893	.4896	.4898	.4901	.4904	.4906	.4909	.4911	.4913	.4916
2.4	.4918	.4920	.4922	.4925	.4927	.4929	.4931	.4932	.4934	.4936
2.5	.4938	.4940	.4941	.4943	.4945	.4946	.4948	.4949	.4951	.4952
2.6	.4953	.4955	.4956	.4957	.4959	.4960	.4961	.4962	.4963	.4964
2.7	.4965	.4966	.4967	.4968	.4969	.4970	.4971	.4972	.4973	.4974
2.8	.4974	.4975	.4976	.4977	.4977	.4978	.4979	.4979	.4980	.4981
2.9	.4981	.4982	.4982	.4983	.4984	.4984	.4985	.4985	.4986	.4986
3.0	.4987	.4987	.4987	.4988	.4988	.4989	.4989	.4989	.4990	.4990

Source: Based on Table 1 of A. Hald, *Statistical Tables and Formulas* (New York: Wiley), 1952.

TABLE II Critical Values of t

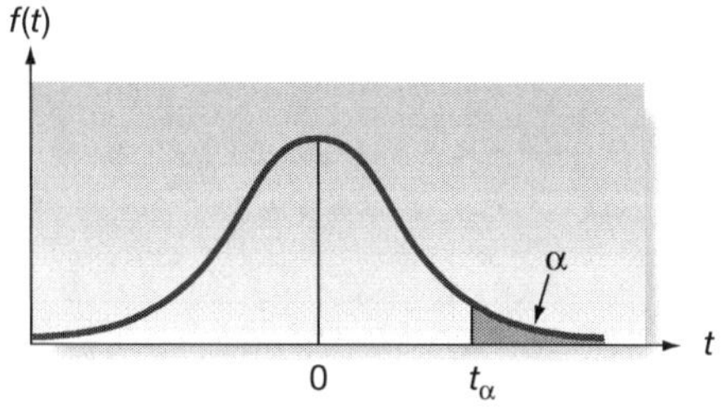

Degrees of Freedom	$t_{.100}$	$t_{.050}$	$t_{.025}$	$t_{.010}$	$t_{.005}$	$t_{.001}$	$t_{.0005}$
1	3.078	6.314	12.706	31.821	63.657	318.31	636.62
2	1.886	2.920	4.303	6.965	9.925	22.326	31.598
3	1.638	2.353	3.182	4.541	5.841	10.213	12.924
4	1.533	2.132	2.776	3.747	4.604	7.173	8.610
5	1.476	2.015	2.571	3.365	4.032	5.893	6.869
6	1.440	1.943	2.447	3.143	3.707	5.208	5.959
7	1.415	1.895	2.365	2.998	3.499	4.785	5.408
8	1.397	1.860	2.306	2.896	3.355	4.501	5.041
9	1.383	1.833	2.262	2.821	3.250	4.297	4.781
10	1.372	1.812	2.228	2.764	3.169	4.144	4.587
11	1.363	1.796	2.201	2.718	3.106	4.025	4.437
12	1.356	1.782	2.179	2.681	3.055	3.930	4.318
13	1.350	1.771	2.160	2.650	3.012	3.852	4.221
14	1.345	1.761	2.145	2.624	2.977	3.787	4.140
15	1.341	1.753	2.131	2.602	2.947	3.733	4.073
16	1.337	1.746	2.120	2.583	2.921	3.686	4.015
17	1.333	1.740	2.110	2.567	2.898	3.646	3.965
18	1.330	1.734	2.101	2.552	2.878	3.610	3.922
19	1.328	1.729	2.093	2.539	2.861	3.579	3.883
20	1.325	1.725	2.086	2.528	2.845	3.552	3.850
21	1.323	1.721	2.080	2.518	2.831	3.527	3.819
22	1.321	1.717	2.074	2.508	2.819	3.505	3.792
23	1.319	1.714	2.069	2.500	2.807	3.485	3.767
24	1.318	1.711	2.064	2.492	2.797	3.467	3.745
25	1.316	1.708	2.060	2.485	2.787	3.450	3.725
26	1.315	1.706	2.056	2.479	2.779	3.435	3.707
27	1.314	1.703	2.052	2.473	2.771	3.421	3.690
28	1.313	1.701	2.048	2.467	2.763	3.408	3.674
29	1.311	1.699	2.045	2.462	2.756	3.396	3.659
30	1.310	1.697	2.042	2.457	2.750	3.385	3.646
40	1.303	1.684	2.021	2.423	2.704	3.307	3.551
60	1.296	1.671	2.000	2.390	2.660	3.232	3.460
120	1.289	1.658	1.980	2.358	2.617	3.160	3.373
∞	1.282	1.645	1.960	2.326	2.576	3.090	3.291

TABLE III Critical Values of χ^2

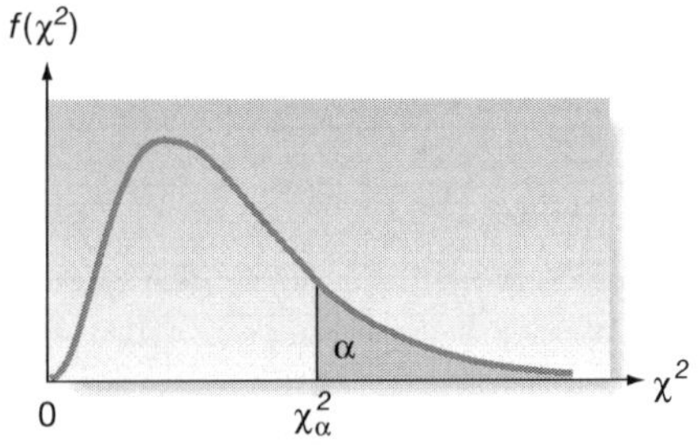

Degrees of Freedom	$\chi^2_{.995}$	$\chi^2_{.990}$	$\chi^2_{.975}$	$\chi^2_{.950}$	$\chi^2_{.900}$
1	.0000393	.0001571	.0009821	.0039321	.0157908
2	.0100251	.0201007	.0506356	.102587	.210720
3	.0717212	.114832	.215795	.351846	.584375
4	.206990	.297110	.484419	.710721	1.063623
5	.411740	.554300	.831211	1.145476	1.61031
6	.675727	.872085	1.237347	1.63539	2.20413
7	.989265	1.239043	1.68987	2.16735	2.83311
8	1.344419	1.646482	2.17973	2.73264	3.48954
9	1.734926	2.087912	2.70039	3.32511	4.16816
10	2.15585	2.55821	3.24697	3.94030	4.86518
11	2.60321	3.05347	3.81575	4.57481	5.57779
12	3.07382	3.57056	4.40379	5.22603	6.30380
13	3.56503	4.10691	5.00874	5.89186	7.04150
14	4.07468	4.66043	5.62872	6.57063	7.78953
15	4.60094	5.22935	6.26214	7.26094	8.54675
16	5.14224	5.81221	6.90766	7.96164	9.31223
17	5.69724	6.40776	7.56418	8.67176	10.0852
18	6.26481	7.01491	8.23075	9.39046	10.8649
19	6.84398	7.63273	8.90655	10.1170	11.6509
20	7.43386	8.26040	9.59083	10.8508	12.4426
21	8.03366	8.89720	10.28293	11.5913	13.2396
22	8.64272	9.54249	10.9823	12.3380	14.0415
23	9.26042	10.19567	11.6885	13.0905	14.8479
24	9.88623	10.8564	12.4011	13.8484	15.6587
25	10.5197	11.5240	13.1197	14.6114	16.4734
26	11.1603	12.1981	13.8439	15.3791	17.2919
27	11.8076	12.8786	14.5733	16.1513	18.1138
28	12.4613	13.5648	15.3079	16.9279	18.9392
29	13.1211	14.2565	16.0471	17.7083	19.7677
30	13.7867	14.9535	16.7908	18.4926	20.5992
40	20.7065	22.1643	24.4331	26.5093	29.0505
50	27.9907	29.7067	32.3574	34.7642	37.6886
60	35.5346	37.4848	40.4817	43.1879	46.4589

(continued)

TABLE III (continued)

70	43.2752	45.4418	48.7576	51.7393	55.3290
80	51.1720	53.5400	57.1532	60.3915	64.2778
90	59.1963	61.7541	65.6466	69.1260	73.2912
100	67.3276	70.0648	74.2219	77.9295	82.3581

Degrees of Freedom	$\chi^2_{.100}$	$\chi^2_{.050}$	$\chi^2_{.025}$	$\chi^2_{.010}$	$\chi^2_{.005}$
1	2.70554	3.84146	5.02389	6.63490	7.87944
2	4.60517	5.99147	7.37776	9.21034	10.5966
3	6.25139	7.81473	9.34840	11.3449	12.8381
4	7.77944	9.48773	11.1433	13.2767	14.8602
5	9.23635	11.0705	12.8325	15.0863	16.7496
6	10.6446	12.5916	14.4494	16.8119	18.5476
7	12.0170	14.0671	16.0128	18.4753	20.2777
8	13.3616	15.5073	17.5346	20.0902	21.9550
9	14.6837	16.9190	19.0228	21.6660	23.5893
10	15.9871	18.3070	20.4831	23.2093	25.1882
11	17.2750	19.6751	21.9200	24.7250	26.7569
12	18.5494	21.0261	23.3367	26.2170	28.2995
13	19.8119	22.3621	24.7356	27.6883	29.8194
14	21.0642	23.6848	26.1190	29.1413	31.3193
15	22.3072	24.9958	27.4884	30.5779	32.8013
16	23.5418	26.2962	28.8454	31.9999	34.2672
17	24.7690	27.5871	30.1910	33.4087	35.7185
18	25.9894	28.8693	31.5264	34.8053	37.1564
19	27.2036	30.1435	32.8523	36.1908	38.5822
20	28.4120	31.4104	34.1696	37.5662	39.9968
21	29.6151	32.6705	35.4789	38.9321	41.4010
22	30.8133	33.9244	36.7807	40.2894	42.7956
23	32.0069	35.1725	38.0757	41.6384	44.1813
24	33.1963	36.4151	39.3641	42.9798	45.5585
25	34.3816	37.6525	40.6465	44.3141	46.9278
26	35.5631	38.8852	41.9232	45.6417	48.2899
27	36.7412	40.1133	43.1944	46.9630	49.6449
28	37.9159	41.3372	44.4607	48.2782	50.9933
29	39.0875	42.5569	45.7222	49.5879	52.3356
30	40.2560	43.7729	46.9792	50.8922	53.6720
40	51.8050	55.7585	59.3417	63.6907	66.7659
50	63.1671	67.5048	71.4202	76.1539	79.4900
60	74.3970	79.0819	83.2976	88.3794	91.9517
70	85.5271	90.5312	95.0231	100.425	104.215
80	96.5782	101.879	106.629	112.329	116.321
90	107.565	113.145	118.136	124.116	128.299
100	118.498	124.342	129.561	135.807	140.169

TABLE IV Percentage Points of the F-Distribution, $\alpha = .05$

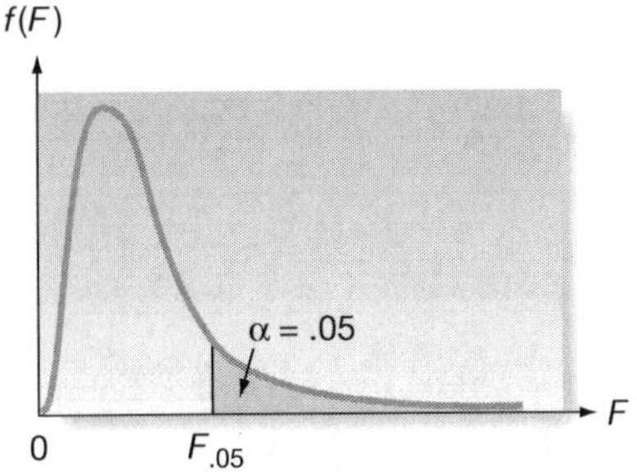

ν_2 \ ν_1 (Denominator Degrees of Freedom \ Numerator Degrees of Freedom)	1	2	3	4	5	6	7	8	9
1	161.4	199.5	215.7	224.6	230.2	234.0	236.8	238.9	240.5
2	18.51	19.00	19.16	19.25	19.30	19.33	19.35	19.37	19.38
3	10.13	9.55	9.28	9.12	9.01	8.94	8.89	8.85	8.81
4	7.71	6.94	6.59	6.39	6.26	6.16	6.09	6.04	6.00
5	6.61	5.79	5.41	5.19	5.05	4.95	4.88	4.82	4.77
6	5.99	5.14	4.76	4.53	4.39	4.28	4.21	4.15	4.10
7	5.59	4.74	4.35	4.12	3.97	3.87	3.79	3.73	3.68
8	5.32	4.46	4.07	3.84	3.69	3.58	3.50	3.44	3.39
9	5.12	4.26	3.86	3.63	3.48	3.37	3.29	3.23	3.18
10	4.96	4.10	3.71	3.48	3.33	3.22	3.14	3.07	3.02
11	4.84	3.98	3.59	3.36	3.20	3.09	3.01	2.95	2.90
12	4.75	3.89	3.49	3.26	3.11	3.00	2.91	2.85	2.80
13	4.67	3.81	3.41	3.18	3.03	2.92	2.83	2.77	2.71
14	4.60	3.74	3.34	3.11	2.96	2.85	2.76	2.70	2.65
15	4.54	3.68	3.29	3.06	2.90	2.79	2.71	2.64	2.59
16	4.49	3.63	3.24	3.01	2.85	2.74	2.66	2.59	2.54
17	4.45	3.59	3.20	2.96	2.81	2.70	2.61	2.55	2.49
18	4.41	3.55	3.16	2.93	2.77	2.66	2.58	2.51	2.46
19	4.38	3.52	3.13	2.90	2.74	2.63	2.54	2.48	2.42
20	4.35	3.49	3.10	2.87	2.71	2.60	2.51	2.45	2.39
21	4.32	3.47	3.07	2.84	2.68	2.57	2.49	2.42	2.37
22	4.30	3.44	3.05	2.82	2.66	2.55	2.46	2.40	2.34
23	4.28	3.42	3.03	2.80	2.64	2.53	2.44	2.37	2.32
24	4.26	3.40	3.01	2.78	2.62	2.51	2.42	2.36	2.30
25	4.24	3.39	2.99	2.76	2.60	2.49	2.40	2.34	2.28
26	4.23	3.37	2.98	2.74	2.59	2.47	2.39	2.32	2.77
27	4.21	3.35	2.96	2.73	2.57	2.46	2.37	2.31	2.25
28	4.20	3.34	2.95	2.71	2.56	2.45	2.36	2.29	2.24
29	4.18	3.33	2.93	2.70	2.55	2.43	2.35	2.28	2.22
30	4.17	3.32	2.92	2.69	2.53	2.42	2.33	2.27	2.21
40	4.08	3.23	2.84	2.61	2.45	2.34	2.25	2.18	2.12
60	4.00	3.15	2.76	2.53	2.37	2.25	2.17	2.10	2.04
120	3.92	3.07	2.68	2.45	2.29	2.17	2.09	2.02	1.96
∞	3.84	3.00	2.60	2.37	2.21	2.10	2.01	1.94	1.88

(*continued*)

TABLE IV (continued)

ν_2 \ ν_1	Numerator Degrees of Freedom									
Denominator degrees of freedom	10	12	15	20	24	30	40	60	120	∞
1	241.9	243.9	245.9	248.0	249.1	250.1	251.1	252.2	253.3	254.3
2	19.40	19.41	19.43	19.45	19.45	19.46	19.47	19.48	19.49	19.50
3	8.79	8.74	8.70	8.66	8.64	8.62	8.59	8.57	8.55	8.53
4	5.96	5.91	5.86	5.80	5.77	5.75	5.72	5.69	5.66	5.63
5	4.74	4.68	4.62	4.56	4.53	4.50	4.46	4.43	4.40	4.36
6	4.06	4.00	3.94	3.87	3.84	3.81	3.77	3.74	3.70	3.67
7	3.64	3.57	3.51	3.44	3.41	3.38	3.34	3.30	3.27	3.23
8	3.35	3.28	3.22	3.15	3.12	3.08	3.04	3.01	2.97	2.93
9	3.14	3.07	3.01	2.94	2.90	2.86	2.83	2.79	2.75	2.71
10	2.98	2.91	2.85	2.77	2.74	2.70	2.66	2.62	2.58	2.54
11	2.85	2.79	2.72	2.65	2.61	2.57	2.53	2.49	2.45	2.40
12	2.75	2.69	2.62	2.54	2.51	2.47	2.43	2.38	2.34	2.30
13	2.67	2.60	2.53	2.46	2.42	2.38	2.34	2.30	2.25	2.21
14	2.60	2.53	2.46	2.39	2.35	2.31	2.27	2.22	2.18	2.13
15	2.54	2.48	2.40	2.33	2.29	2.25	2.20	2.16	2.11	2.07
16	2.49	2.42	2.35	2.28	2.24	2.19	2.15	2.11	2.06	2.01
17	2.45	2.38	2.31	2.23	2.19	2.15	2.10	2.06	2.01	1.96
18	2.41	2.34	2.27	2.19	2.15	2.11	2.06	2.02	1.97	1.92
19	2.38	2.31	2.23	2.16	2.11	2.07	2.03	1.98	1.93	1.88
20	2.35	2.28	2.20	2.12	2.08	2.04	1.99	1.95	1.90	1.84
21	2.32	2.25	2.18	2.10	2.05	2.01	1.96	1.92	1.87	1.81
22	2.30	2.23	2.15	2.07	2.03	1.98	1.94	1.89	1.84	1.78
23	2.27	2.20	2.13	2.05	2.01	1.96	1.91	1.86	1.81	1.76
24	2.25	2.18	2.11	2.03	1.98	1.94	1.89	1.84	1.79	1.73
25	2.24	2.16	2.09	2.01	1.96	1.92	1.87	1.82	1.77	1.71
26	2.22	2.15	2.07	1.99	1.95	1.90	1.85	1.80	1.75	1.69
27	2.20	2.13	2.06	1.97	1.93	1.88	1.84	1.79	1.73	1.67
28	2.19	2.12	2.04	1.96	1.91	1.87	1.82	1.77	1.71	1.65
29	2.18	2.10	2.03	1.94	1.90	1.85	1.81	1.75	1.70	1.64
30	2.16	2.09	2.01	1.93	1.89	1.84	1.79	1.74	1.68	1.62
40	2.08	2.00	1.92	1.84	1.79	1.74	1.69	1.64	1.58	1.51
60	1.99	1.92	1.84	1.75	1.70	1.65	1.59	1.53	1.47	1.39
120	1.91	1.83	1.75	1.66	1.61	1.55	1.50	1.43	1.35	1.25
∞	1.83	1.75	1.67	1.57	1.52	1.46	1.39	1.32	1.22	1.00

TABLE V Percentage Points of the F-distribution, $\alpha = .01$

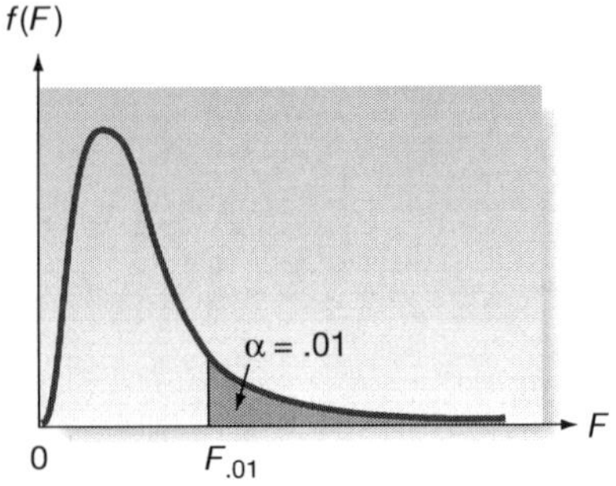

ν_2 \ ν_1	Numerator Degrees of Freedom								
Denominator Degrees of Freedom	**1**	**2**	**3**	**4**	**5**	**6**	**7**	**8**	**9**
1	4,052	4,999.5	5,403	5,625	5,764	5,859	5,928	5,982	6,022
2	98.50	99.00	99.17	99.25	99.30	99.33	99.36	99.37	99.39
3	34.12	30.82	29.46	28.71	28.24	27.91	27.67	27.49	27.35
4	21.20	18.00	16.69	15.98	15.52	15.21	14.98	14.80	14.66
5	16.26	13.27	12.06	11.39	10.97	10.67	10.46	10.29	10.16
6	13.75	10.92	9.78	9.15	8.75	8.47	8.26	8.10	7.98
7	12.25	9.55	8.45	7.85	7.46	7.19	6.99	6.84	6.72
8	11.26	8.65	7.59	7.01	6.63	6.37	6.18	6.03	5.91
9	10.56	8.02	6.99	6.42	6.06	5.80	5.61	5.47	5.35
10	10.04	7.56	6.55	5.99	5.64	5.39	5.20	5.06	4.94
11	9.65	7.21	6.22	5.67	5.32	5.07	4.89	4.74	4.63
12	9.33	6.93	5.95	5.41	5.06	4.82	4.64	4.50	4.39
13	9.07	6.70	5.74	5.21	4.86	4.62	4.44	4.30	4.19
14	8.86	6.51	5.56	5.04	4.69	4.46	4.28	4.14	4.03
15	8.68	6.36	5.42	4.89	4.56	4.32	4.14	4.00	3.89
16	8.53	6.23	5.29	4.77	4.44	4.20	4.03	3.89	3.78
17	8.40	6.11	5.18	4.67	4.34	4.10	3.93	3.79	3.68
18	8.29	6.01	5.09	4.58	4.25	4.01	3.84	3.71	3.60
19	8.18	5.93	5.01	4.50	4.17	3.94	3.77	3.63	3.52
20	8.10	5.85	4.94	4.43	4.10	3.87	3.70	3.56	3.46
21	8.02	5.78	4.87	4.37	4.04	3.81	3.64	3.51	3.40
22	7.95	5.72	4.82	4.31	3.99	3.76	3.59	3.45	3.35
23	7.88	5.66	4.76	4.26	3.94	3.71	3.54	3.41	3.30
24	7.82	5.61	4.72	4.22	3.90	3.67	3.50	3.36	3.26
25	7.77	5.57	4.68	4.18	3.85	3.63	3.46	3.32	3.22
26	7.72	5.53	4.64	4.14	3.82	3.59	3.42	3.29	3.18
27	7.68	5.49	4.60	4.11	3.78	3.56	3.39	3.26	3.15
28	7.64	5.45	4.57	4.07	3.75	3.53	3.36	3.23	3.12
29	7.60	5.42	4.54	4.04	3.73	3.50	3.33	3.20	3.09
30	7.56	5.39	4.51	4.02	3.70	3.47	3.30	3.17	3.07
40	7.31	5.18	4.31	3.83	3.51	3.29	3.12	2.99	2.89
60	7.08	4.98	4.13	3.65	3.34	3.12	2.95	2.82	2.72
120	6.85	4.79	3.95	3.48	3.17	2.96	2.79	2.66	2.56
∞	6.63	4.61	3.78	3.32	3.02	2.80	2.64	2.51	2.41

(continued)

TABLE V (continued)

ν_2 \ ν_1	Numerator Degrees of Freedom									
Denominator Degrees of Freedom	**10**	**12**	**15**	**20**	**24**	**30**	**40**	**60**	**120**	**∞**
1	6,056	6,106	6,157	6,209	6,235	6,261	6,287	6,313	6,339	6,366
2	99.40	99.42	99.43	99.45	99.46	99.47	99.47	99.48	99.49	99.50
3	27.23	27.05	26.87	26.69	26.60	26.50	26.41	26.32	26.22	26.13
4	14.55	14.37	14.20	14.02	13.93	13.84	13.75	13.65	13.56	13.46
5	10.05	9.89	9.72	9.55	9.47	9.38	9.29	9.20	9.11	9.02
6	7.87	7.72	7.56	7.40	7.31	7.23	7.14	7.06	6.97	6.88
7	6.62	6.47	6.31	6.16	6.07	5.99	5.91	5.82	5.74	5.65
8	5.81	5.67	5.52	5.36	5.28	5.20	5.12	5.03	4.95	4.86
9	5.26	5.11	4.96	4.81	4.73	4.65	4.57	4.48	4.40	4.31
10	4.85	4.71	4.56	4.41	4.33	4.25	4.17	4.08	4.00	3.91
11	4.54	4.40	4.25	4.10	4.02	3.94	3.86	3.78	3.69	3.60
12	4.30	4.16	4.01	3.86	3.78	3.70	3.62	3.54	3.45	3.36
13	4.10	3.96	3.82	3.66	3.59	3.51	3.43	3.34	3.25	3.17
14	3.94	3.80	3.66	3.51	3.43	3.35	3.27	3.18	3.09	3.00
15	3.80	3.67	3.52	3.37	3.29	3.21	3.13	3.05	2.96	2.87
16	3.69	3.55	3.41	3.26	3.18	3.10	3.02	2.93	2.84	2.75
17	3.59	3.46	3.31	3.16	3.08	3.00	2.92	2.83	2.75	2.65
18	3.51	3.37	3.23	3.08	3.00	2.92	2.84	2.75	2.66	2.57
19	3.43	3.30	3.15	3.00	2.92	2.84	2.76	2.67	2.58	2.49
20	3.37	3.23	3.09	2.94	2.86	2.78	2.69	2.61	2.52	2.42
21	3.31	3.17	3.03	2.88	2.80	2.72	2.64	2.55	2.46	2.36
22	3.26	3.12	2.98	2.83	2.75	2.67	2.58	2.50	2.40	2.31
23	3.21	3.07	2.93	2.78	2.70	2.62	2.54	2.45	2.35	2.26
24	3.17	3.03	2.89	2.74	2.66	2.58	2.49	2.40	2.31	2.21
25	3.13	2.99	2.85	2.70	2.62	2.54	2.45	2.36	2.27	2.17
26	3.09	2.96	2.81	2.66	2.58	2.50	2.42	2.33	2.23	2.13
27	3.06	2.93	2.78	2.63	2.55	2.47	2.38	2.29	2.20	2.10
28	3.03	2.90	2.75	2.60	2.52	2.44	2.35	2.26	2.17	2.06
29	3.00	2.87	2.73	2.57	2.49	2.41	2.33	2.23	2.14	2.03
30	2.98	2.84	2.70	2.55	2.47	2.39	2.30	2.21	2.11	2.01
40	2.80	2.66	2.52	2.37	2.29	2.20	2.11	2.02	1.92	1.80
60	2.63	2.50	2.35	2.20	2.12	2.03	1.94	1.84	1.73	1.60
120	2.47	2.34	2.19	2.03	1.95	1.86	1.76	1.66	1.53	1.38
∞	2.32	2.18	2.04	1.88	1.79	1.70	1.59	1.47	1.32	1.00

Glossary

adjusted R-squared Modified R-squared that penalizes the inclusion of irrelevant regressors.

adjustment coefficient Contribution of the error correction term to the VEC; over time it corrects the deviations from equilibrium to bring the system closer to the long-run equilibrium relation.

AIC See *information criteria.*

analytical forecast Prediction from a nonlinear (or linear) time series model that is calculated by solving analytical integrals.

ARCH See *autoregressive conditional heteroscedasticity.*

AR(p) Autoregressive model of order p so that the dynamics of the process are a linear function of the last p observations.

asset pricing Finance models that explain the price formation of financial assets.

augmented Dickey-Fulle for unit root Test statistic to assess the presence of unit roots by also taking into account the autocorrelation of the data.

autocorrelation function Collection of correlation coefficients between any two random variables in the stochastic process that are k periods apart for $k = 1, 2, \ldots$

autoregressive conditional heteroscedasticity (*ARCH*) Conditional variance of a random variable specified as an autoregressive function of past squared innovations; (G)ARCH a generalized ARCH model for which the conditional variance is a function not only of past squared innovations but also past conditional variances; (I)GARCH integrated ARCH for which the persistence in variance is equal to 1.

autoregressive representation (AR) Time series model whose dynamics are a linear function of past observations of the process.

beta of an asset Risk of an asset measured as the covariance of the asset return with the market in units of market variance.

bid-ask bounce Movement of an asset price between the ask price (paid by the buyer) and the bid price (received by the seller by the seller).

Black-Scholes formula Most popular option pricing formula based on the assumption that stock returns are normally distributed.

BLUE Best linear unbiased estimator.

call option Derivative that grants the buyer the right to buy the underlying asset at a specific time and at a specific price.

capital asset pricing model (CAPM) Mathematical relationship that explains the expected return of an asset as a linear function of risk.

chain rule of forecasting Recursive relation to obtain each successive multistep forecast of an autoregressive model as a linear function of the immediate previous forecasts.

cob-web model Description of the dynamics of market prices as alternating movements, below and above the equilibrium price, which result from the interaction of suppliers and consumers in the market.

cointegrating relation Linear equation that defines the econometric long-run equilibrium.

cointegration Econometric long-run equilibrium defined as a stationary linear combination of nonstationary processes.

combination of forecasts Linear and nonlinear averages of the forecasts of several models.

conditional mean Average of a random variable Y conditioning on the information set.

conditional probability density function The density function of a random variable Y for a given value of a variable X.

conditional variance Average of the squared deviations of Y with respect to its conditional mean conditioning on the information set.

continuous time model Time series specification in which time is a real number; thus, time flows continuously.

correlation coefficient Measure of linear dependence between two random variables bounded by –1 and 1.

covariance Measure of linear dependence between two random variables.

covariance stationarity Time-invariant first and second moments for the random variables in the stochastic process.

critical value The value of a random variable associated with a given significance level.

cross-sectional sample average Mean of several realizations of a random variable calculated across units.

cumulative distribution function Function that accumulates the probabilities of outcomes of a random variable ordered in an increasing fashion.

cycle Periodic fluctuation in a time series.

Delphi Oracle Prophecies spoken by Pythia, the priestess of the god Apollo, in the city of Delphi in ancient Greece.

density forecast Conditional probability density function of the process at a future date.

deterministic cycle Periodic fluctuations generated by deterministic variables such as a time index.

deterministic seasonality Calendar fluctuations generated by deterministic variables such as seasonal dummies.

deterministic trend Slowly and smoothly upward or downward tendency in a time series generated by deterministic variables such as a time index.

Dickey-Fuller test for unit root Statistic to assess the presence of unit roots.

discrete time series model Time series specification in which time is an integer index as 1, 2, 3, etc.

disequilibrium error Shock that breaks the long-run equilibrium.

diversification gains Benefit (smaller expected loss) derived from combining several forecasts.

economic model Structural representation of the economy summarized by a set of equations; the parameters in these equations are known as *structural parameters.*

equal predictive ability Identical expected losses of two competing forecasts.

error variance Dispersion of the error in a regression model.

estimate Specific value of the estimator based on sample information.

estimation Branch of statistical inference that aims to calculate the parameters of a population model based on sample information.

estimation sample Sample used for estimation of the time-series model.

estimator Mathematical expression to calculate the regression coefficients in a regression model or any other time series model.

event forecasting Predicting a specific occurrence and/or its timing.

expected shortfall Average loss within the α-quantile of portfolio returns.

expected value Measure of centrality of a random variable; also known as *population mean.*

exponentially weighted moving average (EWMA) volatility Estimator of the conditional variance calculated as a weighted moving average of the squared returns (in deviation from the mean) of an asset; also known as *exponential smoothing of squared returns.*

F-distribution Asymmetric probability density function formed as the ratio of two independent chi-square distributed random variables.

first difference Difference between the value of a random variable and its 1-period lagged value.

forecast error Difference between the realized value of the variable of interest and its prediction.

forecast horizon Number of periods into the future for which a prediction is made.

forecast uncertainty Variance of the forecast error.

forecasting Science and art of predicting the future with some degree of accuracy.

forecasting environment Setup of the estimation and prediction samples; a *recursive* environment when the estimation sample increases one observation at the time and the model is re-estimated at every increase of the sample; a *rolling* environment when the estimation sample is of fixed length but rolled forward one observation at the time, the model is re-estimated at every roll of the sample; and a *fixed* environment when the estimation sample is of fixed length and the model is estimated only once but new information is incorporated into the forecast.

F-test Statistic to measure the significance of a joint-valued null hypothesis.

GARCH See *autoregressive conditional heteroscedasticity* (*ARCH*).

Gauss-Markov theorem Mathematical result that explains the statistical properties (BLUE) of the estimators of the regression coefficients.

Granger-causality In a vector autoregression (VAR) system, assessment of which variables are more informative to forecast the system at a future date.

heteroscedasticity Conditional variance of a random variable that is not constant but depends on a set of explanatory variables.

high-frequency data Information collected at short and very short periods of time such as hours, minutes, seconds.

homoscedasticity Constant conditional variance of the dependent variable in a regression model.

house price growth One period percentage change in the price index of residential property.

house price index Aggregate of residential property prices in several locations to provide a global price measure of the residential sector of the economy.

I(0) Integrated process of order zero, which means that the process is stationary.

I(1) Integrated process of order one, which means that the process contains one unit root.

(I)GARCH See *autoregressive conditional heteroscedasticity* (*ARCH*).

Impulse-response Reaction over time for each variable in a VAR system to a shock to any of the variables in the system.

index of volatility (VIX) Calculated from option prices on the SP500 index; also known as the *fear index*.

information criteria (AIC, SIC) Measures to select the best time series model(s) by minimizing the residual variances but taking into account a penalty function to compensate for irrelevant regressors.

Information set Collection of time series information until the present time.

Informational efficiency test Statistical assessment of whether the optimal forecast error is uncorrelated with any variable(s) in the information set.

innovation Shock or unpredictable surprise in a time series model.

in-sample properties Statistical properties related to model specification such as correct dynamics, white noise errors, and correct functional form of the conditional density.

integrated variance Continuous sum of the instantaneous variances over a day.

interval forecast Collection of forecasts enclosed between a lower and upper bounds.

invertibility Property of an MA model that guarantees an equivalent AR representation in which the present is a function of past information.

kurtosis Measure of the tail-density of a random variable.

lag operator Function that delivers the one-period lagged random variable.

lag structure Number of lags for each variable in every equation of a VAR system.

linearity Assumption in a regression model that requires the dependent variable to be a linear function of the regression coefficients.

linearity testing Assessment of whether the dependence of a time series should contain dynamics other than those provided by ARIMA models.

linear regression model Specification of the conditional mean of a random variable Y as a linear function of a set of X variables.

long-run equilibrium Relation among the variables of a system when they reach the steady state; all variables grow at the same rate in the steady state.

loss differential Difference between the losses corresponding to two competing forecasts.

loss function Function that provides the costs associated with forecast errors; is *symmetric* when errors of the same magnitude but opposite signs have the same cost; is *asymmetric* when errors of the same magnitude but opposite signs have different costs.

low-frequency data Information collected at long periods of time such as years, decades, centuries.

MA(∞) Moving average model of infinite order so that the dynamics of the process are a linear function of all past innovations.

MA(q) Moving average model of order q so that the dynamics of the process are a linear function of the last q innovations.

Markov regime switching Time series model that allows for different regimes driven by a latent (nonobservable) variable; is Markov because the transition probability of moving to another state depends only on the most recent state.

mean prediction error test Statistical assessment of whether the expected value of the forecast error is zero in the case of a symmetric loss function or any other constant value in the case of an asymmetric loss function.

mixture of distributions Probability density function of a random variable that results from combining several density functions.

moments Statistical measures that characterize a random variable.

moving average representation (MA) Time series model whose dynamics are a linear function of past innovations.

multistep forecast Prediction for a horizon longer than one period.

natural logarithm Logarithm of a variable in base e, where $e = 2.7182$, such as $e^a = x \rightarrow a = \log(x)$.

nonlinearity Time series model in which the conditional mean of the process does not belong to the class of ARIMA models.

nonstationarity A stochastic process in which the unconditional moments and/or the probability density functions of the random variables depend on time.

nonsynchronous trading Exchanging different assets at different frequencies.

normal probability density Common probability density function also known as the *bell-shaped curve* because the profile of the function resembles a bell; values of the random variable are distributed symmetrically around the mean; it is characterized by a skewness of zero and a kurtosis of 3.

numerical forecast Prediction from a nonlinear (or linear) time series model that is calculated by approximating analytical integrals by their empirical counterparts.

optimal forecast Prediction obtained by minimizing the expected loss function.

optimal weight Weight assigned to each asset in a portfolio allocation problem calculated by minimizing the variance of the portfolio subject to a desired return.

option pricing Models that explain the price of an option as a function of the price of the underlying security, its variance, time to expiration, strike price, and free-risk interest rate.

ordinary least squares Estimation technique to obtain the regression coefficients that consists of minimizing the sum of squared residuals of the model.

out-of-sample properties Statistical properties related to the assessment of the forecasting ability of the model(s).

parsimony principle Preference for models with the smallest number of parameters among those with similar explanatory power.

partial autocorrelation function Collection of correlation coefficients between any two random variables in the stochastic process that are k periods apart for $k = 1, 2, \ldots$ controlling for the information that runs in between periods.

persistence Length of time that a shock remains in the system.

point forecast Single value prediction.

population Collection of information on each and every unit or element of a collective.

portfolio allocation Deployment of capital among assets with different risks.

prediction sample Sample used for assessing the forecast based on the time series model; not used in the estimation stage.

probability density function Function that delivers the probability associated with a given outcome of a random variable.

p-value Smallest significance level at which a null hypothesis can be rejected.

Q-statistic Test to assess the joint statistical significance of several autocorrelation coefficients.

qualitative information set Collection of the forecaster's knowledge and experiences that are not readily quantifiable.

quantile Value of a random variable obtained by finding the inverse of the cumulative distribution function for a fixed probability.

quantitative information set Collection of historical time series until the present time.

random walk Process with a unit root; when the process incorporates a constant, it is a random walk with drift, and when there is no constant, it is a random walk without drift.

realized volatility Estimator of the integrated variance calculated as the sum of the intraday squared returns.

residual variance Estimator of the error variance based on the residuals of a sample regression model.

restricted autoregressive system VAR system with restrictions imposed on the coefficients due, for instance, to the existence of cointegration among the variables in the model.

risk Loss derived from today's decisions involving future events.

risk management Industry practices to assess future losses in a probabilistic fashion.

rolling window volatility Estimator of the conditional variance calculated as a simple moving average of an asset's squared returns (in deviation from the mean).

R-squared Proportion of the sample variation of the dependent variable in a regression model explained by the model's regressor(s).

S-AR Seasonal autoregressive model.

S-ARMA Seasonal autoregressive moving average model.

S-MA Seasonal moving average model.

sample Subset of the population.

sample average Estimator of the expected value.

sample variance Estimator of the population variance.

seasonal cycle Periodic fluctuations associated with the calendar.

seasonality Calendar fluctuations in a time series repeated every year.

serial correlation Time dependence in the errors of a regression model.

short memory Short-lived dynamics so that the conditional mean of a process reverts quickly to the unconditional mean.

SIC See *information criteria*.

significance level Type I error or the probability of rejecting the null hypothesis when it is true.

simulation exercise Generation of artificial data according to a specific model to better understand the properties of the model.

skeleton forecast Biased prediction from a nonlinear time series model.

skewness Measure of asymmetry of a random variable; when the density is symmetric, the skewness is zero.

smoothed price Moving average of present and previous prices.

smooth transition model Time series specification with several regimes in which the transition between the regimes is specified as a smooth continuous function of the state variable.

SP500 index and returns Standard and Poor's 500 index is an aggregate measure of the U.S. stock market based on the stock prices of the 500 largest corporations in United States; returns to the index are the one-period percentage changes.

standardized innovation Shock expressed in units of standard deviations.

standardized residual Residual of a time series model in units of standard deviations.

stochastic cycle Periodic fluctuations generated by random variables.

stochastic process Collection of random variables indexed by time.

stochastic seasonality Calendar fluctuations generated by random variables at the seasonal frequency.

stochastic trend Slow and smoothly upward or downward tendency in a time series generated by random variables.

strong stationarity (first order) Identical probability density function for the random variables in the stochastic process.

Student-t probability density Symmetric probability density function that has fatter tails than the normal with a kurtosis larger than 3.

technical analysis Detection and examination of patterns in prices.

threshold autoregressive model Time series specification that has different autoregressive dynamics (different regimes) below and above a threshold value of the series.

time series Sample of a stochastic process.

time series average Mean of observations calculated over time.

time series forecasting Use of time series information to predict a variable of interest.

time series model Ad hoc representation of the dynamics of a random variable or several random variables based on the time series properties of the data.

time-varying dispersion Dispersion measures such as variance, range, interquartile range, that are functions of time.

***t*-ratio** Statistical test to measure the significance of a single-valued null hypothesis.

trend Slow and smoothly upward or downward tendency in a time series.

trend-stationarity Process with a deterministic tendency in the unconditional mean but with time-invariant second moments.

unbiased estimator Expected value of the OLS estimator that is equal to the population regression coefficient.

unbiased forecast Prediction with an expected forecast error equal to zero.

uncertainty Unknown state of the world; sometimes it is possible to attach probabilities to future events; sometimes the future is completely unknown and completely unpredictable.

U.S. Treasury securities Fixed-income assets guaranteed by the U.S. government.

unit root Linear process with a stochastic trend generated by the sum of all past equal-weighted innovations; it is also known as an autoregressive process with persistence equal to one.

value-at-risk (VaR) Method to assess the potential loss of a portfolio based on the modeling of the α-quantile of portfolio returns for long positions or the $(1-\alpha)$-quantile of portfolio returns for short positions with $\alpha = 0.01$ or 0.05.

variance forecast Prediction of the conditional variance of a random variable.

vector autoregression (VAR) System of linear equations to represent the joint autoregressive dynamics of a set of random variables.

vector error correction model (VEC) Stationary VAR system that includes a correction term for deviations from equilibrium; explains the short-run dynamics of the variables in the VAR.

VIX See *index of volatility*.

volatility Measure of the dispersion of a random variable; commonly referred to as *standard deviation* or *variance* (square of the standard deviation) *of a random variable*.

white noise Stochastic process characterized by lack of autocorrelation at any displacement.

Wold decomposition Theorem stating that, for any covariance-stationary process, there is always a linear MA(∞)representation.

References

The following is a list of textbooks and anthologies that collect the many topics addressed in this textbook. Forecasting is a very fluid field with numerous and relevant contributions appearing almost continuously. With a couple of exceptions, I have limited the number of references to those published in the last two decades in the hope that the reader can always back track to earlier works if he or she feels the need. Although the list is non-exhaustive, it is very comprehensive. Each reference on its own contains a wealth of analysis, and collectively they represent the state of the art in forecasting. Advances in forecasting are first published in academic journals, which address very specialized questions. Through the years, the sum of these focused questions and their solutions amount to large contributions, which become standard practices. The *Handbook* compilations are very detailed descriptions of the state of the art and they are highly recommended to bring the reader up to speed on what is "cooking" in the field. For a deeper technical analysis though, the reader may wish to consult the—literally—thousands of academic journal articles cited in all these works. Happy reading!

Aït-Sahalia, Y. and L.P. Hansen (Eds.), *Handbook of Financial Econometrics* (2005), North Holland, Amsterdam.

Bollerslev, T., M. Watson, and J. Russell (Eds.), *Volatility and Time Series Econometrics. Essays in Honor of Robert F. Engle* (2011), Oxford University Press, New York, NY.

Box, G.E.P, G.M. Jenkins, and G. Reinsel (1994), *Time Series Analysis: Forecasting and Control,* 3rd ed., Prentice Hall, Englewood Cliffs, NJ.

Campbell, J.Y., A.W. Lo, and A.C. MacKinlay (1997), *The Econometrics of Financial Markets*, Princeton University Press, Princeton.

Clements, M.P. and D.F. Hendry (1998), *Forecasting Economic Time Series*, Cambridge University Press, Cambridge.

Clements, M.P. and D.F. Hendry (Eds.), *A Companion to Economic Forecasting* (2002), Blackwell, Oxford.

Cochrane, J. (2001), *Asset Pricing,* Princeton University Press, Princeton.

Cox, J.C. and M. Rubinstein (1985), *Option Markets*, Prentice-Hall, New Jersey.

Elliott, G., C.W.J. Granger and A. Timmermann (Eds.), *Handbook of Economic and Forecasting, vol. 1* (2006), Elsevier, Amsterdam.

Engle, R.F. (1995), *ARCH: Selected Readings*, Oxford University Press, Oxford.

Engle, R.F. and C.W.J. Granger (Eds.), *Long-Run Economic Relationships* (1991), Oxford University Press, Oxford.

Engle, R.F. and D. McFadden (Eds.), *Handbook of Econometrics vol. 4* (1994), Elsevier, Amsterdam.

Engle, R.F. and H. White (Eds.), *Cointegration, Causality and Forecasting. A Festschrift in Honour of Clive W.J. Granger* (1999), Oxford University Press, Oxford.

Fuller, W.A. (1996), *Introduction to Statistical Time Series,* Wiley, New York.

Granger, C.W.J. and P. Newbold (1986), *Forecasting Economic Time Series*, Academic Press, San Diego.

Granger, C.W.J. and T. Teräsvirta (1993), *Modelling Nonlinear Economic Relationships*, Oxford University Press, Oxford.

Gouriéroux, C, and J. Jasiak (2001), *Financial Econometrics*, Princeton University Press, Princeton.

Hamilton, J. D. (1994), *Time Series Analysis*, Princeton University Press, Princeton.

Harvey, A.C. (1993), *Time Series Models*, 2nd ed., MIT Press, Cambridge, MA.

Hendry, D.F. (1995), *Dynamic Econometrics*, Oxford University Press, Oxford.

Hylleberg, S. (Ed.), *Modelling Seasonality* (1992), Oxford University Press, Oxford.

Jorion, P. (2001), *Value-at-Risk: The New Benchmark for Managing Financial Risk*, McGraw-Hill, New York.

Lütkepohl, H. (1991), Introduction to Multiple Time Series Analysis. Springer-Verlag, New York, NY.

Maddala, G.S. and C.R. Rao (Eds.), *Handbook of Statistics, vol. 14* (1996), North Holland, Amsterdam.

NBER Macroeconomics Annual (several years), NBER Book Series, http://www.nber.org.

Stock, J.H. and M.W. Watson (Eds.), *Business Cycles, Indicators, and Forecasting* (1993), University of Chicago Press for NBER.

Stock, J.H and M.W. Watson (2007), *Introduction to Econometrics*, Prentice Hall.

Taylor, S. (1996), *Modeling Financial Time Series*, 2nd ed. Wiley, New York, NY.

Ullah, A. and D.E. Giles (Eds.), *Handbook of Applied Economic Statistics* (1998), Dekker, New York.

Ullah, A. and D.E. Giles (Eds.), *Handbook of Empirical Economics and Finance* (2011), Chapman & Hall, Boca Raton, FL.

White, H. (1994), *Estimation, Inference and Specification Analysis*, Cambridge University Press, Cambridge.

Wooldridge, J.M. (2009) *Introductory Econometrics. A Modern Approach*, South-Western, Mason, OH.

Index